RAND McNALLY

ENCYCLOPEDIA

— OF —

WORLD
RIVERS

Rand M\^{c\}Nally & Company

CHICAGO · NEW YORK · SAN FRANCISCO

A BISON BOOK

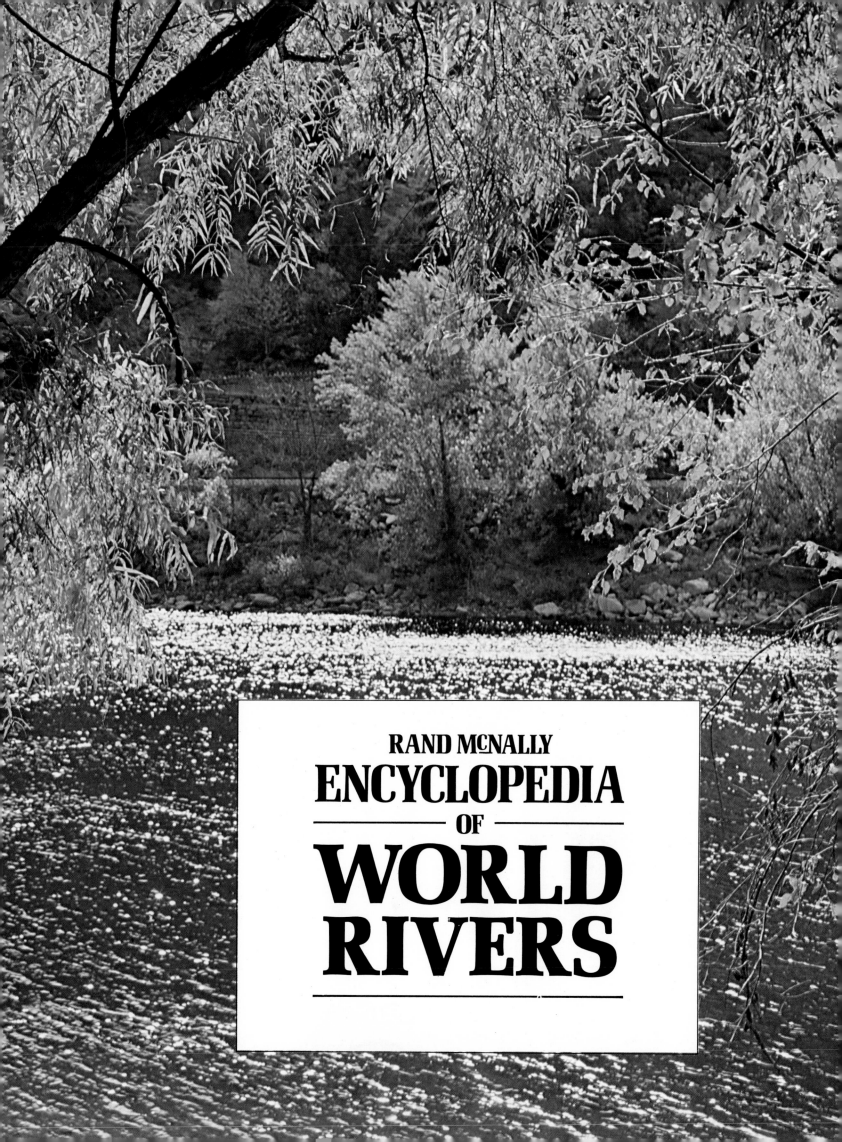

RAND McNALLY
ENCYCLOPEDIA
— OF —
WORLD
RIVERS

Published in the United States by
Rand McNally & Company 1980

First published in the United Kingdom by
Bison Books Limited

Produced by
Bison Books Limited
4 Cromwell Place
London SW 7

Copyright © 1980 by Bison Books Limited

All rights reserved

ISBN: 528-81048-1
Library of Congress Catalog Card Number:
79-87898

Phototypeset in Great Britain by
Filmtype Services Limited, Scarborough

Printed in Hong Kong

Contributors

Catherine Bradley
Susan de la Plain
Susan Garratt
S L Mayer
Janet MacLennan
Thomas A Siefring
Roland Swink

Contents

Introduction

This all-encompassing encyclopedia collects, in a single volume, those rivers which in some way have made a contribution to man's progress and development. The major considerations in selecting the rivers were length, natural beauty and geographic importance. However, a myriad of smaller rivers were also included because their banks provided sites for important towns, they were once significant trade routes or they were the scenes where historic events – battles, conferences and the like – occurred.

The book is arranged by continent: Africa, Asia, Australasia, Europe, North America and South America. Each section is introduced by a map which locates the major rivers and their relationship to the geographic features of the continent. Within each section the rivers are arranged alphabetically and cross referenced where necessary. The larger rivers are treated in depth: each profile includes source, lengths, tributaries, natural features, dams, hydroelectric power stations, industrial activity, agriculture, fauna and flora, history and many other facts of interest.

Of the problems encountered by the team, two are worthy of note. First, the lengths of the rivers recorded in the source materials vary a great deal – some statisticians measure source to outlet in a straight line omitting all meanderings, some measure length from where the river assumes a specific name to where it stops using that name (for example, the Amazon is always measured from its main head stream which is in fact the Marañón); others actually follow every bend to take accurate measurements, and some merely extrapolate lengths based on other known distances. Every opportunity has been taken by the contributors to give as accurate a figure as possible, often averaging several sources. In almost all cases it has been our intention to measure from source to outlet including all meanderings.

Spellings, too, have presented problems. After some discussion it was decided that we would attempt to use the English phonetic spelling closest in sound to the local pronunciation of the name of the river; for example, Huang Pu is used rather than Whampoa. Of course there are exceptions, such as the Donau which we persist in calling the Danube or the Odra which we call the Oder and so on.

Reference sources have included the United States Defense Mapping Agency, the American National Geographical Society, the Royal Geographical Society of Great Britain, governmental departments of many countries and even tourist agencies. Encyclopedias, atlases, foreign embassies, ministries of the interior, universities and high commissions were consulted and the relevant information written into the pages of this volume. Considerable time and effort has gone into producing what we hope will be a valuable and entertaining addition to everyone's library.

The Editors

Africa

Afram, Ghana

The Afram River rises in Ashanti in central Ghana and flows southeast to enter the southwestern arm of Volta Lake. It is 150 miles (240 km) long and nearby are extremely rich deposits of bauxite.

Akobo, Ethiopia

The Akobo rises in the highlands of southwestern Ethiopia. It is 270 miles (430 km) long and flows on a northwesterly course to join the Pibor River, which forms the border with Sudan, near the town of AKOBO. The region near the river is rich in gold deposits.

Alima, Republic of the Congo

The Alima rises in the Crystal Mountains west of DJAMBALA and flows on a wide curve eastward to join the Zaire River southsouthwest of MOSSAKA. The river is 300 miles (480 km) and is navigable for 200 miles (320 km). It is also known as the Leketi and Mpama in its upper courses.

Ankobra, Ghana

The Ankobra rises northeast of WIAWSO in southwestern Ghana. It is 120 miles (190 km) long and runs past PRESTEA to enter the Gulf of Guinea west of AXIM.

Anseba, Ethiopia

The Anseba rises near the city of ASMERA, which has a population of 250,000, in northern Eritrea. It is 215 miles (346 km) long and flows northwest to join the Barka River.

Aruwimi, Zaire

The Aruwimi rises initially as the Ituri River near Lake Albert on the western slopes of the Ruwenzori Mountain Range, Zaire. The river is 620 miles (1000 km) long and flows south, then bends westward before the junction with the Shari River, which is 100 miles (160 km) long, below IRUMU. The primeval forest of Ituri is a natural wonder – the trees shoot up to a massive height of 150 feet (45 m) and, because of the shade provided by the great trees, virtually no undergrowth exists in this region. Also this area is the home of the pygmy tribes who remain apart from the rest of 'civilization' in general. The river assumes the name of Aruwimi at the town of AVAKUBI, then continues, passing through the settlements of PANGA, BANALIA and YAMBUYA to join the Zaire (Congo) River at the port of BASOKO. Of historical interest is the fact that Henry Morton Stanley fought his most important battle with the cannibal tribesmen of the river at the mouth of Aruwimi on 1 February 1877. This fierce attack against Stanley's expedition was the 28th of the journey. The Aruwimi is not navigable for the majority of its course due to the numerous rapids, but below the Yambuya rapids it is navigable for its remaining 75 miles (121 km).

Atbarah, Ethiopia-Sudan

The Atbarah is the chief right-bank tributary of the Nile. It has a length of 800 miles (1290 km) and rises in the Ethiopian highlands not far from GONDER. The river flows through ravines before entering Sudanese territory, where it is reinforced by two tributaries, the Angareb and the Satit Rivers. At KHASHM AL-QIRBAH is located a dam which provides a large proportion of water for various regional irrigation projects. The only large town along the river is ATBARAH which is located near the confluence with the Nile. The Atbarah does not flow all year but is a seasonal river. During the dry season, only shallow rock pools remain to give the traveler any inkling that a river once ran by in the channel. Yet during the wet season the Atbarah contributes slightly more than 22 percent of the Nile's flow. It is believed that in past ages the Atbarah had a much larger flow and capacity but geological change has resulted in the present intermittency of the river.

Athi, Kenya

The Athi rises south of NAIROBI, the capital of Kenya with a population of 500,000. It is 350 miles (560 km) long and flows southeast to enter the Indian Ocean near MALINDI. It is also called the Galana River in its lower course.

Awash, Ethiopia

A river in the eastern Ethiopian plateau, the Awash rises on the northern scarp of the Great Rift Valley to the west of ADDIS ABABA, the Ethiopian capital. The river is 500 miles (800 km) long and flows north, creating a belt of beautiful forests and thick vegetation along its course. The wild life of this area consists of monkeys, crocodiles, hippopotamuses, water buffalo, leopards, hyenas, antelope and numerous species of snakes. The Awash flows into Lake Abe, a salt lake located in the middle of the Danakil Plain. Upon reaching the edge of the desert the river passes the small village of AWASH and then flows through a narrow gorge before running into Lake Abe.

Awash National Park

Bafing, Guinea-Mali

The Bafing River rises south of TIMBO, Guinea and flows for a total of 350 miles (560 km). It is not navigable and flows northeast and north to BAFOULABE in Mali to join the Bakoye River, which is 250 miles (400 km) long, to form the Senegal River. The principal tributary of the Bakoye is the Baoule River which is 300 miles (480 km) long.

Bandama, Ivory Coast

The Bandama rises in the northern highlands of the Ivory Coast, West Africa. It is 450 miles (720 km) long and flows due south to the Gulf of Guinea. Its principal tributaries are the Red Bandama and the Nzi Rivers. The river is navigable by small vessels only for 60 miles (97 km) upstream.

Bani, Ivory Coast

The Bani rises in the mountains of the Ivory Coast when several headstreams merge approximately 100 miles (160 km) east of BAMAKO. The river is 230 miles (370 km) long and runs northeast to become a tributary of the Niger River at MOPTI.

Barka, Ethiopia

The Barka River rises southwest of ASMERA in Eritrea and is also called the Barakar. It is 275 miles (443 km) long, and flows north to the Sudanese border, then runs 125 miles (200 km) to enter the Red Sea. The river is intermittent and only reaches the Red Sea during seasons of intense flooding.

Baro, Ethiopia

The Baro rises south of GORE in southwestern Ethiopia. It is 190 miles (310 km) long and flows due west to join the To Kau River at the Sudanese border. It marks the border until it joins the Pibor River to form the Sobat River.

Batha, Chad

The Batha rises 30 miles (48 km) westsouthwest of ADRE near the Sudanese border with Chad. It is intermittent and flows west to Lake Fitri which is between 20–40 square miles (50–100 sq km) in area, largely depending upon the rainfall. The river is 325 miles (523 km) long when in flow.

Benue, Cameroon-Nigeria

The Benue rises in the Adamawa Mountain Range and flows north initially. On the first leg of its course, it receives the Mayo-Kebbi River which connects the Benue and the Logone Rivers at high water, and there are swamps through which the Niger and the Chad systems are linked together on occasion. The river turns westward flowing toward the Niger after the confluence with Mayo-Kebbi. On the right bank of the Benue is the river port of GAROUA,

The River Benue at Makurdi.

and from here the river is navigable for shallow vessels. Once past the town of YOLA in Nigeria, the Benue is navigable all year for the remainder of its course. The chief tributaries of the Benue are the Gongola, the Faro, the Katsina Ala and the Donga Rivers. The river is 870 miles (1400 km) long and joins the Niger River at the town of LOKOJA. In the 1960s some school boys, while digging around the Katsina Ala River, accidentally discovered some very finely wrought terra cotta statues from a 2000-year-old civilization. The new culture was named the Nok Culture after the nearby town of NOK. Archeologists have continued their research and expanded the digging, but as yet there are no answers as to what ended a promising and culturally advanced civilization more than a thousand years older than any other discovered in West Africa.

Beth, Morocco
The Oued Beth rises in northwestern Morocco and flows north-northwest from the Atlas Mountain Range to join the Sebou River approximately 15 miles (24 km) northeast of PORT LYAUTEY. The river is 120 miles (190 km) long and flows through an area rich in citrus fruit and cotton. This is made possible by the large dam south of SIDI SLIMANE.

Betsiboka, Madagascar
The Betsiboka rises north of the capital TANANARIVE which has a population of 335,000. It is the chief river of Madagascar and is 325 miles (523 km) long. It flows north-northwest past MADIROVALO and MAROVOAY to enter the Mozambique Channel of the Indian Ocean. The Betsiboka Valley is noted for its agricultural value to the country's economy and for the gold discovered nearby.

Bomokandi, Zaire
The Bomokandi rises approximately 40 miles (64 km) south-southeast of WATSA in northeastern Zaire. It is 300 miles (480 km) long and flows northwest and west past GOMBARI and POKO to join the Uele River at the town of BAMBILI.

Bomu, Zaire
Also known as the M'Bomou, it rises near the Sudanese border, approximately 25 miles (40 km) northwest of DORUMA in northern Zaire. It is 450 miles (720 km) long and flows west past the town of BANGASSOU to join the Uele River to form the much larger Ubangi River.

Bou Regreg, Morocco
The Oued Bou Regreg rises in the foothills of the Middle Atlas Mountain Range of northwestern Morocco. It is 110 miles (180 km) long and flows northwest to enter the Atlantic Ocean between SALE and RABAT, the capital of Morocco.

Bou Sellam, Algeria
The Oued Bou Sellam rises near SETIF in the Tell Atlas Mountain Range of northeastern Algeria. The river is 170 miles (270 km) long and flows northwest to Soummam River at AKBOU.

Bubye, Rhodesia (Zimbabwe)
The river rises near WEST NICHOLSON in Rhodesia (Zimbabwe). It is 175 miles (282 km) long and flows southeast to become a tributary of the Limpopo River.

Buffalo, South Africa
The Buffalo rises in the Drakensberg Range of South Africa. It is 200 miles (320 km) long and flows southeast past RORKE'S DRIFT to join the Tugela River. Rorke's Drift, a relatively unknown mission station in the late 19th century, was the scene of one of the most ferocious battles in the annals of the British Army. Here a small detachment of troops and engineers fought against overwhelming odds, the entire might of the Zulu nation, rampant with victory over a British column which had been encamped on the slopes of a sharp plateau not far away. The entire column was wiped out to a man but the gallant defenders of Rorke's Drift held out. Victoria Crosses were awarded to a large number of soldiers from that small detachment.

Bushimaie, Zaire
This river rises northeast of SANDOA in the southern portion of Zaire. It is 240 miles (390 km) long and flows north to join the Sankuru River north of TSHILENGE. The nearby Bushimaie diamond fields are some of the richest in the world.

Busira, Zaire
The Busira is formed by the Lomela and Tshuapa Rivers near BOENDE in western Zaire. It is 170 miles (270 km) long and flows to join the Momboyo River to form the Ruki River.

Caldeon, Lesotho
The Caldeon rises in the Drakensberg Range in Lesotho. It is 300 miles (480 km) long and flows southwest as the border with the Orange Free State, then joins the Orange River just east of BETHULIE.

Cameroon, Cameroon
The Cameroon is an estuarial inlet which takes in 230 square miles (596 sq km) on the Gulf of Guinea. It is 20 miles (34 km) long and 30 miles (48 km) wide. The port city of DOUALA is located at its head. The estuary receives the Mungo and the Wouri Rivers. There are a number of islands located directly in front of the estuary, the largest being Cape Cameroon.

Casamance, Senegal
The Casamance rises in the Fouta Djallon massif of West Africa. It is 200 miles (320 km) long and flows due west through Senegal to enter a wide delta before running into the Atlantic Ocean. The chief port is ZINGUINCHOR which has a population of 30,000 and is 40 miles (64 km) inland.

Cavalla, Ivory Coast-Liberia
The Cavalla rises near the border of the Ivory Coast and Liberia and flows to the Gulf of Guinea east of HARPER. It is 320 miles (510 km) long and is navigable for 80 miles (129 km).

Cess, Liberia
The Cess rises in the Nimba Mountains of Liberia and is alternatively known as the Cestos. It is 200 miles (320 km) long and flows south and southwest to enter the Atlantic Ocean at RIVER CESS TOWN.

Chambeshi, Zambia
The Chambeshi rises north of the town of ISOKA, Zambia. It is 300 miles (480 km) long and flows southwest to enter the swamps of Lake Bangweulu.

Chari, Chad
See Shari, Chad

Cheliff, Algeria
The Cheliff rises in the Djebel Amour Mountains as the Oued Sebgag. It is the most important and longest river in Algeria. It is 450 miles (720 km) long and is dammed to provide a source of hydroelectric power and irrigation for the highly developed agricultural schemes in the lower valley. The river flows from the mountains to join the Oued Nahar Ouassel, then crosses the Tell Atlas Mountain Range through a deep gorge. The river then swings west and meanders past ORLEANSVILLE to finally enter the Mediterranean Sea near MOSTAGANEM. In a country that treasures each and every drop of water, the Cheliff is by far its most important natural asset.

Chicapa, Angola
The Chicapa rises in the northeastern portion of Angola south of ALTO CHICAPA. It is 400 miles (640 km) long and flows due north past VILA HENRIQUE DE CARVALHO and forms a section of the Angola-Zaire border. The Chicapa is noted for the extensive diamond washings along its course. At the moment this river is not being utilized to its full potential.

Chiloango, Zaire
The Chiloango rises approximately 25 miles (40 km) east-northeast of TSHELA in the Crystal Mountain Range of Zaire. It is 90 miles (145 km) long and flows initially southwest, then turns westward to enter the Atlantic Ocean north of CABINDA, Angola.

Congo, Zaire
See Zaire, Zaire.

Corubal, Guinea-Bissau
Alternatively known as the Cocoli, it rises in the Fouta Djallon Range in the Republic of Guinea. The Corubal is the longest river in the country with an overall length of 300 miles (480 km). It flows southwest to join the Geba River estuary.

Cross, Cameroon-Nigeria

The Cross River rises in the southern Bamenda highlands in Western Cameroon. The Cross is 300 miles (480 km) long and runs west and south to enter the Gulf of Guinea just south of CALABAR.

Cuanza, Angola

The Cuanza rises southeast of CHITEMBO on the Bie Plateau of central Angola. It is 600 miles (960 km) long and flows north and west to enter the Atlantic Ocean south of LUANDA. The river is navigable for approximately 120 miles (190 km) below the town of DONDO.

Cuito, Angola

The Cuito rises in the central plateau of southeastern Angola. The Cuito is 400 miles (640 km) long and flows on a southeasterly course to join the Okavango River at DIRICO.

Cunene, Angola

Also spelled Kunene, it rises near NOVA LISBOA (New Lisbon, Angola was originally a Portuguese possession), a city with a population of 110,000, in central Angola. It is 700 miles (1130 km) long and flows south and west to form the Angola-Namibia border. It enters the Atlantic Ocean at FOZ DO CUNENE. This area was the scene of intense fighting during the country's civil war between the Communist and Western factions.

Dabus, Ethiopia

The Dabus rises in the central highlands of Ethiopia. It is 125 miles (201 km) long and flows northeast to join the Blue Nile approximately 25 miles (40 km) northeast of BELFODIO. Extensive gold mining is conducted near AOSSA.

Daka, Ghana

The Daka rises north-northwest of YENDI, Ghana. It is 200 miles (320 km) long and flows south to join the Volta River east-southeast of the town of YEJI.

Dawa, Ethiopia

The Dawa rises in the highlands south of Hula in southern Ethiopia. It is 360 miles (580 km) long and flows southeast to join the Genale Dorya River at DOLO to form the Juba River. Extensive gold mining is conducted in the valley near the town of ADOLA.

Densu, Ghana

The Densu rises northwest of KOFORIDUA in southern Ghana. It is 70 miles (113 km) long and flows due south to enter the Gulf of Guinea south of ACCRA.

Didessa, Ethiopia

This river rises in the central highlands of Ethiopia approximately 30 miles (48 km) northwest of JIMA. The river is 230 miles (370 km) long and runs northwest to join the Blue Nile north of NEJO. The confluence of the Didessa and the Blue Nile is 45 miles (72 km) north of Nejo.

Dinder, Ethiopia

This river rises west of Lake Tana in the Ethiopian highlands. It is 300 miles (480 km) long and flows due west to the Sudanese Plain. The river becomes a tributary of the Blue Nile northeast of HAG ABDULLAH. The Dinder is navigable for 120 miles (190 km) during the flood season; otherwise it is restricted.

The Draa River valley forms part of the boundary between Morocco and Algeria. It is noted for its prehistoric caves and runs through the northern Sahara.

Draa, Morocco

The Oued Draa rises at the confluence of two headstreams on the slopes of the High Atlas Mountain Range in northwest Africa. The river is intermittent and is usually dry. It is 700 miles (1130 km) long and flows southeast past ZAGORA, then swings southwest to form the border with Algeria before entering the Atlantic Ocean southwest of CAPE DRAA.

Eilia, Zaire

The Eilia rises on a plateau northwest of Lake Tanganyika in the eastern region of Zaire. It is 285 miles (459 km) long and flows west passing ITULA and KAMA before joining the Lualaba.

Left: A native village on the Faleme River.

Above: The Gambia River.

Fafan, Ethiopia
This river rises northeast of HARER in southeast Ethiopia. It is 350 miles (560 km) long and flows in spasms to a marsh 35 miles (56 km) southeast of KELAFO. The river is intermittent for the majority of its course.

Faleme, Guinea-Mali
This river rises near FIRGHIA on the border of Guinea and Mali. It is 250 miles (400 km) long and runs north-northeast along the Senegal-Mali border. It becomes a tributary of the Senegal River above BAKEL.

Fatima, Wadi, Saudi Arabia
A small intermittent river of Saudi Arabia, it flows from central Hejaz for 100 miles (160 km) before entering the Red Sea south of JIDDA.

Fimi, Zaire
The Fimi River rises as the Lukenie River east of Katako Kombe, Zaire. It is 550 miles (880 km) long and flows directly into Lake Mai-Ndombe. When it exits the lake, it becomes the Fimi River and flows for a further 110 miles (180 km) to join the Kasai River. It is navigable for 500 miles (800 km) below LODJA.

Fish, Namibia
The Fish is an intermittent river which flows for a total of 500 miles (800 km) to become a tributary of the Orange River.

Gabon, Gabon
The Gabon is a 40-mile (64-km) long estuary just north of the equator. It is nine miles (14 km) wide at the mouth and LIBREVILLE is located on the north side. It is fed by several streams which flow from the Crystal Mountain Range.

Gambia, Senegal-Gambia
The Gambia River rises in the Fouta Djallon Mountain Range of Senegal, West Africa. The Gambia is 700 miles (1130 km) long and flows west through a sparsely populated undeveloped territory. The river passes BARRAKUNDA FALLS and enters the territory of Gambia. It is only 175 yards (160 m) wide at this stage. The town of KOINA is the head of the river's navigational limit for small vessels. This region of Gambia is so flat that the river is tidal as far as Barrakunda Falls. Once past the upper and practically isolated upper reaches, the river is lined with numerous wharves and small towns. The Gambia is the country's chief trade route, and provides the means to export the valuable peanuts which make up 98 percent of the country's total export trade. GEORGETOWN, a port with a population of 2000, is the head of navigation for ocean-going vessels and is located 175 miles (280 km) upstream. The capital of Gambia, BANJUL, with a population of 42,000, is located on a peninsula at the river's mouth.

Gamka, South Africa
This river rises in the Nieuwveld Range in the south Cape Province of South Africa. It is 160 miles (260 km) long and flows south-southwest past BEAUFORT WEST to join the Olifants River below the town of CALITZDORP to form the Gourits River.

Gash, Ethiopia-Sudan
The Gash rises southwest of ASMERA in the northeastern portion of Africa. It is 300 miles (480 km) long and flows west-northwest across the Sudanese border to join the Atbarah River which it only reaches during the rainy season. It flows through an extremely arid and barren section of northeastern Africa.

Geba, Guinea-Senegal
The Geba River rises in Guinea and flows across into southern Senegal. It is 200 miles (320 km) long and flows southwest passing

BAFATA to enter a deep estuary on the Atlantic Ocean at BISSAU. The estuary is 50 miles (80 km) long and five miles (eight km) wide.

Genale Dorya, Ethiopia
This river rises on Mount Guramba in southern Ethiopia. It flows south, east and south again to DOLO, where it joins the Dawa River to form the Juba River. Its chief tributary is the Web River. The river is 380 miles (608 km) long.

Gheris, Morocco
The Oued Gheris rises in the High Atlas Mountains of Morocco. It is 170 miles (270 km) long and flows southeast and south passing GOULMINA before joining Oued Ziz in the Sahara Desert to form the Oued ed Daoura. In bygone ages, these rivers were longer and carried a considerable amount of water but the gradual expansion of the desert rendered this once fertile area non-productive.

Gilo, Ethiopia
Also known as the Gelo, it rises south of GORE in southwestern Ethiopia. It is 170 miles (270 km) long and flows west-northwest to join the Pibor River north-northeast of AKOBO near the Sudanese border.

Giri, Zaire
The Giri rises north-northwest of BUDJALA in the northwest of Zaire. It is also called the N'Giri and is 225 miles (362 km) long. It flows south and southwest to become a tributary of the Ubangi River at the town of GIRI, 70 miles (120 km) above the Ubangi's confluence with the Zaire (Congo) River.

Gogeb, Ethiopia
The river rises about 50 miles (80 km) southeast of GORE in southwestern Ethiopia. It is 140 miles (224 km) long and flows east-southeast to join the Omo River near WAKA.

Gongola, Nigeria
The Gongola River rises on the Bauchi Plateau of northeastern Nigeria. It is 300 miles (480 km) long and flows northeast initially, then swings east and finally south before joining the Benue River at NUMAN. The chief tributary of the Gongola is the Hawal River.

Gorgol, Mauritania
The Gorgol rises in two headstreams west of KIFFA which meet 40 miles (64 km) east of KAEDI. The Gorgol flows for 40 miles (64 km) before joining the Senegal River as its chief tributary.

Gourits, South Africa
The Gourits River rises at the confluence of the Gamka and Olifants Rivers approximately ten miles (16 km) south of CALITZDORP in Cape Province of South Africa. It is 80 miles (129 km) long and flows due south to enter the Indian Ocean southwest of MOSSEL BAY.

Great Berg, South Africa
The river rises east of STELLENBOSCH in Cape Province, South Africa. It is 140 miles (230 km) long and flows northwest to St Helena Bay of the Atlantic Ocean.

Great Fish, South Africa
The Great Fish rises northeast of GRAAFF REINET in southeastern Cape Province, South Africa. It is 400 miles (640 km) long and flows southeast to enter the Indian Ocean east-northeast of PORT ALFRED. Its chief tributary is the Little Fish River.

Great Kei, South Africa
The Great Kei rises at the confluence of the White Kei River, 90 miles (145 km) long, and the Swart Kei River, 120 miles (190 km) long. The river is 140 miles (224 km) long and flows east-southeast of QUEENSTOWN to continue on course until it enters the Indian Ocean northeast of EAST LONDON.

Great Scarcies, Guinea
Also known as the Kolente, it rises north of KINDIA, Guinea. It is 160 miles (260 km) long and flows along the border of Sierra Leone past KAMBIA to enter the Atlantic Ocean north of FREETOWN.

Gwai, Rhodesia (Zimbabwe)
The Gwai rises near the town of FIGTREE in western Rhodesia (Zimbabwe). The Gwai is 260 miles (420 km) long and flows northwest past the town of GWAI to join the Zambezi River approximately 65 miles (106 km) east of Victoria Falls.

Hamman, Algeria
The Oued Hamman is formed by several headstreams in the High Plateaus in the Oran Department of Algeria. It is 160 miles (260 km) long and flows to the Habra lowland adjacent to the Gulf of Arzew. There are large storage dams located at BOU-HANIFIA and at the junction with the Oued Fergoug.

Hartbees, South Africa
The Hartbees River is formed by the confluence of the Mottels and the Zak Rivers near KENHARDT, South Africa. It is 70 miles (113 km) long and flows northwest to join the Orange River near KAKAMAS.

Harts, South Africa
The Harts rises in the Witwatersrand, Transvaal, South Africa. The river flows through some of South Africa's most beautiful countryside. The river is 270 miles (430 km) long and flows southwest to join the Vaal River at DELPORTSHOOP.

Hunyani, Rhodesia (Zimbabwe)
The Hunyani rises west of MARANDELLAS in northern Rhodesia (Zimbabwe). It is 260 miles (420 km) long and flows west initially, then swings north to the Zambezi River in

Mozambique. Ten miles (16 km) from the capital SALISBURY, is the Prince Edward Dam which supplies the city with drinking water.

Ikelemba, Zaire
This river rises 25 miles (40 km) southwest of BEFALE, Zaire. It is 200 miles (320 km) long and flows northwest and southwest to the Zaire (Congo) River at COQUILHATVILLE. The river is navigable by steamer for 85 miles (137 km) below BOMBIMBA.

Imo, Nigeria
The Imo rises west of OKIGWI in southern Nigeria. The river is 150 miles (240 km) long

Juba, Ethiopia-Somalia
The Juba is formed by the confluence of the Genale Dorya and the Dawa Rivers in the mountains of southern Ethiopia at the small village of DOLO, which is situated on the border of Ethiopia and Somalia. This region has seen some of the bitterest fighting of this century. The Juba winds south like a long green snake running along through the scrubland. It is 545 miles (877 km) long and is navigable for approximately 400 miles (640 km). The river is connected with Lake Deshekwama about 30 miles (48 km) from its outlet through a series of channels. The Juba then enters the Indian Ocean through a small mouth which is partially blocked by an extremely dangerous bank.

Kaduna, Nigeria
The Kaduna River rises on the Bauchi Plateau southwest of JOS in central Nigeria. It is 325 miles (523 km) long and flows northwest and southwest to join the Niger River at the town of MUREJI.

Kafue, Zambia
The Kafue rises on the Zaire border, west of ELISABETHVILLE in central Zambia. It is 600 miles (970 km) long and flows on a winding course southeast through a region extremely rich in copper ore. It then swings southwest and finally east to become a tributary of the Zambezi River in Rhodesia (Zimbabwe).

Kagera, Tanzania-Rwanda-Burundi
The Kagera River is formed by the confluence of the Ruvuvu and the Nyawaronga Rivers on the borders of Tanzania, Rwanda and Burundi. It is also called the Alexandra Nile and is 250 miles (400 km) long. It flows north initially, then east to the western shores of Lake Victoria north of BUKOBA. It is the principal tributary of Lake Victoria and as such is regarded by many as the headstream of the Victoria Nile River.

Kasai, Angola-Zaire
The Kasai rises on a plateau in northeastern Angola. It is 1338 miles (2153 km) long and flows north along the border of Angola and Zaire for a distance before crossing over into Zaire territory. It then flows northwest and finally west to enter the Zaire (Congo) River at KWAMOUTH, a large trading center. The Kasai and the other major southern affluents of the Zaire River keep the flow of the main river constant. The chief tributaries of the Kasai are: the Sankuru, which joins it at BASONGO, and its yellow colored waters can be seen for miles; the Fimi, which is navigable for the majority of its course; the Chicapa, which was the very first affluent of the Zaire known to Europeans; and the Kwango, which is also largely navigable. The Kasai itself is navigable between the towns of MAI MUNENE and MAKUMBI, the transhipment location for the railway to CHARLESVILLE which bypasses the obstacle of the Wissmann Falls. Below the Falls the river is again navigable for its remaining 475 miles (760 km) to the Zaire. It is also known as the Cessai in its upper reaches.

and flows south through an oil-palm region to enter the Gulf of Guinea below OPOBO. The river is sometimes called the Opobo River during the last stage of its flow to the gulf.

Itimbiri, Zaire
The Itimbiri rises as the Rubi River, west of NIAPU in the northern Zaire. It is 165 miles (265 km) long and flows due west past BUTA and EKWANGATANA, where it becomes the Itimbiri River. Now the river flows for a further 180 miles (290 km) southwest past AKETI and IBEMBO to join the Zaire (Congo) River as a tributary. The river is navigable for 160 miles (260 km) below Aketi and is an important transportation route.

A native paddles his dugout across the Imo River.

Ivindo, Cameroon-Gabon
The Ivindo rises on the Cameroon-Gabon border just east-northeast of MINVOUL. It is also known as the Livindo. The river is 225 miles (362 km) long and flows due south initially, then moves southwest to join the Ogooue River east of BOOUE.

Jong, Sierra Leone
Formed by the confluence of the Teye and the Pampana Rivers west of Yele in southern Sierra Leone, it is 100 miles (160 km) long and flows due south to join the Sherbro River at BONTHE.

Above: The Kaduna River of Nigeria
Right: The Kingani River winds through the plains of Tanzania.

Kebbi, Nigeria

Also known as the Rima, the Kebbi rises southeast of KATSINA in Nigeria. It is 450 miles (720 km) long and flows northwest, west and southwest to join the Niger River at GOMBA. Its chief tributaries are the Sokoto and the Zamfara Rivers.

Keiskama, South Africa

This river rises in the Amatola Range of southeastern Cape Province, South Africa. It is 160 miles (260 km) long and flows on a winding course to enter the Indian Ocean southwest of EAST LONDON.

Kingani, Tanzania

This river rises in the Uluguru Mountain Range of eastern Tanzania. It is 125 miles (201 km) long and flows past Ruvu to enter the Indian Ocean opposite Zanzibar.

Komati, South Africa

The Komati rises in the north Drakensberg Range of South Africa, north of ERMELO. It is 500 miles (800 km) long and flows eastward through Swaziland, then northeast into Mozambique, then swings due south to enter the Indian Ocean just northeast of MAPUTO (Lourenço Marques). Its chief tributary is the Krokodil River.

Komoé, Upper Volta-Ivory Coast

The Komoé rises southwest of BOBO DIOULASSO, Upper Volta. The river is 475 miles (764 km) long and flows due south to enter the Gulf of Guinea at GRAND BASSAM.

Konkoure, Guinea

The Konkoure rises in the Fouta Djallon Mountain Range, west of MAMOU in Guinea. It is 160 miles (260 km) long and flows west to the Atlantic Ocean at Sangarea Bay north of CONAKRY.

Krokodil, South Africa

This river rises north of BELFAST, Transvaal, South Africa. It is 175 miles (280 km) long and flows east to join the Komati River near the Mozambique border to form the boundary of the Kruger National Park.

Kuruman, South Africa

The Kuruman rises in the Kuruman Hills of northern Cape Province, South Africa. It is 250 miles (400 km) long and flows northwest to join the Molopo River.

Kwando, Angola

Also called the Linyanti, it rises on the great central plateau of Angola. It is 500 miles (800 km) long and flows southeast along the Zambian border to enter the marshes on the Botswana border.

Kwango, Angola

The Kwango River rises south of ALTO CHICAPA in northern Angola. It is 300 miles (480 km) long and flows northwest initially, then swings on course to form the Zaire border for approximately 200 miles (320 km), before turning north to join the Kasai River below BANDUNDU. Its chief tributaries are the Wamba River, 370 miles (600 km) long, and the Kwilu River, 650 miles (1050 km) long. The total length of the Kwango is 700 miles (1130 km).

Limpopo, Rhodesia (Zimbabwe)-South Africa-Mozambique

The Limpopo is the second longest river of Africa to enter the Indian Ocean. The river is 1100 miles (1770 km) long and drains an area of 170,000 square miles (444,300 sq km). The Limpopo is also known as the Krokodil, and rises only 300 miles (480 km) from the Indian Ocean, but flows in a large semi-circle to reach its outlet. The river rises near KRUGERSDORP, in South Africa, on the northern side of the Witwatersrand, and heads northward across the ridges of the bankeveld. The river cuts through these ridges in narrow *poorts* or gaps. Probably the most famous of these *poorts* is Hartebeespoort. Here the river crosses the Magaliesberg ridge, and a large dam in the poort has enabled 33,000 acres of land to be irrigated by the waters of the Limpopo. The chief crops in this area are tobacco and wheat. The river flows from BRIT through 100 miles (160 km) of bushveld until it comes up against another section of quartzite ridges. Cutting through these at Vlieepoort, adjacent to the iron mining center of THABAZIMBI, the river then flows through sandy terrain, heading northwest to its junction with the Marico River. From this confluence, the river is known officially as the Limpopo, and now heads northeast to form the border between Botswana and the Transvaal for over 250 miles (400 km). The river is joined by the Shashi as it begins to make its swing eastward and is the largest of the Rhodesian (Zimbabwe) tributaries. The Limpopo is the boundary between the Transvaal and Rhodesia (Zim-

babwe) for 150 miles (240 km) before it enters Mozambique. The main road between Rhodesia (Zimbabwe) and South Africa crosses the Limpopo at the Beit Bridge, and the river then falls steeply into the plains of Mozambique. It then runs southeast for the last 300 miles (480 km) of its course. The largest tributary of the Limpopo is the Olifants River, which is 450 miles (720 km) long, rising near the South African capital of PRETORIA and which joins the main river 130 miles (210 km) from the mouth. Below the confluence with the Olifants, the Limpopo is navigable to the sea. The river supports a large amount of wildlife, especially crocodiles. The 'great gray green greasy' [Kipling] Limpopo is one of southern Africa's most valued natural resources.

Lindi, Zaire

The Lindi rises approximately 35 miles (56 km) southwest of LUBERO in eastern Zaire. It is 375 miles (603 km) long and flows

northwest, west and finally southwest through a dense forested region to join the Zaire (Congo) River near STANLEYVILLE.

Livironza, Burundi

This river rises to the north of Lake Tanganyika in Burundi. It is 100 miles (160 km) long and flows north-northeast to join the Ruvuvu River at NYAWARONGO to form the Kagera River. It is regarded by some as the farthest headstream of the Nile. It is 4150 miles (6680 km) from the Mediterranean Sea.

Logone, Chad

Formed at the town of BOUMO by the junction of the M'Bere and the Pende Rivers in Chad, the river is 240 miles (384 km) long and runs northwest and then north to join the Shari River at Fort Lamy. Added to the M'Bere River, the Logone has a total length of 500 miles (800 km).

Lomami, Zaire

The Lomami is one of the principal tributaries of the Zaire (Congo) River. It is 800 miles (1290 km) long and rises in the central region of the Katanga Highlands of Zaire. The upper sections of the Lomami borders the boundary of Kasai and Katanga, and is noted for its rather abrupt changes in directional flow. It flows rapidly for its first 200 miles (320 km) before slowing down in its lower reaches. The lower section of the Lomami basin is rich in coal and will provide a considerable energy source for Zaire in future years. As the river heads towards its junction with the Zaire River, it meanders for the last 200 miles (320 km) of its course and is very wide. The river is navigable by steamer for this section. It joins the Zaire River at the town of ISANGI approximately 70 miles (113 km) below KISANGANI (formerly Stanleyville, with a population of 225,000).

Lomela, Zaire

The Lomela rises north of KATAKO KOMBE in central Zaire. It flows for a total of 500 miles (800 km) northwest and west-northwest, passing LOMELA to join the Tshuapa River west of the town of BOENDE. Together they form the Busira River. It is navigable for 400 miles (640 km) below Lomela.

Lopori, Zaire

The Lopori rises approximately 70 miles (113 km) due west of YAKUMA in western Zaire. The river is 380 miles (610 km) long and flows northwest and west to join the Maringa River at BASANKUSU to form the Lulonga River.

Lowa, Zaire

Formed by the confluence of the several headstreams in the Kahusi Mountains of eastern Zaire, the Lowa River is 275 miles (442 km) long and flows due west to join the Lualaba River.

Luanginga, Angola

The Luanginga rises in the central plateau of Angola. It is 250 miles (400 km) long and flows southeast into Zambia and joins the Zambezi River below KALABO.

Luangwa, Zambia

The Luangwa River rises northeast of ISOKA in northeastern Zambia. The river is 500 miles (800 km) long and runs south-southwest to become a tributary of the Zambezi River.

Luapula, Zaire-Zambia

The Luapula River rises in the southern portion of Lake Bangweulu. It flows south initially, then northwest and finally north to Lake Mweru. The river is a headstream of the Luvua River. The Luapula is 350 miles (560 km) long.

Below left: The Beit Bridge across the Limpopo River.
Below: The Luangwa River of Zambia.

Luembe, Angola
The Luembe rises in northeastern Angola near NOVA CHAVES. It is 350 miles (560 km) long and flows due north into Zaire to join the Kasai River. The chief tributary is the Chiumbe River.

Lufira, Zaire
This river rises west-northwest of ELISABETH-VILLE in the highlands of Katanga, Zaire. It is 300 miles (480 km) long and runs northeast and north-northwest to join the Lualaba River at KISALE. The chief power plant in Zaire is located at Cornet Falls which supplies a large amount of the country's hydroelectric power.

Lucas, Morocco
The Lucas rises in the Rif Mountain Range of western Morocco. It is 85 miles (137 km) long and flows west and northwest to enter the Atlantic Ocean at LARACHE.

Lugenda, Mozambique
The Lugenda rises in northern Mozambique in Lake Chiuta. It is 300 miles (480 km) long and flows northeast to Ruvuma River at the border of Tanzania.

Lukuga, Zaire
The Lukuga is the only outlet of Lake Tanganyika. It leaves the lake at KALEMIE and flows 200 miles (320 km) due west to join the Lualaba River.

Lulua, Angola-Zaire
The Lulua rises at the border of Angola and Zaire, south of MALONGA. It is 550 miles (880 km) long and runs north and northwest to join the Kasai River, north of CHARLESVILLE in Zaire.

Lungwebungu, Angola
The Lungwebungu River rises in the central plateau of Angola. It flows for 400 miles (640 km) on a southeasterly course into Zambia to join the Zambezi River just north of MONGU.

Lurio, Mozambique
The Lurio River rises in the Namuli Mountains of Mozambique. It is 335 miles (539 km) long and flows northeast and then eastward to enter the Mozambique Channel.

Luvua, Zaire
The Luvua rises in Lake Mweru in the southeastern region of Zaire. It is 215 miles (346 km) long and flows northwest to the Lualaba River at Ankoro. It is regarded as the eastern headstream of the Zaire (Congo).

Mahajamba, Madagascar
The Mahajamba rises northeast of ANKAZOBE in central Madagascar. It is 200 miles (320 km) long and flows northwest to a large delta at Mahajamba Bay in the Mozambique Channel.

Malagarasi, Tanzania
This river rises in western Tanzania north-northeast of KIBONDO. It runs in a circular course, first southwest, then south-southeast and finally west to enter Lake Tanganyika.

Mangoky, Madagascar
The Mangoky rises in central Madagascar as the Matsiatra River. It is 350 miles (560 km) long and flows north and southwest to BEROROHA, then swings westward and northwest to a wide estuary in the Mozambique Channel. The river is navigable for 160 miles (260 km) below Beroroha.

Mangoro, Madagascar
The river rises south of Lake Alaotra in eastern Madagascar. It is 130 miles (210 km) long and flows south and east to enter the Indian Ocean south of MAHANORO.

Mano, Liberia
The Mano begins near VONJAMA in Liberia and flows for a total of 200 miles (320 km). It runs southwest to enter the Atlantic Ocean at MANO SALIJA.

Mara, Kenya
The river rises in the southwestern portion of Kenya. It is 160 miles (260 km) long and flows due south and then west through Tanzania to enter Lake Victoria at the town of MUSOMA.

Maringa, Zaire
The river rises approximately 70 miles (113 km) southeast of the town of DJOLU in the western region of Zaire. It is 325 miles (523 km) long and runs west and northwest to join the Lopori River at BASANKUSU to form the Lulonga River. The Lulonga flows for a further 130 miles (208 km) to join the Zaire (Congo) River at the town of LULONGA.

Mazoe, Rhodesia (Zimbabwe)
The Mazoe begins to the north of the capital, SALISBURY, in Rhodesia (Zimbabwe). It is 200 miles (320 km) long and flows east-northeast through the Bindura-Shamva gold mining region to become a tributary of the Zambezi River below TETE in Mozambique.

M'Bere, Cameroon
Also called the Western Logone, it rises in Cameroon and flows for 270 miles (430 km) on a northeasterly course past MOUNDOU to join the Pende River.

M'Bridge, Angola
The M'Bridge rises in the central plateau southwest of MAQUELA DO ZOMBO in northwestern Angola. It is 220 miles (350 km) long and runs west-southwest into the Atlantic Ocean north of AMBRIZETE.

Medjerda, Tunisia
The Medjerda rises in the Medjerda Mountain Range of northeastern Algeria and is the principal river of Tunisia. It is 230 miles (370 km) long and flows east-northeast into Tunisia and then into the Gulf of Tunis, only 20 miles (32 km) from the city of Tunis which has a population of 665,000. The chief tributaries are the Oued el Lil, the Mellegue and the Siliana Rivers.

Mekerra, Algeria
The Mekerra rises in the High Plateaus of the Oran Department of northwestern Algeria. It is 150 miles (240 km) long and flows north-northeast passing SIDI-BEL-ABBES and SAINT-DENIS-DU-SIG before crossing the coastal lowlands, where it is ultimately dammed for irrigation purposes.

Miliane, Tunisia
The river rises northeast of SILIANA in central Tunisia. It is 80 miles (129 km) long and flows northeast to enter the Gulf of Tunis six miles (ten km) southeast of TUNIS.

Mina, Algeria
The Mina rises in the High Plateaus of the Oran Department of northern Algeria. It is 150 miles (240 km) long and flows northwest across the Tell Atlas Range to join the Cheliff River.

Modder, South Africa
The river rises in the Orange Free State northwest of WEPENER in South Africa. It is 225 miles (362 km) long and flows northwest and west past the town of PAARDEBERG to join the Riet River south-southwest of KIMBERLEY, a city with a population of 95,000.

Mogalakwena, South Africa
The Mogalakwena rises west of NYLSTROOM in the Transvaal, South Africa. The river is 250 miles (400 km) long and flows north to become a tributary of the Limpopo River.

Molopo, South Africa
The Molopo rises in the Transvaal of South Africa and flows through some of the most scenic and beautiful countryside in this part of the continent. It is 600 miles (960 km) long and assumes a very winding course, flowing west past MAFEKING to become the boundary between Botswana and South Africa. It then turns south to join the Orange River. The siege of Mafeking was a heroic resistance put up by the British during the Boer War.

Momboyo, Zaire
The river rises initially as the Luilaka River southwest of the town of LOMELA in the central and western portion of Zaire. It is 270 miles (430 km) long and flows northwest and north-northwest passing IKALI and MONKOTO, where it becomes the Momboyo River. It continues northwest on course to join the Busira River at the junction town of INGENDE to form the Ruki River. The Momboyo's total length is close to 315 miles (507 km).

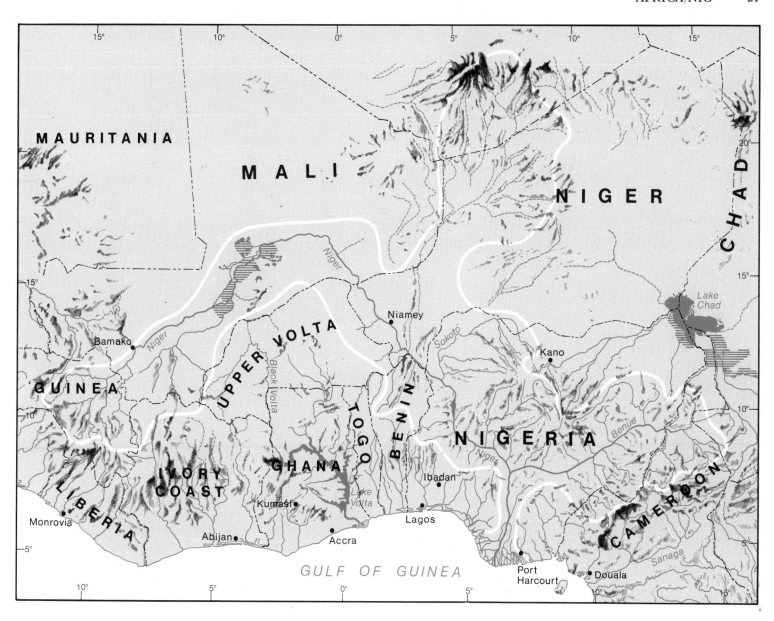

Mongala, Zaire

A river formed by the confluence of three headstreams at the town of BUSINGA in the northwestern region of Zaire. The river is 205 miles (330 km) long and flows due south, then swings to a westerly course before joining the Zaire (Congo) River at GUMBA-MOBEKA. The Mongala is navigable from Businga.

Mono, Togo-Benin

This river rises in Togo south of DJOUGOU in Benin. It is 250 miles (400 km) long and runs due south to enter the Bight of Benin on the Gulf of Guinea west of GRAND POPO.

Moulouya, Morocco

The river rises in the High Atlas Mountain Range, southwest of the town of MIDELT in Morocco. It is 320 miles (510 km) long and runs north-northeast past GUERCIF to enter the Mediterranean Sea approximately 35 miles (56 km) southeast of MEDILLA. The river is not navigable and has a very irregular volume.

Mzimvubu, South Africa

See Umzimbuvu, South Africa

N'Goko, Cameroon

The river rises as the Dja River southeast of the town of ABONG-M'BANG in Cameroon. It assumes a winding course, first running west, then east and finally southeast past MOLOUN-DOU to join the Sanga River at the town of OUESSO.

N'Gounie, Gabon

The river rises approximately 25 miles (40 km) southeast of M'BIGOU in Gabon. It is 275 miles (442 km) long and flows southwest and northwest past MOUILA to join the Ogooue River above LAMBARENE.

Niger, Guinea-Mali-Niger-Nigeria

The Niger is the third longest river in Africa. It has a length of 2590 miles (4170 km) and drains an area of 580,000 square miles (1,502,200 sq km). The Niger rises near the border of Sierra Leone in the Fouta Djallon Mountains of Guinea. It begins at an altitude of 1000 yards (910 m) and flows northeast in a great loop to its most northern point near the ancient city of TIMBUKTU (which today has a population of 15,000) on the edge of the Sahara Desert. The river continues on to BAMAKO (which has a population of 182,000) and is the capital of the Republic of Mali. Bamako is the chief commercial and distributing center of the region; it exports peanuts, corn, rice, livestock and hides. Reaching SEGOU, a town of 27,200 people, the river expands into a maze of channels at flood time; this huge inland delta covers an area of 30,000 square miles (77,700 sq km) between August and November. This entire area was once a large ancient inland sea, and only the few scattered lakes remaining in the area give some indication of how large this sea once was. In 1947 the Sansanding Dam was built which raised the water level by 14 feet (4 m), and helped to control the flow of water in the Niger. This upper section of the river is known as the Joliba River. The system does not assume the name Niger until it reaches its northernmost point which is located at the port city of KABARA.

Kabara is the port section of Timbuktu. At one time Timbuktu was the most notorious and romantic city in the entire African continent. It was famous for its slave markets and rich gold merchants; now it is just a small crumbling town which has only memories of a once great and rather remarkable history.

Once the Niger passes BOUREM, it turns southward leaving the southern edge of the

Tilemsi Valley, which extends north for over 500 miles (800 km) into the northeastern portion of Mali. The river then reaches GAO, (a small town about 200 miles (320 km) past Timbuktu), which was once the capital of the great and magnificent Shonghai Empire. In

Left: The Niger River just after it has been joined by the Benue.
Below: A native river craft sails down the Niger.

this same district close to the edge of the desert, north of the Niger dwell the 'people of the veil,' a nomadic tribe, known as the Tuaregs. Unlike the Moslem world where the women are veiled, the *men* of the Tuaregs wear the veil in their society. Being basically nomadic, they roam all over the desert from one desert oasis to another. They make some of the finest handmade silver crosses in the world, highly prized by the French.

The Niger then crosses into Nigerian territory, and soon after receives the Kebbi River near the town of BAHINDI. It now swings due south past the Bussa Rapids and flows for 60 miles (97 km) to JEBBA, where the middle section of the Niger ends.

From Jebba the Niger is navigable to the delta between July to October when the water is at its highest. Reaching MUREJI, located at the confluence of the Kaduna River, the Niger is navigable the entire year by steamer. The river now flows on to the junction with the Benue River, its only major tributary. Eighty miles (129 km) from the coast at the town of ABO, the Niger enters its deltaic stage which extends over an area of 14,000 square miles (36,260 sq km), and is 200 miles (320 km) wide along the coast. The delta of the Niger is larger than that of the Nile and is made up of 14 separate arms and numerous smaller channels. The four main ports of the Niger delta area are PORT HARCOURT (population 210,000) on the Bonny River, LAGOS, the capital, with a population of 841,000, FORCADOS, situated on the Forcados River and navigable for ocean-going vessels, and CALABAR (population 47,000) on the Cross River. Near Calabar live the primitive Efik and Ibibo tribes, who depend totally upon the oil palm for their livelihood. The products of the oil palm and the newly developed off-shore oil make up 99 percent of the country's economy. The Niger is by far the most important river of northwestern Africa.

Nile, East Africa-North Africa

One of the great rivers of the world, the Nile is also the longest, with a length of 4132 miles (6648 km). Its greatness does not only lie in its size but also in its historical and archeological importance over the last 6000 years. One of the greatest and earliest riverine cultures in the world began to bloom along the Nile – the Egyptian. The Nile Basin covers an area of over 1,100,000 square miles (2,900,000 sq km), and includes parts of Egypt, Sudan, Ethiopia, Kenya, Rwanda, Tanzania, Zaire, Uganda and Burundi. The Nile extends from equatorial Africa, through the magnificent tropical plains of southern Sudan, to the deserts of northern Sudan and Egypt, ultimately to find its way through a massive delta into the Mediterranean Sea.

The Nile provides hydroelectric power and water for irrigation projects, and is one of the prime means of transportation in East Africa. The majority of the population of over 20 million is centered along the banks of the Nile and its delta region. The historical importance of this river is unequaled. Even in Roman times the Nile valley and its civilizations were considered ancient. Before Rome's dominance over 30 dynasties of Egyptian Pharaohs had ruled holding together the kingdoms of the

Upper and Lower Nile for thousands of years, expanding and conquering neighbors and creating one of the first great commercial empires of the world. After the passing of the Pharaohs came Alexander the Great, Ptolemy and his successors, the Romans and Byzantine Empires, and finally Mohammed and the Ottoman Empire.

The Nile is unlike most rivers, because it is a considerable stream even at its source, near JINJA in Uganda. J H Speke and James Grant, two British explorers, discovered the source of the Nile in 1862, and solved what had been one of Africa's great mysteries. It is the chief outlet of Lake Victoria, which is the largest lake in Africa. The Victoria Nile, as it is known here, is controlled at its outlet by the Owen Falls Dam. This dam was constructed in 1954 and now covers what was once the Ripon Falls.

At Lake Kyoga, 50 miles (80 km) from the Owen Falls, the Nile leaves the plateau at Murchison Falls, and enters the northern point of Lake Albert. The river is now known as the Albert Nile or Bahr el Jebel until it reaches NIMULE in the Sudan. The Nile flows through some of the finest parkland in the world which serves as the home for some of Africa's big game – lions, elephants, leopards, giraffes, zebras and gazelles. The river is navigable for steamers throughout south-central Sudan.

Beyond the town of BOR, the river runs for 350 miles (560 km) through the Sudd swamps, which, until 1839–42, stopped all efforts to explore the Upper Nile. The tributaries, Bahr el Ghazal, the river of gazelles, and the Bahr el Ziraf, the river of giraffes, were also explored during this period. Reaching Lake No, the swamps end and the Nile continues, to be joined by the Sobat River, a right bank tributary, close to the town of MALAKAL. From the junction of the Sobat, the Nile flows through a flat wide plain to KHARTOUM; the most significant landmark along the course is the Gebel Aulia Dam. Khartoum exists at the confluence of the Blue Nile and the White Nile.

Once past Khartoum the waters of the clear White Nile can be seen mixing with the bluer and darker waters of the Blue Nile as it flows for another 1900 miles (3060 km) before entering the Mediterranean Sea. The Nile receives only one more tributary as it flows to the sea, the Atbarah River. During the summer flood water, the Blue Nile provides 68 percent, the White Nile 10 percent and the Atbarah 22 percent of the river's water; in the low season the Atbarah dries up and the White Nile provides the majority of the water for the main river. Upon reaching the 6th cataract, the Nile flows through a large gorge, then runs through the clear Shendi reach, and afterwards rapids and cataracts alternate with smooth stretches to Lake Nasser which extends south into Sudan and north to the Aswan High Dam. The river flows through a narrow trench and is bordered by desert all the way to the capital, CAIRO, a city of 4,500,000. The valley of the Nile is only one mile wide (1.6 km) at this stage, but it gradually widens to between 5–12 miles (8–19 km). Along the river the ancient capital cities of Memphis and Thebes which were themselves great metropolis's 5000 years ago were built. Today, small sailing boats can still be seen on the river (they are known locally as feluccas) as well as primitive waterwheels

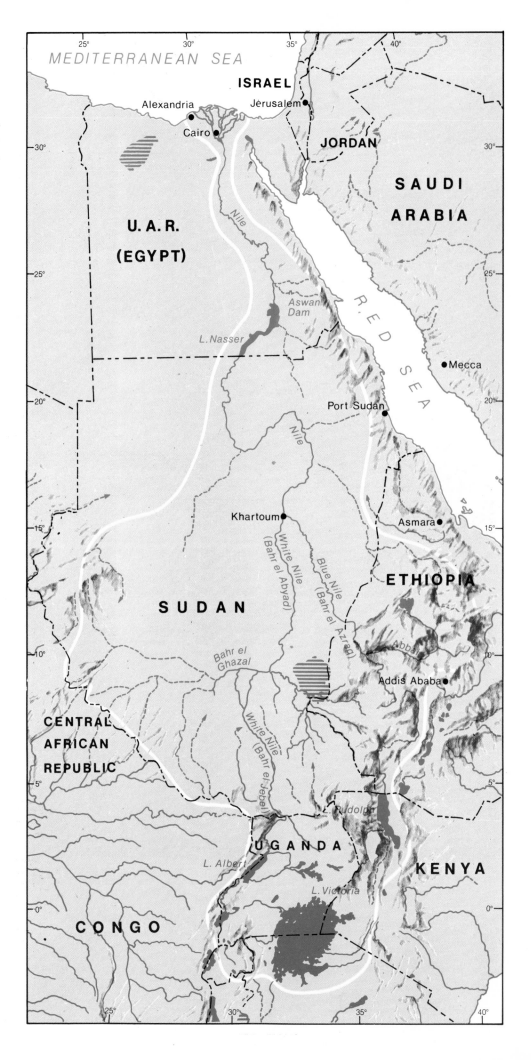

Sail boats on the Nile at Aswan.

Civilization continues to flourish on the banks of the fertile Nile.

which still raise the life-giving water of the Nile to irrigate the nearby stretches of the Nile's river valley. Near ASWAN, a city of 127,000, and SILSILEH are the ancient quarries which provided the talented engineers of the Pharaohs with the stone to build the magnificent pyramids. This section of the valley was the site of the spectacular Abu Simbel Temple, which was flooded over when the Aswan Dam was built. The Egyptian government realizing the archeological importance of this temple has recently raised it piece by piece and is reconstructing it in a safe location. Below Aswan are the other famous temples of Luxor, Edfu and Karnak, which are situated opposite the even more famous Valley of the Kings. As the Nile approaches CAIRO, it passes the great pyramids of Sakkara and Giza. Cairo is the capital city of today's Egypt and has a population of 4,500,000. Finally, once past Cairo, the Nile begins to enter its delta at the head of the Mohammed Ali Barrage. The

entire delta region is crossed and recrossed by numerous irrigation canals. The river flows through the delta in two branches, the Damietta and the Rosetta. The Nile is one of the most studied rivers in world history. Records have been kept since 711 AD. Today there are numerous gauges throughout the valley of the Nile to record water levels at all times of the year. The Nile was one of the cradles of civilization and even today its importance cannot be overstated.

Nosob, Namibia (South West Africa)
The Nosob River rises north-northeast of WINDHOEK in Namibia. It flows southwest forming the border between Botswana and the Cape Province of South Africa. It continues through the Kalahari Desert to join the Molopo River. It is 500 miles (800 km) long and for a large portion of its course is intermittent, especially in the Kalahari Desert.

Nuanetsi, Rhodesia (Zimbabwe)
This river rises about 20 miles (32 km) northeast of FILABUSI in Rhodesia (Zimbabwe). It is 250 miles (400 km) long and flows southeast to join the Limpopo River as a tributary in Mozambique.

Nyanga, Gabon
The Nyanga rises about 50 miles (80 km) due east of M'BIGOU in the southwestern region of Gabon. It is 240 miles (390 km) long and flows west to enter the Atlantic Ocean northwest of the town of MAYUMBA.

Nyawaronga, Rwanda
The river rises due east of Lake Kivu, one of the loveliest of the great African lakes. Lake Kivu is 1600 feet (488 m) deep and at an altitude of 4788 feet (1460 m) is one of the most beautiful lakes in Africa. The Nyawaronga is

Above left: The Nile meanders across the Sudan.
Above: The Fula rapids on the Nile at Nimule.

250 miles (400 km) long and flows eastward to join the Ruvubu River near the Tanzania border to form the Kagera River.

Nyong, Cameroon
The Nyong rises due east of ABONG-M'BANG in the central Cameroon. It is 400 miles (640 km) long and flows due west past the towns of AKONOLENGA and ESEKA to enter the Atlantic Ocean approximately 40 miles (64 km) south-southwest of EDEA.

Nzi, Ivory Coast
The Nzi rises southeast of FERKESSEDOUGOU in the Ivory Coast. It has a length of 280 miles (450 km) and meanders southward to join the Bandama River near TIASSALE.

Nzoia, Kenya
The Nzoia rises in the Cherangany Hills of southwestern Kenya and flows through some of that nation's most scenic countryside. It is 150 miles (240 km) long and runs southwest past MUMIAS to enter Lake Victoria just south of PORT VICTORIA.

Ogooue, Gabon
Also known as the Ogowe, it rises near ZANAGA in Gabon. It is a large river which flows initially northwest past the towns of FRANCEVILLE and LASTOURSVILLE, then swings first west and then south to enter a large delta on the Gulf of Guinea. Its main tributaries are the Leconi, Ivindo and Abango.

Ogun, Nigeria
The Ogun rises in Oyo Province of southwestern Nigeria. It is 200 miles (320 km) long and flows south past the towns of OLOKEMEJI and ABEOKUTA to enter the Lagos Lagoon just north of LAGOS, the capital, with a population of 842,000.

Olifants, South Africa-Mozambique (1)
This Olifants River rises in the southern Transvaal west of WITBANK in South Africa. It is 350 miles (560 km) long and flows northeast and east to enter Mozambique to join the Limpopo River at a point 130 miles (210 km) due north of MAPUTO. It is this river which is an attraction at Kruger National Game Park. In Mozambique the river is known as Rio dos Elefantes.

Olifants, South Africa (2)
The 'lesser' Olifants rises north-northwest of WORCESTER in the Cape Province of South Africa. It is 170 miles (270 km) long and flows north-northwest past the town of CLANWIL-

*Above: fishing baskets in position at a barrier on the
Nzoia River in Kenya.
Below: The Ogooue River seen from the Albert
Schweitzer hospital.*

Left: The Ogun River in Nigeria.

Above: 'Mukolo' dugout crosses the Okavango River.

LIAM to enter the Atlantic Ocean 30 miles (48 km) north-northwest of Lambert's Bay.

Okavango, Angola-Namibia

The Okavango rises as the Cuango in the central region of Angola, east of HUAMBO in the Bie Plateau. The river flows southeast receiving tributaries from the left bank only as it runs along the border of Angola and Namibia. The river is full of rapids in this section and the surrounding region is relatively thinly inhabited. The river is navigable at high water by canoes but this mode of transportation is even dangerous in the quieter sections as it is occupied by crocodiles and hippopotamuses. Once past the Popa Falls the Okavango enters the Ngami basin and then crosses into Botswana at the town of MUHEMBO. Here the river begins to spread out into a huge swamp which stretches to Lake Ngami. The silt brought by the Okavango is the main ingredient in the composition of this huge swamp. Floating vegetation takes root, and then so fills up the various channels that it finally blocks the flow of the river. The river manages to cut its way through various channels only to allow the disused outlets to silt up once again. Nearby Lake Ngami, discovered by David Livingstone in 1849, had a length of 30 miles (48 km) and a width of 12 miles (19 km) but by 1860, it was only a mere trickle in a tremendous area of reeds. This was transformed in 1925, when vast flooding brought this ghost lake back into existence with a length of around four miles (six km). Now the lake has once again disappeared leaving only a wide grassy plain with exceptionally rich black soil which is utilized by the Damara tribesmen to graze their herds of cattle and sheep.

Before flowing through its inland delta, the Okavango divides into three separate channels: the Teoghe, the Ngoga and the Boro Rivers, which themselves further split into even more numerous channels. One of these channels, the Thamalakane River, an eastern branch, is linked with Lake Ngami through the Nghabe Channel which possesses an exceptionally unusual characteristic. Whenever the lake has a considerable volume of water on hand the channel flows in the opposite direction carrying water back into the river. The Okavango River is quite remarkable but remains in need of deeper study. The Okavango is 1000 miles (1600 km) long.

Omo, Ethiopia

The river rises south of Mount Goroken in southern Ethiopia. Its chief tributaries are the Gogeb and the Gibbe Rivers. It flows for 500 miles (800 km) due south before entering Lake Rudolf. The lake itself is long and narrow, encompassing 3500 square miles (9065 sq km), and is one of the lowest and shallowest lakes in East Africa. Except for the Omo River, flowing into the northern end of the lake from the well-watered Ethiopian highlands, all the drainage is seasonal. The fishing in the lake is world renowned.

Onilahy, Madagascar

The Onilahy River rises approximately 20 miles (32 km) due south of BETROKA in the Massif de L'lvakoany in the southwestern region of the Madagascar. It is 250 miles (400 km) long and flows west to enter St Augustin Bay on the Mozambique Channel just north of SOALARY.

Orange, South Africa

The Orange is the longest river in South Africa with a length of 1300 miles (2090 km). It has a drainage basin exceeding 328,000 square miles (849,500 sq km) and rises at a height of 10,000 feet (3050 m) on the flanks of the Mont-aux-Sources in the Drakensberg of South Africa. The source of the Orange is only a mere 200 miles (320 km) from the Indian Ocean, yet the river does not utilize it as an outlet, but flows the width of southern Africa to enter the Atlantic Ocean. The Orange flows south from the gentle surface of the top of the escarpment, and drops through a series of deep valleys and gorges, with many rapids and waterfalls, before turning west into a very wide valley. Flowing for slightly over 200 miles (320 km), the river leaves Lesotho, and becomes the boundary between the Orange Free State and the Cape Province for approximately 300 miles (480 km). During the Boer War, this region (especially around the town of COLESBERG) witnessed continuous bitter and intense

Above: An aerial photograph of the Omo River.
Above right: The Orange River near its mouth.
Right: The Orange River at Norvalspont.

fighting for the first year of the campaign. Eventually the British Army succeeded after numerous engagements against a much smaller force, to advance and capture BLOEMFONTEIN, the capital of the Orange Free State. In this upper section of the river, it receives only one important tributary, the Caledon, which rises close to the source of the Orange, but takes a direct southwesterly route to join the river approximately 54 miles (87 km) below ALIWAL NORTH. The valley of the Caledon has the most fertile land on the plateau. Reaching NORVALSPONT the Orange heads northwest, and keeps to this course for over 200 miles (320 km) until it is joined by its principal tributary, the Vaal. It assumes the general direction of the Vaal for close to 100 miles (160 km) before reverting to its northwesterly course. Upon reaching UPINGTON, it swings

due west toward the Atlantic Ocean. It is interesting to note that between the Atlantic and the confluence with the Vaal, the Orange receives no perennial tributaries. The Orange, with its meagre list of tributaries, drains the entire South African plateau south of WITWATERSRAND, all of Lesotho, large tracts of Botswana and Namibia. From its source high in the Drakensberg where the average annual rainfall is 60 inches (150 cm), the river runs from grassy pastures to true arid desert, with an annual rainfall of less than one inch (2.5 cm). Once the river flows below Upington, it splits into several branches, resulting in a number of islands; this is a distinct character-

istic of the river for the next 70 miles (113 km). This section ceases at the Augrabies Falls, where the river falls over 500 feet (152 m) into a granite gorge with sheer sides through which it flows for a distance. Approximately four miles (six km) below the falls it becomes the border of South Africa and Namibia for the rest of its course before entering the Atlantic Ocean. The Orange, like its cousin far to the north, the Nile, rises in a well-watered area and then flows through a desertlike region without receiving any tributaries. However, whereas the Nile has seen the birth of a great riverine civilization along its course, the Orange has not seen the rise of any major riverside

settlements. Most likely the reason for this is that the high concentration of silt in the various channels coupled with the falls and rapids in some reaches make the river virtually unnavigable. The river is named in honor of the Prince of Orange, who arrived at Cape Town in 1777 and traveled to the river in an exploratory expedition. The Orange is a spectacular and interesting river which has yet to be fully developed and utilized.

Oti, Upper Volta
The Oti rises in Upper Volta and flows south past SANSANNE-MANGO across the border into

Augrabies Falls on the Orange River.

Ghana. It continues on course to join the Volta River south-southeast of KETE-KRACHI. The river is 320 miles (510 km) long.

Ouémé, Benin

Also known as the Weme, it rises in the Atakora Mountains of Benin. The river is 300 miles (480 km) long and flows south past CARNOTVILLE and OUEME to a large delta on the Gulf of Guinea near the town of COTONOU. The principal tributary is the Okpara River which is 150 miles (240 km) long.

Ouergha, Morocco

The Oued Ouergha rises in the Rif Mountain Range of Morocco. It is 120 miles (190 km) long and flows west-southwest to join the Sebou River north of PETITJEAN.

Oum er Rbia, Morocco

The river rises in the Middle Atlas Range northeast of KHENIFRA in western Morocco. It is 345 miles (555 km) long and flows southwest past DAR OULD ZIDOUH, then swings northwest to enter the Atlantic Ocean below AZEMMOUR. There are important hydroelectric dams located on the river.

Pangani, Tanzania

Also known as the Ruva, it rises on Mount Kilimanjaro, a peak which is 19,340 feet (5899 m) high, in northeastern Tanzania. It is 250 miles (400 km) long and flows southeast to enter the Pemba Channel of the Indian Ocean at the town of PANGANI.

Pende, Cameroon

Also known as the Eastern Logone, it rises approximately 25 miles (40 km) south-southwest of BOCARANGA. It is 225 miles (362 km) long and flows due north past the town of DOBA to link up with the M'Bere River to form the Logone River south-southeast of LAI.

Pongola, South Africa
The Pongola rises in the Drakensberg Range of northern Natal, South Africa. It is 350 miles (560 km) long and flows east through Zululand, then north into Mozambique where it is called the Maputo River, and finally into Delagoa Bay of the Indian Ocean south-southeast of MAPUTO.

Pra, Ghana
The Pra rises to the northwest of MPRAESO in southern Ghana. It is 150 miles (240 km) long and flows due south to enter the Gulf of Guinea at SHAMA. The chief tributaries of the Pra are the Birim and the Ofin Rivers.

Pru, Ghana
The Pru River rises in the Ashanti, approximately 33 miles (53 km) west of MAMPONG in central Ghana. It is 120 miles (190 km) long and runs northeast passing PRANG to join the Volta River southeast of YEJI.

Pungue, Mozambique
The Pungue River rises near Mozambique's border with Rhodesia (Zimbabwe). It is 200 miles (320 km) long and flows southeast before entering the Mozambique Channel of the Indian Ocean at BEIRA.

Rahad, Ethiopia
The Rahad rises due west of Lake Tana in Ethiopia. Lake Tana is the largest body of water in Ethiopia with a length of 50 miles (80 km), a width of 40 miles (64 km) and encompassing 1400 square miles (3626 sq km). It is a beautiful lake and has over 60 affluent streams which keep its water level high. The Rahad is 300 miles (480 km) long and flows northwest into the Sudan to join the Blue Nile near WADI MADANI.

Red Volta, Upper Volta
The Red Volta rises northwest of OUAGADOUGOU, the capital of Upper Volta which has a population of over 100,000. It is 200 miles (320 km) long and flows southeast through Ghana to join the White Volta River near the town of GAMBAGA.

Riet, South Africa
The Riet rises in the southwestern region of the Orange Free State of South Africa. It is 250 miles (400 km) long and flows northwest into Cape Province to become a tributary of the Vaal River. Its principal tributary is the Modder River.

Rokel, Sierra Leone
The Rokel rises practically on the Guinea border of central Sierra Leone and is also known as the Seli. It is 250 miles (400 km) long and runs first southwest and south passing BUMBUNA and MAGBURAKA, then turns westward to join Port Loko Creek to form the Sierra Leone River just 17 miles (27 km) southwest of PORT LOKO.

Rufiji, Tanzania
The Rufiji is formed by the confluence of two headstreams in the eastern region of Tanzania. The river is 175 miles (280 km) long and runs northeast and east to enter the very wide delta – 30 miles (48 km) wide – in the Indian Ocean. The principal tributary of the Rufiji is the Great Ruaha River.

Ruhuhu, Tanzania
This small river rises south of NJOMBE in southern Tanzania. It is 100 miles (160 km) long and runs southeast and southwest to enter Lake Nyasa just south of MANDA. Lake Nyasa, also known as Lake Malawi, is the third largest of the great lakes of Africa. It has a length of 360 miles (580 km) and is between 15–50 miles (24–80 km) wide taking in an area of 11,000 square miles (29,000 sq km). The Ruhuhu River is the lake's chief tributary. When David Livingstone found the lake in 1859, he gave it the name of 'Lake of Storms' because of the unpredictable weather in this region.

Ruvuma, Mozambique
The Ruvuma River rises east of Lake Nyasa in the northern Mozambique highlands. The river is 450 miles (720 km) long and its chief tributary is the Lugenda River. The Ruvuma flows north, then turns eastward to form the majority of the Tanzania-Mozambique border, before entering the Indian Ocean just north of CABO DELGADO.

Ruvubu, Burundi
The Ruvubu rises in several headstreams east of MATANA, Burundi. The river is 300 miles (480 km) long when its chief headstream, the Livironza River, is included. It flows north-northeast to join the Nyawaronga River at the Tanzanian border to form the Kagera River.

Sabi, Rhodesia (Zimbabwe)
The Sabi begins approximately 50 miles (80 km) due south of SALISBURY the capital of Rhodesia (Zimbabwe). The river is 400 miles (640 km) long and flows southeast and south to the Mozambique border, then swings east to enter the Mozambique Channel of the Indian Ocean at NOVA MAMBONE.

Saint John, Liberia
The river rises northeast of the town of GANTA on the Guinea border of central Liberia. It is 120 miles (190 km) long and flows southwest to enter the Atlantic Ocean at EDINA.

Saint Paul, Liberia
This river begins at the confluence of two headstreams near the Guinea border of central Liberia. The river is 125 miles (200 km) long and runs southwest past WHITE PLAINS, which is also the head of the river's navigational limit, to enter the Atlantic Ocean north of the capital MONROVIA. The capital of Liberia was named after the American President James Monroe and has a population of over 100,000.

Salonga, Zaire
The Salonga River rises at the confluence of two headstreams west-southwest of BOKWANKUSU in western Zaire. It is 210 miles (340 km) long and runs northwest to join the Busira River.

Sanaga, Cameroon
The Sanaga is formed by the confluence of several headstreams approximately 90 miles (145 km) northwest of BATOURI in Cameroon. It is 325 miles (520 km) long and flows west-northwest to enter the Atlantic Ocean south of DOUALA. Its principal tributary is the M'Bam River, and it is linked to the Cameroon and Nyong Rivers in the lower course.

Sankuru, Zaire
The Sankuru rises initially as the Lubilash River in the highlands of Katanga Province in central Zaire. The Lubilash River is 285 miles (459 km) long and flows north to Mwango where it becomes the Sankuru River. It then moves due north and west passing the town of LUSAMBO before turning north again for a distance. Its final course change is westward to join the Kasai River opposite the town of BASONGO. The total length of the river is 750 miles (1210 km).

Sassandra, Ivory Coast
The Sassandra rises in the uplands near the Guinea border of the western Ivory Coast. It is 350 miles (560 km) long and runs southeast to enter the Gulf of Guinea at the town of SASSANDRA.

Sebou, Morocco
The Sebou begins as the Guigou River in the Middle Atlas Range, south-southeast of AZROU in Morocco. The river is 280 miles (450 km) long and flows north to the outskirts of FES, then swings west to enter the Atlantic Ocean at MEHDIA.

Senegal, Mali-Mauretania-Senegal
The Senegal is formed by the confluence of the Bafing and the Bakoye Rivers, both of which rise in the Fouta Djallon Range and flow westward to meet at the town of BAFOULABE. The river forms the border between Mali and Mauretania between the Karakoro confluence and BAKEL. Once past the town of Bakel, the Senegal is the boundary between Mauretania and Senegal practically to the sea. The river is 1015 miles (1633 km) long and is one of the chief rivers of West Africa. In its upper reaches, the river is beset with rapids – the principal one being the 60-foot (18 m) Gouina – and the Felou Falls. Once through this region, the river slows down and the gradient is

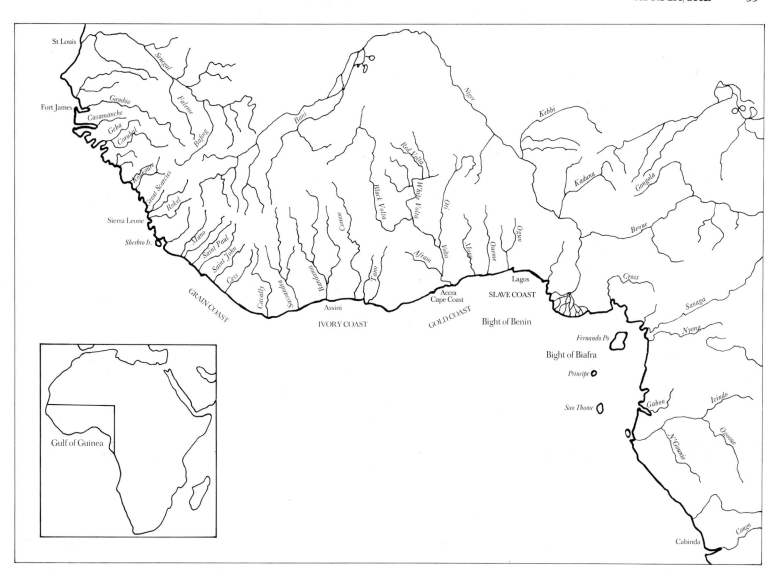

gentle. The Senegal is noted for its many distributaries; the lower section of the river both fills and receives water from Lake Guiers and Lake Rkiz. The Senegal was visited as early as the 3rd century BC by the great Carthaginian, Hanno. In 1455 Bartholomew Dias, a Portuguese explorer sailed up the river's estuary. The town of SAINT LOUIS, with a population of 50,000, was founded in 1658 by the French and has the distinction of being the nearest tropical West African port to the European continent. Below Saint Louis, the Senegal flows for a further 20 miles (32 km) behind the Langue de Barbarie, a large sandpit, before entering the sea. During high water large barges can reach as far as KAYES, 603 miles (970 km) upstream. The Senegal was one of the earliest known rivers of West Africa and in its upper reaches has great potential.

Seybouse, Algeria

The Seybouse rises approximately 20 miles (32 km) east of CONSTANTINE in northeastern Algeria. It is 145 miles (233 km) long and flows due east past GUELMA, then north to enter the Mediterranean Sea south of ANNABA.

Shangani, Rhodesia (Zimbabwe)

The Shangani rises to the south of SHANGANI in Rhodesia (Zimbabwe). It is 220 miles (350 km) long and flows northwest and west to join the Gwai River to the northwest of the town of DETT.

Shari, Zaire

The Shari begins 30 miles (48 km) due west of MAHAGI in the northwestern region of Zaire. The river is 100 miles (160 km) long and flows south-southwest and southwest passing through an extremely hot and torrid zone before joining the Ituri River below IRUMU. The Shari is a prime source for hydroelectric power for the nearby gold fields.

Shari, Chad

The lower portion of the Shari was explored in 1823 by Dixon Denham of the Oudney-Clapperton Expedition and the Frenchman Emile Gentil navigated the river to Lake Chad. The Shari or Chari is 590 miles (950 km) long and rises at the junction of the Bamingui and the Gubingui Rivers, which drain the northern Ubangi-Shari Plateau. The principal tributary of the river is the Logone River which joins it near FORT FOURREAU. Between these two rivers of central Africa are numerous channels and distributaries which spread out in all directions during the rainy season but soon after dry up leaving little or no trace of their course. This region in past geological ages was full of lush vegetation, small streams and rivers but now only a few rivers and practically no vegetation remains. This region is known as the 'Mesopotamia of the Chad,' and together the two rivers provide 915 miles (1472 km) of navigable waterway, for vessels up to a 10-ton limit. The basin is a game hunter's paradise and the freshwater fishing is among the best in the world. The river ends its journey by emptying into Lake Chad. Lake Chad is a rather remarkable lake with a length of 140 miles (225 km) and a width of 90 miles (145 km). It is not exceptionally deep, averaging between two–five yards/meters, but it takes in an area of 10,000 square miles (25,900 sq km) and is dotted with over 980 islands. The water is brackish and the majority of the lake is swampy. Lake Chad is all that remains of a once great ancient lake, which may even have been an inland sea.

Shashi, South Africa

The river rises in northeastern Botswana of South Africa. It is 225 miles (362 km) long and flows south and southeast to join the Limpopo River about 40 miles (64 km) west of the town of BEITBRIDGE.

Shebele, Ethiopia

The river rises on Mount Guramba in the

Ethiopian highlands. The Shebele flows for 1200 miles (1930 km) northeast and southeast into Somaliland, then south by BELET UEN, and finally southwest near the war-torn town of MOGADISHO to enter a large swamp approximately 25 miles (40 km) from the Indian Ocean. Although in length it should be considered one of the chief rivers of Africa, this is not the case, as the river is dry during February and March. It only runs during the rainy seasons, twice a year, and therefore cannot be considered to be a major river. In past geological times, the river probably had a large volume of water and possibly flowed into the Indian Ocean but with the many climatic changes throughout the African continent this is no longer the case.

Shire, Malawi-Mozambique
The Shire River begins at the southern end of Lake Nyasa (Malawi). It is 250 miles (400 km) long and flows due south past LIWONDE and MPIMBE into Mozambique to join the Lower Zambezi River approximately 30 miles (48 km) below the town of SENA. Its most important feature is the Murchison Falls just below Mombe.

Sierra Leone, Sierra Leone
A large estuary on the Atlantic Ocean in the western region of Sierra Leone, the Sierra Leone is 25 miles (40 km) long and between four–ten miles (6–16 km) wide. The estuary is formed by the junction of Port Loko Creek and the Rokel River 17 miles (27 km) southwest of the town of PORT LOKO.

Sobat, Sudan
Formed by the confluence of the Baro and the Pibor Rivers, southeast of the town of NASIR at the Ethiopian border, the Sobat is 205 miles (330 km) long and flows northwest past the town of ABWONG to join the White Nile River as a tributary southwest of MALAKAL in the Sudan.

Sokoto, Nigeria
Also known as the Gandi, it rises near the town of FUNTUA in northwestern Nigeria. The Sokoto is 200 miles (320 km) long and flows northwest to SOKOTO and then south to join the Niger north of BESSE.

Sondags, South Africa
The Sondags River rises north-northeast of GRAAF REINET in the southeastern region of Cape Province, South Africa. It is 250 miles (400 km) long and flows southeast to enter Algoa Bay of the Indian Ocean about 20 miles (32 km) northeast of PORT ELIZABETH, which has a population of 450,000.

Soummam, Algeria
The Oued Soummam rises in the Atlas Tellien Range, east of AUMALE in northeastern Algeria. It is 126 miles (203 km) long and flows northeast to enter the Gulf of Bejaia of the Mediterranean Sea just south of the town of BEJAIA.

Swakop, Namibia
The Swakop River rises on the plateau to the north-northeast of WINDHOEK, the capital city with a population of 38,000. It is 250 miles (400 km) long and is an intermittent river, flowing due west to enter the Atlantic Ocean at SWAKOPMUND.

Tekeze, Ethiopia
The Tekeze rises southeast of Mount Abune Yosef north of DESSYE in northwestern Ethiopia. It is 470 miles (760 km) long and flows on a northwesterly course into the Sudan to join the Atbarah River northeast of AL-QADARIF. The chief tributaries of the Tekeze are the Gheya, Tsellari and the Weri Rivers. The lower course of the river is called the Setit River and is dry nine months out of the year. At one time in past geological ages this river had a tremendous volume of water but climatic changes have made it a ghost of its once great self.

Top: Canoes on the bank of the Sokoto River in Northern Nigeria.
Above: Bond's Drift, a settlement on the Tugela River, east of Lesotho.
Above right: A native canoe, cut out of one solid log, tied up on the Ubangi River.

Tana, Kenya
The Tana rises in the Aberdare Range to the west of NYERI, a town of 10,000 in Kenya. It is 500 miles (800 km) long and flows due east and then south around Mount Kenya, a peak 17,058 feet (5203 m) high, across the famous Ngangerabeli Plain to enter the Indian Ocean at the town of KIPINI.

Tano, Ghana
The Tano rises in the Ashanti, northwest of MAMPONG in the southwestern portion of Ghana. The river is 250 miles (400 km) long and flows due south past TANOSA, the head of the river's navigational limit to enter Lagune Aby north-northwest of HALF ASSINI.

Tonj, Sudan
The river rises on the border of Uganda and flows for over 300 miles (480 km) north-northeast past TONJ and into the Sudd swamps. It then proceeds into Lake Ambadi where it joins the Jur River to form the Bahr el Ghazal.

Tshuapa, Zaire
The Tshuapa River rises southeast of KATAKO KOMBE in central Zaire. It is 600 miles (970 km) long and flows northwest past IKELA, then swings west past BOKUNGU to join the Lomela River due west of Boende to form the Busira River.

Tsiribihina, Madagascar
The river rises at the junction of several headstreams southwest of MIANDRIVAZO in western Madagascar. It is 325 miles (523 km) long and flows west to enter the Mozambique Channel.

Tugela, South Africa
The Tugela rises in the Drakensberg Range on the Lesotho border, Natal, South Africa. The river is 300 miles (480 km) long and flows east through a tremendous gorge and falls 2800 feet (854 m) in a series of large falls before passing BERGVILLE and COLENSO to enter the Indian Ocean south of ESHOWE. The principal tributaries of the Tugela are the Buffalo and the Klip Rivers.

Turkwel, Kenya
The Turkwel rises on Mount Elgon in northwestern Kenya. The river is 200 miles (320 km) long and flows north-northeast past the towns of KUCHELEBAI and LODWAR to enter Lake Rudolf.

Ubangi, Central African Republic-Zaire
The Ubangi is formed by the confluence of the Bomu and the Uele (Welle) Rivers. It is 1400

miles (2253 km) long including the Uele River. The Ubangi is also known as the Oubangui. The Bomu rises near the border of Sudan in the Central African Empire and runs for 450 miles (720 km) west before joining the Uele. The Uele begins as the Kibali River to the north of Lake Albert, in northeastern Zaire. It becomes the Uele at its junction with the Dungu River. The Uele is considered the most important of the two sources of the Ubangi, and flows west for 700 miles (1130 km) to join the Bomu at the trading center of YAKOMA. The Ubangi was discovered by G A Schweinfurt in 1870, who believed that it was a section of the Chad system, but W Junker soon substantiated its link with the Zaire (Congo). It is interesting to note that the great explorer Henry M Stanley did not even record the Ubangi on his epic trip down the Zaire. The reason for this is that the Ubangi is a very deceptive river. It enters the Zaire through a thick maze of wooded islands which conceals its various mouths. The river begins as a very

wide stream, and is navigable from Yakoma to BANZYVILLE. The Ubangi's chief tributaries are the Kolto and the Kouma Rivers. After the confluence with the Kouma, the Ubangi turns south and cuts its way through the Zongo Rapids. From Banzyville to BANGUI, the river is not navigable but at Bangui, the chief transhipment port and commercial center for the region, the river again becomes navigable. Below Bangui the Ubangi's course is filled with numerous small islands and the river is navigable for 375 miles (603 km). It joins the Zaire as its principal northern tributary at the village of IREBU, at the mouth of Irevu Channel. Lake Tumba, which is 23 miles (37 km) long and 8–12 miles (13–19 km) wide, drains through this channel into the Zaire. However, when the Zaire is in flood, the water flows the opposite way, from the river into the lake. The Ubangi is one of the most interesting rivers in central Africa and has great potential in its upper stretches.

Uele, Zaire
Also known as the Welle, it rises as the Kibali River, due west of MAHAGI in northern Zaire. The Uele is the principal headstream of the Ubangi River. It is 700 miles (1130 km) long

and flows north and northwest past TORA to DUNGU, where it is joined by the Dungu River to form the Uele. It then runs due west past BAMBILI and BONDO to join the Bomu River at YAKOMA to form the Ubangi. The Uele is one of the more important rivers of this region.

Umzimvubu, South Africa
The river rises in the Drakensberg Range of the eastern Cape Province, South Africa. It is 300 miles (480 km) long and flows due south to enter the Indian Ocean at PORT ST JOHNS. The chief tributary is the Umzimhlava River, 150 miles (240 km) long.

Vaal, South Africa
The Vaal is the northernmost headwater of the Orange River. In Afrikaans, the name means grayish-brown stream. The Vaal rises on the Sterkfontein Beacon, south of the village of BREYTEN in the southeastern Transvaal, South Africa. The chief tributaries of the Vaal are the Wilge, Riet, Valsch, Vet, Mooi, Harts and Schoonspruit Rivers. The Vaal is 720 miles (1160 km) long and flows west-southwest to become a tributary of the Orange River near the town of DOUGLAS. It serves as a boundary

between the Orange Free State and the Transvaal. The Vaal's tributaries are utilized heavily for irrigation projects, primarily for alfalfa to use for animal fodder, while the unirrigated land is used for raising cattle and sheep. The economic development of the Transvaal has not occurred in agriculture but in gold mining. The gold mines of the Witwatersrand are world famous and are only 35 miles (56 km) from the middle course of the Vaal. The discovery of gold has made the Vaal the most exploited river in the entire country. The Vaal Dam provides water for over three million people and is stored in an area of two million acres. The river is not navigable.

Volta, Upper Volta-Ghana
The Volta is formed by the confluence of the Black Volta and the White Volta Rivers in northern Ghana. It flows south to enter the Gulf of Guinea, and is 710 miles (1140 km) long. The river is seasonal. In the summer, the width of the river is half a mile (two km) and it has a depth of 45–50 feet (14–15 m); but in

sharp contrast, the river shrinks considerably during the dry season. The Volta drains the basin between the Niger and the Gambia Rivers. It has many rapids and is consequently unfit for navigation, except for its last 60 miles (97 km) below AKUSE. The mouth of the Volta is obstructed by a large bar which is dangerous to shipping. The Volta is not only the principal river of Ghana but is the country's future source of hydroelectric power.

Volta, White, Upper Volta-Ghana
The White Volta rises in Upper Volta and then flows across the border into Ghana northwest of BAWKU. It is 550 miles (880 km) long and runs south past YAPEI to join the Black Volta to form the Volta River about 38 miles (61 km) northwest of YEJI. Its chief tributary is the Red Volta River.

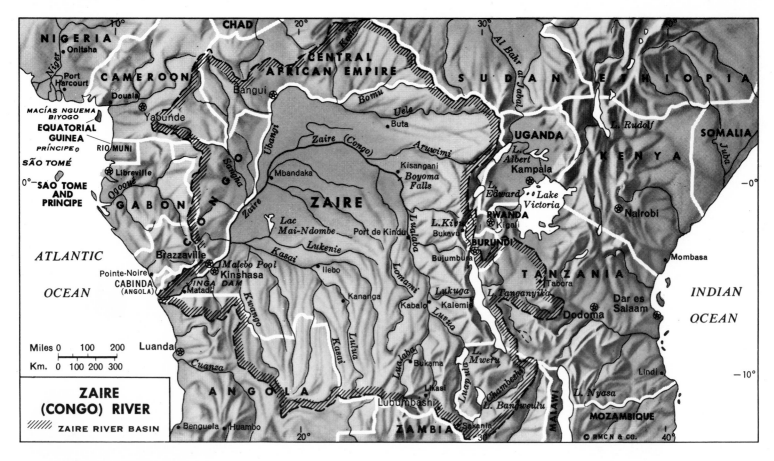

ZAIRE (CONGO) RIVER
///// ZAIRE RIVER BASIN

Zaire, Zaire

The Zaire or Congo is the largest river in Africa with a drainage basin of over 1,425,000 square miles (3,690,000 sq km), and is the second longest river in the continent with a length of 2716 miles (4370 km). The Zaire was discovered in 1482 by the Portuguese navigator Diego Cao who built a commemorative pillar at the place where he landed. It remained virtually uncharted until 1816 when Captain J K Tuckey's British Expedition made it as far upstream as ISANGILA before being forced to turn back. In 1871 Livingstone followed the course of the Chambezi River believing it to be one of the headstreams of the Nile as far as the Lualaba at NYANGWE. But the Zaire was not fully explored until 1874, when the great explorer Henry Stanley arrived at Nyangwe to start one of the greatest exploration journeys of all time. Stanley started out with 350 men, women and children and combated fever, smallpox and numerous savage tribesmen on the way to the mouth of the river. Finally after 999 days, and with only 115 of the original members surviving, the expedition reached the mouth of the Zaire, and an epic journey was completed. The source of the Zaire is the Lualaba River which rises on a plateau, 4650 feet (1418 m) high, in southeastern Katanga. The river flows north and runs through Lake Kisale to be joined by the Lufira River just before the confluence with the Luapula River. Many consider the Luapula River to be a headstream of the Zaire as well. The Luapula is called the Chambezi in Zambia, and passes through Lake Mweru and when it emerges is known as the Luvua. There are numerous spectacular waterfalls along the Luvua's course before it joins with the Lualaba. The combined rivers flow northward and receive the Lukuga River which comes in from Lake Tanganyika. At Kabalo, 50 miles (80 km) downstream, a long navigable section ends as the Lualaba passes through extremely wild rapids known as the 'Portes d'Enfer.' Over the rapids a railway bridge has been erected which runs to Lake Tanganyika, and the interested onlooker is rewarded by a breathtaking view, not equaled anywhere else in the world. The rapids run for 75 miles (121 km). The river then becomes navigable again between the towns of KASONGO and KIBOMBO. This region is savanna, and the chief crops are cotton and peanuts. The river flows through another 75 miles (121 km) of rapids before reaching its next navigable stretch in which there are no interruptions for about 190 miles (310 km) until it reaches the Stanley Falls. Once the river passes the seven cataracts at Stanley Falls, it becomes the Zaire and is navigable for 1000 miles (1600 km). The river now proceeds westward across central Africa, and passes through one of the richest equatorial forests in the world. The Zaire's chief tributaries are the Aruwimi, the Lomami, the Itimbiri and the Mongala Rivers, which enter the main stream during this middle course. The river is now over 10 miles (16 km) wide in places and is studded with numerous wooded islands as it flows north across the equator. It is joined by the Lulonga and the Ruki Rivers above MBANDAKA, and just below the town the Ubangi joins the Zaire. Shortly afterwards the river is reduced somewhat in width to between one–two miles (two–three km) and runs through a stretch which is known as the 'Chenal.' Upon reaching the town of KWA-MOUTH, the Zaire is joined by another tributary, the Kwa River. As the river expands into the Stanley Pool, the navigable portion of the river comes to an end. On opposite sides of the Pool are the cities of KINSHASA, with a

Right: Approaching Hatadi on the Zaire (Congo) River.

population of 1,500,000, and BRAZZAVILLE, with a population of 100,000. Kinshasa is the capital of Zaire, and as Leopoldville, was the old capital of the Belgian Congo. Brazzaville, on the other hand, was the old colonial capital of the French Congo. Leaving the Stanley Pool, the Zaire passes through Livingstone Falls, which is a series of 32 cataracts, and then cuts its way through the Crystal Mountains. A mile or so downstream the large port city of MATADI, (population 110,500) is located. Below Matadi the Zaire widens out to form a large estuary, and flows through a natural obstacle to navigation, the 'Devil's Cauldron,' which is a whirlpool. Early explorers and travelers could not hope to navigate this impediment. Today ocean-going vessels are able to steam upstream as far as Matadi. Further downstream is the historic settlement of BOMA, a town of 34,000, where the Zaire splits into two separate channels around Matoba Island, and then flows into its delta. The Zaire actually enters the Atlantic Ocean at BANANA POINT, which in bygone days was a large and important port, but which has since been superceded by Boma and Matadi. The reddish brown waters of the Zaire can be noticed flowing out into the Atlantic for miles. The river has a submerged submarine canyon which extends far out into the ocean. The Zaire has the honor of being the only river system in the world which flows in both the northern and southern hemispheres.

Zak, South Africa

The Zak or Sak River rises north-north-west of BEAUFORT WEST in the Cape Province of South Africa. The river is 350 miles (560 km) long

Ferries cross the Zaire (Congo) River at Kinshasa.

The waterfront of Kinshasa (Leopoldville) on the Zaire.

and flows in a continuously northward direction joining the Mottels River just southeast of KENHARDT to form the Hartebeest River. This area is prime agricultural country and is noted for its superb crops of gooseberries.

Zambezi, Angola-Zambia-Rhodesia (Zimbabwe)-Mozambique

The Zambezi is ranked fourth of Africa's rivers, is 1700 miles (2740 km) long, drains an area of nearly 513,500 square miles (1,330,000 sq km), and is the longest African river to empty into the Indian Ocean. The river rises at an altitude of 5000 feet (1525 m) in a corner of Angola, bordering Zaire and Zambia, and flows south. The upper portion of

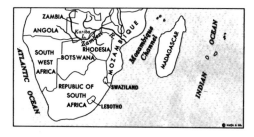

the river has long stretches of gentle gradients, alternating with short sections of rapids. During the rainy season, the Zambezi floods to a width of 20 miles (32 km), especially through the marshy plains of Barotseland. One of the most magnificent spectacles of the whole continent is VICTORIA FALLS where the Zambezi

tumbles over 400 feet (122 m) into a zigzag gorge more than a mile (1.6 km) long. Because it is so narrow at this point it was an obvious and ideal location for the construction of railway and car bridges. At one time, the stretch of the river after the Victoria Falls was one large turbulent mass for its next 600 miles (960 km) but with the construction of the Kariba Dam, the river has been largely controlled. Below KARIBA, the river is joined by two of its principal tributaries the Kafue and the Luangwa Rivers. When the river enters Mozambique, it picks up the drainage of Lake Nyasa through the Shire River. Flowing through Mozambique, the Zambezi is navigable for two long stretches separated by extensive sections of rapids. The lower course of the river is shallow and follows a shifting course surrounded by numerous sandbanks. Finally it reaches the Indian Ocean through a large and very complex delta. Exploration and colonization of the Zambezi was based on the gold and ivory available in the south-central interior. At one time the entire region was exploited by the Arab slave traders. The next to enter the area were the Portuguese. As the Portuguese influence deteriorated, the British became dominant. Livingstone attempted to open up the Zambezi basin but was stopped at the Kebrassa Rapids, located 400 miles (640 km) upstream. The man who opened up the Zambezi basin was Cecil Rhodes, after whom Rhodesia was named.

Africa's fourth longest river, the Zambezi, and its magnificent Victoria Falls.

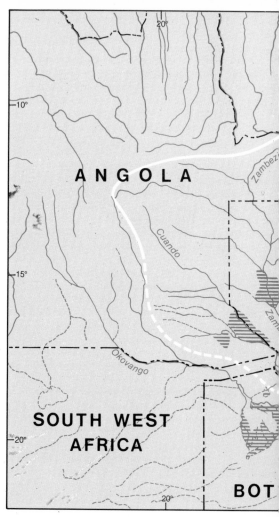

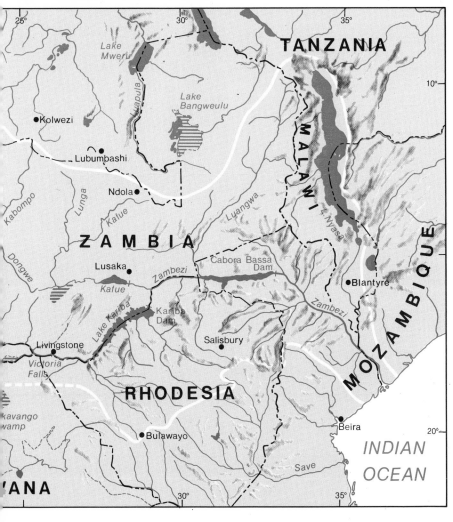

Above: An aerial photograph of the Victoria Falls on the Zambezi River.

Below: The Kariba Dam and reservoir on the Zambezi River.

Right: A waterwheel at sunset on the Euphrates River in Iraq.

Asia

Abakan, Asian USSR

The Abakan rises in the Altai Mountains of Krasnoyarsk Territory. It flows northeast for 350 miles (560 km) before becoming a tributary of the Yenisey River to the south of the town of ABAKAN.

Ab-i-Diz, Iran

This river rises in the Zagros Mountain Range of southwestern Iran. It flows south past the towns of DOW RUD and DEZFUL to join the Karun River approximately 25 miles (40 km) north-northeast of AHVAZ. The river is 250 miles (400 km) long.

Abra, Philippines

Several branches come together to form the Abra River in the mountains of Abra Province in northern Luzon. It is 55 miles (88 km) long and flows southwest to enter the South China Sea near VIGAN.

Abukuma, Japan

The Abukuma River rises northwest of SHIRAKAWA in central Honshū. It flows northeast to enter the Pacific Ocean south of SENDAI. The river is 122 miles (196 km) long.

Adonis, Lebanon

Alternatively called the Nahr Ibrahim, the Adonis rises as a substantial stream in the central region of Lebanon. It has a large volume of water for such a short river, 14 miles (23 km). Initially, the river runs through a series of waterfalls, and once through the mountains flows down an exceptionally large gorge which is totally impassable. The ancient Biblical city of BYBLOS is located near the end of the Adonis. It is over 6000 years old and was one of the chief religious and commercial centers of the ancient world. This ancient city saw the merging of the three major ancient civilizations of that day: the Egyptian, the Asiatic and the Mycenaean. During the month of February each year, the heavy seasonal rains wash so much of the local red soil into the channel that the river takes on the appearance of blood. During this period in ancient times, sacrifices were made to insure that the harvest would be good. The entire river valley is packed with old shrines, sacred groves and other religious places as well as locations with specific archeological significance. The Adonis, although short, is one of the most historical rivers in the Near East.

Afrin, Turkey

The Afrin rises in southern Turkey and for the first 35 miles (56 km) of its course runs through Syria. The river then turns back into Turkish territory and enters Lake Amik to the northeast of the ancient city of ANTIOCH. The river is 100 miles (160 km) long.

Ajay, India

The Ajay is formed by two headstreams near DEOGHAR in Bihār. It runs through the rich rice districts of Bihār. It is 160 miles (260 km) long and flows east through Bengal to join the Bhāgīrathi River at KATWA.

Agusan, Philippines

The Agusan is the largest river in Mindanao Island with a length of 240 miles (390 km). It flows from northeast of Davao Gulf in the southeastern portion of the island on a northerly course past BUTUAN to enter Butuan Bay, Mindanao Sea. The river is navigable by small vessels for over 150 miles (240 km).

Aksu, Asian USSR

This river rises in the Dzhungarian Alatau, Kazakh and flows for a total of 160 miles (260 km). It runs through desert on the initial part of its journey, then through irrigated wheatland and past AKSU before entering Lake Balkhash.

Aldan, Asian USSR

The Aldan rises in the western portion of the Stanovoi Mountain Range of eastern Siberia. The river is 1767 miles (2843 km) long and is one of the least known of the Siberian rivers. It runs north and east through a narrow valley around the Aldan Plateau, and is fed by melting snow and rain in its upper course. As the valley broadens out, the river is utilized extensively for mining and is the center for gold, mica and coal deposits. The chief tributaries are the Amga, the Timpton, the Uchur and the Maya. The river is frozen solid from mid October to May but is navigable during the remainder of the year as far as TOMMOT, a town located 1000 miles (1610 km) from the mouth. The Aldan is abundant in fish and is a primary source for hydroelectric power in the region. It becomes a tributary of another large river, the Lena, approximately 100 miles (160 km) north of YAKUTSK.

Aley, Asian USSR

Sometimes called the Alei River, it rises in the Altai Mountains and flows due west past LOKOT. The river then turns northeast to join the Ob River south of BARNAUL. It is 330 miles (530 km) long.

Amga, Asian USSR

The Amga rises on the Aldan Plateau in the southern Yakut Autonomous Republic. It flows northeast past the town of AMGA parallel to the Aldan River which it joins 170 miles (270 km) northeast of YAKUTSK. The Amga is 1000 miles (1610 km) long.

Amgun, Asian USSR

The Amgun rises in the Bureya Mountain Range in the Khabarovsk Territory. It flows for 490 miles (790 km) on a northeast course past OSIPENKO to join the Amur River above the city of NIKOLAYEVSK. The Amgun is navigable for 265 miles (426 km).

Amu Darya, USSR-Afghanistan

In the ancient world the river was known as the Oxus and as such was one of the most famous rivers of the world. Mention of the Oxus can be found in major historical works predating the birth of Christ. It is formed by the confluence of two large headstreams, the Pyandzh and the Vaksh, which both drain the Pamirs after flowing down from the glaciers on the slopes of the highest mountains in the world, the Himalayas. For the first 170 miles (270 km) the Amu Darya is the boundary between the USSR and Afghanistan and flows through a broad desert basin. In past geological ages the river had the Caspian Sea as its outlet, and this ancient course can still be traced across the wide Turkmen Desert. The river was called the Uzboy during this period when it flowed to the Caspian. It now runs northwest and is between a half mile and one mile (one and two km) wide as it flows through the deserts of central Asia before entering the Aral Sea through a huge delta. The Amu Darya runs through some of the worst desert terrain in the world, an area totally devoid of all growth. The only human habitations are built directly on the banks of the river. The river supports an extremely narrow oasis belt along its course and provides irrigation water for crops. Archeologists have determined that irrigation systems were in use on the lower course of the river since 1200 BC. Herodotus knew the wide Oxus Plain as Bactria which was mentioned in the chronicles of Alexander the Great. The entire area has been dominated by various empires over the ages, the most notable being the Persians under Darius, Alexander the Great, Caliphs of Islam and probably the greatest of them all, Genghis Khan. Zoroaster founded his religion in ancient Bactria. From the sixteenth century the Uzbek khans ruled until the Imperial Russians conquered the region in 1873. The Amu Darya supports one of the most extensive irrigation projects today and one that is continually expanding. The river is 872 miles (1403 km) long.

Amur, USSR-China

The Amur is one of the great rivers of the world and Asia. It flows for a total of 1767 miles (2843 km). The river is formed by the confluence of the Shilka and Argun Rivers and runs southeast and northeast to enter the Tatar Strait of the Sea of Okhotsk and the Sea of Japan. The river forms the border between the USSR and Communist China for most of its course. At KHABAROVSK the river turns to flow for the remainder of its course entirely through the Soviet Union until it reaches its ten mile (16 km) wide estuary which is opposite the Island of Sakhalin. Between May and November the entire length of the Amur is navigable, and because of this it is the most important waterway of the Soviet Union's Far Eastern territory. The chief tributaries of the Amur are the Amgun, Bureya, Zeya, Sungari and the Ussuri Rivers. The majority of farmland in the Soviet Union lies in the Amur and tributary Ussuri River Valleys. Also the forests which run along the river's course provide timber and furs; the neighboring area is rich in coal, iron ore, gold, lead, tungsten and graphite. The river is used to carry foodstuffs and manufactured goods down-

Right: A pleasure boat cruises along the Amur River. The river is used to transport cargo as well as passengers.

The Soviet city of Khabarovsk is located on the banks of the Amur very near the country's westernmost border with China.

stream; the goods carried upstream consist mainly of oil, lumber, fish, coal and other miscellaneous products. The Russians came to the Amur region in the 17th century – the Cossacks were the first settlers. However this area is still a bone of contention between the USSR and China. The Chinese called the Amur the Hei Ho or Black River, and in ancient times it was known as the Heilung Kiang or Black Dragon River. The wealth of the Amur has been one of the causes of the severe border clashes between the forces of China and the USSR.

Anabar, Asian USSR
The Anabar rises on the great central Siberian Plateau in Yakut Autonomous Republic. The river is 560 miles (900 km) long and flows north to the Laptev Sea in the Arctic Ocean. It is navigable for 100 miles (160 km).

Anadyr, Asian USSR
The Anadyr rises in the Kolyma Range of Siberia. It is 694 miles (1117 km) long and flows southeast past MARKOVO and ANADYR before entering the Bering Sea. The chief tributaries of the Anadyr are the Belaya and Bolshaya Rivers.

Anambar, Pakistan
See Nari, Pakistan

Angara, Asian USSR
Chief tributary of the Yenisey River, the Angara rises as the outlet of Lake Baykal, the deepest lake in the world. (It is 5300 feet (1617 m) deep in its central section.) It is navigable for practically all of its 1151 miles (1852 km), except for one 50 mile (80 km) stretch of rapids below the town of BRATSK. The chief tributaries are the Irkut, Oka, Belaya, Taseyeva and Ilim Rivers. Below the Ilim River confluence, it is sometimes called the Upper Tunguska River.

Angren, Asian USSR
The Angren rises in the Chatkal Range of the Uzbek. It is 130 miles (210 km) long, and flows west to join the Syr Darya River southeast of the town of CHINAZ.

Ankara, Turkey
The Ankara rises south-southeast of ANKARA, the capital city of Turkey. It flows due west through the city of Ankara where it meets the Cubuk River, 45 miles (72 km) long, before continuing to the Sakarya River. The Ankara is 85 miles (137 km) long.

Anyui, Asian USSR
The Anyui is formed by the confluence of the Greater Anyui River, 420 miles (676 km) long, and the Lesser Anyui River, 340 miles (550 km) long. It flows due west to enter the Kolyma River at NIZHNE-KOLYMSK. The river is very short as the Greater Anyui and Lesser Anyui do not meet until just before the Kolyma confluence.

This 1953 photograph of the Padun rapids on the Angara River shows an untamed wilderness. This is now the location of one of the world's largest hydroelectric stations, the Bratsk installation.

Aras, Turkey
The Aras River rises on Bingol Dag of Turkish Armenia. It is 550 miles (880 km) long and flows through lava plateaus to form a small section of the Soviet-Turkish border. The river was known in ancient times as the Araxes, and supported an ancient civilization, linguistically close to the Assyrians. The Aras valley also formed a part of the kingdom of Armenia which was an ally of Rome for a time. The Aras valley is believed by many to have been the location of the Garden of Eden from the Bible possibly because different varieties of fruits grow well there. Legend has it that Noah planted the first vineyard in the Aras valley. Also associated with Noah is Mt Ararat where it is believed that his ark came to rest after the flood. The Aras is really a river of many faces. It forms the border between the Soviet Union and Iran for a distance. It drains the Sevan Lake and a large portion of the Yerevan plain on the Soviet side. The river flows through a large gorge near JOLFA, which is an important railway and road crossing. After leaving the gorge, it flows across the Mughan steppe to join the Kura River near the Caspian Sea. Some of the water from the Aras does succeed in flowing into the Caspian Sea independently through a small, separate channel. During the summer the river is fordable but between March-May it is in flood and very dangerous.

Arghandāb, Afghanistan
This river rises in the Indu Kush of southern Afghanistan and is sometimes called the Arachotus River. It is 350 miles (560 km) long and flows southwest to the Helmand River at the town of LASHKAR GAH. The Arghandāb irrigates a large portion of Qandahār Province. The chief tributary is the Arghastan River.

Argun, China-USSR
The Argun rises as the Hailaerh River in the Greater Khingan Mountains of northeastern China. It flows past HAILAERH, then assumes the name of Argun for the remaining 500 miles (800 km) of its course in which it also forms the border between China and the USSR. It joins the Shilka River to form the great Amur River. The Argun runs through a region rich in silver, lead and coal deposits. The total length of the river is 950 miles (1530 km).

Atrai, Bangladesh
The Atrai rises at the foot of the southeastern Nepalese Himalayas. It flows for 240 miles (390 km) on a southerly course through a rich agricultural region of west Bengal in India and eastern Bangladesh. It finally joins the Jamuna River near BERA.

Atrek, Iran
The Atrek rises in the Turkmen-Khurasan Mountains of northeastern Iran. It is 300 miles (480 km) long and flows due west past QUCHAN to the Sumbar River then along the border to enter the Caspian Sea.

Bāghmati, Nepal-India
The Bāghmati is formed from several headstreams near KATMANDU in eastern Nepal. The river is 225 miles (362 km) long and flows south into Bihār, then turns southeast to join the Burhi-Gandak River.

Baitarani, India
The river rises in northeastern Orissa, India. It is 250 miles (400 km) long and flows due north to the boundary of Bihār before turning southeast to join the Brāhmani River. It then flows into the Bay of Bengal.

The Atrek River serves as a boundary between the Soviet Union and Iran for part of its course.

Baksan, Asian USSR
The Baksan rises at the foot of Mt Elbruz, in the Greater Caucasus Mountains in the Kabardian Autonomous Republic. It flows northeast to join the Malka River. Chief tributaries are the Chegem and Cherek Rivers. It is 100 miles (160 km) long and supports a large hydroelectric station near BAKSAN.

Banās, India (1)
The Banās rises in the Arāvalli Range in eastern Rajasthan, India. It is 310 miles (500 km) long and flows east to join the Chambal River near Sheopur.

Banas, India (2)
This Banas River rises east of SIROHI, Bombay in the southern Arāvalli Range of India. It is 169 miles (272 km) long, and flows into the Little Rann of Cutch to the southwest of RADHANPUR.

Bang Pakong, Thailand
Called the Prachimburi River by some natives, it rises in the San Kamphaeng Range of southern Thailand. It is 125 miles (201 km) long and flows on a winding course through the industrial heart of Thailand to BANG PAKONG on the Gulf of Siam.

Barok, India
See Surma, India

Barguzin, Asian USSR
The Barguzin rises on the Vitim Plateau of Buryat-Mongol Autonomous Republic. It is navigable for the last 160 miles (260 km) of its course. The river is 437 miles (703 km) long and flows southwest to enter the deepest lake in the world, LAKE BAYKAL.

Barito, Indonesia
The Barito rises south of the Sarawak border of central Borneo and flows south past BANJERMASIN to enter the Java Sea. The river is 550 miles (880 km) long.

Bassac, Cambodia-South Vietnam
The Bassac forms one of the many branches of the Mekong Delta. During the Vietnam War, the USAF occupied a small tactical airbase at Binh Thuy, a short distance from CAN THO CITY, the fourth largest city in the country. The Bassac flows for 200 miles (320 km) southeast to enter the South China Sea near SOC TRANG.

Bassein, Burma
The Bassein is the westernmost mouth of the great Irrawaddy River in Lower Burma. It is 200 miles (320 km) long and branches off north of HENZADA to flow south-southwest to enter the Andaman Sea. The river is called the Ngawun River in its upper course.

Beās, India
Also called the Biās, it rises at an altitude of over 13,000 feet (3965 m) in the Punjab Himalayas and is one of the five great rivers of the Punjab. The Beās is 325 miles (523 km) long and flows due south through the Kulu Valley, then swings west and south-southwest to join the Sutlej River. The Beās was the eastern limit of Alexander the Great's invasion in 326 BC. It was here that the great commander turned back towards his homeland only to die on the journey.

Beisug, Asian USSR
The Beisug rises northwest of KROPOTKIN in the Krasnodar Territory. It is 110 miles (180 km) long and flows northwest to Beisug Liman, which is a 20 mile (32 km) long lagoon of the Sea of Azov.

Beji, Pakistan
See Nari, Pakistan

Belaya, Asian USSR (1)
This Belaya River (see below) rises in the southern Ural Mountains of Bashkir Autonomous SSR near Iremel Mountain. It is 882 miles (1419 km) long and flows southeast past BELORETSK, then swings due north to the town of STERLITAMAK, and finally northwest to join the Kama River. The chief tributaries are the Ufa, Sim, Dema and Syun Rivers.

Belaya, Asian USSR (2)
This Belaya River rises on the Fisht Peak of the Greater Caucasus Mountains of the Krasnodar Territory. It is 125 miles (201 km) long and runs north past the town of MAIKOP then heads north-northwest to join the Kuban River just east of KRASNODAR. The Belaya has a unique 30-square-mile (78 sq km) reservoir near its mouth.

Bernam, Malaysia
The Bernam rises on the Pahang border in western Malaysia. The river is 100 miles (160 km) long and flows along the Perak-Selangor border. The chief tributary is the Slim River. It passes TANJONG MALIM and HUTAN MELINTANG before entering the Malacca Strait.

Betwa, India
The Betwa rises in the Vindhya Mountain Range, Bhopāl, central India. The Betwa is very important to the region because it supplies a large proportion of the hydroelectric power to the Jhānsi district at DUKWAN and DEOGARH. The river is also utilized to irrigate the fields without which a large part of the population would starve. The Betwa is 380 miles (610 km) long and flows northeast to join the Yamuna River near the town of HAMIRPUR.

Bhāgirathi, India
This Indian river rises in a glacier west of Kumaun Himalayas, India. It runs for 120 miles (190 km) passing the towns of GANGOTRI, TEHRI and DEVAPRAYAG. At Devaprayag it is joined by the Alaknanda River, which is 75 miles (121 km) long, to form the Ganges. The Bhāgirathi River is one of the most sacred rivers in India and is treated with the utmost respect.

Bhavāni, India
The Bhavāni River rises in Western Ghāts of southwest Madras near Coimbatore. It flows for 110 miles (180 km) east-northeast to the Cauvery River at the town of BHAVANI. Its chief tributary is the Moyar River, 90 miles

(145 km) long, which joins it near SATYA-MANGALAM.

Bhima, India
The Bhima rises northwest of POONA in Western Ghāts, India. The chief tributaries are the Mutha Mula, 80 miles (129 km) long, the Kagna, 70 miles (113 km) long, and the Nira, 110 miles (180 km) long. The river itself is 450 miles (720 km) long and runs southeast through the center of BOMBAY, then southwest to HYDERABAD to join the Kistna River north-northwest of RAICHUR.

Biās, India
See Beās, India

Biryusa, Asian USSR
The Biryusa River rises in the eastern Sayan Mountain Range in south Krasnoyarsk Territory. It is also called the Ona River. The Biryusa is 468 miles (753 km) long and flows north and northwest to join the Chuna River, 600 miles (960 km) long, to form the Tasayena River. The Tasayena flows 72 miles (116 km) east-southeast to join the Angara River, 50 miles (80 km) long slightly above the confluence with the Yenisey River, one of the largest rivers of Asia.

Black, China
The Chinese call the Black, the Hei Chiang. It rises at a height of 4000 feet (1220 m) in Yunnan Province of China and flows parallel to the Red River through a series of deep canyons. It is 500 miles (800 km) long, and eventually joins the Red River east of VIET-TRI. Note to readers: The Amur River of Asian USSR was called the Hei Ho or Black River by the Chinese before the USSR established dominance in the area. (See Amur, USSR-China for details.)

Bolshaya, Asian USSR (1)
This Bolshaya River rises in the Kamchatka Peninsula and flows southwest to the town of UST-BOLSHERETSK. It is joined by the Bystraya River to form a large lagoon which widens out to the Sea of Okhotsk. The river is 125 miles (201 km) long.

Bolshaya, Asian USSR (2)
This Bolshaya River rises in the Koryak Range of Siberia. It is 185 miles (298 km) long and flows into Anadyr Bay of the Bering Sea.

Botoma, Asian USSR
The Botoma rises in the northwest Aldan Plateau of southern Yakut Autonomous SSR. It is 300 miles (480 km) long and runs north-northeast to join the Lena River above the town of POKROVSK.

Brāhmani, India
The Brāhmani is formed by the confluence of the, Sankh and South Koel, east of RAJ GANGPUR in Orissa, India. It is over 300 miles

(480 km) long and flows south-southeast initially, then swings due east to enter the Bay of Bengal at PALMYRAS POINT together with the Baitarani River.

Brahmaputra, China-India-Bangladesh
The Brahmaputra is one of the great rivers of the world; it is also called the Tsingpo. The name Brahmaputra in Hindu means, 'son of Brahma.' Its two headstreams rise on a glacier near the Tibetan mountain pass of Mariam La. There were arguments and controversy between many explorers concerning the source of the Brahmaputra. In fact, numerous stretches were still unexplored until 1924 when Captain F Kingdon Ward pressed ahead of his colleagues and discovered the source of the river. The river's chief tributaries are the Tsangpo, the Chu, the Kyi and the Nyanh Chhu Rivers. It is one of the most remarkable inland waterways in the world. Small vessels (coracles) navigate it for 400 miles (640 km) at an incredible altitude of 12,000 feet (3660 m) above sea level. The Brahmaputra is 250 miles (400 km) longer than the Ganges. Rice and sugar cane grow on permanently banked fields around the villages as the river flows through northern India. The river is extremely vulnerable to earthquakes which are known to be quite frequent in this part of the world. It is

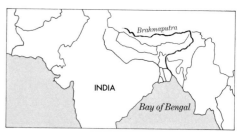

a matter of record that in 1935 during a severe quake, the river actually flowed backward for a few seconds, an event which caused havoc in the surrounding countryside. In the upper regions of the river, navigation has not even today resumed its prequake importance. Furthermore because the Brahmaputra forms a large portion of the boundary between India and Bangladesh, it has become difficult to reach joint agreement on its possible full-scale utilization. Attempts are being made by both countries as they realize that the Brahmaputra is essential to both countries' economies. A tributary of interest is the Tīstā, a right-bank river which at one stage in its history, flowed to the Ganges. The Brahmaputra now reaches its deltaic stage: it dispatches distributaries carrying huge amounts of silt and water to the joint delta. The Brahmaputra contributes more alluvium to the delta area than the Ganges. The river is 1800 miles (2900 km) long and drains an area in excess of 361,000 square miles (935,000 sq km). The river separates to form the Jamuna, which flows south, while the Brahnaputra flows southeast past JAMALPUR to join the Arial Khān. It joins the Meghna River in draining the former course in Mymensingh and the neighboring hills. The combined channel is in fact now an estuary and is named the Meghna. The entire landscape of the delta region is amazingly complex – an ever-changing maze of shifting channels, small pools in hidden hollows and long deserted stream courses. The delta supports crops of rice, numerous vegetables and jute, and is one of the most densely settled rural regions in the world. The only problem occurs during the rainy season when the floods come; the resulting damage is often severe and the loss of life is sometimes exceedingly great.

Brantas, Indonesia
This Indonesian river rises near the southeast coast of Java in the mountains. It runs north and east to its delta in the Madura Strait south of SURABAYA near the mouth of the Kali Mas River.

Bureya, Asian USSR
The Bureya rises in the northern Bureya Mountain Range of southwestern Khabarovsk Territory. It is 445 miles (716 km) long. It flows south-southwest through the large Bureya coal deposits, then past the town of CHEKUNDA to join the Amur River. This region is noted for its gold, tungsten and molybdenum deposits.

Burhi Gandak, India
The Burhi is formed by the confluence of several headstreams to the south of MOTIHARI, Bihār, India. The river is over 200 miles (320 km) long and runs on a southeasterly course to join the Ganges River near MONGHYR.

Cagayan, Philippines
The Cagayan is the largest river in the Philippines. It is 220 miles (350 km) long and rises in the high northern mountains of northern Luzon, 35 miles (56 km) south-southeast of the town of BAYOMBONG. The chief tributaries are the Magat which joins near HAGAN and the Chico which flows 140 miles (230 km) from north-northeast of BAGUIO, the summer capital of the Philippines,

to join 26 miles (42 km) south of APARRI. The climate in the Cagayan basin is governed by the monsoons and by the shape of the mountains. It is navigable for small rivercraft for approximately 70–150 miles (113–240 km) depending upon the state of the river. Upon reaching Aparri, the chief port on the river and the center for the export of rice and tobacco, the Cagayan then flows into the Babuyan Channel of the Luzon Strait.

Calti, Turkey
The Calti rises in central Turkey. This small river flows eastward to become a tributary of the Euphrates River northwest of the town of KEMALIYE. It is 73 miles (117 km) long.

Cau Song, Vietnam
The Cau Song rises near BAC-CAN in Northern Vietnam. It is linked to the much larger Red River by several channels. It is 200 miles (320 km) long and runs southeast past the towns of THAI-NGUYEN and BAC-NINH. On its lower course, below Bac-ninh, the river changes names and becomes the Thaibinh River until it empties into the Gulf of Tonkin.

Cauvery, India
Sometimes spelled Kaveri, this Indian river rises on Brahmagiri Hill in the Western Ghāts and is one of India's sacred rivers. It is 475 miles (764 km) long and flows unnoticed eastward, then northeast and east-southeast. Upon reaching KRISHNARAJASAGARA, 12 miles (19 km) from the city of MYSORE, the Cauvery is dammed to form a large reservoir. The waters from the reservoir are utilized to supply the Irwin irrigation canal. Just below the dam are the Brindavan Gardens, a famous tourist attraction. Reaching Sivasamudram Island, the river falls over the Cauvery Falls, a drop of 320 feet (98 m), and during the rainy season it is 1000 feet (305 m) wide. There are large hydroelectric stations located nearby which were originally built to provide the gold fields

at KOLAR with sufficient power to operate heavy equipment. The river then flows through a series of wild gorges until it reaches Hagenakel Falls. Crossing the Indian state of Madras, the river flows through a narrow gorge near SALEM, where one of the largest dams in the world, the METTUR DAM is located. This dam holds a huge lake encompassing an area of 60 square miles (155 sq km) by a wall 5300 feet (1617 m) long and 176 feet (54 m) high. The river splits into two branches slightly above TRICHONOPOLY, at Srirangam Island which is the principal pilgrimage center for the river. The Cauvery is sacred to the Hindus and is sometimes called the Ganges of the South. Both branches flow on to form a common delta which has been irrigated since the 11th century.

Ceyhan, Turkey
The Ceyhan rises in the Anti-Taurus Mountain Range of southern Turkey. Its chief tributaries are the Ergenez River, 125 miles (201 km) long, and the Goksu River, 115 miles (185 km) long. The river flows past the towns of ELBISTAN and CEYHAN to enter the Gulf of Iskenderun just southeast of the city of ADANA.

Chambal, India
The Chambal rises near the crest of the Vinhya scarp, 20 miles (32 km) southwest of INDORE in Madhya Pradesh, and flows down the northward slope of the lava plateau of Malwa. The chief tributaries are the Sipra, Kali, Parbati and Sindh Rivers. The Chambal and its tributaries are surrounded by jungle-saturated ravines. On reaching KOTAH, the river takes a relatively straight course north towards the Yamuna River. The actual confluence is somewhat delayed as usual in the case of rivers flowing across such large alluvial plains. The Chambal parallels the Yamuna for close to 70 miles (113 km) before actually joining it. The Chambal is 550 miles (880 km) long.

The Cauvery River of India

Changjin, North Korea

This river rises in North Korea and flows northeast to join the Yalu River below Changbai in Manchuria. It is 160 miles (260 km) long.

Chao Phraya, Thailand

The Chao Phraya is the principal river of Thailand. It is formed by four streams in the northern hills of Thailand. The four streams – the Ping, the Wang, the Nan and the Yom Rivers – join in pairs and then join at NAKHON SAWAN to form the Chao Phraya River. The river is 140 miles (230 km) long and flows slowly across the great central plain of Thailand. The river has managed to raise itself above the plain and the surrounding region is one of the great rice-growing areas of the world. Various branches of the Chao Phraya shoot off along the course to the sea. The Tha Chin River leaves the main river above the town of CHAINAT and flows on a basically parallel course before entering the Gulf of Siam at SAMUT SAKHON. The Lop Buri, on the other hand, leaves the river below SINGBURI and flows east but rejoins the main river about 75 miles (121 km) further downstream. Of particular interest for the historian or archaeologist are the magnificent Khmer temples and 17th-century royal palaces along the Lop Buri. The Chao Phraya continues on course and passes through BANGKOK, the capital of Thailand and one of the most fascinating cities in the world. The Chao Phraya is now navigable to the Gulf of Siam by ocean-going vessels. One of the principal tourist sights in Bangkok is the beautiful Temple of Dawn which is located on the

Above: Sunrise over the Bhima River near Poona, India.

Top right: The Cauvery River near Thanjavur in southern India.

Far right bottom: One of the many temples passed by the Chao Phraya River of Thailand.

Right: The sacred Brahmaputra as it flows through Assam province in India.

banks of the Chao Phraya. Residents of Bangkok use the river and its many canals much as the peoples of Venice and Amsterdam use theirs. Temples and houses and shops made out of ornately carved teak line the banks of the Chao Phraya.

Charysh, Asian USSR
The Charysh rises in the Altai Mountains. It flows through a region rich in copper and lead-zinc ores. The river is 268 miles (431 km) long and runs west-northwest past CHARYSHSKOYE and northeast past BELOGLAZOVO to enter the Ob River.

Chaya, Asian USSR
The Chaya rises at the junction of the Parbig and Bakchar Rivers in the Tomsk Oblast. It is 110 miles (180 km) long and runs northeast to the Ob River. It is navigable.

Chenāb, Pakistan
The Chenāb is one of the five rivers of the Punjab. The principal headstream of the Chenāb is the Chandra River which rises in the Great Himalayas and flows south-southeast. The river is 650 miles (1050 km) long and runs northwest through the Himachal Pradesh to cross into Kashmir. It continues on course until it reaches KISHTWAR where it changes direction, now flowing south and west around the Pir Panjāl. The river runs southwest through West Punjab, Pakistan, and is joined by the Jhelum which flows from the north, and the Rāvi which comes in from the east. Together these three rivers form the Trimab

and flow southwest to join the Sutlej just east of the town of ALIPUR. These four together with the Beās, the chief tributary of the Sutlej, form the Five Rivers of the Punjab or Panjnad. The area surrounding these rivers is well populated and utilized extensively to grow wheat, rice, cotton, sugar and oilseeds, as well as other various small crops.

Cherchen, China

The Cherchen rises in central Kunlun in southern Sinkiang Province, China. It is 300 miles (480 km) long and flows northeast past the town of CHERCHEN to border the Takla Makan Desert. It joins the Tarin River west of the Lob Nor Basin.

Cheyyar, India

The Cheyyar rises in the Javādi Hills of central Madras. It is 120 miles (190 km) long and flows northeast through rich agricultural land to join the Palar River southeast of WALAJAPET.

Chientang, China

The Chientang is formed by the confluence of two main branches at LANCHI in Chekiang Province, China. The river is also known as the Tsientang. It is 285 miles (459 km) long and flows north-northeast past CHIENTE and FUYANG to enter Hangchow Bay below the city of HANGCHOW, which has a population of over 1,225,000.

Chi, Thailand

The Chi River rises in the Dong Phaya Yen Range of eastern Thailand. The Chi is 250 miles (400 km) long and runs northeast and southeast through the Korat Plateau to the Mun River north of UBON RATCHATHANI.

Chialing, China

The Chialing rises in the Shensi-Kansu border region south of TIENSHUI, China. It is over 600 miles (970 km) long and flows due south through the Shensi and Szechwan Provinces to join the Yangtze River at the city of CHUNGKING which has a population of over 3,500,000.

Chico, Philippines

The Chico rises north-northeast of the mountain capital of the Philippines, BAGUIO, in northern Luzon. The river drains a rich tobacco region. It is 140 miles (230 km) long and runs northeast to join the Cagayan River approximately 25 miles (40 km) south of APARRI.

Chikoy, Asian USSR

The Chikoy rises in the Borshchovochny Mountain Range, Chita Oblast, in the Buryat-Mongol Autonomous SSR. It flows north and east to join the Selenge River. The Chikoy is 350 miles (560 km) long.

Chikugo, Japan

The Chikugo rises in the mountains of central Kyūshū, Japan. The river is sometimes called the Tikugo. It is 88 miles (142 km) long and flows northwest, then west and finally southwest to enter the Amakusa Sea, just southeast of SAGA. The Chikugo runs through and drains a large rice-growing area of Kyūshū.

Chindwin, Burma

The source of the Chindwin is made up of several streams which run off the Kumon and Patkai Ranges in the northern extremes of Burma. They flow through one of the most densely forested, sparsely populated regions in the world. The Chindwin flows south for the majority of its course. It passes through SINGKALING, HOMALIN, MAWLAIK, KALEWA and MONYWA before joining the Irrawaddy River to the northeast of PAKOKKU. The river is 500 miles (800 km) long, and is navigable for 380 miles (610 km) as far as Homalin by flat-bottomed steamers during the rainy season. In the dry season, the river is only navigable as far as KINDAT, a distance of 240 miles (390 km). The lower reaches of the Chindwin are heavily populated, well cultivated and quite flat compared to the upper stretches of the river.

Ching, China

Formed by the confluence of two headstreams near ENSHIH in southwest Hupeh Province, the Ching River is 150 miles (240 km) long. It runs due east to join the Yangtze River at ITU.

Chip Chap, India

See Shyok, India

Ch'ongch'ōn, North Korea

The Ch'ongch'ōn rises in the mountains of Pyongan Province, North Korea. The river is 124 miles (200 km) long and flows southwest into Korea Bay.

Choshui, Taiwan

The Choshui rises in the central mountains west-northwest of the town of HWALIEN. It is the longest river in Taiwan with a length of 102 miles (164 km). It flows southwest and west to enter the Formosa Straits.

Chu, Asian USSR

The Chu rises in western Terskei Alatau in two branches. It is over 700 miles (1130 km) long and flows due north past KOCHKORKA and through the reservoir at Boom Gorge. Then it swings west-northwest along the foot of the Kirkhiz Range before turning north and west through the Kazakh steppes. It enters a small salt lake but the waters of the Chu all but evaporate before reaching this tiny outlet.

Chulym, Asian USSR

The Chulym rises in the Kuznetsk-Alatau Range of Siberia at a height of 6500 feet (1980 m) above sea level. The river is the chief right bank tributary of the Ob River and is 1177 miles (1894 km) in length which makes it one of the longest rivers in Siberia. It flows due north passing the towns of BOGOTOL and BIRILYUSSY, then swings west-northwest past ASINO to join the Ob River near MOGOCHIN. The river is navigable below ACHINSK but freezes over by the end of October. The river flows rapidly from its source to Achinsk, but then splits up into various channels and a short distance downstream assumes the normal characteristics of a steppe river with numerous sandbanks and bends. The river is quite wide due to the island-like sandbanks between the channels and during the rainy season the valley is subjected to severe flooding.

Chumysh, Asian USSR

The Chumysh rises in the northern Altai Territory of the USSR and is formed by the confluence of two headstreams on Salair Ridge. It is 380 miles (610 km) long and runs west to join the Ob River west of BARNAUL.

Chusovaya, Asian USSR

The Chusovaya is formed by the confluence of two headstreams from the Ural Mountain Range in the Sverdlovsk Oblast. Major tributaries are the Koiva, 112 miles (180 km) long, Usva, 120 miles (190 km) long, and the Sylva 390 miles (630 km) long. It flows through the central Urals on a northwesterly course before swinging west through CHUSOVOY to join the Kama River. The river is navigable seasonally and is 480 miles (770 km) long.

Clear, China

The Clear River rises in Yunnan Province, China at a height of 4000 feet (1220 m). It is 250 miles (400 km) long and flows south-southeast into North Vietnam to join the Red River at the town of VIET-TRI.

Coruh, Turkey-USSR

Also called the Tchoruk, the Coruh rises on Mt Mescit, west of ERZURUN. It flows northeast into the USSR and empties into the Black Sea. The river is 229 miles (368 km) long.

Dadung, Vietnam

See Dong-nai, Vietnam

Dāmodar, India

The Dāmodar begins in Chota Nagpur Plateau of Bihar and West Bengal. It is over 340 miles (550 km) long, and runs east and southeast past RANIGANJ and BURDWAN before turning southwards in several channels to join the Hooghly River southwest of CALCUTTA. The chief tributaries are the Konar-Bokaro River and Barakar River. The 8500 square mile (22,015 sq km) Dāmodar Valley is one of India's principal mining districts and hydro-electric sources.

Dasht, Pakistan

The Dasht River rises in Central Makrān Range of Baluchistan in western Pakistan. It is 265 miles (426 km) long and runs west past the town of TURBAT, then southwest to Gwatar Bay

Right: The Chusovaya River in the Urals.

on the Arabian Sea. It is an intermittent river. Its chief tributary is the Nihing River.

Daubikhe, Asian USSR
The Daubikhe rises in several headstreams in the Sikhote-Alin Range, Maritime Territory, USSR. It is 175 miles (282 km) long and flows north to join the Ulukhe River to form the Ussuri River.

Deduru Oya, Sri Lanka
The Deduru rises northwest of KANDY in Ceylon. It is 87 miles (140 km) long and flows northwest and west to the Indian Ocean.

Delice, Turkey
The Delice rises on the Akdag mountain range in central Turkey. The river runs for 120 miles (190 km) first west and then north to enter the Kizil River.

Dhasān, India
The Dhasān begins in the Vindhya Range, East Bhopāl, central India. It is 235 miles (378 km) long and runs due north to join the Betwa River south of ORAI.

Diyālā, Iran-Iraq
The Diyālā rises in Kurdistan, western Iran as the Sirvān River. It is 275 miles (442 km) long and flows into Iraq to join the Tigris River at DIYALA just southeast of BAGHDAD. This region is one of the centers of ancient Mesopotamia.

Diz, Iran
See Ab-i-Diz, Iran

Dong-nai, Vietnam
The Dong-nai rises in the Annamese Cordillera in South Vietnam as the Dadung River. It is over 300 miles (480 km) long and flows west on its initial course, then changes to a southerly direction, passing BEN HOA to form a joint delta with the Saigon River on the South China Sea.

Dzabkhan, Mongolia
The Dzabkhan rises on the southern slopes of the Khangai Mountain Range of the Mongolian People's Republic. It runs south and northwest for 500 miles (800 km) to enter Airik Nor Lake.

Dzhida, Asian USSR
The Dzhida rises in the eastern Sayan Mountains of the southern Buryat-Mongol Autonomous Republic. The river is 300 miles (480 km) long and flows on an eastward course to join the Selenge River to the south of the town of SELENDUMA.

East, China
Alternatively known as Tung Kiang, the East River rises in two branches in the Kiulien

Mountains of southern China. It is 250 miles (400 km) long and flows southwest and west past LAOLUNG, HOYUN and WAIYEUNG to enter the Canton River delta. Its chief tributary is the Tseng River.

Etsin Gol, China

This Chinese river is formed by the confluence of the Peita and the Hei Rivers at TINGSIN, Kansu Province in northwestern China. The river is also called the Jo Shui. It flows northeast through Inner Mongolia to a huge lake-like depression on the Outer Mongolian border. It is 200 miles (320 km) long.

Euphrates, Western Asia

The Euphrates is one of the most famous and best-known rivers of the ancient world. Along with the Tigris, it formed the ancient 'Land Between the Two Rivers' and was the location of one of man's earliest recorded civilizations.

This 'Land Between the Two Rivers' gave rise to Sumerians, Chaldeans, Babylonians and Assyrians to name but a few of the ancient peoples of Mesopotamia. The Euphrates historically can be rated with the Nile, the Indus and the Huang Ho (Yellow) Rivers as the great givers of life to the first civilizations of the world. The Euphrates is the largest river in Western Asia, and has a length of 2235 miles (3596 km). The ancient Sumerians called it *Buranunu*, the Babylonians, *Purattu*, and the Old Persians, *Ufrat*, all of which when translated mean 'Great River.' The present name of the river dates from around 450 BC. The Euphrates rises in the mountains north of ERZURUM in Turkey, and flows through a series of gorges for the majority of its upper course. The river is called the Kara Su or Firat Su in Turkey, and near the town of MALATYA is joined by Murat Su, the longest left-bank tributary of the river. The Euphrates then leaves the mountains of Turkey and flows across into Syria. It then runs through a narrow trench-like depression bordered by the desert on both sides. Next the river reaches the ancient crossing place of THAPSACUS, used by marauding hoardes and armies for thousands of years. It was used by Xenophon and the 'Ten Thousand' Greeks on their great march and again by Alexander the Great in 321 BC on his magnificent advance through ancient Mesopotamia. The river then turns southwest and maintains this direction for the remainder of its course. The Euphrates was the outer-limit boundary of the Roman Empire under the Emperor Trajan. Further downstream in Syria, the river is joined by two left-bank tributaries, the Balikh and the Khabur Rivers, the last tributaries of the Euphrates. Just beyond the Iraqi border huge cultivated islands are located where large water wheels

lift the precious water from the river to irrigate the nearby fields. The ancient town of HIT which provides bitumen for building today, also supplied bitumen to build the city of BABYLON. Between the towns of Hīt and RAMADI, the Euphrates slowly enters its delta, although still 450 miles (720 km) from the sea. It shares this magnificent alluvial lowland with its sister river, the Tigris; they merge into one channel as far as MUSEYIB. The Euphrates then splits into two branches, the Hindiya and Hilla, for a short distance but becomes a single channel once again at SAMAWA. The river continues on course southwest through Lake Hammar until it reaches the Shatt al-Arab. The river is navigable but the shallowness of Lake Hammar deters large vessels from making an attempt to navigate further upstream. Located on the banks of the Hilla is the ancient city of Babylon, reckoned by some historians to be even greater than Rome. The two holy cities of KARBALA and NEJAF are located west of the Hindiya branch. This entire region of the Euphrates is literally covered with ancient relics and historical sites; one of the most famous is the great Sumerian city of UR, the oldest site in the entire delta area. Shooting off from the Euphrates are large irrigation canals. Some of these canals are extremely ancient and have become derelict but undoubtedly date back to a time when this region was heavily populated and far more developed than it is now. Ancient man, 3500 years ago, turned this region into one of the

The Euphrates River near Siverek in Turkey.

garden spots of the world; today it is a sparsely populated region, virtually a desert. The canals still in use or newly built help to irrigate the nearby fields. The chief crops in this region are cotton, rice, dates and barley.

Fen, China

The Fen rises in the Luya Mountain Range of Shansi Province, China. The river is largely navigable and is 430 miles (690 km) long. It flows south-southwest across the province of Shansi to Sinkiang, then continues to join the Huang Ho River at HANCHENG.

Fu, China

Sometimes called the Suining, the Fu rises on the Kansu border of Szechwan Province. Partly navigable, the river is 350 miles (560 km) long. It runs southeast past the towns of PINGWU, CHANGMING and SUINING to join the Chialing River at HOCHUAN.

Fuji, Japan

The Fuji rises in the mountain ranges of central Honshū near KOFU. The Fuji River flows southward for 100 miles (160 km) past the great mountain of Japan, Mt Fujiyama, which is 12,389 feet (3779 m) high, before entering Suruga Bay.

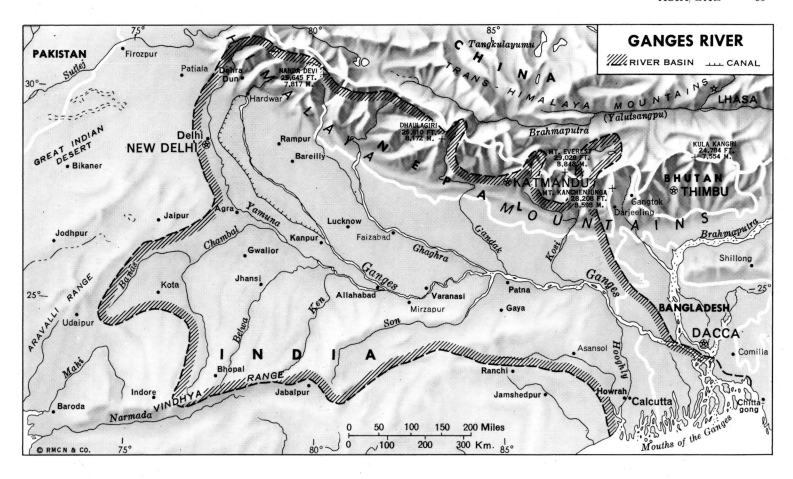

Gal Oya, Sri Lanka

The Gal Oya River rises in the eastern Ceylon hill country to the east of the town of BADULLA. The river is only 62 miles (100 km) long and flows first north, then eastward to enter the Indian Ocean.

Ganges, India

One of the great rivers of India, the Ganges rises at the junction of the Bhāgirathi and the Alaknanda Rivers at the sacred town of DEVAPRAYAG in northern India. The Alaknanda is the greater of the two headwaters, and rises north of Nanda Devi near the border of Garhwal and Tibet. Although the smaller of the two, the Bhāgirathi is considered to be the true source of the Ganges; it rises in an ice cave in the Gangotri glacier at a height of 10,300 feet (3142 m). The Ganges forces its way through the Siwaliks and emerges at HARDWAR where it is slightly over one mile (two km) wide. Hardwār is the scene of great pilgrimages every seventh and fourteenth year as these are especially sacred to the Hindus. The headworks of the Upper Ganges Canal system is also located at Hardwār in the form of a large barrage for lifting water into the canals. The Ganges has a relatively narrow flood plain, but one which has been intensively cultivated for centuries. The Hardwār barrage lifts water from the present river channel to spread it over large alluvial deposits which the river has laid down along its ancient courses and secondary channels for irrigational purposes. This large plain of the Ganges is well developed and heavily populated. It is also spanned by many railway and road bridges. The Ganges passes through the princely capitals of FARRUK-ABAD

and KANAUJ, then on to the great industrial city of KANPUR (Cawnpore), with a population of 1,175,000. The river is slightly incised into the alluvial cone between Kānpur and ALLAHABAD, the latter with a population of 550,000. At Allāhābād the Ganges is joined by one of its chief tributaries, the Yamuna River. This river junction is a sacred one in the eyes of the Hindus, and they believe that a third sacred spiritual river, the Saravasti joins this confluence. In Hindu the name of the city is Prayag, or the 'Place of Sacrifice.' The Ganges is one of India's great rivers not only for volume and length, but for its religious value to the Hindu people. However, there are other great rivers in northern India whose alluvial fans and cones are greater than those of the Ganges: for instance, the Jumna, the Sarda, the Chambal, the Son, the Gogra, the Gandak and the Kosi Rivers are equal to or larger than the Ganges and are of equal economic or commercial import but yet they do not have the religious significance and therefore not the fame. For the majority of the year, the Ganges is a normal, large river but with the coming of the monsoons in June, added to the melting of the snow on the Himalayas it becomes a raging torrent, spreading its flood waters across the narrow flood plains of the basin. Flowing from Allāhābād, the Ganges takes an easterly course, meandering towards the northeastern portion of the peninsular block where it bends around the Rājmahāl Hills before turning southeast into its delta. The chief flood plain tract of the Ganges is between Allāhābād and the river's great southern curve. This plain extends for 400 miles (640 km) in length and is between 10–50 miles (16–80 km) wide in places. This area is heavily populated and one

of the principal rice-growing regions of India. Ancient cities mark the former courses of the river, and meanders, levees, cut-offs, and other features of a flood plain can be found. The Ganges flows through the holy city of BENARES or VARANASI, which has a population of over 620,000, and its banks are lined with temples. Pilgrims of the Hindu faith come from all over India to pray and bathe in the Ganges, wash in the sacred well of Vishnu, which is supposed to have been dug by the god himself and filled with the sweat of his toil. The city is also held in reverence by the Buddhists because it was at Benares that Buddha taught the 'Eightfold Path.' The Ganges continues on to pass once-important river ports and administrative and commercial centers such as BALLIA, GHAZIPUR, PATNA, MONGHYR and BHAGALPUR. The delta of the Ganges begins approximately 220 miles (350 km) from the sea. The Ganges is 1557 miles (2505 km) long, and drains a basin of 188,800 square miles (488,990 sq km). The chief distributary, the Jamuna, flows southeast to join the main Brahmaputra channel, and carries the bulk of the Ganges' water. The channel continues as the Padma, joins the Meghna and finally enters the Bay of Bengal through four separate and distinct mouths. It is ironic that this great river which begins in the high, clean-aired glacier of Gangotri is destined to end its journey in a dirty, muddy, over-populated river delta.

Gazimur, Asian USSR

The river rises in the Nerchinsk Mountain Range of the Buryat-Mongol Autonomous Republic. It is 250 miles (400 km) long and flows north-northeast to join the Argun River,

itself 65 miles (105 km) long, above the
confluence with the great Amur River.

Gediz, Turkey

Also called the Sarabat, the Gediz rises in the
Mural Dag Mountains of western Turkey. It
flows southwest and then west past the towns
of MANISA and MENEMEN to enter the Gulf
of Smyrna near the town of FOCA. It is 215
miles (346 km) long.

Ghaggar, India

The Ghaggar River rises in the Siwalik Range
of Himchal Pradesh in India. It is 215 miles

*Sunrise over the Ganges River at Varanasi
(Benares).*

Three scenes of the Ganges as it passes through the city of Varanasi (Benares). The top photo shows the Ghāts at dawn.

(346 km) long and flows in a southwesterly direction to approximately nine miles (14 km) west-southwest of SIRSA where it feeds two large irrigation canals. At one time the Ghaggar was much longer, over 400 miles (640 km) in length, and was the ancient link between the Indus and the Ganges River systems. It is also linked to Hindu mythology as one of the famous lost rivers of India. The ancient course of this river is extremely interesting to follow for both the amateur and the experienced geologist.

Gharraf, Shatt al, Iraq
Rising in southeastern Iraq, the Gharraf is a connecting channel between the Tigris and Euphrates Rivers in the ancient 'Land Between Two Rivers.' It leaves the Tigris at AL-KUT IMARA and then flows south to the Euphrates after traveling slightly over 70 miles (113 km). It is utilized primarily for irrigation.

Ghātprabha, India
The Ghātprabha River rises in Western Ghāts to the south of the great city of BOMBAY, India. It flows for 140 miles (230 km) east-northeast to join the Kistna River past the town of GOKAK. The river has a large hydroelectric station which provides the region with cheap electricity.

Ghaznī, Afghanistan
The Ghaznī rises in the far Hindu Kush of Afghanistan. It is 100 miles (160 km) long and flows south before emptying into the Ab-e-Istādeh-ye Moqor, a salt lake.

Gilgit, India
The Gilgit begins on a high glacier in the Punjab Himalayas of India. It is 150 miles (240 km) long and runs north, east and southeast before joining the Indus River as a tributary, north of BUNJI.

Gin Ganga, Sri Lanka
Gin Ganga rises in southwestern Sri Lanka east of DENIYAYA. It flows 70 miles (113 km) on a west and south-southwest course before running into the Indian Ocean at GINTOTA.

Girna, India
The Girna rises in Western Ghāts, central Bombay, India. It runs for a total distance of 200 miles (320 km), east, northeast and finally west-northwest before becoming a tributary of the Tāpi River, south of the town of CHOPDA.

Godāvari, India
One of India's sacred rivers, the Godāvari rises in the Western Ghāts about 80 miles (129 km) north-northeast of BOMBAY. The river is 900 miles (1450 km) long and flows southeast down the eastern slopes of Western Ghāts. It continues eastward crossing Hyderābād through a highly cultivated region. Continuing eastward, the river runs through the alluvial plains of Paithan and Nander, then runs

southeast again along the borders of Hyderābād to force its way through the Eastern Ghāts into Madras through a steep gorge. The river flows through the northern Circars, which were ruled by the kings of Golconda in 1575 and for a short time by the French. The Mogul Emperor granted it to the East India Company shortly afterwards. Upon reaching the town of RAJAHMUNDRY, the river begins to form its delta. The Godāvari is a sacred Hindu river and there are shrines at TRIMBAK, BHADRACHALAM and Rājahmundry. The river ends at the Bay of Bengal.

Gogra, Tibet-Nepal-India
The Gogra rises in the Great Himalayas south of Lake Manasarowar in Tibet. It is 600 miles (970 km) long, has a catchment area of 10,000 square miles (25,900 sq km) and flows through the Siwalik foothills near RAJAPUR in Nepal, then across the border into India. The Gogra is also known as the Chagra. For some unknown reason it has not built up an alluvial cone like its sister rivers the Rāpti and the Sārda. The Gogra flows between the two cones of these sister rivers in a shallow gutter-like channel. This region is sparsely populated compared to the densely-peopled plains to the east and west. The Gogra ends its run as a tributary of the Ganges.

Gokase, Japan
The Gokase River rises in eastern Kyūshū, and runs for 83 miles (134 km) on a southeasterly course into the Hyūga Sea of the Pacific Ocean at NOBEOKA.

Goksu, Turkey
Also called the Gok, it rises in the Taurus Mountain Range of southern Turkey. The river runs for 150 miles (240 km) southeast past SILIFKE before entering the Mediterranean Sea. During the Crusades Frederick Barbarossa, Emperor of the Germans, attempted to cross the Goksu River unaided and was drowned.

Gomati, India
The Gomati rises in Uttar Pradesh, India and flows for over 500 miles (800 km). It runs southeast past the famous town of LUCKNOW, then SULTANPUR and KIRAKAT to become a tributary of the Ganges River near SAIDPUR.

Greater Naryn, Asian USSR
See Naryn, Asian USSR

Gorgān, Iran
The Gorgān rises in the Ala Dagh of northeastern Iran. It is utilized primarily for irrigation projects. It is 150 miles (240 km) long and flows west to the southeastern corner of the Caspian Sea.

Gundlakamma, India
This Indian river begins in northeastern Madras in the Eastern Ghāts of India. It flows northeast past the Cumbum Reservoir, then

swings southeast past ADANKI to enter the Bay of Bengal east of ONGOLE. The river is 140 miles (230 km) long.

Hab, Pakistan
The Hab rises in the Pab Mountain Range of southeastern Baluchistan. The river is 250 miles (400 km) long, and flows south-southeast initially, then turns to a south-southwest course, flowing along the Sind border to enter the Arabian Sea north of Cape Muān.

Hagari, India
This river is formed by the confluence of two small headstreams southeast of KADUR. The river actually rises in the Baba Budan Range, Mysore, India, and flows for 100 miles (160 km) as the Vedavati River. Once past the town of HIRIYUR, it becomes the Hagari River, and flows for a further 170 miles (270 km) to enter the Tungabhadra River west-northwest of ADONI.

Halīl, Iran
The Halīl River rises south of KERNAN in the Zāgros Mountain Range of southeastern Iran. It is 200 miles (320 km) long and runs southeast to the large salt lake depression known as Jaz Mūriān.

Hailar, China
See Argun, China

Han, China
The Han rises in southern China on the Fukien-Kiangsi Province border. The river is 210 miles (340 km) long, and flows in a southerly direction into Kwangtung Province. The Han is navigable for 100 miles (160 km) upstream from its mouth. It enters the South China Sea after forming a delta.

Han, Korea
The Han rises over 100 miles (160 km) east of SEOUL, the capital of South Korea. It flows 292 miles (470 km) on a southwest course, then moves northwest past CH'UNGJU and Seoul before entering the Yellow Sea at Kanghwama Island. Chief tributary is the Pukhan River, itself 110 miles (180 km) long. The river is navigable by small vessels for slightly over 185 miles (298 km). During the 1950–51 Korean War, the river was the scene of intense fighting between US and Communist Forces.

Han Shui, China
This Han begins in Shensi Province, China. The river is 750 miles (1210 km) long, and

flows east-southeast into Hupeh Province. It is navigable only during the summer season and is subject to very severe flooding. It joins the Yangtze River at WUHAN.

Hari, Indonesia
The Hari rises in the Padang Highlands of South central Sumatra. It is also known alternatively as the Jambi or Djambi River. The river is navigable for 55 miles (88 km) from its mouth to the town of DJAMBI. It has a total length of 250 miles (400 km), and runs northeast past Djambi to enter the Berhala Strait of the South China Sea.

Hari Rūd, Afghanistan
The Hari Rūd rises in Koh-i-Baba Mountain Range and runs through Turkmen SSR, Iran and Afghanistan. On its upper course it is known as the Tedžen River, and irrigates one of the richest agricultural regions of Herāt Province in Afghanistan. The river is over 700 miles (1130 km) long, and runs due west initially, then swings north to disappear under the sands of the Kara-Kum Desert.

Harşit, Turkey
The Harşit rises in the Gumusane Mountains of northeastern Turkey. The Harsit is 83 miles (134 km) long, and runs northwest to enter the Black Sea near TIREBOLU.

Hārūt Rud, Afghanistan
Alternatively known as the Adraskand, Hārūt Rud rises approximately 80 miles (129 km) southeast of HERAT in western Afghanistan. It is 250 miles (400 km) long, and flows southwest to the Hāmūn-e-Sābārī Lagoon in the Sistan depression.

Hei Chiang, China
See Black, China

Helmand, Afghanistan
The Helmand is 700 miles (1130 km) long, and is the largest river to flow entirely within the borders of Afghanistan. It rises in the western slopes of the Paghman Mountains in the Hindu Kush, approximately 35 miles (56 km) due west of KABUL, the capital of Afghanistan and which has a population of 475,000. The upper reaches of the river are barren and unpopulated. It flows through a sparsely populated area called Hazāra, which is peopled by the descendants of the Mongol hordes of Genghis Khan. The Helmand Valley is fertile and divides the desert wastes of Sistan on the west from the deserts of Rīgestān on the east. Below the town of GIRISHK, at Qala Bist, the river is joined by the Arghandāb, Arghastān and Tarnak Rivers. The Helmand swings in a great loop through the desert area, westward through RŪDBĀR, then northwest through KILA-E-FATH to enter the marshy Sistan lake depression. This large depression is really a lagoon which is 70 miles (113 km) long in the rainy season but is only the size of a few small lakes in the dry season. It sits on the Iran-Afghanistan border, and was quite large in past ages.

Hingol, Pakistan
The Hingol rises in the central Brahui Range south-southwest of KALĀT, in Baluchistan, west Pakistan. The river is the longest in Baluchistan at 350 miles (560 km). It flows due south through the gorge which Alexander the Great utilized in 325 BC in the Makrān Coast Range, to finally enter the Arabian Sea east of the town of ORMĀRA.

Hoang Ho, China
See Huang Ho, China

Hooghly, India
The Hooghly River is an arm of the Ganges delta and is formed by the confluence of the Bhāgīrathi and the Jalangi Rivers at NABAD-WIP. It forms the western boundary of the Ganges delta. The Hooghly is 160 miles (257 km) long, and flows into the Bay of Bengal. From the town of HOOGHLY, north past CALCUTTA for 18 miles (29 km) to the sea, the river is navigable, the center of one of the most industrialized areas in India which provides for 50 percent of the population of West Bengal. Between Calcutta and Hooghly are the large towns of NAIHATI, BHATPARA, CHANDAN-NAGAR, BARRACKPORE and BARANAGAR; and this stretch of river saw prosperous English, Dutch, Portuguese, French, Danish and Austrian settlements thrive until the complete domination of the region by the English at Calcutta in 1692. Calcutta became important because ocean-going vessels can navigate for 120 miles (190 km) up the estuary. Calcutta was the capital of British India until 1910 and the headquarters of the East India Company.

Hotien (Hhotan), China
The Hotien rises in two headstreams in the Kunlun Mountains of southern Sinkiang Province. It is 400 miles (640 km) long and flows north through the Takla Makan Desert. The river is intermittent and in a good year sometimes reaches the Tarim Danya.

Hovd, Mongolia
The Hovd rises in the Altai Mountains of western Mongolia. The river is 330 miles (530 km) long, and flows east past ULEGEI and southeast to Lake Khara Usu near JIRGALANTA.

Hsi, China
The Hsi is the longest river in southern China with a length of 1300 miles (2093 km). It constitutes South China's principal river artery, and has a drainage area of over 150,000 square miles (400,000 sq km). It is to South China what the Huang Ho and the Yangtze Rivers are to the North. The river rises in eastern Yunnan Province as the Pahtah Ho River, and flows south initially, then turns north to the Kweichow border. It changes its name to the Hungshui or Red River, and flows around the Kweichow-Kwangsi border for approximately 160 miles (258 km) before bending southeast to run through central Kwangsi and Kwangtung. The chief tributaries of the Hsi Kiang are the Yu or Hsiang,

which rises also in Yunnan Province and flows parallel to the main channel, before swinging in a huge bend to join the Hsi 100 miles (160 km) above the city of WUCHOU, at KWEIPING; the Liu and the Kwei Rivers. Hsi Kiang means West River in Chinese to set it apart from the Pei Kiang or North River and the Tung Kiang or East River. The three rivers all converge on the Cantonese delta. The Hsi Kiang is used to describe the entire basin of the river which rises in Yunnan, while the Kweichow tableland and Chu Kiang refer to the eastern branch of the Hsi Kiang downstream from CANTON. The upper reaches of the Hsi Kiang are sparsely populated mountainous country, and the opposite of the lowlands through which the river flows in its lower reaches. The lowlands of the Hsi Kiang are one of the most heavily populated regions in China. The chief western course of the Hsi enters the sea just west of MACAO. The majority of the delta region lies between the Hsi and the Chu Kiang, the latter being the eastern course of the river, between both of these outlets, an area of 1500 square miles (4000 sq km) is covered. The principal port on the Hsi Kiang is Canton with a population of 2,500,000, it has been the chief port of China for over 2000 years and was the main point of contact with the rest of the known world. The river is navigable for a large part of its course, except for those places which are obstructed by rapids and falls.

Hsiang, China
The Hsiang rises at HAIYANGPING and flows through a series of deeply cut valleys in Kwangsi Province, China. It is 715 miles (1150 km) long, drains an area of 37,000 square miles (95,830 sq km) and flows in its upper course through mountainous terrain ranging from between 3000–4000 feet (915–1220 m) high. Reaching the town of LINGLING the river enters its middle course and is joined by the Tao River. Below HENGYANG the extensive lowlands take over from the hilly terrain. The river is now joined by its chief tributaries the Lei, Mi and the Chungling Rivers. The region surrounding the river is one of intensely cultivated rice fields which always bring in a bumper crop. The Hsiang has an easy and gentle gradient making it a joy to navigate for large steamers and small vessels alike. Finally the Hsiang enters the much larger Yangtze through a shallow storage lake, Tungting Lake. The valley of the Hsiang is the main link between south and central China, and with the Kiangsi is the major route for migratory people moving southward. The most important town on the river is the provincial capital of CHANGSHA, which is also the commercial and trading center of the region.

Huai, China
It rises in the Tungpeh Mountains of central China. The Huai is 600 miles (970 km) long, and flows east-northeast past Honan and Anhwei Provinces to enter Hungtze Lake.

Huang Ho, China
Also known as the Hwang Ho and the Yellow River, it is the second longest river in China, with a length of 2901 miles (4668 km). The

Huang Ho has its source west of Kyaring Nor and Ngoring Nor, two lakes situated in the highlands of Tsinghai, at an altitude of over 14,000 feet (4270 m). The river links both lakes together and then flows eastward into neighboring Kansu Province. Upon reaching the city of LANCHOU, which has a population of 1,750,000, it turns northeast to Ningsia, then north through the fabulous Great Wall of China and into Inner Mongolia. It changes direction yet again, running eastward and passing the town of PAOTOU, before swinging south again and through the Great Wall for the second time. The Huang Ho is the border between Shensi and Shansi Provinces, and flows east toward the city of KAIFENG, which has a population of 345,000, then turns northeast to wind across the North China Plain. Because the silt has been deposited on the river bed, the river level is constantly rising which has resulted in the river becoming a wide but shallow channel. Numerous dikes have been built to reclaim some of the land previously inundated by the river but this has only limited the silt deposition to the actual channel. The result has been that the surface of the Huang Ho is many feet above the plain through which it flows – during the low season it is approximately 15 feet (5 m) higher, and in the rainy season it is more than 35 feet (11 m) higher. The Huang Ho threatens the countless hundreds of thousands of people who live along it. When the snows melt high in the mountains near the source and the monsoons

Left: The Howrah Bridge over the Hooghly River at Calcutta.
Below: Sunset on the Hooghly River taken from Strand Road in Calcutta.

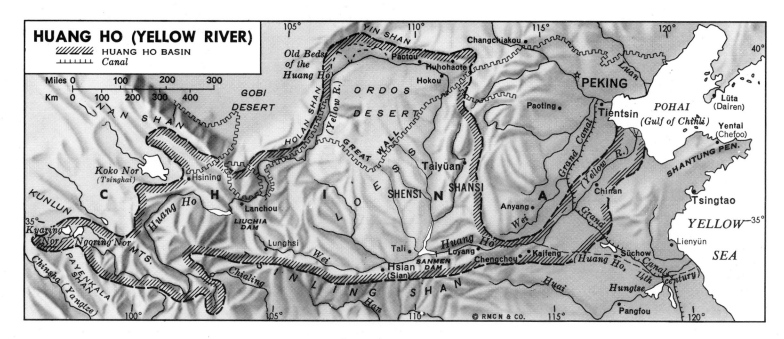

HUANG HO (YELLOW RIVER)
////// HUANG HO BASIN
⊥⊥⊥⊥⊥⊥ Canal

come, then the dikes are breached and a flood let loose on the defenseless plain. The great floods which have occurred in this basin have earned the river the names of 'The Scourge of the Sons of Han,' 'China's Sorrow' and 'The Ungovernable.' The Huang Ho has changed course quite a few times during recorded history: first in 602 BC; then in 1194, when it flowed into the Yellow Sea north of Shantung; in 1853 when it ran into the Gulf of Chihli; in 1938 it was diverted as a defensive maneuver to its former mouth in the East China Sea; and 1947 when the river once again was re-routed to the Gulf of Chihli. The river is virtually unnavigable except for a few sections, between TUNGKUAN and HOKOW, and for approximately 30 miles (48 km) upstream from the mouth. The Huang Ho is too shallow and wide. Although the Huang Ho has sustained millions of Chinese for at least 6000 years, no large cities have developed along its course, except for Lanchou and Kaifeng. The river runs across SHANTUNG and enters the Yellow Sea through the Gulf of Chihli, just north of the Shantung Peninsula. The chief tributaries of the Huang Ho are the Fen, the Lo, and the Wei Rivers. At the confluence of the Wei-ho, the Huang Ho moves through the Tungkuan gorges, which form the historic gateway into the rich and fertile lowlands of North China. A large dam has been built here to store water and control the flow of the river to impede the massive flooding of the lower river. The river deposits gargantuan loads of yellow-colored silt along its course, and this is where it has derived its name. The first great Imperial dynasties of ancient China were established in this region, and the capital was located at Hsian, only a short distance from the Huang Ho. The river has many historic associations and is still one of the natural assets of North China.

Huang-Pu, China
The Huang-Pu rises in a network of canals in the Kinshan area in southern Kiangsu Province, China. Alternatively known as the Whangpoo or Whampoa, it is 60 miles (97 km) long and flows northeast and north past the city of SHANGHAI, which has a population of 8,500,000, to join the Yangtze River at Wa Sung. Ocean-going vessels travel up a large canal as far as Shanghai.

Hulun, China
The Hulun rises in the Lesser Khingan Mountains of central Manchuria. The river is over 250 miles (400 km) long, and flows southwest and south through a prosperous agricultural district before joining the Sungari River below the farming town of HAILAERH (HULUN).

Hung Ho, Vietnam
See Red, Vietnam

Hungshui, China
See Hsi Kiang, China

Hunza, India-Pakistan
The Hunza is formed by the confluence of two small headstreams which flow out of northern Karakoram in northern Kashmir. It is 120 miles (190 km) long, and flows south, west and south to become a tributary of the Gilgit River east of the town of GILGIT.

Huto, China
The Huto rises on the northern slopes of the Wutai Mountain Range in northeastern China. Alternatively known as the Tzeya, it flows due south and then east before joining the Pai River near the famous city of TIENTSIN. The river is over 400 miles (640 km) long, and runs through Shansi and Hopeh Provinces on its way to the Pai.

Ichamatic, India-Bangladesh
See Jumuna, India-Bangladesh.

Idenburg, Indonesia
See Taritalu, Indonesia

Iderijn, Mongolia
The Iderijn rises in the Khangai Mountains of Mongolia. It runs 281 miles (450 km) on an east-northeast course before joining the Mörön River to form the Selenge River approximately 35 miles (56 km) southeast of Mörön.

Ilek, Asian USSR
Rises in the Mugodzhary Mountains northeast of KANDAGACH. The river is 330 miles (530 km) long, and flows north and northwest to join the Ural River at the town of ILEK. This river is not navigable.

Ili, Asian USSR
This medium-sized river flows for a total of 540 miles (870 km) from its source in the Tien Shan Mountains. The Ili is formed at the confluence of the Kunges, which is 140 miles (230 km) long, and the Tekes, which is 270 miles (430 km) long; both rivers meet 65 miles (105 km) due east of KULDJA. The Ili flows west past the town and then heads northeast through a sandy desert and forms a small delta as it enters Lake Balkhash, approximately 320 miles (510 km) due west of the Chinese boundary. This region is not densely populated and communications are still poor; but Kuldja is the chief commercial center of the Ili River Basin and even boasts a small airport. The Ili is navigable in its middle section to BAKAMAS; and its principal tributaries are the Kaskelan and the Chilik Rivers. Mining is done on a small scale along the lower slopes of the Tien Shan and oil fields in the area are being expanded, although realistically speaking the yields will never be great.

Ilim, Asian USSR
The Ilim rises in the Ilim Mountain Range of the Irkutsk Oblast, USSR. It is 225 miles (362 km) long, and flows due north through the Angar-Ilim iron ore region to join the Angara River near the town of BADARMA. It is partly navigable for 125 miles (200 km) below the town of ILIMSK.

Indigirka, Asian USSR

The river rises on the Oymyakon Plateau in Yakut at the confluence of two small mountain streams. It is 113 miles (182 km) long, and one of the many large rivers of Siberia. The Indigirka flows northward across the plateau, running through several mountain ranges and is an untapped hydroelectric resource. It flows over an extremely rocky bed which causes rapids and makes the floating of timber down river impractical. Once past the rapids, the speed of the river drops and it becomes wider and deeper. It is joined by its two principal tributaries the Moma and the Selennyach Rivers shortly afterwards. The river is navigable as far as the confluence with the Moma. Its level fluctuates and is high in the summer and low in the winter. During the winter months, when it freezes over, the water in the channel is frozen solid for large stretches of the river. This entire region is sparsely inhabited; but the river is extremely rich in fish, and the valley has many natural resources which are being rapidly developed, lumber and fur to name the two most important. The river finally enters the East Siberian Sea through its delta which has many channels, the largest being the Srednii, the middle channel.

Indragiri, Indonesia

Alternatively known as the Kuantan, it rises in the Padang Highlands of central Sumatra, Indonesia. The river is 250 miles (400 km) long, and runs due east to the Berhala Strait of the South China Sea.

Indus, Tibet-Pakistan

The Indus is 1800 miles (2900 km) long, drains 372,000 square miles (963,500 sq km), has a catchment area of 103,000 square miles (266,800 sq km) and is by far the greatest river in the Indian subcontinent. The huge Indus Plain was the home of one of the earliest civilizations in the world between 2500–1500 BC. This rich region has always lured invaders down from the north and the west. The most

notable was Alexander the Great, who in 325 BC defeated a local army but chose not to follow up his victory and returned to Persia. The Indus civilization centered around two large and highly developed cities, MOHENJO-DARO and HARAPPA, and over 100 towns of various sizes. The river has its source high in the glaciers of the Kailas Range at a height of 17,000 feet (5185 m). The Indus runs northwest into central Kashmir through a tremendous cleft two miles deep between Karakoram and the Himalayas. It then turns southwest almost at the borders of the Soviet Union. The Indus then forces itself through an enormous gorge three miles (five km) deep and succeeds in pushing through the Great Himalayas west of Nanga Parbat. Emerging from the mountains at a height of 1100 feet (335 m) at ATTOCK, it receives the waters of the Kabul-Swat river

The Lloyd Barrage (bars placed in a watercourse to increase its depth for irrigation) at Sukkur on the Indus River.

systems. Now the Indus becomes a many-channeled, ever-changing river which during flood peaks carries over 60 times the low water flow. The river deposits a tremendous load of sandy alluvium along its course which is extremely susceptible to wind erosion and deposition. The braided flood plain of the Indus runs either due south or southwest. About 50 miles (80 km) from the Indus and running parallel to it, is the dry and ancient bed of the Ghaggar River. This practically unknown ancient river bed may be followed for slightly over 400 miles (640 km) northwest to HISSAR in the Punjab; and this dried-up river bed is the only remnant of a link which existed in past geological times between the two great river systems of the Indus and the Ganges. West of the flood plain is a huge desert, the only farming done is around the fertile oases,

using dams to catch whatever water runs down from the Kirthar and Brahui Ranges. In modern times, various schemes have been concocted to fully utilize the obvious power of the Indus but most of them have been fraught with disaster. In 1929 the British who were the rulers of India, built the huge Lloyd Dam at SUKKUR which helped to irrigate an area of 5,500,000 acres. The huge benefits of this stupendous project were undermined by subsequent errors; seepage from the extremely permeable canal beds led to a high watertable, resulting in waterlogging. Immediately the

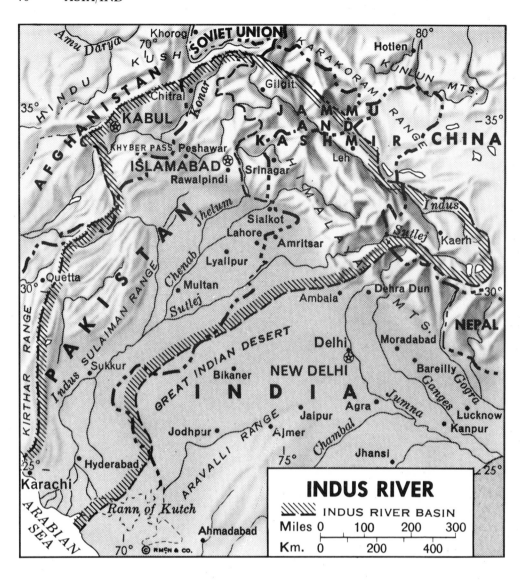

incidence of malaria shot up, as this marshy region became a prime breeding ground for the mosquito. The majority of the problems have been successfully dealt with but only through stubborn perseverance. Unlike the Nile, the Indus has its great delta at its beginning and upon reaching the Arabian Sea is dominated by the extreme desert-like conditions surrounding it.

Ingoda, Asian USSR

The Ingoda River rises in Borshchovochny Range of the Chita Oblast, USSR. It is over 500 miles (800 km) long, and follows a northeasterly course before joining the Onon River to form the Shilka River approximately 15 miles (24 km) above the town of SHILKA.

Inya, Asian USSR

The Inya rises in the central Kuznetsk Basin of the USSR. The river is 331 miles (533 km) long, and flows west-northwest to join the Ob River above NOVOSIBIRSK.

Irrawaddy, Burma

The principal river of Burma, the Irrawaddy rises in several headstreams in the hilly, evergreen forests on the borders between Burma and China. The actual beginning of the

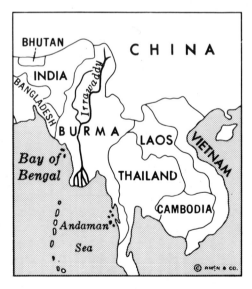

main stream is the confluence of the Mali Hka and the Nmai Hka. The Mali is narrow, deep and approximately 150 yards (138 m) wide above the confluence with the Nmai, and navigable by river launch upstream for 45 miles (72 km). The Nmai is some 400 yards (368 m) wide but is not navigable. From the confluence to the sea the Irrawaddy runs through hilly terrain, until it reaches the large terraced plains of the dry zone close to MANDALAY. The river runs due south initially

Top and above: Two views of the Indus River as it flows over the flood plain.

Top right: This aerial view of the Irrawaddy shows the patchwork nature of the surrounding farmland.

through a region covered in tropical evergreens, then a deciduous monsoon forest famous for its teak until it reaches the river port of BHAMO. This city was the start of the ancient trade route to Yunnan in China. The Irrawaddy swings west to its junction with the Kaukkwe River, then it turns south again, running on this course as far as Mandalay practically in a straight line. It is now a powerful river with a current to be reckoned with; the river steamers can navigate as far as MYITKYINA, although there are three rough spots which have to be taken carefully. These rough areas are in reality defiles which range from 250 feet (76 m) in depth and 100 yards (92 m) wide to 40 miles (64 km) long, 50 yards (46 m) wide between cliffs which rise from 60 feet (18 m) upwards. The river passes the ancient imperial capital of Mandalay which is dominated by the famous Golden Pagoda. Just six miles south of Mandalay, is AVA, the ancient capital of Burma which is situated in Sagaing district on the left bank of the Irrawaddy, where the Myitnge River joins the main river.

It was the last royal capital of Burma and is now only a desolate site. Now the river swings westward, diverted from a former course in the Sittang Valley by recent geological action in the form of severe volcanic activity. The river flows through beautiful villages, the majority of the small houses being built on stilts in large orchard gardens. Each separate village is capable of supporting itself and has its own crops of rice, fruits and various vegetables. The next major tributary to join the Irrawaddy is the Chindwin, which is a major river in its own right and navigable for slightly over 200 miles (320 km). During the reconquest of Burma during World War II this region saw some of the hardest fighting in the theater. The delta of the Irrawaddy is the great Rice Bowl of Asia and provides Burma with its largest export. The river has now completed its run from the mountains and enters the Andaman Sea. The Irrawaddy is 1300 miles (2090 km) long, its delta over 150 miles (240 km) wide and has a catchment basin of 158,500 square miles (410,500 sq km).

The Irtysh River in Siberia supplies hydroelectricity.

Irtysh, Asian USSR

The Irtysh rises in the glaciers of the southwestern slopes of the Altai Mountains in Sinkiang Province, China. It flows initially as the Black Irtysh due west to enter Lake Zaysan, which is 60 miles (97 km) long and covers an area of 700 square miles (1810 sq km). On leaving the lake it becomes the Irtysh and heads north and northwest, flowing through a flat steppe region, with low banks, before it turns west cutting its way through the western Altai Mountains. It passes the town of SEMIPALATINSK, then flows through the western Kulunda steppe and past the towns of PAVLODAR and TOBOLSK, and enters the Ob River at Khanty-Manisk. Between Pavlodar and Tobolsk is the most important town on the river, OMSK, which is the chief administrative center of western Siberia. Hydroelectric resources are outstanding on the Irtysh, it is extremely rich in fish, and numerous minerals are found throughout its basin – gold, silver, and coal to name but a few. The chief affluents of the Irtysh are the Bukhtarma, Om, Narym, Tara, Osha, Ishim, Konda, Tobol and Vagai Rivers. The river is navigable during the summer from the Ob confluence to Semipalatinsk by steamer, and to Lake Zaysan by small vessels. The Irtysh is 2640 miles (4250 km) long, including the Black Irtysh, and drains a basin of 616,000 square miles (1,595,400 sq km).

Iset, Asian USSR

The Iset begins in the central Ural Mountain Range northeast of Bilimbai in southwestern Siberia. The Iset is 330 miles (530 km) long, and runs southeast to join the Tobol River south of YALUTOROVSK.

Ishikari, Japan

The Ishikari is the second longest river in Japan at 227 miles (365 km). It rises on Asahidake in western Hokkaido and flows due west to enter the Sea of Japan at the town of ISHIKARI.

Ishim, Asian USSR

The Ishim rises north of KARAGANDA in the Kazakh SSR, and is the largest left bank tributary of the Irtysh River. The Ishim is 1123 miles (1807 km) long, and flows due west past ATBASAR, then swings north past PETRO-PAVLOVSK, then on to the Ishim Steppe to join the Irtysh River approximately 110 miles (180 km) east-southeast of TOBOLSK. The chief tributaries of the Ishim are the Nura and the Koluton Rivers.

Izhma, Asian USSR

The Izhma rises in the south Timan Ridge of the Komi Autonomous Republic. It is 320 miles (510 km) long and runs north to become a tributary of the Pechora River at UST-TSILMA.

The river is navigable for 190 miles (310 km) below the great oil fields of UKHTA.

Jambi, Indonesia

See Hari, Indonesia

Jamuna, India-Bangladesh

The Jamuna River is approximately 100 miles (160 km) long and joins India's Brahmaputra River to Bangladesh's Ganges River near its mouth. The river, like its two fellow rivers is regarded as sacred by the citizenry. The Jamuna breaks away from the Brahmaputra near BAHADURABAD GHAT, forms a wide flat river and joins the Ganges near DACCA. It is navigable for its entire length.

Jhelum, Pakistan

The Jhelum rises in the Pir Panjāl Range of Pakistan. This river is the westernmost of the five great rivers of the Punjab. It is 480 miles (770 km) long and runs northwest through the Vale of Kashmir and Wular Lake, then it turns west, south and finally southwest past JHELUM CITY to join the Chenāb River.

Jinzū, Japan

The Jinzū rises west of Mt Hotaka in central Honshū. It is 78 miles (126 km) long, and flows west-northwest past TOYAMA to enter

The Jordan River entering the Sea of Galilee (above), and two aerial photographs (right and below) showing the lush valley and the Jordan River snaking through the arid wastes.

Toyama Bay, an inlet of the Sea of Japan. It is also called the Zinzū River on its upper course. Hydroelectric plants along the upper course provide a substantial amount of the region's electric power.

Jordan, Israel
The Jordan is the great river most often mentioned in the Bible and means so much historically that it defies adequate description.

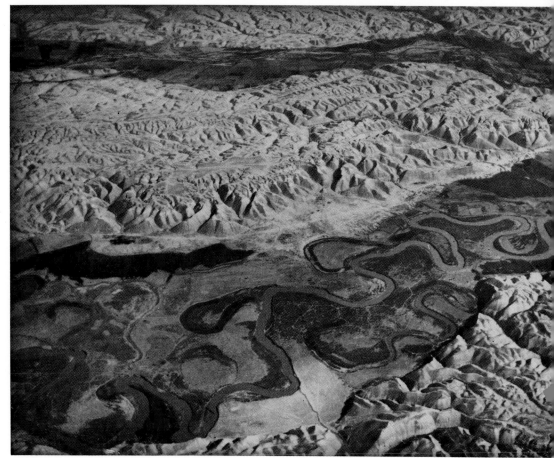

Although only 200 miles (320 km) long and small when compared to the Amazon, Orinoco, Mississippi, Danube, Indus, Huang Ho, Tigris and Euphrates Rivers; it is still one of the greatest rivers of the world. The river rises in various sources around the Hula Basin: the Nahr Banias rises in Syria at the southern base of Mt Hermon; the Nahr Leddan, the major source, rises on Mt Hermon and meets the Banias at HULIOT; the Nahr Hasbani, the winter source, rises in Lebanon on the western slopes of Mt Hermon, parallels the Litani River, and joins the Leddan at SDEH NEHEMIA in Israel. The river flows due south through the famous Sea of Galilee and The Ghor – a great depression forming a section of the Great Rift Valley – before entering the Dead Sea.

Three views of the Kābul River as it flows through Afghanistan.

The only tributary of any note is the Yarmūk River. The Jordan is basically fast during its initial steep and abrupt course, but in the middle and lower courses it is sluggish. The principal crossings are the B'nat Ya'akov-Bridge to DAMASCUS, the Gesher railroad bridge, el Manshiya, a pipeline, and the Allenby Bridge, the main route between JERUSALEM and AMMAN. The Jordan is called Nahr al Urdunn in Hebrew, and means 'river of Dan.'

Kābul, Afghanistan-Pakistan
The Kābul rises at the foot of the Unai Pass, in the Paghman Mountains. It flows eastward along the northern slopes of the Safed Koh Range and is 320 miles (515 km) long. Only 45 miles (72 km) from its source is the ancient city of KABUL, the present capital of modern Afghanistan, and the principal trade center of

the region with a population of well over 600,000. This once great city was the former capital of the Mogul Empire under the Emperor Baber. At Kābul the river receives one of its tributaries, the Loger River. In Afghanistan the river's primary use is for irrigation of the Jalalabad Valley, and the large river station at WARSAK controls the irrigation system of Peshāwar in Pakistan. The region is extremely mountainous, with many gorges, but the Kābul continues eastward to enter the Vale of Peshāwar. The Vale is an oasis rich in beautiful groves of willow, tamarisk and mulberry trees. The principal crops are maize, cotton, wheat, sugar and tobacco. The chief tributaries of the river are the Chentral, the Konar and the Swat Rivers. The Kābul swings south to join the Indus River at the town of ATTOCK.

Kafirnigan, Asian USSR
The Kafirnigan rises in the eastern Gissar Range of the Tadzhik Autonomous Republic. It is 220 miles (350 km) long and flows west-northwest and then south to join the Amu Darya River. The river is linked to the Surkhan Darya by the Gissar Canal. The chief tributary is the fast-flowing Dyushambinka River.

Kajan, Indonesia
The Kajan rises in the Iran Mountains on the border between Indonesia and Malaysia in eastern Borneo. It is 250 miles (400 km) long, and flows east and east-northeast to enter the Celebes Sea. It has an alternative name of Bulungan in its upper course.

Kaladan, Burma
The Kaladan rises in the Chin Hills near the Indian border of Lower Burma. It is 200 miles (320 km) long, and flows past the towns of PALETWA and KYAUKTAW to enter the Bay of Bengal at AKYAB. The Kaladan is linked to the Lemro and Mayu Rivers and together they form a quite substantial waterway which is used for irrigation and transportation.

Kali Gandak, Nepal
Alternatively known as the Krishna, this river rises in the Nepal Himalayas. The Kali Gandak is 200 miles (320 km) long and flows south-southwest, then eastward to join the Trisuli River, approximately 55 miles (88 km) west of KATMANDU, thus forming the Gandak River.

Kalindi, India-Bangladesh
See Jamuna, India-Bangladesh

Kali Sindh, India
The Kali Sindh rises in the Vindhya Range of central India. It is over 220 miles (350 km) long and flows east-southeast of INDORE, then north to join the Chambal River just southeast of LAKHERI.

Kalni, Bangladesh
See Meghna, Bangladesh

Kalni, India
See Surma, India

Kamchatka, Asian USSR
The river rises in the Kamchatka Peninsula of the USSR. It is 335 miles (539 km) long and flows due north past the town of MILKOVO, then turns eastward to enter the Pacific Ocean at UST-KAMCHATSK.

Kampar, Indonesia
The Kampar rises in the Padang Highlands of central Sumatra east of Mt Ophir. The river is 200 miles (320 km) long and runs east to the Strait of Malacca almost directly across the channel from Singapore.

Kan, Asian USSR
The Kan rises in the eastern Sayan Mountain Range of south Krasnoyarsk Territory of the USSR. It is 318 miles (512 km) long and runs past the town of KANSK, then swings west to join the Yenisey River northeast of KRASNOYARSK.

Kan, China
This Kan rising in Kiangsi Province, China, at the confluence of two headstreams, the Kung Shui and the Chang Sui Rivers which meet at KANCHOU. Its course is impeded by rapids as it passes through a mountainous area. Near the town of WANAN are the famous 'Eighteen Rapids' of the Kan. Despite the rapids small vessels manage to reach Kanchou, a city of 140,000. Once the Kan flows below CHANGSHU it enters the plains, and the surrounding land is protected by dikes as the river is subject to flooding. The chief tributary is the Chi River. It enters Lake Poyang at WUCHENG, and leaves it from the southern end to flow to the Yangtze River. The river is 540 miles (870 km) long and has a great hydroelectric potential, which will be fully developed by the late 1980s.

Kapuas, Indonesia
The Kapuas rises in the Kapuas Mountain Range of central Borneo. The river is alternatively known as the Kapoeas, it is 710 miles (1140 km) long and flows west-northwest past the town of SINTANG to enter the South China Sea southwest of PONTIANAK.

Karasuk, Asian USSR
The Karasuk rises on the eastern Baraba Steppe of the USSR. The river is 220 miles (350 km) long and runs southwest past the town of KOCHKI to the Karasuk salt lakes.

Karkheh, Iran
The Karkheh River rises in the western Zāgros Mountains at the confluence of two headstreams in southwestern Iran. The river is 200 miles (320 km) long and flows south-southeast to disappear into the Tigris marshes near the Iraq border.

Karnaphuli, India-Bangladesh
The Karnaphuli River rises in the Lushai Hills of Assam and flows south initially, then turns southwest through Bangladesh finally to enter the Bay of Bengal south-southwest of the town of CHITTAGONG. The river is 146 miles (235 km) long.

Kārūn, Iran
The Kārūn rises on the Zardeh Kuh Mountain in southwestern Iran. It is 470 miles (760 km) long, and flows as a raging mountain torrent through deep gorges in the Zāgros Range. The entire upper valley is practically inaccessible, and the only inhabitants are nomadic tribesmen. The Kārūn leaves the mountains near the town of SHUSHTAR, and separates into two channels, and does not reunite until the confluence with the Ab-i-Diz River. The river winds in a great meander through the south-eastern portion of the Tigris-Euphrates lowland to join the Shatt al-Arab at KHOR-RAMSHAHR. It is navigable for small vessels to Dar-i-Khazineh. The Kārūn is susceptible to flooding during late November to June.

Kas, Asian USSR
The Kas rises in the Krasnoyarsk Territory of the USSR. It is sometimes called the Greater Kas and flows northeast for 165 miles (265 km) to join the Yenisey above the town of YARTSEVO. The Kas is linked by the Lesser Kas and the Ket Rivers to the Ob-Yenisey Canal system.

Katun, Asian USSR
The Katun rises in the Altai Mountains of the USSR. The river is 386 miles (621 km) long, and flows due west, then swings northward to join the Biya River at the town of KATUN to form the Ob River. The Katun's chief tributaries are the Chuya and Maima Rivers.

Kaveri, India
See Cauvery, India

Kelantan, Malaysia
The Kelantan rises in several headstreams in the Kelantan Mountains of northern Malaya. It is 150 miles (240 km) long, and flows north to the South China Sea at TUMPAT.

Kelkit, Turkey
The Kelkit rises in the Erzincan Mountains of northern Turkey. The Kelkit is 220 miles (350 km) long, and flows west-northwest to join the Yesil Irmak River northwest of the town of ERBAA.

Ken, India
The Ken rises in the Vindhya Range of central India. It is 235 miles (378 km) long, and runs north to the Yamuna River southwest of FATEHPUR. Its chief tributary is the Sonār River.

Kerulen, Mongolia
Also known as the Cherlen, it is 785 miles (1263 km) long and rises on the southern slopes of the Henteyn Mountains, north of ULAN BATOR in Mongolia. The river runs south to the Mongolian Plateau, then flows east and northeast past ONDOR HAAN and BAIN-TUMEN to enter Lake Dalai in the Inner Mongolian Autonomous Region of China. The Kerulen flows parallel to the edge of the great Gobi Desert, the location of some of Rider Haggard's best stories, and along an excellent strip of land which separates Mongolia and China. This large grassland region is sparsely inhabited, although steps have been taken by various administrations to open it up for settlement. But the rigorous conditions, compounded by the high altitudes, blistering Siberian winds and uncertain rainfall make this region extremely difficult to cultivate. Only the very hardiest of plants and animals will survive.

Ket, Asian USSR

The Ket rises approximately 60 miles (97 km) due north of Krasnoyarsk in the USSR. It is 845 miles (1360 km) long and is a quite substantial river. It flows northwest initially, then swings due west to join the Ob River south of the town of NARYM. The Ket is linked with the Ob-Yenisey Canal system via the Kas River.

Khābūr, Turkey-Syria

The Khābūr rises in the southeastern region of Turkey. The river is 200 miles (320 km) long and runs southeast and south through Syria to join the Euphrates River north of AL-MAYADIN.

Khāsh Rūd, Afghanistan

The Khāsh Rūd rises in the Hindu Kush of southwestern Afghanistan. It is 250 miles (400 km) long, and flows on a southwesterly course to Sistan lake which is a large depression in the earth's surface.

Khatanga, Asian USSR

The Khatanga rises at the confluence of the Kotui River, 233 miles (375 km) long, and the Moyero River, 312 miles (502 km) long, in the northeastern section of Krasnoyarsk Territory of the USSR. The river is 412 miles (663 km) long and flows north and northeast to enter the Khatanga Gulf of the Laptev Sea.

Khilok, Asian USSR

The Khilok rises northwest of Chita in the southern Buryat-Mongol Autonomous SSR. It is 380 miles (610 km) long and flows southwest to join the Selenge River.

Kien, China

The Kien River rises near the Yunnan border in Kweichow Province, China. The river is called the Wu for the first part of its journey. It is 700 miles (1130 km) long and flows due east across Kweichow into Szechwan to join the Yangtze near FOULING.

Kinabatangan, Borneo

The river rises in the central highlands and flows over 350 miles (560 km) northeast to enter the Sulu Sea approximately 30 miles (48 km) east-southeast of SANDAKAN. The Kinabatangan is the longest river in Borneo.

Kirenga, Asian USSR

The Kirenga rises in the Baykal Mountain Range of the Irkutsk Oblast of the USSR. It is 340 miles (550 km) long and runs due north to join the Lena River at KIRENSK.

Kishon, Israel

This is an intermittent river with a length of approximately 45 miles (72 km). It rises on Mt Gilboa east of JENIN, near the southern edge of the Plain of Jezreel. The Kishon is wholly within the small borders of the state of Israel. It winds northwest across the Plain of Jezreel, then swings northeast by Mt Carmel, with all its Biblical and historical connotations, to enter the Bay of Haifa of the Mediterranean Sea at the port of HAIFA. The Israelis have built locks, reservoirs and dams along its course to aid in the expansion of nearby agricultural projects. It is also known as the Qishon.

Kiso, Japan

The Kiso rises near the Ōtaki peak in central Honshu, Japan. The river is 135 miles (217 km) long, and flows east, then swings southwest before entering Ise Bay. The Kiso's chief tributaries are the Nagara and the Ibi Rivers.

Kistna, India

Sometimes called the Krishna, it rises near MAHABALESHWAR in the Western Ghāts approximately 40 miles (64 km) from the Arabian Sea. It is 800 miles (1290 km) long, and flows southeast down the steep slopes past the town of SANGLI and enters Hyderābād west of RAICHUR. The river is liable to severe flooding during the rainy season and consequently the large towns and villages have been built away from the river. The chief tributaries of the Kistna are the Bhīma, which joins near Rāichūr, and the Tungabhadra, which joins at ALAMPUR. The river then turns east-northeast to run along the Hyderābād-Madras border. The Kistna flows through a valley which was formed by an outcrop of the Nallamalai Hills, and then heads in a large semi-circle across the Godāvari-Kistna Plain of the northern Circars to empty into the Bay of Bengal through a small delta. The principal port in the delta is BEZWADA. The river carries an enormous amount of silt which it discharges in the delta, which makes this area an excellent location for rice growing. In its upper reaches near SIDDESWARAM, a large hydroelectric station has been built which is providing the much-needed power for this area.

Kiya, Asian USSR

The Kiya rises east of the town of Pezas in the Kemerovo Oblast of the USSR. It is 315 miles (507 km) long, and runs north and northwest to join the Chulym River at the town of ZYRYANSKOYE.

Kizil Irmak, Turkey

The Kizil begins near the Kizil mountain in central Turkey and flows in a large arc first southwest past SIVAS, then swings northwest, north and finally northeast before entering the Black Sea to the north of BAFRA. The river is 715 miles (1150 km) long and its principal tributaries are the Balaban, Delice and the Devrez Rivers.

Kokcha, Afghanistan

The Kokcha begins in the Hindu Kush of northeastern Afghanistan. The Kokcha is 200 miles (320 km) long, and flows north and west before joining the Panj River.

Kokshaga, Lesser, Asian USSR

See Lesser Kokshaga, Asian USSR

Kolva, Asian USSR

Rises in the northern Ural Mountains of the Molotav Oblast of the USSR. It is 290 miles (470 km) long, and flows south and west past CHERDYN to join the Vishera River. The Kolva's principal tributaries are the Berezovaya and the Vicherka rivers.

Kolyma, Asian USSR

The Kolyma is formed by the confluence of several headstreams in the Cherskiy Range of northeastern Siberia. It is 1335 miles (2148 km) long, and is one of the longest rivers in Siberia. The Kolyma flows north through mountainous terrain covered in forests. The upper reaches of the river are an extremely rich gold mining region. It is navigable for 1000 miles (1610 km) from its mouth, for approximately one-third of the year, and the remainder of the year is frozen. It continues northward and enters the East Siberian Sea, forming a delta mouth west of the Bay of Ambarchik. The town, AMBARCHIK, used to transfer merchandise from the sea to river transport. The delta is divided into several channels, the most important are the Kamennaya, the Kolyma and the Zemlyanaya. The chief resources of this region are fur, fisheries and reindeer.

Konar, Pakistan

The Konar rises in the eastern Hindu Kush of West Pakistan. It flows southeast for 250 miles (400 km) before joining the Kābul River below the town of JALALABAD in Afghanistan.

Konda, Asian USSR

The Konda rises in the swamps of the Tyumen Oblast of the USSR. It is 715 miles (1510 km) long, and flows west, south-southeast, east and northeast before finally joining the Irtysh River at REPOLOVO.

Kông Se, Laos

The Kông Se rises in the Annamese Cordillera southwest of HUE, Laos. The river flows for 300 miles (480 km) south-southwest through Cambodia to become a tributary of the Mekong at the town of STOENG TRENG.

Kondoma, Asian USSR

The Kondoma rises in the Abakan Range of the southwestern Kemerovo Oblast of the USSR. It is 265 miles (426 km) long and runs due north past TASHTAGOL to join the Tom River at STALINSK.

Kuantan, Indonesia

See Indragiri, Indonesia

Kuban, Asian USSR

The Kuban rises on the western slope of Mt Elbrus in the Greater Caucasus Mountains of the Georgian SSR. The river is 584 miles (940 km) long and navigable for 150 miles (240 km). It flows north and west through large swampy delta region of the Sea of Azov on the Black Sea.

Kūm, South Korea

The Kūm rises southeast of Ch'ungju in South Korea. It is 247 miles (397 km) long and flows north, northwest and southwest to enter the Yellow Sea at KUNSAN.

Kuma, Asian USSR

The Kuma rises in the central Greater Caucasus Mountains of the USSR. It is 360 miles (580 km) long and flows east-northeast into a large swampy region approximately 50 miles (80 km) from the Caspian Sea. During exceptionally heavy flooding the river will on occasions actually reach the Caspian.

Kumano, Japan

The Kumano rises in the Kii Peninsula of Honshū, Japan. The river is 100 miles (160 km) long, and flows south past the town of HONGU, then moves southeast to enter the Kumano Sea at SHINGŪ. The chief tributary is the Kitayama River which is 40 miles (64 km) long.

Kunduz, Afghanistan

The Kunduz rises in the Hindu Kush of northeastern Afghanistan. It is 250 miles (400 km) long and flows due east and north through Shikari Pass to join the Amu Darya River on the borders of the USSR.

Kura, Turkey-Asian USSR

The Kura rises in the eastern mountains of Turkey, and is the principal river of the Soviet Transcaucasia. It is 940 miles (1510 km) long, and flows through a barren plateau region, before crossing into the Georgian SSR of the Soviet Union. The valley of the Kura links the Black and Caspian Seas through a corridor between the Armenian highlands and the Caucasus Mountains. As it flows through Georgia, the region becomes more and more scenic, with beautiful orchards and vineyards. Along the river is built the ancient city of TBILISI, which has a population of 890,000, and was founded in AD 379 by the Persians. Also not far away is the town of GORI, with a population of 45,000, which was the birthplace of Stalin, the autocratic ruler of the Soviet Union from 1924 until 1953. At MINGECHAUR there is a large dam and hydroelectric station which provides electric power and water for irrigation projects throughout Georgia. The river is navigable for small vessels only for 150 miles (240 km) upstream to YEVLAKH. Its outlet is the Caspian Sea.

Kureyka, Asian USSR

The Kureyka rises in the northern Krasnoyarsk Territory of the USSR. It is 500 miles (800 km) long and flows due west to join the Yenisey River at UST-KUREYKA.

Kwei, China

The Kwei rises near the Hunan border of western Kwangsi Province, China. It is 200 miles (320 km) long and flows southeast to join the Sun River at WUCHOU. It is linked to the Hsiang River by a canal.

Kwo, China

The Kwo rises near KAIFENG in Honan Province, China. It is 220 miles (350 km) long and flows southeast to join the Huai River in Anhwei Province.

Labuk, Malaysia

The Labuk rises south of Mt Kinabalu, a peak which is 13,455 feet (4104 m) high and located in the easternmost region of Sabah (Northern Borneo). It is 200 miles (320 km) long and flows east-northeast to enter the Sulu Sea approximately 40 miles (64 km) west-northwest of SANDAKAN.

Langat, Malaya

The Langat rises in the central Malayan Mountains of Selengor Province in western Malaya. It is 100 miles (160 km) long and flows southwest, and then west past KAJANG to enter the Malacca Strait southwest of PORT SWETTENHAM.

Lei, China

The Lei rises near KUEITUNG in Hunan Province, China. It is over 200 miles (320 km) long and flows southwest and northwest past the towns of JUCHENG and LEIYANG to join the Hsiang River at the town of HENGYANG.

Lemro, Burma

The Lemro rises in the southern Chin Hills of Lower Burma. The Lemro flows 180 miles (290 km) south to MYAUNGBWE which is the head of the river's navigation. It enters the Bay of Bengal at MYEBON.

Lena, Asian USSR

The Lena is one of the great rivers of the world and the longest in eastern Siberia with a length of 2650 miles (4260 km). It has a drainage area of 936,300 square miles (2,425,000 sq km), which is one of the largest in the Asian continent. The river rises on the western slope

of the Baykal Range, near Lake Baykal, and at an altitude of 4700 feet (1433 m). The upper section of the Lena is characteristic of any mountain stream; the banks are high and the valley is very narrow. Below the confluence with the Vitim River, the volume of water in the channel increases noticeably and islands begin to appear scattered along its course. The valley opens up and the slopes are much lower. Once the river passes the confluence with the Aldan River, the valley is now a large and broad plain, for the most part swampy and filled with lakes. Finally, past the junction where the Vilyuy River joins the main channel, the valley narrows once again, before branch-

Above: Dolomite rocks overlook the Lena River.

ing out into a delta. The chief arms of the Lena delta are the Bykov, (which is the most important for navigation, linking the Lena to the Bay of Tiksi,) the Olenek and the Trofimov. The river is navigable for 2450 miles (3940 km) as far as KACHUGA, in June-October. The basin of the Lena is not as populated as some of the regions in western Siberia, mainly because the winter is very severe. There are large deposits of gold, coal and mica along the river's course.

Lepsa, Asian USSR

The Lepsa rises in the Dzungarian Alatau, Kazakh SSR. It flows for 210 miles (338 km) northwest past LEPINSK to enter Lake Balkhash.

Lesser Kokshaga, Asian USSR

The Lesser Kokshaga rises west-northwest of Novy Toryal in the Mari Autonomous Republic. It is 125 miles (200 km) long and flows on a southward course to join the Volga River as a tributary at Mariinski Posad. Chief tributary is the Lesser Kundysh River which is 50 miles (80 km) long.

Li, China

Rises on the Hupeh border in northwestern Hunan Province, China. The river is 250 miles (400 km) long, and runs southeast initially, then swings due east to enter Lake Tungting near ANSIANG.

Liao, China

The Liao is formed by the confluence of two large headstreams southeast of SHUANGLIAO in

Above: The Mahaweli Ganga River of Sri Lanka.

northeastern China. It is 900 miles (1450 km) long and flows south past the towns of TIEHLING and LIAOCHUNG to enter the Gulf of Liaotung at YINGKOU.

Litani, Lebanon

One of the trouble spots of the late 1970s, the Litani has seen bitter fighting between the PLO (Palestinian Liberation Organization) and the invading Israeli troops in the invasion of Lebanon in March 1978. This historic river rises near BAALBEK in Lebanon and flows through a region which is steeped in history. It is only 90 miles (145 km) long, and enters the Mediterranean Sea north of Tyre and south of Sidon. Both of these great ancient cities were the seats of enormous political and commercial power in ancient times.

Luan, China

The Luan rises in Chahar Province of northern China as the Shangtu River. It is 500 miles (800 km) long and flows north past the town of SHANGTU, then southeast through CHENGTE (JEHOL) and crosses into Hopeh Province before entering the Gulf of Chihli.

Lopburi, Thailand

See Chao Phraya, Thailand

Loralei, Pakistan

See Nari, Pakistan

Luang, Thailand

See Tapi, Thailand

Lungchwan, China

See Schweli, China

Lūni, India

The Lūni rises in the Arāvalli Range of southwestern India and flows for a total of 330 miles (530 km). It runs through a semi-barren landscape, where the only vegetation which stands these conditions is millet. The Lūni is a seasonal river and the average rainfall in this area is less than ten inches (254 mm) annually. The river enters the Arabian Sea through the Rann of Cutch salt crusted marshes of southwestern India.

Lupar, Malaysia

The Lupar rises in the Kapuas Mountains of south Sarawak. It is 142 miles (228 km) long and flows southwest to Lubok Antu and then west-northwest to the South China Sea just east of KUCHING.

Madhumati, India

A large distributary of the Ganges delta, it leaves the Padma River just north of KUSHITA. It is 190 miles (310 km) long, and flows south-southeast through the Sundarbans to enter the Bay of Bengal.

Mae Klong, Thailand

The Mae Klong begins in the mountains of central Thailand near the Burmese border. The river is 250 miles (400 km) long, and flows due south and southeast to enter the Gulf of Siam at SAMUTSONGKHRAM. The chief tributary of the Mae Klong is the Khwaer Noi River which is 150 miles (240 km) long.

Mahakam, Indonesia

The Mahakam rises in the central mountains of Indonesian Borneo and is known also as the Kutai River. It is 450 miles (720 km) long and runs southeast to enter the Makassar Strait east of SAMARINDA.

Mahānadi, India

The Mahānadi is 560 miles (900 km) long and rises in the Eastern Ghāts of eastern Orissa, India. The river flows due north, then swings east, and makes a horseshoe loop to run northeast where the river has been dammed to form the Hirakūd Reservoir. Beyond the dam is a region rich in untapped coal seams which is being developed, but the land is cultivated mainly for rice. The principal tributaries are the Hasdo, the Tel, and the Seonāth Rivers. At the town of CUTTACK, it is dammed to control flooding of the delta before it enters the Bay of Bengal. The Mahānadi's delta is large and is also fed by the Baitarani and the Brāhmani Rivers. The width of the delta is 125 miles (200 km). At flood time, the Mahānadi's discharge is the greatest of any other river in the entire subcontinent.

Mahānanda, Nepal

The Mahānanda River is formed by the confluence of headstreams in the southeastern Nepalese Himalayas. It is 225 miles (362 km) long and flows south-southwest and south-southeast to join the Ganges River at GODAGARI.

Mahaweli Ganga, Sri Lanka

The Mahaweli Ganga rises on the Hatton Plateau of Sri Lanka, formerly Ceylon, just off the southeastern tip of India. It is the longest river in the country with a length of 206 miles (331 km). It flows through the beautiful scenery of Sri Lanka, passing tea and rubber plantations, and small Sinhalese villages with their rice fields, orchards and spice gardens. The river flows east through the highlands past the town of PERADENIYA, the location of the University of Sri Lanka. It then flows past KANDY, a city of 68,000, the center of the Sinhalese culture and the former capital of the ancient kingdom of Ceylon. The Dutch, French and Portuguese all captured Kandy, but the Sinhalese always recaptured it, until the British finally pacified the country around 1815. Leaving Kandy the river flows east, then turns north and finally enters Koddiyar Bay of the Indian Ocean.

Mahi, India
The Mahi rises south of SARDARPUR in western Vindhya Range. The Mahi is 360 miles (580 km) long and flows north and southwest to enter the Gulf of Khambhāt in the northern Arabian Sea.

Mali, Burma
The Mali rises near Putao in Upper Burma and flows for 200 miles (320 km) in a southerly direction to join the Nmai River, north of MYITKYINĀ to form the Irrawaddy River.

Mama, Asian USSR
The Mama rises northeast of Lake Baykal in the Buryat-Mongol Autonomous Republic. The river is 200 miles (320 km) long, and runs northeast to join the Vitim River at the town of MAMA. It flows through an area rich in mica deposits.

Mamberamo, Indonesia
This river rises at the junction of the Taritatu and Tariku Rivers in western Irian Yaya. The Mamberamo is the largest river in New Guinea with a length of 500 miles (800 km). It flows northwest to enter the Pacific Ocean near Cape Tandjung Perkam. The river is also known as the Rochussen in its upper course.

Mana, Asian USSR
The Mana rises in the eastern Sayan Mountains of southern Krasnoyarsk Territory of the USSR. It flows 330 miles (530 km) on a northwest course to join the Yenisey River west of the town of KRASNOYARSK.

Manās, Tibet
The Manās rises north of the town of TSONA in Tibet. It is 220 miles (350 km) long and flows basically south and southwest through BHUTAN where it is called the Dangme Chu River. It then continues south-southwest to join the Brahmaputra River opposite GOĀLPĀRĀ, India. Its largest tributary is the Tongsa River.

Mand, Iran
Sometimes called the Mond, it rises in several headstreams in the Zagros Mountains west of Shīrāz in southern Iran. It is 300 miles (480 km) long and flows southeast, south and finally west before entering the Persian Gulf south-southeast of Būshehr.

Manipur, India
The Manipur rises as the Imphāl or Achauba River, in the northern Manipur Hills of India. It is 200 miles (320 km) long, and flows due south past IMPHAL to join the Myittha River, which is 150 miles (240 km) long, just east of FALAM in Upper Burma.

Mānjra, India
The Mānjra rises on the Deccan Plateau of central Hyderābād, India, just southwest of the town of BĪR. It is 385 miles (619 km) long and flows east-southeast and north to Godāvari River, northwest of NIZĀMĀBĀD.

Manych, Asian USSR
The Western Manych rises near Divnoye, in the northern Caucasus Mountains. It is 200 miles (320 km) long and flows northwest to become a tributary of the Don River southwest of the town of BAGAYEVSKAYA.

Maya, Asian USSR
The Maya rises in the Dzhugdzhur Range of the Khabarovsk Territory of the USSR. It is 660 miles (1062 km) long, and flows south-southwest past the town of NELKAN which is also the head of the river's navigational limit. It continues northwest to join the Aldan River at UST-MAYA.

Meghna, Bangladesh
The Meghna rises in Bangladesh, the river is really a continuation of the Surma River. It is 132 miles (212 km) long and flows south-southwest to join the Padma River northwest of CHANDPUR. It then continues for a further 90 miles (145 km) as the Meghna River to the Bay of Bengal. In its upper course it is known as the Kalni River. The river forms the eastern boundary of the Ganges delta.

Mekong, Southeast Asia
The Mekong is 2500 miles (4020 km) long and has a drainage basin of some 313,000 square miles (810,700 sq km). It is one of the longest rivers in Asia, and the chief river of Southeast Asia. It rises in the highlands of Tsinghai Province, China very near the border with Tibet, in the Tanglha Mountain Range. This

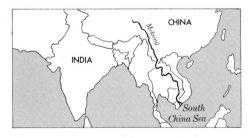

high mountainous region is also the source of the Salween, the Huang Ho (Yellow) and the Yangtze Rivers. The river flows southeast initially, then heads south running through China, Tibet, Laos, Cambodia and the southern part of Vietnam to where it enters its delta in the South China Sea south of HO CHI MINH CITY, formerly Saigon. During its first 200 miles (320 km) or so, the river falls from

16,700 feet (5090 m) to 10,000 feet (3050 m) at CHIAMDO. The river then veers to the south, crosses into Yunnan Province and is spanned by the famous Burma Road near the town of PAO SHAN. It continues southward leaving Chinese territory to become an Indo-Chinese river. The Mekong now runs parallel to the Salween and the Yangtze River for 600 miles (970 km), a raging torrent virtually imprisoned by high and rocky walls, and flowing through gorges and deep ravines as it rushes southward. As the river flows out of the mountainous regions, it enters a beautiful region covered in jungle and tropical vegetation. Its wilder nature left behind for the time being the river flows on toward the sea. During the rainy season, the turbulent nature of the river returns as it becomes swollen, often dangerous, and floods its banks at the height of the southwest monsoons. In the summer the river barely covers its bed; a natural flood reservoir is located at the Tônlé Sab, a lake connected to the river at PHNOM PENH, the capital of Cambodia. Below Phnom Pénh is the beginning of the Bassac River, the principal delta arm of the Mekong. The river is navigable to an extent for shallow draft vessels,

Left and below: Settlements along the Mekong River of Southeast Asia.

but hazards do exist, whirlpools, deep ravines and rapids. The river's chief asset is the rich alluvial soil which it deposits throughout the delta area making this region one of the 'rice baskets' of the world.

Menderes, Turkey
The Menderes is 250 miles (400 km) long and rises in the Anatolian Plateau of western Turkey. It is also called the Büyük or Great Menderes to distinguish it from the Little Menderes to the north, which was known as the ancient Scamander. The Menderes is the longest river which rises in Anatolia. It flows initially through a short marshy stretch, then runs through a deeply carved valley and becomes even deeper below its confluence with Banaz River. In ancient times the river was known as the Maeander and because of the extremely winding course of the river in its lower courses, the English word to meander was derived from it. Upon reaching SARAYK-HOY, the river swings west, and although its valley is very narrow, it soon opens up into a wide Mediterranean type landscape. The valley is trench-like and continues for a further 80 miles (129 km) to the sea. Near the old market town of AYDIN, the river makes one of its many course changes, this time heading southwest and soon enters the Aegean Sea. Near its mouth is the site of the once great, ancient port city of MILETUS, which was abandoned long ago due to the silting up of the Menderes. Miletus was one of the Ionian Greek city-states which refused to bow to Darius, the Persian King and consequently asked the mainland Greek city-states for help, which resulted in the long running battle between the Greeks and the Persians, culminating in the destruction of the Persian Empire by Alexander the Great.

Miass, Asian USSR
The Miass rises in the southern Ural Mountain Range of the southwestern Siberian area. It is 390 miles (630 km) long and flows due north through a rich gold-mining region, then east-northeast to join the Iset River.

Min, China (1)
The Min rises at the junction of the Kien, Sha and Futun Rivers in Fukien Province, China. The river is 350 miles (560 km) long and runs southeast by NANPING and SHUIKOW to enter the East China Sea below FUCHOU (Foochow).

Min, China (2)
This Min rises in the Min Shan of western Szechwan Province, China. It is 500 miles (800 km) long and flows due south past the towns of SUNGPAN, KUANHSIEN and LOSHAN to finally enter the Yangtze River at IPIN.

Moesi, Indonesia
See Musi, Indonesia

Mogami, Japan
The Mogami is formed by the confluence of two headstreams in northern Honshū, Japan.

It is 134 miles (216 km) long and flows north-northeast past YACHI and OISHIDA, then moves northwest to the Sea of Japan at SAKATA.

Mon, Burma
The Mon rises in the southern Chin Hills of Upper Burma. The river is 150 miles (240 km) long and flows southeast and east to join the Irrawaddy River north of MINBU.

Mor, India
The Mor rises at the junction of several headstreams in Bihār Province of India. The river is 100 miles (160 km) long and runs southeast and east to join the Dŵarka River, which is a tributary of the Bhāgīrathi River, just east of KĀNDI.

Moyar, India
The Moyar rises in the Nilgiri Hills of southwestern Madras, India. It is 90 miles (145 km) long and flows due north past the falls and hydroelectric power station at PYKARA, before turning east to join the Bhavāni River.

Muleng, China
Also known as the Muren, it rises in the highlands south of Muleng in northeastern China. It is 250 miles (400 km) long and flows north and northeast through a large coal mining region to join the Ussuri River south of HULIN on the border of the Soviet Union.

Mun, Thailand
This river rises in the San Kamphaeng Range at a height of 1500 feet (457 m) in eastern Thailand. The river is 300 miles (480 km) long and runs due east through the large Korat Plateau to join the Mekong River northwest of PAKSĒ. Its chief tributary is the Chi River.

Muar, Malaysia
The Muar rises east of Seremban in southern Malaya. It is 140 miles (230 km) long and flows east past KUALA PILAH, then turns south through the northwestern section of Johore and one of the largest rubber growing districts in the country before entering the Strait of Malacca at MUAR.

Murat, Turkey
The Murat rises southwest of Mt Ararat, a peak which is 16,946 feet (5169 m) high and in Turkish called Buyuk Agri, in northeastern Turkey. The river runs for 380 miles (610 km) in a westerly direction passing KARAKOSE, TUTAK, MALAZGIRT and PALU before joining the western headstream of the Euphrates.

Murgab, Afghanistan
The Murgab rises in the western portion of the Hindu Kush in northwestern Afghanistan. It is 530 miles (850 km) long and is a medium-sized river. It flows west and northwest past BALA MURGHAB, then enters the Turkmen Autonomous Republic at MARUCHAK, and flows north to disappear into the Kara-Kum Desert.

Mūsi, India
The Mūsi rises on the southern Deccan Plateau, southeastern Hyderābād, India. It is 180 miles (290 km) long and flows due east past VIKARABAD and HYDERABAD before turning south to join the Kistna River.

Musi, Indonesia
Alternatively known as the Moesi, it rises in the Barisan Mountain Range of southern Sumatra, Indonesia. It is 325 miles (520 km) long and is navigable by ocean-going vessels as far as PALEMBANG. It flows north-northeast past TEBINGTINGGI, then swings due east to Palembang and then north through the delta to the Bangka Strait of the South China Sea.

Mutan, China
The Mutan rises in the hills southwest of TUNHUA in northeastern China. The river flows north-northeast through Kingpo Lake, then past NINGAN and MUTANCHIANG to join the Sungari River at SANSING. The river is 415 miles (668 km) long.

Mutha Mula, India
The Mutha Mula begins at the junction of two headstreams at POONA which flow from the Western Ghāts in India. The river is 80 miles (129 km) long and flows east to join the Bhima River just northwest of DAUND. It is utilized for important irrigation projects and is a chief source of hydroelectric power for the region.

Myitnge, Burma
The Myitnge rises in the Shan Plateau east of LASHIO in Upper Burma. It is 250 miles (400 km) long and flows southwest to join the Irrawaddy River at SAGAING. It is also called the Nam Tu River in its upper course.

Nadym, Asian USSR
The Nadym rises in Lake Numto in northwestern Siberia. It is 155 miles (250 km) long and runs north into Ob Bay west of NYDA.

Nāgāvali, India
The Nagavali River rises in the Eastern Ghāts, south of Orissa, India. It is 150 miles (240 km) long and flows south-southeast to enter the Bay of Bengal approximately five miles (eight km) from CHICACOLE.

Nahr Ibrahim, Lebanon
See Adonis, Lebanon.

Naktong, Korea
The Naktong is the largest river in Korea. It rises in the mountains of central South Korea southwest of SAMCH'OK. It is 326 miles (525 km) long and flows south, west and southeast past the town of SAMNANGJIN to enter the Korean Strait near the city of PUSAN which has a population of 1,425,000. The Naktong is navigable for 214 miles (344 km) of its course and as such is the most important river in South Korea.

Nan, Thailand
The Nan rises near the Laos border in the northern Luang Prabang Range of northern Thailand. It is 500 miles (800 km) long and flows due south past UTTARADIT, the head of the river's navigational limit. The Nan joins the Ping River near NAKHON SAWAN to form the Chao Phraya River. The Nan forms a common flood plain with its sister river the Yom.

Nantu, China
The Nantu rises in the mountains of Hainan Island, which is in the Gulf of Tonkin. It is 170 miles (270 km) long and flows northeast to enter HAIKOU (Hohow) Bay of the Hainan Strait.

Naoli, China
The Naoli rises in the hills of northeastern China north of TSINING. It is 250 miles (402 km) long and flows northeast to join the Ussuri River south-southwest of KHABAROVSK.

Nāri, Pakistan
The Nāri rises as the Loralei River in the central Brāhui Range of eastern Baluchistān. It flows east initially, then moves south as the Anambar River, west-southwest as the Beji River and finally due south as the Nari River. As the Nari it passes through the Kachhi Plain, past BHAG to the Northwestern Canal of the Sukkur Barrage system near USTA MUHAMMAD. The river is 325 miles (523 km) long.

Narmada, India
The Narmada is only second to the Ganges in the eyes of the Hindus. It rises near the village of Amarkantak in the southeast Vindhya Pradesh close to the border with Madhya Pradesh, at an altitude of 3493 feet (1065 m), in the Maikala Hills of central India. The river is 775 miles (1247 km) long and flows mainly west-southwest to northern Bombay, to form a large estuary below BROACH and entering the Gulf of Khamblāt, an arm of the Arabian Sea. The river is only navigable for 60 miles (97 km) above its mouth during the rainy season. Like the Tāpi the Narmada is unusual in that it flows west to enter the Arabian Sea, while the other rivers which rise above the east coast in the Western Ghāts flow across India into the Bay of Bengal. Pilgrimages are a regular occurrence along the Narmada, and some consider it to be more important religiously even than the Ganges.

Naryn, Asian USSR
The Naryn rises as a headstream of the Syr Darya River in Kirghiz and Uzbek SSR. It is 449 miles (722 km) long and flows west as the Greater Naryn, then receives the Lesser Naryn River east of the city of NARYN before continuing northward. It runs on this course for a distance before changing again, this time to a westerly direction past TOKTOGUL and southwest through the Fergana Valley and eventually joining the Kara Darya River near BALYKCHI to form the Syr Darya River. The chief tributaries of the Naryn are the Son Kul and the Kokomeren Rivers.

Ngawun, Burma
See Bassein, Burma

Nīra, India
The Nīra rises in Western Ghāts south of POONA. It is 115 miles (185 km) long and flows east-southeast to join the Bhīma River to the southeast of INDAPUR. The river is noted for the famous Lloyd Dam to the north of BHOR.

Nmai, Burma
Chief headstream of the Irrawaddy River, the Nmai rises in the high mountains north of PUTAO, in northern Upper Burma. The river is 300 miles (483 km) long and runs due south to join the Mali River in forming the Irrawaddy.

Nonni, China
The Nonni rises in the Ilkuri Mountains of northeastern China. The Nonni is 740 miles (1190 km) long and flows due south along the eastern foot of the Greater Khingan Mountain Range past the towns of MUNKIANG and CHICHIHAERH (Tsitsihar) to join the Sungari River approximately 100 miles (160 km) west-northwest of HARBIN.

North, China
This river rises in Kwangtung Province, China at the confluence of the Cheng and the Wu Rivers at KUKONG. It is 200 miles (320 km) long and flows due south past YINGTE and SANSHUI to enter the Canton River delta.

Nura, Asian USSR
The Nura rises southeast of KARAGANDA, in the Kazakh SSR. It is 445 miles (720 km) long and flows northwest past TEMIR-TAU, and through Lake Kurgaldzhino to Lake Tengiz.

Nyang Chu, Tibet
The Nyang Chu rises in a small lake in the southeastern region of Tibet, at an altitude of 14,800 feet (4514 m). The river is 110 miles (177 km) long, and flows north and northwest along the Indian-Tibet trading route, past GYANGTSE and SHIGATSE to join the Brahmaputra River northeast of Shigatse.

Ob, Asian USSR
The Ob is one of the great rivers of Siberia and one of the longest in the world. It is 2287 miles (3680 km) long, and flows from its source in the

Altai Mountain Range northwest and then north into Ob Bay, a large inlet of the Kara Sea of the Arctic Ocean. The Ob is actually formed at the confluence of the Biya and the Katun

Top: The turbulent Nmai River of Burma.

Above: Ob Bay at the mouth of the Ob River.

Rivers near the town of BIYSK. The largest tributary of the Ob is the Irtysh River, itself 2640 miles (4250 km) long. The other tributaries are the Tom, 522 miles (840 km) long, the Ket, 845 miles (1360 km) long, the Chulym, 1177 miles (1894 km) long, the Vakh, 560 miles (900 km) long and the Vasyugan, 625 miles (1006 km) long. The river flows through a forested, steppe zone of the western Siberian lowlands below the town of KAMEN-NA-OBI. When the Irtysh joins the Ob, the river becomes a tremendous stream with a width of slightly over 12 miles (19 km), and a complex network of deep channels. At this stage the Ob is like a large inland sea, with high right banks and low left banks covered in shrubs and water meadows. In its lower course the Ob receives two large tributaries, the Kazym, a right-bank stream, and the Northern Sosva from the left. The river is the chief means of transportation for a very large region. It is navigable from

Biysk and shipping services are provided for the entire length of the river and its subsidiary streams. The river freezes by the middle of October and remains frozen until the spring thaws, approximately six months out of the year. The region is not very heavily populated but it does have excellent farming land, and there are a number of collective farms dealing primarily in beef, dairy products and wheat. The Ob is extremely rich in fishing and is the center of the region's hydroelectric power resources. The principal port on the Ob is NOVOSIBIRSK, with a population of 135,000, which is built on both sides of the river and is the chief industrial center of the region and junction of the Trans-Siberian Railroad. Once the Ob reaches its delta it divides into two branches, and at the mouth is a huge shallow bar formed by the river's great deposits which prevent ocean-going vessels from going up the river. This is one of the relatively unknown rivers outside the Asian continent but this should be rectified as it is an important asset to the Soviet Union and to the region through which it flows. It drains an area of 1,131,000 square miles (2,929,290 sq km).

Okhota, Asian USSR
The Okhota rises in the mountains south of the Oymyakon Plateau in the Khabarovsk Territory of the USSR. The river is 220 miles (354 km) long and flows due south to enter the Sea of Okhotsk near the city of OKHOTSK.

Olekma, Asian USSR
The Olekma rises in the Yablonovy Range of the USSR. It is 794 miles (1278 km) long and flows due north through an area rich in gold to join the Lena River below the town of OLEKMINSK. The chief tributaries are the Chara, the Tungir and the Nyukzha Rivers.

Olenek, Asian USSR
The Olenek rises on the Central Siberian Plateau in the northwestern Yakut Autonomous Republic. It is 1500 miles (2410 km) long, and flows east and north passing Olenek to enter the Laptev Sea of the Arctic Ocean at UST-OLENEK. The river is navigable for 500 miles (800 km).

Om, Asian USSR
The Om rises in the Vasyuganye marshes of the USSR. It is 475 miles (764 km) long, and flows due west past the towns of KUYBYSHEV and KALACHINSK to join the Irtysh River at Omsk. The river is navigable for 200 miles (320 km) above the mouth.

Omolon, Asian USSR
The Omolon rises in the Kolyma Range of the USSR. It is 715 miles (1150 km) long and flows due north to join the Kolyma River approximately 60 miles (97 km) southwest of Nizhne-Kolymsk.

Ona, Asian USSR
See Biryusa, Asian USSR

Onon, Mongolia-Asian USSR
The Onon rises in the Henteyn Mountains of northeastern Mongolia. The river is 592 miles (953 km) long and flows generally east and then northeast into the Soviet Union to join the Ingoda River, 15 miles (24 km) southwest of SHILKA to form the Shilka River.

Orhon, Mongolia
The Orhon is 700 miles (1130 km) long and rises in the heavily wooded slopes of the Khangai Mountains of the Mongolian People's Republic. The rainfall is uncertain in this region and added to the severe winters, agriculture in this area is strictly limited to subsistence farming. The chief tributaries of the Orhon are the Tuul, the Khara Gol and the Iro Rivers. The Orhon is separated from the Selenge River by a massif as both rivers flow

northeast to meet at SUKHE BATOR. The town of Sukhe Bator is a well-known trading center and transit point for cargo, it is ideally situated on the ancient caravan route southward into China from Russia. The town is now connected by railway to the Trans-Siberian railroad at ULAN-UDE near Lake Baykal. An item of note is that with all the modern conveniences and means of rapid transport, it is still not unusual to see camels, oxcarts and horsemen riding or moving across the steppes and deserts as a part of the daily routine.

Orontes, Lebanon-Syria
The Orontes is one of the rivers of the ancient world. It was also known in history as the Draco, the Typhon and the Axius. Today, it is also known as the Nahr al-Asi, and although not a particularly long river, it is of interest to the historian and the archeologist. The river is 355 miles (570 km) long and flows through varied as well as beautiful scenery. The river irrigates an area of 85,000 acres, and its valley was an important military and commercial route between Egypt and Asia Minor. The river rises in springs west of BAALBEK close to a cave believed to be the retreat of St Maron, the founding father of the Maronites. At Baalbek is located the ancient temple of the Roman God Jupiter. The Romans named Baalbek Heliopolis, or the city of the sun. Entering Syria the river runs through the artificial lake of Homs and located in the middle of the lake is the ancient ruins of a Hittite fort. Once past Homs, the river narrows into a ravine but only for a short distance as it widens out as it reaches HAMAH. The Orontes turns westwards and enters the coastal plain in Turkey. Located on the banks of the river is the ancient city and crossroads of ANTIOCH. It was founded in 300 BC by the Greeks and was one of the richest and largest cities of the old world.

Ou Nam, Laos
Ou Nam rises on the Chinese frontier of northern Laos and is 280 miles (450 km) long, and flows due south to join the Mekong River north of the city of LUANG PRABANG.

Padas, Malaysia
The Padas rises in the mountains of northwestern Sabah and flows due north through a beautiful scenic gorge. The river is 150 miles (240 km) long and after passing BEAUFORT swings west to enter Brunei Bay.

Pahang, Malaysia
The Pahang is formed by the confluence of two headstreams the Jelai and Tembeling Rivers, the Pahang flows south past TEMERLOH, then swings east to enter the South China Sea below PEKAN. The river is 200 miles (320 km) long and is the principal river of Malaya.

Pai, China
The Pai rises southeast of KHYUAN in Hun Province, China. It is 300 miles (483 km) long and flows southeast past the towns of MIYUN and TING-SIEN. The river joins the Grand

Canal, Yungting and Huto Rivers at the Tientsin area to enter the Gulf of Chihli between TAKU and TANGKU.

Palār, India
The Palār begins on the Deccan Plateau to the east of KŌLAR, India. It is 230 miles (370 km) long and flows south-southeast, northeast past ĀMBŪR and east-southeast past ARCOT to enter the Bay of Bengal south-southwest of MAHABALIPURAM.

Pampanga, Philippines
The Pampanga rises in several headstreams near CARRANGLAN on Luzon. The Pampanga is the second largest river on Luzon with a length of 120 miles (190 km). It flows southwest past CABANATUAN and CABIAO to a wide delta on Manila Bay approximately 25 miles (40 km) northwest of MANILA.

Panj, Asian USSR
The Panj rises on the boundary between Afghanistan and the Soviet Union. It is a headstream of the Amu Darya River and is formed by the confluence of the Pamir and Vākhān Rivers near QALA PANJA. It flows west and north past KHOROG, then through the Darvaza Gorge and finally west-northwest to Vakhsh River to form the Amu Darya River. The Panj is 400 miles (640 km) long.

Panjnad, Pakistan
The Panjnad is formed by the confluence of the Sutlej and the Chenāb Rivers, which combines the water of all five rivers of the Punjab, east of ALPUR in Pakistan. The river is 60 miles (97 km) long and flows southwest to become a tributary of the Indus River.

Pārbati, India
The Pārbati rises in the Vindhya Range of central India. It is 270 miles (430 km) long and flows due north to join the Chambal River approximately 15 miles (24 km) northwest of SHEOPUR.

Pa Sak, Thailand
Rises in the Phetchabun Range of central Thailand. It is 250 miles (400 km) long and flows due south through ŁOM SAK and SARA BURI to join the Lop Buri River, an arm of the Chao Phraya River.

Pasig, Philippines
The Pasig rises in the Laguna de Bay in southern Luzon. It is only 14 miles (23 km) long and flows northwest through the center of the capital, MANILA, dividing the city in two. It continues on course into Manila Bay. The river has very important commercial activities on its banks.

Penganga, India
The Penganga rises in the Ajanta Hills west of BULDANA on the Hyderābād-Madhya Pradesh border of central India. It is 340 miles (550 km)

long and flows east-southeast past MEHEKAR, then proceeds eastward to join the Wardha River approximately ten miles (16 km) southwest of CHANDRAPUR.

Penner, India

Rises on the Deccan Plateau of eastern Mysore, India. It is 350 miles (560 km) long and flows due north past the town of GAURIBIDANUR, then swings east past TADPATRI and finally east-southeast to the Coromandel Coast of the Bay of Bengal north of MADRAS.

Perak, Malaysia

The Perak rises in the Kalakhiri Range of northern Malaya. The Perak is 170 miles (270 km) long and flows due south to enter the Strait of Malacca at BAGAN DATOH.

Peri, Turkey

The Peri rises on the Palandöken Daǧlan approximately 25 miles (40 km) south of ERZURUM in central Turkey. The river is 145 miles (233 km) long and flows west and southwest to join the Murat River.

Phet Buri, Thailand

The Phet Buri rises in the Tenasserim Range on the Burma frontier of southern Thailand. It is 100 miles (160 km) long and flows east and north-northeast to enter the Gulf of Siam.

Ping, Thailand

The Ping rises in the Daen Lao Range of northern Thailand. The Ping is 300 miles (483 km) long and flows due south past the towns of CHIANGMAI and KAMPHAENG PHET to join the Nan and the Yom Rivers to form the Chao Phraya River near NAKHON SAWAN.

Pit, Asian USSR

The Pit rises in the Krasnoyarsk Territory of the Soviet Union. The river is 245 miles (394 km) long and flows southwest to join the Yenisey River below YENISEYSK.

Ponnaiyār, India

The Ponnaiyār rises in eastern Mysore, India. Also called the Southern Penner, it is 250 miles (400 km) long and flows southeast of CHIK BALLAPUR. The river continues south and southeast past the towns of KAVERIPATNAM and TIRUKKOYILUR to finally enter the Bay of Bengal just north of CUDDALORE.

Porsuk, Turkey

The Porsuk rises south of SABUNGU in central Turkey. It is 170 miles (270 km) long and flows north and east passing ALPU and ESKISEHIR to join the Sakarya River approximately 11 miles (18 km) northwest of POLATLI.

Pulang Pulangi, Philippines

Alternatively known as the Rio Grande De Mindanao it rises in northern Mindanao, Philippines. It flows 200 miles (320 km) through swampy terrain north of Lake Būluan, then turns northwest to enter Illana Bay of the Moro Gulf.

Pulvar, Iran

The Pulvar rises in central Iran west of ABADEH. The river is 150 miles (240 km) long and flows southeast and southwest through the Zogros Mountain Range to meet the Kār River approximately 25 miles (40 km) northeast of SHIRAZ. The river flows through a region rich in archeological treasures for the ruins of the ancient cities of Persepolis and Pasargadae were built close to the river. Numerous archeological expeditions and surveys of this region have been conducted to uncover the remains of the once important and great centers of the ancient world.

Pūrna, India (1)

The Pūrna rises in the Ajanta Hills of northwestern Hyderābād, east of the town of CHALISGAON, India. The river is 220 miles (350 km) long and flows southeast and south past PURNA to join the Godāvari River.

Pūrna, India (2)

This Pūrna rises in the Western Ghāts of Mahārāshtra, India. It is 125 miles (200 km) long and flows westward past the towns of ALCHAPUR and BHUSAWAL till it joins the Tapi at Jālgaon and flows to the Gulf of Cambay of the Arabian Sea south of SURAT.

Pyasina, Asian USSR

The Pyasina rises near NORILSK in the Krasnoyarsk Territory of the USSR. It is 660 miles (1060 km) long and flows due north through Lake Pyasino to enter the Kara Sea.

Qaisar, Afghanistan

The Qaisar rises in BAND-E-TURKESTAN, Northern Afghanistan. It is 150 miles (240 km) long and flows due north past MAIMANA and ANDKHUI only to disappear into the desert north of Andkhui.

Qareh Chai, Iran

Alternatively known as the Qareh Sū, it rises in several headstreams in the Hamadān region of central Iran. It is 150 miles (240 km) long and flows eastward passing NOWBARAN and SAVEH to enter the salty Lake Namak.

Qezel Owzan, Iran

The Qezel Owzan is reputed to be the longest river in northwestern Iran, and rises in the high Kordestān Mountains due north of SANANDAJ. The river flows through mountain gorges with extremely steep sides eastward, then swings north and finally southeast before joining the Shāhrūd at MANJIL to form the Safid Rud River.

Rajang, Malaysia

The Rajang rises in the mountains east of BINTULU in Sarawak, western Borneo. It is the largest river in Sarawak and is 350 miles (560 km) long. It is navigable for 80 miles (129 km) by ocean-going vessels as far as SIBU. The river flows southwest and west to enter the South China Sea through a large delta.

Rakhshān, Pakistan

The Rakhshān rises in the eastern Siāhān Range of western Baluchistan. The river is 160 miles (260 km) long and flows west-northwest passing PANJGUR, then northwest to join the intermittent Māshkel River, which is 200 miles (320 km) long when it flows, near the Iranian border. The Rakhshān is noted for the remarkable date palms which grow along its course.

Rangoon, Burma

The Rangoon is a marine estuary of the Pegu and Myitmaka Rivers in Lower Burma. It is 25 miles (40 km) long and flows southeast to enter the Gulf of Martaban of the Andaman Sea. The estuary is linked with the Irrawaddy delta by the Twante Canal. Also the capital RANGOON is made accessible for ocean-classed vessels via a large canal.

Rāpti, Nepal

The Rāpti rises in the Nepal Himalayas and is 400 miles (640 km) long. It flows south-southeast, west and southeast into India to join the Gogra River near BARHAJ.

Rāvi, India

The Rāvi rises in the Pir Panjāl Range of the Himalayas in northwestern India. The Rāvi is one of the five rivers of the Punjab. It is 475 miles (764 km) long and flows west-northwest and southwest past LAHORE to join the Chenāb River.

Red, Vietnam

The Red River rises in Yunnan Province, China at a height of 6500 feet (1982 m). It is the longest river of North Vietnam and is also known as the Hung Ho or Yuan Kiang. It is 750 miles (1210 km) long and flows southeast past YUANJIANG and MANHAO into Vietnam. The river continues on course passing the capital city of HANOI to a huge delta on the Gulf of Tonkin. The chief tributaries of the Red River are the Black and Clear Rivers.

Rewa, Fiji

The Rewa rises in the mountains near VATUKOULA and is the largest river in Fiji. It is 90 miles (145 km) long and flows southeast to enter Lauthala Bay near SUVA.

Rioni, Asian USSR

The Rioni rises south of the crest line of the main Caucasus Range in Georgia, SSR. It is 179 miles (288 km) long, drains an area of 5200 square miles (13,470 sq km) and flows west across the Kolkhida (Land of the legends of the Golden Fleece, sometimes called Colchis) lowlands to enter the Black Sea at POTI.

Above: The Ravi River of India near Lahore.　　　　*Below: A typical scene along the Salween River.*

Rokan, Indonesia

The Rokan rises in the Padang Highlands on Mt Ophir in Sumatra, Indonesia. It is 175 miles (282 km) long and flows north and northeast to the Strait of Malacca at BAGANSIAPI-API. The river is navigable for practically its full length.

Sābari, India

The Sābari rises in Eastern Ghāts, approximately 30 miles (48 km) south of JEYPORE, India. It is 260 miles (420 km) long and flows northwest and south-southwest past KONTA to join the Godāvari River. The chief tributary of the Sabari is the Machkund River which is 190 miles (310 km) long and joins it at the small town of KONTA.

Sābarmati, India

Rises west of UDAIPUR in the southern Arāvalli Range of India. It is 250 miles (400 km) long and flows due south past AHMADABAD to enter the Gulf of Khombhāt of the Arabian Sea.

Sai, India

Rises 15 miles (24 km) southeast of SHALIJA-HANPUR, in central Uttar Pradesh, India. It is 280 miles (450 km) long and flows southeast to join the Gomati River southeast of JAUNPUR.

Saigon, Vietnam
The Saigon rises west of LOC-NINH on the Cambodian border of southern Vietnam. It is 140 miles (230 km) long, and flows south and southeast past HO CHI MINH CITY to form a common delta with the Dong-nai River on the South China Sea.

Sakarya, Turkey
The Sakarya rises north-northeast of AFYON-KARAHISAR in central Turkey. The river is 490 miles (790 km) long and flows east, north, west and finally north again before entering the Black Sea at KARASU.

Sal, Asian USSR
The Sal rises at the junction of two small headstreams in the Yergeni Hills southeast of Rostov Oblast in the USSR. It is 400 miles (640 km) long and flows due west past DUBOVSKOYE to join the Don River.

The Sabarmati River near Ahmadabad, Gujarat Province, India. The rivers of India serve many functions.

Salween, Tibet, China and Burma
The Salween is 1750 miles (2820 km) long and is one of the longest rivers in South Asia. It has been called by some the most picturesque and yet the wildest river in the world. The Chinese believe that the river is unkind, if not outright inhospitable to strangers, and can be deadly. The Salween rises south of KUEN-LUN in the Tanglha Range of eastern Tibet. This region is barren and windswept, yet it is also the source for three other large rivers: the Huang Ho, the Mekong and the Yangtze. The river flows southeast and for a time parallels the Mekong and the Yangtze, before swinging south through Yunnan Province to cross over into Burma. The Salween cuts through the Shan Plateau and the Karenneni Hills to enter the Andaman Sea, through two separate mouths, north and south of Bilugyun Island in the Gulf of Martaban. The most important mouth is the

southern one which is utilized by ocean-going vessels to reach MOULMEIN. The river dissects the great Yunnan Plateau of China and then flows into the Shan States. During the dry season there are white sandy stretches along the banks of the river, but the rains bring a dramatic change to the Salween. The torrent comes raging down the channel rising to an incredible height of between 50–90 feet (15–27 m). The rapids in the Salween are extremely dangerous and very numerous, but more hazardous still are the sections of the river where reefs shoot out into the stream without any warning, creating raging back-waters. On the other hand, stretches of the Salween are so quiet as to make navigation a joy to the natives who utilize the river quite regularly. The Burma Road crosses and recrosses the river successively, but there are no large settlements to be found along the river. The nearest villages and towns are built at a safe height of over 1000 feet (305 m). The most dangerous section of the Salween is the gorge between the mouth of the Yunzali and Kyaukhyat. It forms a short portion of the Burma-Thailand border before heading toward the sea. During its lower course light steamers can navigate as far as SHWEGUN, which is located 63 miles (101 km) from the port.

San Se, Cambodia

The San Se is formed by several headstreams at a height of 1600 feet (490 m) near the city of KONTUM in Vietnam. It is 200 miles (320 km) long, and flows south-southwest to the Cambodian Plain where it is joined by the Srêpôk River. The San Se then continues on to join the Se Khong River above the town of STOENG TRENG.

Sārda, Nepal-India

The Sārda is 310 miles (500 km) long and rises in the great Nanda Devi Range of the Himalayas in Nepal. The river is actually formed by the confluence of the Kali and the Ramganga Rivers. It then runs in a winding course southwesterly through the outer Himalayan Plain, between KUMAON and the western portion of Nepal. It forces its way through the Siwalik Hills, and emerges near the town of TANAKPUR. The Sārda has built up a large alluvial fan which is some 5000 square miles (12,950 sq km) in area, and is crossed by spillbanks and former channels as it flows southeast to join the Gogra River northeast of LUCKNOW, which has a population of 850,000. The Sārda irrigates over one million acres of land, and is a major hydroelectric source for the region.

Segama, Malaysia

The Segama rises in the central highlands of Sabah and flows for 300 miles (480 km) east-northeast to the Sulu Sea.

Selemdzha, Asian USSR

The Selemdzha rises in the northern Bureya Range of the Amur Oblast of the USSR. It is 425 miles (684 km) long and flows southwest past EKIMCHAN, the head of the river's navigational limit. It continues on to join the Zeya River near the town of NOVO-KIYEVSKA. Extensive gold mining operations are conducted in the upper regions of the river.

Selenge, Mongolia

The Selenge is the principal river of the Mongolian People's Republic and has a length of 980 miles (1580 km). It is formed by the confluence of the Ideriin and the Mörön Rivers in the northwestern region of Mongolia. The river runs east-southeast, then swings northeast, and due north across the border into the Soviet Union near the town of SUKHE BATOR. The Selenge runs parallel to the railway line from Peking until it swings west to enter Lake Baykal, the deepest lake in the world. Lake Baykal is unique in that it has species of fish, seals, plankton and other marine species which do not exist anywhere else in the world. The river forms a small delta just north of KABANSK. The Selenge is navigable below Sukhe Bator

from May to October when it is free of ice. The principal tributaries are the Chikoy, the Uda, the Or hon, the Egij and the Dzhida Rivers.

Selety, Asian USSR

The Selety rises near TSELINOGRAD in the northern Kazakh Hills of the USSR. It is 180 miles (290 km) long and flows north-northeast to enter the Seletytengiz salt lake which takes in an area of 350 square miles (906 sq km) approximately 100 miles (160 km) south of OMSK.

Sên, Stung, Cambodia

The Stung Sên rises west of MELOUPREY when several headstreams meet after flowing down from the Dangrek Mountains near the Thailand border. It is 200 miles (320 km) long and flows due south past KAMPONG THUM to the Tônlé Sab.

Send Rud, Iran

The Send Rud rises in the Elburz Mountain gorge at MANJIL when the Qezel Owzan and the Shāhrūd meet. It flows through northern Iran for 60 miles (97 km) to a large delta on the Caspian Sea east of RASHT.

Seyhan, Turkey

The Seyhan rises in the Anti-Taurus Mountains of central Turkey as the Yenice Irmak River. It is 320 miles (510 km) long and runs south-southwest passing PINARBASI and ADANA to enter the Mediterranean Sea east of MERSIN. The chief tributary is the Goksu River.

Shilka, Asian USSR

The Shilka rises at the confluence of the Ingoda and Onon Rivers in the Chita Oblast of the USSR. It is 345 miles (555 km) long and flows east-northeast passing the towns of SHILKA, SRETENSK and UST-KARSK before joining the Argun River to form the Amur River on the borders of the USSR and China. The Shilka is entirely navigable. Its chief tributaries are the Nercha and Amazar Rivers.

Shimanto, Japan

The Shimanto rises northeast of NOMURA in southwestern Shikoku, Japan. It is 112 miles (180 km) long and flows south, west and finally southeast before entering Tosa Bay at SHOMODA.

Shimsa, India

The Shimsa rises east-southeast of TUMKUR in southern Mysore, India. It is 140 miles (225 km) long, and runs west past GUBBI and then south past MADDUR to join the Cauvery River. A major hydroelectric station is located above the mouth of the river at Shimsa Falls which are 310 feet (95 m) high.

Shinano, Japan

The Shinano rises north of KOFU and is the longest river in Honshū, Japan. It is 229 miles

(369 km) long, and flows north-northeast past SENJU, NAGAOKA and SANJO to enter the Sea of Japan at NIIGATA.

Shweli, China

The Shweli rises as the Lungchuan River in Yunnan Province of China. It is a tributary of the Irrawaddy River which it joins after flowing 400 miles (640 km) south and southwest into Burma at INYWA.

Shyok, India-Pakistan

The Shyok rises as the Chip Chap River in the Aghil-Karakoram Range of central Kashmir. It is 340 miles (550 km) long and flows west, south and northwest to join the Indus River east-southeast of the town of SKARDU. The principal tributary of the Shyok is the Nubra River.

Simav, Turkey

Alternatively known as the Susurluk, it rises six miles (ten km) east of SIMAV in northwestern Turkey. The river is 160 miles (258 km) long and flows west and north to enter the Sea of Marmara. The principal tributaries are the Koca, Nilufer and Kirmasti Rivers.

Sind, India

The Sind rises in the northeast Madhya Bhārat, India, west-northwest of SIRONJ. It is 320 miles (515 km) long, and flows north-northeast to join the Yamuna River west of AURAIYA.

Sittang, Burma

The Sittang rises on the Shan Plateau northeast of YAMETHIN in Burma. The Sittang is one of the primary rivers in Burma. It is 350 miles (563 km) long and flows past TOUNGOO to enter the Gulf of Martaban of the Andaman Sea.

Solo, Indonesia

The Solo rises approximately 40 miles (64 km) southeast of Solo. It is the longest river in Java at 335 miles (539 km). The river is also known as the Bengawan. It flows north past SOLO, east past NGAWI and northeast past TJEPU and BODJONEGORO to enter the Java Sea opposite Madura Island. For navigational reasons the river is canalized for 15 miles (24 km) above the mouth.

Son, India

The Son rises in northeastern Madhya Pradesh of central India. It is 475 miles (764 km) long and flows east to the Kaimur Hills, then swings east-northeast into Bihār and finally northeast to the Ganges River southeast of CHAPRA. The chief tributaries are the Rihand and North Koel Rivers. The Son achieves a width of between two to three miles (three and five km) during its lower course.

Sosva, Asian USSR (1)
The Sosva rises in the central Ural Mountains of the Sverdlovsk Oblast, USSR. It is 345 miles (555 km) long and flows north, east and south-southeast passing MASLOVO and FILKINO, then northwest past SOSVA and GARI to join the Lozva River which is 265 miles (426 km) long to form the Tavda River.

Sosva, Asian USSR (2)
The Sosva rises on the eastern slopes of the northern Ural Mountains. It is also called the Northern Sosva. It is 400 miles (640 km) long and flows east past the town of NYAKSIMVOL, the head of the river's navigational limit, then turns north, east-southeast and finally east-northeast to join an arm of the Ob River.

South Koel, India
The South Koel rises on the Chotanāgpur Plateau in southern Bihār and northern Orissa, India. It is 200 miles (320 km) long and flows west, south and west again to join the Sankh River to form the Brāhmani River.

Subarnarekha, India
This small river in northeastern India rises on the Chotanāgpur Plateau. The river is 290 miles (470 km) long and flows east passing RANCHI as a sandy-bedded stream between beautiful bluffs. It runs across the steep edge of the plateau in lovely cascades, then it turns south through the lower section of the plateau and passes the towns of JAMSHEDPUR and TATANAGAR. The river now flows along the western edge of the Ganges delta and finally enters the Bay of Bengal, through sandbars, mangroves and high mudbanks.

Sungari, China
The Sungari is the longest river entirely within the physical boundaries of Manchuria, with a length of 1150 miles (1850 km). The source of the Sungari is high in the Changpai Mountains, a tremendous mountain range in the southern highlands of Manchuria. It is formed by the confluence of the Erhtao and the Towtao Rivers; the river then flows northwest passing the towns of FENGMAN and CHILIN (Kirin). At Chilin the river becomes navigable. The chief tributary is the Nen Chiang or Nonni River, which joins the main stream at FUYU. The river then turns east-northeast passing HARBIN and KIAMUSZE to join the Amur River at TUNGKIANG. The Sungari provides power to FUSHUN, CHANGCHUN and Harbin, through the Hsiao-Fengman Dam, which is 300 feet (90 m) high and 3500 feet (1070 m) across. Together with the Yalu River, the Sungari provides practically all the hydroelectric power for Manchuria. Together with the Liao River, the Sungari drains approximately half of all Manchuria. The river freezes over between October-April.

Sun Kosi, Nepal
The Sun Kosi rises on the Gosainthan Peak in eastern Nepal. It is 160 miles (260 km) long and flows south-southwest and east-southeast to join the Arun and Tamur Rivers in forming the Sapt Kosi River. The chief tributary is the Dudh Kosi River, which has the most terrible rapids in the world.

Surma, India-Bangladesh
The Surma rises as the Barak River in the Manipur Hills, northwest of UKHRUL in Assam. It is 320 miles (510 km) long and flows west and south-southwest, then swings north and west through the Surma Valley, before turning south-southwest to join the Meghna River. For part of its course, the river is known as the Kalni.

Sutlej, Pakistan
The Sutlej rises in Rakas Lake on the southern slopes of Mt Kailas at an altitude of 15,000 feet (4575 m). It is the longest of the Five Rivers of the Punjab, with a length of 850 miles (1370 km). The source is somewhat disputed because the Indian geographer Swami Pranavanada once saw a river winding from Lake Ma'nasluowochi to the Sutlej. He therefore rightly assumed that the actual source is Lake Ma'nasluowochi even though this shallow river is for the most part dry, yet it has been discovered recently that the river flows underground for quite a distance. It is safe to assume that Lake Ma'nasluowochi is the real source of the Sutlej. The river flows northwest in a very narrow and deep channel. Reaching Shipki Pass the Sutlej swings southwest and cuts its way through the Zāskār Range of the Great Himalayas in a magnificent gorge about 20,000 feet (6100 m) deep. Gradually descending the river is still 10,000 feet (3050 m) high at Shipki, and 3000 feet (915 m) at the town of RAMPUR. Further downstream the river is dammed by the Bhākra Dam which is a deep storage reservoir, covering 200 square miles (518 sq km) and about 40 miles (64 km) of the Sutlej course. Also located eight miles (13 km) further along the channel is another large dam, the Nangal Dam. From this point the river flows southeast for some time along the Jaswan Dun, a fertile valley situated between the Siwalik Hills and the outer Himalayas. The five rivers of the Punjab have been utilized for centuries for major irrigation projects, and their waters have turned semi-arid and barren land into crop-bearing soil. After the confluence with the Beās, the Rājasthān Canal takes some of the waters of the Sutlej far into the desert. The next major tributary is the Chenāb, which has already absorbed the Rāvi and the Jhelum. The final stretch of the river from the Chenāb confluence to the junction with the Indus is called the Panjnad, the Five Rivers.

Swāt, Pakistan
The Swāt rises in the Hindu Kush of Pakistan. It is 200 miles (320 km) long and flows south, southwest and finally southeast past UTMANZA to join the Kābul River near the mountain town of CHARSADDA.

Sylva, Asian USSR

The Sylva rises in the central Ural Mountains, approximately seven miles (11 km) east of Shalya in the USSR. It is 390 miles (630 km) long and runs northwest, south-southwest and north-northwest to join the Chusovaya River east-northeast of MOLOTOV. The chief tributary is the Iren River.

Syr Darya, Asian USSR

The Syr Darya is one of the longest rivers in central Soviet Asia with a length of 1660 miles (2670 km). The river drains an area of 84,600 square miles (219,100 sq km). In ancient history it was known as the Jaxartes. The Syr Darya is formed by the confluence of the Kara Darya and the Naryn Rivers, which both rise in the Tien Shan Mountains. The two rivers meet in the wide Fergana Valley, which has rich soil and is densely populated. The land here is irrigated by the waters of all the smaller, as well as the larger rivers, resulting in the Syr Darya losing much of its previous volume. The main crop in this region is cotton, and the Syr Darya and its headstream the Kara Darya also contribute water to the Great Fergana Canal which carries the valuable water to the far-away irrigation projects. The Fergana Valley was the home of the Tartar khans throughout medieval times to the middle 19th century when it was assimilated into Russia. Two large reservoirs have been formed where the Syr Darya finally cuts its way out of the basin by the construction of two large dams. The power stations here provide much of the electrical power for the region. The river now flows north and meanders slowly, changing direction to the northwest before running into the Aral Sea. The Syr Darya is unstable, branching into numerous channels and changes direction numerous times. The river is very shallow and unnavigable, running through a desert lowland which saps its vital water resources. The river enters the Aral Sea through a large delta on its eastern shore. The delta is utilized to grow rice and is swampy.

Taedong, North Korea

Rises in the mountains northwest of HUNGNAM, in North Korea. It is 245 miles (394 km) long and runs southwest past PYONGYANG and SONGNIM to Korea Bay at NAMP'O.

Tanshui, Taiwan

The Tanshui rises as the Szeshe River at the foot of Mt Morrison and is the second longest river in Taiwan. It is navigable for 30 miles (48 km) in its lower course. It flows south-southwest to join the Nansinien River, then continues as the Tanshui to enter the Formosa Strait at TANSHUI.

Tao, China (1)

The Tao rises on the Tsinghai border of Kansu Province, China. It is 280 miles (450 km) long and flows east and north to become a tributary of the mighty Huang Ho River southwest of the city of LANCHOU.

Tao, China (2)

This Tao rises in the Great Khingan Mountains of northeastern China. It flows for 250 miles (400 km) east-southeast to join the Nonni River.

Tapi, Thailand

Alternatively known as the Luang, it rises in the Malay Peninsula of southern Thailand. It is 100 miles (160 km) long and flows from the Sithammarat Range north past SURAT THANI to enter the Gulf of Siam.

Tāpi, India

The Tāpi rises south of the Mahādeo Hills, in Madhya Pradesh, India. The entire course of the river is in the Deccan lavas, and the upper course is the refuge of the Gonds. Near BURHANPUR the Tāpi passes through a region of rich black soil which supports crops of cotton, wheat, sorghum, linseed and pulses. The chief tributary is the Pūrna, which gives the river a route east to the coalfields of Nāgpur and the Godāvari basin. The river enters a wide valley between the Sātpura-Mahādeo Ranges and the Ajanta Range, which is known as the East and West Khandesh. The river is 450 miles (720 km) long and empties into the Gulf of Khambhāt of the Arabian Sea.

Above: Surat Castle and fishing boats on the Tapi River in India.

Tarim, China

The Tarim rises in the Karakoram Range of Sinkiang, China. It is 1300 miles (2090 km) long and flows eastward across a large depression along the northern edge of the Takla Makan Desert and ends at Lop Nor Lake. This ancient lake, practically an inland sea in bygone ages, has been reduced to several small periodic lakes which greatly fluctuate in size and are fed by the Tarim. Its maximum size is believed to be in the region of 60 miles (97 km) long, and between 15–25 miles (24–40 km) wide.

Taritalu, Indonesia

Alternatively called the Idenburg, it rises in the northeastern Orange Range of western New Guinea. The river is 230 miles (370 km) long and flows northwest to join the Tariku River in forming the Mamberamo River.

Tarnak, Afghanistan

The Tarnak rises approximately 45 miles (72 km) southwest of GHAZNI in southeastern Afghanistan. It is 210 miles (340 km) long and flows southwest along the Kabul-Qandahar highway to the Arghastān River near QANDAHAR.

Tarum, Indonesia

Sometimes called the Chitarum, this Indonesian river rises in the mountains south of BANDUNG in western Java. The Tarum is utilized extensively for irrigation works near the town of KRAWANG. The river is over 170 miles (270 km) long and flows northwest to enter the Java Sea near Batavia Bay.

Tatu, China

The Tatu rises in KUNLUN in eastern Szechwan Province, China. It is 400 miles (640 km) long and runs south to join the Min River at LOSHAN.

Tavda, Asian USSR

The Tavda is formed by the confluence of the Lozva and Sosva Rivers north of GARI in western Siberia, USSR. It is 450 miles (720 km) long and runs southeast to join the Tobol River approximately 45 miles (72 km) southwest of TOBOLSK. The chief tributary is the Pelym River. The Tavda is navigable.

Tenasserim, Burma

This river rises when two small headstreams meet east-northeast of TAVOY in Lower Burma. It is 280 miles (450 km) long and flows south and northwest to the Andaman Sea at MERGUI.

Tenryū, Japan

The Tenryū rises in Lake Suwa near OKAYA in Honshū, Japan. It is 135 miles (217 km) long and flows south past INA and IIDA to enter the Philippine Sea near HAMAMATSU.

Tes, Mongolia

The Tes River rises in the northern Khangai Mountains of northwestern Mongolia. It is 353 miles (568 km) long and flows into the USSR, then along the border to Lake Ubsa Nor.

Teshio, Japan

The Teshio rises in the mountains northeast of ASAHIKAWA in Hokkaidō, Japan. It is 188 miles (302 km) long and runs north-northwest past the cities of NAYORO and BIFUKA, then south-southwest to enter the Sea of Japan at TESHIO.

Tigris, Southwestern Asia

The Tigris rises in Lake Golcuk in the Kurdistan region of east-central Turkey approximately 15 miles (24 km) southeast of the town of ELAZIG, and not far distance from the Euphrates River. Along with the Euphrates, the Tigris formed the ancient 'Land Between the Two Rivers' where the ancient civilizations of Mesopotamia rose and fell over 4000 BC. The primitive agriculture of Mesopotamia largely depends upon the rich

Above: A kalek laden with bags of wool crosses the Tigris near Baghdad.

Right: An aerial photograph of the Tigris near Baghdad in the province of Diyala where it is joined by the Diyala River.

alluvium which both rivers brought down their courses in the past and the life-giving water which is utilized for irrigation. The Tigris is navigable by shallow-draft steamers as far as BAGHDAD. The river is 1181 miles (1900 km) long.

The Tigris flows southeast along the southwestern edge of Armenian Knot. Nearby is the town of DIYARBAKIR in Turkey which was founded by the Romans in AD 230. Today the town is populated by Kurds and is the chief center for the agriculturally rich region which grows wheat, millet, barley and rice, and exports large quantities of wool and mohair. The river continues on course through a barren area for approximately 20 miles (32 km) forming the border between Turkey and Syria. It then turns southeast to run into Iraq. The Tigris flows onto the Eski Mosul Dam very close to the Mosul Oilfield. This area is extremely rich in agricultural products, but the trade in cotton has declined sharply since the ancient days of the muslin trade. In the tenth century MOSUL was an independent kingdom ruled by its own caliph. Directly across the river are the ancient ruins of the capital of the Assyrian Empire, NINEVEH, one of the truly magnificent cities of the ancient world. Nineveh was the center of ancient Mesopotamia civilization until it fell to the sword in 612 BC. The massive ruins extend for over three miles (five km) in length which gives

the onlooker an idea of its once great size.

The Tigris is joined by the Great Zab and the Little Zab Rivers below Mosul. The river flows southeast to SAMARRA and finally reaches the great Tigris-Euphrates Plain. The ruins of Sāmarrā, the seat of the Abbasid caliphs, extend along the banks of the Tigris for over 20 miles (32 km). Mesopotamia seems to have had more than its share of great and powerful cities but only the shells remain of these once proud metropolises. Here a great barrage is built across the river to provide water for the storage area of Lake Tharthār via a 40 mile (64km) long canal. The principal purpose of this scheme was originally to protect the capital of Iraq, Baghdād, with a population of over 1,750,000, from flooding. Below Sāmarrā, the Tigris runs east-southeast, then south to Baghdād, the city founded by Mansur in AD 762 and which rose to be one of the greatest of all Islamic cities. Caliph Harun-el-Rashid, the greatest and most powerful of all Caliphs described in the 'Thousand and One Nights,' ruled from Baghdād. The commercial prosperity of the city declined and it was captured and sacked by the Mongols in 1258. Baghdād was also destroyed and the populace put to the sword in 1400 by the great Tamerlane, then by the Persians in 1524, and later captured after hard fighting by the Ottoman Turks in 1638 and in 1917 by the British Army of Mesopotamia. In 1921 the Kingdom of Iraq was established and later a republic in 1958. The Iraqis have turned their attentions now to the development of their natural resources and have reestablished Baghdād as one of the great world commercial centers. Passing the Kut Barrage, the Tigris now quite unstable in its course, sends out a main branch, the Shatt al Gharraf, which gradually falls away from the main channel on a south-southeast course and links up with the Euphrates. The Tigris flows on eastward, then turns southeast to join the Euphrates at Al Qurnah, which many believe to be the traditional site of the Garden of Eden, located 40 miles (64 km) above the town of BASRA. The combined river is referred to as the Shatt al Arab, which continues for a further 120 miles (190 km) through extremely marshy countryside before entering the Persian Gulf. The climate in this area is very hot and dry. The rise of world crude oil prices in past years has enabled the Arab States to make much more out of their oil revenues than previously, and this is being poured into the control of the Tigris and Euphrates River systems which have been ignored in the wake of other world events.

To, China
River rising in several headstreams in Szechwan Province, China. It is also known as the Chung Kiang and Lu Ho River. The river is 300 miles (480 km) long and flows past KIENGANG, TZECHUNG and FUSHUN to join the Yangtze River at LUCHOU (Luhsien).

Tobol, Asian USSR
The Tobol rises in the Mugodzhary Mountains of northern Kazahkstan. Initially the river is a mountain stream, but in its middle and lower courses has a wide valley, as it flows through the western Siberian lowland. During

Sunday afternoon on the banks of the Tobol River in Siberia.

extremely hot and dry seasons the river becomes dry above KUSTANAY. The Tobol has a very winding course, and in its northern parts has numerous swamps and lakes. The chief tributaries are the Iset, Ili, Tura, Tavda, and the Ubalan Rivers. The river's primary use is for timber floating and is navigable below the confluence of the Tura River. The Tobol is 1042 miles (1677 km) long, and one of the longest rivers in Siberia.

Tokachi, Japan
The Tokachi rises southeast of ASAHIKAWA, Hokkaidō, Japan. It is 122 miles (196 km) long and runs south, east-southeast and south-southeast to enter the Pacific Ocean at OTSU.

Tom, Asian USSR
The Tom rises in the Kuznetsk Alatau Mountains of the USSR. The river is 522 miles (840 km) long and runs west and north through the Kuznetsk Basin to join the Ob

River approximately 30 miles (48 km) north-northwest of the city of TOMSK. The principal tributaries are the Usa, the Mras-Su and the Kondoma Rivers.

Tone, Japan
The Tone rises in the mountains north of MAEBASHI, Honshū, Japan. The river has a length of 230 miles (370 km) and runs south and southeast past the towns of TORIDE and SAWARA to enter the Pacific Ocean at CHOSHI.

Tônlé Sab, Cambodia
The Tônlé Sab or Great Lake as it is known in Cambodia is the natural flood reservoir of the Mekong River. In flood season the lake inundates an area of 2500 square miles (6475 km), which is quite an increase from its normal low water area of 1000 square miles (2590 sq km). The lake is connected to the Mekong River by the Tônlé Sab River which is 70 miles (113 km) long. The lake has an average depth of three to ten feet (one to three m) in the dry season and 30–40 feet (nine to twelve m) in the west season. The Tônlé Sab

reverses its flow in the dry season, running into the Mekong instead of vice versa. This is one of nature's most interesting and unusual natural reservoirs.

Traing, Malaya
The Traing rises in the central Malaya Mountains and flows due south and then west passing KUALA LUMPUR, the capital and a city of 325,000. The river then continues on past KELANG before entering the Strait of Malacca at PORT SWETTENHAM. The Traing is 60 miles (97 km) long.

Tsingpo, Tibet-India-Pakistan
See Brahmaputra, Tibet-India-Pakistan

Tumān, Korea
The Tumān rises on Changpai Mountain and forms the border between Korea and China, and Korea and the Soviet Union. It is 324 miles (521 km) long and runs northeast past the cities of MUSAN and HOERYONG, then turns eastward and southeast to enter the Sea of Japan.

Tungabhadra, India
This river rises in numerous headstreams in the Western Ghāts in northwestern Mysore. The two main headstreams, the Tunga and the Bhadra Rivers join at KUDALI, approximately seven miles northeast of Shimoga to form the Tungabhadra. The river is 400 miles (640 km) long and flows northeast to form the boundary between Hyderābād and Madras, then bends eastward to join the Kistna River after flowing for 220 miles (350 km). The lowlands between the Kistna and the Tungabhadra is known as the Raichur Doab and is noted for its tobacco and rice crops. This region is not very prosperous and the river is only navigable by small coracles for 200 miles (320 km).

Tunguska, Lower, Asian USSR
The Lower Tunguska or Nizhnyaya is the longest tributary of the Yenisey River. It is also one of the longest rivers in Siberia, with a length of 1671 miles (2689 km). The river rises in the south Central Siberian Plateau, and runs north for its first phase. It then changes direction, flowing due west to join the Yenisey 537 miles (864 km) from its mouth. The Lower Tunguska is unnavigable due to the numerous rapids and shallows which beset its entire course. The whole course of the river is winding, through a deep and narrow valley. This entire region is sparsely populated only supporting a few Evenki reindeer herdsmen.

Tunguska, Stony, Asian USSR
The Stony or Verkhnaya Tunguska rises in the Central Siberian Plateau. It is 962 miles (1548 km) long and flows across the Central Siberian Plateau to join the Yenisey after flowing through numerous rapids. The region is only inhabited by a few Evenki herdsmen who manage on the very barest of necessities. The river is totally frozen from October-May.

Tura, Asian USSR
The Tura rises in the central Ural Mountains of southwestern Siberia. It is 625 miles (1006 km) long and flows east and north past MALOMALSK, then east past VERKHOTURYE, southeast past TURINSK, and finally east to the Tobol River. The Tura's chief tributaries are the Nitsa, Tagil, Is, Pyskma and Aktai Rivers.

Turukhan, Asian USSR
A river rising near the Arctic Circle approximately 80 miles (129 km) south-southwest of Igarka in the Krasnoyarsk Territory of the Soviet Union. It is 320 miles (510 km) long and joins the Yenisey River at TURUKHANSK.

Tuul, Mongolia
The Tuul rises in the Henteyn Mountains of northern Mongolia. The river is 437 miles (703 km) long and runs southwest past the capital ULAN BATOR. It then moves northwest to the Orhon River.

Tzu, China
The Tzu rises in the Kwangsi border of Hunan Province, China. It is 460 miles (740 km) long and flows north and northeast past the cities of SHAOYANG and YIYANG to Lake Tungting at YUANKIANG. The Tzu forms a joint delta with the Hsiang River.

Uda, Asian USSR
The Uda rises in the Stanovoi Range in the Khabarovsk Territory of the Soviet Union. The Uda flows east-northeast for 330 miles (530 km) to enter the Sea of Okhotsk at CHUMIKAN. The principal tributary is the Maya River.

Ural, European-Asian USSR
The Ural is a very unique river in that it is regarded as the boundary between Europe and Asia. It is one of the longest rivers in the Soviet Union with a total length of 1575 miles (2534 km). It rises at a height of 2010 feet (613 m) in the Ural Mountain Range, and flows south as a torrent, rushing along the eastern margins of the mountains. The Ural becomes more gentle and leaves the forests of the mountains to flow through the open steppes past Mt Magnitnaya, which has some of the best quality iron ore in the world. Nearby on the banks of the Ural, the town of MAGNITOGORSK has grown since 1930 to become one of the Soviet Union's largest steel and iron works. Two large reservoirs have been built on the Ural to provide the town with the much needed cheap hydroelectric power. The Ural now flows toward IRIKLINSKIY where there is another large dam and hydroelectric station. It then continues on to ORSK where the river swings to a westerly direction and cuts through the low southern section of the Ural Mountains in a narrow gorge, called the 'Orsk Gates.' The Ural receives only one major tributary, the Sakmara River at the city of ORENBURG. It was originally built as a fortress in 1743 to guard Russia's trade gateway to central Asia. The Ural Horde of the Cossacks had its center located at Orenburg. Upon reaching URALSK, the river turns south once again, it is now about one-third of a mile (530 m) across and begins to meander across a wide flood plain. Below Uralsk the river flows through a semi-arid region with no tributaries reaching it, in fact distributaries take water from the main channel, only to die in the Caspian lowlands. These small distributaries of the Ural only reach the Caspian Sea during the rainy seasons. On the main channel near its mouth is located the town of GURYEV which is the center of a small but valuable oilfield. The Ural is navigable only to Uralsk, except during the spring flood when small vessels can reach as far as Orenburg.

Ussuri, Asian USSR-China
The Ussuri is formed by the confluence of the Ulukhe River – 165 miles (265 km) long – and the Daubikhe River – 175 miles (282 km) long – on the border of the Soviet Union and China. The river is 365 miles (587 km) long and runs due north along the border past the cities of LESOZAVODSK, IMAN and BIKIN to meet the Amur River in two arms at FUYUAN and KHABAROVSK. The Ussuri is one of the most important rivers of this region.

Vakh, Asian USSR
The Vakh rises in the Ob-Yenisey Divide in the Tomsk oblast of the Soviet Union. The river is 560 miles (9202 km) long and flows west past LARYAK to become a tributary of the Ob River.

Vasyugan, Asian USSR
The Vasyugan rises in the Vasyuganye Marshes of the Tomsk Oblast of the Soviet Union. It is 625 miles (1006 km) long and flows northwest, north and finally east to join the Ob River near KARGASOK.

Vilyuy, Asian USSR
The Vilyuy rises on the central Siberian Plateau in the Yakut Autonomous SSR. The river is 1512 miles (2433 km) long and flows east past the cities of SUNTAR and VILYUYSK to join the Lena River approximately 180 miles (290 km) northwest of YAKUTSK. The region along the river's course is rich in gold and platinum. The river is navigable for 500 miles (800 km).

Vitim, Asian USSR
The Vitim rises on the Vitim Plateau and has a length of 1132 miles (1821 km). It flows north-northwest past BODAYBO and MAMA to join the Lena River at VITIM. The river is navigable below the town of Bodaybo.

Wainganga, India
This river rises in the central Sātpura Range of Madhya Pradesh, India. It is 360 miles (580 km) long and flows north, east and south past PAUNI to join the Wardha River approximately 40 miles (64 km) southeast of CHANDA to form the Pranhita River. The Pranhita is a considerable tributary of the Godāvari River.

Walawi Ganges, Sri Lanka
The Walawi rises in the hill country of southern Sri Lanka and flows for 83 miles (134 km) east and southeast to enter the Indian Ocean south of HAMBANTOTA.

Wardha, India
The Wardha rises near PANDHURNA, Madhya Pradesh, India. It is 250 miles (400 km) long and flows southeast through large cotton fields to join the Wainganga River southeast of CHANDA to form the Pranhita River.

Wei, China
The Wei rises in southeastern Kansu Province, China. The Wei is the chief right-bank tributary of the mighty Huang Ho River. It is 540 miles (870 km) long and runs east, north of the Tsinling Mountains past the city of TIENSHUI and into Shensi Province. The river continues past HSIENYANG and WEINAN to join the Huang Ho near TUNGKUAN. The principal tributaries of the Wei are the Lo and the King Rivers.

Wu, China
The Wu is formed by the confluence of two headstreams near LISHUI in Chekiang Province, China. The river is 285 miles (459 km) long and flows east-southeast past TSINGTIEN and WENCHOU to enter the East China Sea.

Yalu, China
The Yalu is 500 miles (800 km) long and rises on the southern slopes of Changpai Mountain. It flows southeast past the town of CHANGPAI, then runs westward to LINKIANG, and southwest passing TSIAN, and SUPUNG to TANTUNG, where it enters Korea Bay of the Yellow Sea. The Yalu is only navigable in its lower reaches and is utilized primarily for logging. Located at Supung is a huge hydroelectric dam which provides power to the capital of North Korea, PYONGYANG, and Tantung, LUTA (Dairen) and MUKDEN. In Korean the Yalu is called the Amnok-Kang, and in Japanese the Oryokko. It forms an integral portion of Manchurian-North Korean boundary and was in dispute after World War II and was fought over during the Korean War. The upper reaches of the Yalu are extremely cold, with bitter winds and climate has restricted the farmers to one crop a year.

Top left: A modern bridge spans the Ural River at Guriev, a city which is shared by two continents, Europe and Asia. The bridge is 1800 ft (550 m) long. Above and right: Two views of the Vakh River. This rapid and unpredictable river is capable of changing its course every year.

Yalung, China
The Yalung rises in the Bayan Kara Mountains of Sinkiang Province, China. The river is 880 miles (1420 km) long and flows south past SHIHCHU and YAKIANG to join the Yangtze River on the Yunnan border.

Yamuna, India

The Yamuna rises at an altitude of 11,000 feet (3355 m), approximately five miles (eight km) north of the hot spring at JAMNOTRI, in the western Kumaon Himalayas. It cuts deep into the mountains forming the boundary between Uttar Pradesh and Himachal Pradesh, and flows southwest through a gorge in the Siwalik Hills. It then enters the Indo-Gangetic Plain, and has built a cone over 100 miles (160 km) wide, and has cut a narrow flood plain into the surface of the plain. The Yamuna is 860 miles (1380 km) long, and is one of the chief tributaries of the Ganges. It provides drinking water for DELHI and is utilized for irrigation projects upstream. It is joined by the Chambal River above ALLAHABAD, before entering the Ganges. The Chambal and the Yamuna are both sacred rivers to the Hindus, and the exact spot where they meet is considered to be especially holy. The water of the Yamuna is quite clear and blue, while the Ganges is brown; for a distance below the confluence the difference is visible.

Yana, Asian USSR

The Yana rises in the Verkhoyansk Range of the Yakut Autonomous Republic of the Soviet Union. It is 667 miles (1073 km) long and flows north past the cities of VERKHOYANSK and KAZACHYE to enter the Laptev Sea through a very large delta below the city of UST-YANSK. The Yana is navigable below Verkhoyansk between June and September when the river is free of ice. The principal tributaries of the Yana are the Bytantai and the Adycha rivers. The Verkhoyansk area is the center of the coldest region on earth. The lowest recorded temperature was a biting −92 degrees F.

Yangtze, China

This is the great river of China and the longest in the continent of Asia with a length of 3434 miles (5525 km). In Chinese it is called the

Ch'ang Chiang River. The Yangtze drains an enormous area of 756,000 square miles (1,958,000 sq km). It rises in several head-streams in the Tanglha Range very near the border of Tibet. The river runs east and south through the province of Sinkiang on a parallel course with the Mekong and the Salween Rivers, two of Asia's other great rivers. It enters Yunnan Province and passes within 40 miles (64 km) of the canyon through which the Mekong flows. The Mekong and the Salween Rivers follow on in their southward direction toward the tropical zones; the Yangtze is checked by the high Chinese tableland, and consequently veers eastward and then northward through the Taliang Shan to enter Szechwan Province. From Tibet through the mountains of Sinkiang and Yunnan Provinces, the river has a long and precipitous descent through a series of deep ravines and gorges. The river falls in its first 600 miles (970 km) from an altitude of 16,000 feet (4900 m) to 8500 feet (2590 m) at the town of BATANG. By the time it reaches WA-WU, it has fallen to 1900 feet (580 m), and at CHUNGKING, in the Red Basin of Szechwan Province, China's most densely populated province, it is 630 feet (190 m).

Once again forced to run through a series of deep gorges the river breaks out at ICHANG at only 130 feet (40 m) above sea level. Below the city of SUCHOW the river runs through the southern edge of Red Basin of Szechwan, and past the cities of LUCHOU, Chungking and WANHSIEN. Afterwards the Yangtze receives two large tributaries, the Min and Chialing Rivers, it is along this stretch that the population of Szechwan is centered with an unbelievable density of 1000 people per square mile (2.7 sq km). The region is rich in tea, medicinal plants, ramie, silk and tobacco. The city of ICHANG is located at the border of Szechwan-Hupeh, and is the head of the Yangtze's navigational limit. It is the limit for

The Yangtze River at Wuhan in Hupei Province of central China.

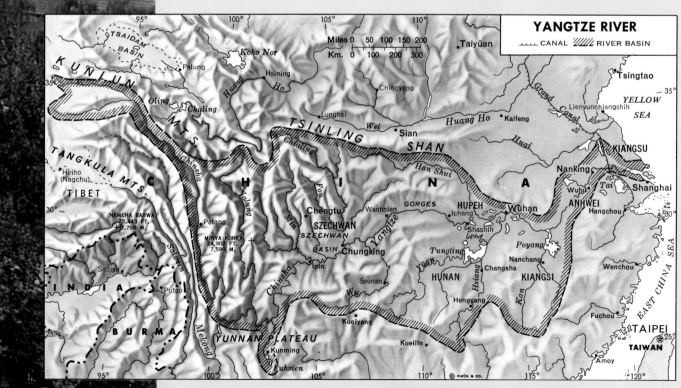

ocean-going vessels and serves the lake-filled basin of Hupeh. The Yangtze serves the cities of HANYANG, WUCHANG and HANKOW. The conurbation is known as Wuhan, and it is here that the Peking-Canton railway crosses the Yangtze by a bridge finished in 1958. This railway junction has now made Wuhan a great commercial transfer point as it is accessible for ocean-going vessels. The vessels can sail up to Wuhan, offload their cargo, which in turn can be loaded onto railway cars and redistributed throughout the region. Above Wuhan, the river is navigable by shallow-bottomed craft only, therefore all of the transshipments are accomplished at Ichang. Other tributaries of note are the treacherous Yalung, the To, the Han, and the Wu Rivers. Upon reaching ANHWEI the Yangtze runs through lowlands sprinkled with lakes and flows through the Kiangsu flats formed by the alluvial deposits of the Yangtze, Huang Ho and the Huai Rivers. In the lower reaches of its course, the river serves the cities of ANKING, WUHU and NANKING. Nanking is a city with a population of 2,000,000, and means 'southern capital,' it has been the seat of the Chinese government on several occasions: the last time under Chiang Kai-shek. The Yangtze is navigable for 1000 miles (1610 km) by ocean-going vessels, and for 1500 miles (2410 km) by smaller vessels and is China's greatest internal waterway. Its banks are the most densely populated area in the entire world. In its last stage, the Yangtze is linked by the Whangpoo River to the great port city of SHANGHAI and the East China Sea.

Yarkand Soche, China

The Yarkand or Soche rises near K2 peak in the main Karakoram Range in southwestern Sinkiang Province, China. The river is 500 miles (800 km) long and runs northeast past YARKAND and MERKET to join the Aksu River in forming the Tarim River.

Yeloguy, Asian USSR

The Yeloguy rises in the marshes which are the source of the Vakh River in Krasnoyarsk Territory, Soviet Union. It is 350 miles (560 km) long and runs north and northeast to become a tributary of the Yenisey River.

Yenisey, Asian USSR

The Yenisey is one of the great rivers of Siberia and the world. It is 2566 miles (4129 km) long

and drains an area of 1,003,474 square miles (2,599,000 sq km). The Yenisey is formed at the confluence of the Bol'shoy (Great) Yenisey and the Malyy (Little) Yenisey Rivers at KYZYL in a deep mountain basin of the Tuva Autonomous Republic of the Soviet Union. The two main headstreams flow through a large tectonic basin westward to form the Yenisey. The river manages to cut its way out of this large basin through the high Western Sayan Mountain Range to the north in a very deep, long gorge, literally strewn with rapids. This gorge is now the site of a huge hydroelectric project and supplies the region with a large proportion of its electricity needs. After escaping one mountain basin, the Yenisey immediately enters another, but it exits from this second gorge through the Eastern Sayan Mountain Range. At the mouth of this second gorge is located the important city of KRASNOYARSK which is also the site of a large hydroelectric project. Krasnoyarsk is the largest settlement on the river, with engineering works, food-processing industries and timber yards. Once below the city the Yenisey flows due north for over 1000 miles (1610 km). From the left bank the river does not receive any tributaries of note and is mainly covered by vast swamps and great forests. The difference in the right bank is remarkable. From the very edge of the river rises the Central Siberian Plateau, and numerous tributaries flow into the Yenisey from this plateau. The principal tributaries are the Angara or Upper Tunguska River, the Stony Tunguska and the Lower Tunguska Rivers. The Central Siberian Plateau has been the scene of large-scale mining endeavors for centuries. The following minerals are found in abundance: nickel, gold, copper, platinum and cobalt. The chief mining town in the region is NORILSK in the Putoran Mountains and is connected to the Yenisey by the port of DUDINKA on the main railway line. IGARKA is another important river port located 130 miles (210 km) above Dudinka and is one of the largest sawmilling and timber exporting ports in the entire Soviet Union. Once below Dudinka the Yenisey finally enters its estuary which is an unbelievable 300 miles (480 km) long. The lower course of the river is through a desolate and unpopulated tundra region, except for the roaming Nentsy reindeer herders who travel throughout this region practically unnoticed. The entire river below the town of Angara is only sparsely populated. The Yenisey is the one and only routeway in the region and is navigable along its full length of 2566 miles (4129 km). The only problem is the long periods when the river is frozen over, in the lower reaches up to six months while in the upper reaches it can be as long as nine months. The river has one of the heaviest discharges of water of any river in the world with 4,500,000 cubic feet (128,600 cu m) of water every second.

Yeşil, Turkey

The Yeşil begins in the Kizil Dag Mountains north-northeast of Zara in northern Turkey. It is 260 miles (420 km) long and flows west-northwest to enter the Black Sea at Cape Civa.

Ying, China

The Ying rises in the Sung Mountains of northwestern Honan Province, China. The Ying is 300 miles (480 km) long and flows southeast past YUHSIEN and CHOUKOUCHEN into Anhwei Province, then continues past FOUYANG to join the Huai River at CHENG-YANGKUAN. The chief tributary of the Ying is the Sha River.

Yom, Thailand

The Yom rises near the Laos border in northern Thailand. It is one of the headstreams of the Chao Phraya River. It is 400 miles (640 km) long and flows south past SAWANKALOK and SUKHOTHAI to form a joint flood plain with the Nan River. It joins the Ping River near NAKHON SAWAN to form the Chao Phraya River.

Zab, Turkey

Also called the Great Zab, it rises in the Turkish Kordestān hills near the Iranian border. It is 265 miles (430 km) long and flows south-southwest past COLEMERIK into Iraq. It then moves due south to become a tributary of the Tigris River south-southeast of MOSUL.

Zeravshan, Asian USSR

The Zeravshan rises in eastern Turkestan Range of the Tadzhik and Uzbek SSR. The river is 460 miles (740 km) long and flows due west past MATCHA and PENDZHIKENT before dividing into two separate arms the Kara Darya and the Ak Darya Rivers between the ancient city of SAMARKAND and KHATYRCHI, then southwest past BUHARA to only disappear into the desert north of Chardzhou.

Zeya, Asian USSR

The Zeya rises in the Stanovoi Range of the Amur Oblast of the Soviet Union. It is 750 miles (1210 km) long and flows southeast and south to join the Amur River at BLAGOVESHCHENSK.

Zohreh, Iran

Alternatively known as the Tab, it rises in the Zāgros Mountains approximately 90 miles (140 km) northwest of SHIRAZ in southwestern Iran. The river is 200 miles (320 km) long and flows west and south to enter the Persian Gulf 80 miles (129 km) east-southeast of the town of ABADAN.

Right: The Derwent River at New Norfolk in Tasmania.

Australasia

Ashburton, Western Australia, Australia

This intermittent river of northwestern Western Australia rises east of MUNDIWINDI. The river runs on a westerly course to MT VERNON, then swings northwest to the town of GLENROY at Exmouth Gulf of the Indian Ocean. The Ashburton's chief tributaries are the Hardey and Henry Rivers. The river is 400 miles (640 km) long and for the most part consists of waterholes.

Balonne, Queensland, Australia

The Balonne rises in the McPherson Range and flows for 495 miles (796 km). It has two tributaries: the minor Dogwood River and the stronger Condamine River, the true source, which runs northwest past the town of WARWICK. As the Balonne shifts to a southwesterly direction at Sunnybank where it is joined by the Bungil River. Just above DIRRANBANDI the river branches into two separate channels: the first called the Culgoa River runs into the Darling River and the second is the Narran River which enters Lake Terewah.

Bogan, New South Wales, Australia

The Bogan River has its source in central New South Wales near the town of PARKES. The river is 451 miles (726 km) long and becomes a tributary of the Darling River (also called Barwon) approximately 25 miles (40 km) northeast of the town of BOURKE.

Brisbane, Queensland, Australia

The source of the Brisbane is in southeastern Queensland in the Australian Great Dividing Range. It runs for a total of 201 miles (323 km) on a southerly course, then it swings northeast through the city of BRISBANE which is the capital of Queensland and has a population of 649,500. The river then heads for Moreton Bay which is its final destination. It is navigable to Brisbane.

Buller, South Island, New Zealand

The Buller rises in Lake Rotolti in the northwestern portion of South Island. It has a length of 105 miles (169 km) and runs in a southwesterly direction to the Tasman Sea.

Burdekin, Queensland, Australia

The Burdekin rises in the hills west of the town of INGHAM in eastern Queensland. It is 440 miles (710 km) long and runs southeast, then north before flowing into Upstart Bay.

Burnett, Queensland, Australia

The Burnett can be classified as a medium-sized river. It flows for a total of 250 miles (400 km) from the Auburn Range of Queensland, first south to the town of EIDSVOLD, then turns east and finally northeast to Hervey Bay on the Pacific Ocean. The principal tributaries of the Burnett are the Auburn River, named for the mountain range from which it flows, and the Nogo and Boyne Rivers. The Burnett is important for irrigation purposes.

Campaspe, Victoria, Australia

The Campaspe rises south of KYNETON in the Great Dividing Range and heads north to join the Murray River. The Campaspe is utilized primarily for irrigation projects and runs for 100 miles (160 km) from its source to its outlet.

Canning, Western Australia, Australia

The Canning is 52 miles (84 km) long and lies in the Darling Mountain Range of southwestern Western Australia. It runs in a northwesterly direction on its way to the Swan River estuary at the city of FREEMANTLE on the Indian Ocean. Freemantle has a population of 21,980 and is situated very near Perth.

Castlereagh, New South Wales, Australia

A river which rises in the Liverpool Mountain Range of New South Wales. The river runs for a total of 341 miles (549 km) past COONAMBLE to join the Darling River approximately 30 miles (48 km) west of the town of WALGETT. The Castlereagh drains a substantial area primarily utilized by sheepherders.

Clarence, New South Wales, Australia

The Clarence is 245 miles (394 km) long. It rises in the McPherson Range of New South Wales and flows southeast, then northeast passing GRAFTON. The river is navigable below GRAFTON for 45 miles (72 km) where steamers carry produce and other supplies. It enters the Pacific Ocean 11 miles (18 km) from Maclean.

Clutha, South Island, New Zealand

The Clutha is the principal river of South Island. It begins to flow from Lake Wanaka and runs for a total of 210 miles (340 km) passing the towns of CROMWELL and ALEXANDRA on its way to enter the South Pacific near KAITANGATA. The river is navigable for a short distance up river from its mouth by small steamers.

Cooper's Creek, Queensland, Australia

Formerly known as the Barcoo River, Cooper's Creek is formed by the confluence of the Barcoo and Thompson Rivers. This river like the majority of Australian rivers is intermittent. It has a length of 880 miles (1420 km) and empties into LAKE EYRE. It really is a continuous line of deep waterholes which during the monsoon season are linked together giving it the appearance of a river. In 1847 Sir Thomas Mitchell believed it to be the great north-flowing river which he had been seeking for years. This misconception was put right 11 years later when another renowned Australian explorer Sir A C Gregory proved beyond a shadow of a doubt that the misnamed river was only the intermittent stream called Cooper's Creek.

Daly, Northern Territory, Australia

The Daly is 225 miles (362 km) long and runs from the hills west of the small town of KATHERINE northwest to enter the Timor Sea via Anson Bay.

Darling, Eastern Australia

The Darling is one of the three principal river systems of Australia. It has a length of 1704 miles (2742 km). The Darling rises on the western slopes of the Great Australian Divide where the Barwon and Culgoa Rivers come together just north of the town of BOURKE in New South Wales. In any other continent, the

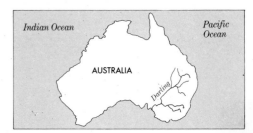

Darling would have a huge capacity and great channel, but this is not the case in Australia. The river has absolutely no snow near its headwaters and consequently must rely totally upon the fickle waters of the monsoons to feed itself. It does receive tributaries: the Condamine, Macintyre Brook, Gwydir, Castlereagh, and Bogan to name the major ones, but these do not substantially increase the shallow waters of the Darling. Once the river passes Bourke, the Warrego and Paroo Rivers are the only tributaries of note; and the Paroo only adds its waters to the Darling two or three times in 100 years. The Darling flows through some of the most arid country in Australia resulting in the majority of its water evaporating as fast as it gets into the main channel. When the floods come to the Darling region, the backwater channels fill rapidly forming over 70 lakes which all link up through the river's many channels. The rains bring life to the arid area surrounding the Darling; brilliant grasses and flowers bloom for a short

Above: 'Dead Man's Crossing' on Cooper's Creek in Queensland. Usually a chain of waterholes, floods occur suddenly and have been known to sweep many a stranger to his death.
Above right: Gum trees mark the course of the Darling River near Broken Hill in western New South Wales.

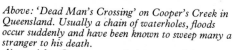

while before the waters dissipate and then the region returns to its arid state. Although the Darling has a very sporadic flow, many ranchers have drilled artesian wells into the bed of the river to supply their sheep with adequate fresh water all year. The Darling region is excellent sheep country and the early Australian settlers took advantage of this by making it into one of the great sheep-raising areas in the world. The Darling is probably best noted for being the principal tributary of the Murray River which is Australia's premier river. Although river traffic never flourished on the Darling as on the Murray, small steamers still plowed up the treacherous riverbed to ship wool to the large cities on the coast. An item of note for the interested historian is that the first vessel up the Darling to Bourke in 1861 was the *Gemini* which hauled a load of hard liquor to the parched men of the town. The last vessel to steam up the Darling was in 1943, and believe it or not, it carried another load of hard liquor to a small garrison of thirsty soldiers in Queensland. The Darling is one of the most underestimated rivers in the world and most likely in past geological ages was even greater than the Murray.

Dawson, Queensland, Australia
The Dawson rises in the Carnarvon Mountain Range in Queensland. It flows for 312 miles (502 km) first eastward, then northeast before turning north to meet the MacKenzie River to form the larger Fitzroy River.

DeGrey, Western Australia, Australia
The DeGrey River rises in the hills to the southeast of MARBLE BAR. The DeGrey is an intermittent river, which flows for 190 miles (310 km) before emptying into the Indian Ocean just east of PORT HEDLAND.

Derwent, Tasmania, Australia
The Derwent River rises in LAKE ST CLAIR in southern Tasmania, the island located off the southeastern corner of Australia and separated from the mainland by the Bass Strait. The principal tributaries of the Derwent are the Clyde, Jordan and Ouse Rivers. The Derwent runs southeast past the towns of CLAREMONT, BELLERIVE and HOBART, the latter being the capital of Tasmania. It has a length of 107 miles (172 km) and enters Storm Bay of the Tasman Sea through a wide estuary approximately four miles (six km) wide.

Diamantina, Queensland, Australia
The Diamantina rises in the Selwyn Range of Queensland and flows for a total of 560 miles (900 km). Like the majority of Australian rivers it is intermittent. The river received its name in 1866 after the wife of the Governor of Queensland, Sir G Brown. Charles Sturt, the great Australian explorer, had crossed its stony and dry channel on his trek across the continent in 1844 and did not even deem the dry riverbed worth naming. The river only flows during the wet season but its waterholes and tree-lined channels break the monotony of the arid countryside. Further along the Diamantina is the town of BIRDSVILLE, one of the primary bases for the Flying Doctor Service. The river finally empties into the Warburton River at Lake Willand, an intermittent body of water near CLIFTON HILLS.

Digul, Papua New Guinea
The Digul rises on the southeastern slopes of the Orange Range and is alternatively known as the Digoel. It is 400 miles (640 km) long and flows south and west to enter the Arafura Sea north of Frederik Henrik Island. The river drains a large marshy jungle region.

Drysdale, Western Australia, Australia
The Drysdale rises in the Kimberley Range of the extreme northeast corner of Western Australia. It flows north to enter the Timor Sea near Cape Talbot and is an extremely intermittent river during its initial stages.

Fitzmaurice, Northern Territory, Australia
The Fitzmaurice rises in the northwest position of the Northern Territory and flows 104 miles (167 km) on a westerly course before entering Joseph Bonaparte Gulf. This is another intermittent Australian river.

Fitzroy, Queensland, Australia
The Fitzroy is formed by the confluence of the Dawson and Mackenzie Rivers. The river is 174 miles (280 km) long and flows north for a short distance before turning southeast past the town of ROCKHAMPTON to enter Keppel Bay of the Pacific Ocean at the port of ALMA. The Fitzroy is navigable for approximately 50 miles (80 km) above Rockhampton.

Fitzroy, Western Australia, Australia
Rising in the Kimberley Plateau of north Western Australia, the Fitzroy is 350 miles (560 km) long and runs west. Its major tributaries are the Margaret River and

Above: Barrage on the Fitzroy River in Western Australia.
Left: The Derwent River of Tasmania
Right: The flood plains of Queensland's Diamantina River are extensive even though the river itself is intermittent, flowing only in the rainy season.

Christmas Creek. Although it too relies upon the wet season for most of its water supply, the Fitzroy is a valuable river especially to the sheepherders who need the outstanding spring pastures which it provides. The river was named for a captain of the *Beagle*, by Captain Stokes who was the skipper at the time. The river is the hideaway of ibis, geese and pelicans during dry season when it is only a series of deep waterholes dotted along the northwestern Australian hills. It finally empties into King Sound of the Indian Ocean.

Flinders, Queensland, Australia
The Flinders River rises west of Charters Towers in the Great Dividing Range of northern Queensland. The river is 520 miles (840 km) long and flows west passing HUGHEN-DEN and RICHMOND before changing direction to the northwest. The Flinders runs on this northwesterly course then turns north to enter the Gulf of Carpentaria.

The broad waterless bed of sand called the Gascoyne River. It runs but once to thrice a year yet supplies water to the locals.

Fly, Papua New Guinea

The Fly River rises in the perpetual mists and forests of the New Guinea Highlands. It flows through thick jungle-clad hills to the place where it receives its chief tributary, the Strickland River. (The Strickland rises in the high mountains near Mt Hagen.) Captain Blackwood named the Fly after his vessel HMS *Fly* while he was charting the Gulf of Papua. An Italian naturalist, Albertis explored the river in 1876. The Fly is 700 miles (1130 km) long and is navigable for 500 miles (800 km) upstream. After flowing through swampy lowlands and the numerous changing mouths of the mangrove-surrounded delta, the Fly finally enters the Gulf of Papua.

Fortescue, Western Australia, Australia

The Fortescue is 340 miles (550 km) long and begins northwest of the small township of MUNDIWINDI in northwestern Western Australia. It runs northeast to ETHEL CREEK, then turns northwest past Mt Bruce and into the Indian Ocean approximately 80 miles (129 km) southwest of ROEBOURNE. The Fortescue like most Australian rivers is intermittent.

Gascoyne, Western Australia, Australia

The Gascoyne River rises in the Robinson Range of the western corner of Western Australia. It flows for 475 miles (760 km) and its major tributary is the Lyons River which itself is 225 miles (360 km) long. The Gascoyne runs due west to enter Shark Bay on the Indian Ocean at CARNARVON.

Gawler, South Australia, Australia

The Gawler rises above the town of GAWLER where it is joined by the intermittent South Para River. It then flows into the Gulf of St Vincent, north of PORT ADELAIDE.

Gilbert, Queensland, Australia

The Gilbert begins near the junction of the Great Dividing and Gregory Mountain Ranges of northern Queensland. It has a length of 312 miles (500 km), and flows northwest through thick grazing land and into the Gulf of Carpentaria.

Goulburn, Victoria, Australia

The Goulburn has its source in the Great Dividing Range just southeast of WOODS POINT in central Victoria. It is 280 miles (450 km) long and passes through the Eildon Weir, then swings northward past the power station at SHEPPARTON and into the Murray River near ECHUCA. The Goulburn is one of the few rivers in Australia which usually has water in its channels all year.

Grey, South Island, New Zealand

This river rises in the Spenser Mountain Range of South Island. It is 75 miles (121 km) long and runs southwest to GREYMOUTH where it enters the Tasman Sea.

Haast, South Island, New Zealand

The Haast rises in the Southern Alps of South Island and flows for a total of 60 miles (97 km). It runs southwest to enter the Tasman Sea.

Hastings, New South Wales, Australia

The Hastings begins in the Great Dividing Range of eastern New South Wales. It flows 108 miles (174 km), south and then east to enter the Pacific Ocean at PORT MACQUARIE.

Hawkesbury, New South Wales, Australia

The Hawkesbury rises in the Great Dividing Range of eastern New South Wales. It flows 293 miles (471 km) northeast past Goulburn to enter BROKEN BAY on the Tasman Sea.

Hopkins, Victoria, Australia

The Hopkins River rises in the Great Dividing Range, southwest of the town of ARARAT in southern Victoria. It flows for 135 miles (217 km) on a southerly course to enter the Indian Ocean east of WARRNAMBOOL.

Hotham, Western Australia, Australia

The Hotham rises east of the town of PINGELLY in southwestern Western Australia. It runs intermittently on a westerly course to join the Williams River in forming the Murray River.

Hunter, New South Wales, Australia

The Hunter rises in the Liverpool Range, an offshoot of the Great Dividing Range. It runs for a total of 290 miles (470 km) in a generally eastward direction. The Hunter's main tributaries are the Goulburn, Paterson, Williams and Wollombi Rivers. The entire region in which the river flows is prime farming land. The river empties into the Pacific Ocean near the port of NEWCASTLE.

Huon, Tasmania, Australia

The Huon rises approximately 50 miles (80 km) west of HOBART, the capital of Tasmania. The river flows for 105 miles (169 km) on an easterly course passing the towns of HOUNVILLE and FRANKLIN to enter the Tasman Sea.

Lachlan, New South Wales, Australia

The Lachlan rises in the Cullarin Range of the Great Dividing Range. The river is 920 miles (1480 km) long and the fourth longest river in Australia. It was discovered by G W Evans and named for the then Governor Lachlan Macquarie in 1815. Once the river leaves the wide eucalyptus forests near its headwaters, it runs northwest, then southwest entering extremely arid country and without any tributaries of note. The district through which the Lachlan flows was made famous by Australian 19th century bushrangers who robbed the miners during the Australian Gold Rush. The Lachlan is the chief tributary of the Murrumbidgee River.

Leichardt, Queensland, Australia

The Leichardt River rises near the town of MARY KATHLEEN in northern Queensland. The 300 mile (480 km) long intermittent river flows north to enter the Gulf of Carpentaria.

Limmen Bight, Northern Territory, Australia

The Limmen Bight rises on the Barkly Tableland of Australia's northeastern Northern Territory. This intermittent river runs for 140 miles (230 km) on a northeasterly course before entering the Gulf of Carpentaria.

McArthur, Northern Territory, Australia

This river rises on the northern end of the Barkly Tableland in northeast Northern Territory. It has a length of 125 miles (201 km), and flows on a northeasterly course to PORT MCARTHUR on the Gulf of Carpentaria.

MacKenzie, Queensland, Australia

The MacKenzie River is formed by the confluence of the Nogoa and Comet Rivers. It flows for 170 miles (270 km) before emptying into the Pacific Ocean.

Macleay, New South Wales, Australia

The Macleay rises in the New England Range of eastern New South Wales. It runs for 250 miles (400 km). The river flows first southeast, then northeast to enter the Pacific Ocean near Smoky Cape.

Macumba, South Australia, Australia

The Macumba River rises as the Alberga River in the Musgrave Range of South Australia. It flows on a southeasterly course to enter Lake Eyre, Australia's largest ghost lake, at its northern-most head. Lake Eyre is a huge salt lake in central South Australia which is between 20–40 miles (32–64 km) wide, 130 miles (210 km) long and encompasses 3500 square miles (9065 sq km). In the bygone Cretaceous Age a huge inland sea covering 500,000 square miles (1,295,000 sq km) spread out over this entire area. Today the lake is for the most part dry but whenever an extremely wet season occurs, Lake Eyre can be filled to capacity in a very short time. This was proved in 1949 when the lake filled rapidly due to heavy rains in far northern Queensland. The Macumba and Warburton Rivers are the main channels which bring this life-giving water to the dry lake.

Manawatu, North Island, New Zealand

This river rises in the Ruahine Range in the southern portion of North Island. It flows for 100 miles (160 km) southwest past PALMERSTON NORTH to the Cook Strait northeast of the WELLINGTON. The town of Palmerston North is a good sized town of over 50,000.

Manning, New South Wales, Australia

The Manning River rises in the Great Dividing Range of eastern New South Wales. The Manning is 139 miles (224 km) long and runs east to the Pacific Ocean southwest of CROWDY HEAD.

Markham, Papua New Guinea

The Markham River is 200 miles (320 km) long. It rises in the Finnisterre Range and flows southeast to enter the Huon Gulf of the Solomon Sea at LAE. The Markham River was the scene of several battles during World War II as General MacArthur attempted to retake New Guinea.

Mary, Queensland, Australia

The Mary River begins in the low hills of southeastern Queensland. It is 165 miles (265 km) long, and runs past the towns of GYMPIE, 11,000 and MARYBOROUGH, 20,000 to enter Hervey Bay. The river is navigable for a short distance below the town of Maryborough.

Mataura, South Island, New Zealand

Rising south of Lake Wakatipu in the southern portion of South Island, the Mataura River is 120 miles (192 km) long and flows southeast to enter Toetoes Bay of the Foveaux Strait.

Mitchell, Queensland, Australia

The Mitchell rises in the Great Dividing Range near RUMULA in northern Queensland. It runs for 350 miles (560 km) and receives the Palmer and Lynd Rivers. The Mitchell runs west by northwest to enter the Gulf of Carpentaria.

Mokau, North Island, New Zealand

The Mokau rises south of TE KUITI, North Island. It is navigable for a distance of 25 miles (40 km) as far as the Mokau coal mines. The river is 75 miles (121 km) long and runs into the North Taranaki Bight on the Tasman Sea on the western side of the island.

Murchison, Western Australia, Australia

The Murchison rises in the southeastern Robinson Ranges near Mt Hale which is 2400 feet (732 m) high, in the western central portion of Western Australia. It is 440 miles (710 km) long and runs on a very intermittent course southwest to enter the Indian Ocean.

Murray, Western Australia, Australia

The Murray River is formed by the confluence of the Hotham and Williams Rivers near Mt Keats in Western Australia. The Murray enters the Indian Ocean approximately 50 miles (80 km) from the city of PERTH.

Murray, New South Wales, Australia

The Murray is the principal river system of Australia, and has a total length of 1609 miles (2589 km). It forms a large part of the boundary between Victoria and New South Wales. It drains an area in excess of 415,000 square miles (1,075,000 sq km). The Murray rises in the alpine meadows of the Snowy Mountain Range of the Australian Alps and is the only Australian river that can be compared to other major river systems of the world. The

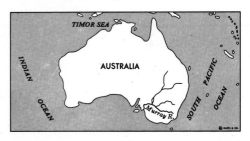

river flows from its source high in the Snowy Range fed by twin headwaters, the Indi and Swamp Plains Rivers, through hills covered by eucalyptus forests and swampy flats. In its first 200 miles (320 km), the Murray falls 5000 feet (1525 m) descending into the foothills and heading toward the town of ALBURY. The river flows through a great plain, cutting its way here and there, with billabongs, (distributary channels) branching off into backwaters along the river's course. These backwater channels are the breeding grounds for the famous 'Murray cod.' The banks of the Murray are lined with redgums which provide timber and honey. Although the Murray is a perennial river, it has been dry in at least three places during recorded Australian history. The great Murray Valley provides fruit farms, vineyards, pastures and grazing land which is the heartland of Australian economy. The river has been utilized for irrigation to such an extent that over one million acres of previously arid land is now plush farming land. The Murray's principal tributaries are the Darling, Murrumbidgee, Edward, Goulburn, Ovens, Lodden, Avoca and Campaspe Rivers, the majority of which run from the Victorian Alps southward. The Darling River joins the Murray approximately 500 miles (800 km) from the sea. Although sporadic in nature, the Darling in past eons most probably outflowed the Murray. The land between the confluence of the two great rivers of Australia was prime settlement land and the early settlers took advantage of it and called it *Riverina*. As the

river continues it cuts through a Tertiary sedimentary deposit which proves that during that age, a large sea gulf existed over this area. The Murray then runs into a wide lagoon named Lake Alexandrina. This lake could have been the site of the principal seaport of the continent but any plan to do this has been frustrated by the treacherous shoals and unmanageable tides. Leaving Lake Alexandrina, the Murray's final destination is Encounter Bay of the Indian Ocean. Steamers plied up the river carrying sheep, wool, timber

Mildura on the Murrav River is noted as the center of the fruit growing area and for its timber. Still used as a river port, paddle wheelers are now more for tourists than for trade.

and whatever cargo was requested by the settlers in the backwater country of the Murray for years but with the coming of the railroads in 1864 the river trade abruptly came to a halt. The Murray, Darling and Murrumbidgee Rivers provide the majority of water, irrigation and hydroelectric power for the southeastern portion of the continent.

Murrumbidgee, New South Wales, Australia

The aborigines called this river the 'big waters,' and in 1824 the two Australian explorers Hamilton Hume and W H Hovell discovered what was to be the only major river system of the island continent. The Murrumbidgee is 1050 miles (1690 km) long, and rises in the high meadows of the Snowy Mountain Range of New South Wales. The river runs south initially, then turns northward into the Australian Capital Territory to within

Trout fishing on the Murray River in Koskiusko National Park.

Bridge over the flooded Murray River at Barham, Victoria.

15 miles (24 km) of the Federal Capital of CANBERRA. The walks along the sandy banks of the Murrumbidgee are very pleasant during the summer months. The river is joined by Goodradigbee and Tumut Rivers, both noted for their excellent trout fishing above WAGGA WAGGA. This region in which the Murrumbidgee flows is full of orchards, vineyards and rice fields. The river runs through one of

Australia's few areas which has enough natural water resources to irrigate and expand the region's agricultural output a hundredfold. The Murrumbidgee Irrigation Area has already reclaimed over 420,000 acres of land for farming and grazing, quite an achievement for a continent so lacking in good water resources. It finally ends its long run and becomes a tributary of the Murray River.

Namoi, New South Wales, Australia
The Namoi River rises in the Liverpool Range of central New South Wales as the Peel River. It is 526 miles (846 km) long and runs on a northwesterly course past TAMWORTH and NARRABRI to meet the Darling River at WALGETT.

New, South Island, New Zealand
Rising just south of Lake Wakatipu in South Island, the New, sometimes called the Oreti,

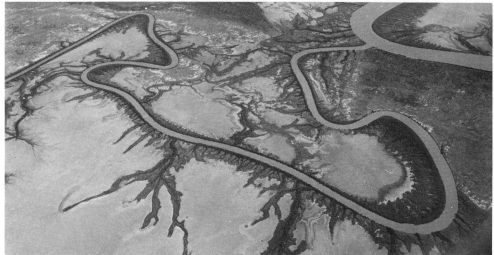

Top: The meandering course of a tributary to the Murrumbidgee River is marked by eucalyptus trees.
Above: The Norman River approaches its mouth at the Gulf of Carpentaria.
Left: The Murrumbidgee River

flows for 105 miles (168 km) southeast to enter the Foveaux Straits south of INVERCARGILL.

Nicholson, Northern Territory, Australia

Another of Australia's many intermittent rivers, the Nicholson rises in the Barkly Tableland of the eastern Northern Territory. It runs for 130 miles (210 km) on an easterly course until it enters the Gulf of Carpentaria close to the mouth of the Albert River.

Nogoa, Queensland, Australia

The Nogoa begins in central Queensland southwest of the town of SPRINGSURE in the Great Dividing Range. It is 180 miles (290 km) long, and flows northeast joining the Comet River near the town of Comet to form the Mackenzie River.

Norman, Queensland, Australia

The Norman rises in the Gregory Range of northern Queensland near the town of WOOLGAR. The Norman receives the Yappar and Clara Rivers on its way to the Gulf of Carpentaria. The river is 260 miles (420 km) long and is intermittent.

Ohau, South Island, New Zealand

The Ohau is a small river of central New Zealand's South Island. It flows through Lake Ohau, which is located 65 miles (105 km) west of TIMARU and is ten miles by three miles (16 km by five km). The Ohau River drains the lake and continues eastward to join the Tekapo River.

Onkaparinga, South Australia, Australia

This river begins just northeast of WOODSIDE in South Australia. It runs southwest into the Gulf of St Vincent below ADELAIDE.

Ord, Western Australia, Australia

The Ord rises in the King Leopold Range in the northeastern corner of Western Australia. The Ord is extremely intermittent, although in the past it was a large and flowing stream as witnessed by its channel. It passes the town of ORD RIVER and runs close to the border of the Northern Territory and Western Australia. The Ord empties into the Timor Sea near WYNDHAM. It is 300 miles (480 km) long and is infested with man-eating crocodiles.

Ovens, Victoria, Australia

The Ovens River is 110 miles (180 km) long and runs from the Australian Alps in northeastern Victoria to become a tributary of the Murray River. The Ovens passes through some of Australia's most beautiful scenic countryside.

Paroo, Queensland-New South Wales, Australia

The Paroo rises in central Queensland, and

flows intermittently southward toward the Darling River but never actually reaches it. It flows through extremely arid countryside but during the rainy season can become swollen with torrential rain.

Pieman, Tasmania, Australia
This Tasmanian river rises approximately five miles (eight km) from Rosebery in western Tasmania where two small streams come together. The river is 40 miles (64 km) long and runs southward to the Indian Ocean.

Pukaki, South Island, New Zealand
The Pukaki River drains Pukaki Lake which is situated 55 miles (88 km) west of TIMARU. The lake is ten miles by two miles (16 km by three km). The Pukaki River continues southward until it joins the Tekapo River.

Purari, Papua New Guinea
The Purari rises in the Bismarck Range of the Territory of New Guinea. It is 170 miles (270 km) long, and runs south to enter the Gulf of Papua. The Purari is navigable for 120 miles (190 km) from the mouth. The width of the river at the mouth reaches up to two miles (three km).

Rakaia, South Island, New Zealand
One of New Zealand's most beautiful rivers, the Rakaia River rises in the Southern Alps, southwest of ARTHUR'S PASS. The Rakaia is 95 miles (153 km) long and enters the Canterbury Bight near CHRISTCHURCH.

Ramu, Papua New Guinea
The Ramu rises in the Kratke Range of northeastern New Guinea. It is also known as the Ottilien, and flows for 400 miles (644 km) northwest to enter the Bismarck Sea.

Rangitikei, North Island, New Zealand
This river rises in the Kaimanawa Mountain Range of southern North Island. It runs for 115 miles (185 km) southwest to enter the Cook Straits.

Richmond, New South Wales, Australia
The Richmond rises in the McPherson Range of northeast New South Wales. It has a length of 163 miles (262 km) and flows past the town of CORAKI on the way to enter the Pacific Ocean at BALLINA. The Richmond is navigable for approximately 70 miles (113 km) of its course below the town of LISMORE.

Ringarooma, Tasmania, Australia
The Ringarooma rises southwest of the town of the same name and flows 62 miles (100 km) past DERBY and GLADSTONE. The area is noted for its substantial deposits of tin ore. It enters Ringarooma Bay of the Bass Straits.

Right: The Bandicoot Bar diversion dam on the Ord River should transform a barren cattle-ranching area into fertile farmland.

Roper, Northern Territory, Australia
The Roper is a river in the north central portion of the Northern Territory. It rises near the great aboriginal reserve and runs eastward for its entire intermittent length of approximately 420 miles (680 km). It empties into the Gulf of Carpentaria.

Sepic, Papua New Guinea
The Sepic rises in northeastern New Guinea and drains the entire northern Victor Emmanuel and southern Torricelli Ranges. It flows for 700 miles (1130 km) northeast to enter the Bismarck Sea. The river is navigable for 180 miles (290 km) of its course.

Snowy, Victoria, Australia
The Snowy is one of the most scenic rivers of Australia, and is unusual in that it has water all year. It rises on the slopes of Mt Kosciusko, a peak 7316 feet (2231 m) high, in the Snowy Mountain Range of southeastern Australia. The river is 270 miles (430 km) long and is amalgamated into the Murray-Darling River system for irrigation purposes. The Snowy Mountain Project is costing the Australian people £375 ($750) million and the cost is still rising. But the project is well worth the price as it will provide approximately 1500 square miles (3885 sq km) of agricultural land, nine power dams and more than 11 power stations to provide hydroelectric power to southeastern Australia's growing population. The huge project has provided countless jobs and increased the population of the local area by 40,000 people since the early 1960s. The Snowy finally flows into the Bass Strait.

South Esk, Tasmania, Australia
The South Esk is the longest river in Tasmania with a length of 120 miles (190 km). It receives the Lake River, 73 miles (117 km) long, as its chief tributary. The South Esk rises in the mountains of Tasmania near Ben Lomond. It runs southeast, southwest and northwest before finally joining the North Esk River, itself 45 miles (72 km) long, to form the Tamar River at LAUNCESTON.

Swan, Western Australia, Australia
The Swan River rises in the Avon Hills of southwestern Western Australia, near the

Inset: The Ord River near Kununurra in Western Australia.

town of CORRIGAN. It is 240 miles (390 km) long, and flows past YORK and PERTH to enter the Indian Ocean at FREMANTLE. The Swan's chief tributary is the Helena River, 40 miles (64 km) long. An item of note is that the SWAN RIVER SETTLEMENT founded in 1829 was the first colonial settlement in Western Australia.

Taieri, South Island, New Zealand
The Taieri River rises in the Rock and Pillar Range to the east of the town of ROXBURGH in South Island. It is 125 miles (200 km) long and flows north, then southeast to enter the Pacific Ocean near DUNEDIN.

Tamar, Tasmania
The Tamar rises in northern Tasmania at the confluence of the North and South Esk rivers at LAUNCESTON. It is a navigable river much utilized by steamers. The river flows for a total of 40 miles (64 km) northwest to PORT DALRYMPLE on the Bass Straits.

Tekapo, South Island, New Zealand
The Tekapo River rises in Lake Tekapo, 12 miles by four miles (19 km by six km), and running 40 miles (64 km) to join the Ahuriri River to form the Waitaki River.

Thames, North Island, New Zealand
The New Zealand Thames rises to the west of Lake Rotorua and flows northward to enter the

Firth of Thames of the Hauraki Gulf. The river is 90 miles (145 km) long, and runs through some of New Zealand's most scenic countryside.

Victoria, Northern Territory, Australia
The Victoria is 350 miles (560 km) long and rises in the hills west of POWELL CREEK. It flows northeast, then northward, and finally westward before entering Queens Channel of the Joseph Bonaparte Gulf.

Waikato, North Island, New Zealand
The Waikato is the longest river in New Zealand with a total length of 220 miles (350 km). It rises in Lake Taupo, North Island and runs northwest past the town of HAMILTON to enter the Tasman Sea. The river is navigable by steamer for 80 miles (129 km) of its course.

Waitaki, South Island, New Zealand
The source of the Waitaki River is the junction of the Ahuriri and Tekapo Rivers. It flows southeast for 95 miles (153 km) before entering the Pacific Ocean.

Wanganui, North Island, New Zealand
The Wanganui rises northwest of Lake Taupo, North Island and runs south for 140 miles (230 km). It passes TAUMARUNUI and finally enters the Pacific at PUKEURI.

Warburton, South Australia, Australia
The Warburton River rises in intermittent Lake Willard which is fed by the waters from

the Diamantina River in northern South Australia. It flows southeast through the Lake Eyre Basin into Lake Eyre itself. The Warburton is approximately 180 miles (289 km) long.

Warrego, Queensland, Australia
The Warrego begins in the Carnarvon Mountain Range of Queensland. It flows southwest past CHARLEVILLE and CUNNAMULLA to become a tributary of the Darling River just southwest of Bourke. The principal tributaries of the Warrego are the Angellala and Ward Rivers. It is 495 miles (796 km) long.

Wenlock, Queensland, Australia
This river rises in the Sir W Thompson Range of northern Queensland to the southwest of Cape Direction. The Wenlock flows for 160 miles (260 km) on a northwesterly course to enter the Gulf of Carpentaria at PORT MUSGRAVE. It is only navigable for 25 miles (40 km) and then only by small vessels.

Williams, Western Australia, Australia
The Williams rises northeast of the town of WILLIAMS and runs intermittently on a due west course before joining the Hotham River to form the Murray River.

Yarra, Victoria, Australia
The Yarra River rises in the Great Dividing Range of southern Victoria. It runs past MELBOURNE to enter Port Phillip Bay. The river is 115 miles (185 km) long.

Europe

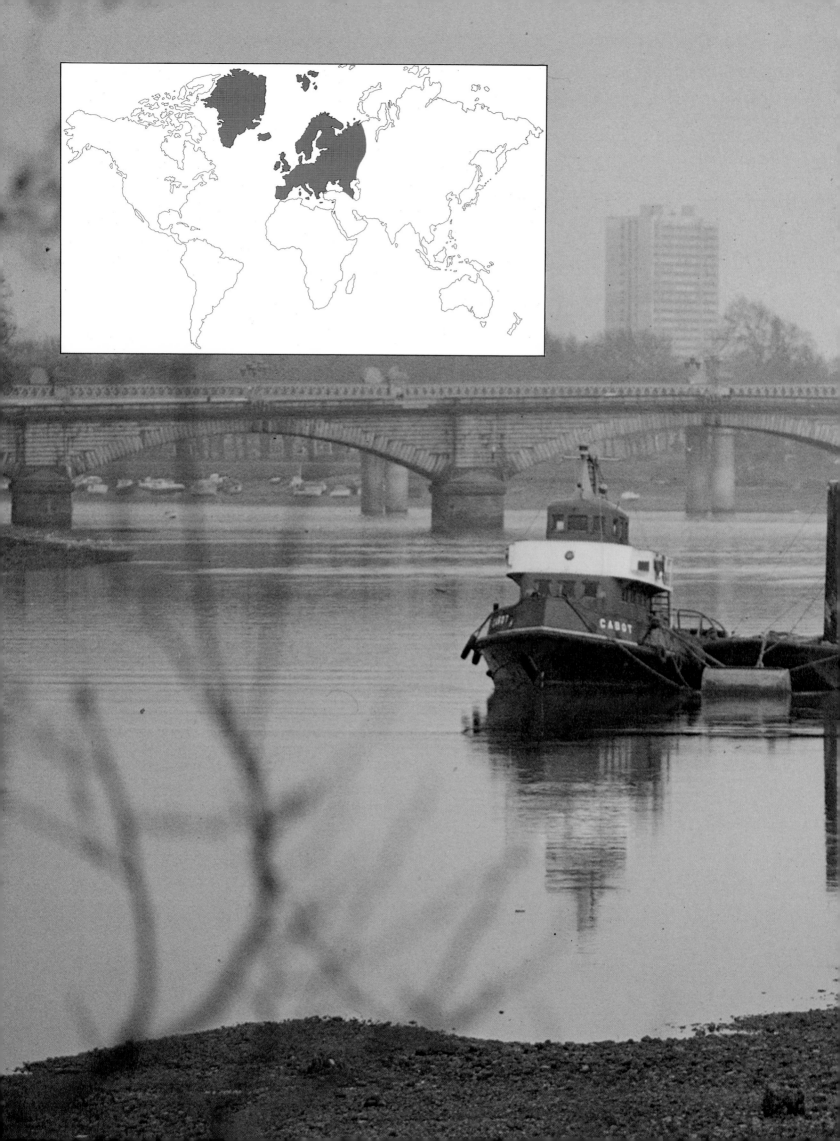

Aare, Switzerland

The Aare is the longest and most important river wholly within the boundaries of Switzerland. It is 180 miles (290 km) long. Rising high in the snows of the Bernese Oberland, it receives run-off water from the Oberaare and Unteraare glaciers before flowing north through MEIRINGEN and the eastern end of Lake Brienz. The most picturesque and spectacular stretch of the Aare is at Meiringen, where it slices its way through the Gorge of the Aare. The Swiss, ever careful of their tourist attractions, have built causeways very close to the foaming, racing waters, where visiting tourists can safely witness this fantastic natural wonder. Safely on its way, it passes INTERLAKEN and continues on to its next destination, the Lake of Thun. The Aare then flows out at the northern end of the Lake Thun and heads for BERN. Shortly after Bern the river is dammed to form the Wohlensee. The Aare's next stop is Lake Biel, where it enters as the Hagneck Canal and departs as the Aare Canal near NIDAU. It then flows northeast to SOLOTHURN and OLTEN, and ultimately joins the mighty Rhine near WALDSHUT.

Abbey, Devon, England

This West Country river rises east of HARTLAND and flows past the remains of Hartland Abbey into the Atlantic Ocean between Hartland Point and the Quay.

Abel, Powys, Wales

This small stream rises in the east to join the River Fyllon at LLANFYLLIN, thus forming the River Cain.

Acheron, Epirus, Greece

The river is 36 miles (58 km) long and is famous in Greek mythology for being the boundary of Hades. It flows in a southwesterly direction to enter the Ionian Sea near PARGA.

Adaja, Spain

The river is 120 miles (190 km) long. It rises in central Spain and flows in an easterly direction to the famous city of AVILA. It then changes direction and flows north to join the Douro River.

Add, Strathclyde, Scotland

The Add River rises northwest of FURNACE on the western shore of Loch Fyne, flowing in a southwesterly direction to Crinan Loch and ultimately to the Sound of Jura.

Adda, Italy

Several small lakes in the Rhaetian Alps of northern Italy form the source of the Adda, approximately nine miles (14 km) northwest of BORMIO. The river flows through majestic scenery along the southern portion of Stelvio Pass between Italy and Switzerland. Picking up numerous small mountain streams, the Adda's volume increases a hundredfold. It changes course to the southwest and heads through the Valtellina Valley. This area is quite fertile and is particularly known for its vineyards, corn and rye. The Adda provides a considerable amount of the available hydroelectric power for this area. Its next stop is Lake Como, Italy's third largest lake. It flows through the lake, leaves it at LECCO and continues down through the Lombard Plain. The Adda has witnessed many battles along its banks because it was once the feudal border between the warring states of Milan and Venice. Near the ancient city of CREMONA, the Adda is received by the Po. The Adda is 150 miles (240 km) long.

Adige, Italy

The Adige rises in three small beautiful Alpine Lakes which are just south of Passo di Reisia. This spot is unique in that the borders of Austria, Italy and Switzerland meet here. This high Alpine valley has for hundreds of years been a major access point for trade and travel between Italy and the north. The Adige flows southeasterly through breathtaking natural scenic wonderlands. The first town which the river passes is MERANO, previously an Austrian possession until 1918 but which reverted back to the Italians at that time. Merano is a much sought after tourist resort during the holiday season. The next stop the river makes is south at ROVERETO. It then passes into a narrow valley and runs parallel with the eastern shore of the famous Lake Garda, turns southeast and flows through the Po River Plain. As the Adige continues on its course, the only city of major importance which it passes is VERONA. A major commercial center on the Brenner Pass route between central Europe and northern Italy, it has museums and churches which tourists travel the world to come and see. It was also the scene for the tragic feud between the Ghibelline and Guelph families in the Middle Ages which Shakespeare used for the background of his play, *Romeo and Juliet*. The city has the second largest Roman Amphitheater still in existence. After leaving Verona, the Adige continues on its course toward the Adriatic which it enters five miles (eight km) southeast of the town of CHIOGGIA, a seaport at the southern end of the Venice Lagoon. The Adige is 225 miles (362 km) long.

Adour, France

The Adour rises in the Pyrénées near Pic du Midi de Rigorre. It is 210 miles (340 km) long and navigable as far as DAX. It initially flows north but changes to a westerly course and enters the Bay of Biscay below BAYONNE.

Adur, West Sussex, England

The Adur rises west of HORSHAM, flows in a southerly direction and enters the English Channel at SHOREHAM-BY-SEA. It is a small river but one which flows through some of the best-loved English countryside in the southeast section of the country.

Aegospotamos, Greece

The Aegospotamos flows across the Gallipoli Peninsula and then into the Dardanelles. The Bay of Aegospotamos was the scene of a major sea battle in 405 BC when the Spartan Admiral Lysander defeated the Athenian fleet.

The Thoré is a tributary of the Agout River.

Aeron, Dyfed, Wales

The Aeron rises west of BLAENPENAL, a small hamlet seven miles (11 km) northwest of TREGARON and flows in a loop southward into Cardigan Bay at ABERARON, a small town and port.

Afton Water, Strathclyde, Scotland

The Afton Water rises a mile (1610 m) south of the Afton Reservoir and flows north through the reservoir to its final destination at NEW CUMMOCK where it joins the River Nith. The fishing, as in most Scottish rivers, is excellent.

Agout, France

The river rises in the southern portion of France in the Tarn Department. The Agout is 112 miles (180 km) long and its major tributaries are the Dadou and the Thoré. Flowing in a westerly direction for the entire course it joins the Tarn River at SAINT SULPICE.

Agri, Italy

The Agri is 68 miles (109 km) long and rises in the Italian Apennines south of the town of POTENZA. This river supplies the majority of drinking water for this part of Italy. It flows southeast for the majority of its course and ends in the Gulf of Taranto.

Agueda, Spain

The Agueda is a tributary of the Douro and is 80 miles (129 km) long. It flows in a northwesterly direction and passes CIUDAD RODRIGO in western Spain before joining the Douro at the Portuguese border.

Ain, France

The river rises in the Jura Mountain range. It is 118 miles (190 km) long and is navigable during parts of the year. The primary tributary of Ain is the Bienne River. The Ain provides a major source of hydroelectric power for this region of France, before joining the Rhône River as a tributary itself.

Aire, North Yorkshire, England

The Aire is 70 miles (113 km) long. The river has its source in the limestone area near Malham Tarn. The river actually comes to the surface at the bottom of Malham Cove and then flows in an easterly direction, receiving the River Calder as its major tributary. It passes through SKIPTON, KEIGHLEY, BINGLEY, SHIPLEY and LEEDS on the way to join the River Ouse above BOOTHFERRY BRIDGE at GOOLE.

Aisne, France

The Aisne is 165 miles (265 km) long and rises in the plateau of western Lorraine. The Aisne is not a very navigable river because of its fluctuating depths and extremely winding course. In places it has been made navigable by numerous locking weirs, which are expensive to maintain. During World War I the main battle line ran extremely close to the Aisne throughout the war. It empties into the Oise River.

Aiviekste, European USSR

This Latvian river is 80 miles (129 km) long and the primary outlet of Lubana Lake, the largest body of fresh water in this small country. The Aiviekste flows southwest and joins the Western Dangava River at the town of PLAVINAS.

Akhelóös, Greece

The Akhelóös, which means 'white river' in Greek, is 140 miles (230 km) long and is named 'white' because it is an extremely muddy river. Ancient legend tells how the great hero Hercules attempted to drain the marshes in the lower course of the river. The river flows in a southerly direction for its full course to empty into the Ionian Sea opposite ITHAKI. A particularly notable fact is that the river carries over two hundred times more water in the winter months than in the corresponding summer period because over 80 inches (200 cm) of rain falls in the winter months, and only a very small rainfall is recorded during the summer. Various attempts have been made to control this excessive winter flow which annually threatens to flood the lower regions of the river. It is hoped that it will also provide cheap hydroelectric power.

Akhtuba, European USSR

Actually a distinct part of the mighty Volga River, the Akhtuba leaves the Volga to run on a parallel course for all of its 320-mile (510-km) length. Its outlet is the Caspian Sea which it enters through the Volga Delta. On its last leg, the Akhtuba is known as the Kigach River.

Alagon, Spain

The Alagon is 130 miles (210 km) long. It rises southwest of PENA DA FRANCIA in western Spain and is a major tributary of the Tagus River which it joins at ALCANTARA.

Alberche, Spain

The Alberche is 110 miles (180 km) long. A secondary tributary of the Tagus River, it rises in Castile, one of the ancient kingdoms of old Spain, and flows in a northeasterly direction through Avila, one of Spain's most fertile provinces. The Alberche joins the Tagus approximately three miles (five km) east of TALAVERA DE LA REINA.

Alcantara, Sicily

The Alcantara is only 30 miles (48 km) long. This short river provides the majority of hydroelectric power and irrigation for the entire island. It flows north of Mt Etna, one of the most active volcanos in the world, into the Ionian Sea.

Alfios, Greece

This is the major river of the Greek Peloponnesus. This region was dominated in ancient times first by the might of Mycenae and then by the soldiers of Sparta. The Alfios rises in the Taygetus Mountain Range and flows northwest through Olympia to the Gulf of Kiparissiakós. It is 69 miles (111 km) long and is supposed to have been utilized by Hercules in his 12 labors, one of which was to clean out the Augean stables.

Aliákmon, Greece

The Aliákmon is 195 miles (314 km) long and the longest river in Greece. It rises in the Grammos Mountain Range near the Albanian border and enters the Aegean Sea 20 miles (32 km) southwest of SALONIKA.

Allier, France

The Allier is 225 miles (362 km) long and rises in the Lozère Department of central France and flows past ISSOIRE, VICHY and MOULINS, before becoming a tributary of the Loire River at NEVERS. The Allier itself receives three major tributaries: the Dore, Alagnon and Sioule Rivers.

Alma, European USSR

The Alma is 45 miles (72 km) long and rises in the Crimean Mountain Range. Initially it flows in a northwesterly direction before changing course to a more westerly flow. Only 16 miles (26 km) north of where it enters the Black Sea is SEVASTOPOL, a Russian fortress. Sevastopol was the scene of an extended siege by the Germans during World War II.

Almanzore, Spain

Near the mouth of this obscure river the French forces of Napoleon inflicted a crushing defeat upon the Spanish. The length of the river is 80 miles (129 km). It rises in the Sierra de los Filabres of southern Spain and flows in a southeasterly direction until it enters the Mediterranean Sea.

Alster, Sweden

The Alster is 80 miles (129 km) long. Rising southwest of ASEDA, a small Swedish town in the southeast of the country, it flows east to the Kalmar Sound in the Baltic Sea.

Alt, Merseyside, England

The Alt rises at ROBY in Merseyside and flows northwest into the Crosby Channel approximately three miles (five km) south of FORMBY.

Alta, Norway

This small river is 120 miles (190 km) long. It flows from the Finnish border region past KAUTOKEINO to the Alta Fjord and has some breathtaking scenery along its course.

Altmühl, West Germany

The Altmühl River of Bavaria rises northeast of ROTHENBURG. It is 137 miles (220 km) long and flows southeast initially before changing its course to a more easterly direction. At the town of KELHEIM it becomes a tributary of the mighty Danube River.

Alun, Clwyd, Wales

This river rises on the north slopes of the Maesyrychen Mountain just north of LLANGOLLEN, a tourist center in North Wales. The Alun flows northward to RHYD-Y-MWYR, then changes direction and heads southeast to BRADLEY, north of Wrexham and finally becomes a tributary of the River Dee at ROSSETT.

Alun, Dyfed, Wales
This river rises four miles (six km) northeast of ST DAVID'S, a town known for its famous cathedral. It flows southwest through St David's into St Brides Bay, only a mile (1610 m) southwest of the village.

Alwin, Northumbria, England
This Cheviot Hills river rises near CUSHAT LAW in an area noted for its border warfare for centuries. It was in this corner of northern England that two great border families, the Percys of Northumberland and the Stewarts of Scotland, fought many a minor skirmish as well as full scale battles which for years bled the North Country dry. The river flows south into the River Coquet at Low Alwinton near the village of ALWINTON in Coquetdale.

Amber, Derbyshire, England
This tiny river rises southwest of the town of CHESTERFIELD. It flows in a southerly direction for the rest of its course before joining the River Derwent at AMBERGATE.

Amman, Dyfed, Wales
This river rises in the Black Mountains of Dyfed. It is formed by the joining of two streams, the Aman Fawr and Aman Fach, at RHOSAMAN. It then flows in a westerly direction before becoming a tributary of the River Loughor on the south side of AMMANFORD, a town on the edge of the revenue producing South Wales coalfields.

Amstel, Netherlands
The Amstel divides AMSTERDAM, the capital city of the Netherlands, and the so-called 'Venice of the North,' into two main sections. Fifty miles (80 km) of canals create a city made up of 70 islands connected by 500 bridges. This beautiful city is one of the great treasures of Europe. Amsterdam's fame as an international port can be credited to the existence of the Amstel River. The most famous beer in the Netherlands is named Amstel after the lifegiving river.

Angerman, Sweden
This beautiful river rises in the mountains near Sweden's border with Norway and flows in a southeasterly direction for the initial portion of its course before changing to a more southerly course for the remainder of the journey to the Gulf of Bothnia. It is 280 miles (450 km) long. The Angerman has its source at the southern end of Fjallfjallet, a mountain peak which is 4600 feet (1400 m) high. The river follows a course through a U-shaped valley previously gouged out by a glacier but long since abandoned. As the river descends, it passes through some of the finest mountain scenery in the world. With its leveling off, the Angerman becomes wider and slower, providing much of the necessary hydroelectric power for this part of Sweden. The main trade in this area is lumbering and the trees are cut and floated down the river to the pulp and paper mills at KRAMFORS. The river is not navigable except for its last 20 miles (32 km).

Aniene, Italy
The river is 61 miles (98 km) long; its alternative name is the Teverone River. This river rises in the Apennines and joins the Tiber River above ROME. The place where it joins the Tiber was a major stopping place for Roman legions on their homeward journey.

Aóös, Greece
This river rises near METSOVON in northwestern Greece. It is 125 miles (200 km) long and is known on part of its course as the Vijosé River. It flows across the Albanian frontier into the Adriatic Sea approximately 15 miles (24 km) from the city of VLORE.

Aragon, Spain
This river rises in the Pyrénées near the French border. It is 120 miles (190 km) long and its major tributary is the Arga River which flows 100 miles (160 km) past PAMPLONA. It flows in a southwesterly direction through Huesca, Saragossa and Navarre provinces to join the Ebro River northwest of TUDELA.

Aran, Powys, Wales
The Aran River rises four miles (six km) northeast of LLANBISTER, a village on the River Ithon, and flows in a southerly direction to join the River Ithon north of PENYBONT.

Aray, Strathclyde, Scotland
The Aray River rises in Argyll. It flows south to Glen Aray, and then on to its outlet at Loch Fyne at INVERARAY. It is a good trout stream.

Arbogaån, Sweden
Beginning its life as the Hork River in central Sweden and flowing for a distance of 100 miles (160 km), the Arbogaån flows in a southeasterly direction to Lake Malar, a major waterway connected with Lake Hjalmar. Together they encompass an area of 190 square miles (490 sq km). Both lakes are interconnected by the Arbogaån Canal, eight miles (13 km) long.

Arc, France
The Arc River flows from the Grées Alps through the Savoie Department and is 90 miles (145 km) long. The river flows in a great arc through the Maurienne valley which can boast of 18 hydroelectric power stations and chemical plants. Its outlet is the Isère River.

Arda, Bulgaria
The Arda River rises near SMOLJAN in the Rhodope Mountain Range of Bulgaria. Its length is 180 miles (290 km). It flows eastward into Thrace and joins the Marica River near the ancient Imperial city of ADRIANOPLE.

Ardèche, France
This river rises in Monts du Vivarais in the southern portion of France and is 70 miles (113 km) long. The river flows to its outlet, the Rhône River, near PONT-SAINT-ESPRIT.

Argens, France
This river rises in the Lower Provence Alps of southeastern France. It is 72 miles (116 km) long and flows in an easterly direction to a few miles south of the town of FREJUS where it enters the Mediterranean Sea.

Arges, Rumania
A major tributary of the Danube River, it is 180 miles (290 km) long and is formed by two headstreams in the Făgăras Mountain Range. The Arges flows southeasterly until it reaches the Danube. It is linked to BUCHAREST, the Rumanian capital, by a 13-mile (21-km) canal which supplies the city with a continuous supply of fresh water.

Ariège, France
The Ariège rises in the eastern Pyrénées of southern France and flows past the towns of TARASCON and PAMIERS before it enters the Garonne River as a tributary above the major city of TOULOUSE. Its length is 106 miles (171 km). The Ariège provides a large part of this district's hydroelectric power.

Arno, Italy
This river rises at a height of 4500 feet (1370 m) in the Etruscan Apennines. The entire area was dominated centuries ago by the Etruscans, a people which has left its history shrouded in mystery. The Arno is 150 miles (240 km) long. It flows north initially before turning abruptly to a westerly direction passing the great medieval city of FLORENCE before it enters the Ligurian Sea below PISA and its famous leaning tower.

Arrow, Midlands, England
This Midlands river rises only eight miles (13 km) southwest of the city of BIRMINGHAM, the second city of England. It flows south to become a tributary of the River Avon, five miles (eight km) northeast of EVESHAM, a town known for the remains of its abbey and the battle fought nearby in 1265 which was a turning point in English history.

Arrow, Powys, Wales
This river rises near GLASCWM, a tiny Welsh hamlet. It flows in an easterly direction through KINGTON, a town close to the border, before entering the River Lugg as a tributary just two miles (three km) southeast of LEOMINSTER.

Arun, Sussex, England
This river is only 37 miles (60 km) long. It flows past Arundel Castle, the country home of the Dukes of Norfolk. It enters the English Channel at the resort town of LITTLEHAMPTON. This area is one of the main tourist attractions of southeastern England.

Ash, Hertfordshire, England
This small river rises just east of BUNTINGFORD, and it flows south into the River Lea about a mile (1610 m) southeast of the town of WARE.

Atran, Sweden

The Atran is a small river of Sweden which is 145 miles (233 km) long. The river rises east of ULRICEHAMM in southwestern Sweden and flows southwest past ATRAN to enter the Kattegat.

Aube, France

This scenic river is navigable and begins in the Plateau of Langres in the Department of the Haute Marne. The Aube is 140 miles (230 km) long and joins the Seine at ROMILLY-SUR-SEINE after flowing in a northwesterly direction for the majority of its course.

Aveyron, France

The river rises in the Aveyron Department of southern France. It is 155 miles (249 km) long and its primary tributary is the Viaur River. The Aveyron flows in a westerly direction past the towns of RODEZ and VILLEFRANCHE-DE-ROUERGUE to enter the Tarn River just below MONTAUBAN.

Avon, Central Region, Scotland

This good fishing river rises three miles (five km) south of FALKIRK. It flows westerly toward CUMBERNAULD, then easterly to AVONBRIDGE and then northeast to LINLITHGOW, famous for the ruins of its Royal Scottish Palace, the birthplace of Mary, Queen of Scots in 1542. The river enters the Firth of Forth between GRANGEMOUTH and BO'NESS near the remains of the Antonine Wall.

Avon, Devon, England

The Avon River rises in Dartmoor and flows in a southerly direction entering Bigbury Bay a mile (1610 m) northwest of the picturesque village of THURLESTONE.

Avon, Grampian Region, Scotland

This excellent fishing river rises in the Cairngorm Mountains. It flows easterly through the Loch of Avon and the Glen of Avon, and then proceeds to TOMINTOUL as the Strath Avon finally joining the River Spey below the famous Ballindalloch Castle.

Avon, Leicestershire, England

This river rises on the border between Northamptonshire and Leicestershire near SOUTH KILWORTH. It flows in a southwesterly direction past the town of RUGBY made famous by *Tom Brown's School Days*. Leaving Rugby it passes WARWICK, STRATFORD, EVESHAM and PERSHORE, finally joining the River Severn as a tributary at TEWKSBURY, famous for its abbey church and the site of a major battle during the English War of the Roses.

Avon, Wiltshire, England (1)

The Avon River of ancient Wessex rises west of SHERSTON, a small town north of MALMESBURY. It flows through the ancient Roman city of BATH and then past BRISTOL to join the River Severn at AVONMOUTH. The river is navigable to Bristol for large ships.

Avon, Wiltshire, England (2)

Rising in the Vale of Pewsey, this picturesque river flows directly south through AMESBURY, the cathedral city of SALISBURY, quiet FORD-

Above: Two views of the Pulteney Bridge over the River Avon (1) at Bath.

INGBRIDGE and small RINGWOOD. The Avon ends at CHRISTCHURCH HARBOUR in Dorset.

Above: The River Avon (1) near Bristol.

Axe, Somerset, England

This beautiful river rises under the Mendip Hills of Somerset, and comes to ground at WOOKEY HOLE, a set of underground caverns which are the primary tourist attraction of the area. Guided tours are given of the underground caves. From Wookey the Axe flows northwest into the Bristol Channel at Weston Bay just south of the major resort town of WESTON-SUPER-MARE.

Aydar, European USSR

The Aydar or Aidar River is 120 miles (190 km) long and rises east of VEIDELEVKA, Ukraine. It flows in a southerly direction through the prime wheat country of the Ukraine. It joins the Northern Donets River near VOROSHILOVGRAD.

Bain, North Yorkshire, England

This small northern river which rises in the moors south of the town of HAWES flows in a northeast direction through SEMER WATER and BAINBRIDGE before it enters the River Ure.

Baise, France

This river rises in the Hautes-Pyrénées of southwestern France. It is 118 miles (190 km) long and flows in a northerly direction passing NERACON its way to join the Garonne near PORT-SAINT-MARIE.

Balder, Cumbria, England

This northern river rises on Stainmore Common. It flows eastward and passes through the reservoirs of Balderhead, Blackton and Hury on its way to join the River Tees at COTHERSTONE, Durham.

Baldwin, Isle of Man

The Baldwin rises in the central portion of the island and runs southward into the Glass River just north of the capital, DOUGLAS.

Bann, Northern Ireland

The Bann River rises high in the Mourne Mountain Range of Northern Ireland. It is 80 miles (129 km) long. On its first leg, it flows through Down and Armagh Counties toward the southern shore of Lough Neagh. The river flows through this huge lake (lough) and exits on the opposite side, continuing on its journey past the town of COLERAINE and on into the Atlantic Ocean.

Bannock Burn, Scotland

The Bannock Burn is a very famous Scottish river. In 1314 a battle was fought between Robert Bruce, Norman-Celtic King of Scots, and the forces of Edward II, King of England – victory insured an independent Scotland. The river flows through BANNOCKBURN village, located only a few miles southeast of STIRLING and its famous castle. It flows into the River Forth a few miles east of Stirling.

Left: The River Avon (2) at Amesbury, Wiltshire, England.

Barbon Beck, Cumbria, England
The Barbon Beck River rises as a small stream called Barkin Beck, northeast of KIRKBY LONSDALE, and flows in a southwesterly direction until it reaches BARBON. A short distance further on it enters the River Lune.

Barle, Somerset, England
The Barle River rises on Exmoor at PINKERY POND. It flows practically unnoticed through WITHPOOL and DULVERTON, and joins the River Exe as a tributary just northeast of EXEBRIDGE.

Barvas, Western Isles, Scotland
The Barvas rises in the lakes south of the village of BARVAS on the Isle of Lewis. It flows in a northerly direction down Glen Mor Barvas to reach Loch Mor Barvas and shortly after the Atlantic Ocean.

Beaulieu, Hampshire, England
The Beaulieu rises in the New Forest, an area where William Rufus, King of England and the favorite of his father William the Conqueror, was slain while hunting in the 11th century. It flows past BEAULIEU, best known to tourists for its ruined abbey and grounds and its motorcar museum. It ends, a short distance away, in the Solent.

Bega, Rumania-Yugoslavia
The Bega is 130 miles (210 km) long. It begins in the Poiana Ruscăi Mountain Range of Rumania. The Bega flows west and southwesterly across the border into Yugoslavia. It becomes a tributary of the River Tisza at KNICANIN.

Belah, Cumbria, England
The Belah River rises in the moors area east of KIRKBY STEPHEN. It flows in a northwesterly direction until meeting the River Eden a few miles southwest of the village of BROUGH as a tributary.

Bele, Dyfed, Wales
The Bele rises southeast of NEWCASTLE EMLYN and flows southeast to CWMDUAD where it becomes a tributary of the River Duad. It is noted for its fishing.

Beli Timok, Yugoslavia
This small river in eastern Serbia is 30 miles (48 km) long and flows on course to join the Crna River which is 50 miles (80 km) long at ZAJECAR, to form the Timok River.

Bellart, Isle of Mull, Scotland
The river runs northwest to Loch na Cuilce about five miles (eight km) due west of TOBERMORY, the chief town and resort of the Isle of Mull.

Berezina, European USSR
The Berezina rises in the Lithuanian-White Russian uplands. It is 365 miles (587 km) long

The Beaulieu River in Hampshire, England

and navigable for 330 mile (530 km). It flows south to join the larger Dnepr River approximately 14 miles (23 km) northwest of RECHITSA. It runs through a low lying and heavily wooded area. The Berezina is linked to the Western Dvina, the Neman and the Bug through a system of small canals which connect the Baltic and Black Sea. Small river barges ply back and forth on a regular basis. The river has not favored conquerors over the years: Napoleon during his fateful retreat from Moscow suffered severe losses at the Berezina crossing and in 1944 the armies of Adolf Hitler were practically annihilated on the banks of this otherwise small and inconsequential river.

Berkel, West Germany-Netherlands
The Berkel rises in northwest Germany close to the town of BILLERBECK. It is only 60 miles (97 km) from source to outlet. It becomes a tributary of the Ijssel River in the Netherlands at the town of ZUTPHEN.

Beult, Kent, Southern England
The Beult rises in the ASHFORD area of Kent. It flows westward and joins the River Medway at the town of YALDING.

Beuvron, Central France
This small river of central France is 80 miles (129 km) long. It flows from GIEN across the Sologne River and becomes a tributary of the Cosson River, which flows into the River Loire just below BLOIS, a famous medieval city.

Bewl, East Sussex, England
This tiny river rises near FLIMWELL, a small village in Sussex. It flows west initially and then changes its course north to run through the Bewl Bridge Reservoir on the way to join the River Teise.

Biebrza, Poland
The Biebrza is 112 miles (180 km) long from its source near GRODNO in northeast Poland to

where it joins the Narew River just east of LOMZA. It is navigable below the Augustow Canal which joins the Biebrza to the Czarna Hancza River.

Bishopdale Beck, North Yorkshire, England

This river rises north of BUCKDEN PIKE. It flows in a northeasterly direction until it meets the River Ure east of AYSGARTH, a small village in Wensleydale.

Biss, Wiltshire, England

This river rises south of WESTBURY, a town at the foot of the Great Salisbury Plain of ancient Wessex. Westbury is known for the famous Westbury White Horse carved into the nearby chalk hills. The Biss flows north passing TROWBRIDGE before it meets the River Avon.

Bistrita, Rumania

This river rises at Prislop Pass in the Carpathian Mountains of northeastern Rumania. It flows in a southeasterly direction 175 miles (282 km) to become a tributary of the larger Siret River. It is known for its lumber industry and extensive hydroelectric power stations.

Bityug, European USSR

The Bityug is a tributary of the much larger Don River and is 220 miles (350 km) long. It rises northeast of TOKANEVKA and flows west initially but changes to a more southerly course as it travels to join the Don at PAVLOVSK.

Black Bourn, Suffolk, England

This scenic river rises southeast of the old abbey town of BURY ST EDMUNDS, which boasts of a shrine of a martyred king, a Benedictine Abbey and Roman remains. The river flows north through the village of IXWORTH and becomes a tributary of the River Little Ouse a few miles southeast of THETFORD.

Black Cart Water, Strathclyde, Scotland

This river rises in the Strathclyde region and flows northeast from Castle Semple Loch. It joins the White Cart Water a short distance due north of the town of PAISLEY and then flows into the much larger River Clyde the major Scottish river.

Black Esk, Dumfries and Galloway, Scotland

This small Scottish river runs south through the Black Esk Reservoir to meet the River White Esk to form the River Esk. The upper portions of the river are excellent for fishing and related sports.

Blackwater, Republic of Ireland

The first part of the Blackwater River flows through the rugged heights of Kerry and Cork Counties. The river's course becomes more relaxed as it passes through north Cork and

County Waterford. The surrounding terrain is remarkably wooded and the river is noted for its stretches of prime salmon fishing. Centuries ago, English settlers found the Blackwater Valley an ideal location to establish permanent homes, and some of the fine estates which grew in the valley survived the wars of later years. The river abruptly changes its course from east to south, flows through the woods of Dromana and gradually widens to reach the sea at YOUGHAL. Its length is 90 miles (145 km).

Blackwater, Essex, England

This river rises in one of the most beautiful parts of Britain north of BRAINTREE. This entire area is one where tourists come to relax and enjoy the English countryside. The river flows in a southeasterly direction into the North Sea just south of Mersea Island.

Blackwater, Hampshire, England

The river rises near ALDERSHOT and flows northward to SANDHURST, the home of the Royal Military Academy. The river changes course to the west and joins the River Loddon at the town of SWALLOWFIELD a short distance from READING.

Bleng, Cumbria, England

The Bleng River rises in the high Cumbrian Mountains. It flows in a southwesterly direction to WELLINGTON, then changes course eastward to join the River Irt northwest of SANTON BRIDGE.

Blithe, Staffordshire, England

This river rises east of STOKE-ON-TRENT in the middle of the English 'Potteries.' It flows southeasterly through Blithfield Reservoir and joins the River Trent near KING'S BROMLEY.

Blyth, Northumberland, England

This northern river rises west of KIRKHEATON. It flows in an easterly direction across flat open country towards BEDLINGTON and enters the North Sea at BLYTH.

Blyth, Suffolk, England

This Blyth River rises near LAXFIELD and flows east through the village of BLYTHBURGH into the North Sea. It is tidal to just below BLYFORD.

Bobr, Poland

The Bobr River rises at the foot of Riesenberge in southwest Poland. It flows northeast to KAMIENNA GORA, then changes course northwesterly to join the Oder River as a tributary west of KROSNO RODZANSKIE. It is 160 miles (260 km) long.

Bode, West Germany

This small river flows from the Upper Harz Mountain Range to join the Saale River at the town of NIENBURG. Its length is 100 miles (160 km) and the river flows in an easterly direction for its entire course.

Bollin, Cheshire, England

The Bollin River rises a few miles southeast of MACCLESFIELD. It flows in a northwesterly direction through Macclesfield and WILMSLOW to join the River Mersey just east of WARRINGTON in Lancashire.

Bosna, Yugoslavia

This river is 191 miles (307 km) long and navigable for the first 96 miles (154 km) of its course. Its major tributary is the Lasva River which is only 30 miles (48 km) long. It flows through an area known for its metallurgical industry. The river rises at the foot of the Treskavica Mountain Range, 12 miles (19 km) from the town of SARAJEVO, a place remembered for the assassination of Archduke Franz Ferdinand and his wife which resulted in the start of World War I. It becomes a tributary of the Sava River at the town of SAMAC.

Bovey, Devon, England

The Bovey River rises in the northern portion of Dartmoor. It flows in a northeasterly direction before changing its course to a southeasterly direction and passing BOVEY TRACEY. It enters the River Teign south of CHUDLEIGH KNIGHTON.

Box, Suffolk, England

The Box River rises south of LAVENHAM and flows southeast to within one mile (1600 m) of HIGHAM where it joins the River Stour.

Boyd, Avon, England

The Boyd rises south of the town of CHIPPING SODBURY and flows south to join the River Avon as a tributary just above KEYNSHAM.

Boyne, Republic of Ireland

The Boyne is probably best remembered for the famous Battle of the Boyne, the site of which lies between the towns of SLANE and DROGHEDA. The Stuart line of kings ended with the defeat of James II by William of Orange. The Boyne actually begins close to EDENBERRY in a low-lying nondescript country, only 300 feet (100 m) above sea level. On the first half of its course the river is extremely sluggish as it passes through a plain of glacial deposits. The next stop for the Boyne is the thriving market town of TRIM, or 'The Town of the Ford of the Elder Tree,' as the Irish call it. The town lies in the center of a fertile plain. It can boast one of the earliest religious settlements in the country, and contains a greater concentration of antiquities than any other parish of comparable size. Here at TRIM St Patrick is believed to have founded a monastery on the banks of the Boyne. After the Anglo-Norman invasion of Ireland, the county of Meath was given over to Hugh de Lacy as his share of the spoils of war. De Lacy realized the importance of Trim, made it his capital and began building a large fortified castle in 1173 to protect his interests. Trim Castle became the largest Anglo-Norman fortress in the entire country and today still provides a spectacular sight. Leaving Trim the Boyne continues slowly on

The River Bollin near Wilmslow in Cheshire, England.

its way to pass through the rich pasture lands of County Neath until it reaches NAVAN. The town itself is set in the middle of beautiful countryside that extends to the banks of the river. At this stage in its course, the Boyne is a picture of sylvan beauty as it flows onward. At Navan the Boyne is joined by one of its tributaries, the Blackwater, which drains the southern portion of County Navan. After Navan the Boyne begins to deepen and cuts a small gorge at BEAUPARE near Slane. The river continues now in a broad and well-defined valley as it moves through Slane on its way to the Irish sea. The Boyne is well noted for its salmon fishing. The Boyne is 62 miles (100 km) long.

Bradano, Italy
The Bradano begins in the Apennines, 13 miles (21 km) north of POTENZA. It is 73 miles (117 km) long and flows southeasterly to enter the Gulf of Taranto.

Brain, Essex, England
The Brain River rises near the town of BRAINTREE, a spectacular town noted for its old streets and horse-racing. It flows southeast and joins the River Blackwater near WITHAM.

Braint, Anglesey, Wales
This tiny river on the Isle of Anglesey rises east of PENTRAETH and flows southwest into the Menai Strait on the eastern side of NEW-BOROUGH WARREN.

Bran, Powys, Wales (1)
The Bran River rises east of Llyn Brianne Reservoir practically on the borders of Dyfed and Powys. It flows in a southerly direction until it joins the River Towy (Tywi) close to LLANDOVERY.

Bran, Powys, Wales (2)
This river rises on Mynydd Epynt and flows southeast joining the River Usk at ABERBRAN, a town west of BRECON.

Bray, Devon, England
The Bray rises on the Exmoor and flows in a southerly direction becoming a tributary of the River Mole three miles (five km) southwest of MOLTON.

Brda, Poland
This river rises near MIASTKO in the northwestern section of Poland. It flows southeast through several lakes, then changes direction to a more southerly course past the town of KORONOWO and changes direction once again, this time to an easterly course. It finally joins the Vistula River five miles (eight km) east of BYDGOSZCZ.

Brede, East Sussex, England
This river rises near BATTLE, a town in East Sussex near where William the Conqueror defeated Harold in 1066, thus changing the

entire course of Anglo-Saxon history. It joins the River Rother at the resort town of RYE, an old-world town renowned throughout the Southeast coast of England.

Brenig, Clwyd, Wales
The Brenig River rises in Llyn Bran and flows south through the Brenig Reservoir. It joins the River Alwen east of the Alwen Reservoir.

Brenne, France
The Brenne River is in one of the most poorly drained areas of France between the Indre and Creuse Rivers in central France. The area is full of lakes of which only a few have outlets.

Brent, London, England
The Brent River begins as DOLLIS BROOK in the borough of Barnet in north London. The river flows southward through the borough of Brent and forms the Brent Reservoir between Barnet and Brent. It becomes a tributary of the River Thames at BRENTFORD above Kew Bridge.

Brenta, Italy
The Brenta begins its short 100 mile (160 km) journey to the Adriatic in two Alpine lakes, the Caldonazzo and Levico, a short distance southeast of TRENTO. This river is a very rapid mountain stream which flows through VAL-SUGANA, a valley noted for its raw silk and forestry industries. It is also a very important tourist area. The Brenta turns southeast and

enters the Venetian Plain passing the old town of CITTADELLA, still completely surrounded by its ancient medieval town walls. The Brenta is linked to the chief city in this area, PADOVA, by a system of canals, which also links it to the Po, Adige and Bacchiglione Rivers. The lower section of the Brenta is navigable. The river enters the Adriatic just southeast of CHIOGGIA, a port and fishing center joined to the mainland by a bridge. The Brenta used to enter the Lagoon of Venice but in 1896 its mouth shifted to its present location.

Brett, Suffolk, England
The Brett rises north of BRETTENHAM, a small village north of LAVENHAM and flows south into the River Stour south of HIGHAM.

Bug (Southern), European USSR
The Southern Bug is 533 miles (858 km) long. It rises in the Volyno-Podolsk uplands of the Ukraine. The course of the river is swift and winding for the majority of its length and it is only at VOSNESENSK that the Bug becomes navigable. The river is partly frozen from December to the middle of March. It enters the Black Sea by a very long and winding estuary which was formed by a drowned river valley. On the eastern shore of this large estuary is NIKOLAYEV, a major port, important for its huge shipbuilding yards.

Bug (Western), European USSR-Poland
The Western Bug is 484 miles (779 km) long.

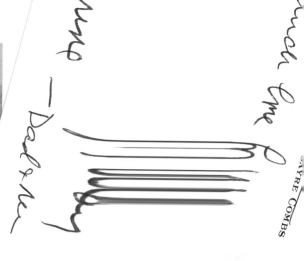

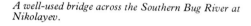

A well-used bridge across the Southern Bug River at Nikolayev.

This river rises in the undulating hills of the Volyno-Podolsk, east of the city of LVOV and forms the border between Poland and the USSR for about 150 miles (240 km). It flows through the fortress town of BREST. Just below Brest, the Bug changes its course and flows west into Poland. Shortly thereafter it receives the Narew River, its only large tributary. It is navigable to Brest but only for small vessels. The final destination of the river is the Baltic Sea.

Bure, Norfolk, England
The Bure is 50 miles (80 km) long. It rises west of FAKENHAM, a village in Norfolk. The river flows southeast past AYLSHAM, then through the Norfolk Broads and joins the Breydon Water at GREAT YARMOUTH, a seaside town noted for its fishing fleet.

Buzau, Rumania
The Buzau rises in the Buzau Mountain Range in central Rumania. It is 125 miles (201 km) long and flows in a continuous curve to enter the Siret River as one of its tributaries.

By, Norway-Sweden
The river rises in eastern Norway and flows across the border into Sweden. It is 80 miles (129 km) long and flows south past SAFFLE to enter Lake Vänern.

Cabriel, Spain
The Cabriel River rises in central Spain near the source of the Tagus River. It has a length of 125 miles (201 km) and flows southeast to join the Júcar River as a tributary.

Cader, Gwynedd, Wales
The Cader River rises on the western slope of Cader Idris, a peak with a height of 2927 feet (893 m). The river runs southwest to join the River Dysynni northeast of LLANEGRYN.

Cain, Powys, Wales
The Cain River is formed by the confluence of the Rivers Abel and Fyllon at LLANFYLLIN. It flows in an easterly direction to join the River Vyrnwy on the east side of LLANSANFFRAID-YM-MECHAIN, a small village five miles (eight km) from LLANFYLLIN.

Calder, Cumbria, England
The Calder begins its run at the west end of Ennerdale Fell. It flows southwest past the atomic power station at Calder Hall and into the Irish Sea northwest of SEASCALE.

Calder, Highlands, Scotland
This small river runs east to join the River Spey, one mile (1610 m) southwest of the village of NEWTONMORE, a holiday and skiing center. Newtonmore is also the headquarters of the Clan Macpherson and is the home of the Macpherson Museum.

flows east by HEBDEN BRIDGE, SOWERBY BRIDGE, BRIGHOUSE, DEWSBURY and WAKEFIELD. The Yorkshire Calder joins the River Aire at the town of CASTLEFORD.

Caldew, Cumbria, England
The Caldew rises on the eastern slopes of SKIDDAW and flows north to join the River Eden on the north side of CARLISLE.

Cale, Somerset, England
The Cale rises north of the town of WINCANTON in Somerset. It flows south through the town and continues on its course and becomes a tributary of the River Stour west of MARNHULL.

Calore, Italy
The Calore rises in the Appenines Mountains of Campania in southern Italy northeast of the town of SALERNO. The Calore has a length of 60 miles (97 km) and flows north then west to join the Volturno River northeast of CASERTA.

Cam, Cambridgeshire, England
The Cam rises in northwestern Essex and flows for 40 miles (64 km) into the Great Ouse River. At TRUMPINGTON, a suburb of the university city of CAMBRIDGE, two small rivers meet, the Rhee and the Granta. The Granta rises in the chalk hills of Essex and is sometimes called the Cam by local people. The Rhee rises near ASHWELL in Huntingdonshire and flows northeast until it meets the Granta to form the Cam. Along the banks of the Cam as it flows through Cambridge are the great colleges of the University of Cambridge. The River Cam is navigable up to Cambridge but only by small vessels. It joins the Great Ouse just above the cathedral town of ELY.

Camddwr, Powys, Wales
This small river rises three miles (five km) northeast of LLANBISTER in Powys. It flows southwest to join the River Ithon just north of LLANDDEWI YSTRADENNI.

Camel, Cornwall, England
The Camel flows through some of the most picturesque scenery in the West Country. It rises near DAVIDSTOW and flows south and then

Punters on the Backs pass King's College, Cambridge on the Cam River.

northwest past the charming little town of WADEBRIDGE. It then passes the town of PADSTOW and enters Padstow Bay. It is navigable to small craft.

Carbones, Spain
The Carbones rises in the Sierra de Yeguas in Andalusia in southwestern Spain. Its length is 75 miles (121 km). It flows in a northwesterly direction to join the Guadalquivir River and is primarily utilized for irrigation as this area of Spain is very dry.

Carew, Dyfed, Wales
The Carew rises west of SAUNDERSFOOT, Dyfed. It continues westward until it reaches the village of CAREW and the imposing ruins of Carew Castle. The castle, magnificent even in ruins, was formerly one of the eight royal demesnes belonging to the Princes of South Wales. Also nearby is one of the finest Ogham Crosses in Wales, the Carew Cross, which is believed to date from the 7th or 8th centuries. The river forms an estuary which continues northwest to merge with the River Cresswell. The Carew finally flows into the Daugleddau River at JENKINS POINT, Pembrokeshire.

Carey, Devon, England
The Carey rises near HALWILL and flows into the Tamar River on the border of Devon and Cornwall northeast of LAUNCESTON and its imposing ruined castle.

Carfan, Powys, Wales
The Carfan rises four miles (six km) northeast of CEMMAES, Powys and flows south to meet with the Twymyn River to form the Rhiw Saeson River near LLANBRYNMAIR.

Carrión, Spain
The Carrión River rises in the Cantabrian Mountains of central Spain and is 120 miles (190 km) long. It flows past the town of PALENCIA to become a tributary of the Piseurga River near DUENAS.

Carron, Scotland (1)
The Carron rises in Sutherland and flows east down Strath Carron to the Kyle of Sutherland at BONARBRIDGE, a small village at the head of Dornoch Firth 14 miles (23 km) west of Dornoch.

Carron, Scotland (2)
This Carron River rises in the Campsie Fells on the borders of the Central and Strathclyde regions and flows east through the Central Valley Reservoir and into the Firth of Forth.

Carron Water, Scotland
This small river rises in Lowther Hills and flows south to the River Nith at CARRONBRIDGE which is noted for its remains of a Roman Fort.

Caseg, Gwynedd, Wales
This tiny river runs west into the River Llafar southeast of BETHESDA. The Casey is noted for its fishing.

Cassley, Scotland
The river rises in the Sutherland area. It flows southeast down Glen Cassley into the River Oykel, eight miles (13 km) southwest of LAIRG, a small village at the southeast end of Loch Shin.

Caundle Brook, Dorset, England
The Caundle Brook River rises west of BUCKLAND NEWTON in Dorset. It flows north and then slightly changes course to the northeast before joining the River Lydden, just north of LYDLINCH, a small village in Blackmoor Vale.

Cennen, Dyfed, Wales
The river rises southeast of LLANDEILO in the Black Mountains, flowing west and then changing its course to a northward direction before joining the River Towy (Tywi) just south of Llandeilo. It passes close to the Welsh castle of Carreg Cennen, an impressive ruin on limestone cliffs.

Cephissus, Greece
This ancient river rises on Mount Parnassus. It is 71 miles (114 km) long and flows in an east/southeast direction through ancient PHOCRIS, LOCRIS and BOEOTIA to the Gulf of Euboea ten miles (16 km) from KHALKIS.

Cère, France
The Cère rises in the Massif du Cantal near LE LIORAN in central France. It is 70 miles (113 km) long and its only major tributary is the small Jordanne River which is 22 miles (35 km) long. The Cère flows in a westerly direction to join the Dordogne River below the town of BRETENOUX.

Ceri, Dyfed, Wales
This small river rises southeast of LLANGRANOG in Dyfed. It heads south to become a tributary of the larger River Teifi at the village of CWMCOY.

Cerne, Dorset, England
The river rises near UP CERNE in Dorset. It flows into the River Frome on the north side of DORCHESTER, the county town of Dorset.

Cessnock Water, Strathclyde, Scotland
The river rises south of DARVEL in the Strathclyde region. This portion of Scotland is noted for its excellent fishing rivers and streams. The Cessnock Water flows in a circuitous direction proceeding northwesterly to join the River Irvine between the towns of KILMARNOCK and GALSTON.

Cetina, Yugoslavia
The river rises in the Dinara Range of South Croatia. It is 70 miles (113 km) long and has a major hydroelectric station at Gubarvic Falls. The river flows southeast past SESTANOVAC, then changes course westward to OMIS where it enters the Adriatic Sea.

Charente, France
The river rises four miles (six km) southwest of ROCHECHOUART in western France. The Charente is 220 miles (350 km) long and is navigable below the city of ANGOULEME. Its major tributaries are the Tardoire, 62 miles (100 km) long, the Touvre and Seugne, 47 miles (76 km) long and the Boutonne, 58 miles (93 km) long. The river flows in a westward direction past Angoulême, COGNAC and ROCHEFORT, before entering the Bay of Biscay.

Chater, Leicestershire, England
The river rises south of Whatborough Hill east

Câvado, Portugal
The river has its source near the Spanish border. It is 73 miles (117 km) long and is not navigable. It flows westward past the towns of AMARES and BARCELOS to enter the Atlantic Ocean at ESPOSENDE.

Cedig, Gwynedd, Wales
The Cedig rises six miles (ten km) southeast of BALA and flows south into Lake Vyrnwy, Powys, a large reservoir.

Cefni, Isle of Anglesey, Wales
The Cefni rises in the center of Anglesey and flows southward through the Cefni Reservoir. The river then passes LLANGEFNI, changes direction to the southwest through Maltraeth Marsh and the Maltraeth Sands before entering Caernarvon Bay.

Cegidog, Clwyd, Wales
The Cegidog flows eastward along a very short course and enters the River Alun on the

The Hennessy warehouses at Cognac on the Charente River.

southern side of Cefn-bedd, Clwyd, only a mere four miles (six km) from the town of WREXHAM.

Ceiriog, Clwyd, Wales
The Ceiriog rises in the Berwyn Mountains to the southeast of the town of CORWEN and flows east by GLYN CEIRIOG and CHIRK. Chirk is a small town located five miles (eight km) from OSWESTRY. Near the old church is located the remains of a Norman Castle built in the 11th century, and a mile to the west is a 14th century castle which is open to the public. The Ceiriog becomes a tributary of the River Dee just northeast of Chirk.

Ceirw, Clwyd, Wales
The Ceirw rises to the south of PENTREFOELAS, a small village in Clwyd. It flows east to join the River Alwen on the southeast side of MAERDY.

of TILTON and flows into the River Welland two miles (three km) east of STAMFORD.

Chelt, Gloucestershire, England
The Chelt rises east of CHELTENHAM SPA, noted for its waters, and flows west through the town center. The Chelt joins the River Severn about five miles (eight km) north of GLOUCESTER, a town noted for its fine cathedral.

Chepino, Bulgaria
The Chepino rises in southwest Bulgaria and is formed by the confluence of various streams from the Rhodope Mountains. It is 56 miles (90 km) long. It flows past VELINGRAD and KAMENICA to the Marica River. The basin of the Chepino is a much noted resort area, famous for its many thermal springs.

Cheptsa, European USSR
The Cheptsa is 310 miles (500 km) long. It rises in the west foothills of central Ural Mountains and flows to the Vyatka River at KIROVO-CHEPETSKI. The river is used extensively as a channel for floating lumber from the forests to the mills.

Cher, France
The Cher is 200 miles (320 km) long. It rises in the Massif Central, about 14 miles (23 km) east of AUBUSSON. The river is navigable from NOYERS to its mouth. It receives the Tardes, Arnon, Yèvre and Sauldre Rivers as tributaries. It flows past MONTLUCON and VIERZON to the Loire below TOURS.

Cherwell, Oxfordshire, England
The Cherwell is 30 miles (48 km) long. It rises 12 miles (19 km) northeast of BANBURY. The river flows south to join the Thames near the university of Oxford. This beautiful little river has excellent boating and fishing facilities.

Chet, Norfolk, England
The Chet rises northwest of EAST PORINGLAND and flows east into the larger River Yare, about three miles (five km) north of LODDON.

Chew, Somerset, England
The Chew rises near CHEWTON MENDIP and flows through the small Chew Valley Lake into the River Avon at KEYNSHAM. Keynsham is noted for its chocolate and paper products and is midway between BATH and BRISTOL.

Chiese, Italy
The Chiese River of northern Italy rises in the high glaciers of the Adamello Mountains. It is 100 miles (160 km) long and flows in a southerly direction for the majority of its course through Lago d'Idro, passing VOBANRO and ASOLA before it reaches the Oglio River.

Cigüela, Spain
The river is 125 miles (201 km) long. It begins to the west of CUENZA in central Spain. It continues in a southwesterly direction to flow through the swamps northeast of CIUDAD REAL. The lower course of the Cigüela River is known alternatively as the Zàncara River.

Chir, European USSR
This river is not navigable. It rises south of MIGULINSKAYA and flows 215 miles (346 km) southeast to the Don at NIZHNE-CHIRSKAYA.

Churnet, Staffordshire, England
This river rises near UPPER HULME in Staffordshire. It flows southwest of LEEK, a town noted for its textile mills, and then swings in a loop to the west. Again changing direction the river flows southeast until it joins with the River Dove south of ROCESTER.

Claerwen, Dyfed-Powys, Wales
This Welsh river rises on the border between Dyfed and Powys southeast of CWMYSTWYTH, a small hamlet close to DEVILS BRIDGE. The river flows south to the Claerwen Reservoir and then southeast through it, and on to the head of Caban Coch Reservoir. The Claerwen then turns northeast to join the River Elan in the reservoir. The fly fishing is excellent.

Clun, Shropshire, England
This river rises at ANCHOR, Shropshire on the Welsh border. It flows east to ASTON-ON-CLUN, then, changing direction, it heads south to join the River Teme at LEINTWARDINE, a village on the site of the Roman Bravonium.

Clwyd, Clwyd, Wales
This river rises in the Clogaenog Forest. The Clwyd flows south to MELIN-Y-WIG, and then heads northeast to RUTHIN and passes near the ruins of its 13th century castle which is now in the grounds of a hotel. It then flows north to the coast on the west side of RHYL. The entire valley between Ruthin and ST ASAPH (noted for the ruins of its 13th century cathedral) is popularly known as the Vale of Clwyd.

Clydach, Dyfed, Wales
The river rises four miles (six km) south of LLANBYDDER. It continues south through GWERNOGLE in the Forest of Brechfa, a national forest ten miles (16 km) north of the previous county town of CARMARTHEN. The Clydach eventually flows into the River Cothi a mile (1610 m) east of BRECHFA, a town named for and in the center of the famous forest. This area is a very popular tourist center.

Clyde, Scotland
The Clyde is Scotland's most important river and is formed by the confluence of two small streams: the Daer Water and the Potrail Water which rises in the Scottish Borders area noted for its green hills. It is 80 miles (129 km) long. As the river flows down to its outlet at the Firth of Clyde, it passes through numerous valleys which are dammed to supply drinking water for the cities and towns on the Lower Clyde. The river flows northeasterly as an average-

The Clyde River in the Lowther Hills of Scotland.

sized stream and is noted for its trout fishing. The region around the Clyde is utilized by farmers as winter feed grazing for their dairy herds and sheep.

At SYMINGTON, a small railroad junction, the Clyde heads northwest and stays on this course for 15 miles (24 km) before shifting to a southwesterly course. The Clyde changes course once again near the confluence with the Douglas Water and heads in a northeasterly direction. This northeast direction is maintained by the river for the remainder of its journey to the estuary of the Firth of Clyde.

The river has a drop of slightly over 300 feet (90 m) in the next five miles (eight km) of its course, through a series of waterfalls at Bonnington Linn, Cora Linn, Dundaff Linn and Stonebyres Linn. The Clyde reaches the

Colne, Essex, England
The river rises in northwestern Essex and then flows southeast through the ancient Roman town of COLCHESTER. Leaving Colchester, the Colne flows into the North Sea between BRIGHTLINGSEA and Mersea Island.

Corfe, Dorset, England
The river rises just south of the Purbeck Hills in Dorset. It flows northwest of KIMMERIDGE, and then eastward and northward until it passes between the gap in the hills at the famous CORFE CASTLE, a Norman fortification which was besieged during the English Civil War. The Corfe finally flows into Poole Harbor and ends its short run.

Cover, Yorkshire, England
This river rises north of KETTLEWELL in North Yorkshire. It flows southeast through COVER-DALE until it joins the River Ure just east of MIDDLEHAM, a town noted for its 12th century ruined castle and its modern racing stables.

Crane, Dorset, England
The Crane rises near CRANBORNE in Dorset. It flows southeast through the village and then continues until it reaches the Moors River just southeast of the village of VERWOOD.

Crane, Middlesex, England
This Greater London river begins as Yeading Brook in HARROW, a London borough noted for the Harrow Boys' School which was attended

flood plains of the Lower Clyde at CROSSFORD. The river next passes WISHAW and LARKHALL on its way to GLASGOW. Leaving Larkhall the river flows through the Lanarkshire coalfield.

Upon reaching the city of Glasgow, once the heart of the shipbuilding industry, the river flows past the engineering works and ship-building yards of GOVAN, RENFREW, CLYDE-BANK, BOWLING and DUMBARTON. Past these, the Clyde passes the small ports of GREENOCK and PORT GLASGOW. Now the river has broadened into the huge estuary of the Firth of Clyde which turns southward after GOUROCK. The United States Navy has port facilities for its Atlantic Fleet in the Firth of Clyde, especially for the nuclear powered Polaris submarines. The area surrounding the Firth of Clyde is noted for its natural beauty.

Cocker, Cumbria, England
This lakeland river rises in the Cumbrian Mountains. It flows north through BUTTER-MERE and Crummock Water, and meets the River Derwent at COCKERMOUTH, a town noted for its 13th century castle, clothing industries and as Wordsworth's birthplace.

The bustling city of Glasgow sprawls on the banks of the Clyde River.

by such personages as Winston S Churchill. It flows in a loop through SOUTH RUISLIP, RUISLIP MANOR and on to HOUNSLOW. In the London flood of 1977 this river overflowed its banks and severely damaged local housing. It meets the Thames at ISLEWORTH.

Crasna, Rumania-Hungary
See Kraszna, Rumania-Hungary

Crati, Italy
The river rises in the La Sila Mountains of southern Italy. It is 50 miles (80 km) long. It flows north past COSENZA, and then shifting ever so slightly, heads in a northeasterly direction until it enters the Gulf of Taranto.

Craunfurdland Water, Strathclyde, Scotland
This Scottish river rises in Strathclyde and flows southwest to join with Fenwick Water northeast of KILMARNOCK, an industrial town 19 miles (31 km) southwest of Glasgow. The river is known from this point as Kilmarnock Water and continues on its course until it joins the River Irvine on the south side of the town.

Cresswell, Dyfed, Wales
The river rises northwest of SAUNDERSFOOT, a small coastal resort town, only three miles (five

A picturesque stream leading to the Cocker River in Cumbria, England.

km) north of TENBY. It flows west to the small village of CRESSWELL, and forms an estuary. The Carew river joins it soon after and together they flow into the Daugleddau River at JENKINS POINT.

Creuse, France
The river rises a short distance west of LA COURTINE. It flows northwest past AUBUSSON, ARGENTON and LE BLANC to the Vienne river. There is a hydroelectric plant near EGUZON which provides power for the local district. The Creuse's major tributaries are the Petite Creuse, Claise and Gartempe Rivers. Its length is 160 miles (260 km).

Crimple Beck, Yorkshire, England
This river rises southwest of HARROGATE, a town noted for its spas and conference centers. It flows in an easterly direction and passes the towns of PANNAL and SPOTFORTH on its way to join the River Nidd west of WALSHFORD.

Crna, Yugoslavia
The Crna is 127 miles (204 km) long and rises northwest of the town of KRUSEVO in Macedonia. It flows southeast, then northeast to join the Vardar River near GRADSKO.

Crouch, Essex, England
This is an English east-coast river which rises west of the town of BASILDON and flows east into the North Sea just north of Foulness Island. This area is a well-traveled tourist spot and is noted for its fine yachting in the Crouch estuary.

Cynrig, Powys, Wales
This river flows down the east side of the Brecon Beacons, a small mountain range noted for its unspoiled natural beauty. The Cynrig flows northeast until it joins the River Usk approximately two miles (three km) east of the town of BRECON.

Cywyn, Dyfed, Wales
The Cywyn River rises a few miles east of Trelech, a village seven miles (11 km) south of NEWCASTLE EMLYN. It flows south and joins the river Taf three miles (five km) southeast of St Clear, a village which still has the traces of a moat and bailey castle.

Daer Water, Strathclyde, Scotland
The river rises in the Lowther Hills. It flows north through the Daer Reservoir and joins Potrail Water to form the River Clyde two miles (three km) south of ELVANFOOT, a Scottish village at the confluence of Elvan Water and the River Clyde, south of ABINGTON.

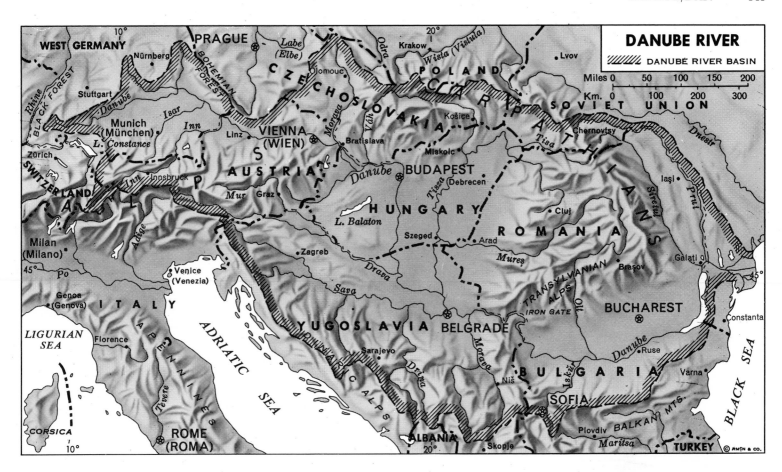

DANUBE RIVER
///// DANUBE RIVER BASIN

Miles 0   50   100   150   200
Km.   0   100   200   300

Dahme, East Germany
The Dahme River is 60 miles (96 km) long. It rises in the lower portion of Lusatia and flows in a northerly direction through several small lakes. It joins the Spree River in the southeast sector of BERLIN.

Dal, Sweden
The Dal River is 330 miles (530 km) long and has its source in the confluence of two headstreams, the Osterdal (East Dal) and the Vasterdal (West Dal). They both rise on the Norwegian border and fall from a height of over 3400 feet (1040 m). These two head-streams flow through deep, glacier cut valleys with spectacular views. The mountains are completely barren but their slopes are covered with indigenous forests at a lower level. After proceeding for over 100 miles (160 km) along its course the Osterdal gradually begins to widen out into the most beautiful lake in Sweden, Lake Siljan. The lake itself is 530 feet (161 m) above sea level, 25 miles (40 km) long and has an average width of six miles (ten km). Once the Osterdal leaves Lake Siljan it flows through an important agricultural area and is met 15 miles (24 km) downstream by the Vasterdal to form the Dal. The river narrows considerably as it approaches the industrial town of BORLANGE, where the largest steel works and paper mills in Sweden are located. The Dal also produces a large proportion of the much needed Swedish hydroelectric power. The river continues on course and next passes SATER, located on the narrow Säterdal. Ten miles (16 km) further on the Dal reaches the oldest town on its banks, HEDEMORA. It then passes AVESTA, a town also noted for its steel manufacturing capability. The river then

changes direction to flow east and gradually arcs to the west, flowing in a northerly direction by the time it reaches the coast at SKUTSKAR on the Gulf of Bothnia.

Dane, Cheshire-Derbyshire, England
The Dane rises on the border between Cheshire and Derbyshire, southwest of the town of BUXTON, noted for its spa and which the Romans called Aquae Arnemetiae. It flows in a westerly direction to the town of MIDDLEWICH, Cheshire and then continues northwesterly until it joins the River Weaver at NORTHWICH.

Danube River, Europe
The Danube is Europe's second longest river after the Volga and throughout the turbulent history of the continent, it has been an important avenue of conquest, migration and trade. At DONAUESCHINGEN, two small streams, the Breg and Brigach which rises in the Black Forest, join to form the beginning of the mighty 'Blue Danube.' The actual name of the river is a derivative of the Latin word Danuvius. The river flows through the Schwäbische Alb and follows the northern edge of the Bavarian plateau. At ULM the Danube becomes navigable for small craft, and ultimately at REGENSBURG is able to accommodate regular traffic. Some of the tributaries of the Danube which flow from the Alps are the Iller, the Inn, the Isar and the Lech. Reaching PASSAU the river enters Austrian territory and flows between the Austrian Alps and Bohemian Forests along the rim of the Bohemian Basin. This is, beyond a doubt, the most beautiful and breath-taking portion of the

Two views of the Danube as it passes Budapest.

Danube. The picturesque river valley with its quaint villages and castles are a thing of the past. One such castle is Durnstein, the castle which became famous as the prison of Richard the Lion-Hearted in 1192–93. Modern dams have been constructed along the Danube to

The Danube River delta near the Black Sea in Rumania.

harness its great hydroelectric potential and more are programmed for the future. On leaving the gorge of Wachau, the Danube reaches VIENNA, the renowned capital city of Austria, known also for the famous 'Blue Danube' waltz by Johann Strauss. Once past Vienna the river begins to branch out and is noted for its surrounding woodlands and numerous wild birds. In this low-lying area the Danube receives one of its major tributaries, the Morava, and this divides the Upper Danube from the Middle Danube. Further down river the Danube is fully within the borders of Czechoslovakia, then it divides itself into three branches, the central one forming the border between Hungary and Czechoslovakia, until finally at KOMARON the river is united again. At the mouth of the Ipel River, the Danube enters Hungarian territory, and then twisting sharply southwards at VAC, reaches BUDAPEST, the capital of Hungary. The river takes on a majestic air as it flows gracefully through the center of this twin city – BUDA on the right bank and PEST on the left bank. Badly damaged during World War II, the city is completely rebuilt and is once again

a source of pride for its people. The river continues its southward meander, frequently splitting into two distinct branches, until it enters Yugoslavia near MOHACS. (At Mohàcs in 1526, a great battle was fought between the Turks and the Hungarian Army; the latter were severely defeated, and the Turks were allowed to proceed to the very gates of Vienna.) The Danube receives its three major tributaries the Drava, the Tisza and Sava (the largest) during the middle stage. It passes through the ancient fortress city of BELGRADE, the capital of Yugoslavia, which claims to have been destroyed and rebuilt 34 times. The next section of the Danube constitutes its major navigational hazard, the cataracts. This stretch which extends for over 75 miles (121 km), rises to a height of 1000 feet (305 km) in places, and narrows from 550 yards (500 m) to a mere 160 yards (146 m). The major obstacle is at the very end and is called the Iron Gate: it is really a rock bar in the bed of the river. This natural hazard has been overcome since 1896 by an artificial channel. The Iron Gate also denotes the beginning of the Lower Danube. From BAZIAS to SILISTRA the river

forms the natural boundary between Rumania and Bulgaria. A matter of geographical note here is the sharp contrast between the opposite banks. The northern shore is flat, while the southern shore rises to 300 feet (90 m) to the plateau surface. The remaining section of the Danube before it enters the Black Sea is a great resort for naturalists. There are over 70 species of fish in the Danube, including sturgeon and others whose very fine roe make an excellent grade of caviar. Also wildfowl such as cranes, cormorants, herons, pelicans and even flamingoes exist throughout the region. Before the river turns eastward at GALATI lies BRAILA, the chief Rumanian grain port. Beyond Galati the Danube receives its tributary, the Prut, which since 1940 has been the boundary with the USSR. From this point downstream, the Danube forms the natural boundary between Russia and Rumania. Near TULCEA the Danube delta begins, a marshy no man's land of about 1000 square miles (2700 sq km), built up by three main distributaries, the Chilia, Sulina and St Gheorghe. The Danube exceeds all other rivers in Europe in the volume of water carried. It is 1750 miles (2820 km) long.

The village of Grein on the Danube in Austria.

Dart, Devon, England

The Dart rises in Dartmoor among the peat bogs and granite plains and is 46 miles (74 km) long. It has many headstreams, the primary ones being the Black Brook, Cherry Brook, the Cowsie, Walla, Swinscombe, Webbern and Yeo. The main streams, the East and West Dart, join at Dartmeet and the river flows in a generally southeasterly direction. It courses under some unique pre-Celtic stone bridges and passes some of the finest scenery in southern England. Dartmoor is noted for its summer survival march which is world renowned for its toughness. The river itself is a typical plains river, bursting its banks during the winter months. Reaching TOTNES, the Dart. becomes tidal and the surrounding country-side changes noticeably. It is during this later stage that the old Celtic name for the river is fully realized, for the banks are covered by thick oak trees and the river is called the oak-tree river. After running in loops for a few miles, the Dart begins its last leg, running into a sunken river valley drowned by the rising sea over 15,000 years ago. The river next passes DARTMOUTH, a small port and resort noted for the Royal Naval College which overlooks the Dart estuary, before it flows finally into the English Channel.

Darwen, Lancashire, England

The Darwen rises near the town of DARWEN, noted for its wallpaper and paint products. It flows north and passes BLACKBURN, a town known for its local football club, 'the Blackburn Rovers.' The Darwen then flows west to join the River Ribble at WALTON-LE-DALE.

Dean, Cheshire, England

The Dean rises four miles (six km) east of MACCLESFIELD, a town known for its silk and textiles. It flows in a northwesterly direction through BOLLINGTON to meet the River Bollin on the north side of WILMSLOW, a large residential town.

Deben, Suffolk, England

The Deben rises close to DEBENHAM, a small Suffolk village tucked away in a beautiful portion of Britain. It is 30 miles (48 km) long and flows southeast past WICKHAM, then shifts slightly southward to pass WOODBRIDGE. The river is navigable below Woodbridge. It then forms an estuary and flows south into the North Sea at WOODBRIDGE HAVEN, just northeast of FELIXSTOWE, one of the major ports in East Anglia.

Dee, Dumfries and Galloway, Scotland

The Dee has its source in Loch Dee in Glentrool Forest Park. It flows southeast through the Loch of Clatteringshaws to Loch Ken before passing south to Kirkcudbright Bay.

Dee, Grampian, Scotland

The river rises in the Pools of Dee in the Cairngorm Mountain range. The Dee is 90 miles (145 km) long and flows eastward for its entire journey to the North Sea, passing Braemar Castle on its way. Braemar was utilized by the Hanoverian forces to restrain

the Highlanders after the Scottish Earl of Mar started a rebellion in 1715. The Dee next passes close to Balmoral Castle, the favorite home of Queen Victoria and her Prince Consort Albert. The river is noted for its salmon fishing. The Dee ends its flow at ABERDEEN, now the most important port on the east side of Scotland, especially since the discovery of North Sea oil.

Dee, Gwynedd, Wales

The River Dee rises at the base of a 600-foot (183-m) cliff which is the eastern portion of Mt Dduallt, a peak which stands 2155 feet (657 m) high. The Dee is 110 miles (180 km) long and descends swiftly in the first 1000 feet (305 m) of its seven mile (11 km) course into Bala Lake. Leaving Bala the river flows to CORWEN, a small market town. It then changes direction and moves eastward at a very rapid pace due to the steepness of the gradient. It passes LLANGOLLEN, a town famous for its annual musical eisteddfod, and makes three meanders which cut a swaith in the valley floor. The Dee then heads for CHESTER on its final leg and becomes an estuary before it empties into the Irish Sea. This river is a naturalists' paradise.

Dema, European USSR

The Dema rises in the southern Ural Mountains just northwest of FEDOROVKA. It flows in a westerly direction past PONOMAR-EVKA, then changes to a northeasterly flow until it reaches the Belaya River at UFA.

Top left: A pastoral setting for the meeting of the East and West Dart to form the Dart River at Dartmeet in Devon.
Bottom left: Deeside near Balmoral Castle, one of the Queen's holiday retreats, in Scotland. Balmoral was one of Queen Victoria's favorite summer residences.
Below: A bridge over the Dee (Wales) at the beautiful city of Chester.

Demer, Belgium

The Demer rises near BILZEN, in the central portion of Belgium and is 60 miles (97 km) long. It flows past DIEST and then joins the Dyle River at WERCHTER. It is mainly a nondescript river but major fighting took place along its banks during World War II.

Derwent, Cumberland, England

The Derwent is a northern river which rises in the Cumbrian Hills, northeast of SCA FELL, and has a length of 35 miles (56 km). It flows north to pass through Derwent Water, then changes course slightly to the northwest and flows through Bassenthwaite Lake. The Derwent receives the River Cocker at COCKERMOUTH and then proceeds on its journey to the Solway Firth.

Derwent, Derbyshire, England

This is a Midland river which rises on the northeast slopes of Bleaklow Hill, east of GLOSSOP. It flows south through the Derwent and Ladybower Reservoirs, passes BASLOW, MATLOCK (noted for its baths and Roman lead mines) and BELPER. The Derwent then flows through the city of DERBY, an avid football city, home of Derby County Football Team. Finally it joins the River Trent at GREAT WILNE, three miles (five km) southwest of LONG EATON. It is 60 miles (96 km) long.

Derwent, Yorkshire, England

The Derwent is a Moors river which rises in the famous Fylingdales Moor region, just south of the resort town of WHITBY. It flows south through the Vale of Pickering, an area known for its beauty. The river then flows southwest to MALTON and continues south to STAMFORD BRIDGE to meet the River Ouse southeast of SELBY, which is noted for the ruins of a once-fine abbey church.

Desna, European USSR

The Desna rises near the town of YELNYA and flows in a southerly direction past the cities of BRYANSK and NOVGOROD-SEVERSKIY. It is 737 miles (1186 km) long and is navigable for slightly over 500 miles (800 km) of its course below Bryansk. The Desna then changes its course to the southwest, flows past CHERNIGOV and continues on to join the Dnepr River, of which it is a major tributary.

Deveron, Scotland

The Deveron rises in the southern portion of Banffshire and flows northeast past the town of HUNTLY to the North Sea between the towns of BANFF and MACDUFF. It is a quiet river with excellent fishing and is 61 miles (98 km) long.

Devoll, Albania

The Devoll rises in the Grammos Mountains, just south of KORITSA, in the central portion of Albania. It has a length of 100 miles (160 km). The river flows in a westerly direction through Lake Maliq, past the towns of GRAMSH and KUCOVE. It meets the Osum River near BERAT and they jointly form the Seman River.

Devon, Scotland

The river rises on the border of the Central Region and Tayside. It flows east down Glen Devon to the village of GLENDEVON and then changes course to a southeasterly direction to the Crook of Devon. The river again shifts direction to run almost due west, to the south side of MENSTRIE. Its final path takes it to the River Forth a few miles west of ALLOA, a town noted for its wool and distilleries.

Diebidale, Sutherland, Scotland

The Diebidale rises in the Sutherland district of Scotland. It flows northeast down the Glen of Diebidale to the head of Glen Calvie.

Dimbovita, Rumania

The Dimbovita River is 155 miles (250 km) in length and rises in the Făgăraș Mountain Range, southwest of the town of ZARNESTI. It flows initially in a northeasterly direction, but changes course and proceeds south across Transylvanian Alps, a region noted for its vampire legends and local superstitions. The river then flows southeast very close to the capital of BUCHAREST and enters the Arges River at the town of BUDESTI. The river is actually linked with the capital city by a 13-mile (21-km) long canal.

Disna, European USSR

The river of former Lithuania rises in Lake Disna, a small lake south of the town of DOKSTOS. It has a length of 95 miles (153 km). It flows westward to join the Western Dvina River at DISNA.

Divelish, Dorset, England

The Divelish rises near the small village of WOOLLAND. It flows north to join the River Stour as a tributary one mile (1610 m) northwest of STURMINSTER NEWTON.

Dives, France

The river rises near EXMES in the Orne Department of northern France. It has a length of 60 miles (97 km). The Dives flows north through marshy terrain in the Auge Valley and enters the English Channel below the small town of DIVES-SUR-MER. Here in 1066, William, Duke of Normandy embarked on his conquest of the kingdom of Saxon England.

Dnepr, European USSR

The Dnepr, or the ancient Borysthenes, is 1420 miles (2280 km) long and is the third largest river in Europe. It has its source in the southern end of the Valday Hills at a height of 722 feet (220 m) in a peat bog. This is also the source of the Western Dvina River. The Dnepr's initial run is southward through a low and marshy area past DOROGOBUZH, where it changes direction to a westerly course. It passes the ancient city of SMOLENSK, a former center for trade routes between the East and West. Leaving Smolensk the river cuts its way through a great limestone ridge and creates the Kobelyak rapids. On its way to the Black Sea the Dnepr receives the following tributaries,

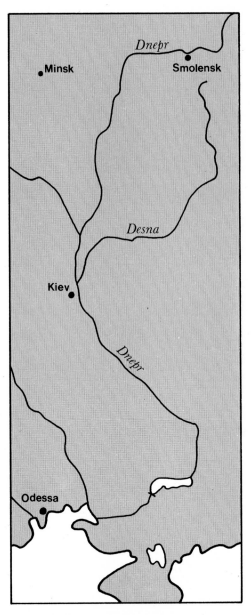

the majority of which are large rivers in their own right: Berezina, 365 miles (587 km) long; Pripyat, 498 miles (801 km) long; Teterev, 227 miles (365 km) long; Ingulets, 342 miles (550 km) long; Sazh, 403 miles (648 km) long; Desna, 738 miles (1187 km) long; Psel, 501 miles (806 km) long; Vorskla, 307 miles (494 km) long and the Samara, 244 miles (393 km) long. Upon reaching ORSHA the river turns to the west once again and continues on to MOGILEV, another historic Russian city. The Dnepr then encounters the head of Volyno-Podolsk upland and heads southeast to run along the foot of this great upland region. The river is surrounded on all sides by great forests of birch, oak, pine and spruce trees as far as the ancient city of KIEV. This city was the capital of Russia from the ninth to the 13th centuries. Kiev is located on the right bank of the Dnepr and derived its great wealth from the river trade. It is still the capital city of the Ukraine and is inhabited by over one million people. Leaving Kiev the Dnepr flows into the huge Kremenchug Reservoir, formed by the massive dam of the same name. The river flows through a series of dams, the Zaporozhe, the Kakhovka and finally the Dneprodzerzhinsk, the latter completed in the mid-1960s. The river again changes direction as it enters the

Right: Ships pass through the Kakhovka Lock near the mouth of the Dnepr River.
Below: The Paton bridge across the Dnepr River at Kiev.
Below right: The winding course of the Dnestr as it passes through the northern part of the Moldavian Republic.

huge flood plains of the delta which eventually turns into the tremendous Dnepr-Bug estuary at the Black Sea. The Dnepr provides water for irrigation as far away as the Crimea. It is now navigable to Orsha and many of its numerous tributaries are also navigable.

Dnestr, European USSR

The Dnestr has its source in the central Carpathian Mountain Range near the borders of the Soviet Union, Poland and Czechoslovakia. It starts as a small but rapid mountain stream as it flows northeast through a small, stony valley in the foothills of the Carpathians. It passes the town of SAMBOR as it leaves the mountains and then heads in a southeasterly direction. Numerous tiny tributaries flow into the Dnestr from the high ground on both sides of the river. The Dnestr meanders so wildly that it cuts an incision deep into the floor of its valley. The valley of the Dnestr has a flourishing agricultural economy based on maize, wheat, sugar beets and tobacco. It is the most densely populated region in the entire Soviet Union. Surprisingly, the Dnestr supports no large towns on its banks, but its tributaries have a large number of cities on their banks. The river changes course frequently from east to southeast on the remainder of its journey to the Black Sea. It is characterized by a very slow current, shallows and sandbanks. The Dnestr enters the Black Sea through a sunken valley which was drowned by the sea in some past geological age and is now in the shape of a huge estuary. The river is navigable as far as the border between the Ukrainian and Moldavian Republics. It is 877 miles (1411 km) long and drains an area covering 27,795 square miles (71,989 sq km).

Doe, Yorkshire, England

The River Doe rises east of Whernside. It flows underground in the general area of CHAPEL LE DALE and joins Kingsdale Beck at INGLETON to form the River Greta. The Doe is famous for its waterfalls at Snow Falls and Beezley Falls, both of which are major tourist attractions.

Dommel, Netherlands

The river has a length of 51 miles (82 km). It rises northwest of the town of WEERT in the southern Netherlands. The Dommel flows in a north-northwest direction and joins the Aa River, 50 miles (80 km) long, and the Zuid Willemsvaart Canal, which has a length of 76 miles (122 km), at HERTOGENBOSCH. The three together form the River Dieze which flows five miles (eight km) northwest to become a tributary of the Maas River.

Don, European USSR

The Don is one of the major rivers of Russia and flows for a length of 1224 miles (1969 km). The ancient name for the Don was the Tanais. This was derived from the ancient fortress city of AZOV, which was founded in the sixth century BC as a Greek colony and called Tanais. The Don is the fifth longest river in Europe and drains an area of 170,849 square miles (442,499 sq km). The river begins in the northern area of central Russia near the town of NOVOMOSKOVSK, a town important for its chemicals. The Don flows in a southward direction along the edge of the central uplands. Throughout its length the Don only falls an average of 634 feet (193 m), giving it one of the lightest falls of any major European river. The Don flows so gently that its most popular nickname is the 'Quiet Don.' One of Russia's great novelists Sholokhov called his famous novel by that title although it has been

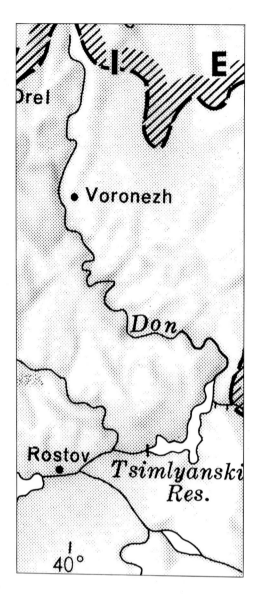

mistranslated by various individuals. At the city of DANKOV, the Don begins to widen and is joined south of the city by two of its major tributaries, the Sosna and Krasivaya Mecha. Before receiving its next large tributary the Don flows through an area of forest steppe, an area constantly put to the plow and so fertile that it produces bumper crops of wheat and sugar beets, the principal agricultural products of the region. The next tributary is the Voronezh, and only a few miles away stands the important industrial town of VORONEZH. The Don only becomes a navigable river at LISKI, 60 miles (97 km) below the confluence with the Voronezh. This is because plowing has led to severe erosion along the once fertile belt of the right bank and this material has been blown into the Don, causing shallows and sandbanks where none had previously existed. Leaving Liski the Don flows through one of the most famous areas in all of Russia, the region once occupied by the Don Cossacks, extraordinary horsemen and renowned fighters. The Don Cossacks were constantly at war with the Tartars until the Tzars eventually brought them into their sphere of jurisdiction. Along the flood plain of its valley, the Don is joined by the Khoper River which is 626 miles (1007 km) long and a little further on the Medveditsa River which is 475 miles (764 km) long. Past the confluence with the Medveditsa, the Don turns into a large bend or elbow and flows southwest. This area was the scene of the most ferocious fighting of World War II. It was here on the 'Don Elbow' that the Battle of Stalingrad, now VOLGOGRAD, was fought in August 1942. Here at the bend the Don is joined to the Volga only 40 miles (64 km) away by a ship canal, from the town of KALACH on the Don to KRASNOARMEYSK on the Volga. The canal is made up of 13 locks which can admit the largest ocean-going ship, as well as cargo vessels carrying lumber, petroleum, coal and metallurgical supplies from the Donbass area. A huge dam was constructed at the city of TSYMLYANSK along with a hydroelectric power plant. The Don is joined by the Donets River, 631 miles (1015 km) long, and the Manych River, 162 miles (261 km) long, below the dam as it stretches across its broad flood plain. As the Don progresses towards its mouth it flows past the industrial city of ROSTOV-ON-DON, population 650,000. From this port the Don flows to its delta and the Gulf of Taganrog, the northeastern portion of the Sea of Azov.

Don, Grampian, Scotland

The river rises seven miles (11 km) south of TOMINTOUL and runs east by the town of ALFORD. It continues past INVERURIE to the North Sea, north of ABERDEEN. The Don is 82 miles (132 km) long and is noted for its fishing.

Don, Yorkshire, England

The river rises west of DUNFORD BRIDGE and has a length of 70 miles (113 km). It flows east to PENISTONE, then changes course to the southeast and heads for SHEFFIELD. It shifts again to a northeasterly direction and passes ROTHERHAM, MEXBOROUGH and DONCASTER to join the River Ouse at GOOLE in Humberside.

Left: Rostov on the banks of the Don River.

Donets, European USSR

The Donets River is one of the major tributaries of the Don River. The Donets rises in the southern portion of central Russia and flows for 631 miles (1015 km) before joining the Don. It flows south through the rolling hills of the Russian uplands before reaching the 17th-century fortress city of BELGOROD which today is a primary agricultural center.

The river is not naturally navigable, but for 138 miles (222 km) upstream from its confluence with the Don to GUNDOROVKA, the river can take barge traffic due to the construction of canals. The first tributary of consequence to join the Donets is the Udy, and at this location the important industrial city of KHARKOV is situated. At this point the river begins to widen considerably as it flows southeast to join the Don. The remainder of the Donets' course is a relatively slow and meandering one. Further on the Donets is joined by the Oskol River, 287 miles (462 km) long, and numerous small tributary streams from the uplands. The Donets then flows through the wheat belt of the Soviet Union. On the right bank of the river and running parallel to the river is the Donets Ridge. Beneath this ridge and extending to the very banks of the river is the Soviet Union's largest indigenous coalfield. The major towns along the river's course are LISICHANSK and KAMENSK-SHAKHTINSK, large mining towns. KONSTANTINOVKA and KRAMATORSK, steel and iron towns, are on the tributary Torets River, and LUGANSK, which is noted for its engineering works, is located on the tributary Lugan River.

Dordogne, France

This river rises high in the northwestern flanks of Le Mont-Dore, an extinct volcano in the Auvergne Mountains of the Massif Central. The river begins at a height of 5620 feet (1714 m) where the annual precipitation is over 52 inches (one and one-third m). The majority of the run-off is from melting snow in the spring which becomes a raging torrent further down the steep slopes. The length of the Dordogne is 290 miles (467 km). In the upper reaches of the river, the Dordogne flows through deep mountain gorges with steep walls. Its waters are augmented on its flow by numerous tributaries such as the Cère and Marenne Rivers which, like the Dordogne, have been dammed to prevent the turbulent flow of the rivers and to provide hydroelectric

power. The lower reaches of the river are totally different; it flows through open valleys and the river is relatively placid for the remainder of its course. The final destination of the Dordogne is BEC D'AMBES where it becomes a major tributary of the Gironde River.

Doubs, France

The Doubs rises in the Jura Mountain Range above the town of MOUTHE in eastern France and has a length of 270 miles (430 km). It flows northeast through the lakes of Saint-Point and Brenets. Then it makes a short loop into Switzerland and flows westward into the metallurgical area of MONTBELIARD. Passing through it turns southwest and joins the Saône River 55 miles (88 km) from its source.

Top: The Dordogne River from Beynac in France.
Above: View of Oporto down the Douro River from Vila Nova, Portugal.
Right: The Dovey River of Northern Wales.

Douro, Spain

The Douro rises on Pico de Urbion at a height of over 5000 feet (1525 m), in the Iberic Mountain Range and flows for a distance of 490 miles (790 km). The river drains the northern basin of Meseta. It flows first southward for a short time, but then changes slightly to the west as it loses altitude and heads for the Spanish-Portuguese border. The Douro forms the border between the two countries of the Iberian Peninsula for

approximately 75 miles (121 km). The river has a fast current during its course through the deep gorges cut into the crystalline rock formations and is filled with numerous rapids which makes navigation impossible at this stage. The Douro does not become navigable until well within the Portuguese border and 121 miles (195 km) from the Atlantic Ocean. A few miles above the primary port of Portugal, PORTO, the Douro widens out into an estuary. Only small vessels can still reach Porto due to the sand bar which stretches across the mouth of the estuary and only flat bottomed boats can go above the city.

Dove, Derbyshire, England

This river rises on the border between Derbyshire and Staffordshire, southwest of the town of BUXTON. It flows south past UTTOXETER, then turns slightly to the southeast to join the River Trent at the country village of NEWTON SOLNEY.

Dovey (Dyfi), Gwynedd, Wales

The river begins as several small streams north of LLANYMAWDDWY. It flows southwest past MACHYNLLETH, a beautiful little town located in Powys. It then flows into Cardigan Bay west of ABERDOVEY.

Drac, France

The Drac begins its course in the Dauphiné Alps in southeastern France and has a length of 95 miles (153 km). Its major tributaries are the Romanche River, 48 miles (77 km) long and the Bonne River, 20 miles (32 km) long. The river is known for its very important hydroelectric stations. The Drac itself becomes a tributary of the Isère River below the alpine city of GRENOBLE.

Drammen, Norway

This is one of Norway's most beautiful rivers. It is 170 miles (270 km) long. The Drammen begins as the Hallingdalselvi River, in the Hallingskarv Mountains, in southeastern Norway. It flows east through Lake Kroderen which is 27 miles (43 km) long and two miles (three km) wide. When the river exits the lake it becomes the Drammen River and flows the rest of the way into the Drammen Fjord very near Oslo.

Drava, Italy-Austria-Yugoslavia

The Drava begins in the Carnic Alps, not too distant from DOBBIACO, in Italy. The Drava is 450 miles (720 km) long and is one of the longest rivers in central Europe. The Isel River joins the Drava at LIENZ in the South Tyrol. With its new addition, the river flows on to SPITTAL, a town in the province of Carinthia, well known for its breweries and huge paper mills. Just above the village of DRAVOGRAD the Drava crosses the Yugoslavian border, where it is joined by another tributary river, the Meza. This stretch of the Drava is very popular with the canoeing enthusiasts of the world who consider this piece of the river as their personal testing ground. The river continues through Slovenia and Croatia. It

picks up its next tributary, the Mur River, at LEGRAD, and for a distance acts as the border between Hungary and Yugoslavia until just east of the town of OSIJEK it joins the mighty Danube.

Drawa, Poland

The river rises north of CZAPLINEK, in northwestern Poland. It flows south and west through a series of small lakes on its 100 mile (160 km) journey to join the Notec River.

Drin, Albania

The river rises at KUKES where the Black and White Drin Rivers meet to form the Drin. It is 175 miles (282 km) long. The Drin flows west through a series of gorges through the plain of Scutari. Then it changes direction to the south and passes the town of LESH. The Drin has two arms: the first empties into the Drin Gulf of the Adriatic Sea and the second joins the Bojana River as a tributary.

Drina, Bosnia, Yugoslavia

The Drina is formed by the confluence of the Piva and Tara Rivers, northeast of Mt Malgic. It is 285 miles (459 km) long. Its major tributaries are the Foca and Lim rivers, which together are 136 miles (219 km) long and the Cotina River, itself 75 miles (121 km) long. It flows in a northeasterly direction past the towns of VISEGRAD, FOCA and ZVORNIK and becomes a tributary of the Sava River, approximately 12 miles (19 km) from the town of BIJELJINA.

Driva, Norway

This beautiful river rises on the slopes of Mt Snohetta, in western Norway. This is truly scenic countryside at its very best. The Driva flows 100 miles (160 km) into its outlet at the head of Sunndals Fjord which connects with the North Sea.

Dronne, France

This river rises in the Dordogne Department of southwestern France. It is 115 miles (185 km) long. The Dronne passes the towns of BRANTOME and SAINT-AULAYE on its way to become a tributary of the Isle River just below COUTRAS.

Drut, European USSR

This partly navigable river of the eastern portion of White Russia is 180 miles (290 km) long. It rises north of TOLOCHIN in the Smolensk-Moscow Uplands. The Drut is a tributary of the Dnepr River which it joins at ROGACHEV.

Drweca, Poland

The Drweca is a tributary river of the Vistula which flows 152 miles (245 km). Its source is southeast of OSTRODA, in northern Poland. Initially, the Drweca flows northwest but changes to a southwesterly direction and passes through several lakes before finally joining the Vistula.

Duddon, Cumbria, England

The river comes to life at Wrynose Pass in Cumbria. The Duddon flows south to run between Haverigg Point and the Furness peninsula into the Irish Sea. Its course is unmarked by anything of great note, but some of the scenery along its banks is worth seeing.

Dudwell, East Sussex, England

The Dudwell rises east of the town of HEATHFIELD. It flows eastward to join the River Rother below ETCHINGHAM, a small village seven miles (11 km) north of BATTLE near which William the Conqueror defeated King Harold in 1066.

Dugoed, Gwynedd and Powys, Wales
The Dugoed rises on the borders between these two ancient kingdoms of Wales, approximately five miles (eight km) northeast of MALLWYD in Gwynedd. It continues first south and then changes to a westerly course before flowing into the River Dovey.

Duisk, Strathclyde, Scotland
The Duisk has its headwaters in the Strathclyde region of Scotland. It flows northwest to pass the village of BARRHILL before joining the River Stinchar at PIN-WHERRY, a small village at the confluence of both rivers.

The River Duddon in Cumbria.

Dulais, Dyfed, Wales
The river has its headstreams northeast of LLANFYNYDD in Dyfed. The Dulais flows in a southerly direction until it joins the River Tywi east of the village of RHOSMAEN, northeast of LLANDEILO.

Dulais, West Glamorgan, Wales
The river rises near the SEVEN SISTERS village located only eight miles (12 km) northeast of NEATH, famous for the remains of its abbey. The Dulais joins the River Neath just northeast of the town of Neath.

Dulas, Dyfed, Wales (1)
This River Dulas rises near the hamlet of BLAENFFOS, south of CARDIGAN. It flows east until it runs into the River Cych to the west of NEWCASTLE EMLYN.

Dulas, Dyfed, Wales (2)
This excellent fishing river begins south of LLANGEITHO, in Dyfed. It heads south to flow into the River Teifi at LAMPETER.

Dulas, Powys, Wales (1)
The river comes to life south of the Caban Coch Reservoir, in Powys and flows in a

southerly direction to join the River Irfon as a tributary at GARTH.

Dulas, Powys, Wales (2)
This River Dulas rises a few miles southeast of LLANGURIG in Powys. It runs east then changes to a northwest course before flowing into the River Severn southwest of LLANIDLOES.

Dulas, Powys, Wales (3)
The river flows south on an uneventful course. It becomes a tributary of the River Dovey northeast of the town of MACHYNLLETH.

Dulas, Powys, Wales (4)
The river rises east of RHAYADER and flows south initially, shifting to a southeast direction before entering the River Ithon close to LLANDRINDOD WELLS, a popular resort town of Wales.

Dullan Water, Grampian Region, Scotland
This tiny river begins in the Grampian region. It flows northeast down Glen Rinnes to eventually join the River Fiddich at DUFFTOWN.

Dulnain, Highlands, Scotland
The river rises in the Monadhliath Mountains at a height of 3000 feet (915 m). It runs northeasterly to join the River Spey southeast of the BRIDGE OF DULNAIN.

Dunajec, Poland
This river is formed by the confluence of the Black and White Dunajec rivers at NOWY TARG, in the Krakow Province of southern Poland. The two headstreams of the Dunajec rise in the High Tatra and flow through a natural scenic wonderland. The Dunajec is 128 miles (206 km) long and flows in an easterly direction. Along its course are several large power dams which provide a large proportion of the hydroelectric power for the area. The river then changes direction slightly to the northeast and continues on this basic course till it reaches the Vistula near the town of ZABNO.

Duneaton Water, Strathclyde, Scotland
The river rises on the slopes of Cairn Table, at a height of 1944 feet (593 m). It flows east to join the River Clyde a few miles north of the town of ABINGTON. It is a good fishing river.

Durance, France
The Durance begins its 180-mile (290 km) journey to the Rhône River at the foot of the Montgenèvre Pass, in the southeastern section of France. It receives quite a large number of tributaries: the Asse, Bléone, Buech, Cuisane, Ubaye and Verdon rivers. It flows in a generally southwesterly direction passing through the Provence Alps. It moves past the town of BRIANCON and then changes direction to a westerly flow and enters the Rhône River

slightly southwest of AVIGNON. This town was famous for the great division in the ranks of the Catholic Church when there were two Popes, one in Rome and the other in Avignon.

Dvina, Northern, European USSR
The Northern Dvina is 466 miles (750 km) long, is navigable for 342 miles (550 km) of its course and drains an area of 140,000 square miles (362,600 sq km). The river is formed by the meeting of the Yug and Sukhona Rivers and after only 35 miles (56 km) of its course is joined by its primary tributary the Vychegda River, 665 miles (1070 km) long. The river flows in a northwesterly direction until it enters the Dvina Gulf, an arm of the White Sea, through a delta. The Northern Dvina sees a large amount of traffic on its waters and is utilized primarily for floating timber. At its mouth is the largest sawmilling and timber exporting city in the entire Soviet Union, ARCHANGEL. This river is one of the most important waterways in Russia.

Dvina, Western, European USSR
The Western Dvina is 634 miles (1020 km) long and drains an area of 32,900 square miles (85,200 sq km). This river rises in the Valday Hills, only a few miles from the beginnings of two great rivers the Volga and Dnepr. The upper section of the Western Dvina flows in a southwesterly direction, past ZAPADNAYA DVINA, a small river town, where the actual head of navigation begins for the river. The river then flows on to VITEBSK, a fortress city of medieval times and the scene of many a siege. From Vitebsk the Western Dvina meanders in a northwesterly direction to pass POLOTSK. The

lower reaches of the river flow through the former Latvian Republic, one of the old Baltic Sea countries which the Soviet Union annexed during World War II. The principal tributary of the Western Dvina is the Mezha which is 161 miles (259 km) long. The river then flows through the city of RIGA and finally on to its outlet the Baltic Sea a few miles further on.

Dwyfor, Gwynedd, Wales
This small river rises in Cwmdwyfor below the village of TRUM Y DDYSGL. It flows in a southerly direction into its outlet TREMADOC BAY just west of CRICCIETH and the remains of its 13th-century castle.

Dwyryd, Gwynedd, Wales
The river rises near BLAENAU FFESTINIOG, a town noted for its slate quarrying. It only flows 14 miles (23 km) before entering its outlet Cardigan Bay. On its way the Dwyryd passes through the much loved Vale of Ffestiniog where it is joined by the River Cynfal. Although only a short river it passes through some of the most scenic areas in Wales.

Dyje, Austria-Czechoslovakia
This river is formed by the confluence of the Austrian and Moravian branches of Dyje in Lower Austria. The Dyje is the major tributary of the Morava River and is 175 miles (282 km) long. Its principal tributary is the Svratka River, which is 106 miles (171 km) long, close to the town of DOLNI VESTONICE. It flows in a northeasterly direction into Czechoslovakia, then turns to a more easterly course and passes BRECLAV to join the Morava.

Above: Two views of the Durance River: (left) south of Sisterton and (right) at Sisterton.

Below: Sailing is a popular pastime on the Northern Dvina.

Eachaig, Strathclyde, Scotland

The river rises in Argyll and flows south through Loch Eck. It continues on until it reaches the head of Holy Loch, the home of the US Navy Nuclear submarine fleet in Britain.

Earn, Tayside, Scotland

The Earn is only 55 miles (88 km) long. This well-known river has its source in western Perthshire. There the headstreams of the Earn run down the mountain slopes into Loch Earn, an excellent water skiing center. Loch Earn itself is six and a half miles (ten km) long and four square miles (ten sq km) in area and is located in one of the most beautiful spots in Scotland. Departing from the loch, the river flows on past COMRIE and then on to the holiday resort town of CRIEFF. The river meanders the rest of its way toward its outlet, the River Tay, cutting deeply into the plains. The Earn is best remembered in the various Scottish ballads which sing about the daring deeds of those two lawless clans the Campbells and MacGregors. It was just above the Loch of Earn that the famous Rob Roy MacGregor was captured by the Duke of Montrose but succeeded in making good his escape.

Eau, Lincolnshire, England

The river rises east of the town of GAINS-BOROUGH. It flows first north and then eastward before entering the River Trent as a tributary south of EAST BUTTERWICK.

Eau, Great, Lincolnshire, England

A sister river of the Eau above, it rises south of the village of DRIBY in Lincolnshire. It flows in a northeasterly direction to enter the North Sea at SALTFLEET HAVEN.

Ebbw, Powys, Wales

The river rises three miles (five km) north of the town of EBBW VALE in Gwent. It flows south into the estuary of the River Usk south of the town of NEWPORT. This area in Wales is a coal mining, steel and brick manufacturing industrial area.

Ebro, Spain

This river of northeastern Spain has a length of 580 miles (930 km). The Ebro drains the largest area in the Iberian Peninsula. It rises in the Cantabrian Mountains at a height of over 2800 feet (848,000 m) and maintains a southeasterly course for its entire run to the Mediterranean Sea. The river flows through the driest regions of Spain but with the aid of priceless water for irrigation from its tributaries the Arga, Aragon, Gàllego and Segre, agriculture is possible. Once the Ebro passes

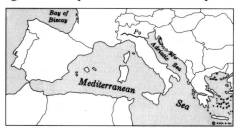

The Eden River rises near Kirkby Stephen (background) in Cumbria.

through the gorges of the Catalan Mountains it enters the coastal plains near TORTOSA, the scene of some of the bitterest fighting of the Spanish Civil War. General Franco's much talked about Ebro Offensive decisively split Catalonia from the rest of Spain and thus effectively eliminated the major source of revolution by his drive to the sea. It is not navigable except for very shallow bottomed vessels.

Eden, Cumbria, England
The Eden is 65 miles (105 km) long and rises south of Kirkby Stephen on Black Fell Moss. It flows in a southwesterly direction to the village of AISGILL, then shifts direction northward and passes APPLEBY and CARLISLE. It enters the Solway Firth west of Bowness-on-Solway.

Eden, Gwynedd, Wales
This small Welsh river rises south of the village of TRAWSFYNDD on the east side of LLYN TRAWSFYNDD. It flows south to join the River Mawddach a few miles northeast of LLAN-ELLTYD, a village a mile from the town of DOLGELLAU and very close to the ruins of Cymer Abbey. The scenery here is some of the most beautiful in Wales.

Eden, Surrey, England
The Eden rises near OXTED, a town due west of WESTERHAM. It flows southeast past EDEN-BRIDGE and Hever Castle, the home of Ann Boleyn, the favorite wife of Henry VIII and mother of Queen Elizabeth I. It joins the River Medway at PENSHURST, in Kent.

Eden, Tayside, Scotland
The river rises north of the town of KINROSS. It flows east through the Earldom of Fife, one of the ancient Celtic kingdoms of Scotland. Its final destination is the North Sea at St Andrews Bay. ST ANDREWS is world famous for being the birthplace of golf, and has some of the finest golf courses in the country.

Eder, West Germany
This river is 110 miles (180 km) long. It rises on the Ederkoft Mountain of West Germany. The Hemfurth Dam on its course forms a huge reservoir which provides a regulated water supply to the Weser River and the Ems-Weser Canal. The Eder flows east to join the Fulda River near the town of GRIFTE.

Edw, Powys, Wales
The Edw is a good fishing river which rises five miles (eight km) west of NEW RADNOR in Powys. The river flows first south and then southwest before it enters the River Wye near the village of ABEREDW. This small Welsh village has the remains of a baronial castle.

Ega, Spain
The Ega, one of the tributaries of the Ebro River, rises in the Cantabrian Mountain Range of northern Spain southeast of the town

Right and below: The Elbe River at Dresden.

of VICTORIA. It flows first by the town of ESTELLA then swings south on its 75 mile (121 km) journey to join the Ebro River at SAN ADRIAN.

Eger, Bavaria, Germany
This river is 159 miles (256 km) long and rises in the Fichtelgebirge, in Bavaria. It flows in an easterly direction through Czechoslovakia, and then shifts to a northerly course to where it joins the Elbe River at LITOMERICE.

Ehen, Cumbria, England
The Ehen begins its journey as the River Liza in the Cumbrian Mountains, on the northern slopes of Great Gable, a peak which is 2949 feet (899 m) high. It flows west into the Ennerdale Water, a small lake in Cumbria and emerges as the Ehen. The Ehen then flows by ENNERDALE BRIDGE and the village of EGREMONT before it runs into the Irish Sea with its sister river the Calder just northwest of SEASCALE.

Eider, Germany
This river is 118 miles (190 km) long and is for the most part navigable on its entire course. The Eider rises approximately eight miles (12 km) south of the city of KIEL. It flows north to the Kiel Canal, and then slowly meanders eastward to enter the North Sea below the town of TONNING. The Eider River represents the historic boundary between the provinces of Schleswig and Holstein. These two provinces have been the bone of contention between the Danes and the Germans for centuries.

Elan, Dyfed, Wales
The river rises a few miles east of CWMYS-TWYTH in Dyfed. It flows in an easterly direction to enter Powys, then changes to a southeasterly direction to PONT AR ELAN, located at the head of the Craig Coch Reservoir. The river then flows south through two large reservoirs to enter the Caban Coch Reservoir. The Elan then heads southeast to join the River Wye as a tributary south of the village of RHAYADER.

Elbe, Czechoslovakia-Germany
The Elbe is one of Germany's most important rivers, only second to the Rhine in historical and economic significance. The Elbe is formed by the running together of many small streams at a height of 4600 feet (1400 m) on the southern side of Riesengebirge near the Bohemian and Silesian frontier. The Elbe is 706 miles (1136 km) long and drains an area in excess of 56,000 square miles (145,000 sq km). The Elbe is a great commercial waterway and of great importance to Germany and Central Europe. Along its course, the Elbe receives numerous tributaries but the most significant are the Havel, the Saxonian Saale, the Black Elster and the Vltava rivers. The river makes an arc over 225 miles (362 km) long as it flows through Czechoslovakia passing large and small cities alike. Above the large industrial and mining center of USTI NAD LABEM, the Elbe

changes direction to a more northerly course and enters Germany. It passes the famous city of DRESDEN, devastated by bombing during World War II. The Elbe continues on and passes WITTENBERG, DESSAU and MAGDEBURG, all cities with significant historical backgrounds. The river now heads for the great port city of Germany, HAMBURG. Below Hamburg the Elbe has a width from over four to nine miles (six to 14 km). The Elbe can accommodate the largest ocean liners at Hamburg although the city itself is 55 miles

(88 km) from the sea. The remainder of the river's journey to the North Sea is uneventful.

Elster, Black, Germany
This river, which is 116 miles (187 km) long, rises in the Upper Region of Lusatia, in central Germany. It flows in a northwesterly direction to become a tributary of the mighty Elbe River near the city of JESSEN.

Elster, White, Czechoslovakia-Germany
This river flows through some of the most scenic parts of Germany. It is 153 miles (226 km) long and has its source in the northwestern portion of Czechoslovakia adjacent to the German border. The stream is beautiful as it cascades through thick forests on its way through eastern Germany. The White Elster flows through one of the most gorgeous valleys in all Germany, the Vogtland.

Above: Craig Goch Dam, Elan River, Wales.

It passes numerous industrial towns, the most important being OELSNITZ, PLAUSEN, GREIZ and ZEITZ. Upon reaching LEIPZIG, one of East Germany's most important cities, it changes direction and flows northwesterly into Saxony. The river separates here at Leipzig into two distinct streams. The main branch flows northwest and joins the Saale River, south of the ancient city of HALLE. The secondary branch is called the Luppe, and it parallels the main branch until it joins the Saale at MERSEBURG. The White Elster's principal tributaries are the Parthe and Pleisse Rivers in Saxony.

Elwy, Clwyd, Wales
The river is formed by the confluence of the Rivers Cledwen and Gallen near the village of LLANGERNYW in Clwyd. The Elwy flows in an easterly direction initially before changing to a more northerly flow. It joins the River Clwyd just north of the small village of ST ASAPH, noted for the remains of a 13th-century cathedral. It is a very popular tourist area.

Ema, European USSR
This river, of the former Baltic country of Estonia, is on one of the old medieval trade routes. It has a length of 109 miles (175 km). The Ema rises in the Otepaa Hills and flows first southwesterly, then west to pass through Lake Vortsjarv. The Ema then heads eastward past the town of TARTU into Lake Peipus.

Emba, European USSR
This Russian river is 384 miles (618 km) long. It rises in the southern Mugodzhar Hills of Kazakh. It flows in a southwesterly direction to pass through the oil producing region on its way to the Caspian Sea. Its major tributary is the Temir River.

Emme, Switzerland
This Swiss river is only 50 miles (80 km) long but flows through some of the finest scenic regions of Switzerland in its short journey. The Emme rises six miles (ten km) northeast of INTERLAKEN in central Switzerland and passes through the Emmental to join the River Aare near the town of SOLOTHURN.

Ems, Germany
The river rises in the vicinity of PADERBORN in northwestern Germany. It flows in an easterly direction then proceeds northward for a total of 250 miles (400 km), forming an estuary of the North Sea.

Endrick Water, Stirlingshire, Scotland
This Scottish river flows 20 miles (32 km) from its source in the Fintry Hills of central Scotland to the end of Loch Lomond, a mile (1610 m) south of the village of BALMAHA. It forms the border between the Central Region and Strathclyde on its lower course.

Enns, Austria
The Enns rises south of the town of RADSTADT, in central Austria. It has a length of 160 miles (260 km) and is navigable below the town of STEYR. It flows eastward through a gorge in the Ennstal Alps surrounded by fantastic scenery for the remainder of its journey to meet the Danube just southeast of the city of LINZ.

Eresma, Spain
The Eresma River rises in the Sierra de Guadarrama Mountains of central Spain. It is 105 miles (169 km) long and flows in a northwesterly direction to join the Adaja River as a tributary near the town of VALDESTILLAS.

Ergene, European Turkey
The river begins its course in the Istranca Mountains of European Turkey, the small portion of Turkey which is on the western side of the Bosphorus. It flows 125 miles (201 km) first west and then southwest to join the Marica River near the town of IPSALA.

Erne, Republic of Ireland
This Irish river rises in the hills of central County Cavan, a county also noted for its excellent quality crystal. It has a length of only 72 miles (116 km) but drains an area of over 1600 square miles (4144 sq km), a sizeable area for such a small river. The Erne links several waterways in County Cavan and County Fermanagh in an area abundant in lakes and small streams. The two largest of these freshwater lakes are Lough Oughter and Upper Lough Erne. This entire region of Ireland is a prime agricultural producing area much renowned for its cattle and dairy products. It is at the town of BELLEEK near the outlet of Lower Lough Erne that the river runs through a series of rapids towards BALLYSHANNON. At Ballyshannon is a hydroelectric station which produces a large proportion of the region's power. The Erne finally empties into the Atlantic Ocean at the end of its run.

Esk, Dumfries and Galloway, Scotland
The river rises at the confluence of the Black Esk and White Esk Rivers. It flows past LANGHOLM, a town noted for its woolen manufacturing industry, and then on to CANONBIE, a small village. The Esk then flows on a southerly course and passes across the border into England. It then heads past the town of LONGTOWN to enter the Solway Firth on the Irish Sea.

Esk, Lothian, Scotland

The other Scottish Esk is a river which is also formed by the confluence of two other smaller streams: the North Esk and the South Esk. The South Esk rises in the Moorfoot Hills and flows northward to join the North Esk north of the town of DALKEITH. The Esk flows in a northerly direction to the Firth of Forth at the town of MUSSELBURGH.

Esk, North Yorkshire, England

This Esk River rises on Farndale Moor of the North Yorkshire Moors National Park, a favorite area for hikers. It flows northward to the town of CASTLETON, then changes slightly to the east and flows into the North Sea at the resort town of WHITBY.

Esla, Spain

The river rises in the Cantabrian Mountains of northwestern Spain and is 175 miles (282 km) long. Its major tributaries are the Cea, Bernesga and Orbigo Rivers. The Esla flows in a westerly direction and joins the Douro River approximately 15 miles (24 km) west of the city of ZAMORA.

Etive, Strathclyde, Scotland

This Scottish river flows down Glen Etive southwesterly near the Glenetive National Forest. It continues on its rather short course to the head of Loch Etive, a sea loch which extends 18 miles (29 km) from Ledaig Point to the very foot of Glen Etive. The entire region is very wild and mountainous, but exceptionally beautiful.

Ettrick Water, Borders Region, Scotland

The river rises five miles (eight km) east of the town of MOFFAT. It flows northeast through Ettrick Forest, made famous during the fighting for Scottish independence when it served as a hideout for Sir William Wallace, one of Scotland's greatest heroes. The Forest of Ettrick is a large moorland region mainly utilized today for grazing cattle and sheep. The river flows on to enter the River Tweed as a tributary stream northeast of the town of SELKIRK.

Eure, France

This French river is 140 miles (230 km) long and rises in the Perche Hills of northwestern France. The major tributaries of the Eure are the Avre and Iton rivers. The Eure passes the city of CHARTRES famous for its spectacular medieval cathedral which towers over the city proper. Then it proceeds to flow in a northerly direction past the towns of MAINTENON and LOUVIERS to become a tributary of the Seine above PONT-DE-L'ARCHE.

Evan Water, Dumfries and Galloway, Scotland

This river rises in the Lowther Hills and flows south to join the River Annan a few miles south of the small resort town of MOFFAT. Here at Moffat, the River Annan is also joined by the much smaller Moffat Water. This area is an excellent tourist attraction.

Evenlode, Gloucestershire, England

This English river is only 35 miles (56 km) long. The Evenlode rises near MORETON-IN-MARSH, a small town made of Cotswold stone northwest of CHIPPING NORTON. The river flows on a southerly course, changing to a southeasterly flow after a few miles and passes CHARLBURY to become a tributary of the River Thames near the university city of OXFORD.

Exe, Somerset, England

This river of southeastern England has a length of 54 miles (87 km). The Exe rises high on Exmoor near the Atlantic seaboard of Somerset. It flows southeast on a very winding and twisting course. The Exe is joined by the River Barle just above the market town of DULVERTON. It then crosses the border between Somerset and Devon, and now heads south to rendezvous with the River Loman just below the town of TIVERTON, a well-known market and manufacturing center. Its next tributary is the Little Dart, after which the Exe flows through some very rich agricultural country. The Culm River is the next addition to its waters, as it swings westward in a wide curve to enter the cathedral city of EXETER. At Exeter it changes into a tranquil stream with no resemblance to its upper reaches. Below Exeter, the river forms a tidal estuary which is a drowned valley and is a naturalists' paradise abounding in waterfowl and seabirds. The river actually enters the English Channel at EXMOUTH, a beautiful little holiday resort town with excellent beaches. The Exe is world famous for its salmon fishing.

Ey Burn, Grampian, Scotland

The river begins in the Grampian Region of Scotland and flows in a northerly direction down Glen Ey. It joins the River Dee as a tributary stream at the village of INVEREY west of BRAEMAR.

Eye Brook, Leicestershire, England

This small English Midlands river rises southwest of the town of TILTON in Leicestershire, nine miles (14 km) northwest of UPPINGHAM. The Eye flows southeasterly through the Eye Reservoir and then continues on to meet the River Welland east of the small village of CALDECOTT.

Eye Water, Borders, Scotland

This small river begins in the Lammermuir Hills, a few miles southwest of the village of OLDHAMSTOCKS. It flows east by the two villages of GRANTSMOUTH and AYTON and finally enters the North Sea at the town of EYEMOUTH.

Eynort, Highlands, Scotland

This river on the beautiful isle of Skye heads south at the beginning of Loch Eynort on the island's southwest coast. The area is a favorite tourist haunt.

Fairham Brook, Leicestershire, England

This English Midlands river rises near the village of OLD DALBY in the fox-hunting country of Leicestershire. It flows in a northwesterly direction to join the River Trent as a tributary at the town of WEST BRIDGFORD, noted for its coach-building industry.

Fal, Cornwall, England

This beautiful Cornish river rises on the north side of Goss Moor near ST DENNIS. It flows first south and then southwest to form an estuary at CARRICK ROADS below Turnaware Point. It then flows past the port of FALMOUTH with its deep natural anchorage. Falmouth is noted as a tourist resort but is just as famous as a fishing port. At the entrance to Carrick Roads at Falmouth Bay, are the two castles of Pendennis and St Mawes built to protect the harbor and town from the French enemy. The view from the old battlements of Pendennis Castle out to sea and across the Fal estuary is well worth the trip and the River Fal offers some beautiful boating trips.

Falloch, Central Scotland

This river rises on the west side of Reinn a' Chroin. It then heads north and southwest down the Glen of Falloch. The river then flows south to enter the famous Loch Lomond in the Strathclyde region. Also famous are the Falls of the Falloch which are only four miles (six km) southwest of the picturesque village of CRAINLARICH.

Farigaig, Highlands, Scotland

The Farigaig River flows initially northward before turning to a westward direction and entering Loch Ness at the town of INVER-FARIGAIG, a few miles from FOYERS, a village at the mouth of the River Foyers. Loch Ness is of course world famous for being the home of the elusive Loch Ness Monster, supposedly witnessed by many sightseers and locals but with little concrete evidence to back up the sightings.

Farrar, Highlands, Scotland

The Farrar River runs eastward from the Loch of Monar which is eight miles (13 km) long and a source for hydroelectric power for the district. The Farrar flows on to join the River Glass as a tributary at the village of STRUY, just below the city of INVERNESS. The Farrar is noted for its excellent fishing.

Fathew, Gwynedd, Wales

The Fathew River rises a mile (1610 m) southwest of the village of ABERGYNOLWYN in Gwynedd. It continues on its southwesterly course and enters the River Dysynni just west of the small village of BRYCRUG.

Fekete, Hungary

The river rises south of the town of KADARKUT in southern Hungary. It has a length of 75 miles (121 km). It flows southeasterly to join the larger Drava River southwest of the town of SIKLOS.

Feshie, Highlands, Scotland

This scenic little Highland river rises on the south side of the beautiful Glen Feshie Forest which stretches across the top of Glen Feshie and is a natural deer forest. The small Feshie River then flows northward down Glen Feshie and into the River Spey close to the village of KINCRAIG.

Fiddich, Grampian Region, Scotland

The river rises in the Corryhabbie Hill, a mountain 2563 feet (782 m) high, located six miles (ten km) east of Glen Livet. This area of the Grampian region is noted for making the finest malt whisky in the world such as Glen Livet and Glen Fiddich. The small rivers in this part of Scotland provide the primary ingredient for these famous whiskys: excellent fresh mountain water. The Fiddich flows northeast through Glen Fiddich, then shifts course slightly to the west to pass DUFFTOWN. It then heads northwest to join the River Spey at the distillery village of CRAIGELLACHIE near Rothes-on-Spey.

Findhorn, Highlands, Scotland

This is another beautiful Scottish river which comes to life in the Monadhliath Mountains, a range which runs northeast to southwest across the border of Inverness and Badenoch and Strathspey districts. The highest peak in this range is Carn Dearg, 3100 feet (950 m). The length of the Findhorn is only 62 miles (100 km) but again it flows through a beautiful region of Scotland's Highlands noted world-wide for its scenery. The river flows west of KINGUSSIE and heads northeast down Strath Dearn to pass into Findhorn Bay and finally into the North Sea. On the east side of Findhorn Bay is the small village of FINDHORN, noted for its fishing fleet. These Scotsmen are great fishermen and well respected across the seas.

Finglas Water, Central Region, Scotland

Finglas Water rises in the Central Region and flows southeast down Glen Finglas. It passes through the big Glen Finglas reservoir to join the Black Water practically between Loch Achray and Loch Venachar to the west of the town of CALLANDER.

Finlas Water, Strathclyde, Scotland

The Finlas flows down the Glen of Finlas in a southeasterly direction. It heads for its outlet Loch Lomond, the famous Scottish loch just south of ROSSDHU. Rossdhu, noted for its castle and as the seat of the Colquhoun Clan, is situated on the western banks of Loch Lomond, one of the most beautiful and famous of Scottish lakes.

Finnan, Highlands, Scotland

One of the numerous Scottish rivers of the Highland region, it flows in a southward direction down Glen Finnan. It ends its journey at the head of Loch Shiel, a very narrow lake, slightly over 17 miles (27 km) long. The Finnan is well noted for its sports fishing.

Fiora, Italy

The river rises in Monte Amiata in the central area of Italy near the town of SANTA FIORA. The Fiora has a length of 51 miles (82 km). It flows southward to enter the Tyrrhenian Sea to the northwest of TARQUINIA, an ancient Etruscan town of great importance prior to the rise of Rome.

Fivehead, Somerset, England

The river rises in the eastern portion of the Blackdown Hills of Somerset, the English 'Summer County.' It flows eastward eventually joining the River Isle a few miles from the village of CURRY RIVEL.

Flumendosa, Sardinia

The river rises in southeastern Sardinia in Monti del Gennargentu. The Flumendosa is 79 miles (127 km) long and empties into the Tyrrhenian Sea.

Font, Northumberland, England

The River Font is formed by a number of small streams which flow into the Font Reservoir, south of the town of ROTHBURY. It leaves the reservoir and flows in a southeasterly direction by NETHERWITTON, a small Northumbrian village with an 18th-century hall. The Font continues to join the River Wansbeck at MITFORD which has the remains of a Norman castle.

Forsa, Isle of Mull, Scotland

The ISLE OF MULL is one of Scotland's most beautiful isles. The river begins its course down Glen Forsa to enter the Sound of Mull at the village of SALEN just southeast of the town of TOBERMORY.

Forss Water, Highlands, Scotland

The river begins in the Caithness district and flows northward from Loch Shurrery. The Forss continues on its northward course to the west of THURSO before it enters the North Sea. The Bridge of the Forss is a road bridge which carries the A-836 highway over the river five miles (eight km) west of the town of Thurso.

Forth, Central Region, Scotland

This river is world famous for the great bridges which span it. The best known is the one at QUEENSFERRY, approximately eight miles (13 km) northwest of EDINBURGH, the capital city of Scotland. Edinburgh itself is often remembered for the view from the top of Edinburgh Castle overlooking the entire city and the FIRTH OF FORTH out to the sea. The length of the Forth is 104 miles (167 km). It is formed high on BEN LOMOND – 3192 feet (974 m) – by two headstreams which meet at ABERFOYLE, a small village located on the banks of the Forth between Achray and Loch Ard Forest just below the southwest section of the Mentieth Hills. The river then flows east, passing STIRLING and its imposing castle set on a high crag overlooking the town. It then continues onward to pass ALLOA and then KINCARDINE where it widens into the Firth of Forth, a large estuary of the North Sea. The Forth has been visited by enemy fleets on numerous occasions during the past 2000 years or more, as its natural harbor furnished a good anchorage for ships of war as well as commercial vessels. The Royal Navy utilized this roadstead on numerous occasions in the past 50 years. During World War II, the first engagement between the Royal Air Force and the Luftwaffe occurred above the Firth of Forth. The Forth is as much a part of Scotland's history as Robert Burns, Robert the Bruce and Bonnie Prince Charlie.

Foulness, Humberside, England

This river rises near the town of MARKET WEIGHTON in Humberside. It flows southward in a loop taking it into the Market Weighton Canal, a few miles north of the town of NEWPORT, and eventually joins the River Humber as a tributary near FAXFLEET.

Fowey, Cornwall, England

One of the most popular rivers of England's southwest region, it has a length of only 30 miles (48 km) but flows through the beautiful southwest coast. The Fowey actually rises near the Cornish town of CAMELFORD on Bodmin Moor. The Moor was made famous by the authoress Daphne du Maurier, who wrote 'Jamaica Inn,' a novel about the Cornish shipwreckers who preyed on helpless ships caught in the dangerous nearby coastal waters. The river flows south past the town of LOSTWITHIEL before entering the English Channel at the resort town of FOWEY.

Foyers, Inverness, Scotland

The river flows southeast of LOCH NESS. It has two waterfalls called the Falls of Foyers which provide much needed hydroelectric power for this region of the Highlands.

Foyle, Northern Ireland-Republic of Ireland

The Foyle is an excellent fishing river in Northern Ireland. Although only 24 miles (38 km) long, the Foyle is part of an enormous river system which drains the majority of County Tyrone and all of southern County Donegal. The Foyle actually begins at the confluence of the Finn and Mourne Rivers near the town of STRABANE. The Mourne itself flows down from the most beautiful section of northern Ireland, the Mourne Mountains. The tributaries of the Mourne are numerous for a small river and drain the large Omagh Basin of northern Ireland. The river flows past OMAGH, and between the peaks of Bessy Bell, 1387 feet (362 m) and Sperrins, 828 feet (253 m). The Foyle is a tidal river for several miles above the city of LONDONDERRY, once alive with industries and much frequented by tourists. Unhappily this is no longer the case with the continuation of the insurmountable troubles which have beset the province since 1970. The Foyle widens out into Lough Foyle, a large estuary which is practically landlocked by the Magillgan headland. This headland approaches to within a mile of the town of GREENCASTLE on the Donegal side of the lake.

Top: The Esk River at Grosmont, North Yorkshire.
Above: An Aerial shot of Scotland's Forth River.
Top center: The Foyers River.

Top right: Loch Lomond is fed by the Falloch River.
Right: The Frome River at Wareham in Dorset.

Freshney, Humberside, England
The river flows in a southwesterly direction after rising near the town of GRIMSBY. It continues on through the western part of Grimsby itself and joins the River Humber as a tributary.

Frome, Dorset, England
The river rises to the south of the town of YEOVIL, which hosts an annual Royal Naval Air Show. The river then flows southeast past the county town of DORCHESTER to WAREHAM. It joins the English Channel at Poole Harbor ending its short run.

Frome, Hereford, England
This river rises north of the old market town of BROMYARD which is located to the west of WORCESTER. It flows south to join the River Lugg approximately four miles (six km) east of the town of HEREFORD. Hereford is a beautiful county town noted for its cathedral which is one of the primary tourist attractions of the area.

Frome, Somerset, England
The river rises approximately six miles (ten km) south of the medieval town of FROME with its steep streets and 18th-century wool merchants' houses. It flows in a northerly direction to join the River Avon as a tributary a few miles west of BRADFORD-ON-AVON.

Fruid Water, Borders Region, Scotland
The river flows from the Borders region of Scotland northward through the Fruid Reservoir. Leaving the reservoir it flows to within 1 mile (1610 m) southwest of the town of TWEEDSMUIR to join the River Tweed.

Gade, Hertfordshire, England
The Gade rises in the beautiful CHILTERN HILLS, the majority of which lies within the county of Buckinghamshire. The Chilterns are of particular interest to tourists because of the walks in the country, natural scenic beauty and antique shops in the numerous villages, such as WEST WYCOMBE, tucked away in the secluded hillsides. The Gade flows from northwest of HEMEL HEMPSTEAD in a southerly direction to join the River Colne just east of the town of RICKMANSWORTH.

Gail, Austria
The Gail is a tributary of the Drau River and is 75 miles (121 km) long. It is not one of Austria's major rivers but flows through some of the finest scenery in the country. The Gail rises in the Carnic Alps of southern Austria. It flows east and meets the Drau River at the town of VILLACH.

Gairn, Grampian, Scotland
The river rises in the Invercauld Forest. It heads east and joins the River Dee as a tributary one mile northwest of BALLATER, a small village and holiday resort.

Gala Lane, Dumfries and Galloway, Scotland
The Gala Lane rises three miles east of MERRICK. It flows north along the border with Strathclyde and into the southern end of Loch Doon. The Loch of Doon is very large and forms a reservoir at the head of the River Doon.

Gàllego, Spain
The river rises high in the Pyrenees near the Pourtalet Pass of northeastern Spain. It is 130 miles (210 km) long. It flows southwest first but then changes course to the south and joins the Ebro River as one of its many tributaries. The Gàllego provides a considerable amount of water for irrigation projects and hydroelectric power stations.

Gannel, Cornwall, England
The river begins at FRADDON in Cornwall. It flows to the Atlantic Ocean northeast of Pentire Point just southwest of the resort town of NEWQUAY. The RAF Station of ST MAWGAN is only a few miles away.

Garbh Ghaoir, Tayside Region, Scotland
This Scottish river begins in Tayside and flows from Loch Laidon to the head of Loch Eigheach. The North of Scotland Hydroelectric Power Board has a huge reservoir at Loch Eigheach.

The Gade River at Waterend.

Garonne, France
One of the major rivers of France, the Garonne rises high in the Spanish Val d'Aran in the central Pyrenees Mountains. Its source is formed by two headstreams, the first beginning in the eastern portion of the Val d'Aran, and the second coming from an underground cavern near the western end as an underground stream. The river leaves the Val d'Aran via the Pont du Roi gorge, an impressive landmark. It flows across the foothills of the Pyrenees and quickly enters the Aquitainian basin. Aquitaine, a former duchy and a great feudal power in medieval France, is noted for its wine-producing vineyards. It was also the home of Eleanor, first Duchess of Aquitaine, and later Queen of England, wife of Henry II, mother of Richard Coeur du Lion and King John. Reaching the town of PORTET, only a short distance from the city of TOULOUSE, the Garonne receives its first major tributary stream, the Ariège, which also rises in the crestline of the eastern Pyrenees. The river next runs past TOULOUSE, the center of the region's industries; at this stage in its course the river is only 450 feet (136 m) above sea

level. As the Garonne flows on, it receives many tributaries from its left bankside including the Louge, Nère, Touch, Save, Gimone, Arrats and Gers, to name the principal ones. The largest tributaries of the Garonne flow from the eastern side and drain off the Massif Central Range of France, notably the Lot, the Tarn and the Dordogne Rivers. The Garonne itself is not a very navigable river and vessels can only travel as far as CASTETS. Numerous small towns line the banks of the river on its way to the Gironde estuary: VALENCE, AIGUILLON, AGEN, MAR-MANDE and MACAIRE to name but a few. Between Macaire and BORDEAUX is a region rich in beautiful meadows and vineyards. The Garonne passes through Bordeaux only 60 miles (97 km) from the sea and now changes its course to a westward direction. The Dordogne enters the Garonne to become the Gironde only 15 miles (24 km) below Bordeaux at BEC D'AMBES, the very tip of the Entre-deux-Mers peninsula. The length of the Garonne is 450 miles (720 km).

Garry, Tayside Region, Scotland

This river runs southeast from Loch Garry, a reservoir and hydroelectric station of the North of Scotland Hydroelectric Power Board, which is five miles (eight km) long. The Garry flows through Glen Garry to become a tributary of the River Tummel northwest of PITLOCHRY also noted for its fishing.

Right: The Forth River near Edinburgh.
Below right: The Garonne weaves through the checkerboard French countryside.

Gartemple, France
The Gartemple rises in the Plateau de Millevaches of central France. It is 120 miles (190 km) long and flows west initially, then turns north to join the Creuse River.

Gauja, European USSR
This river rises in the Vidzeme Hills and is the longest river in Latvia at 260 miles (420 km). The Gauja winds and curves first east by northeast, then shifts to a north by northwesterly course and finally moves to a southwesterly course as it nears the capital and port of RIGA. The river is connected with the Western Dvina River by canals and various waterways and is utilized to float timber down the coast. It empties into the Gulf of Riga and the Baltic Sea.

Gaula, Norway
The Gaula is 90 miles (140 km) long. It rises north of ROROS in the central region of Norway. It flows in a northwesterly direction to become a tributary of the Sokna River at the town of STOREN. The river changes direction to the north as it begins to enter the Trondheim Fjord, its final destination.

Gaunless, Durham, England
The Gaunless rises north of BARNARD CASTLE, a town on the River Tees famous for the remains of its 12th-century castle. It flows eastward to join the River Wear as a tributary north of BISHOP AUCKLAND.

Gelt, Cumbria, England
The river rises in Geltsdale in Cumbria, very close to the Northumbrian border. It flows northwest to join the River Irthing as a tributary just three miles (five km) west of the town of BRAMPTON.

Genil, Spain
The river is 150 miles (240 km) long. It begins high on the glaciers of the Sierra Nevada in southern Spain. It flows north to join the Guadalquivir River as a tributary near the town of PARMA DEL RIO.

Gers, France
This French river rises on the Lannemezan Plateau in southwestern France and has a length of 110 miles (180 km). It flows north to meet the Garonne River at the town of AGEN.

Gill Burn, Highlands, Scotland
The river starts in the far northeastern corner of Caithness near the village of BRABSTERMIRE. It flows east into the Bay of Freswick approximately four miles (six km) from the most northern portion of the British mainland at JOHN O'GROATS.

Gipping, Suffolk, England
The Gipping rises six miles (ten km) to the northeast of STOWMARKET, a small town in Suffolk. It flows south to the city of IPSWICH. The Gipping then forms part of the estuary which is known as the River Orwell.

Gironde, France
The Gironde is a famous estuary on the Bay of Biscay in southwestern France. It is 46 miles (74 km) long and, on average, 2–7.5 miles (3–12 km) wide. The Gironde is formed by the confluence of the Garonne and Dordogne Rivers, two of the largest and most important rivers in France. The Gironde flows through the Medoc wine district, famous for its great vineyards. It is navigable to the city of BORDEAUX, known for its wines and tapestries.

Glåma, Norway
The Glåma is the longest river in Scandinavia. It rises at an altitude of 2700 feet (818 m) on a

Below: The tidal Gironde River.
Right: Aberglaslyn Pass on the Glaslyn River, Wales.

plateau of eastern Norway and flows for 365 miles (587 km). The Glåma gathers numerous tributaries as it flows down through the mountainous regions of Norway. It flows through the ancient town of ROROS which has been a leading copper exporter for the past 350 years or more. The valley of the Glåma is called the Osterdal. It continues on course to pass through ALVDAL, then flows southeast in a straight line for 150 miles (240 km). The principal tributaries of the Glåma are the Atna, Rena and the Vorma Rivers. The river passes through ELVERUM, a very important town noted for its sawmills and lumber yards. Elverum also has a large military training establishment which has been the primary reason for the town's growth. The last session of the Norwegian Parliament was conducted at Elverum, as they fled from the invading Germans. The river turns west at the town of KONGSVINGER after traveling 50 miles (80 km) from Elverum. The Glåma now enters Lake Oyeren in the heart of Norway's great timber region, only 15 miles (24 km) from the capital, OSLO. The Glåma next passes through the chief timber town of SARPSBORG which is 40 miles (64 km) from Kongsvinger. The river flows over the Sarps Falls, which furnishes hydroelectric power for the entire area. The river then heads for the sea, which it enters only a short distance from Oslofjord at FREDRIKSTAD, an important shipbuilding town. The river is navigable only as far as Sarpsborg because of the waterfall.

Glaslyn, Gwynedd, Wales

The river rises on the eastern side of Mt Snowdon, the highest peak in Wales at 3560 feet (1085 m). Snowdon gives its name to the surrounding mountain range and the region, Snowdonia. It flows through LYN GLASLYN and LYN LLYDAW, then changes course to the southeast and passes through LYN GWYNANT to the village of BEDDGELERT. The river then goes through the Pass of Aberglaslyn to the town of PORTMADOC before reaching its final destination, the Bay of Tremadoc, at Harlech Point.

Glass, Highlands, Scotland

This River Glass begins to flow in the Inverness district. It runs in a northeasterly direction down Strathglass, the valley of the river, eventually to join the River Farrar just southeast of the Struy Bridge. The Glass is a good fishing river.

Glass, Isle of Man

This river rises in the central Manx mountains and flows south to become a tributary of the River Dhoo to the west of the capital city of DOUGLAS. The river then flows through the city and into the harbor.

Glaven, Norfolk, England

The Glaven rises in what used to be one of the most powerful medieval earldoms and later dukedoms of the kingdom. The river begins north of Baconsthorpe and flows southward in a loop passing HUNWORTH and LETHERINGSETT villages, then it turns northward by the town of GLANDFORD. It enters the North Sea north of the village of CLEY NEXT THE SEA.

Glen, Borders, Scotland

This river starts as the Bowmont Water in Scotland very close to the English border. It flows by YETHOLM and MINDRUM to its confluence with the College Burn at WEST-NEWTON, Northumbria. Here it assumes the name of the River Glen until it joins the River Till west of DODDINGTON.

Glen, Lincolnshire, England

The river rises near the village of OLD SOMERBY in Lincolnshire. It flows past ESSENDINE southward, then moves northeast through GREATFORD and crosses the Fens to become a tributary of the River Welland six miles (ten km) to the northeast of SPALDING.

Glengarriff, County Cork, Republic of Ireland

The river rises in the hills above the town of GLENGARRIFF and descends from one set of dark pools to another on its picturesque course through the thick oak woods along its path. To walk along the banks of this beautiful little river is a naturalist's dream come true. The Glengarriff passes under a bridge built by the famous English Lord Protector, Oliver Cromwell, and finally flows into the salt expanses of BANTRY BAY. This river is noted for its fine fishing.

Glyme, Oxfordshire, England

This beautiful and quiet little English river has some wonderful scenery along its banks. The fishing is good and on walks along the banks one can admire the swans sailing freely. The river rises east of CHIPPING NORTON and flows southeast to the village of WOOTON. Then it flows south through the manmade lake in the fantastic parks of BLENHEIM PALACE outside the village of WOODSTOCK. Blenheim was the birthplace of the great 20th century statesman, politician and leader, Sir Winston S Churchill. The palace was originally built for John Churchill, Duke of Marlborough by Vanbrugh by a grateful people in memory of his great victories during the 18th century. The Glyme continues and flows into the River Evenlode at the southern section of the park.

Glynde Reach, East Sussex, England

The river has its origins in the numerous streams which rise in the locale of RIPE, a small Sussex village. The Glynde Reach flows west down the South Downs through the village of GLYNDEBOURNE, home of the famous Glyndebourne summer opera season and meets the River Ouse southeast of LEWES.

Goch, Gwynedd, Wales

This river forms the upper portion of the River Rhaeadr Fawr. It flows north into Conway Bay, a few miles west of the village of LLANFAIRFECHAN. Conway is a well-known holiday resort area of Wales and is famous for its bridge and fortress castle.

Golo, Corsica

The Golo is 45 miles (72 km) long and as such is the longest river on the island of Corsica, the birthplace of Napoleon Bonaparte. It rises south of Monte Cinto and flows through the Corsican mountains into the Tyrrhenian Sea near the seaport of BASTIA.

Goryn, European USSR

This Ukrainian river is 404 miles (650 km) long. It begins northeast of the town of ZOLOCHEV, meanders east by northeast, shifts to north by northwest for a short while, and finally changes to a northerly direction and passes into Byelorussia. It passes STOLIN, the head of its navigation to join the Pripyat River as a tributary.

Goyt, Derbyshire, England

The River Goyt rises on the High Peak south of BROWN KNOLL in Derbyshire. It flows in a westerly direction to the village of NEW MILLS, then changes direction to a northwesterly course to join the River Tame north of the industrial town of STOCKPORT. The confluence of River Goyt and River Tame form the River Mersey.

Grannell, Dyfed, Wales

The river rises near the Welsh hamlet of DIHEWYD in Dyfed. The Grannell flows southward to become a tributary of the larger River Teifi west of the small market town of LAMPETER which is approximately 20 miles (32 km) northeast of CARMARTHEN.

Greater Cheremshan, European USSR

The river rises south of SHUGUROVO and has a length of 245 miles (394 km). It flows northwest past the town of CHEREMSHAN, then changing direction heads southwest past NIKOLSKOYE. Its largest tributary is the Lesser Cheremshan which is 65 miles (105 km) long. The Greater Cheremshan ends as a tributary of the much larger Volga River.

Greater Irgiz, European USSR

With a length of 335 miles (539 km), the Greater Irgiz rises southwest of the town of BUZULUK, in the Obshchi Syrt Mountains of the southeastern USSR. It joins the Volga river at VOLSK.

Greeba, Isle of Man

The river rises on the west side of the Greeba Mountains of Man. It flows south to join the larger River Dhoo at the village of CROSBY.

Greeta, Western Isles, Scotland

This river of Lewis begins in the lochs approximately six miles (ten km) northwest of STORNOWAY, the principal town of Lewis and its chief port, situated on the east coast 22 miles (35 km) south of the Butt of Lewis. It continues southeast to flow into Stornoway Harbor, a large natural anchorage on the south side of the town. The chief industries are tweed manufacturing and fishing.

Greta, Cumbria, England
This river rises in Stainmore Forest to the east of the town of BROUGH. It flows eastward past BOWES and BRIGNALL to GRETA BRIDGE. Then it continues north until it joins the River Tees toward the northside of ROKEBY PARK to the southeast of BARNARD CASTLE.

Greta, North Yorkshire, England
The Greta is formed by the confluence of the Rivers Doe and Kingsdale Beck at INGLETON. It flows west to join the River Lune north of the village of MELLING in the county of Lancashire.

Grwyne Fawr, Powys, Wales
The river begins high in the Black Mountains, a few miles north of WAUN FACH. The Grwyne Fawr flows south to its confluence with the Grwyne Fechan. It continues on a southerly course until it meets the River Usk, southeast of the village of CRICKHOWELL where there are the ruins of an ancient castle fortification.

Grwyne Fechan, Powys, Wales
Together with its sister river, the Grwyne Fawr, the Grwyne Fechan combines to make a healthy sized tributary of the River Usk. It also rises on Waun Fach in Powys at a height of 2660 feet (811 m).

Gryfe, Strathclyde, Scotland
The river rises in the hills south of GREENOCK. It flows north into the Gryfe Reservoir which is really a pair of reservoirs, three miles (five km) south of Greenock. Then it flows southeast through STRATH GRYFE to the BRIDGE OF WEIR and finally joins the Black Cart Water to the northwest of the town of PAISLEY.

Guadajoz, Spain
The Guadajoz is 125 miles (201 km) long. It flows from near ALCALA LA REAL in the province of Andalusia. The Guadajoz continues westward to join the Guadalquivir River south of the famous city of CORDOBA.

Guadalete, Spain
The Guadalete begins in the Cadiz province of Spain, one of the strongholds of the Moors in bygone days and home of such legends as El Cid. The river flows for 85 miles (137 km) southwest and eventually makes a wide curve into Cadiz Bay on the Atlantic Ocean. The chief tributary of the Guadalete is the Majaceite River.

Guadalhorce, Spain
The Guadalhorce begins in Granada province in southern Spain. It flows for 75 miles (121 km) passing through the Chorro Gorge and entering the Mediterranean Sea near the town of MALAGA.

Guadalope, Spain
The Guadalope River is 123 miles (198 km) long and flows from northeast of TERUEL in

eastern Spain to the Ebro River near the town of CASPE.

Guadalquivir, Spain
The Guadalquivir has its source in the Sierra Morena Mountains at a height of 4600 feet (1400 m), only 45 miles (72 km) from the Mediterranean Sea. It has a length of 420 miles (680 km) and flows first in a northwesterly direction to the town of BAEZA. The river here is actually a flowing torrent, raging down steep gorges and picking up tributaries along the way, the most important being the Guadalamar River. In its next 100 miles (160 km) the Guadalquivir falls over 800 feet (244 m) as it begins to achieve a quieter flow. The region

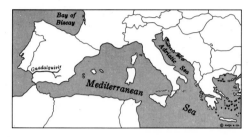

around the river is mainly agricultural, growing oranges, sugar cane, grapes and numerous vegetables. From CORDOBA to SEVILLE the river meanders its way across the most extensive lowland in the Iberian peninsula. Exactly midway between Cordoba and Seville the river receives its principal tributary, the Genil River. Upon reaching the port of Seville, which is only 54 miles (87 km) from the sea and 28 feet (nine m) above sea level, it is on the last leg of its long journey. Seville can be reached by large sea-going vessels through channels which are being constantly dredged to keep the waterway open to traffic. Just to the southwest of Seville the Guadalquivir breaks up into small distributaries and feeds the huge tidal marshes called by the Spanish, *Las Marismas*. This entire area was once a huge lake. The river now has reached its final destination, the Gulf of Cadiz, on the Atlantic Ocean.

Guadarrama, Spain
The tributary of the Tagus, the Guadarrama has a length of 90 miles (145 km) and flows from high in the Sierra de Guadarrama, northwest of the capital city of Spain, MADRID. The river continues northwest and then south to join the Tagus seven miles (11 km) west of TOLEDO.

Guadiana, Spain
The source of the Guadiana is the uplands of La Mancha in southeastern Spain. It has a length of 510 miles (820 km). The exact source of this river is difficult to discover because most of the headstreams which form it disappear for 75 percent of the year. The Záncara River is considered to be the real source and assumes the name, Guadiana, near the town of CIUDAD REAL. Here the river takes on a more permanent look as it always has water from this point onwards. The river passes through a very wide flood plain which during the winter months is usually com-

pletely underwater. The river is so wide near the town of MERIDA that it is spanned by a bridge made of 64 arches. Reaching the town of BADAJOZ the river turns to a southwesterly direction as it nears the Gulf of Cadiz. The Guadiana is navigable by sea-going vessels as far as POMARAO, where it is joined by the Chança River, 30 miles (48 km) upstream. The Guadiana enters the Gulf of Cadiz at Ayamonte.

Gudena, Denmark
The Gudena River is the longest river in Denmark with a length of 98 miles (158 km). It rises in the eastern portion of Jutland famous for its ancient Viking civilization. It flows north past the town of SILKEBORG and enters the Randers Fjord. RANDERS is a principal Danish port and the Gudena is navigable in its lower course.

Gwash, Leicestershire, England
This Midlands river, rising near the village of KNOSSINGTON, flows easterly through Empingham Reservoir and joins the River Welland as a tributary a mile to the east of STAMFORD, an ancient stone-built town on the banks of the Welland, 12 miles (19 km) northwest of PETERBOROUGH.

Gwendraeth Fâch, Dyfed, Wales
The river rises southeast of the village of LLANARTHNEY located six miles (ten km) west of the town of LLANDEILO. It heads southwest to KIDWELLY, a small town on its banks. The remains of Kidwelly Castle built in the 12th-14th centuries are visible from the river.

Gwendraeth Fawr, Dyfed, Wales
The river rises near GORSLAS, a village located northeast of CROSS HANDS. It flows southwest to join its sister river the Gwendraeth Fâch to form the estuary leading into CARMARTHEN BAY. The scenery in this part of South Wales is beautiful and the fishing is excellent.

Gwenfro, Clwyd, Wales
This northern Welsh river flows from near BWLCH-GWYN, a village five miles (eight km) northwest of WREXHAM. The river continues eastward to flow through Wrexham, a town noted for its chemical industries and being the center of the local coal mining region. It enters the River Clywedog southeast of Wrexham.

Gwili, Dyfed, Wales (1)
Rising east of the village of LLANPUMSAINT, Dyfed, the Gwili flows westward to become a tributary of the larger Tywi just east of the town of CARMARTHEN, a town noted for its spring fairs and hospitality. The fishing is outstanding in this region of Wales.

Gwili, Dyfed, Wales (2)
The river rises near CROSS HANDS, in Dyfed. Its course is practically straight south into the River Loughor just to the west of PONTARDULAIS, a small town in West Glamorgan.

Gwydderig, Powys, Wales
The river rises as the Nant Gwared River, north of the town of TRECASTLE in Powys. It flows south to join the River Llywel then changes to a northwesterly course and becomes a tributary of the River Tywi at the town of LLANDOVERY.

Roman bridge over the Guadalquivir, Cordoba, Spain.

Gwyrfai, Gwynedd, Wales
The river rises on the western slopes of MT SNOWDON, the highest peak in Wales. It flows in a northwesterly direction through the Llyn Cwellyn, a small lake and past WAUNFAWR. It then heads westward and passes by BONT-NEWYDD before it enters Foryd Bay.

Gwys, Powys, Wales
The source of the Gwys is two small mountain streams, the Gwys Fawr and Gwys Fàch, both of which rise in the southern foothills of the Black Mountains of ancient Powys. Both streams join to form the Gwys north of YSTALYFERA, a small village. The Gwys then flows southwest to become a tributary of the River Twrch at CWMTWRCH-UCHAF.

Hase, Germany

The Hase River rises in the TEUTOBURG FOREST of northwestern Germany. It flows north, then gradually shifts westward passing OSNABRUCK and QUACKENBRUCK, the latter being the head of navigation for the Hase. It runs into the Dortmund-Ems Canal at the city of MEPPEN. The Hase has a length of 80 miles (129 km).

Haddeo, Somerset, England

The river rises three miles (five km) west of the Clatworthy Reservoir. It flows in a south-westerly direction and joins the larger River Exe just north of EXBRIDGE.

Haine, Belgium

This river is 40 miles (64 km) long. It rises near the town of ANDERLUES in the southwestern portion of Belgium. It flows first northward but swings to a westerly course, flowing through the Hainault coal mining region. It becomes a tributary of the Scheldt River at the French town of CONDE-SUR-L'ESCAUT.

Halse Water, Somerset, England

The river rises on the eastern slopes of the Brendon Hills near the village of BROMPTON RALPH. It runs in a southeasterly direction to join the River Tone at BISHOP'S HULL very close to the famous cider-making town of TAUNTON.

Hamble, Hampshire, England

The river rises near BISHOP'S WALTHAM, a small town noted for the remains of a 13th century bishop's palace. The Hamble flows into the Southampton Water between the towns of HAMBLE and WARSASH. The river is well known for its yachting.

Hamps, Staffordshire, England

The Hamps starts its run near the town of LEEK in Staffordshire. It flows southward to pass WINKHILL, a small hamlet, then changes to an eastward course past the village of WATERHOUSES. The Hamps then flows north to its eventual confluence with the River Manifold just east of the town of GRINDON.

Hansag, Hungary

Although not a river, this bog land of northwestern Hungary is mentioned because of the rivers which cross its path. The entire area is swamp and encompasses an area of 218 square miles (565 sq km). The Hansag is fed by the Ikva and Répce Rivers, and is partially drained by the Ferto Canal. Peat is a byproduct of the bogs and is cut for fuel.

Harbourne, Devon, England

This river rises on Dartmoor a few miles west of the market and manufacturing town of BUCKFASTLEIGH. The Harbourne flows southeast to STOKE POINT where it joins the River Dart. The country walks in this region are spectacular.

Harley Brook, Salop, England

This river begins as the Hughley Brook northwest of the hamlet of PLAISH. It flows first southeast, then shifts to a northeasterly course before it enters the village of HUGHLEY. It enters the River Severn one mile (1610 m) south of LEIGHTON.

Hart Burn, Northumbria, England

A river of one of the ancient Anglo-Saxon kingdoms of Britain, the Hart Burn rises in the endless moors to the north of KIRKWHELP-INGTON, a small village nine miles (14 km) southeast of OTTERBURN. The river flows in an easterly direction to join the River Wansbeck west of the town of MORPETH.

Havel, Eastern Germany

The source of the Havel is in the lake region of Mecklenburg in the marshy lowlands of northern Germany. This area is also the source for two other major rivers, the Oder and the Vistula. The Havel flows in a southerly direction passing ZEHDENICK, then ORANIEN-BURG, where the river becomes a part of the Berlin-Stettin Canal. This canal was once a major waterway. Completed in 1914 it is capable of handling ships up to 600 tons. Upon reaching the western perimeter of SPANDAU, the Allied prison in which such Nazi war criminals as Rudolph Hess were incarcerated, the Havel achieves its independence once again. Here it widens to become the scenic Havel Lakes. In the center of this beautiful area is the former home of the Prussian kings and German emperors, POTSDAM. The Havel continues on its course westward to pass BRANDENBURG. The river is 215 miles (346 km) long and is navigable for 205 miles (330 km) of its course. It finally becomes a tributary of the larger Elbe six miles (ten km) from the town of HAVELBERG.

Hayle, Cornwall, England

This river rises south of the Cornish industrial town of CAMBORNE which was once the center of the Cornish tin-mining industry. The river flows past the town of HAYLE, a fishing community and resort three miles (five km) southeast of St Ives Bay across the Hayle estuary. This part of Cornwall is a prime tourist area from April to October.

Hebble Brook, West Yorkshire, England

This northern river rises in the Oxenhope Moor of West Yorkshire. It flows in a southerly direction and joins the River Calder at the large industrial town of HALIFAX, known for its textiles and engineering works.

Helford, Cornwall, England

The river begins near the town of HELSTON where a large fair is held every summer. The Helford flows eastward into the English Channel between Mawnan and Dennis Points. This area of Cornwall is famous as a tourist center and fishing paradise.

Helge, Sweden

This river rises to the northeast of the town of LJUNGBY in southern Sweden. The length of the Helge is 200 miles (320 km). It flows in a southerly direction to pass through Lake Mockel and then proceeds to Hano Bay, an arm of the Baltic Sea, its final destination.

Helme, Germany

The Helme rises in the foothills of the southern portion of the Hartz Mountains of central Germany. It has a length of 55 miles (88 km). It flows southeast to become a tributary of Unstrut River near the town of ARTERN.

Henares, Spain

The river rises in the Guadalajara province of central Spain. It is 91 miles (146 km) long. The Henares flows in a southwesterly direction to join the Jarama River, itself a tributary of the much larger Tagus, approximately nine miles (14 km) east of the Spanish capital of MADRID.

Hérault, France

The river begins in the Cévenne Mountains of southern France. It has a length of 100 miles (160 km). It flows south to the Gulf of Lion just below the town of AGDE.

Hernad, Czechoslovakia

A medium-sized river of Czechoslovakia, the Hernad is 165 miles (265 km) long. It rises in the Low Tatra Mountains and flows in an easterly direction initially, then changes to a southerly course crossing the Hungarian frontier to join the Sajó River as a tributary southeast of the town of MISKOLC. Together the rivers join the Tisza River ten miles (16 km) further on.

Hilton Beck, Cumbria, England

Hilton Beck starts on Murton Fell in Cumbria and runs southwest to the village of HILTON. Then it flows on to join the River Eden a few miles southeast of the small town of APPLEBY which has the remains of a 12th century Norman castle.

Hindburn, Lancashire, England

The Hindburn rises on the northern slopes of the Forest of Bowland. It flows on a northwesterly course, eventually joining the River Wenning to the east of HORNBY.

Hinnisdal, Highlands, Scotland

The Hinnisdal only runs for a short distance. It flows west into Loch Snizort, a large bay on the northern coast of Skye, at the entrance of Loch Snizort Beag, a long and narrow inlet of the bay at its southeastern corner.

Hirwaun, Dyfed, Wales

This river rises to the southeast of the town of ABERPORTH. It flows on a southerly course joining the River Teifi a few miles west of the market town of NEWCASTLE EMLYN.

Hiz, Hertfordshire, England

The river rises to the southwest of HITCHIN, a small town northeast of LUTON. The River Hiz flows through the town and proceeds northward to meet the River Ivel at HENLOW, also a Royal Air Force Station which hosts an annual air show, a short distance from the town of BIGGLESWADE in Bedfordshire. Biggleswade is renowned for being the home of Old Warden, an antique aircraft museum which is a prime tourist attraction.

Hodder, Lancashire, England

The river rises in the Forest of Bowland and runs south through the Stocks Reservoir. It passes the village of SLAIDBURN and joins the River Ribble just southwest of the town of CLITHEROE.

Hodge Beck, North Yorkshire, England

This Yorkshire river begins in the Cleveland Hills. It heads south down Bransdale and becomes a tributary of the River Dove to the south of KIRKBYMOORSIDE. The Hodge Beck flows through some of North Yorkshire's most scenic countryside.

Hoff Beck, Cumbria, England

The river begins approximately one mile (1610 m) to the south of GREAT ASHBY, a village in Cumbria. It takes a northward course to pass through the village of Hoff on its way to join the River Eden north of COLBY.

Hogsmill, Surrey, England

The river rises near the town of EWELL. This town, only five miles (eight km) southeast of KINGSTON, is the site of Nonsuch Palace, a huge mansion built by Henry VIII. The Hogsmill continues on to join the River Thames at Kingston.

Holme, West Yorkshire, England

The river rises southwest of HOLMFIRTH, a town noted for its textiles and engineering works. It carries on northward to enter the River Colne at HUDDERSFIELD.

Honddu, Powys, Wales (1)

This river begins at Mynydd Eppynt, a wild moorland area to the southwest of the town of BUILTH WELLS which is also utilized as an artillery range. The Honddu flows south to enter the River Usk at the town of BRECON.

Honddu, Powys, Wales (2)

The second Welsh river to be called by that name rises in the Black Mountains on the southern slope of Hay Bluff at a height of 2199 feet (666 m). It flows generally in a southerly direction for the first leg of its journey, passing LLANTHONY on the way to join the River Monnow just north of PANDY in Gwent.

Hope, Sutherland, Scotland

The Hope rises in the Sutherland district of the Highlands. It flows north to enter Loch Eriboll, approximately nine miles (14 km) long and two miles (three km) wide. Its final destination is the Atlantic Ocean. It is a good fishing river for the interested angler.

Hortobagy, Hungary

This medium-sized river rises 15 miles (24 km) northwest of MAJDUBOSZORMENY. It runs for 70 miles (112 km) in a southerly direction, varying at times to a more southeasterly course. The Hortobagy drains the district of the same name before linking up with the Berettyó Canal to form the Berettyó River.

Housay, Western Isles, Scotland

This river on the Isle of Harris (famous for its tweed) begins as the River Ulladale in the Forest of Harris. It heads in a northeasterly direction to flow to the head of Loch Resort.

Hron, Czechoslovakia

The Hron begins on the southeastern slopes of the Kralova Hola Mountain Range. It has a length of 170 miles (270 km). It flows first westward, then shifts to a southerly course before running into the Danube River near the Hungarian town of ESZTERGOM.

Hudeshope Beck, Durham, England

This river of northeastern England starts on Middleton Common. It runs in a southerly direction to become a tributary of the River Tees at MIDDLETON IN TEESDALE.

Huerva, Spain

The river rises in Teruel province of northeastern Spain. The Huerva flows 90 miles (145 km) north to the Ebro River, passing through some of the finest olive orchards in the Iberian peninsula. It actually meets the Ebro at ZARAGOZA, one of Spain's most famous ancient cities. Zaragoza was the capital city of the kingdom of Aragon.

Huisne, France

This tributary of the Sarthe River rises southwest of MORTAGNE in the Orne Department of France. It has a length of 80 miles (129 km) and flows southwest to join the Sarthe at LE MANS, noted for its famous race track.

Hull, Humberside, England

The river rises at ELMSWELL in Humberside. The Hull flows east to WANSFORD, then south to BEVERLEY and finally enters the River Humber at the town of HULL.

Humber, Humberside, England

This estuarial river is 40 miles (64 km) long and between one to eight miles (two–13 km) wide. It is navigable and the principal ports are GRIMSBY and HULL. It is formed by the junction of the Rivers Trent and Ouse which flow into the North Sea between Northcoates Point in Lincolnshire and Spurn Head in Humberside. It is one of the major ports of the eastern coast of England.

Hunte, Germany

The Hunte is 120 miles (190 km) long and begins in the Wiehen Mountain Range of northwestern Germany approximately four miles (six km) from the town of MELLE. It flows through the old town of OLDENBURG to the Weser River at ELSFLETH. It forms a part of the Ems-Hunte Canal on its lower course, which serves to connect the larger Ems and Weser Rivers.

Huntspill, Somerset, England

One of England's West Country rivers, the Huntspill flows through the Glastonbury area, famous for the ruins of its abbey church and the burial site of King Arthur and Queen Guinevere. It flows into the estuary of the River Parrett just west of the village of HUNTSPILL.

Hvita, Iceland

The river is 80 miles (129 km) long. It rises in Hvitarvatin Lake in southwestern Iceland. The Hvita flows southwest to join the Sog River and their confluence forms the Olfusa River. The river is very beautiful to walk along during the short summer months.

Ialomita, Rumania

This eastern European river rises in the Bucegi Mountains of central Rumania. It has a length of 200 miles (320 km). The Ialomita's principal tributary is the Prahova River. The river flows first south and then east before it becomes a tributary of the much larger Danube near the picturesque agricultural market village of HIRSOVA about 90 miles (145 km) from Bucharest.

Ibar, Yugoslavia

The river begins in the Mokra Planina, southeast of the town of BERANE. It flows for a total of 152 miles (245 km) before entering the Western Morava River below the town of RANKOVICEVO. The principal tributary of the Ibar is the Sitnica River.

Idle, Nottinghamshire, England

The Idle is formed by the confluence of the Maun and Polter Rivers approximately four miles south of EAST RETFORD, a town noted for its engineering and dyeing plants. The river flows in a northward direction through East Retford to BAWTRY, then changes course to the east and joins the River Trent at WEST STOCKWITH.

Idoch Water, Grampian, Scotland

The Idoch Water has its source in the Grampian region of Scotland. It flows southwest through CUMINESTOWN, then changes to a northwesterly course near the town of TURRIFF. It becomes a tributary of the River Deveron at Turriff which is the center of the agricultural region in this part of Scotland.

Ii, Finland

The Ii rises in the lake region of central Finland. It is 150 miles (240 km) long and runs in a southwesterly course to enter the Gulf of Bothnia at the town of II.

Ik, European USSR

The Ik has a length of 326 miles (525 km). It rises in the southern Ural Mountain Range near the town of BELEBEJ. The Ik flows in practically every direction but east. Its outlet is the Kama River and its principal tributaries are the Menzelaya and Usen Rivers.

Ill, France

The source of the Ill is high in the Jura Mountain Range of eastern France. It flows northeast past the towns of MULHOUSE and STRASBOURG. It is 127 miles (204 km) long. Its principal tributaries are the Fecht, Thur and Bruche Rivers which all flow down from the Vosges Mountains. The Ill becomes a tributary of the Rhine below Strasbourg.

Iller, Germany

The Iller is 91 miles (146 km) long. Its source is the Allgäu Alps near the Austrian border. The river flows north to join the Danube at the town of NEUULM a satellite of the industrial city of Ulm, southeast of Stuttgart.

Above: Ferry on the Humber River, Yorkshire.

Ilm, Germany

The Ilm has its source in the Thuringian Forest of central Germany just southwest of ILMENAU. It has a length of 75 miles (121 km). The Ilm flows northeast to where it joins the Thuringian Saale River to the west of NAUMBERG.

Ina, Poland

The Ina is a medium-sized river with a length of 70 miles (113 km), and flows first south, then westward until it finally enters the Damm Lake near the town of POLICE.

Indal, Sweden

The river is 220 miles (350 km) long. The Indal rises in the mountains south of STORLIEN in central Sweden. It takes a winding course as it flows through Stor Lake to enter the Gulf of Bothnia approximately ten miles (16 km) northeast of the town of SUNDSVALL, noted for its timber industry.

Ingrebourne, Essex, England

The river begins near BRENTWOOD, a town southwest of CHELMSFORD in Essex. It flows south to become a tributary of the River Thames just southwest of RAINHAM in the borough of Havering in London.

Inn, Switzerland-Austria-Germany

The source of the Inn is GRAUBUNDEN in Switzerland. The headwaters form just below Maloja Pass as it comes forth from Lake Lunghino. On the first portion of its run, the river is made to appear insignificant by the huge and towering shapes of the glacier-covered Rhaetian Alps to the north and the ever-impressive Bernina Alps to the south. The famous Swiss Alpine resort of ST MORITZ lies here in this spectacular scenic region. As the Inn approaches the Austrian frontier, it becomes a fast moving torrent running through the Finstermunz Pass. It forms the border between Austria and Switzerland for a few miles before turning towards Innsbruck. The valley is called the *Oberinntal* in German or the Upper Inn Valley. The Inn continues to twist and turn as it heads first southwest and then northeast. As it proceeds toward the junction of the Kauner valley, the river shifts to a northerly direction, then practically due west before entering another narrow and precipitous gorge. (It was at this point that Tyrolean peasants successfully ambushed enemy troop movements attempting to force their way through the pass in 1703 and 1809.) The valley now widens as the river once again changes direction, this time to an easterly course. The Inn flows through the center of INNSBRUCK, the skiing capital of Austria. The beautiful city of Innsbruck attracts its share of honeymooning couples and offers a superb selection of hotels. Upon leaving Innsbruck, the river valley is known as the Unterinntal or the Valley of the Lower Inn. The Inn passes the old mining town of SCHWAZ noted for its rich copper and gold mines during the 15th century, then proceeds on to WORGL flowing northward. The river forms a section of the border between Austria and Germany before it actually enters German territory. The Inn now flows eastward and forms the boundary between Bavaria and Austria. There are three huge hydroelectric dams on the river's course which provide the region with a large proportion of its power. This was accomplished as a joint Austro-German undertaking and has proved to be valuable for all concerned. The Inn becomes a tributary of the Danube below the once large river port of PASSAU. It is 320 miles (510 km) long.

Iorsa Water, Strathclyde, Scotland

The source of Iorsa Water is to the west of CASTEAL ABHAIL on the Isle of Arran. It flows southwest down the Glen Iorsa into Kilbrannan Sound at the northern end of Machrie Bay.

Right: The Humber's waterfront at Hull.

Ipel, Czechoslovakia

The source of the Ipel is found in the Ore Mountain Range of southwestern Slovakia. The Ipel has a length of 152 miles (245 km). It flows first in a southerly direction but shifts to a southwesterly course, east of the town of ESZTERGOM before it becomes one of the many tributary rivers of the Danube.

Iput, European USSR

The Iput rises east of KLIMOVICHI in the Smolensk-Moscow Upland. It is 295 miles (475 km) long. The river heads west by southwest passing through the towns of SURAZH and DOBRUSH before entering the Sozh River at GOMEL.

Irfon, Powys, Wales

The river rises a few miles southwest of the Claerwen Reservoir. The Irfon flows southward to LLANWRTYD WELLS, a small spa which has an excellent tweed factory. The river then flows east by LLANGAMMARCH WELLS, whose springs contain barium chloride, unique in the British Isles. Leaving Llangammarch Wells the river passes CARTH on its way to join the River Wye as a tributary on the northwest side of BUILTH WELLS.

Irk, Greater Manchester, England

The streams which form the Irk join at MIDDLETON in Greater Manchester. The Irk then carries on to join the River Irwell at the port city of MANCHESTER.

Irthing, Cumbria, England

The source of the Irthing is the confluence of the Gair Burn and Tarn Beck on the borders of Cumbria and Northumberland on the western side of Wark Forest. The Irthing flows southwest to join the River Eden five miles (eight km) east of the town of CARLISLE.

Irwell, Lancashire, England

The Irwell is 40 miles (64 km) long. Its principal tributary is the Roch River. Its source lies north of BACUP in Lancashire. It flows south through RAMSBOTTOM and then BURY, and passes MANCHESTER and SALFORD before swinging to a westerly course to join the River Mersey at IRLAM.

Isar, Austria-Germany

The Isar is a Bavarian river which rises in the Karwendelgebirge of northern Austria at a height of 5840 feet (1780 m). It flows through some of the most spectacular scenery in Bavaria which the Isar enters at the Scharnitz Pass. The fresh trout of the Isar were noted as a delicacy in Roman times and they still are today. It flows eastward initially, then shifts direction northward as it reaches BAD TOLZ, a German summer resort and winter sports recreation area. The Isar now enters the large Bavarian plain as it heads for the center of the largest city in Bavaria, MUNICH. The river is extremely fast at this stage of its flow and contains several hydroelectric power stations. The river is not really navigable except for shallow-bottomed boats and canoes. The Isar becomes a tributary of the Danube on the western fringe of the beautiful Bavarian Forest. It is 163 miles (262 km) long.

Isbourne, Gloucestershire, England

The river rises near the town of WINCHCOMBE in the Cotswold Hills, a popular and scenic holiday center. The river flows north until it joins the River Avon at EVESHAM, the center of a large fruit and vegetable growing area.

Ise, Northamptonshire, England

The Ise River of the English Midlands rises north of NASEBY, a small village which marks the site of the last major battle in the English Civil War. It flows east past the town of KETTERING and enters the River Nene on the southeast side of the town of WELLINGBOROUGH known for its shoe factories and clothing manufacturers.

Isère, France

The source of the Isère is found high in the Graian Alps above Val d'Isère in southeastern France. It is 180 miles (290 km) long. The river flows westward through the Savoy Alps then shifts to a southwesterly course and finally to a northwesterly direction at the foot of Grande Chartreuse. Passing on to the town of VALENCE, it joins the Rhône as a tributary. The Isère provides a substantial amount of the local hydroelectric power.

Iskâr, Bulgaria

The Iskâr rises at the confluence of three small headstreams which flow down from the Rila Mountain Range of northwestern Bulgaria. It has a length of 250 miles (400 km). The major tributaries of the Iskâr are the Malki Iskâr and the Panrga Rivers. The river flows northward through the large Sofia Basin and the Balkan Mountains, before it turns northeast to become a tributary of the Danube at the town of BORIL.

Isla, Grampian Region, Scotland (1)

This Scottish river of the Grampian Region rises three miles (five km) northeast of the town of DUFFTOWN. The Isla flows northeast to the town of KEITH then proceeds east to join the River Deveron approximately five miles (eight km) north of HUNTLY. The Isla is another excellent Scottish fishing river.

Isla, Grampian Region, Scotland (2)

This Isla begins on the border of the Grampian and Tayside Regions south of BRAEMAR. It heads south down the Glen Isla to AIRLIE CASTLE where the Ogilvy residence was located before being sacked by the notorious Campbell family in 1640. The river carries on to enter the River Tay west of COUPAR ANGUS. It has a length of 46 miles (74 km).

Isle, France

This French river is 145 miles (233 km) long. It rises in the Monts du Limousin in southwestern France. The river flows past the towns of PERIGUEUX and GUITRES on its southwesterly course before becoming a tributary of the Dordogne River at LIBOURNE. The principal tributaries of the Isle are the Dronne and Auvézère Rivers.

Isonzo, Yugoslavia

A series of battles were fought along this Yugoslavian river between 1915–1917 by the Austro-Italian armies. The river rises in the Triaglav Mountains of northwestern Yugoslavia and heads in a southerly direction to enter the Gulf of TRIESTE, a port on the Adriatic Sea. The river is 84 miles (135 km) long.

Itchen, Hampshire, England

The Itchen is 25 miles (40 km) long. It flows from west of HINTON AMPNER northward to NEW ALRESFORD. The river then proceeds west to KING'S WORTHY, a small country village, before heading south to pass through the cathedral city of WINCHESTER. The city of Winchester has the honor to have once been the capital of England as it was the main city of the West Saxons and Wessex. The cathedral is well worth traveling to see and the streets of the town are busy but still retain their old-world look. The Itchen is very famous as a trout stream. The river enters Southampton Water at SOUTHAMPTON, England's major south-coast port.

Ithon, Powys, Wales

This Welsh river rises south of NEWTOWN in Powys. It flows southward to LLANDRINDOD WELLS, a very popular Welsh resort town. The Ithon then joins the River Wye as a tributary just to the south of NEWBRIDGE ON WYE.

Iwrch, Clwyd, Wales

The Iwrch rises at a height of 2712 feet (827 m) on Cadair Dorwyn, a mountain in Clwyd. It heads southeast to join the River Tanant southeast of LLANRHAEADR-YM-MOCHNANT. The walks along the banks of this river are a naturalist's delight.

Jabalón, Spain

The Jabalón rises to the southeast of the town of MONTIEL in central Spain. It is 100 miles (160 km) long. The river heads first on a westerly course, then shifts slightly to the northwest before joining the Guadiana River near the town of CIUDAD REAL.

Jagst, Germany

This winding river is 101 miles (163 km) long. The source of the Jagst is found east of ELLWANGEN in southern Germany. The river flows north and then west in its attempt to reach the Neckar River at BAD FRIEDRICHSHALL.

Jalón, Spain

The Jalón is 145 miles (233 km) long and traverses a region noted for its lush vineyards and olive groves. The river has its source south of MEDINACELI in central Spain and flows northeast to become a tributary of the Ebro at Alagon.

Jarama, Spain

The Jarama rises in the Somosierra Mountain range of central Spain. It is just over 100 miles (160 km) long. During the Spanish Civil War, the Jarama River region bore mute witness to one of the most savage battles of the conflict in 1937 with heavy casualties. The major tributaries of the Jarama are the Lozoya, Manzanares, Henares and Tajuna Rivers. It becomes a tributary of the much larger Tagus River near ARANJUEZ.

Jiu, Rumania

The Jiu rises to the south of PETROSANI at the confluence of two headstreams and then cuts a gorge through the Transylvanian Alps (of Count Dracula fame) of southwestern Rumania. The upper valley of the Jiu is the major coal mining district of the country. The river is 135 miles (217 km) long. It flows southward for the majority of its journey until it eventually becomes a tributary of the Danube, 28 miles (45 km) to the west of the town of CORABIA.

Júcar, Spain

The Jucar comes to life at a height of 6000 feet (1800 m) on the slopes of the Sierra de Albarracin in the Montes Universales range of southeastern Spain. The source of the Júcar is only slightly less than 20 miles (32 km) from the beginning of the Tagus. Some of the most majestic scenery in all of Spain lies along the path of the rugged Júcar. It flows through deep gorges, numerous rapids and a large number of small waterfalls as it winds its way in a great curve, first south, then east. The main tributary is the Cabriel. During the winter months the river is susceptible to flooding, but in the summer the water supply rapidly dwindles. On its last leg the Júcar flows through one of Spain's agricultural belts noted for vegetables and fruit. The river enters the Gulf of Valencia on the Mediterranean Sea near the town of CULLERA thus ending its run. It is 310 miles (500 km) long.

Kale Water, Borders, Scotland

The Kale Water rises in the famous Cheviot Hills. It flows in a northerly direction past the villages of HOWNAM and MOREBATTLE. The river turns to the west and heads for the junction with the River Teviot approximately four miles (six km) south of the market town of KELSO. Kelso is located at the confluence of the rivers Teviot and Tweed, northeast of HAWICK and southwest of BERWICK-UPON-TWEED. It is the center of a large agricultural region with large corn and livestock markets. A principal tourist attraction is the ruins of the 12th century abbey located at Kelso.

Kala, Finland

The Kala has its source east of KOKKOLA in the western portion of Finland. The river is 80 miles (129 km) long. It flows northwesterly to enter the Gulf of Bothnia at KALAJOKI.

Sluices of the Kama hydroelectric station. The Kama is Europe's fourth largest river.

Kalix, Sweden

The river rises west by northwest of the town of KIRUNA in Lapland. The Kalix is 270 miles (430 km) long which makes it one of the principal rivers of Scandinavia. It flows southeast initially, then shifts to a more southerly course as it enters the Gulf of Bothnia at KALIX.

Kama, European USSR

The Kama is relatively unknown outside the European continent, although it is the fourth largest river in Europe and one of the most important in the Soviet Union. The Kama begins in the central Ural Mountains and flows north initially: during the remainder of its travels the river flows east, south and finally southwest. This entire region is one of the Soviet Union's most industrialized. The Kama is one of Europe's most scenic rivers and it attracts tourists throughout the spring and summer months. The river is only navigable for six months of the year. It is 1262 miles (2031 km) long and empties into the Volga River near KAZAN.

Kamienna, Poland

The Kamienna rises southwest of the Polish town of SZYDLOWIEC in central Poland. It has a length of 81 miles (130 km). The river flows easterly to join the Vistula near PULAWY.

Kara, European USSR

The river begins in the northern Ural Mountain Range of European Russia. The Kara is 130 miles (210 km) long and its primary tributary is the Silova River. The river flows north to enter Baydaratskaya Bay of the Arctic Ocean. It forms part of the boundary between European USSR and Asiatic USSR.

Kelvin, Strathclyde, Scotland

The Kelvin rises approximately three miles (five km) to the east of the town of KILSYTH. It flows west then southwest through the northwest section of GLASGOW. The river joins the River Clyde just a few miles west of the city center.

Kemi, Finland

The Kemi rises high in the Lapland fells. Three small streams come together to form the Kemi – the Kitinen, Kemihaara and Luiro. The river is 300 miles (480 km) long and is the second largest in Finland but is only navigable for small vessels. It is a primary source for hydroelectric power and provides a large proportion of the country's power. Its principal tributary is the Ounas River which rises in the Enontekiö Fells. During the summer months the Kemi is utilized as Finland's major floating route for softwood. It empties into the Gulf of Bothnia.

Kemp, Salop, England
The Kemp rises near the small town of BISHOP'S CASTLE on the Welsh border. The town has a small brewery and the remains of a medieval castle. The river flows southeast to join the River Clun four miles (six km) west of the railway junction town of CRAVEN ARMS.

Kenfig, Glamorgan, Wales
The river rises north of Cefn Cribwr, a small hamlet northwest of BRIDGEND. The Kenfig flows west into Swansea Bay to the south of Margam, a district of PORT TALBOT, noted for its huge steelworks. Although a small river it serves as the boundary between Mid Glamorgan and West Glamorgan.

Kennet, Wiltshire, England
The Kennet rises on the Marlborough Downs near UFFCOTT in eastern Wiltshire. The river is 44 miles (71 km) long. The Kennet flows south, in places underground, to the town of AVEBURY, famous for its neolithic stone circles. The river then flows through MARLBOROUGH, HUNGERFORD and NEWBURY, a town famous for its stud farms and horse racing. The Kennet continues its eastward journey to enter the River Thames at READING, a short distance from the Queen's residence of Windsor Castle.

Kensey, Cornwall, England
The Kensey is a West Country river which rises near the Cornish town of TRENEGLOS. It heads east flowing through the northern section of the Cornish border town of LAUNCESTON. Overlooking the town is the remains of a medieval castle, built soon after the Norman Conquest. Here the Kensey enters the River Tamar as a tributary.

Kent, Cumbria, England
This beautiful river of northeastern England rises high in the Lake District, a picturesque and popular tourist area. The Kent flows south through the Kentmere Reservoir, then proceeds to the lakeland town of KENDAL and finally heads to MORECAMBE BAY where it enters the sea off HUMPHREY POINT.

Kent Water, East Sussex, England
The river rises to the east of EAST GRINSTEAD, a town in East Sussex. The Kent Water is, for a time, the boundary between Kent and East Sussex. It flows eastward and joins the River Medway as a tributary north of the village of ASHURST.

Kershope Burn, Cumbria, England
Kershope Burn rises on the border between England and Scotland just east of NEW-CASTLETON. The river heads southwest to flow into the Liddel Water at the village of KERSHOPEFOOT in Cumbria.

Khoper, European USSR
The Khoper rises southwest of the town of PENZA. It has a length of 626 miles (1007 km). It flows first southwest, then proceeds south to join the Don River to the west of SERAFI-MOVICH. The main tributaries of the Khoper are the Buzuluk and Vorona Rivers.

Kingie, Highlands, Scotland
The Kingie flows down Glen Kingie in the Lochaber district of the Highlands. It joins the River Garry a few miles southeast of the Loch Quioch dam.

Kinglas, Strathclyde, Scotland
The Kinglas rises on the southern side of Glas Bheinn Mhor in Argyll. It proceeds southward, then westward down Glen Kinglas to enter Loch Etieve on the south side of Ardmaddy Bay. It is an excellent river for fishing.

Kingsdale Beck, North Yorkshire, England
The Kingsdale Beck rises to the west of WHERNSIDE. It flows south to join with the River Doe at INGLETON to form the River Greta. The Beck is noted for its scenic waterfalls at PECKA FALLS and THORNTON FORCE.

Kinnel Water, Dumfries and Galloway, Scotland
An excellent fishing river, the Kinnel Water rises to the north of QUEENSBERRY. It flows southeast to join the River Annan northeast of the town of LOCHMABEN. This region, once known as the Lordship of Annandale, was the home of Robert the Bruce, prior to his assuming the Earldom of Carrick.

Klar, Norway-Sweden
This river begins as the Trysil River which emerges from the Femund Lake in eastern Norway. It is 201 miles (323 km) long. The Klar flows south into Sweden where it enters its outlet Lake Väner at the Swedish town of KARLSTAD.

Klyazma, European USSR
The Klyazma rises to the east of SOLNECHNO-GORSK in central European USSR. The upper course of the river is connected with the Moscow Canal. It has a length of 390 miles (628 km). It flows east to join the Oka River to the southwest of the manufacturing city of VOLODARY.

Kokemäen, Finland
The Kokemäen begins as the outlet for Nasijärvi Lake and its associated water systems. The river is continuously being developed as a further source for the much needed hydroelectric power required for the region. The Kokemäen is the major river of western Finland. It empties into the Gulf of Bothnia through a wide estuary. It is 90 miles (145 km) long.

Kolbäck, Sweden
This Swedish river is 100 miles (160 km) long. It flows southeast to LAKE MALAR. The Kolbäck forms the Strosholm Canal, a major waterway below the town of SMEDJEBACKEN.

Koros, Hungary
The Koros is formed by the confluence of the White and Rapid Koros Rivers, approximately seven miles (11 km) east of the town of GYOMA in southeastern Hungary. The Koros is 50 miles (80 km) long. It flows west and then southwesterly to join the Tisza River east of the town of CSONGRAD.

Koros, Rapid, Hungary
The Rapid Koros rises to the southeast of HUEDIN, a village in Transylvania. It has a length of 120 miles (190 km).

Koros, White, Hungary
The White Koros rises high in the Metalici Mountain Range of Rumania. It flows west by northwest to where it joins with the Rapid Koros to form the Koros. The White Koros is 150 miles (240 km) and its principal tributary is the Black Koros which is 85 miles (137 km) long.

Kosely, Hungary
The river rises to the north of DEBRECCEN in eastern Hungary. The Kosely flows first south, then proceeds in a more westerly direction to join the Hortobagy River southwest of the town of NADUDVAR. It is 100 miles (160 km) long.

Kovda, European USSR
The Kovda rises in Lake Top and heads north passing through Lake Pya. The river then flows through Lake Kovd to enter the Kandalaksha Bay of the White Sea. The Kovda is 137 miles (220 km) long.

Kraszna, Rumania-Hungary
The Kraszna rises in the Apuseni Mountain Range of northwestern Rumania to the southwest of the town of ZALAU. It is 125 miles (201 km) long. The river flows north and then northwest passing into Hungary where it enters the Szames River below its confluence with the larger Tisza River.

Kymi, Finland
The Kymi drains an area in excess of 14,000 square miles (37,000 sq km). It is the fourth largest river system in all of Finland. The Kymi drains the entire Paijanne Lake system to the Gulf of Finland, a large track of land. The river is still utilized as a prime route for floating timber down river. It is also a primary source for hydroelectric power and is being rapidly developed to increase further its present potential. The largest exporting city of softwoods in Finland, KOTKA, is located at the Kymi's mouth. The river is 90 miles (145 km) long and empties into the Gulf of Finland at Kotka.

Kupa, Yugoslavia
The river begins northeast of FIUME (Rijeka), in Yugoslavia. It has a length of 185 miles (298 km). The principal tributaries of the Kupa are the Glina and Dobra Korana Rivers. The Kupa flows east to join the Sava River at the town of SISAK.

Kyle, North Yorkshire, England
The Kyle rises to the north of EASINGWOLD in North Yorkshire. It flows southwards to become a tributary of the River Ouse at NEWTON-ON-OUSE.

Kym, Northamptonshire-Cambridgeshire, England
This Midlands river begins as the River Til southeast of the village of RUSHDEN. It flows northeast to TILBROOK, a village in Cambridgeshire, then turns southeast to become the River Kym and flows through the village of KIMBOLTON, a village noted for its castle. It flows into the River Ouse on the north side of the town of ST NEOTS, about 18 miles (30 km) from Cambridge.

Laba, European USSR
The Laba is formed by the junction of the Great and Little Laba Rivers in the Caucasus range to the southeast of the town of MOSTOVSKOYE. The river is 219 miles (352 km) long. It becomes a tributary of the Kuban River at UST-LABINSKAYA midway between Krasnadar and Kropotkin.

Laborec, Czechoslovakia
The Laborec is 80 miles (129 km) long. It rises east of BARDEJOV near the Polish frontier in the Beskid Mountains of eastern Czechoslovakia. It flows southward to become a tributary of the Latorica River.

Lagan, Northern Ireland
The Lagan rises southwest of BALLYNAHINCH. It has a length of 45 miles (72 km). It flows by DROMORE, then turns north for a few miles before changing direction to the northeast passing LISBURN on its way to Belfast Lough. The river is connected by canal to LOUGH NEAGH.

Lagan, Sweden
The river rises south of the town of JONKOPING in southwestern Sweden. It is 170 miles (270 km) long. It flows in a southerly direction to the town of MARKARYD, then shifts westward to the Kattegat near LAHOLM. The Lagan is an excellent salmon river.

Lahn, Germany
The Lahn is 160 miles (260 km) long. Its major tributary is the Dill River, itself only 30 miles (48 km) long. The Lahn flows from Ederkopf south and then west past the town of MARBURG. It then flows through GIESSEN, the head of the river's navigation, LIMBURG and BAD EMS to finally join the Rhine at LAHNSTEIN.

Lambourn, Berkshire, England
One of the tributaries of the River Kennet, the Lambourn comes to life on the Berkshire Downs above the town of LAMBOURN. It flows in a southeasterly direction to NEWBURY where it meets the Kennet.

Lambro, Italy
The river rises between two arms of Lake Como, south of the town of BELLAGIO in northern Italy. The Lambro is 80 miles (129 km) long. It flows southeast to become a tributary of the much larger Po, northwest of PIACENZA.

Lamone, Italy
The Lamone rises in the ETRUSCAN APENNINES of central Italy. This area was once the heartland of the ancient Etruscan people who were well established in the Italian peninsula long before the coming of the Romans. The river flows northeast, then eastward to its destination the Adriatic Sea at MARINA DI RAVENNA. The Lamone is 60 miles (97 km) long.

Land Yeo, Avon, England
The river rises at BARROW GURNEY to the southwest of the cathedral city of BRISTOL. It flows west to enter the mouth of the River Severn to the southwest of CLEVEDON.

Lark, Suffolk, England
The Lark rises south of the old town of BURY ST EDMUNDS in Suffolk. Bury St Edmunds boasts of an abbey church, the shrine of a martyred English king and later a cathedral market town. The Lark is 26 miles (42 km) long and flows through one of the most historic regions of Britain. The Lark joins the River Ouse just south of LITTLEPORT in Cambridgeshire.

Latoritsa, European USSR-Czechoslovakia
The Latoritsa rises high in the Beshchady Mountain Range of the Ukraine. It has a length of 96 miles (154 km). The river flows south initially, then changes direction to the west as it passes into Czechoslovakia. The Latoritsa joins the Ondava River southeast of the town of KOSICE to form the Bodrog River.

Laver, North Yorkshire, England
This river in the north of England rises on Dallowgill Moor to the north of PATELEY BRIDGE. The Laver proceeds on an eastward course to join the River Skell on the western side of the cathedral town of RIPON. The Laver flows through some of the most scenic countryside of North Yorkshire.

Lay, France
The Lay is 80 miles (129 km) long. The river rises to the north of LA CHATAIGNERAIE and heads in a southwesterly direction. The major tributary of the Lay is the Yon River. The river enters the Bay of Biscay approximately ten miles (16 km) southwest of the town of LUCON.

Lea, Bedfordshire, England
The River Lea rises at the village of LEAGRAVE to the north of the town of LUTON. The principal tributary of the Lea is the River Stort. The Lea is 46 miles (74 km) long and flows in a southeasterly direction. The Lea supplies a large proportion of London's fresh water through a system of reservoirs below WALTHAM ABBEY. It passes HERTFORD and HATFIELD before entering the River Thames at BLACKWALL.

Leam, Northamptonshire, England
The Leam rises at HELLIDON and flows first in a northward direction. It then shifts to the west before joining the River Avon between the towns of LEAMINGTON and WARWICK, the latter noted for its famous castle.

Leba, Poland
The Leba River rises to the west of KARTUZY in northwestern Poland. The Leba is 80 miles (129 km) long. It passes through Lake Leba on the way to enter the Baltic Sea near the town of LEBA.

Lech, Austria-Germany
The Lech rises ten miles (16 km) east of the Austrian town of BLUDENZ. It has a length of 175 miles (282 km). The Lech's main tributary is the Wertach River. The Lech flows northeast to Germany, then moves north past the towns of FUSSEN, LANDSBERG and AUGSBURG. It enters the Danube close to the town of RAIN.

Ledwyche Brook, Salop, England
The Ledwyche Brook rises on the south side of the hill known as Brown Clee. It flows south to join the River Teme at the town of BURFORD.

Lee, Republic of Ireland
The river Lee is only 60 miles (97 km) long. It rises at a height of 1600 feet (488 km) on the Derrynasageart Mountains of southern Ireland. The river cascades down to the bottom of the valley, then flows through a boggy stretch before entering Gouganebarra Lake. In the center of the lake is a small island which was the oratory of the founder of the city of Cork, St Finbar, a 7th century monk. The next stop for the Lee is LOUGH ALLUA where it is joined by two tributary rivers, the Bunsheelin and Owengarriff. The Lee passes on eastward through the bog country to DROMCARRA, then turns north to a wide lake near CARRIGADROHID, which is formed by a dam built to harness the river's water for hydroelectric power. It is here at this reservoir that the Lee's main tributaries the Laney and Sullane join to add their water to the main river. The Lee flows on to its next major stop, the city of CORK. The river is tidal to just above Cork. The Lee eventually runs into its estuary and the Atlantic Ocean.

Leidle Water, Strathclyde, Scotland
This beautiful river rises on BEINN NA CROISE, on the Isle of Mull, an island of the Inner Hebrides with a 350 square mile (910 sq km) area. The Leidle Water heads south, then west

and finally northwest down Glen Leidle before entering Loch Scridain.

Leine, Germany
This river of northeast, Western Germany rises near the town of WORBIS. The Leine has a length of 120 miles (190 km). It heads on a northerly course past the towns of GOTTINGEN and HANNOVER to join the Aller River.

Leith, Cumbria, England
The Leith rises high near Shap Summit in Cumbria. SHAP is noted for the remains of

An aerial photograph of Waltham Abbey, a town on the Lea River in Bedfordshire.

its 13th-16th century abbey. The river flows north to MELKINTHORPE, then changes to a more eastward course and enters the River Lyvennet east of the village of CLIBURN.

Leith Water, Midlothian, Scotland
The Leith Water rises to the southeast of WEST CALDER. It has a length of 23 miles (37 km). It flows northeast past BALERNO, then by the capital city of Scotland, EDINBURGH, to enter the Firth of Forth at LEITH.

Leitha, Austria
The Leitha is formed by the confluence of the Pitten and Schwarza Rivers near the town of ERLACH in eastern Austria. It heads first on a northeasterly course, then changes to a more easterly course passing BRUCK to join the Danube. It is 112 miles (180 km) long.

Lek, Netherlands
The Lek is really an arm of the Rhine delta. This arm leaves the main river at WIJK and flows southwest to join the Noord River, which together form the New Maas River. The Lek is 40 miles (64 km) long.

Tranquility as the Lee River passes the town of Cork in the Republic of Ireland.

Lenne, Germany
The Lenne is 60 miles (97 km) long. It draws its first breath high in the Kahle Asten Mountains. The river heads northwest past the town of ALTENA to join the Ruhr at HAGEN.

Let, Sweden
The Let is a river of central Sweden and rises south of VANSBRO. It is 100 miles (160 km) long. It flows south through Lake Möckel to its final destination, Lake Skager.

Leven, Cumbria, England
The Leven rises in LAKE WINDERMERE in Cumbria in northwestern England. It flows southwest to the Leven estuary at HAVER-THWAITE, then passes south into MORECAMBE BAY. This area, called the Lake District, is one of the most popular tourist areas in England.

Leven, North Yorkshire, England
The river rises on Kildale Moor, North Yorkshire and flows westward through the towns of KILDALE, LITTLE AYTON, GREAT-AYTON, STOKESLEY, HUTTON RUDBY and CRATHORNE to finally join the River Tees to the east of YARM.

Leven, Strathclyde, Scotland
This Leven rises at the foot of LOCH LOMOND. The river flows south to join the River Clyde at the town of DUMBARTON, famous for its distilleries, shipbuilding and manufacturing industries. Dumbarton is 10 miles (16 km) downstream from Glasgow.

Lew, Devon, England
The Lew rises in the Halwill Forest. It flows on a northerly course through NORTHLEW and into the River Torridge just northwest of HATHERLEIGH. This small river flows through beautiful West Country landscape.

Newby Bridge on Lake Windermere signifies the beginning of the Leven River of Cumbria.

Lewis Burn, Cumbria, England
This river of northwestern England rises on the border between Cumbria and Northumberland. It flows from the western edge of the Kielder Forest northeast to join the River Tyne approximately one mile (1610 m) west of the village of PLASHETTS, Northumberland.

Liddel Water, Borders, Scotland
This river rises in the famous Cheviot Hills only eight miles (13 km) from CARTER BAR. It heads southwest down Liddesdale to where it meets the English-Scottish boundary at KERSHOPEFOOT. The Liddel Water then flows southwest along the border to become a tributary of the River Esk.

Lielupe, European USSR
The Lielupe begins at the confluence of the Mūša and Mémele Rivers at BAUSKA in central Latvia, SSR. It has a length of 74 miles (119 km). The river flows northwest past the town of JELGAVA. Then it heads north and northeast to the mouth of Western Dvina River in the Gulf of Riga.

Liffey, Republic of Ireland
The Liffey rises in County Wicklow and flows for a total of 70 miles (113 km) before entering the Irish Sea. The source of the river is in the 1700-foot (515-m) high peat-covered granite hills south of the capital, DUBLIN. Running initially as a small stream, the river soon expands as it is joined by Ballydonnell and Cloghleagh streams. The Liffey then leaves the hills and flows through a wide valley until it enters the Pollaphuca Reservoir. Here a dam floods the Liffey valley as well as its principal tributary, the Kings River. The reservoir provides a portion of Dublin's fresh water, and hydroelectric power. The river passes KILCULLEN, then swings north to CLANE, and finally shifts eastward to LEIXLIP about ten miles (16 km) downstream. The Liffey now heads for its final destination, first flowing through Dublin on its way. The river is tidal as far as the city's 18th century custom house. One of the main attractions here is O'Connell Street and the bridge over the Liffey, which is wider than its overall length. Leaving Dublin, the Liffey enters the Irish Sea.

Lim, Devon, England
The river rises a few miles north of UPLYME. It runs south through LYME REGIS, a resort on the Devon coast. The Lim enters Lyme Bay.

Lim, Yugoslavia
The river rises in Lake Plav in the northern Albanian Alps. It heads north by northwest to enter the Drina River southwest of VISEGRAD. The river is 136 miles (219 km) long.

Lima, Spain-Portugal
This river of northwestern Spain rises in Antela Lake and flows for 70 miles (113 km) before ending its run in the Atlantic Ocean. The Lima passes through northern Portugal on its way to the sea near VIANA DO CASTELO.

Linth, Switzerland

The Linth is formed by the headwaters of two small mountain streams north of the town of LINTHAL in northern Switzerland. The Linth is only 87 miles (140 km) long but flows through some of Switzerland's most scenic regions. It heads north through the Escher Canal to enter Lake Walen, then it exits into the Linth Canal to the Lake of Zürich. Leaving the Lake of Zürich, the river is known as the Limmat River which becomes a tributary of the Aare.

Lippe, Germany

The Lippe rises in the Teutoburger Forest of northwestern Germany and flows for a total of 147 miles (237 km). It runs west past the town of LIPPSTADT which is the head of navigation, then passes HAMM to join the Rhine at WESEL.

Liri, Italy

This river of central Italy rises west by southwest of AVEZZANO. It flows initially southeast, then shifts to a southerly flow past the town of ISOLA DEL LIRI. The river changes direction again and flows past PONTECORVO and on to the Gulf of Gaeta a short distance from the town of the same name. The Liri is 98 miles (158 km) long.

Livenza, Italy

The river rises north of SACILE in northeastern Italy and is 70 miles (113 km) long. It flows southeast transversing the Venetian Plain to enter the Adriatic Sea near the town of CAORLE.

Livet Water, Grampian, Scotland

This small Scottish river rises in the Grampian region. The Livet Water flows down GLEN LIVET on its way to join the River Avon near the distillery town of TOMINTOUL. Glen Livet is a famous Scottish malt whiskey.

Ljunga, Sweden

The Ljunga River rises southeast of the town of TRONDHEIM in northern Sweden. It has a length of 200 miles (320 km). The river flows

The River Liffey and Dublin in the Republic of Ireland.

southeasterly through a series of small lakes before passing the power station located at LGUNGAVERK. It then flows on to MATFORS and the Gulf of Bothnia near SUNDSVALL.

Ljusnan, Sweden

The Ljusnan is 270 miles (430 km) long and flows southeast from ROROS in central Sweden. Its major tributary is the Voxnan River. The Ljusnan heads on its southeasterly course until it enters the Gulf of Bothnia.

Llobregat, Spain

The Llobregat rises in the Sierra de Cadi of northeastern Spain. It has a length of 105 miles (169 km). The river flows first south, then swings to the southeast before entering the Mediterranean Sea south of BARCELONA.

Llynfi, Powys, Wales

The river rises northwest of BWLCH in Powys

Salmon fishing in the Lochy River of Scotland.

and between the towns of BRECON and CRICKHOWELL. The Llynfi runs north through Llangorse Lake. After leaving the lake it continues northward to become a tributary of the River Wye at GLASBURY.

Lochy, Inverness, Scotland
The Lochy is a river of the LOCHABER district of the Highlands. It runs through a beautiful and picturesque section of Scotland. The river leaves Loch Lochy and ends its run when it flows into Loch Linnhe.

Loddon, Hampshire, England
The river rises east of BASINGSTOKE and heads northeast to become one of the many tributaries of the River Thames just west of WARGRAVE in the county of Berkshire.

Logan Water, Strathclyde, Scotland
The Logan Water rises in the Strathclyde region. It heads eastward to join the River Nethan southwest of the small town of LESMAHAGOW which is also known as ABBEY GREEN and noted for its hosiery manufacturing industries.

Loing, France
The river rises near Saint-Sauveur in central France and is 100 miles (160 km) long. Its principal tributary is the Ouanne River. It flows north past the towns of MONTARGIS and NEMOURS to join the Seine.

Loir, France
The Loir rises north of the town of ILLIERS in central France. It has a length of 193 miles (311 km). It flows west by southwest to join the Sarthe River near ANGERS.

Loire, France
The Loire rises at a height of 4600 feet (1400 m) in the southeast portion of the Massif Central. The river flows through steep gorges and then more open basins but at a very rapid pace. The first basin through which the Loire flows is the Le Puy. Leaving this basin, it continues through the winding gorge of Peyredeyre, then entering the basin of Forez. The river again leaves the basin through a gorge named for the nearby town of ROANNE. Flowing past the town of NEVERS, the Loire is

joined by the Allier River and after another 40 miles (64 km), it finally departs the mighty Massif Central Range near COSNE. The river now takes a wide curving course northwest to ORLEANS, before turning west to the Bay of Biscay. The next stage of the river's course is 220 miles (350 km) to the town of ANGERS, the former ducal city of Anjou. The Loire is joined during its course by the Cher, Vienne and Indre Rivers. The river is so choked up with sediment and flood waters that by the time it reaches TOURS, it is 1250 feet (380 m) wide. Tours was the scene of a major battle during the Moorish penetration of Western Europe from their fortresses in Spain. Charles Martel, the commander of the Frankish army, defeated the Moors and ended, once and for all, their northward push. The Loire valley is one of the best farming regions in France. The river runs through the Val d'Orleans, the Val de Blois, the Val de Touraine and the Val d'Anjou. Finally, reaching NANTES, the Loire estuary

filters out to the Bay of Biscay for a length of 30 miles (50 km). The channel is constantly dredged to insure that deep-water vessels can safely anchor at Nantes. The outport of the city is ST NAZAIRE, which served as a primary German submarine pen during World War II. The Loire is 625 miles (1006 km) long.

Lonja, Yugoslavia
The Lonja is a small river of Yugoslavia rising near VARAZDIN in northern Croatia. It heads south to become a tributary of the Sava River near the town of KUTINA. The Lonja is 100 miles (160 km) long.

Lot, France
This medium-sized French river rises near Mont Lozère in southern France. It has a length of 300 miles (480 km). The Lot's principal tributaries are the Célé and Truyère

The Lovat River in the Velikiye Luki region of the USSR.

Rivers. The river flows on a westerly course to join the larger Garonne River at AIGUILLON.

Loud, Lancashire, England
The Loud rises on the southern slopes of the Forest of Bowland in the County of Lancashire. It flows east into the River Hodder at Doeford Bridge, near CHIPPING.

Lovat, European USSR
The Lovat is a river of western Russia, rising southeast of the town of NEVEL. It has a length of 335 miles (539 km) and is classed as a medium-sized river. Its main tributaries are the Kunya and Polist Rivers. The Lovat flows northward to join the Pola River to form joint deltas as both rivers enter Lake Ilmen.

Lowman, Devon, England
The Lowman rises near HOCKWORTHY in Devon. It flows southwest to join the River Exe at the quaint little town of TIVERTON.

The Chateau and old town of Saumur on the Loire River.

Lowther, Cumbria, England
The Lowther rises on the Shap Fells of Cumbria, close to the summit of Shap. The river heads north to join the River Eamont a few miles southeast of PENRITH.

Lox Yeo, Avon, England
The Lox Yeo rises just below the scenic Mendip Hills, near the country town of WINSCOMBE. The Mendip Hills are one of southwestern England's principal tourist areas. The river flows into the River Axe near LOXTON.

Loy, Highlands, Scotland
The Loy begins in the Lochneil Forest of the Lochaber district of the Highlands. It heads southeast down Glen Loy to join the River Lochy a few miles southwest of GAIRLOCHY.

Lozva, European USSR
The Lozva River begins in the central Ural Mountain Range of the Soviet Union. It has a length of 265 miles (426 km). The river flows southeast to meet the Sosva River near the town of GARI to form the Tavda River.

Luga, European USSR
The Luga rises near the city of NOVGOROD. It flows 215 miles (346 km) on a southerly and then northwesterly course to enter Luga Bay in the Gulf of Finland. The Luga's principal tributary is the Oredezh River.

Lugg, Powys, Wales
The Lugg rises eight miles (13 km) west of the town of KNIGHTON. It has a length of 40 miles (64 km). It flows past LEOMINSTER in Herefordshire. It joins the River Wye near the cathedral town of HEREFORD, the county town of Herefordshire.

Lule, Norway
This medium-sized river of Norway rises southwest of NARVIK, a town famous during World War II for the military operations carried out in its vicinity. The river is 280 miles (450 km) long. It flows southeast through Stora Lule Lake, then over the majestic falls at Porjus and Harspranget, both of which are principal hydroelectric power stations in the Norwegian grid. The Lule now heads northwest to enter the Gulf of Bothnia at LULEA.

Lune, Cumbria, England
A river rising in the northern spur of the Pennines of northwestern England. The Lune has a total length of 55 miles (88 km), not a very long river, but a scenic one. Thousands of years ago, the Lune had a northerly course to CARLISLE but for an undetermined reason, the river shifted to a southerly course through the moorland of SEDBERGH. Next the Lune passes through KIRKBY LONSDALE, famous for its superb 14th century bridge which is still utilized for pedestrian traffic across the river. The river meanders for a substantial distance before flowing through the narrow Halton Gorge. The Lune passes LANCASTER, an important town in Roman times; realizing its strategic value, the Normans built a strong castle at Lancaster. The bitter rivalry between the house of Lancaster and the house of York caused the Wars of the Roses. After leaving Lancaster, the Lune becomes tidal and enters Morecambe Bay and finally flows into the Irish Sea. The Lune is navigable as far as Lancaster for small coastal vessels.

Luther Water, Grampian Region, Scotland
The Luther Water rises in Drumtochty Forest of the Grampian Region of Scotland. It heads south to join the River Esk a few miles west of the town of MARYKIRK.

Luznice, Austria-Czechoslovakia
This small Austrian river rises southeast of the town of KAPLICE. The Luznice flows east, then shifts to a northeasterly course crossing over into Bohemia. Then it travels northwest for a short distance before turning southwest to become a tributary of the Vltava River near the town of TYN.

Lyd, Devon, England
The river rises on Dartmoor and flows west past the town of LYDFORD and through the Lydford Gorge. It continues on to join the River Thrushel at the small town of LIFTON before proceeding to its final destination, the River Tamar, a few miles east of the Cornish border town of LAUNCESTON.

Lyna, Poland
The Lyna rises south of OLSZTYN in northeastern Poland. It has a length of 137 miles (220 km). It flows north to cross the USSR's frontier, passing DRUZHBA, the junction for the Masurian Canal, before joining the Pregel River at the town of ZNAMENSK.

Lynher, Cornwall, England
The Lynher rises on Bodmin Moor near the village of ALTARNUM. It flows southeast to become a tributary of the River Tamar below the town of SALTASH.

Lys, France-Belgium
This very beautiful river of northern France rises in the hills of Artois. It has a length of 135 miles (217 km). The Lys flows northeast past AIRE, which is the junction with the Flanders Plain canal system, and into Belgium. It continues on to join the Scheldt River at the old town of GHENT.

Maas, Belgium-Netherlands
See Meuse.

Main, Germany
The Main is formed by the confluence of the Red and White Main Rivers at MAINLEUS, a small village in northern Bavaria. The Main is 307 miles (494 km) and one of the major trade routes of Europe. The river is linked with the Rhine and Danube Rivers by the great Ludwig Canal at the ancient city of BAMBERG. The main tributaries of the Main are the Regnitz, Franconian Saale and Tauber Rivers. The Main is full of bends which adds to its natural beauty. The river passes SCHWEINFURT and WURZBURG, a very old and lovely city. The Main continues on course passing the great city of FRANKFURT and then enters the Rhine.

Maira, Italy
The Maira rises in the Cottian Alps in northwestern Italy near the town of ACCEGLIO. A major hydroelectric power generating station is located at Acceglio. The river then flows east and northeast to join the Po River east of the town of PANCALIERI. The Maira is only 65 miles (105 km) long.

Main Water of Luce, Strathclyde, Scotland
This river rises four miles (six km) southeast of BALLANTRAE, a small town made famous by the Hollywood movie *Master of Ballantrae*. The Main Water of Luce flows south into the Dumfries and Galloway region to join the Cross Water of Luce at the village of NEW LUCE, to form the Water of Luce.

Marica, Bulgaria-Greece-Turkey
The river rises in the Rila Mountain Range of Bulgaria. The Marica is 300 miles (480 km) long and flows easterly between the lowlands of the Balkan and Rhodope Mountains. The river forms the boundary between Greece and Bulgaria for a time before crossing wholly into

Greece. Then for approximately 115 miles (185 km) the river is the boundary between Turkey and Greece. This frontier region was once the ancient Kingdom of Thrace noted for its horsemen and gold carvings. The river is not navigable except for small boats and empties into the Aegean Sea.

Marne, France
The Marne rises on the Plateau of Langres and drains an area of slightly more than 8000 square miles (20,700 sq km). It is one of the major tributaries of the Seine. The river is navigable from SAINT-DIZIER to its confluence with the Seine. The Marne receives as

tributary rivers, the Rognon, Saulx, Ourcq, Grand-Morin and Somme-Soude. The river is one of France's most important commercial waterways, as canals link it with the Aisne, the Saône and the Rhine. It does not carry a lot of water because of the chalky terrain through which it flows, especially in Champagne. The river is noted for excellent fishing with a variety to interest all freshwater fishermen. During World War I, the Marne was the scene of bitter fighting.

Maun, Nottinghamshire, England
The Maun rises near the town of MANSFIELD in Nottinghamshire. It runs through Mansfield, then changes course to pass EDWINSTOWE and OLLERTON before joining the River Meden to form the River Idle just south of the town of EAST RETFORD.

Mayenne, France
The river rises on Mont des Avaloirs in western France. The Mayenne's principal tributaries are the Oudon, 40 miles (64 km) long and the Varenne, 30 miles (48 km) long. It is 125 miles (201 km) long and flows first west, then south passing the town of MAYENNE located at the head of the river's navigation. The confluence of the Mayenne and Sarthe Rivers forms the Maine River at ANGERS.

Mease, Leicestershire-Staffordshire, England
A river of the English Midlands rising east of the town of ASHBY-DE-LA-ZOUCH. It heads first south, then west into Staffordshire, and finally northwest to become a tributary of the River Trent near CROXALL.

Meavy, Devon, England
The Meavy rises near the town of PRINCETON on Dartmoor, which was originally built next to a prison utilized to accommodate French captives of the Napoleonic Wars. It flows

southwest through the Burrator Reservoir and the tiny village of MEAVY. It changes direction to run south and enter the River Plym at the end of Bickleigh Vale.

Medina, Isle of Wight, England
The Medina rises at CHALE GREEN near the south coast of the island. It flows north to enter the Solent at the yachting town of COWES.

Medway, West Sussex-Kent, England
The Medway is the major waterway of the Northern Weald and is 70 miles (113 km) long. The various streams which rise at a height of 600 feet (180 m) on the northern slopes of the Ashdown Forest form the headwaters of the Medway. The river flows eastward to cross the Kent boundary near the town of ASHURST, then continues on to TUNBRIDGE WELLS. The river now turns northward to the town of TONBRIDGE in the Vale of Kent, a beautiful lush area in southern England. The Medway then receives two of its main tributaries, the River Eden and the River Beult. It now remains on its northeasterly course passing YALDING, then makes an eastward loop towards MAIDSTONE where it is joined by the River Len. This region around the city is known for its large orchards and hop fields which provide a substantial quantity of fresh fruit and hops for local brewers. The next obstacle the river overcomes is the North Downs as it gets ready to enter its own estuary and pass the surrounding towns of ROCHESTER, CHATHAM and GILLINGHAM. The Medway estuary was once a huge naval base but all of the facilities are now closed, and the large dockyards in a state of disrepair. The estuary narrows as it reaches out between the Isle of Grain and SHEERNESS before opening out into its final destination, the massive Thames estuary.

Memele, European USSR
The Memele rises north of ROKISKIS in the old Baltic Sea country of Lithuania. It has a length of 118 miles (190 km). It runs west by northwest to meet the Musa River at BAUSKA in Latvia to form the Lielupe River.

Meon, Hampshire, England
The river rises south of EAST MEON. It flows northwest through the villages of East and WEST MEON, then, changing direction to a more southwesterly flow, it runs through WICKHAM and TITCHFIELD before entering the Solent west of HILL HEAD.

Mersey, Lancashire, England
The Mersey is 70 miles (113 km) long and is formed by the confluence of two small rivers the Goyt and Tame which come together in the town of STOCKPORT. Both of these rivers have their sources high in the Pennines at a height of 1650 feet (500 m). The Mersey flows along the southern portion of England's third city, MANCHESTER. At a point seven miles (11 km) downstream, the Mersey is diverted into the Manchester Ship Canal and provides the majority of water for that manmade innovation. Four miles (six km) further downstream the Mersey is joined by the River Bollin. The overflow of water from these two rivers escapes into the Mersey's old bed and once again the stream acquires its lost identity. The river next passes through the town of WARRINGTON, an industrial site noted for its wire trade, steel and iron works, breweries and paper mills. Once the Mersey leaves Warrington it becomes tidal, and is joined shortly after by its last two major tributaries, the Irwell and the Weaver. The Mersey, at this stage, becomes what is known as the Inner Mersey, covering an area of 30 square miles (78 sq km) altogether and which is 19 miles (31 km) long. The river has the important cities of LIVERPOOL (home of a famous football team) and BOOTLE, both on the east bank, while on the west bank are located BIRKENHEAD and WALLASEY. These four cities on the mouth of the Mersey on the Irish Sea together make up one of the greatest ports in the world.

Mesta, Bulgaria-Greece
The Mesta rises in the Rila Mountain Range of Bulgaria, where two headstreams meet to form the river. These two streams are the Bela Mesta and Cherna Mesta. The river runs southeast through a narrow valley separating the Pirin and Rhodope Ranges from each other. The river has a total length of 150 miles (240 km). It crosses into Greece upstream from DHELTA. The Mesta forms the boundary between the Greek provinces of Makedhonia and Thraki on its way to the Aegean Sea.

Metauro, Italy
The Metauro has its source in two headstreams in the Etruscan Alps in central Italy, northeast of the town of SANSEPOLCRO. It has a length of 70 miles (113 km). The river flows past URBANIA to enter the Adriatic Sea near the town of FANO.

Meurthe, France
The river rises in the Vosges Range of northeastern France. It is 105 miles (169 km) long. Its major tributaries are the Mortagne and Vezouze Rivers. The Meurthe flows in a northwesterly direction past the town of

The Medway River east of Tonbridge, Kent.

LUNEVILLE which is the head of navigation for the river. It goes on to pass NANCY to enter the Moselle River.

Meuse, France-Belgium-Netherlands

The Meuse has its source in southern Lorraine. It runs north past the fortress city of VERDUN, a military garrison since the time of the Romans and which was heavily defended by the French in one of the costliest battles of World War I. The major tributaries of the Meuse are the Sambre, the Chiers and the Sormonne Rivers. The river runs for a total length of 580 miles (930 km) before entering the North Sea. At GIVET the Meuse enters Belgium and becomes a much more navigable river than in France. The Belgian government has built a series of locks to regularize the river to accommodate barges. It makes a loop to MAASTRICHT and the river is within the confines of the Netherlands for eight miles before turning once more toward the town of MAASBRACHT. In the Netherlands it is called the Maas.

Left: Ferry crossing the Mersey near Liverpool.
Below: View of the Maine taken from the castle at Angers.

The Meuse-Maas has been an international problem for the Belgian and Dutch governments for years because both would like the river to be fully navigable at this stage but that would mean co-operation between both the countries. As yet this has not happened because the Dutch would have the advantage for their huge port of ROTTERDAM which would be a disadvantage to the Belgian port of ANTWERP. Both countries tried to remedy this by constructing canals within their territorial limits to by-pass this unnavigable section: the Dutch built the Juliana Canal and the Belgians the Albert Canal. Once below Maasbracht, the river is called the Maas by the Dutch as it is totally within their territory; the river now heads west to link up with the huge Scheldt, Maas and Rhine delta. The river finally enters the North Sea through a manmade channel, the Bergsche Maas, to by-pass the Waal distributary.

Mezen, European USSR
The Mezen rises in the swampy area of the Timan Hills of northern European USSR. It is

Below: The Freyr Rocks on the Meuse near Dinant in the Namur district of Belgium.

533 miles (853 km) long and flows on a northwesterly course across a large flat plain on its way to enter the White Sea. The Mezen is only navigable on its lower course. It is utilized primarily to float timber down river to the sawmills of the town of MEZEN at the mouth of the river.

Mijares, Spain
The Mijares rises to the west of the town of TERUEL in eastern Spain. It is 65 miles (105 km) long. It flows southeast to enter the Mediterranean Sea southeast of CASTELLON DE LA PLANA.

Mincio, Italy
The Mincio River begins as the Sarca River, approximately 12 miles (19 km) east of the city of EDOLO in northern Italy. The total length of the river, including the first section (which is called the Sarca) is 88 miles (142 km). The Sarca runs in every direction but west on its way to Lake Garda. Leaving the lake it becomes the Mincio at PESCHIERA and continues on course to MANTOV. It becomes a tributary of the River Po shortly after leaving the city.

Moldava, Rumania
The Moldava rises in the Carpathian Mountains of Moldavia in eastern Rumania. It has a length of 110 miles (180 km). The Moldava runs east past CIMPULUNG, then southeast past ROMAN, finally joining the Siret River to the northwest of BACESTI.

Mole, Devon, England
The river rises on Exmoor just a few miles north of TWITCHEN. It runs southwest past NORTH and SOUTH MOLTON, a small village and market town respectively, before joining the River Taw at JUNCTION POOL.

Mole, West Sussex-Surrey, England
The Mole rises at CRAWLEY in West Sussex in one of England's most beautiful country areas. The river flows past the towns of HORLEY, DORKING, LEATHERHEAD and ESHER before

becoming a tributary of the River Thames opposite HAMPTON COURT PALACE. One of the Royal residences, it was built by Cardinal Wolsey during the reign of Henry VIII. Its famous maze and gardens are open to the public.

Mologa, European USSR
The Mologa rises west of BEZHETSK. The river is 203 miles (327 km) long. It heads in every direction but south, past PESTOVO, the actual head of the river's navigation, before flowing past USTYUZHNA to the Rybinsk Reservoir north of VESYEGONSK.

Mondego, Portugal
The river rises in the Sierra da Estrela, north of the town of COVILHA in central Portugal. The Mondego has a length of 137 miles (220 km).

Left: The Mole River meanders through Surrey.

Its major tributary is the Dão River. It flows southwest through the Coimbra Plain to enter the Atlantic Ocean at FIGUEIRA DA FOZ.

Montone, Italy
The river rises in the Etruscan Apennines, southeast of the town of MARRADI in central

Italy. Its chief tributary is the Rabbi River. The length of Montone is only 53 miles (85 km). The river flows northeast to meet the Ronco River near the ancient town of RAVENNA and together they form the Fiume Uniti River.

Moraca, Yugoslavia
The Moraca is formed by the confluence of headstreams rising in the Stozac Mountains of Montenegro. The river is 60 miles (97 km) long and its chief tributary is the Zeta River. The Moraca flows south past the town of TITOGRAD to its outlet Lake Scutari, west of PLAVNICA.

Morava, Czechoslovakia
The Morava River rises on Kralicky Sneznik, northwest of STARE MESTO in central Czechoslovakia. It has as principal tributaries the Becva, Dyje and Hana Rivers. The Morava is 227 miles (365 km) long. It flows initially south by southeast, then swings south by southwest and finally moves to a straight southerly course before it enters the Danube at DEVIN.

Morava, Yugoslavia
Called the Great Morava, it is the chief river of Serbia in Yugoslavia. The Morava is formed by the confluence of the Southern and Western Morava Rivers near the town of STALAC. The Great Morava is 134 miles (216 km) long. It flows north past CUPRIJA to the mouth of the Danube northeast of SMEDEREVO.

Mornos, Greece
The Mornos rises in the Oeta Massif of central Greece. It is noted for its hydroelectric power stations which provide a substantial amount of regional power. The Mornos is only 38 miles (61 km) long. It flows southwest from its source to enter the Gulf of Corinth southeast of the Greek town of NAVPAKTOS.

Mörrum, Sweden
The river rises east of VARNAMO in southern Sweden. It is 80 miles (129 km) long. The Morrum flows south past ALVESTA, then by RYD before it enters the Baltic Sea near KARLSHAMN.

Moselle, France-Germany
The Moselle is 330 miles (530 km) long and runs from the slopes of the Ballon d'Alsace in the Vosges Mountain Range on a northwesterly course. The river passes the Pont-St-Vincent in southern Lorraine, then on to TOUL, before making a swift turn to the northeast as it approaches FROUARD. At one stage in a past geological age, the Moselle was a tributary of the Meuse but due to erosion, the upper Moselle was eventually diverted into the Meurthe-Moselle catchment. The former valley of the Moselle can be seen in the Toul Gap which is today utilized by the Marne-Rhine Canal. This junction gave great importance to the city of Toul which has been a military fortress town for centuries. The next important strategic town on the banks of the Moselle is METZ. The river is not a naturally navigable river but it has been regularized and canalized to make it accessible by small vessels.

Summer on the Moskva River.

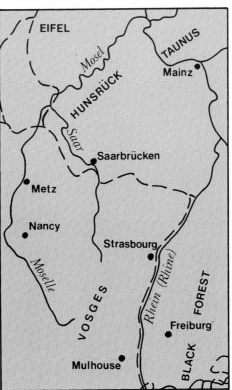

Between the towns of SCHENGEN and WASSER-BILLIG, the Moselle forms the boundary between the tiny country of Luxembourg and West Germany. Finally the river becomes an entirely German river and continues on a northeasterly course as it heads for TRIER, the birthplace of the great founder of Communism, Karl Marx. The Moselle finally joins the Rhine at the city of KOBLENZ. Just before its confluence with the Rhine the river flows through an area noted for its production of magnificent Moselle wines.

Moskva, European USSR
The Moskva begins west of UVAROKA in the Smolensk-Moscow Upland. It has a length of 315 miles (507 km). The chief tributaries are the Kolocha, Pakhra, Ruza and Istria Rivers. It flows northwest initially, then swings easterly to pass the town of ZVENIGOROD, finally proceeding southeast past the large cities of MOSCOW, KOLOMNA and BRONNITSY to join the Oka River opposite SHCHUROVO. The major Battle of Borodino was fought at the confluence with the right bank Kolocha River during the Napoleonic Wars. The Moskva is

Right: Origins of the Narew River in Estonia.

joined to the Volga River by the Moskva Canal.

Moy, Republic of Ireland
The Moy rises in County Sligo in the Republic of Ireland. It has a length of 40 miles (64 km). The river flows southwest across the border into County Mayo, then turns northward passing FOXFORD and BALLINA on its way to Killala Bay on the Atlantic Ocean.

Msta, European USSR
The Msta begins in a small lake northwest of VYSHNIY VOLOCHEK. It is 275 miles (442 km) long. The Msta is connected with the Tvertsa and Volkhov Rivers by a system of canals. The river flows northwest, then west to the delta at Lake Ilmen approximately seven miles (11 km) from the city of NOVGOROD.

Muick, Grampian Region, Scotland
The Muick rises in the Grampian region of Scotland. It flows northeast from Loch Muick down the Glen Muick to join the River Dee just south of the village and resort of BALLATER, near Balmoral Castle, the holiday home of the British Royal family.

Mulde, East Germany
The Mulde River rises north of COLDITZ, a former Allied prisoner of war camp, made famous by the television series *Colditz*. The river is formed by the confluence of Freiberger Mulde and Swickauer Mulde Rivers. The Mulde has a length of 81 miles (130 km). It flows northwest past GRIMMA and WURZEN to become a tributary of the Elbe at DESSAU.

Mur, Austria-Yugoslavia
The river rises in the Hohe Tauern Mountain Range of Austria. The Mur has a length of 300 miles (480 km) and is navigable below the city of GRAZ. A large proportion of regional hydroelectric power is provided by the Mur at the power stations located at Graz, PEGGAU and MIXNITZ. It flows east to pass the city of BRUCK, then proceeds south past Graz to enter Yugoslavia just below the town of RADKERS-BURG. The Mur continues southeast to join the Drava River at LEGRAD.

Mures, Rumania-Hungary
The river rises in the Carpathian Mountains of Moldavia near the town of GHEORGHENI. The Mures flows for a total of 550 miles (880 km) before flowing into the larger Tisza river at SZEGED. The river is navigable for approximately 200 miles (320 km) of its course to DEVA, a town which was a Roman settlement centuries ago. The upper reaches of the river are utilized mainly for floating timber. It runs through historical regions of Rumania and Hungary before joining the Tisza.

Murz, Austria
The Murz rises in the Schneealpe Mountains

of Austria. It is 80 miles (129 km) long. It is a tributary of the Mur at BRUCK.

Nab, Germany
The Nab actually rises as the Waldnab River a few miles south of BARNAB. It is 100 miles (160 km) long. The river heads south passing WEIDEN and SCHWANDORF before it enters the Danube to the west of the city of REGENSBURG. The principal tributaries of the Nab are the Vils and Fichtelnab Rivers.

Nalón, Spain
The Nalón rises in the Cantabrian Mountains of northwestern Spain. It flows northwest through one of Spain's principal coal and iron-ore regions. The river is 80 miles (129 km) long and enters the Bay of Biscay five miles (eight km) northeast of PRAVIA.

Nams, Norway
The Nams River rises in Lake Nams in central Norway, ten miles (16 km) north-northeast of GJERSVIKA. It is 120 miles (190 km) long, and flows southwest and west to enter Nams Fjord.

Narew, European USSR-Poland
The Narew rises northwest of PRUZHANY. It is 275 miles (442 km) long. Its major tributary is the Western Bug River. The Narew flows west by northwest crossing into Poland past the town of LOMZA. It continues southwest past PULTUSK and then enters the Vistula River near NOWY DWOR.

Neath, Powys, Wales
Sometimes called the Nedd, the Neath is one of the most beautiful rivers of Wales. It flows from the Black Mountains southwest of BRECON, down the gorgeous Vale of Neath to the town of NEATH. Neath is a small Welsh town much visited for its famous abbey remains which lie adjacent to the river. It is well worth walking along this stretch of the river during the spring and summer months.

Neb, Isle of Man
The Neb rises in the central mountains east of LITTLE LONDON. It flows through that village, then proceeds southwest down Glen Helen to ST JOHN'S. The Neb then flows to PEEL and enters Peel Bay.

Neckar, Germany

The Neckar rises in the Black Forest of Western Germany. It is one of the most beautiful rivers in the world. It has a length of 228 miles (367 km). It starts as a tumbling mountain stream at an altitude of 2287 feet (698 m) high. The river flows down through ROTTWEIL, then turns north to the town of HORB. The Neckar swings northeast to ROTTENBURG, then on to the old imperial city of TUBINGEN. Upon reaching ESSLINGEN, the river becomes much wider and deeper and flows through a valley of exceptional scenic beauty. Next the river passes through MARBACH, the birthplace of the German poet, Schiller. Here the Neckar becomes navigable for small vessels. The river's principal tributaries are the Enz, Fils, Elsenz, Rems, Kocher and Jagst Rivers. The next stops are STUTTGART and then HEILBRONN. The river is canalized at Heilbronn and vessels up to 1200 tons have access this far. The next major stop for the river is the university city of HEIDELBERG. The Neckar's destination is the Rhine at MANNHEIM.

Neisse, Glatzer, Czechoslovakia

The Glatzer Neisse rises in the Sudeten Mountains on the Czechoslovakian border to the northeast of MIEDZYLESIE. It has a length of 121 miles (195 km). The upper portion of the river is used only for floating timber because of its turbulent character. The river flows south by southwest passing BYSTRZYCA, KLODZKA and GLATZ, before turning eastward. It then heads through PACZKOW and the Otmuchow hydroelectric station prior to passing NEISSE. The Glatzer Neisse finally becomes navigable at LWIN BRZESKI. The river is a fisherman's delight and has an overabundance of fish. It finally ends as a tributary of the Oder River, ten miles (16 km) southeast of the port of BRIEG.

Neisse, Lusatian, Czechoslovakia-East Germany-Poland

Called the Gorlitzer Neisse, it rises on the Isergebirge of Czechoslovakia at a height of 1150 feet (350 m). The river's main function has been to form the boundary between Eastern Germany and Poland since 1945. The river flows northwards through the towns of GORLITZ, FORST and GUBEN, the latter the head of navigation. It then enters the Oder River, nine miles (14 km) north of Guben.

Above: The university city of Heidelberg on the Neckar River in Germany.

Neman, European USSR

The Neman rises 30 miles (48 km) southwest of the capital of White Russia, MINSK. The river is 597 miles (961 km) long. Its principal use is to float timber. The Neman flows west, then changes to a more northerly course as it enters Lithuania, one of the old Baltic Sea countries prior to its annexation by the Soviet Union. The chief port of the Neman is the town of KAUNAS at the confluence with the Viliya River in Lithuania. The river ends at the Courland Lagoon on the Baltic Sea. In 1807 Napoleon and Czar Alexander I met on a raft in the center of the Neman to agree to a very short alliance.

Nene, Northamptonshire, England

The Nene rises three miles (five km) southwest of the midland town of DAVENTRY in Northamptonshire. It has a total length of 90 miles (144 km). The river flows past NORTHAMPTON, WELLINGBOROUGH, OUNDLE, PETERBOROUGH and WISBECH. It crosses the Fens to enter the Wash north of SUTTON BRIDGE.

Nera, Italy
The Nera is 80 miles (129 km) long. Its major tributary is the Velino River. This central Italian river rises on Monte Sibillini and flows southwest past TERNI to join the Tiber River.

Neretva, Yugoslavia
The source of the Neretva is high in the Dinaric Alps, north of GACKO. The river flows for 135 miles (217 km) north by northwest, then shifts to a south by southwest course to enter the Adriatic Sea at the town of KARDELJEVO. The Neretva's principal tributaries are the Bregava and Rama Rivers.

Nervion, Spain
This small river of northern Spain flows for 45 miles (72 km) from its source in the Cantabrian Mountains northward. It passes BILBAO to a broad estuary in the Bay of Biscay. Bilbao is noted for its fine metallurgical industries. The Nervion is navigable to Bilbao by medium-sized sea-going vessels.

Neto, Italy
The source of the Neto is located in the La Sila Mountains of Calabria in southern Italy. The Neto is 52 miles (84 km) long. Its major tributaries are the Arvo and Ampollino Rivers which together provide a large quantity of the region's hydroelectric power. The river runs southeast, then east to enter the Gulf of Taranto, in the boot of Italy, just north of the town of CROTONE.

Neva, European USSR
The Neva begins in Lake Ladoga at the town of PETROKREPOST. It is 46 miles (74 km) long. The river is connected with the Volga and White Sea by a system of canals. The Neva flows west to the Gulf of Finland forming the delta mouth at the Russian city of LENINGRAD.

Nid, Sweden-Norway
The Nid rises northeast of ROROS in Sweden. It is 100 miles (160 km) long. The river flows northwest through Selbu Lake to enter Trondheim Fjord at the town of TRONDHEIM.

Above: Heidelberg on the Neckar River.
Right: The Neman River in Lithuanian SSR.

Nidd, North Yorkshire, England
The Nidd rises on the northern slopes of Great Whernside in Yorkshire. It flows east through Angram and Scar House Reservoirs, then changes to a southeasterly flow passing PATELEY BRIDGE. The river passes KNARES-BOROUGH and enters the River Ouse northwest of YORK. The Nidd is 50 miles (80 km) long.

Niers, West Germany-Holland
The Niers rises just a few miles south of WICKRATH in West Germany. It has a length of 80 miles (129 km). The river heads northeast past RHEYDT into Holland and joins the Maas River north of the Dutch town of GENNEP.

Nisava, Bulgaria-Yugoslavia
The Nisava is 102 miles (164 km) long and flows from the Berkovitsa Mountains in northwestern Bulgaria. It becomes a tributary of the Morava River northwest of NIS.

Nissa, Sweden
The Nissa River begins southwest of JONKOP-ING in southwestern Sweden. It has a total length of 100 miles (160 km). It runs southwest past the towns of GISLAVED and OSKARSTROM to the Kattegat at HALMSTAD.

Nith, Strathclyde, Scotland
The source of the Nith is two miles northeast of DALMELLINGTON. It has a length of 80 miles (129 km). The river flows through NEW CUMNOCK, then eastward to SANQUHAR and THORNHILL to Dumfries and Galloway and the Solway Firth.

Nitra, Czechoslovakia
The river rises in the mountains of south-western Slovakia, 13 miles (21 km) north of PRIEVIDZA. It heads 150 miles (240 km) south to pass NITRA and NOVE ZAMKY. It becomes a tributary of the Váh River near KOMARNO.

Noguera Pallarese, Spain
The river rises in the central Pyrenees of northeastern Spain. It is 105 miles (169 km) long and flows southward until it joins the Segre River above the town of CAMARASA.

Nore, Republic of Ireland
The river rises southwest of ROSCREA in County Tipperary. It is 70 miles (113 km) long. The Nore flows northeast, then changes direction to the southeast, passing into County Kilkenny to join the Barrow River near NEW ROSS.

Notec, Poland
The Notec begins in central Poland northeast of KOLO. The river is 273 miles (439 km) long. It is canalized below Lake Goplo and is linked with the Brda River by the Bydgoszcz Canal. It joins the Warta River east of LANDSBERG.

Numedalslagen, Norway
This river of southern Norway rises at a height of over 4000 feet (1220 m) on the Hardanger-vidda. It is only 190 miles (310 km) long but is one of the most beautiful rivers of southern Norway. The Lagen flows down the Numedal on a northerly course, then enters Lake Palsbu and immediately afterwards, Lake Tunhovd. Leaving the latter lake, it flows over a medium-sized waterfall which is utilized to provide a substantial amount of the region's hydro-electric power. As the river continues down Numedal, it assumes a southeasterly direction and flows through the lakes of Nore and Kravik. The two major towns on the river are KONGSBERG, noted as a mining center for silver in the early 17th century, and LARVIK, an important timber, shipbuilding and glass-works town. The river enters Larvik Fjord off the Skagerrak near Larvik where one can take a ferry to Denmark.

Oak Beck, North Yorkshire, England
The Oak Beck is a small northern river which rises on Stainburn Moor southwest of HARROGATE. The river flows northeast through Ten Acre Reservoir, past the western side of Harrogate and finally into the River Nidd east of KILLINGHALL.

Obra, Poland
The Obra River has its source near KOZMIN, in western Poland. The length of the Obra is 150 miles (240 km). It flows past KOSCIAN, then heads west and north past ZBASZYN and MIEDZYRZECZ to become a tributary of the Warta River at SKWIERZYNA.

Odense, Denmark
The Odense rises in Arreskov Lake on Fyn Island in Denmark. It flows past the town of ODENSE to enter Odense Fjord. It is 40 miles (64 km) long.

Oder, Czechoslovakia-Poland
The source of the Oder is approximately 11 miles (18 km) northeast of OLOMOUC in the Oder Mountains of Moravia. It is 563 miles (906 km) long. The Oder heads eastward initially to the town of OSTRAVA and then crosses the Polish frontier. It changes direction to the north and northwest as it heads for WROCLAW. The Oder meets the Lusatian

Neisse just past GLOGOW and forms the border between East Germany and Poland. The principal tributaries of the Oder are the Olza, Klodnica, Barycz, Warta and Ina Rivers on the right bank; and from the left bank the Glatzer Neisse, Olawa, Kaczawa, Lusatian Neisse (mentioned above) and the Bobr. The river once again turns north passing FRANKFURT-AN-DER-ODER and KOSTRZYN, to enter the Oder Marshes. Further along the river separates into two distinct arms: the West Oder, canalized as an integral portion of the Berlin-Stettin Canal, and the East Oder. Both arms flow through the town of STETTIN and enter Damm Lake to the north of the city; they finally link up again to head into the Stettin Lagoon. This large lagoon drains directly into the Baltic Sea through three rivers: the Swine and Peene to the west and the Dievenow to the east. At WROCLAW the Oder becomes navigable because of the numerous manmade weirs and canals along the river. These have brought prosperity to the region, though the river is not utilized as much for shipping of coal, iron-ore and coke as it once was. (The Poles prefer the railroad.) The Oder has the warmest climate in Poland and passes through some of the loveliest and most scenic areas in the country before emptying into the Baltic Sea.

Odiel, Spain
The river begins near ARACENA in the Sierra Morena of southwestern Spain. The Odiel is 92 miles (148 km) long. It receives its major tributary, the Rio Tinto, a few miles south of HUELVA. The Odiel flows southwest, then south to a wide estuary on the Atlantic Ocean.

Ofanto, Italy
The Ofanto rises in the Apennines near TORELLA DE LOMBARDI in southern Italy. The river is 83 miles (134 km) long. It flows in every direction but south to enter the Adriatic Sea approximately four miles (six km) northwest of BARLETTA. The Ofanto has the distinction of being the southernmost river on the Italian east coast.

Og, Wiltshire, England
The Og rises near the village of Ogbourne St George located three miles (five km) north of MARLBOROUGH. It flows south to join the River Kennet to the east of Marlborough.

Oglio, Italy
The source of the Oglio is found at the confluence of various mountain streams at PONTE DI LEGNO in northern Italy. The river is 170 miles (270 km) long and flows in a southwest direction to pass EDOLO through Lago d'Iseo. The Oglio then proceeds south for a short distance before turning to a southeasterly course over the Plains of Lombard to become a tributary of the Po approximately ten miles (16 km) southwest of the city of MANTOVA.

Ogmore, Mid Glamorgan, Wales
This Welsh river rises on the south side of the Craig Ogwr to the west of RHONDDA. It runs south to BRIDGEND and then turns southwest to enter the sea east of PORTHCAWL.

Ognon, France
The river rises in the Vosges Range of eastern France near LE THILLOT. The Ognon is 115 miles (185 km) long and runs southwest to its junction with the Saône River above the town of PONTALLIER-SUR-SAONE. This river flows through some beautiful French countryside on its way to the much larger Saône.

Ogosta, Bulgaria
The Ogosta rises west of BERKOVITSA in northwest Bulgaria. Its major tributary is the Botunya River. The Ogosta is 91 miles (146 km) long and flows northeast to become a tributary of the mighty Danube a few miles west of ORJAHOVO.

Ogwen, Gwynedd, Wales
The Ogwen rises south of Carnedd Llewelyn in Gwynedd. It runs south into Llyn Ogwen, then turns to assume a northerly course to BETHSEDA on its way to CONWAY BAY a few miles east of the Welsh city of BANGOR.

Oise, Belgium-France
The river Oise rises in the Ardennes of

The Oka River approaching Gorki.

Belgium at a height of 1000 feet (300 m). The river is not naturally navigable, but because of man's ingenuity and a system of locked barrages, it can take barges as far as JANVILLE. The Oise flows for a short distance near the border of Belgium and France before actually crossing into France. It flows southwest, then shifts gradually to a more southerly course as it prepares itself to join the River Seine near PARIS. The Oise's principal tributary is the Aisne. The river provides a major route between Paris and FLANDERS. Also because of the trade which used to ply between the capital and the outlying districts a series of towns grew up along the Oise; NOYON, CHANY, COMPIEGNE, CREIL and MONTATAIRE. The river valley is flat and supports a large thriving dairy industry. The Oise is 190 miles (310 km) long.

Oka, European USSR

The Oka is a relatively large river of central European USSR. It has a total length of 918 miles (1477 km). The river flows initially north past OREL to KALUGA, then heads eastward and northeast to pass KOLOMNA where it is joined by the Moskva. The Oka valley is very narrow and is surrounded by water-meadows and marshes. The river is navigable below

Kolomna for large vessels. It continues on its course passing RYAZAN, DZERZHINSK and finally enters the Volga at GORKI. The river's potential is underestimated and its assets as yet underdeveloped.

Olona, Italy

The Olona rises north of VARESE in northern Italy. It has a length of only 65 miles (105 km). The river runs south by southeast past the towns of LEGNANO and MILAN to become a tributary of the Lambro River at SAINT'-ANGELO-LODIGIANO. Near MILAN the Olona is connected by a series of canals to PAVIA and the Po near STRADELLA.

Olt, Rumania-Bulgaria

The river rises east of GHEORGHENI in the Moldavian-Carpathian Mountains of southern Rumania. The Olt is 348 miles (560 km) long. It flows south to SFANTU-GHEORGHE, then proceeds west past FAGARAS, shifting slightly to flow south through the Transylvanian Alps. It enters the Danube at NIKOPOL in Bulgaria.

Olza, Poland-Czechoslovakia

The river rises in the western Beskid Mountains of southern Poland. It is only a small river with a length of 40 miles (64 km). The river heads past JABLUNKOV in Czechoslovakia, then turns east and finally northwest to become a tributary of the larger Oder River to the northwest of NOVY BOHUMIN. The Olza provides a substantial amount of hydroelectric power for the neighboring region.

Ombrone, Italy

The main tributaries of the Ombrone are the Orcia and Arbia Rivers. It has a length of 100 miles (160 km). The Ombrone rises in the Monti Chianti, northeast of SIENA in central Italy. The river flows southwest to enter the Tyrrhenian Sea about ten miles (16 km) from GROSSETO.

Ondava, Czechoslovakia

The river rises in eastern Slovakia on the southern slopes of the Beskid Mountains northeast of BARDEJOV. The Ondava has a length of 85 miles (137 km). It flows south to the confluence with the Latoritsa River to form the Bodrog River southeast of TREBISOV.

Onega, European USSR

The Onega begins in Lake Lacha approximately 150 miles (240 km) north of the town of VOLOGDA in northern European Russia. It has a length of 252 miles (405 km). The rapids of the Onega make it impossible for river traffic and its only use is for timber floating. The river is tidal for up to 20 miles (32 km) from its mouth. The only settlement of any size on its banks is the town of ONEGA noted for its sawmills.

Onny, Shropshire, England

The Onny rises three miles northwest of RATLINGHOPE as the East Onny. Its other branch, the West Onny, rises near SHELVE in Shropshire. Both of these rivers run south eventually to join at EATON, approximately three miles (five km) east of BISHOP'S CASTLE. The Onny, as it is now called, flows southeast to BROMFIELD where it joins the River Teme.

Orchy, Strathclyde, Scotland

This river of Argyll runs southwest from Loch Tulla, located two miles (three km) north of the Bridge of Orchy. It continues down Glen Orchy to enter the northeast end of Loch Awe, a very narrow lake 24 miles (39 km) long which has a maximum depth of 300 feet (100 m).

Ore, Fife, Scotland

The Ore begins when it flows from Loch Ore, a small lake located north of the Scottish town of COWDENBEATH in the Fife region. The river heads east to join the River Leven west of WINDYGATES, a village noted for its distillery.

Orkla, Norway

The river rises northeast of DOMBAS in central Norway. It flows for a total length of 100 miles (160 km), first east to KVIKNE, then turns northeast passing the towns of RENNEBU and MELDAL before entering the Trondheim Fjord at ORKANGER.

Orne, France

The Orne rises near the town of SEES in the Orne Department of northwestern France. It runs for a total of 95 miles (153 km) from source to outlet. The river flows westward, northwest and finally north passing ARGENTAN and CAEN to enter the English Channel at OUISTREHAM. The area in and around Caen was the scene of extremely heavy fighting during the Allied invasion of 1944 in World War II.

Orrin, Highlands, Scotland

The Orrin rises in the East Monar Forest of the Ross and Cromarty District of Scotland. It flows on an easterly course to join the River Conon to the southwest of DINGWALL. The Orrin has some beautiful waterfalls located just a few miles from its confluence with the Conon.

Orwell, Suffolk, England

The River Orwell rises as the River Gipping. It has a length of 21 miles (34 km). The river flows southeast passing the towns of STOWMAR-KET, NEEDHAM and IPSWICH to join the River Stour estuary at HARWICH. It then flows into Harwich Harbor, and finally into the North Sea.

Orzyc, Poland

This Polish river begins as a small stream near MLAWA in northern Poland. It is only a minor river, flowing for a total of 84 miles (135 km). It heads north by northeast, then shifts to a south by southeast course flowing into the Narew River to the northeast of PULTUSK.

Osam, Bulgaria

The Osam is formed by the confluence of the Beli Osam and Cherni Osam Rivers, north of TROYAN in northern Bulgaria. The Osam is 207 miles (333 km) long. It flows from its confluence north past LOVECH, then LEVSKI to become a tributary of the Danube.

Oskol, European USSR

This river of European Russia rises northeast of KURSK in the Central Russian Uplands. Kursk was the site of the largest and most important tank battle of World War II, and was the decisive turning point for the Soviet Armies who totally destroyed the German tank divisions at Kursk. The Oskol is 285 miles (459 km) long. It flows south to pass STARY OSKOL, VALUIKI and KUPYANSK to enter the Donets River east of the town of IZYUM.

Otter, Somerset-Devon, England

The Otter rises on the southern slopes of the Blackdown Hills in the County of Somerset. It proceeds southwest through the towns of HONITON and OTTERY ST MARY in Devon. The river then flows into the English Channel on the east side of BUDLEIGH SALTERTON.

Ottery, Cornwall, England

The river rises near JACOBSTOW in Cornwall. It flows southeast to become a tributary of the River Tamar northeast of LAUNCESTON.

Ouche, France

The Ouche rises in the Côte d'Or Department of central France. It has a length of 60 miles (97 km). The river flows east past the French town of DIJON to the Saône River.

Oude, Strathclyde, Scotland

The river begins in Argyll and flows west from Loch Tralaig, a small lake and reservoir at the head of Loch Melfort. The Oude continues to where it enters the head of Loch Melfort.

Oulu, Finland

The Oulu River runs from LAKE OULU, Finland's fourth largest lake with an area of 387 square miles (1002 sq km). The river is only 65 miles (106 km) long but is one of the principal rivers of northern Finland. It drains an area of 9000 square miles (23,300 sq km). The river is only navigable for very short stretches due to rapids and turbulent waterfalls. The waterfalls provide a large proportion of northern Finland's hydroelectric power. The river empties into the Gulf of Bothnia.

Ounas, Finland

The Ounas is a river of Lapland in Finland which rises on the Norwegian border west of Lake Inari. It flows south on a winding course to join the River Kemi. The Ounas is 210 miles (340 km) long.

Ourthe, Belgium

The river rises initially as two small streams in eastern Belgium which meet west of HOUFFAL-IZE to form the Ourthe. It is 100 miles (160 km) long. The Ourthe flows northwest, then north past ESNEUX and ANGLEUR to join the Meuse River at LIEGE. The Ourthe's principal tributaries are the Amblève and Vesdre Rivers.

Ouse, Great, Northamptonshire, England

The Great Ouse rises north of BRACKLEY in Northamptonshire in the English Midlands. It is 156 miles (251 km) long. The river flows east, northeast and north past the towns of BUCKINGHAM, OLNEY (noted for its furniture manufacturing trade), the county town of BEDFORD (home of John Bunyan), the quaint village of ST NEOTS, the county town of HUNTINGDON and the cathedral town of ELY. The Great Ouse finally enters the Wash slightly northwest of KING'S LYNN.

Ouse, Little, Norfolk-Suffolk, England

The Little Ouse rises on the border between Norfolk and Suffolk to the north of REDGRAVE. It flows west through THETFORD and BRANDON, then joins the Great Ouse at BRANDON CREEK four miles (six km) northeast of LITTLEPORT.

Ouse, North Yorkshire-Humberside, England

The Ouse is formed by the confluence of the Rivers Swale and Ure east of BOROUGHBRIDGE in North Yorkshire. It drains the Vale of York, an area 30 miles (48 km) wide, at its broadest point. The river is only 61 miles (98 km) long but one of England's major rivers. The major tributaries of the Ouse are the Derwent which joins it from the east, and the Nidd, Aire, Don and Wharfe which flow from the Pennines west of the Ouse. The river is tidal to within one mile (1610 m) of NABURN. The Ouse flows southeast by the cathedral city of YORK famous for its minster and medieval walls, then to CAWOOD, SELBY and GOOLE, the chief port.

The Yorkshire Ouse River (left) near York and (below) north of Goole.

The Great Ouse near Roxton, Bedfordshire.

Approximately seven miles (11 km) east of Goole the Ouse joins the River Trent to form the Humber River estuary. For the tourist, Fountains Abbey lies along the Ouse's path.

Ouse, West Sussex, England
The river rises in St Leonard's Forest to the east of Horsham in West Sussex. It flows east then south through the resort of LEWES in East Sussex and finally into the English Channel at NEWHAVEN.

Oust, France
The Oust rises in the Armorican Massif northeast of CORLAY in Brittany. It is 80 miles (129 km) long. The river flows southeast past the towns of ROHAN and JOSSELIN to the Vilaine River near REDON. The Oust is an integral part of the Brest-Nantes Canal.

Ouzel, Bedfordshire, England
The Ouzel rises near DUNSTABLE, the sister town of LUTON and proceeds west, then northward past LEIGHTON BUZZARD and BLETCHLEY. The Ouzel joins the River Ouse at NEWPORT PAGNALL in Buckinghamshire.

Oykel, Highlands, Scotland
The Oykel begins south of Ben More Assynt, a peak rising to a height of 3273 feet (998 m) at the foot of Loch Assynt. The river flows southeast to the Oykel Bridge, then runs down the Strath Oykel to join the River Shin in the Kyle of Sutherland approximately four miles (six km) northwest of BONAR BRIDGE.

Pang, Berkshire, England
The Pang rises to the north of HAMPSTEAD NORRIS, a village six miles (ten km) northeast of NEWBURY. The village is known for the remains of a Roman Villa which is nearby. The river becomes a tributary of the River Thames at the town of PANGBOURNE.

Panaro, Italy
The source of the Panaro is two small headstreams which come together on Monte Cimone in the Etruscan Apennines of central Italy. The river is 103 miles (166 km) long. It runs past the towns of VIGNOLA and BONDENO to the Po near FERRARA.

Park Burn, Northumbria, England
The Park Burn rises in the ancient kingdom of Northumbria. The river is formed by the confluence of the Coanwood Burn and Fell Burn approximately three miles (five km) northwest of the town of HALTWHISTLE. The river runs into the River South Tyne to the southwest of Haltwhistle.

Parnu, European USSR
The Parnu rises in the marshlands near PAIDE in southwestern Estonia, one of the old Baltic Sea countries. The river flows for 90 miles (145 km) before entering Parnu Bay on the Baltic Sea.

Parret, Dorset-Somerset, England
The River Parret rises near CHEDDINGTON in Dorset. The river is only 35 miles (56 km) long. It runs first north, then northwest passing LANGPORT and BRIDGEWATER to enter Bridgewater Bay in the Bristol Channel west of BURNHAM-ON-SEA. The Parret's major tributaries are the Rivers Yeo and Tone.

Pechora, European USSR
The Pechora River rises in the northern Ural Mountains. The river is 1112 miles (1789 km) long. It flows northward through the Pechora Basin and is joined by its two chief tributaries the Izhma and Usa Rivers. The river is broad and slow moving on the majority of its course to the PECHORA GULF of the Barents Sea. The region through which the Pechora flows is utilized mostly for reindeer herding, although rich deposits of coal, petroleum and natural gas have been found in recent times.

Pedias, Cyprus
The Pedias is the largest river on the island of Cyprus. It is 60 miles (97 km) long. The river rises in the Olympus Mountains. It runs initially northeast, but changes direction shortly after to a more easterly course passing the beautiful Cypriot resort city of NICOSIA. The Pedias forms irrigation reservoirs to the west of Cyprus' principal resort city, FAMAGUSTA.

Peene, East Germany
The river is formed when several streams come together in the Mecklenburg area of northern Germany. The Peene is 97 miles (156 km) long and flows eastward through Kummerow Lake before entering the Pomeranian Bay on the Baltic Sea at PEENEMUNDE.

Pembroke, Dyfed, Wales
The Pembroke has its source five miles (eight km) east of the town of PEMBROKE. The river runs west through the town, and is overshadowed by the tremendous fortifications of Pembroke Castle where the powerful Norman Earls of Pembroke ruled an extensive territory in medieval times. The river forms an estuary past the town which continues westward for a short distance before turning north into MILFORD HAVEN (in Welsh – Aberdaugleddyf), this port and natural harbor is a major refinery and oil depot for large tankers.

Pendle Water, Lancashire, England
The Pendle rises on Pendle Hill at a height of 1831 feet (558 m) in the Forest of Pendle to the east of the town of CLITHEROE. The river flows into the River Calder north of the industrial town of BURNLEY.

Penklin Burn, Dumfries and Galloway, Scotland
This small river begins on the southern slopes of Lamachan Hill, a mountain in the Glentrool Forest Park, at a height of 2349 feet (716 m). The Penklin Burn flows south to join the River Cree at NEWTON STEWART.

Pescara, Italy

The Pescara begins in the Apennines near the town of AMATRICE in central Italy. The river is 90 miles (145 km) long. It flows southwest past AQUILA, then changes direction to a northeasterly course towards POPOLI. The Pescara's chief tributaries are the Orte, Sagittario and Tirino Rivers. It finally empties into the Adriatic Sea at the town of PESCARA.

Piave, Italy

This Italian river rises in the Carnic Alps of northern Italy. It flows north, then shifts to an east by northeast course past the town of BELLUNO. The Piave's principal tributaries are the Boite and Cordevole Rivers. The river is 137 miles (220 km) long. After Belluno, the Piave flows southeast past SAN DONA DI PIAVE to enter the Adriatic Sea approximately 20 miles (32 km) to the northeast of VENICE.

Piddle, Dorset, England

The river has its source near ALTON PANCRAS. The Piddle heads southeast through PUDDLE-TOWN, a village northeast of DORCHESTER, then moves north of WAREHAM to enter Poole Harbor.

Piddle Brook, Hereford-Worcester, England

Piddle Brook rises east of WORCESTER, famous for its cathedral and china industry. The river flows south to join the River Avon between the village of Wyre Piddle and the town of PERSHORE.

Pilica, Poland

The source of the Pilica is northwest of WOLBROM in central Poland. The river has a length of 195 miles (314 km). It flows north, then northeast to become a tributary of the Vistula River, approximately 20 miles (32 km) south of the capital city of WARSAW.

Piltanton Burn, Dumfries and Galloway, Scotland

This river rises on the Rinns of Galloway, an anvil shaped peninsula at the southwest extremity of Scotland. This region in ancient Celtic times was the Princedom of Galloway, and the ruler was a man of great wealth and power. The river runs southeast to join the Water of Luce at Luce Bay to the south of GLENLUCE.

Pinega, European USSR

This river rises approximately 67 miles (108 km) north of KOTLAS. The Pinega is 407 miles (655 km) long. It flows northwest, then southwest to become a major tributary of the Northern Dvina River. It is navigable for more than half of its total length.

Piniós, Greece

The river rises east of METSOVON in the Pindus Mountains. It is 135 miles (217 km) long and flows swiftly to the town of KALABAKA where it enters the large Thessalian Plain. This

portion of Greece was noted in ancient times for its horsemen and wild warriors. The river continues eastward and passes TRIKALA, a market center for local produce and the ancient city of LARISA. Leaving Larisa the river flows through the Vale of Tempe situated between the mountains of Olympus and Ossa. In ancient times the Vale was associated with the God Apollo and during the Pythian Games, laurels were gathered in the Vale to bestow upon the victors of the competitions, a far cry from today's money- and status-oriented world. The gorge through the Vale of Tempe was the primary invasion route for Alexander the Great's army when he invaded Greece from Macedonia. The river's final destination is the Aegean Sea.

Pite, Sweden

The Pite is a river of Lapland in northern Sweden. It is 230 miles (370 km) long and rises near the Norwegian border at the foot of Mt Sulitelma. There are several large hydroelectric power stations along its course which provides a substantial amount of power for the local region. The river continues until it enters the GULF OF BOTHNIA.

Platani, Sicily

The Platani is formed by the confluence of several streams southeast of the town of PRIZZI in southwestern Sicily. The river is 70 miles (113 km) long. It runs south for a very short distance, then west and finally southwest to enter the Mediterranean Sea near Cape Bianco. The Platani was known by the ancient Greeks as the Halyais River.

Po, Italy

The Po is the principal river of Italy. It is 405 miles (652 km) long. It rises at a height of 6000 feet (1800 m) in the Cottian Alps very near the French border. By the time the turbulent river has flowed down to the city of TURIN, some of its major tributaries have already swollen its waters, namely the Chisone, Maira and Varaita. At Turin the river turns eastward and by the time it reaches the great Lombardy Plain it has been joined by the Dora Baltea, Orco, Riparia and Stura Rivers. The Po now is at the western edge of the Lombardy Plain which extends for 235 miles (378 km) to the

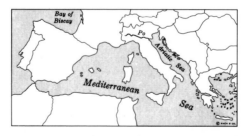

Adriatic coast. As the Po heads toward the coast, it is joined by quite large tributaries from the Swiss Alps – the Ticino, the Lambro, the Adda, the Oglio and the Mincio. The only other major river which joins the Po is the Adige. The river now progresses through a series of natural levées along its banks which have been built up over centuries so that the river is actually higher than the surrounding

land. This has resulted in floods of catastrophic proportions, but modern engineering has cured this to some extent. The river is divided into several distributary channels approximately 25 miles (40 km) from the sea. In past centuries, these distributaries were a distance of 30 miles (48 km) upstream but as the Po continues to bring silt down, the channels silt up and extend themselves further outward at a very rapid rate, each year advancing more and more into the sea. Along the Adriatic coast are numerous lagoons caused by the massive Po delta over the centuries. One of these ancient lagoons contains VENICE, an important historic landmark and once a great maritime power. The Po finally empties into the Adriatic Sea now at TAGLIO DI PO, a village midway between VENICE and RAVENNA.

Pola, European USSR

The Pola rises in the Valdai Hills to the west of Lake Seliger in the western portion of European Russia. The river is 90 miles (145 km) long. It flows northwest to join the delta of the Lovat River at Lake Ilmen.

Polmaddy Burn, Dumfries and Galloway, Scotland

This Scottish river rises on the eastern slopes of Corserine at a height of 2668 feet (814 m) in the Rinns of Kells. It flows east past Dundaugh Castle to the Water of Ken between CARSPHAIRN and DALRY. This region is noted for its superb fishing.

Pont, Northumberland, England

The river rises near the village of LITTLE WHITTINGTON, and flows east past MATFEN, HAWKWELL and STAMFORDHAM and finally joins the River Blyth a few miles north of PONTELAND.

Poprad, Czechoslovakia-Poland

The river rises in the High Tatra Mountains northeast of STARY SMOKOVEC. The Poprad flows southeast, northeast and finally northwest before crossing the Polish frontier and joining the Dunajec River near NOWY SACZ. The river is 95 miles (153 km) long.

Potrail Water, Strathclyde, Scotland

The Potrail Water rises in the Lowther Hills at the foot of Ballencleuch Law at a height of 2000 feet (600 m). The river runs north to join the Daer Water and form the River Clyde a few miles south of ELVANFOOT.

Poulter, Derbyshire, England

The source of the Poulter is to the southeast of BOLSOVER, famous for the remains of a Norman castle rebuilt in the 17th century, and an industrial center for chemical products and oil refining. It flows east through Clumber Park in the Dukeries to become a tributary of the River Idle south of EAST RETFORD in Nottinghamshire.

Two photographs of the Prut River in the Carpathian Mountains.

Prahova, Rumania

The source of the Prahova is in the Translyvanian Alps. The river flows in a southerly direction past the town of SINAIA, then southeast past CAMPINA to join the Ialomita River southeast of the oil refinery city of PLOESTI. During World War II, Ploesti was one of the principal targets for the American Strategic Bomber Command because it supplied the Third Reich with a large proportion of its oil requirements. The Prahova is 80 miles (129 km) long.

Pregel, European USSR

The river is 180 miles (290 km) long and formed by the confluence of the Angerapp and Inster Rivers below the town of CHERNYAK-HOVSK. It runs west past ZNAMENSK to the Vistula Lagoon just below the city of KALINGRAD. The Pregel is joined to the Courland Lagoon by the canalized Deima River.

Pripyat, European USSR

This Ukrainian river rises near the Bug River. It has a length of 500 miles (800 km). The head of navigation for the river is PINSK. Its major tributaries are the Goryn, Ptich, Sluch, Styr and Uzh Rivers. The Pripyat is joined to the Bug and Neman Rivers by canals. The river continues eastward to where it enters the Dnepr about 50 miles (80 km) north of KIEV, the capital of the Ukrainian SSR.

Prosen Water, Tayside, Scotland

The Prosen Water rises near Mayar, a peak in the mountains of Tayside, at a height of 3043 feet (928 m). The river runs down Glen Prosen and is joined by a few small tributary streams from the northeast as it runs southeast. It joins the River South Esk a few miles southeast of the town of KIRRIEMUIR.

Prosna, Poland

This Polish river rises northeast of OLESNO in central Poland. It is 135 miles (217 km) long. The river flows northwest past WIERUSZOW and KALISZ to join the Warta River close to PYZDRY.

Prosnica, Poland

The length of the Prosnica is 102 miles (164 km). It runs northwest from SZCZECINEK to enter the Baltic Sea at KOLOBRZEG.

Prut, Rumania-European SSR

The Prut rises in the Carpathian Mountains on the north side of Goverla peak in the Ukraine. The river flows on an easterly course through the important commercial town of CHER-NOVTSÝ. Continuing on course for a further 20 miles (32 km), the Prut becomes the boundary between the Soviet Union and Rumania. In bygone days, the river was entirely within the boundaries of Rumania, dividing Bessarabia from Moldavia, but in 1940 the former was lost to the Soviet Union. The Prut is navigable as far as the town of LEOVO. It is 530 miles (850 km) long. The Prut runs into the Danube near the town of RENI.

Psel, European USSR

The Psel rises in the Russian Upland of western European Russia. It heads southwest initially, then turns south to join the Dnieper River at KREMECHUG. The Psel is 435 miles (700 km).

Ptich, European USSR

The Ptich rises in central White Russia to the west of the city of MINSK. It is 260 miles (414 km) long and flows southeast and then south to join the Pripyat River west of MOZYR.

Quioch Water, Grampian Region, Scotland

This river rises in the beautiful and dangerous CAIRNGORM MOUNTAINS of northern Scotland. The highest peak in the Cairngorms is Ben Macdui which stands at 4296 feet (1310 m). The Quioch Water heads south to join the River Dee to the west of the village of BRAEMAR. The village is noted for hosting the 'Gathering,' the most famous Highland Games in Scotland, and for its 17th-century castle. Braemar is a popular tourist resort.

Raab, Austria

The river rises in the scenic Fischbach Alps northwest of the town of WEIZ. The Raab is 100 miles (160 km) long. It flows northeast across the Hungarian frontier to GYOR where the Répce River joins it to run into the Danube.

Rance, France

The river rises slightly west of COLLINEE in the western region of France. It runs for a total length of 60 miles (97 km). The Rance heads northeast past DINAN and forms a long estuary, approximately 13 miles (21 km), to the town of ST MALO where it enters the English Channel.

Rapido, Italy

The Rapido rises east of ARINA in the Apennines of central Italy. It is 20 miles (32 km) long. The river joins the Liri River past the town of CASSINO where thousands of Allied troops lost their lives in World War II.

Ray, Wiltshire, England

The Ray rises southwest of SWINDON, an industrial town west of London noted for its aircraft and railway engineering works. The river runs north to become a tributary of the River Thames below CRICKLADE.

Rede, Northumberland, England

The Rede rises on Carter Fell in the famous Cheviot Hills of Northumberland near the English-Scottish border. The river is only 21 miles (34 km) long but flows through an interesting region of northeastern England. It runs southeast through the Catcleugh Reservoir, the Redesdale Forest and the village of ROCHESTER before entering the North Tyne River near the town of BELLINGHAM.

Top: The Reuss River in central Switzerland.
Right: The Reuss River at Lucerne.

Rega, Poland

This Polish river rises in the lakes northeast of the town of DRAWSKO in northwestern Poland. The Rega is 118 miles (190 km) long and runs southwest, then turns northwest before entering the Baltic Sea near KOLBERG.

Reno, Italy

The source of the Reno is in the Etruscan Apennines of central Italy. The river runs for a total length of 131 miles (211 km). It flows north and easterly past the towns of PORRETTA TERME, CENTO and ARGENTA before changing course to a southeasterly direction. The Reno's main tributaries are the Idice, Sillaro, Senio and Santerno Rivers. It finally enters the Adriatic Sea near the city of RAVENNA.

Répce, Austria-Hungary

The river rises near ASPANG in the Lower Austrian regions. It is 100 miles (160 km) long. It flows southeast entering Hungary slightly northeast of KOSZEG. The river is connected by a canal to the Lake of Neusiedler. It turns east to join the Raab River at GYOR.

Reuss, Switzerland

The Reuss is formed by the confluence of two streams running from the St Gotthard and Furka Passes, southwest of ANDERMATT in central Switzerland. It is 99 miles (159 km) long and runs north through Lake Lucerne to become a tributary of the Aare River.

Reut, European USSR

The river rises northwest of the town of TYRNOVO in Moldavia. It is 122 miles (196 km) long. The Reut is the principal tributary of the Dnestr River which it joins at DUBOSSARY.

Rheidol, Dyfed, Wales

The Rheidol rises in the hills north of PLYNLIMON in Cardiganshire. The river is only 24 miles (38 km) long. It runs south to the Devil's Bridge where it turns to a westerly course. The river flows on to enter Cardigan Bay at the lovely Welsh town of ABERYSTWYTH.

Rhin, East Germany

The Rhin rises in the lake district to the west of FURSTENBERG in East Germany. The Rhin is 65 miles (105 km) long. It flows south through Lake Ruppin, then southwest as a canal to join the Havel River west of RHINOW.

Rhine, Switzerland-West Germany-Holland

The Rhine is one of Europe's most important and scenic waterways. It is a river which has witnessed numerous battles and campaigns from Roman times to the present. The legions of Rome had garrison stations along the Rhine to warn of the Teutonic tribes' encroachment upon Imperial territory. The Rhine has a total length of 820 miles (1320 km). It actually has two principal sources: the Hinter Rhine which

Right: The Rheidol River near Pont-erwyd in central Wales.

From the cathedral at Basel looking towards the city's industrial center showing the bridges over the Rhine which link upper and lower Basel.

The Rhine Falls near Schaffhausen in Switzerland are the largest in Europe. Laufen Castle is in the background.

runs out of a glacier at the foot of the Rheinwaldhorn in the Adula Alps; the other is the Vorder Rhine which flows from the extremely deep mountain lake of Toma situated near the summit of the 10,000-foot (3000 m) Piz Badus. Both of these mountain streams link up at REICHENAU to form the Alpine Rhine.

The Rhine is already an important and great river at this stage. It runs north to pass the ancient Roman encampment of CHUR which is noted for green meadows, vineyards and huge orchards.

Flowing on a straight course, the Rhine next serves as the border of the tiny country of Liechtenstein and Austria. It then enters Lake Constance which settles down the flow of the river considerably. The color of water when the river leaves Lake Constance is a shimmering green. The river flows on a westerly course to the town of SCHAFFHAUSEN; it then runs over a series of cataracts which provide the neighboring industries with

hydroelectric power. The Rhine now heads for the important Swiss city of BASEL, a major transportation and communication center. (The river is navigable from Basel to its mouth.) For a considerable proportion of its course the Rhine marks the boundary between France and Germany. The surrounding countryside includes the Vosges Range, Black Forest and the Odenwald which are some examples of natural beauty which makes this region one of the most popular tourist areas in Europe. The principal tributaries of the Rhine are the Neckar, Nahe, Moselle and Lahn Rivers. Between KARLSRUHE and KOBLENZ the Rhine is flanked by vineyards surrounding romantic castles. It flows past MANNHEIM, the second largest inland harbor in Europe; WORMS, the center of the *Nibelungenlied* legend and the heroic Siegfried; MAINZ, where it changes direction to a westerly course; and KOBLENZ, one of Germany's commercial centers and port. Now the river leaves the mountains and passes the capital of West

The Rhine from Drachenfels mountain.

Germany, BONN, Beethoven's birth place. The river has now widened to 3000 feet (1000 m) and passes the industrial heartland of West Germany: COLOGNE, DUSSELDORF, ESSEN and DUISBURG, the latter being the head of deep sea navigation. The Rhine proceeds now to cross the Dutch border and divides into two separate rivers, the Lek and Waal. The Rhine then breaks up into numerous arms and channels which when added together with the Dutch system of canals provide access to AMSTERDAM, ROTTERDAM, ANTWERP and the HOOK OF HOLLAND before flowing into the North Sea.

Rhondda, Glamorgan, Wales

The Rhondda begins at the confluence of the Afon Rhondda Fawr and Afon Rhondda Fach, two streams which rise on the hills west of ABERDARE. These two streams flow parallel to each other until they join together at PORTH. The Rhondda finally becomes a tributary of the River Taff at PONTYPRIDD.

Rhône, France

The Rhône rises at a height of 6000 feet (1800 m) on the Rhône glacier in the Central Alps. This fast-flowing river runs south through a steep-sided limestone gorge, then shifts to a southwesterly course heading towards MARTIGNY. The Rhône is joined by three glacial rivers in its main valley: the Visp, Dixence and Navigenze. Directly after Martigny the Rhône turns northwesterly and heads for Lake Geneva, cutting its way through the mountains in the St Maurice Gorge which is approximately 12 miles (19 km) long. The Rhône deposits a tremendous load of silt in Lake Geneva before leaving the lake as a beautifully clear river. At a position located 31 miles (50 km) downstream the Rhône is dammed to form a lake 14 miles (23 km) long. This dam provides a large percentage of France's hydroelectric power. The river journeys on to the city of LYONS where it picks up the Saône, its principal tributary. For approximately two to three miles (three to five

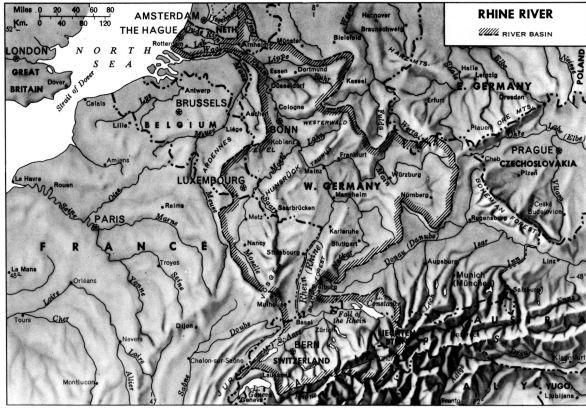

Top center: Le Pont D'Avignon on the Rhône in southern France.

Below: Vineyards and a castle on the Rhine.

Center bottom: Basle's harbor on the Rhine.

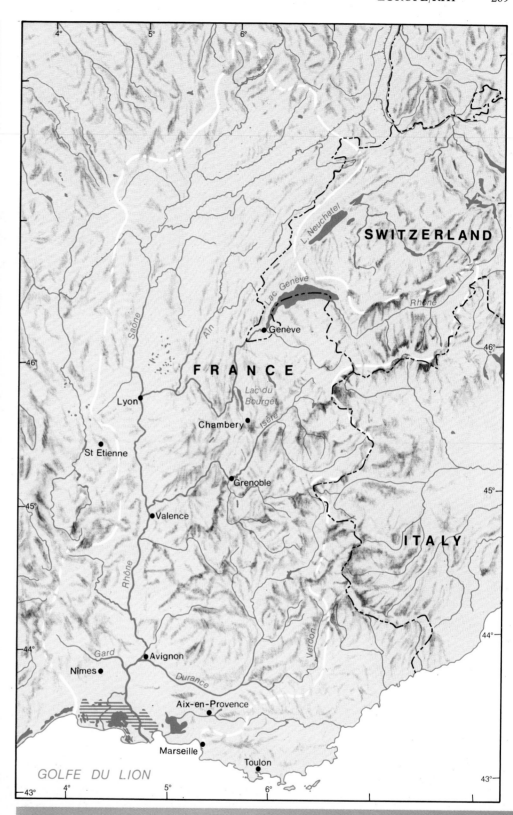

Right: The Rhône at Arles.

Above: The Rhône at Annecy.
Right: Furka Pass above the Rhône.

km) downstream from its confluence, the waters of the left bank are distinctly blue, characteristic of the Rhône, while the right bank is a brownish color, a characteristic of the Saône. The total length of the Rhône is 510 miles (820 km). It is extremely difficult to navigate because of its swift current and fluctuating depths. After being joined by the Saône the Rhône heads south for ARLES, passing the towns of VIENNE, VALENCE, MONTELIMAR and AVIGNON, the latter famous as the seat of the French Popes during the great internal division of the Roman Catholic Church. The Rhône also receives three chief tributaries from the left banks: the Isère, Drôme and Durance Rivers. The Isère alone increases the volume of the Rhône by 25 percent. The delta of the river begins three miles (five km) above the town of Arles. The river separates into two channels – the Grand Rhône and the Petit Rhône. When these channels enter the Gulf of Lion, their mouths are 26 miles (42 km) apart. The delta of the Rhône is called the Camargue, and is composed of marshes, sand deltas and lagoons.

Above: The Rhône near Valance, France.
Left: Lake Geneva. The Rhône flows into the north end of the lake and flows out of the southern end.

Ribble, North Yorkshire, England
The Ribble begins on Gayle Moor in North Yorkshire. It is 100 miles (160 km) long and flows south to SETTLE and LONG PRESTON before shifting to a southwesterly course through PRESTON. It enters the Irish Sea between SOUTHPORT and LYTHAM ST ANNE'S. The Ribble is navigable to large sea vessels from Preston.

Rion, European USSR
The Rion is the principal river of the Georgian USSR and rises in the Caucasus Mountains near the Mamison Pass. It is 180 miles (290 km) long. It runs south, then west past the town of ONI and enters the Black Sea at POTI.

Risle, France
This river in northwestern France rises to the north of COURTOMER. The Risle flows northward past LAIGLE, BRIONNE and PONT-AUDEMER to enter the Seine estuary at the port of HONFLEUR. The river is 75 miles (121 km) long.

Roch, West Yorkshire, England
The source of the Roch is near the borders of Greater Manchester and West Yorkshire just north of LITTLEBOROUGH. The Roch flows southwest through Littleborough and ROCH-DALE, the latter known for its textiles and engineering works. The river proceeds on course until it enters the River Irwell south of BURY.

Roding, Essex, England
The Roding begins near CHAPEL END to the northeast of BISHOP'S STORTFORD. It heads south to become a tributary of the River Thames at Barking Creek in the East End of London.

Roer, Belgium-Holland
The Roer begins in Belgium and flows for a total of 110 miles (180 km). It crosses into Germany and heads past the towns of DUREN and JULICH, then turns southeast to VLODROP and enters the Netherlands. It runs into the Meuse River west of ROERMOND.

Above: Near the mouth of the Ribble River.

Ros, European USSR
The Ros rises southeast of KAZATIN in the central Ukraine. It runs on an easterly course past BELAYA TSERKOV and BOGUSLAV to join the Dnepr River southeast of the town of KANEV. The Ros has a length of 172 miles (277 km).

Rositsa, Bulgaria
This Bulgarian river begins in the Kalofer Mountains of northern Bulgaria. It is 112 miles (180 km) long. The Rositsa flows past SEVLIYEVO before joining the Yantra River northwest of DRAGANOVO.

Rothay, Cumbria, England
The Rothay rises a few miles north of the village of GRASMERE in Cumbria. It flows southwards to Grasmere Lake, then swings eastward to Rydal Water, and finally turns southeast to enter the River Brathay near the resort town of AMBLESIDE at the head of Lake Windermere.

Rother, Derbyshire, England
The river rises near CLAY CROSS, a small town noted for its coal and iron works. It runs north through CHESTERFIELD and STAVELEY to join the River Don at ROTHERHAM midway between Sheffield and Doncaster.

Rother, East Sussex, England
This river runs from just south of ROTHERFIELD to the English Channel southeast of the coastal town of RYE. Rye was one of the ancient towns of the Cinque Port Confederation and is still a very popular summer resort town.

Rother, Hampshire-West Sussex, England
The Rother rises near SELBORNE in Hampshire. It runs south to SHEET, then eastward past MIDHURST, a beautiful country village, noted for one of the most famous inns in the country, the Spread Eagle built in 1430, and for its polo grounds. The Rother River joins the River Arun at PULBOROUGH in West Sussex. The Rother is about 25 miles (40 km) long.

Right: The Sava meets the Danube at Belgrade.

Rubicon, Italy

This river rises in the Etruscan Apennines, northwest of SAN MARINO in central Italy and flows for only 15 miles (24 km). The Rubicon enters the Adriatic Sea near RIMINI. The River was made famous when Julius Caesar disobeyed the order of the Senate not to cross the Rubicon and marched on Rome.

Ruhr, West Germany

The Ruhr lies in the industrial heartland of Germany. It rises on the northern slopes of the Sauerland. The prime usage of the Ruhr is not for navigation or even hydroelectric power but for drinking water which is piped to the industrial cities of the Ruhr Valley. The river is 130 miles (210 km) long. It empties into the Rhine at the river port of RUHRORT.

Rye, North Yorkshire, England

The river rises in the Cleveland Hills of North Yorkshire. The Rye runs southeast past the famous abbey of Rievaulx; Helmsley and Nunnington before emptying its waters into the River Derwent four miles (six km) northeast of MALTON.

Saale, Saxonian, West-East Germany

The Saxonian Saale rises in the Fichtelbirge at a height of 2400 feet (730 m) very close to the Czechoslovakian-German frontier. The river has a length of 265 miles (426 km). It flows north through the industrial city of HOF, which is one of the traffic checkpoints between East and West Germany. Flowing through East Germany the Saxonian Saale's next stop is the Bleiloch Reservoir and dam which contains an area slightly in excess of 3.5 square miles (nine sq km).. The river then moves on to the Hohenwarte Reservoir and dam which provides a large amount of the area's hydroelectric power. It flows through the old river town of SAALFELD which is a good blend of the old and new before passing on to RUDOLSTADT and JENA, the latter famous as the location of one of the major battles of the Napoleonic Wars. Today, Jena is famous for its optical factories. The river continues through one of the rich fruit regions of Germany which is famous for its vineyards. The Saxonian Saale's major tributary, the Unstrut River, joins it at NAUMBURG where the Saale becomes navigable. The Saale proceeds north by northeast passing numerous old German castles before reaching its destination, the Elbe River, between DESSAU and MAGDEBURG.

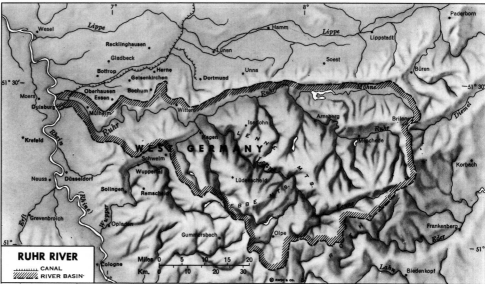

RUHR RIVER
······· CANAL
////// RIVER BASIN

Saar, France-Germany

The Saar rises in the Vosges, when two mountain streams come together near LE DONON, a mountain peak in close proximity to the Franco-German border. The Saar is 150 miles (240 km) long. It proceeds north through the northeastern region of France, crossing over into the Saar Territory at SAAREGUEMINES. The river passes through rolling hills, covered with thick forests before it makes a wide double loop famous the world over for the spectacular scenery on its banks.

This region of the Saar has always been one of the prime reasons why France and Germany have been continuously at loggerheads over it for the past thousand years. After World War I the Saar was taken from Germany and controlled very loosely by the League of Nations from 1918 to 1935. The French government assumed control of the Saar for six years from 1945 to 1951. The Saar was restored to Germany on both occasions because of plebiscites which were held showing that it was the wish of the people to

remain an integral part of the West German Republic. The Saar becomes a tributary of the Moselle River at the town of KONZ southwest of TRIER.

Sado, Portugal

The Sado rises in southern Portugal near OURIQUE. It is 110 miles (180 km) long. It flows northward past ALCACER DO SAL to widen into a large estuary on the Atlantic Ocean at SETUBAL south of Lisbon.

Sajo, Czechoslovakia-Hungary
The river rises in the Slovak Ore Mountains of Czechoslovakia. It flows for 125 miles (201 km) from its source to head south past DOBSINA and ROZNAVA, then southeast into Hungary. The Sajo then passes MISKOLC to join the Tisza River southwest of TOKAJ.

Sakmara, European USSR
The Sakmara rises in the southern Ural Mountains to the southwest of the town of ASKAROVO. It is 440 miles (710 km) long. The river runs south, then turns to a westerly course to join the Ural River west of CHKALOV.

Salor, Spain
This Spanish river rises near MONTANCHEZ in Sierra de Guadalupe, central Spain. The Salor is 78 miles (126 km) long. It flows northwest to join the River Tagus southwest of ALCANTARA at the Portuguese frontier.

Salso, Sicily
The Salso begins in the Madonie Mountains of Sicily, north of the town of PETRALIA SOTTANA. It is 70 miles (113 km) long. It flows south to enter the Mediterranean Sea at LICATA.

Salwarpe, Hereford and Worcester, England
The river rises near BROMSGROVE. It runs southwest into the River Severn three miles (five km) north of the city of WORCESTER, famous for its porcelain china and cathedral.

Samara, European USSR
The Samara rises in the southern Ural Mountain Range to the northwest of the town of PAVLOVKA. The river is 365 miles (587 km) long. It flows west past PEREVOLOTSKOYE and SOROCHINSK. The Samara receives the Buzuluk and Tok Rivers as its major tributaries. The river continues on to where it joins the Volga near KUYBYSHEV.

Sambre, France-Belgium
The river rises near LE NOUVION in northern France. It is 120 miles (190 km) long. The Sambre has been canalized to a great extent to make use of its length. The river flows northeast past LANDRECIES and MAUBEUGE into Belgium, then passes CHARLEROI and CHATELET to join the Meuse River at NAMUR.

San, Poland
The San rises in the Beshchady Mountains of southeastern Poland. It runs for a total of 247 miles (397 km) first past the towns of LESKO and SANOK, then east past PRZEMYSL and finally northwest through JAROSLAW and NISKO. The chief tributaries of the San are the Wisznia, Wislok and Tanen Rivers. The river finally runs into the Vistula.

Sana, Yugoslavia
The Sana is 102 miles (164 km) long. Its source is found to the west of JAJCE in northwestern Bosnia. The river heads north past the towns of KLJUC and PRIJEDOR to join the Una River.

Saône, France
One of the major rivers of France, the Saône rises as a group of headstreams in the Vosges of southern Lorraine at a height of over 1300 feet (400 m). The river is 300 miles (480 km) long. It flows southwest through several small towns namely, GRAY AUXONNE, and ST JEAN-DE-LOSNE, built initially at bridge points over the river.

The river receives its share of tributaries of which the most important are the Seille, Veyle, Reyssouze, Ognon and Doubs Rivers. The valley of the Saône is well defined and broad; the river has a steady flow and the precipitation annually is constant resulting in a stable river. The river flows with the Côte d'Or on one side and the Massif Central on the other. It continues on through the beautiful vineyards of Burgundy to join the Rhône at LYONS.

Sark, Dumfries and Galloway, Scotland
The Sark begins in the Dumfries and Galloway region of Scotland. It flows on a southerly course along the border between the two old enemies, England and Scotland. It runs to the head of the Solway Firth southeast of the town of GRETNA.

Sarthe, France
The river rises in the Perche Hills, north of the town of MORTAGNE in western France. The river has a length of 175 miles (282 km). The Sarthe flows south for a distance before turning to a more southwesterly course, flowing past ALENCON and LE MANS (the latter is the head of navigation) before it meets with the Mayenne River to form the Maine River. The Maine is only seven miles (11 km) long but is one of the tributaries of the much larger Loire.

Sava, Yugoslavia
The Sava rises high in the Julian Alps of Yugoslavia. It has the distinction of being the longest river in the country, with a length of 583 miles (938 km). The river flows initially as two headstreams, the Sava Dolinka and the Sava Bohinjka, which meet in the Alpine tract before running down to the Ljubljana Basin. Upon reaching the city of LJUBLJANA, the Sava turns to an easterly course and heads for a narrow gorge 15 miles (24 km) long which it passes through on the way to the Lower Sava Valley. Once out of the gorge, the Sava enters the large Plain of Posavina. This entire area was once the gulf of the sea in bygone days and is now filled with sediments and alluvial deposits. Crossing this large plain the Sava receives some of its chief tributaries, notably

the Una, Kupa, Bosna and Drina Rivers. The Sava drains an area slightly in excess of 34,000 square miles (88,000 sq km). The river becomes a tributary of the Danube at the capital of Yugoslavia, BELGRADE, the ancient fortress city. The Sava is navigable from the town of SISAK to Belgrade, a length of 367 miles (591 km), which makes it the longest navigable river in the middle Danube basin. This area is a prime tourist attraction with access to MITROVICA, located at the confluence with the Drina, by swift passenger vessels.

Sazava, Czechoslovakia
The Sazava rises in the Bohemian-Moravian heights. It is 135 miles (217 km) long. The river flows west past the towns of PRIBYSLAV and SAZAVA to enter the Vltava River at DAVLE.

Scheldt, Low Countries
The Scheldt is only 270 miles (430 km) long but flows through one of Europe's most historic areas. It rises in a tiny lake near the old abbey of St Martin in Picardy in France. The river then flows northeast past VALENCIENNES, then across the Belgium border and through the towns of TOURNAI, GHENT and the great port city of ANTWERP. The port of Antwerp is 55 miles (88 km) from the sea but due once again to the ingenuity of man and with the help of inland waterways, it serves eastern France, parts of central Europe and western Germany. At the last count over 250 shipping lines were actively utilizing the docks at Antwerp. Leaving Antwerp, the Scheldt enters the

*Above: An aerial photograph of the Saône River.
Right: The Sava River at Zuzemberg, Yugoslavia,
30 miles (50 km) from Zagreb.*

Netherlands. The river has always been a geographical headache to the Dutch who have to cross through Belgium territory to gain access to Zealand Flanders. The river carries on to its estuary and is now called the Western Scheldt.

Secchia, Italy
The river rises in the Etruscan Apennines of central Italy. It is 97 miles (156 km) long. It runs north to enter the Po west of OSTIGLIA.

Segre, France-Spain
The Segre rises above SAILLAGOUSE in the Pyrenees of southern France. The river is 167 miles (269 km) long. It flows southwest entering Spain at PUIGCERDA, continuing on past LERIDA to join the Ebro at MEQUINENZA.

Segura, Spain
The river rises in the Spanish province of Jaen. It flows for 200 miles (320 km) east, past the towns of ALBACETE and MURCIA. Its major tributary is the Mundo River. The Segura enters the Mediterranean Sea approximately 20 miles (32 km) southwest of ALICANTE.

Seine, France
One of the primary rivers of France, the Seine rises at a height of 1500 feet (460 km) on the Plâteau of Langres. During its first few miles, the Seine runs underground and reappears quite frequently, more like a 'jack in the box' than a river. Also it runs dry as far as CHATILLON during exceptionally hot seasons. The river drains the majority of northern France and is the principal river of the Paris Basin. Of course, to the tourist the Seine remains one of the main attractions of France. The river is divided into three distinct sections: the first runs from its source to the tiny town of ROMILLY; the middle course heads from Romilly to FONTAINEBLEAU, the former palace and retreat of the kings of France; the lower course runs northwesterly to the English Channel. The Seine flows through Paris for approximately eight miles of its course, and the Greater Metropolitan Area for twenty miles. Lutetia, the Roman name for the city of Paris and capital of France, was only a tiny settlement on the river's two islands, the Ile de la Cité and the Ile St-Louis, still the heart of this famous metropolis. The Ile de la Cité is probably best remembered for its cathedral of Nôtre Dame, one of the most famous cathedrals in the world. The river divides Paris into two parts; the university and the Latin Quarter are on the left bank, while on the right bank are the shopping centers and public buildings. As one progresses downstream, close to the right bank are the Louvre and the Tuileries, both royal palaces, but now utilized as museums of art. The embankments along

The Scheldt River of Belgium. Below is the Pont des Trous over the river at Tournai. The three photographs along the bottom of the page show the various activities of the vital harbor of Antwerp.

the Seine are the book enthusiast's delight for here the stalls have old and rare books as well as manuscripts in numerous languages which the avid buyer can pick up for a reasonable price. The Seine has a total of 29 bridges over it within the city limits. On a nice spring and summer day, the tourists line up to watch the fishermen. As the river leaves Paris, the banks are lined with huge industrial plants and factories. The river then proceeds towards the English Channel, and is tidal as far as the great port city of ROUEN, a much sought-after city during the seemingly everlasting wars fought between the once great enemies the English and French. Between Rouen and the sea is LE HAVRE, a crude oil port and depot and the second largest port in France. Now the river enters its estuary and together with various small tributaries runs into the sea. The Seine is 482 miles (776 km) long.

Seiont, Gwynedd, Wales

The Seiont rises near LLANDEINIOLEN in Gwynedd. It runs southwest, then north to enter the Menai Straits west of CAERNARVON. The town of Caernarvon is noted for its famous castle fortification which was built to contain the Welsh during the English conquest of Wales.

Below: Paris and the River Seine.

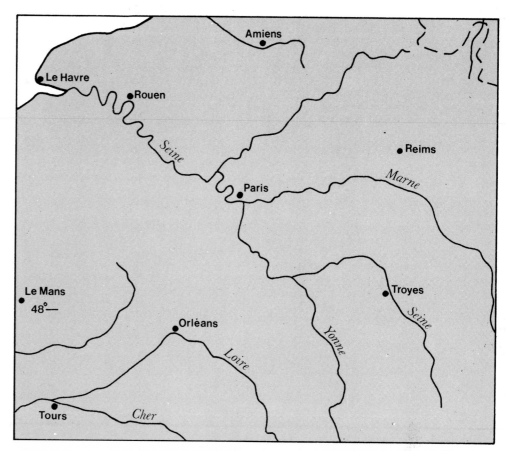

Right: The largest of the bridges across the Severn.
Bottom left: The Severn railway bridge at Sharpness, Gloucester, England.
Far right: Bridgnorth, Salop, England and the Severn River.
Bottom right: Bridge over the Severn at Ironbridge.

Sem, Wiltshire-Dorset, England
The Sem rises in Wiltshire near the Dorset border. It runs east to SHAFTESBURY, then continues on its easterly course until it meets the River Nadder southwest of TISBURY.

Sence, Leicestershire, England (1)
The River Sence rises on the western slopes of the Charnwood Forest in Leicestershire. This area of the famous 'Fox Hunting County' is noted for its scenic beauty. The river continues southwest to join the River Anker northeast of ATHERSTONE.

Sence, Leicestershire, England (2)
The river rises near BILLESDON in Leicestershire. It runs southwest, then west to its confluence with the larger River Soar at the village of Enderby near the city of LEICESTER.

Serchio, Italy
The river rises in the Etruscan Apennines of central Italy. It is 64 miles (103 km) long. The Serchio flows south to enter the Ligurian Sea northwest of the city of PISA, famous for its leaning tower.

Serein, France
The Serein rises northwest of ARNAY-LE-DUC in central France. The river heads northwest past CHABLIS to join the Yonne River northwest of AUXERRE. It is 115 miles (185 km) long.

Sesia, Italy
The river begins on the slopes of Monte Rosa in northern Italy. The Sesia is 86 miles (138 km) long. It runs south and east past VARALLO, then south again past VERCELLI to join the Po River east of CASALE MONFERRANTO.

Severn, Yorkshire, England
This North Yorkshire river rises in the Cleveland Hills to the northwest of Rosedale Abbey set in a beautiful location. It flows south to the River Rye one mile (1610 m) southeast of BRAWBY.

Severn, Wales-England
The Severn rises on the eastern slopes of Plynlimon Fawr in the central part of Wales. It runs for a total length of just over 200 miles (320 km). The river flows northeast to the Vale

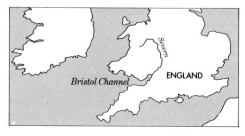

of Powis, an area noted for its agricultural products. The largest town in the Vale is WELSHPOOL. On leaving the vale, the Severn heads east receiving the River Vyrnwy on the way, the Vyrnwy is the chief tributary from the mountain region of Montgomeryshire. The river now flows on towards the town of SHREWSBURY. The Severn in ancient times used to flow north to join the River Trent. But eons ago, the River Dee extended southwards through erosion and managed to secure the Severn as well as the river which forms its upper course. The coming of the last Ice Age witnessed the deposit of moraines across the then Severn-Dee valley to the north of Shrewsbury. This caused the Severn to be dammed and its waters were caught in the Shropshire Basin. The river then made its way through the Ironbridge Gorge escaping southwards to take up its present-day course. The Severn now heads for WORCESTER, the old cathedral town of the district and just past the town is joined by one of its major tributaries, the River Teme. Directly after, at TEWKESBURY, the Severn is again reinforced by another principal tributary, the River Avon flowing down from Warwickshire. The river now is fairly large. The river runs south to the old town of GLOUCESTER, famous for its beautiful cathedral, before entering its estuary. The Severn has tremendous rise in tidal water during the spring tides. The water has risen on occasions by more than 40 feet (12 m) as it pushes up the narrow and very shallow section of the river. This famous solid wall of water is called the Severn Bore, and it was for this reason that the docks at AVONMOUTH, CHEPSTOW and CARDIFF had to be enclosed. The Severn is one of the most important waterways of England.

Sèvre Niortaise, France
This river runs from northeast of MELLE in western France for a total of 95 miles (152 km). It flows west past the town of NIORT to enter the Bay of Biscay near the ISLE DE RE.

Shader, Western Isles, Scotland
The Shader begins in the northern part of the Isle of Lewis. It runs northwest into the Atlantic Ocean between BARVAS and BORVE just west of LOWER SHADER, an ancient village.

Shannon, Republic of Ireland
The Shannon is the largest and by far the most important river in the Republic. The energetic traveler will find the source of the river in the pools at the foot of Mt Toltinbane, a 1881-foot (574 m) peak, in County Cavan. A few miles along it enters Lough Allen and then proceeds south through large expanses of marsh and *callow*, the latter a local term for water meadow. These meadows are utilized to graze cattle in the dry years, but during the wet years, the entire area is more like a primeval inland sea than a river. From North of CARRICK to ROOSKY, the river flows through drumlins, speckled with bogs and marshes. The main stream and its tributaries, the Mountean and Rinn, broaden out into lakes, such as Bodery and Bofin. Near Roosky, the drumlins begin to fade and the river flows through ground

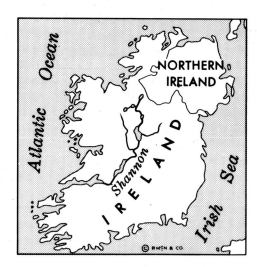

moraine country, and crossings are infrequent. Above Carrick-on-Shannon, the river is only crossed by bridges at LEITRIM and Carrick-on-Shannon. The village of Roosky itself stands at the junction of three county boundaries. From Roosky, the Shannon follows the provincial boundary between Connacht and Leinster through Lough Forbes and between the hills to BALLYCLARE, at the beginning of Lough Ree, the second largest of all the river's lakes. It is shared by three counties – Roscommon in Connacht, and Longford and Westmeath in Leinster. It is 15 miles (24 km) long and up to six miles (ten km) wide. The land between Carrick and Lough Ree is a part of the famous 'Goldsmith Country,' so-named because it was known and loved by the celebrated Irish poet Oliver Goldsmith. After leaving Lough Ree, the Shannon passes through ATHLONE, the so-called 'gateway' town, or BAILE ATHA LUAIN, the Town of the Ford of Luan. Athlone is a busy commercial and communications center on the main road between DUBLIN and GALWAY, and has one of the most important crossings of the river. This crossing was the scene of frequent battles against the western tribes, who always attempted to force their way into the rich Irish midland plains. In 1001, Brian Boru, High King of Ireland marched his army from his palace at Kincora to a great gathering at Athlone. His vessels sailed via Lough Derg and the Shannon.

After leaving Athlone the Shannon flows south and passes what some people believe to be the exact center of Ireland, CLONMACNOISE. Here St Cieran founded a monastery which eventually grew to become the most important ecclesiastical and learning center in the country. The river then leaves Roscommon, and flows along the eastern border of County Galway to MEELICK. At Meelick, three counties and the provinces of Connacht, Munster and Leinster meet on a small island. The river now changes its direction slightly to a south-westerly course, and passes along the boundary of Connacht and Munster, until it enters Lough Derg. Derg is the largest of the Shannon's lakes, and has some of its most breathtaking scenery. The Shannon finally flows through LIMERICK and enters a long estuary before it enters the sea. Limerick is the capital of its county and the third largest city in Ireland. It has a small but very busy port, and 13 miles (21 km) away is Shannon International Airport named after the famous river. The total length of the Shannon is 161

Thomond Bridge at Limerick over the Shannon.

miles (259 km) and it drains 6060 square miles (15,700 sq km).

Shchara, European USSR
The Shchara rises north of BARANOVICHI in White Russia. The River is 200 miles (320 km) long and flows south, west and north-northwest passing BYTEN and SLONIM on the way to join the Neman River near MOSTY. The Shchara is an integral part of the Dnepr-Neman waterway.

Sheshupe, Poland-USSR
This river begins north of the town of SUWALKI in northeastern Poland. It is 191 miles (307 km) long. The Sheshupe flows north through the Lithuanian USSR, then west and northwest by Krasnoznamensk to join the Neman River east of the town of NEMAN.

mountain streams come together. It is 70 miles (113 km) long. The Simeto flows south along the foot of Mt Etna, one of the most active volcanoes in the world, and finally empties into the Gulf of Catania south of CATANIA.

Siret, European USSR
The Siret has its source in the eastern slopes of the Carpathian Mountains of the Ukrainian SSR. The major tributaries of the river are the Barlad, Suceava, Moldava, Bistrita, Trotus, Ramnic and Buzau Rivers, all of which flow from the Carpathians, except for the Barlad. The Siret flows southward through Rumania as it heads for the lower course of the valley. The middle region is very swampy and not suitable for settlement. As the river gets closer to its confluence with the Danube, the heavy concentration of silt becomes more noticeable. In fact, it is so bad that it causes navigational hazards through the formation of sandbanks in the Danube near GALATI called the Tsiglina Shoals. The Siret is 280 miles (450 km) long.

Skat, Bulgaria
The Skat rises in the western Balkan Mountains of northwestern Bulgaria. The Skat flows north past the town of BYALA SLATINA to enter the Danube River at ORYAKHOVO. It is 75 miles (121 km) long.

Skell, Yorkshire, England
The River Skell is a beautiful trout stream. It runs from Dallow Moor north of PATELEY BRIDGE in North Yorkshire, eastward past FOUNTAINS ABBEY. The remains of this abbey are beautiful and set in a spectacular location. The river flows through RIPON and into the River Ure.

Skellefte, Sweden
A river in Lapland, the Skellefte rises on the Norwegian border. It is 255 miles (410 km) long and flows southeast through several large lakes into the Gulf of Bothnia at RONNSKAR.

Skirfare, Yorkshire, England
The River Skirfare rises on the moors of North Yorkshire. The valley of the Skirfare is called the Littondale. The river flows through HALTON GILL, LITTON and ARNCLIFFE before joining the River Wharfe a couple of miles south of the town of KETTLEWELL.

Shiel, Highlands, Scotland
The Shiel rises in the Lochaber district of the Highlands. It runs northwest down Glen Shiel to the BRIDGE OF SHIEL. The river flows into the head of Loch Duich. The fishing in this area of the Highlands is world renowned.

Shkumbin, Albania
The Shkumbin is the principal river of central Albania. It is 90 miles (145 km) long. The river flows from Lake Ochrida on a northwesterly, then westerly course to enter the Adriatic Sea near the town of DURAZZO (DURRES) near the Albanian capital city of Tirana.

Shuya, European USSR
The Shuya rises in Lake Suoyarvi. It is 145 miles (233 km) long. The river runs southeast, then east to Lake Onega north of the city of PETROZAVODSK in the Karelia District of the USSR.

Sieg, West Germany
The river begins on Ederkopf in West Germany. It is 80 miles (129 km) long. The river heads west past the towns of SIEGEN and SIEGBURG to join the Rhine River near the capital of BONN.

Silo, Dyfed, Wales
The Silo is one of Wales' smallest rivers. It runs west into the River Stewy on the western side of PENRHYNCOCH in Dyfed.

Silver Burn, Isle of Man
The Silver Burn rises on the east side of South Barrule. It runs south into Castletown Bay at the town of CASTLETOWN.

Simeto, Sicily
The Simeto is the principal river of Sicily. It rises in the Nebrodi Mountains when several

Slaney, Ireland
The Slaney rises in the Wicklow Mountains of Ireland. It has a length of 60 miles (97 km). The river runs through County Carlow and County Wexford. Its major tributary is the Bann River. The Slaney enters WEXFORD HARBOR which is its final destination.

Slea, Lincolnshire, England
The river rises on Willoughby Heath to the southwest of Ancaster in Lincolnshire. It flows east through the town of SLEAFORD into the River Witham south of the small town of TATTERSHALL.

The Shannon River at Limerick in Ireland.

Sluch, European USSR

The Sluch rises west of Brazaliya in the northwestern Ukrainian SSR. It is 273 miles (440 km) long and flows east, north, north-northwest and finally north to join the Goryn River nòrth-northeast of DUBROVITSA.

Smite, Leicestershire, England

The River Smite rises near AB KETTLEBY and flows between the villages of UPPER and NETHER BROUGHTON northward. It then heads towards NEWARK-ON-TRENT. The Smite flows through the western section of the Vale of Belvoir. It joins the River Devon six miles (ten km) from Newark-on-Trent.

Soar, Leicestershire, England

The River Soar rises six miles (ten km) southeast of the midland town of HINCKLEY. It flows 40 miles (64 km) northeast, then swings to a more northwesterly course as it passes through the city of LEICESTER. The Romans called Leicester Ratae and it was then the home canton of the Coritani tribe. They were not a very rich or prosperous tribe and one Roman Governor stated that they were probably not worth conquering. Modern Leicester is historically important because it is here that King Richard III's body is believed to lie after the fateful Battle of Bosworth Field. The city is noted for its hosiery industry and is also one of the principal shoe manufacturing centers in the Midlands. Leaving Leicester, the Soar flows on to LOUGHBOROUGH and then enters the River Trent midway between Derby and Nottingham.

Soden, Dyfed, Wales

The River Soden rises approximately four miles (six km) south of NEWQUAY. It runs northwest into Cardigan Bay southwest of the town of CARDIGAN itself.

Sog, Iceland

The Sog has its source in Lake THINGVAL-LAVATN. The river flows out of the lake for approximately 15 miles (24 km) in a southerly direction before joining the Hvita River to form the Olfusa River, itself only 18 miles (29 km) long. The river has the largest power station in Iceland located on its course at the Ljosafoss, a large waterfall.

Soham Lode, Cambridgeshire, England

The river rises initially as the River Snail at the village of SNAILWELL. The river flows northwest to the village of SOHAM located five miles (eight km) southeast of ELY. From Soham, the river assumes the name of Soham Lode and continues into the River Ouse three miles (five km) south of Ely.

Sok, European USSR

The Sok rises approximately 20 miles (32 km) south of the town of BUGULMA. It is 210 miles (338 km) long and its major tributary is the Kondurcha River. The Sok proceeds west past ISAKLY, then heads southwest to join the Volga River north of KUYBYSHEV.

Sokna, Norway

The Sokna is a small river of central Norway. It rises north of the town of KVIKNE and flows north to become a tributary of the Guala River at STOREN. The river is 80 miles (129 km) long.

Solva, Dyfed, Wales

The Solva rises southwest of MATHRY in Dyfed. The river flows on the same course into St Bride's Bay on the south side of the village of SOLVA located between the cathedral at ST DAVID'S and HAVERFORDWEST.

Somes, Rumania-Hungary

This river is formed by the confluence of the Great and Little Somes Rivers at DEJ in northern Rumania. It follows a northwesterly course into Hungary where it becomes the Ecsed Marsh. The chief tributary of the Somes is the Kraszna River. The Somes runs into the Tisza River at the town of VASAROSNAMENY near the Hungary-USSR border. The river is 145 miles (233 km) long.

Somme, France

The Somme is probably best remembered for the four-month-long Battle of the Somme fought for a two-mile (three-km) stretch of territory in 1916, the total casualties for both sides running into millions. The river has been a cradle of civilization of man for thousands of years dating back as far as Neolithic Man. The name of the river is Celtic in origin, coming from the Celt word *samara*, which means 'tranquil.' The Somme is 150 miles (240 km) long and flows from FONTSOMME in Picardy through the entire length of the Department of Aisne. The principal tributary of the Somme is the Avre River which joins the main stream in Picardy. The valley of the Somme is covered in marshes which provide numerous obstructions to navigation. The river is well stocked with fish, snipe and wild ducks, and agriculturally the adjacent tablelands are extremely fertile. The most important town on the Somme must be AMIENS, the so-called 'Venice of France.' The river finally ends its run into the English Channel at the Bay of the Somme which actually begins slightly above SAINT-VALERY-SUR-SOMME, a town midway between Dieppe and Boulogne.

Southern Morava, Yugoslavia

The river rises in the southern region of Serbia. It is formed by the confluence of the Binacka Morava and Moravica Rivers at the foot of Crna Gora. The length of the river is 125 miles (201 km). It flows north to STALAC where it is joined by the Western Morava River to form the Morava River.

Sowe, Warwickshire, England

The Sowe rises to the west of BEDWORTH in Warwickshire. It flows south through the eastern portion of COVENTRY, a city which was almost totally destroyed during World War II by the German Luftwaffe. The city has a brand new cathedral adjacent to the ruins of the old one and is an example of excellent modern craftsmanship. The Sowe enters the

River Avon east of KENILWORTH. Kenilworth is the site of one of the most famous castles of Elizabethan England, for it was here that Robert Dudley, Earl of Leicester, built palatial style accommodation to entertain his Queen. The ruins of the castle are well worth visiting and are in the capable hands of the Department of the Environment.

Sozh, European USSR

The Sozh rises in the Moscow-Smolensk Upland near the town of SMOLENSK. It is 402 miles (647 km) long. The river flows southwest past the towns of KRISHEV, SLAVGOROD and GOMEL before joining the Dnepr River at LOYEV. The river is navigable to Krishev.

Spey, Highlands, Scotland

The River Spey rises in the Monadhliath Mountains of the Grampians in the principal Cairngorm watershed. The river is 107 miles (172 km) long, and is famous for its superb salmon fishing. Besides being one of the finest salmon rivers in Scotland, the Spey is also noted for its whiskey distilleries located at ABERLOUR, CRAIGELLACHIE and ROTHES. The winter sporting region of Scotland is located near the Spey with the villages of AVIEMORE, NEWTONMORE, KINGUSSIE and NETHYBRIDGE sharing in the revenues. The river enters the Spey Bay just east of the Moray Firth at KINGSTON.

Spree, East Germany

The Spree River flows through BERLIN, the 'walled city' of Germany. The source of the Spree is located in the Lusatian Mountains to the north of NEUGERSDORF. It flows north past the towns of BAUTZEN and COTTBUS. The river is 250 miles (400 km) long. Below the Cottbus, the Spree begins to change, it divides into several small channels and swings in a great curve to the west, and is the principal feature of the surrounding marsh. This depression which is 27 miles (43 km) long and seven miles (11 km) wide, and takes in an area of 106 square miles (275 sq km) is named the Spree Forest. It is extremely hard to visualize that such a relatively small river has at this point some 200 separate arms and is open to flooding at any time. The river offers excellent fishing for the avid enthusiast. The Spree continues north flowing through the Schwielock and Muggel lakes. It flows through BERLIN, and becomes a tributary of the Havel River at SPANDAU.

Steeping, Lincolnshire, England

The Steeping rises first as the River Lymm near SCAMBLESBY, a small village northeast of HORNCASTLE. The Steeping flows southeast through WAINFLEET and into the North Sea on the western side of Gibraltar Point three miles (five km) south of Skegness.

Stokhod, European USSR

The Stokhod rises north-northwest of TOR-CHIN and flows for 123 miles (198 km) northward to join the Pripyat (Pripet) River eight miles (13 km) northeast of LYUBESHOV.

Right: Dorset's Stour River at Durweston.

Stort, Essex, England

The Stort is an east coast river which rises seven miles (11 km) west of SAFFRON WALDEN in Essex. The river heads south to join the River Lea southeast of WARE in Hertfordshire.

Stour, Dorset, England

The river rises northwest of the town of GILLINGHAM and is 55 miles (88 km) long. The Stour flows southeast past the towns of STURMINSTER NEWTON, BLANDFORD and WIMBORNE MINSTER before joining the River Avon at CHRISTCHURCH to enter the English Channel.

Stour, Cambridgeshire-Suffolk, England

The Stour rises four miles (seven km) northwest of HAVERHILL in Cambridgeshire. It is 47 miles (76 km) long. The river flows southeast through CLARE, CAVENDISH, BURES and DEDHAM to form an estuary at MANNINGTREE. It turns to an easterly course as it heads to HARWICH where it joins the River Orwell. The Stour then proceeds into Harwich Harbor and the North Sea. Constable painted many scenes of this portion of the English countryside, making it eternally famous.

Stour, Great, Kent, England

The Great Stour has its beginnings near LENHAM. The river runs southeast to the town of ASHFORD where it is joined by the East Stour, then flows northeast through the cathedral town of CANTERBURY to PLUCKS GUTTER. Here it is joined by the Little Stour to form the Stour River.

Stour, Oxfordshire, England

This Stour rises in the Cotswolds north of CHIPPING NORTON. The river flows west to BURMINGTON, then heads north through SHIPSTON ON STOUR, and finally joins the River Avon southwest of STRATFORD-UPON-AVON.

Stour, West Midlands, England

The Midlands Stour rises to the south of Dudley. The river runs southwest through STOURBRIDGE and KIDDERMINSTER before joining the River Severn at STOURPORT.

Struma, Bulgaria-Greece

The Struma rises in the Vitosha Mountains of Bulgaria and is one of the principal rivers of the Balkan Peninsula. The river has a total length of 215 miles (346 km). It assumes a southerly course and heads for the GULF OF ORPHANOS in the Aegean Sea. The Struma flows through a countryside filled with vineyards and tobacco fields. It enters Greek Macedonia near the Rupel Gorge. The river continues on course through this region of Greece until it runs into the sea.

Styr, European USSR

The Styr rises south of Brody in the northwestern Ukrainian SSR. The River is

Willy Lott's cottage, near Flatford Mill on the Stour in Suffolk, made famous by John Constable.

280 miles (450 km) long. It runs north past the towns of LUTSK and KOLKI, the latter the head of the river's navigation. The Styr then joins the Pripyat River approximately 20 miles (32 km) to the east of PINSK.

Suir, Ireland

The Suir begins high in the Devil's Mountains of County Tipperary and is 85 miles (137 km) long. It flows south past the towns of THURLES and CAHIR, then changes to an easterly direction past CLONMEL, CARRICK-ON-SUIR and finally WATERFORD, the latter known for its exceptionally fine hand made crystal. The Suir joins the River Barrow at the head of Waterford Harbor.

Sukhona, European USSR

The Sukhona rises in Lake Kubeno, Vologda Oblast, USSR. It is 358 miles (576 km) long and flows east-northeast to join the Yug River at VELIKIY USTYUG to form the Lesser Northern Dvina River. Its chief tributary is the Vologda River.

Sula, European USSR

The Sula rises southwest of SUMY in the Central Russian Upland of the northern Ukraine. It is 250 miles (400 km) long and flows southwest, then south to finally join the

The Swale River near Keld in North Yorkshire.

Dnepr River to the west of the town of GRADIZHSK.

Sura, European USSR
The Sura rises northeast of the town of KUZNETSK in the central European Russian SSR. It runs for a total length of 537 miles (864 km) and is classed as a medium sized river. The Sura flows northeast, then turns to a more northerly course to become a tributary of

the Volga River at VASILSURSK. Its major tributaries are the Alatyr, Pyana and Inza rivers. The Sura is navigable for approximately 400 miles (640 km) of its course.

Sus, Denmark
The Sus is the major river of Sjaelland. It rises southwest of the town of FAKSE and runs for 52 miles (84 km) passing NAESTVED on the way to the Smålandsfarvand Strait which is only eight

miles (12 km) from its source. The reason for this is that the river winds for its entire length before emptying into the Strait.

Sventoji, European USSR
This river rises in a series of small lakes south of ZARASAI in central Lithuania. The Sventoji is 152 miles (245 km) long. The river runs southwest past ANYKSCIAI and UKMERGE to join the Viliya River.

Svir, European USSR

The Svir begins from Lake Onga in the Leningrad Oblast. The river is 140 miles (230 km) long. It is navigable through its entire course as part of the Mariinsk Canal system. It flows west past the two power stations of Podporozhyo and Svirstroi to enter Lake Ladoga at the town of SVIRITSA.

Sviyaga, European USSR

The river rises to the northeast of the town of KUZOVATOVO. It flows by ULYANOVSK and north to ISHEYEVKA and finally enters the Volga River 16 miles (26 km) to the west of KAZAN.

Svratka, Czechoslovakia

The Svratka is 106 miles (171 km) long from its source in the Bohemian-Moravian Heights to the southeast of HLINSKO to where it finally becomes a tributary of the Dyje River. It flows through some of the best regions of Czechoslovakia.

Swale, North Yorkshire, England

The River Swale rises on the moors to the west of the small village of Keld. It runs southeast down Swaledale and through REETH, RICHMOND and CATTERICK BRIDGE to meet the River Ure east of the town of BOROUGHBRIDGE to form the River Ouse.

Swere, Oxfordshire, England

The Swere begins near the village of HOCK NORTON. It flows on an easterly course into the River Cherwell five miles southeast of the town of BANBURY.

Swift, Leicestershire, England

The River Swift, one of Leicestershire's own rivers, rises northwest of the town of HUSBANDS BOSWORTH. It runs southwest into the River Avon at BROWNOVER on the northern side of the town of RUGBY. Rugby is best remembered for the book *Tom Brown's School Days* about an English boy's experience at a public school. The Swift runs directly under the motorway just south of the city of LEICESTER.

Swiftgate, Gloucester, England

The river rises near the spa town of CHELTENHAM. The river flows north to where it meets the River Avon at TEWKESBURY, a town noted for its famous abbey.

Swincombe, Devon, England

The Swincombe rises south of PRINCETOWN on the large expanse of Dartmoor. The moor is the location for the annual Dartmoor survival run which is entered by enthusiasts from all over Europe.

Swindle Beck, Cumbria, England

The Swindle Beck begins on Warcop Fell to the north of Brough in Cumbria. It runs south to join the River Eden at GREAT MUSGRAVE. This small river flows through one of England's most scenic areas.

Syfynwy, Dyfed, Wales

A Welsh river which begins on Mynydd Preseli, north of ROSBUSH, a hamlet north of the reservoir of the same name. The river runs through Rosbush and Llys-f-fran reservoirs to become a tributary of the Eastern Cleddau River north of CANASTON BRIDGE.

Taf, Dyfed, Wales

A Welsh river rising at CRYMMYCH ARMS, the Taf runs by LLANFYNACH, LOGIN and WHITLAND. It continues on course past ST CLEARS where it forms an estuary running past LAUGHARNE. The Taf estuary then joins the Towy estuary and flows into CARMARTHEN BAY.

Taff, Powys, Wales

The source of the River Taff is the confluence of the Great Taf and Little Taf rivers near MERTHYR TYDFIL in Mid Glamorgan. The Taff is 40 miles (64 km) long and 200 years ago was considered a fine river. Today it is probably the dirtiest river in Wales. The salmon which used to spawn up the Taff have long since abandoned it. The river proceeds southward to enter the River Severn at the town of CARDIFF.

Tagliamento, Italy

The source of this river is found high in the Carnic Alps northwest of AMPEZZO in northeastern Italy. It is 106 miles (171 km) long. The river flows east, then south past LATISANA to enter the Adriatic Sea near GRADO.

Tagil, European USSR

The Tagil rises in the central Ural Mountains to the south of KIROVGRAD. It is 260 miles (420 km) long. The Tagil runs north and northeast to join the Tura River.

Tagus, Spain

The Tagus is the longest river in the Iberian Peninsula with a length of 625 miles (1006 km). The river rises southwest of ALBARRACIN in Teurel Province of eastern Spain. It flows a considerable portion of its length below the level of the surrounding countryside because of its deep valleys. As the river flows through the fertile plain south of the Spanish capital city of MADRID, it heads westward toward the ancient town of TOLEDO. This legendary town is practically encased by the Tagus as the river twists and turns first one way and another. Toledo is famous for its superb steel. Upon reaching ALCANTARA, the Tagus becomes the boundary between Spain and neighboring Portugal for approximately 30 miles (48 km). The river then crosses into Portugal and becomes navigable for small vessels at ABRANTES. The Tagus finally empties into the Atlantic Ocean through LISBON BAY. The river has very little navigational use for the majority of its length and is for the most part also unsuited for irrigation projects, but it is a prime source of hydroelectric power.

Tajuna, Spain

The river rises southeast of MEDINACELI in central Spain. It is 152 miles (245 km) long and runs southwest past BRIHUEGA to join the Jarama River, six miles north of ARANJUEZ.

Tamar, Cornwall, England

The Tamar is the principal river of Cornwall in the West Country of England and is 60 miles (97 km) long. The Tamar rises four miles east of MORWENSTOW on the northern Cornish coast. It forms the border between Cornwall and Devon for almost its entire length. It empties into PLYMOUTH SOUND.

Tame, Greater Manchester, England

The river rises on the moors north of JUNCTION. It runs south to join the River Goyt on the northern side of STOCKPORT to form the River Mersey.

Tame, West Midlands, England

The River Tame flows southeast to Perry Barr, a district of the city of BIRMINGHAM approximately three miles from the city center. The river then turns east to head towards COLESHILL where it joins the River Blythe.

Tana, Norway

The Tana forms the boundary between Norway and Finland. It is a noted salmon river. The length of the Tana is 201 miles (323 km). It runs northeast to enter TANA FJORD off the Barents Sea.

Tanaro, Italy

The river rises in the Ligurian Alps of northwestern Italy. It is 171 miles (275 km) long, and flows northeast to become a tributary of the Po river at BASSIGNANA.

Tanat, Gwynedd, Wales

The river rises in the Berwyn Mountain Range on the borders of Gwynedd and Powys. The Tanat runs east to join the River Vyrnwy south of the village of LLANYBLODWEL.

Tarn, France

The Tarn rises in the Cevennes of central France and is 235 miles (378 km) long. The river has many tributaries, the main ones being the Aveyron, Jonte, Dourbie and Agout rivers. The Tarn runs on a westward course passing MILLAU and ALBI before finally entering the Garonne River near MOISSAC.

Taro, Italy

The Taro rises in the Ligurian Apennines of central Italy. It flows for 78 miles (126 km) before entering the Po River west of CASALMAGGIORE.

Tarrant, Dorset, England

The source of the Tarrant is near the hamlet of TARRANT GUNVILLE approximately five miles (eight km) southeast of BLANDFORD FORUM. It flows south to join the River Stour at TARRANT CRAWFORD only a further two miles closer to Blandford Forum.

Tarset Burn, Northumberland, England
Beginning as the Smallhope Burn in the eastern portion of the Kielder Forest, this river runs southeast to join the much larger River North Tyne west of BELLINGHAM.

Tas, Norfolk, England
The Tas in the easternmost county of east Anglia just south of CARLETON RODE. The Tas runs northeast into the River Yare southeast of the picturesque and photogenic cathedral city of NORWICH.

Tauber, West Germany
The Tauber rises northeast of the town of CRAILSHEIM in southern Germany. It is 78 miles (126 km) long and runs northwest past ROTHENBURG to become a tributary of the Main River at WERTHEIM.

Tavy, Devon, England
This river rises in the heart of Dartmoor in the West Country. The Tavy flows southwest through the town of TAVISTOCK to join the River Tamar at LANDULPH.

Taw, Devon, England
Another river rising in the expanse of Dartmoor which runs north to BARNSTABLE. It then flows west to join the River Torridge and continues on, passing into Barnstable Bay. The Taw is 50 miles (80 km) long.

The River Tay at Dowally, Perthshire, Scotland.

Tay, Grampian, Scotland
The Tay rises in the western region of Perthshire when two mountain streams, the Lochay and the Dochart meet at the village of KILLIN. The Tay now enters Loch Tay located six miles (nine km) southwest of ABERFELDY, which is 15 miles (24 km) long by one mile (1610 m) wide, with a depth of 508 feet (155 m). Upon departing the loch which it drains, the Tay proceeds over a flat plain and passes the towns of ABERFELDY, GRANDTULLY, DUNKELD and PERTH, the latter the ancient capital city of the Picts. The Tay has a total length of 120 miles (190 km). It finally flows into the FIRTH OF TAY. The river is navigable for small boats. Its principal tributaries are the

Lyon, Tummel, Isla and Earn rivers. The river is a well-known salmon stream and provides a considerable amount of hydro-electric power for Scotland.

Tees, Cumbria, England
The River Tees rises at a height of 2500 feet (760 m) on Cross Fell which is the highest mountain peak in the Pennines. The river is 96 miles (154 km) long and is navigable as far as STOCKTON. The Tees runs southeast by MIDDLETON in Teesdale to BARNARD CASTLE, then heads east to Stockton-on-Tees and the town of MIDDLESBROUGH, finally turning northeast to enter the North Sea at TEES BAY in North Yorkshire.

Teifi, Dyfed, Wales
The Teifi, one of the most beautiful rivers of west Wales, begins on the western slopes of the Cambrian Mountains. The river flows through a peat bog for the initial portion of its course, but then turns southwest through green countryside passing the market town of LAMPETER. The river flows through a sequence of gorges as it passes the villages of PENTRECWRT, CENARTH, CILGERRAN, and the towns of LLANDYSSUL and NEWCASTLE EMLYN. The fishing on the Teifi is extraordinary and the salmon excellent. The river is famous for its coracle races held every year near Cilgerran. It finally empties into the Irish Sea at CARDIGAN BAY.

Above: The Tay River at Dunkeld.
Top center & top right: The Tees River at Stockton (center) and near Abbey Bridge (right).
Right: The Teme River at Ludlow, Shropshire.
Far right: The Test River near Mottisfont in Hampshire.

Teign, Devon, England
The river rises in the northern portion of Dartmoor. The Teign flows east past CHAGFORD and DUNSFORD, then shifts southward by NEWTON ABBOT. It forms an estuary which flows into the English Channel at TEIGNMOUTH.

Teise, Kent, England
The Teise runs from south of TUNBRIDGE WELLS to LAMBERHURST. It joins the River Beult in two separate channels, the eastern branch meeting the Beult at HUNTON and the western branch at YALDING.

Teme, Powys-Hereford and Worcester, UK
The Teme rises south of NEWTON on the Radnor and Montgomery border. It is 60 miles (97 km) long and runs southeast past KNIGHTON and TENBURY to enter the River Severn south of WORCESTER.

Ter, Spain
This Spanish river rises above CAMPRODON in the Pyrenees of northeastern Spain. It runs for

a total length of 105 miles (169 km). The Ter flows south, then eastward to the GULF OF ROSAS in the Mediterranean Sea northeast of GERONA. There are three major hydroelectric power stations on the Ter at RIPOLL, MANLLEU and EL PORTORAL.

Tern, Staffordshire, England

The river rises near MADELEY and runs through MARKET DRAYTON in Shropshire. The Tern then turns south to become a tributary of the River Severn between the towns of ATCHAM and WROXETER.

Test, Hampshire, England

The river rises at ASHE, a hamlet near OVERTON in Hampshire and flows for a total of 30 miles (48 km). The River Test is a well-known trout stream. It runs southwest to STOCKBRIDGE, then proceeds south to TOTTON and finally to Southampton Water at the city of SOUTHAMPTON.

Tet, France

The Tet River rises in the Pyrenees of southern France. It flows for a total of 75 miles (121 km) on a northeasterly course, passing the towns of MONT LOUIS, PRADES and PERPIGNAN to finally enter the Gulf of Lion below Perpignan.

Teterev, European USSR

A river of the Ukraine which rises to the west-southwest of BERDICHEV. The length of the Teterev is 220 miles (350 km). The river flows northeast past ZHITOMIR and IVANKOV to become just another tributary of the Dnepr River approximately 35 miles (56 km) north of KIEV.

Teviot, Borders Region, Scotland

The Teviot rises in rolling upland country near the border with Dumfries and Galloway six miles east of ESKDALEMUIR. The river is not very long with a total distance of 38 miles (61 km). It flows past TEVIOTHEAD, HAWICK and ROXBURGH to join the River Tweed at KELSO.

Thame, Buckinghamshire, England

The river rises east of the country town of AYLESBURY and flows into the River Thames south of DORCHESTER, Oxfordshire.

Thames, England

The premier river of England, the Thames is one of the best known rivers of the world. Although in length (209 miles: 336 km) it is not classed as one of the great rivers of the world it still rates as one of the most important in Europe. During the last stage of the Pliocene 7000 years ago Britain was still connected to mainland Europe. At this time a huge river ran north through the now submerged English Channel to its outlet in the North Sea. The chief tributaries of this ancient river were the much smaller Thames and Rhine. From its source at SEVEN SPRINGS the river assumes a very winding course as it proceeds through the

English 'clay vale'; running southwest, then northeast through the Cotswolds and Chilterns. The Thames now heads for the University city of OXFORD and picks up numerous small tributaries on the way, the Coln, Windrush and Evenlode to name the chief ones flowing down the southeastern slopes of the Cotswold. The Thames receives its chief tributary, the River Cherwell, near the city center of Oxford and numerous bridges are built over both throughout the city. The Cherwell runs south from its source near Northamptonshire until it joins the Thames at Oxford. 'Father Thames' as it is frequently called flows through English countryside at its very best, passing through small villages lined with willow trees and flowing through broad and scenic meadows. All of these villages and market towns have taken into account the river's habit of flooding across its plain and therefore have built themselves far enough away to combat any flood waters which the mighty river might decide to throw their way. The city of Oxford was built between the confluence of both the Thames and the Cherwell and the university is situated here on the interfluve. The city is the end of the river's commercial navigational limit, but small boats can make it as far as LECHLADE. The Thames now runs through the low ridge of the Oxford Heights in the Sandford Gap. It passes the village of SANDFORD-ON-THAMES, located three miles southeast of Oxford, before heading towards WALLINGFORD. In Norman days this small town was garrisoned by a handpicked troop to control the upper reaches of the Thames Valley and Wallingford Castle was a fortress to be reckoned with; now all that remains is rubble. The river now runs across the chalk downs and on occasions splits into several channels which make islands in the main stream. The countryside here is beautiful and much frequented by tourists. The Thames is joined by two smaller tributaries, the Thame and Ock rivers, which drain the Vale of Aylesbury and the Vale of the White Horse before emptying into the Thames. Finally, the Thames makes its way through the Goring Gorge and into the London Basin and its lower reaches. Reaching the town of READING noted for its superb university colleges, the river is joined by the River Kennet which flows west from the Marlborough Downs. Once leaving Reading, the Thames heads for HENLEY, a beautiful river town world famous for its regatta in the summer. The next stop for the Thames is MARLOW, another lovely town set on the banks with an excellent view of the waters from the bridge over the river. During the summer, the river is full of boats which ply their way here and there. Also the fishing is quite good on this stretch of the river. The Thames runs through the town of MAIDENHEAD, then continues on to the Royal residence at Windsor Castle, the largest occupied fortress in Europe. At Windsor, one can take a boat trip up or down river. After leaving Windsor, the river runs through ETON, noted for its college, SLOUGH, STAINES, WALTON, HAMPTON, noted for its famous palace (Hampton Court) built by Cardinal Wolsey in the time of King Henry VIII, KINGSTON and TEDDINGTON. The tidal limit of the Thames is marked at Teddington. The Thames now flows for 25 miles (40 km) through GREATER

Chelsea Bridge over the River Thames.

LONDON and the CITY OF LONDON. The river is spanned by 18 road bridges, the most famous being Twickenham, Kew, Hammersmith, Putney, Wandsworth, Battersea, Vauxhall, Westminster, Waterloo, Blackfriars, Southwark, London Bridge, Tower and Lambeth. The river is also crossed by six railway bridges and three tunnels run underneath it. The Thames provides a perfect setting for the Houses of Parliament (the former old palace of the kings of England before the great fire which destroyed it) and Big Ben nearby. The Thames finally reaches Tower Bridge. The famous Tower of London can be seen from the river. This was once a Royal prison and residence during times of tension as it is the largest fortification within the city and in times gone by whoever controlled the keys to the Tower controlled London, and therefore the kingdom. Now the river proceeds past the older settlements, DEPTFORD, GREENWICH, WOOLWICH, GREENHITHE and GRAVESEND, before heading out to the English Channel. The principal tributaries of the Thames are the Loddon, Lea, Mole, Darent, Coln and Medway. Upon reaching Gravesend, the river is more than 700 yards wide, and still increases as it approaches the estuary of the Thames. At its widest, the Thames is 5.5 miles (eight km) wide running from SHOEBURYNESS to SHEERNESS. The river's official end is the lighthouse at NORE, where it enters the North Sea.

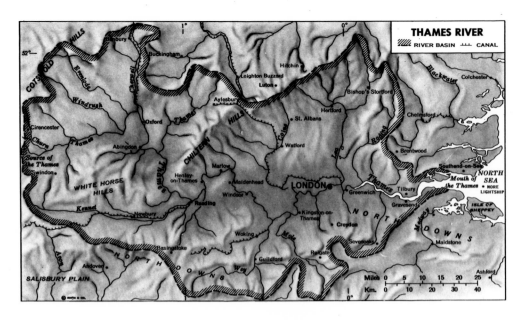

Below: the bridges of London over the Thames: Tower Bridge, Old London Bridge, Cannon Street Bridge, Southwark Bridge, Blackfriars Bridge and in the distance, Waterloo Bridge.

Top right: Swans at Henley on the Thames in early Spring.

Center bottom: the chapel and Eton College from the River Thames.

Bottom right: Picturesque English countryside on the Thames before it reaches London.

Thaw, South Glamorgan, Wales

Rises north of COWBRIDGE and proceeds on a circular course through the small town of Cowbridge. It then heads south passing into the Bristol Channel east of BREAKSEA POINT.

Thet, Norfolk, England

The tiny river Thet rises near the town of ATTLEBOROUGH in Norfolk. It runs southwest to join the River Little Ouse at the town of THETFORD.

Thrushel, Devon, England

Dartmoor has its share of small rivers and the River Thrushel is one of these. It runs west to join the River Lyd at LIFTON, then continues to become a tributary of the River Tamar, three miles east of the border town of LAUNCESTON which was previously the capital of Cornwall.

Thurne, Norfolk, England

Rises near the village of HAPPISBURGH in Norfolk. The River Thurne flows south through Horsey Mere, a lake southwest of the village of the same name, and then into the River Bure south of the village of THURNE.

Tiber, Italy

This is Italy's most historic river, not as important as the Po in the north but still one of the world's most famous rivers. It was on the banks of the Tiber, thousands of years ago, that the twin brothers Romulus and Remus, castaways from the Royal House of Alba Longa, founded the city of ROME. The city was destined to rule the majority of the then civilized world. The Tiber rises on Mt Fumaiolo at a height of 4160 feet (1270 m) in the Etruscan Apennines. The river itself serves no commercial purpose to the capital city as it is prone to flooding, but forms a perfect setting for the city. Rome was originally built upon the Seven Hills on the eastern bank of the Tiber. This was because these small hills provided an easy defense to enemy tribes nearby and it was relatively free of malarial swamps which at that time were common in the surrounding area. Modern Rome is free of these swamps as the Tiber marshes were drained years ago providing Rome with an excellent climate. The river flows through the city past the Vatican on the right bank and the center of modern Rome on the left bank, the Piazza Venezia. Proceeding from Rome, the Tiber heads for the Tyrrhenian Sea and the port of OSTIA which was an important port in the days of ancient Rome, but which serves no practical purpose today. The Tiber has a total length of 251 miles (404 km), 34 miles (55 km) longer than its English counterpart, the Thames.

Ticino, Italy

The Ticino actually rises in Switzerland west of AIROLO. It is 154 miles (248 km) long, and heads south through Lake Maggiore across the Italian border to join the Po River near PAVIA.

Tiddy, Cornwall, England

Rises near the village of Pensilva below the 1213 feet (370 m) Caradon Hill. It flows southeast into the St Germans River below ST GERMANS QUAY, a small village located eight miles southeast of LISKEARD.

Till, Northumberland, England

The Till rises as the Breamish River in the southern Cheviot Hills, then flows eastward to BEWICK, a parish southeast of WOOLER, containing the hamlets of Old and New Berwick. The river then turns north flowing to CHATTON, swinging northwest and into the River Tweed a few miles north of CORNHILL.

Tilt, Tayside, Scotland

The Tilt rises between the Glen Ey Forest and Mar Forest in Loch Tilt. It flows south past the Falls of Tarf, where the Tarf Water joins it, then continues on a southwesterly direction down Glen Tilt. It enters the River Garry at BLAIR ATHOLL.

Timis, Rumania

The Timis River begins southeast of the town of RESITA, in the Translyvanian Alps. It flows southeast to TEREGOVA and turns westward passing CARANSEBES and LUGOJ before crossing the Yugoslavia border. The Timis proceeds by the towns of BOKA and ORLOVAT to enter the Danube River to the east of the capital, BELGRADE. It is 202 miles (325 km) long.

Tirso, Sardinia

This is the principal river of Sardinia. It rises west of the town of BUDDUSO and runs southwest through Lake Tirso. The river is 93 miles (150 km) long. Its main tributary is the Flumineddu River. The Tirso is noted for its irrigation, fisheries and hydroelectric power. Leaving Lake Tirso the river flows to the GULF OF ORISTANO.

Tisza, European USSR-Hungary-Yugoslavia

The Tisza rises at the confluence of the Black and White Tisza rivers above the town of RAKHOV and flows for a total of 803 miles (1292 km). It runs southwest, then turns west

passing SIGHET near the Ukrainian-Rumanian frontier before reentering the Ukraine. Now the river flows toward the Great Hungarian Plain which it irrigates with its water. The next stop on the river's course is the wine-growing town of TOKAJ, then on to SZOLNOK, a large industrial town. From here the river twists and turns although keeping to a roughly parallel course with the Danube. The Tisza flows through SZEGED, the second largest city in Hungary before crossing over into the Vojvodina Plain of western Yugoslavia. During the 1879 flood, the Tisza destroyed Szeged in Europe's worst flood for hundreds of years. The river is navigable for small boats for approximately half of its total length. The main tributaries are the Mures, Somes and Koros rivers. It enters the Danube 23 miles (37 km) northwest of BELGRADE.

Tone, Somerset, England

The river rises in the Brendon Hills of Somerset, an extension of the Exmoor Forest, an integral part of the Exmoor National Park. It runs south to GREENHAM, then turns eastward to pass through the town of TAUNTON, noted for its cider. It continues on course to join the River Parrett at BURROW BRIDGE.

Tormes, Spain

The Tormes rises southwest of AVILA in western Spain as the Sierra de Grados. It is 176 miles (283 km) long and runs past SALAMANCA to enter the Douro River at the Portuguese border.

Torne, Finland

This Scandinavian river rises in Lake Torne in Lapland, located approximately 30 miles (48 km) northwest of the town of KIRUNA. The lake is 40 miles (64 km) long and between one–six miles (two–nine km) wide. The river is 250 miles (400 km) long and drains the lake. Its principal tributaries are the Muonio and Tenglio river systems. The Torne flows to its confluence with the Muonio near the GULF OF BOTHNIA its outlet. The river is geologically young as ascertained by its numerous waterfalls and rapids. It has an excellent hydroelectric potential but due to the borders with Sweden it will take a joint commission before it can be developed fully.

Torne, South Yorkshire, England

The Torne begins west of TICKHILL and flows on a northeasterly course to join the River Trent at the country town of ALTHORPE in Humberside.

Torridge, Devon, England

The River Torridge actually rises on the borders of Cornwall and Devon. It runs east to HELE BRIDGE just north of HATHERLEIGH. Continuing on course, it flows past GREAT TORRINGTON to the town of BIDEFORD, then turns north to join the mouth of the River Taw and head into Barnstaple Bay (which is often called Bideford Bay) on the Bristol Channel.

Touques, France

The river rises in the Perche Hills above GACE in northwestern France. It has a length of 67 miles (108 km). The river flows past LISIEUX and PONT-L'EVEQUE to enter the English Channel at TROUVILLE-DEAUVILLE.

Towy (Tywi), Dyfed, Wales

The Towy is 65 miles (105 km) long and rises in the Cambrian Mountains of southwestern Wales. It runs south through Brianne Reservoir to LLANDOVERY, then heads southwest past LLANDEILO, turning west to pass through CARMARTHEN before entering the Bay of Carmarthen.

Traun, Austria

The source of the Traun is the Totes Gebirge, northeast of OBERTRAUN, in Upper Austria. It has a total length of 80 miles (129 km). It passes through Lakes Hallstadt and Traun before entering the Danube River southeast of the town of LINZ.

Trent, Staffordshire, England

The River Trent rises near BIDDULPH MOOR in Staffordshire and flows by STOKE-ON-TRENT. Stoke is noted for its potteries, factories and huge slag-heaps. The principal tributaries of the Trent are the Sow, Tame, Dove, Derwent and Erewash rivers. It is 168 miles (270 km) long. The Trent has several thermal power stations on its banks and cool water is drawn from its waters. On its downstream course the river has been canalized to make it accessible as far as Cromwell Lock, the extreme tidal limit of the river. The River Trent joins the River Ouse at TRENTFALLS to form the River Humber.

Tromie, Highlands, Scotland

The Tromie rises in Loch an Seilich in the Gaick Forest of the Grampian Mountains in the Badenoch and Strathspey district. The river flows north and is joined by the Allt Bhran just below Meallach Mhor which stands at a height of 2521 feet (769 m). It runs down Glen Tromie and joins the River Spey to the east of KINGUSSIE.

The Black Tisza River in the Ukrainian SSR. The Black Tisza is one of the sources of the 803-mile (1284-km) long Tisza River.

Rome's Castel San Angelo guards the Tiber.

Right: Bridges over the Tyne River at Newcastle.

Tsna, European USSR

The Tsna, a river of central European Russia, rises northwest of RZHAL. The Tsna is 130 miles (210 km) long and flows north past TAMBOV to join the Moksha River near SAVORO.

Turia, Spain

The Turia has spectacular falls at Chulilla which are 500 feet (150 m) high. The river rises near ALBARRACIN in eastern Spain. It has a length of 150 miles (240 km), and flows past the important city of VALENCIA to finally enter the Mediterranean Sea at VILLANUEVA DEL GRAO.

Tweed, England-Scotland

The Tweed rises at TWEED'S WELL in Peeblesshire. The river flows through some of Sir Walter Scott's most loved country. It has been called for some centuries the 'silver Tweed,' more a term of endearment than anything else. It forms part of the English-Scottish border with grim reminders south at Flodden Field where a Scottish army met a disastrous fate and just north at Coldstream where the famous Guards were raised by General Monk. The main tributaries of the Tweed are the Leithen, Quair, Ettrick, Gala, Leader and Teviot. The Tweed is one of the finest salmon and trout rivers in the entire island. It is 97 miles (156 km) long and empties into the North Sea.

Twymyn, Powys, Wales

The Twymyn starts to flow near Glasly Lake and parallels the road for a short distance before heading for DYLIFE, a location southwest of PENNANT. The river then swings north to LLANBRYNMAIR before turning west to enter the River Dovey.

Tyne, Lothian Region, Scotland

The Tyne is known in the upper region of the river as the Tyne Water. It runs from the northern slopes of Moorfoot Hills through HADDINGTON and EAST LINTON to enter the North Sea near DUNBAR.

Tyne, Northumberland, England

The North and South Tyne Rivers join together northwest of the town of HEXHAM in Northumberland to form the Tyne. This river flows through one of the heaviest industrial areas of Great Britain. It passes NEWCASTLE-UPON-TYNE, FELLING, WALLSEND and JARROW, the latter the start of a march to find work in London in the days of severe unemployment. The river is navigable to Newcastle. The Tyne enters the North Sea between SOUTH SHIELDS and TYNEMOUTH.

Tyne, North, Northumberland, England

The North Tyne rises in the Kielder Forest of Northumberland and runs southeast through FALSTONE and WARK before joining the River South Tyne at HEXHAM to form the Tyne.

Tyne, South, Northumberland, England
The South Tyne rises on the Tynehead Fell in Cumbria and runs north by ALSTON. It proceeds to HALTWHISTLE in Northumberland, then turns eastward past HAYDON BRIDGE to join the River North Tyne at HEXHAM to form the Tyne.

Ufa, European USSR
The Ufa rises in a small lake east of KARABASH in the southern Ural Mountain Range. It runs for 599 miles (964 km) before entering the Belaya River at UFA. The river is utilized for lumber floating.

Uisge Labhair, Highlands, Scotland
The river rises east of Aonach Beag, a mountain 3656 feet (1115 m) high in the Badenoch and Strathspey district. The river runs southwest to join the River Ossian near the foot of LOCH OSSIAN.

Ume, Sweden
The Ume is 285 miles (459 km) long and rises southeast of MO in Lapland. It heads southeast through Storuma Lake and passing several power stations towards VANNAS. The Ume's chief tributary is the Vindel River. The river continues on course past Umeå to enter the Gulf of Bothnia at HOLMSUND.

Una, Yugoslavia
The Una rises approximately 11 miles (17 km) east of GRACAC in western Yugoslavia. It flows for a total of 159 miles (256 km) on a northeasterly course past DUBICA to join the Sava River at JASENOVAC.

Unstrut, Germany
The Unstrut begins northwest of the town of DINGELSTADT in central Germany. The river is 116 miles (187 km) long and runs east past ROSSLEBEN and FREYBURG before joining the Thuringian Saale River. The principal tributaries of the Unstrut are the Gera, Helme and Wipper Rivers.

Unzha, European USSR
The source of the Unzha is at the confluence of the Kema and Yuza rivers, southwest of MIKOLSK in the northern Ural Mountains. The river is 340 miles (547 km) long and runs south to become a tributary of the Volga River at YURYEVETS.

Ure, North Yorkshire, England
The river rises on Abbottside Common northwest of HAWES. The Ure flows southeast passing Hawes, MASHAM, RIPON and BOROUGHBRIDGE before entering the River Swale at a location just east of the town of Boroughbridge where it forms the River Ouse.

Urr Water, Dumfries and Galloway, Scotland
The Urr Water rises at Loch Urr and flows southwards past DALBEATTIE. Then it heads to Rough Firth and finally enters the SOLWAY FIRTH.

Usk, Powys, Wales
The river rises southwest of the town of TRECASTLE on the border between POWYS and DYFED; flows north to the Usk Reservoir, then turns east to pass through Trecastle and the county town of BRECON. It then runs past ABERGAVENNY, USK and CAERLEON to enter the Bristol Channel at NEWPORT. The Usk has a total length of 60 miles (97 km).

Vaga, European USSR
The Vaga rises west of TOTMA in northern European Russia. It flows for 330 miles (530 km) northeast passing the towns of VERKHOVAZHYE, VELSK and SHENKURSK to finally enter the Northern Dvina River. The Vaga is navigable for 235 miles (376 km) below Velsk.

Left: The Tweed serves as a border between Scotland and England for part of its length.

Vah, Czechoslovakia

The Vah is formed by the confluence of the Biely Vah and the Cierny Vah rivers in the Low Tatra Mountains of western Slovakia. The river is 245 miles (394 km) long and runs westerly, then southwest, before turning south to join the Danube at KOMARNO. The Vah receives three large tributaries the Little Danube, Orava, and Nitra rivers.

Var, France

The river rises in the Maritime Alps of southeastern France. The Var runs 84 miles (135 km) southeast to where it joins the Mediterranean Sea a few miles southwest of the resort city of NICE.

Vardar, Macedonia

The Vardar is the principal river of Macedonia. The ancient Greeks named it Axiós. It rises in the Shar Mountains of southwestern Yugoslavia which together with the Pindus Range form a lower section of the Dinaric Alps. It flows past GOSTIVAR, SKOPJE, the chief town of Macedonia, TITOV VELES and DJEVD-JELINA. The Vardar Gap has been a primary route for invaders into Greece proper from the time of Philip (King of Macedon and father of Alexander the Great) to the time of the Germans in 1941. The total length of the Vardar is 230 miles (370 km). It enters the Gulf of Salonika, an arm of the Aegean Sea, southwest of the town of SALONIKA.

Venta, Lithuania-Latvia, European USSR

The river rises southeast of the town of TELSIAI. It is 125 miles (200 km) long. It flows eastward initially, then changes to a northwest course past KURSENAI and crosses the border into Latvia and flows past KULDIGA. It finally enters the Baltic Sea at the town of VENTSPILS.

Ver, Hertfordshire, England

The river rises at REDBOURN in Hertfordshire. It flows south past the town of ST ALBANS at the very foot of the abbey church and the remains of the ancient Roman city of Verulamium. Verulamium was sacked during the Iceni Uprising led by the warrior Queen Boudicca. It joins the River Colne between WATFORD and St Albans.

Rolling hills surround the Usk River valley in Wales (both photos).

Vesle, France

The Vesle rises northeast of CHALONS-SUR-MARNE and is 89 miles (143 km) long. It flows northwest past the city of RHEIMS, remembered for its cathedral, to join the Aisne River just six miles (ten km) east of SOISSONS.

Vetluga, European USSR

This Soviet river rises in the northern Ural Mountain Range. It flows 500 miles (800 km) north, west and finally south to join the Volga River as one of its main tributaries directly opposite KOZMODEMYANSK.

Vienne, France

The Vienne rises on the Central Plateau of MILLEVACHES in France, six miles (ten km) west of the town of SORNAC. Its length is 235 miles (378 km). Its major tributaries are the Clain, Creuse and Taurion Rivers. It flows west past the city of LIMOGES, and north past CHATEL-LERAULT and CHINON to join the Loire River at SAUMUR.

Vilaine, Brittany, France

The Vilaine is the largest river in Brittany. It is 140 miles (230 km) long. Its major tributaries are the Ille, Meu, Oust and Don Rivers. It flows in a southwesterly direction past the towns of RENNES and REDON to enter the Bay of Biscay 19 miles (31 km) north of ST NAZAIRE which during World War II was one of the main targets of the Royal Air Force and USAAF in their Strategic Bombing Offensive.

Viliya, European USSR

The Viliya rises southwest of BEGOMI. It is 317 miles (510 km) long. It flows past VILAN in Lithuania to join the Neman River at KAUNAS.

Vindel, Lapland, Sweden

The Vindel rises east of MO and is noted for its excellent salmon fishing and logging industries. It flows 280 miles (450 km) southeast to join the Ume River at VANNASBY.

Vistula, Poland

The Vistula is 678 miles (1091 km) and the longest river in Poland. It has its source on the slopes of Barania Gora in the Beskid Mountain Range at a height of over 3000 feet (900 m). The river has an asymmetric pattern, gathering its tributaries from the right and not from the left. It flows eastward and northeast through the city of CRACOW to the confluence with the San River. Then it changes course taking a northerly direction to the capital city of Poland, WARSAW. Leaving Warsaw the

Vistula flows west and northwest through the towns of WLOCLAWEK and TORUN. The width of the Vistula varies from 450 yards (410 m) at Cracow, to 1320 yards (1210 m) at Warsaw and one mile (1610 m) at Torun. It splits into two distinct streams about 30 miles (48 km) from the sea. The Nogat River is the eastern stream of the Vistula and flows northeast through the Marsh Lands. The Leniwka, the main branch, flows north directly into the Gulf of Danzig. The Vistula is only navigable for small vessels upstream from the San River, below this it is accessible for steamers carrying varying cargo. It empties into the Baltic Sea.

Vit, Bulgaria

This river is formed by the confluence of the Beli Vit and Cherni Vit Rivers which rise in the Teteven Mountain Range. The Vit flows 120 miles (190 km) in a northerly direction until it finally joins the Danube River at SOMOVIT.

Vltava, Bohemia, Czechoslovakia

The river is formed by the confluence of two streams which meet at VOLARY. It is 267 miles (430 km) long. Its major tributaries are the Berounka, Luznice, Malse, Otava, and Sazava Rivers. It flows southeast initially, then changes to a northerly direction as it passes PRAGUE to eventually join the Elbe River opposite the town of MELNICK.

Volga, European USSR

This river is called 'Mother Volga' and is the greatest of all Russian rivers. It is 2292 miles (3688 km) and the longest river in Europe, even longer than the mighty Danube. This river has more historical events associated with it than any other comparable river. Economically, it is impossible to value. The Volga rises in the Valday Hills, an extremely swampy area, and then flows through a series of six small lakes. The numerous small streams in this area not only flow into the Volga but also find their way to join the Dnepr and Western Dvina Rivers. The river flows first in a southeasterly direction. When the river reaches the ancient town of KALININ, it becomes navigable for large vessels. Leaving Kalinin, the Volga immediately enters the huge Ivankovo Reservoir which is over 34 miles (55 km) long. This is only the first of a series of dams and reservoirs which the Volga passes on its course to the Caspian Sea, its final destination. The Volga flows out of the reservoir and heads southeast through a narrow but steeply banked valley on its way to the historic town of YAROSLAVL. This town is at the beginning of a tremendously huge reservoir over 250 miles (400 km) long with an enormous dam at GORODETS. The river then receives its main right-bank tributary the Oka River, itself over 918 miles (1477 km) long, at GORKI. The town of Gorki once was the center of a great fur trade in the old days but now is completely modernized and the home of numerous industries. The Volga continues on its way to the next and largest of all the man-made reservoirs, the Kuybyshev. It was completed in late 1957, and encompasses 2300 square miles (5950 sq km), is 370 miles (600 km) long and 25 miles (40 km) wide. Joining the Volga at

Sunset over the Gorkiy reservoir on the Upper Volga, USSR.

A summer settlement of a collective fishery on the Volga near the Caspian Sea, Astrakhan Region, USSR.

A Russian Orthodox church on the banks of the Volga.

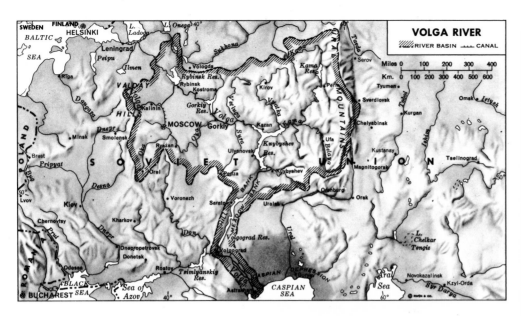

the Kuybyshev is its greatest tributary the Kama River, itself over 1262 miles (2031 km) long and with its own distinct series of reservoirs and dams. On the banks of the great reservoir stands the town of ULYANOVSK, the birthplace of Lenin. Further down is the town of KAZAN which Ivan the Terrible took from the Tartars in 1552. Passing Kazan, the river flows southward through open and intensely cultivated steppes on its way to the Zhigulevsk dam. Here the Volga makes a great loop, known as the Samara Bend, named after the Samara River which joins the Volga at KUYBYSHEV, a town noted for its great refineries. The next stop for the river is at SARATOV where the Volga enters another huge reservoir, the Volgograd. This reservoir covers 1200 square miles (3100 sq km) and is over 370 miles (600 km) long. It was here at Volgograd (STALINGRAD) that one of the greatest battles of World War II was fought between the Soviet Army and the Germans. Further south is the beginning of the Volga-Don canal; completed in 1952, it opened the Volga to ocean-going ships. The next stage of the Volga or the lower course flows through a semi-arid region. The delta of the Volga actually begins about a hundred miles (160 km) from the Caspian Sea which gives an idea how large the delta system really is. This area of the river is rich in natural beauty, including rare plants and wildlife. The Volga is noted for its great variety of sturgeon, producing top grade caviar.

Volkhov, European USSR

The river rises in Lake Ilmen, in northwest Russia. The Volkhov's length is 140 miles (230 km). It flows northeast past the ancient city of NOVGOROD, KIRISHI and VOLKHOV to enter Lake Ladoga.

Volturno, Italy

The Volturno rises in the Apennine Mountains north of the town of VENAFO. The Volturno is the chief river of the boot of Italy. It is 109 miles (175 km) long. It flows past Capua to enter the Tyrrhenian Sea 23 miles (37 km) northwest of the city of NAPLES, once the capital of the Kingdom of Naples and Sicily.

Voronezh, European USSR

This river is formed by the confluence of two headstreams south of MICHURINSK. It has a length of 225 miles (362 km). It flows in a southerly direction past LIPETSK to join the Don River below the city of VORONEZH.

Vorskla, European USSR

The Vorskla river rises southeast of Oboyan in the central Russian Upland. It has a length of 200 miles (320 km). It flows in a southwesterly direction past the towns of GRAIVORON, POLTAVA and KOBELYAKI and joins the Dnepr River southeast of KREMENCHUG.

Vrbas, Bosnia, Yugoslavia

The Vrbas rises southwest of FOJNICA and flows north past the town of JAJCE to become a tributary of the Sava River ten miles (16 km) from GRADISKA. It is 149 miles (240 km) long.

Vuoksi, Finland

This river is one of the most turbulent in Europe with a length of 93 miles (150 km). It has the largest drainage area of any river in Finland. The Vuoksi is the major outlet for Lake Samimaa in the eastern portion of Finland to Lake Ladoga in the Soviet Union. The lower reaches of the river have become famous for the impressive rapids and falls at TAINIONKOWSKI, ENSO and ROUHIALA. They have been included in all major guide books for the past 110 years.

Vyatka, European USSR

This large central Russian river rises in the central Ural Mountain Range. It is 849 miles (1366 km) long. It flows in three directions, north, southwest and south/southwest to join the Kama River as a tributary.

Vychegda, European USSR

This large river rises in the south Timan Ridge. It is 700 miles (1130 km) long. It flows in a westerly direction and passes UST-KULOM and YARENSK to join the Lesser Northern Dvina River at KOTLAS to form the Northern

Dvina River. The Vychegda River has a thriving lumber industry along its banks.

Vyrnwy, Powys, Wales

The origin of Vyrnwy River is in a group of little streams which run into Lake Vyrnwy in Powys. It flows in an easterly direction to join the River Severn northeast of WELSHPOOL.

Waller's Haven, East Sussex, England

The river rises on the high ground south of HEATHFIELD and continues past BATTLE, the site of the battle between William the Conqueror and Harold of England in 1066. William as the victor commemorated the site by building an abbey next to the spot where King Harold died. The river flows into the English Channel at PEVENSEY Sluice. The Waller's Haven receives the Nunningham Stream, Hugletts Stream and the Ash Bourne.

Wansbeck, Northumberland, England

The Wansbeck begins near Sweethope Loughs and flows east picking up the River Font at the town of MORPETH. It then heads for the North Sea between the resorts of BLYTH and NEWBIGGIN-BY-THE-SEA.

Warks Burn, Northumberland, England

Warks Burn rises near Great Watch Hill near the Cumbrian border. It heads eastward through the Wark Forest to join the River North Tyne below the village of WARK.

Warnow, East Germany

The Warnow has its source near PARCHIM in northern Germany. It runs west, then north before turning northeast past the town of BUTZOW and ROSTOCK. The river is 79 miles (127 km) long and enters the Baltic Sea near WARNEMUNDE via the seven mile (11 km) long estuary of the Warnow.

Warta, Poland

The Warta rises 80 miles (129 km) northwest of the Polish city of CRACOW in the Carpathian Mountain Range. It is 445 miles (716 km) long and flows north by northwest to join the Oder River at the town of KOSTRZYN in northern Germany. The Warta is the principal tributary of the Oder and is linked with the Vistula River by the Bydgoszcz Canal and the Notec River. The river is navigable from the city of KONIN in the western region of Poland to POZNAN.

Water of Fleet, Dumfries and Galloway, Scotland

The river rises on the eastern side of the Cairsmore of Fleet at a height of 2331 feet (711 m) as the Big Water of Fleet which meets with the Little Water of Fleet at the tiny hamlet of CASTRAMONT to form the Water of Fleet. The river flows past the Gatehouse of Fleet to enter the BAY OF FLEET.

Top: The Smetana museum across the Vltava River, Prague.

Left: Another view of Prague and the Vltava River.

Wear, Durham, England

The Wear is 75 miles (121 km) long and rises on the peat moors of the Pennine Hills where numerous small streams come together in the vicinity of WEARHEAD. The river flows northward and creates a series of small meanders which cut deeply into the surrounding countryside. The city of DURHAM is noted for its extensively fortified Norman castle and its beautiful cathedral. The meanders of the Wear gave the region a superbly defensive position and Durham castle provided the defense for the city. The Wear enters the North Sea at SUNDERLAND, a great industrial town, also noted for its football team.

Water of Girvan, Strathclyde, Scotland

The Water of Girvan rises in Loch Girvan Eye and flows north through the Glentrool Forest Park. The river then runs through Loch Bradan Reservoir to the town of STRAITON. It then turns around the northern side of Crosshill and swings southwest past DAILLY to the coast at Girvan.

Water of Ken, Dumfries and Galloway, Scotland

This river rises near the borders of Strathclyde and Dumfries and Galloway, just northwest of CARSPHAIRN. It runs south through Carsfad and Earstoun Lochs, then past New Galloway to the Loch of Ken and finally joins the River Dee.

Water of Minnoch, Dumfries and Galloway, Scotland

This region of Scotland is noted for its numerous rivers and excellent fishing streams. The Water of Minnoch is no exception,

Sluice gate on the Waveney River, Ellingham, Norfolk.

running south through Glentrool Forest to join the River Cree northwest of NEWTON STEWART.

Water of Nevis, Highlands, Scotland

The river rises in the Lochaber district in the Mamore Forest. It runs first northeast, then swings to a westerly course past Ben Nevis, the highest mountain of Britain at 4408 feet (1344 m). Ben Nevis is an imposing sight even from a distance. The river heads northwest to enter Loch Linnhe at FORT WILLIAM.

Waveney, Norfolk-Suffolk, England

The Waveney rises near the borders of Norfolk and Suffolk, the two easternmost counties of East Anglia. The river is 50 miles (80 km) long. The Waveney runs past BECCLES and a few other small towns before entering the River Yare at BREYDON WATER. The river is navigable as far as BUNGAY.

Weaver, Cheshire, England

The Weaver rises south of Peckforton and runs southeast to where it is joined by the River Ducknow near the village of Audlem. The river then runs north past WINSFORD, then northwest to the Manchester Ship Canal to finally enter the River Mersey south of RUNCORN.

Webburn, Devon, England

The Webburn is formed by the confluence of the East and West Webburn rivers which rise on Dartmoor. They flow west of MANATON, then head south and join to form the Webburn just east of PONSWORTHY. The river then runs through a heavily wooded valley to join the River Dart south of the charming village of BUCKLAND IN THE MOOR.

The Welland River at Colly Weston on the Northamptonshire border.

Welland, Leicestershire, England

This Midland river rises near MOWSLEY, west of the town of MARKET HARBOROUGH. It runs northeast of STAMFORD, MARKET DEEPING and SPALDING in Lincolnshire before entering the Wash seven miles (11 km) north of HOLBEACH.

Wensum, Norfolk, England

The Wensum rises near the village of HORNINGTOFT, four miles (six km) south of FAKENHAM. It runs westward through Fakenham, then turns southeast towards the cathedral city of NORWICH where it becomes a tributary of the River Yare.

Weser, Germany

The Weser is formed by the confluence of the Fulda and Werra rivers in northwestern Germany. It is 300 miles (480 km) long and flows northward as a shallow river until it reaches the historic city of HAMELIN. Every child knows the nursery story of *The Pied Piper of Hamelin*. The Weser runs through the North German Lowlands, then crosses the rich agricultural area to the town of NIENBURG. After receiving the Aller River, it turns west to BREMEN. The river flows for a distance of 40 miles (64 km) and reaches the great port of BREMERHAVEN. The Weser is not navigable for large commercial vessels. It runs into the Heligoland Bight, part of the North Sea.

Wharfe, North Yorkshire, England

The Wharfe is 60 miles (97 km) long and runs from south of HAWES on an easterly course, then changes direction to a more southeasterly course before resuming its original course at ILKLEY. It carries on to CAWOOD where it becomes a tributary of the River Ouse.

White Cart Water, Strathclyde, Scotland

The White Cart Water has its source south of East KILBRIDE. It runs north to CATHCART, Glasgow, then moves slightly northwest to PAISLEY to link up with the Black Cart Water and run into the River Clyde.

White Esk, Dumfries and Galloway, Scotland

The White Esk rises at a height of 2269 feet (692 m) on Ettrick Pen and flows south through ESKDALEMUIR to join the Black Esk River. The confluence of these two form the River Esk eight miles northwest of LANGHOLM.

White Lyne, Cumbria, England

The White Lyne rises in the Lake district, an area noted for some of the most beautiful English scenery. It runs from the fells north of BEWCASTLE to southwest where it meets the Black Lyne to form the River Lyne five miles west of the town of Bewcastle.

Whitewater, Hampshire, England

The Whitewater rises at SPRING HEAD east of the town of BASINGSTOKE. The river runs north to join the Blackwater near SWALLOWFIELD.

Wieprz, Poland

The Wieprz rises north of Tomaszow Lubelski and runs for a total of 194 miles (312 km). The river flows northwest and then west to the Vistula River near the town of PULAWY.

Windrush, Gloucestershire, England

This beautiful little river rises in the Cotswold Hills east of WINCHCOMBE, and then flows southeast to join the Thames at NEWBRIDGE.

Wissey, Norfolk, England

This river rises southwest of DEREHAM in Norfolk. The Wissey runs west into the River Ouse near DOWNHAM MARKET.

Witham, Leicestershire, England

This winding river begins near WYMONDHAM, a small village in Leicestershire. It flows through GRANTHAM to the cathedral city of LINCOLN, which in Roman times was the fortress of the Ninth Legion. Lincoln is a beautiful city and has a splendid cathedral as well as nearby castle. The Witham enters the Wash southeast of BOSTON.

Wkra, Poland

The Wkra River has its source four miles (six km) northwest of the town of NIDZICA in

northeastern Poland. The river is 164 miles (264 km) long and runs southeast to the Narew River at NOWY DWOR.

Wolf Water, Devon, England

This small river rises in the Halwill Forest of Devon. It flows south into the River Thrushel a mile (1610 m) northeast of the small village of LIFTON, northeast of LAUNCESTON.

Wooler Water, Northumberland, England

This river rises originally as the Harthope Burn on the eastern slopes of the Cheviot Hills of Northumberland. The Wooler Water runs northeast past the town of WOOLER and joins the River Till, a mile (1610 m) northeast of the town.

Worfe, Shropshire, England

The river rises near SHIFNAL and runs south, then west to join the River Severn a couple of miles north of BRIDGNORTH.

Worth, Lancashire, England

The Worth rises on the borders of Lancashire and West Yorkshire west of the town of HAWORTH. It runs east, then shifts slightly to a northeasterly course through KEIGHLEY to join the River Aire.

Wreake, Leicestershire, England

The Wreake rises initially as the River Eye, just northeast of WALTHAM ON THE WOLD, a small village. The river runs south, then west to MELTON MOWBRAY and from here on it is known as the Wreake until its confluence with the River Soar north of the city of LEICESTER.

Wye, Buckinghamshire, England

The Wye rises northwest of WEST WYCOMBE, a quaint, rural English village, noted for its old world look and nearby caves made by the laborers of Sir Francis Dashwood. His famous 'Hell Fire Gang' was noted for its orgies and delvings into the occult in the 18th century. The Wye flows nine miles (14 km) southeast through HIGH WYCOMBE, a town noted for its furniture trade, and then flows through LOUDWATER, and reaches the Thames near HEDSOR.

Wye, Wales-England

The Wye rises on Plynlimon Fawr, Wales, at a height of 2000 feet (600 m). The river is 130 miles (210 km) long and runs only a few miles from the source of the River Severn through a V-shaped valley. The Wye's principal tributaries are the Elan from which the Midland city of BIRMINGHAM draws its water supply through a series of reservoirs; the Lugg joins the main river at the important market and cathedral town of HEREFORD; and the last major tributary is the Monnow, which the Wye picks up near the town of MONMOUTH. The river flows through some of the most beautiful gorges in England and Wales. Once past ROSS-ON-WYE, the river runs through the Forest of

Left: A gorge on the Wye in the heart of Wales.
Below: The Wye near Aberedw, Wales.

Dean and passes by the spectacular remains of Tintern Abbey which is a great tourist attraction.

Yar, Isle of Wight, England

The river rises near FRESHWATER BAY on the southwest coast of this beautiful resort island located just off the southern English coast. The Isle of Wight is separated from the mainland by a narrow channel called the Solent, and ferries reach it from LYMINGTON, SOUTHAMPTON and PORTSMOUTH. The Yar flows on a northerly course and enters the Solent at the town of YARMOUTH. King Henry VIII built a castle here for coastal defense during his reign.

Yar, Isle of Wight, England

A second river also named Yar, it rises near NITON close to the south coast. It flows first northward, and then eastward into Brading Harbor which is just west of the town of BEMBRIDGE.

Yare, Norfolk, England

This river gives its name to the seaport town of GREAT YARMOUTH at its mouth. Great Yarmouth has grown extensively since the discovery of North Sea oil. The Yare has its source near SHIPDAM in Norfolk. It flows east around the cathedral city of NORWICH and into the North Sea at GORLESTON, Great Yarmouth.

Yantra, Bulgaria

The source of the Yantra is three small headstreams which meet south of GABROVO in the Shipka Mountains. The river is 168 miles (270 km) long. It flows northeast by the town of TIRNOVO, then changes course slightly to the northwest and passes BIALA. The main tributaries of the Yantra are the Bregovica and Rosica Rivers. Its final destination is the Danube which it enters near SVISTOV.

Yarty, Devon, England

The river rises to the north of YARCOMBE, a village located at the foot of a very steep hill west of the town of CHARD. It flows south to enter the River Axe a mile (1610 m) southwest of the town of AXMINSTER.

Ydw, Dyfed, Wales

The river begins a few miles southeast of LLANDOVERY. The Ydw flows in a southwesterly direction to join the River Bran as a tributary just east of LLANGADOG.

Yeo, Avon, England

The river begins at the village of COMPTON MARTIN laying at the north foot of the Mendip Hills. The Yeo heads in a northwesterly direction through Blagdon Lake, sometimes called the Yeo Reservoir, and on to CONGRESBURY. Next the river reaches its final destination, the mouth of the River Severn near CLEVEDON.

Yeo, Devon, England

The Yeo has its source near Whiddon Down on the very northern edge of Dartmoor. The river proceeds eastward to join the River Exe below Cowley Bridge just north of the city of EXETER.

Yeo, Dorset-Somerset, England

The Yeo rises east of SHERBORNE in Dorset. Sherborne is the center of a large agricultural district. The town has a medieval abbey and school and, to the east, the remains of a Norman castle. The river passes through town and continues to YEOVIL, then enters the River Parrett south of LANGPORT in Somerset.

Yonne, France

The Yonne is 182 miles (293 km) long. It rises in the Morvan massif of central France. The river flows northwest through the towns of

Below: The mouth of the Wye River at the Severn River below Chepstow.

AUXERRE, located at the head of the river's navigation, JOIGNY and SENS. The Yonne becomes a tributary of the Seine near MONTEREAU-FAUT-YONNE.

Yscir, Powys, Wales

This river has its source high on Mynydd Epynt in Powys in the form of two mountain streams, the Yscir Fawr and Yscir Fechan. These two small streams flow on a somewhat parallel course southward to PONT-FAEN. The streams then join together to make the Yscir which heads south to enter the River Usk at ABERYSCIR.

Ysgethin, Gwynedd, Wales

The Ysgethin, a river of the ancient kingdom of Gwynedd, flows west through Llyn Dulyn and Llyn Bodlyn. After leaving Llyn Bodlyn the river proceeds to enter Cardigan Bay six miles (ten km) northwest of the town of BARMOUTH.

Ystrad, Clwyd, Wales

The river flows northeast of the tiny hamlet of NANTGLYN and past the south side of the hill town of DENBIGH. The town of Denbigh is located high on the slopes of a steep hill, and off to the side is a Norman fortification, Denbigh Castle. The Ystrad then joins the River Clwyd approximately three miles (five km) to the east of Denbigh.

Ystwyth, Dyfed, Wales

The Ystwyth, a good fishing river of Dyfed, rises east of CWMYSTWYTH and then flows west by the hamlet of Cwmystwyth about seven miles (11 km) from the Devil's Bridge. It carries on past PONTRHYDYGROES to the south side of the town of LLANAFAN. The river enters Cardigan Bay with the River Rheidol south of ABERYSTWYTH, a market town which has the remains of a medieval castle.

Ythan, Grampian Region, Scotland

This scottish river has its source in the Wells of Ythan. This little stream heads east to METHLICK, then proceeds to the North Sea which it enters at NEWBURGH BAR.

Yuryuzan, European USSR

This river is 265 miles (426 km) long. It flows generally northeast initially, then shifts to a northwesterly direction, and flows past the towns of YURYUZAN VYAZOVAYA and MALOYAZ. It enters the Ufa River as a tributary near the town of KARAIDEL.

Zezere, Portugal

This medium-sized Portuguese river begins in the Sierra da Estrela of central Portugal. It has a length of 130 miles (210 km). The Zezere flows southwest to become a tributary of the Tagus at the town of CONSTANCIA.

Right : Once the scene of massive logging operations, the Androscoggin River is now the venue for water sports such as canoeing and fishing.

North America

Abitibi, Ontario, Canada

The name of this river is derived from an Algonquian Indian word describing Lake Abitibi's central location between the Ottawa Valley and Hudson Bay. The river flows out of the lake northward to join the Moose River. It is 230 miles (370 km) long and has four large hydroelectric stations which provide power for local mining developments.

Acaponeta, Mexico

The Acaponeta River rises in the Sierra Madre Occidental of western Mexico. It is 120 miles (190 km) long and flows south to Acaponeta, then swings west to enter the Pacific Ocean.

Agua Fria, Arizona, USA

The river rises in western Arizona and flows south to join the Gila River. The Lake Pleasant Dam is 45 miles (72 km) south-southeast of the old territorial capital of PRESCOTT. The river is 120 miles (190 km) long and flows through very scenic countryside.

Aguán, Honduras

The Aguán rises near the town of Yorito in northern Honduras. It is 150 miles (240 km) long and flows east-northeast to enter the Caribbean Sea. Its chief tributary is the Yaguale River.

Aguanaval, Mexico

This river rises northwest of Zacatecas in central Mexico. The Aguanaval is 250 miles (400 km) long and flows due north into Laguna de Viesca. The river irrigates the fertile Laguna district, a prime agricultural area.

Alabama, Alabama, USA

The river is formed by the confluence of the Coosa and Tallapoosa Rivers, seven miles (11 km) northeast of the capital, MONTGOMERY. The name Alabama is of Choctaw origin and means 'thicket-clearers' or 'vegetation gatherers.' The river runs due west to SELMA, then south before emptying into the Tombigbee River. The Alabama is 305 miles (491 km) long, drains an area of 22,600 square miles (58,500 sq km), has an average depth of between three to seven feet (one to two m) and is navigable for most of the year. It is utilized primarily for the transportation of bulk goods such as gravel, lumber, sand, cotton, fertilizers and gasoline.

Albany, Ontario, Canada

The Albany rises in Lake St Joseph in northern Ontario. It is 320 miles (510 km) long and flows east to enter James Bay. The river flows over a clay soil deposited by the melted Continental Ice Sheet. The river is one of Canada's most interesting and historic. The Hudson Bay Company established Fort Albany at the mouth of the river in 1684 for the transaction of their various business enterprises in the region. The fort was lost to the French in 1686 but was returned to the company in 1693. The chief tributary of the Albany is the Kenogami River.

Alatna, Alaska, USA

The Alatna rises in the Brooks Range of central Alaska. It is 200 miles (320 km) long and flows southeast to join the Koyukuk River at the gold mining village of Alatna. The temperature in this part of the world is extremely cold in the winter months and in October the river is frozen.

Allegheny, Pennsylvania-New York, USA

One of the main headwaters of the Ohio River, it rises at an altitude of 2250 feet (686 m) in the hilly, plateau region of Potter County, Pennsylvania. It flows northwest into New York, abruptly turns southwest for 120 miles (190 km), then swings southeast and southwest before meeting the Monongahela at Point Park and the 'Golden Triangle.' This confluence is one of the most spectacular river junctions in North America. The Allegheny is 325 miles (523 km) long and drains an area of 11,410 square miles (29,550 sq km). The chief tributaries are the Clarion, Conemaugh-Kiskiminetas Rivers.

Almendares, Cuba

The Almendares rises near TAPASTE in western Cuba. It is 27 miles (43 km) long, and flows into the Gulf of Mexico near HAVANA. It supplies drinking water to Havana, the capital city of Cuba.

Alsek, Yukon, Canada

The Alsek rises on the eastern slopes of the St Elias Mountains in the southwestern Yukon. The Alsek has a very winding course, and flows for 160 miles (260 km) south-southwest into the Gulf of Alaska.

Altamaha, Georgia, USA

This river is formed by the confluence of the Ocmulgee and the Oconee Rivers in east-central Georgia. It flows southeast for 137 miles (220 km) to enter Altamaha Sound of the Atlantic Ocean.

Ameca, Mexico

The Ameca rises approximately 14 miles (22 km) due west of Guadalajara in western Mexico. The river is 140 miles (230 km) long and enters the Pacific Ocean at Banderas Bay after flowing westward for the majority of its course.

Ammonoosuc, Vermont, USA

The Ammonoosuc rises in southern Coos County, Vermont. It flows west past TWIN MOUNTAIN, LITTLETON and BATH to join the Connecticut River at WOODSVILLE.

Anderson, Northwest Territories, Canada

The Anderson rises north of the Great Bear Lake in the Canadian Northwest Territories. It is 465 miles (748 km) long and flows northward to enter Wood Bay which then enters Liverpool Bay.

Androscoggin, Maine-New Hampshire, USA

The Androscoggin rises in the Rangeley, Richardson and Umbagog Lakes in Maine near its border with northeastern New Hampshire. The river is 175 miles (282 km) long and drains an area of 4000 square miles (10,360 sq km), quite a large region for such a small river. The river is joined by the Magalloway River, then heads southwest and south through New Hampshire. The Androscoggin heads towards Mt Adams, a peak standing 5798 feet (1768 m) high and Mt Washington nearby at 6288 feet (1918 m). Reaching the little town of GORHAM, the river swings east back into Maine, then south to LEWISTON, and finally southeast to join the Kennebec River to form an estuary called Merrymeeting Bay. The valley of the Androscoggin provides support to the local logging industry, pulp and paper factories, and the river has an abundance of fresh water fish.

Angelina, Texas, USA

The river rises near the town of TYLER in eastern Texas. It is 200 miles (320 km) long and flows southeast to join the Neches River, 12 miles (19 km) west of JASPER. The Angelina has very important flood control projects along its course and supplies drinking water for the nearby area.

Animas, Colorado, USA

The Animas rises north of SILVERTON in southwestern Colorado. It is 110 miles (180 km) long and flows due south passing Animas City and Durango to join the San Juan River in northern New Mexico. The river flows through some of the highest mountains in North America. A large hydroelectric station is located near the town of DURANGO, which has a population of 10,333.

Apalachicola, Georgia-Florida, USA

This river is formed by the confluence of the Flint and the Chattahoochee Rivers in southwestern Georgia. The Flint river flows down from southwestern Georgia while the Chattahoochee runs along the Alabama-Georgia borders, before joining up in Lake Seminole. The Apalachicola flows south through the northwestern section of Florida, forming the boundary of Liberty, Gulf and Franklin Counties before entering the Gulf of Mexico at the small seaport town of Apalachicola which has a total population of 3102. From the farthest headstream the river is 500 miles (800 km) long and drains 19,500 square miles (50,500 sq km).

Apishapa, Colorado, USA

The Apishapa rises near Trinchera Peak, 13,623 feet (4132 m) high, in the Sangre de Crisco Mountains in southeastern Colorado. It flows northeast passing Gulnare, which only has a population of 100, and AGUILAR before joining the Arkansas River between FOWLER and MANZANOLA, some 40 miles (64 km) upstream from PUEBLO. The Apishapa is 117 miles (188 km) long and passes through breath-taking scenery.

Appomattox, Virginia, USA

This river rises in central Virginia and flows east past FARMVILLE and PETERSBURG, the head of navigation, and finally reaches HOPEWELL to join the James River as a tributary. The river rises in Appomattox County, and nearby is Appomattox Court House where General Robert E Lee, Commanding General of the Army of Northern Virginia surrendered to General Ulysses S Grant to bring the American Civil War to an end. The river is 137 miles (220 km) long.

Arctic Red, Northwest Territories, Canada

The Arctic Red rises in the Mackenzie Mountains of the Canadian Northwest Territories. The Arctic Red is 230 miles (370 km) long and flows north to become a tributary of the Mackenzie River, which is the second largest river system on the North American continent. Although virtually uninhabited, this region is very scenic in parts.

Arecibo, Puerto Rico

Also called the Rio Grande de Arecibo, this river is 40 miles (64 km) long and runs from the central Cordillera in Puerto Rico to the Atlantic Ocean. This river provides a large proportion of the Island's hydroelectric power through the Dos Bocas Dam. The Arecibo is also linked with the Caonillas Dam on the river of the same name.

Arikaree, Colorado-Nebraska, USA

The Arikaree rises in northern Lincoln County, Colorado. It is 129 miles (208 km) long and flows east-northeast to join the North Fork Republican River at HAIGLER, Nebraska to form the Republican River.

Arkansas, Colorado-Kansas-Oklahoma-Arkansas, USA

The Arkansas River is one of the largest rivers in the United States. It is 1450 miles (2330 km) long and has a drainage area of 157,900 square miles (409,000 sq km). The river rises near LEADVILLE, Colorado on the Sawatch and Mosquito Ranges at an altitude of 10,000–14,000 feet (3050–4270 m) in the Rocky Mountains. The Arkansas is only

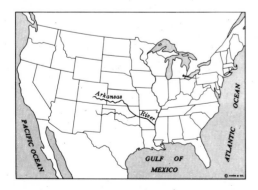

second to the Missouri among the many tributaries of the Mississippi. For its initial run through the Rocky Mountains between LEADVILLE and SALIDA, the river flows through a heavily forested area, carving a deep canyon

through the Rocky Mountain front called Royal Gorge. For its first 150 miles (240 km), the Arkansas flows generally southeast and drops a total of 6750 feet (2060 m) before leaving the Rockies at CANON CITY, Colorado. The chief tributaries of the Arkansas are the Canadian, Cimarron, Neosho, Verdigris, White and the Purgatoire Rivers. The river passes PUEBLO, then flows east across the dry plains of eastern Colorado. This area is one of flat topped mesas and arid landscapes. The main agricultural crops of this region are sugar beets, fruit and grain. The river crosses into Kansas and the valley is made up of hickory and oak forests and broad sandy country. For the majority of its course through Kansas, the river flows through one of the world's greatest wheat growing areas. The principal granaries are DODGE CITY, made famous by the old western movies and television programs, as well as GARDEN CITY, KINSLEY, GREAT BEND, HUTCHINSON and WICHITA. The river makes a great bend northward in central Kansas before swinging southeast and into Oklahoma. Although passing through wheat country adjoining corn and cotton fields, the river runs very near the oil refining city of TULSA. The river is restricted by levees as it passes through eastern Oklahoma and western Arkansas in the wide valley between the forested Boston and Ouachita mountains. This old trail was utilized by Indians, trappers, traders, settlers and the railways, and is now a land full of corn, cotton, livestock and large farms. Once past the city of LITTLE ROCK, the Arkansas meanders past PINE BLUFF to just south of ARKANSAS POST where it splits into two distributaries. These two arms of the Arkansas flow into the Mississippi within a few miles of the division. Much of the Arkansas's water is drawn off for various irrigation projects throughout its course, reducing the river to a trickle during the dry season. The Arkansas is one of the most important rivers in the southwestern United States.

Armeria, Mexico

This river, which rises in Jalisco, western Mexico, is known as the Ayutla River in the upper course and the San Pedro in the middle course. It is 140 miles (230 km) long and flows southeast and south through the fertile Colima Plain to enter the Pacific Ocean below the town of ARMERIA.

Aroostook, Maine-New Brunswick, USA-Canada

The Aroostook rises in north central Maine and is one of the most winding rivers in the eastern United States and Canada. It is 140 miles (230 km) long and flows east, northeast, south, north, east, north, northeast and east passing OXBOW, MASARDIS, SQUA PAN, SHERIDAN, WASHBURN, CROUSEVILLE, CARIBOU and FORT FAIRFIELD. The river joins the St John River at Aroostook Junction in New Brunswick about six miles (ten km) east of Fort Fairfield, just over the border.

Artibonite, Dominican Republic-Haiti

The Artibonite rises in the Dominican Republic and runs for 150 miles (240 km)

before entering the Gulf of Gonarves in Haiti. The US Marines crossed and recrossed this river numerous times during their long police action in the Dominican Republic in the 1900s.

Ashuanipi, Newfoundland, Canada

See Hamilton, Newfoundland, Canada.

Ashuapmuchan, Quebec, Canada

The Ashuapmuchan rises south-southeast of Chibougamau Lake in central Quebec. It is 170 miles (270 km) long and is a very winding river as it flows to its outlet St John Lake or Lac Saint Jean.

Assiniboine, Manitoba-Saskatchewan, Canada

The Assiniboine rises in eastern Saskatchewan and is 450 miles (720 km) long. It is named after the Indian tribe of that name, who are also called the Stone Indians. The principal tributaries of the river are the Qu'Appelle and the Souris Rivers. These three rivers have cut wide valleys in the surface of the prairies before flowing into the lowlands of the ancient Ice Age glacial Lake Agassiz, which was once a huge inland sea. The bluffs along the river provide a change from the low-lying prairies. The two chief cities on the Assiniboine are WINNIPEG, population 540,262, and BRANDON, population 31,000. Winnipeg is the railway center of the Canadian west and handles most of the grain from the prairie provinces. The Assiniboine empties into the Red River of the North at Winnipeg, which continues north to flow into Lake Winnipeg.

Athabasca, Alberta, Canada

The Athabasca River rises in the Jasper National Park of the Rocky Mountains. It flows generally northeast through Lake Jasper, past FORT MCMURRAY and enters Lake Athabasca. The river is 765 miles (1231 km) long and flows through the heartland of central Alberta. The chief tributaries are the Wildhay River, Sakwatamau River, Freeman River, McLeod River, Pembina River, Lesser Slave River and the Clearwater River.

Atoyac, Mexico

See Baloas, Mexico.

Attawapiskat, Ontario, Canada

The Attawapiskat rises in the central region of Patricia district in northern Ontario. It is known initially as the Otoskwin River and flows through a forested area into Lake Attawapiskat. Emerging from the lake it becomes the Attawapiskat and runs for 465 miles (748 km) first north and then east before entering James Bay. The mouth of the river supports a large population of ducks and geese which use this area as a migratory stopover; and the marshy region provides that type of grass known as 'wild rice.' The mouth of the river has a small Crow Indian settlement and small trading posts are located nearby. The principal towns on the river are situated on the headwaters in the gold producing region.

Athabasca Falls in Jasper National Park in the Rockies, Alberta.

Au Sable, New York, USA

The Au Sable River is formed by the confluence of the West Branch which rises near Lake Placid, and the East Branch which flows northeast past Mount Skylight, 4926 feet (1502 m) high, at the town of AU SABLE in northeastern Essex County. The Au Sable flows east-northeast forming the boundary between Essex and Clinton Counties before entering Lake Champlain.

Ayutla, Mexico

See Armeria, Mexico.

Babine, British Columbia, Canada

The Babine River rises in central British Columbia and flows northwest through Babine Lake to emerge near the town of BABINE. The river then swings west-northwest to join the Skeena River as one of its principal tributaries.

Back, Northwest Territories, Canada

The Back rises in Contwoyto Lake of the Northwest Territories. The river was named after Admiral Sir George Back, an expedition commander to this part of Canada between 1833–35. The river is slightly longer than 600 miles (960 km) and flows through a series of small lakes before tumbling over numerous rapids. The valley widens out into a large plain and the river forms Lakes Pelly, Garry and Macdougall, then cuts through rocky terrain into Lake Franklin. The Back finally ends its run into Chantry Inlet.

Balsas, Mexico

The Balsas is 450 miles (720 km) long and rises in the mountains of Tlaxcala State. The river

is wild and in its upper reaches is called the Atoyac. It flows south and southwest through Puebla State, then turns into Guerrero State where it is called the Mescala. The Balsas continues along the borders of Guerrero and Michoacan, both of which are mountainous states, before entering the Pacific Ocean. The river is virtually unnavigable because it runs through innumerable rapids. The valley of the Balsas on the other hand is one of the richest agricultural regions in the country.

Banana, Florida, USA

The Banana is not really a river but a shallow lagoon 30 miles (48 km) long on the eastern coast of Florida. This lagoon is situated between Merritt Island and Cape Canaveral beaches. Merritt Island is separated from the mainland by the Indian River which is just off its western beaches. This entire stretch of land is one continuous beautiful beach.

Barren, Kentucky, USA

The Barren is formed by the confluence of several small streams near FOUNTAIN RUN in southern Kentucky. It is 130 miles (210 km) long and flows generally northwest past BOWLING GREEN, the head of navigation, to join the Green River.

Bavispe, Mexico

The Bavispe rises in the Sierra Madre Occidental southwest of BACERAC in northwestern Mexico. It is 200 miles (320 km) long and flows northward circling the mountains, then swings south past Granados to join the Yaqui River.

Bayou Bartholomew, Arkansas-Louisiana, USA

This river rises near PINE BLUFF, Arkansas. It is 300 miles (480 km) long and flows south to join the Ouachita River in northern Louisiana.

Bear, Utah, USA

The Bear River rises in the Uinta Mountains of northeastern Utah. The river is not navigable, but it irrigates over 50,000 acres of otherwise arid land in Idaho and Utah. It flows north, then northwest around the northern portion of the Wasatch Range and south to the Great Salt Lake, about 13 miles (21 km) due west of BINGHAM CITY, Utah. The Bear is 350 miles (560 km) long.

Beaverland, Montana, USA

See Jefferson, Montana, USA.

Belize, Guatemala-Belize

The Belize rises near the town of DOLORES in Guatemala. It then crosses into British Honduras which is now called Belize. The river is 180 miles (290 km) long and enters the Caribbean Sea at the town of BELIZE.

Bersimis, Quebec, Canada

The Bersimis River rises south of Lake Pletipi

in central Quebec. It is also known as the Betsiamites and flows generally south to enter the St Lawrence River at the town of BETSIAMITES. The river rises in the same general area as the larger Outardes and Manicouagan Rivers and is 250 miles (400 km) long.

Big Blue, Nebraska-Kansas, USA

The Big Blue rises in several headstreams in southeastern Nebraska. Its chief tributary is the Little Blue River which is 206 miles (331 km) long. The river is 250 miles (400 km) long and flows south passing the town of BEATRICE on its way to join the Kansas River near MANHATTAN, Kansas.

Bighorn, Wyoming-Montana, USA

The Bighorn is formed by the confluence of the Popo Agie River which is 60 miles (97 km) long, and the Wind River which is 110 miles (180 km) long, at the town of RIVERTON, Wyoming. It flows north through Freemont County and the Boysen Reservoir, where it is joined by Muskrat Creek, Muddy Creek, Fivemile Creek and Badwater Creek. The Bighorn then flows past the town of BOYSEN, through the Owl Creek Mountains and the Wind River Canyon as it continues northward. The Bighorn is noted for its important irrigation projects at RIVERTON and BIGHORN. It is 461 miles (742 km) long and finally flows into the Yellowstone River at the town of BIGHORN, Montana.

Big Sioux, South Dakota-Iowa, USA

The Big Sioux rises in northeastern South Dakota at a height of 1760 feet (537 m), just north of WATERTOWN. It is 420 miles (680 km) long and flows south, draining the Coteau des Prairies of southwestern Minnesota and northwestern Iowa. The Sioux Indians occupied this region for centuries before the coming of the white man. At PIPESTONE, Minnesota are located the famous catlinite quarries, where the smooth pinkish-red stone was cut into ceremonial pipes. The chief tributary of the Big Sioux is the Rock River. The Big Sioux Valley is located on the very edge of the great American corn belt. West of the Big Sioux Valley is prime cattle country and SIOUX FALLS, South Dakota and SIOUX CITY, Iowa have grown into important meat-packing centers of the mid-western United States. The river takes a fall at Sioux Falls for approximately 20 feet (6 m), and a hydroelectric power station is situated here to provide power to the city. Between Sioux Falls and Sioux City the river forms the border between South Dakota and Iowa. The Big Sioux and the Floyd Rivers join the Missouri River at Sioux City.

Black, Missouri, USA

The Black River rises in Reynolds County, Missouri and meanders southeast and southwest through Arkansas to join the White River near the town of NEWPORT. The Black River is 300 miles (480 km) long and its chief tributary is the Current River which is 225 miles (362 km) long.

Black, New York, USA

The Black rises in Herkimer County, north-central New York. It flows southwest, northwest and west past ALDER CREEK, PORT LEYDEN, LYONS FALLS, GLENFIELD, CASTORLAND, GREAT BEND and DEXTER, to enter Sacketts Harbor, Lake Ontario.

Black Warrior, Alabama, USA

The Black Warrior rises in the southern Appalachian Mountains of northern Alabama. It flows southwest through Jefferson County, passing the towns of TRAFFORD, KIMBERLEY and SAYRE before running into Bankhead Lake. It leaves the lake at its southwest extremity continuing through Tuscaloosa County to Demopolis Lake. It joins the Tombigbee River near the Demopolis Dam.

Blue, Colorado, USA

The Blue rises in Summit County in the Rocky Mountains of central Colorado. It flows northwest through Green Mountain Reservoir to join the Colorado River in Grand County. The surrounding countryside is some of the loveliest in the state.

Boeuf, Arkansas, USA

The Boeuf River rises near PINE BLUFF located in southeastern Arkansas. It flows for 230 miles (370 km) in a southwesterly direction through northeastern Louisiana to join the Ouachita River.

Boise, Idaho, USA

The Boise rises in Lucky Peak Reservoir, Ada County, west-central Idaho. It runs west past the state capital of BOISE, GARDEN CITY, STAR EAGLE and NOTUS before joining the Snake River on the Oregon border.

Bow, Alberta, Canada

The Bow rises on the borders of British Columbia and Alberta in the Rocky Mountains of Canada. It is 315 miles (507 km) long and flows southeast through one of the most scenic and beautiful regions in Alberta, the Banff National Park. It then runs through Lake Louise and the town of BANFF, which is the center of a resort area. The river turns eastward through the magnificent Bow River Pass and heads for CALGARY, which has a population of 403,319, and is the home of the famous Calgary Stampede. Leaving Calgary the Bow turns southeast once again to join the Oldman River about 45 miles (72 km) west of MEDICINE HAT to form the South Saskatchewan River. Southeast of Calgary the Bow is dammed by one of the longest irrigation project dams in the world, the Horseshoe Bend Dam, also known as the Bassano. The Bow is an interesting river and flows through some of the finest ranching country in Canada.

Boyer, Iowa, USA

The Boyer rises close to STORM LAKE, a town in western Iowa with a population of 2104. It is 139 miles (224 km) long and flows south and southwest to join the Missouri River about 13 miles (21 km) due north of COUNCIL BLUFFS, Iowa.

Calgary, the home of Canada's famous Calgary Stampede, as seen from the Bow River.

Brandywine Creek, Pennsylvania-Delaware, USA

The Brandywine Creek is formed by two small branches which come together in Chester County, Pennsylvania, approximately ten miles (16 km) southeast of COATESVILLE. This little river is important in American history because it was the scene of one of General George Washington's defeats at the hands of the British in September 1777. The river flows for 20 miles (32 km) southeast, passing CHADDS FORD, and then runs through northern Delaware to join the Christina River, near that river's junction with the much larger Delaware. The Brandywine was once famous for its spawning fish and was utilized very early as a source of water power for the colonists. Gunpowder and flour became America's great early industries along the banks of the Brandywine. WILMINGTON, the great port city of Delaware, is located at the double estuary of the Brandywine and the Christina Rivers and is an important commercial trading center.

Brazos, Texas, USA

The Brazos is a typical 'western' river, rising on the rolling plains and mesquite woodlands of Stonewall County, Texas, at the confluence of the Salt and Double Mountain Forks. The river is 870 miles (1400 km) long and flows southeast across Texas. The chief tributary of the Brazos is Clear Fork which is 220 miles (350 km) long, and joins the river in Young County. This region is largely agricultural, but has dairies, mining centers and oil producing areas as well. The Brazos passes WACO, named after the Huaco Indians who lived in this region hundreds of years ago. Waco was only a ferry landing on the Brazos in bygone days but it has since grown to be an important commercial center for this area of the Lone Star State. The river enters the Gulf of Mexico at FREEPORT, a town of 11,997, which serves the area as its principal deep-water port and port of entry to the Gulf Intercoastal Waterway. One of the most famous tourist attractions in Texas, Inspiration Point, is on the Brazos about eight miles (13 km) south of Mineral Wells. Also of interest is the beautiful Yellowstone Canyon of the Brazos, which has since been incorporated into the Mackenzie State Park near the city of LUBBOCK. This river is noted throughout its length as one of the state's most scenic natural resources.

Buffalo, Arkansas, USA

The Buffalo rises in the Ozarks of northwestern Arkansas. It is 150 miles (240 km) long and flows east-northeast through the Ozarks to join the White River just southeast of YELLVILLE, with a population of 860, in Arkansas.

Bulkley, British Columbia, Canada

The Bulkley River rises in the Coast Mountains west of Babine Lake in central British Columbia. The Bulkley is 120 miles (190 km) long and flows due west past TELKWA and SMITHERS to join the Skeena River near SOUTH HAZELTON.

Cacapon, West Virginia, USA

The Cacapon begins in Hardy County, West

Mt Rundle overlooking the Bow River.

Virginia as the Lost River and flows past the towns of MATHIAS, LOST CITY and LOST RIVER. After 25 miles (40 km) the water disappears for no apparent reason and does not reappear until WARDENSVILLE. There it is known as the Cacapon River and flows northeast past CAPON BRIDGE and GREAT CACAPON before entering the Potomac River. The river is approximately 85 miles (136 km) long.

Cache, Missouri-Arkansas, USA
The Cache rises in southeastern Missouri and crosses into Clay County, Arkansas. It is 213 miles (343 km) long and flows south-southwest, passing PITTS, ALGOA, PATTERSON and GREYS before joining the White River at CLARENDON.

Cache La Poudre, Colorado, USA
The Cache La Poudre River rises north of the Rocky Mountain National Park in northern Colorado. It is 126 miles (203 km) long and flows past the towns of BELLVUE, LAPORTE, FORT COLLINS, TIMNATH and GREELEY, heading north, east and southeast, before linking up with the South Platte River just past Greeley. The Cache La Poudre receives water from the Laramie River through a two-mile (three-km) tunnel which is an integral part of a large-scale irrigation scheme in the adjacent area.

Cahaba, Alabama, USA
The Cahaba rises in St Clair County, central Alabama, northeast of BIRMINGHAM. It is 200 miles (320 km) long and flows southwest past CENTREVILLE, SUTTLE and CAHABA before joining the Alabama River. The Cahaba supplies a large part of Birmingham's fresh water.

Calaveras, California, USA
The Calaveras rises as the North Fork River in central California and flows for 25 miles (40 km) before joining the South Fork River west of SAN ANDREAS. It flows southwest to join the San Joaquin River slightly west of STOCKTON. The river is very important as it is an integral part of the Central Valley irrigation and hydroelectric schemes. It is 75 miles (121 km) long including the North Fork River.

Calcasieu, Louisiana, USA
The Calcasieu River rises in Vernon parish, west-central Louisiana. It is 215 miles (346 km) long and flows south-southwest through Allen, Calcasieu and Cameron parishes, then Lake Calcasieu before entering the Gulf of Mexico at the town of CAMERON. The lake is connected by a 30-foot (nine-m) wide shipping channel to link with LAKE CHARLES city.

Caloosahatchee, Florida, USA
The Caloosahatchee River rises in Lake Hicpochee in southern Florida. It is 75 miles (120 km) long and flows west-southwest past FORT MYERS and into the Gulf of Mexico. The river is over one mile (1610 m) wide for the last section of its course as it begins to run into the Gulf.

Calumet, Illinois, USA
The Calumet is a short stream which is kept dredged because, along with Lake Calumet, it is a very important part of the Chicago Harbor and Illinois Waterway system. This area is the most densely populated in the state.

Canadian, New Mexico-Texas-Oklahoma, USA
The Canadian River rises near the northeastern border of Colorado and New Mexico. It is 900 miles (1450 km) long and flows southeast initially from its source high in the Sangre de Cristo Mountains. The river runs through Colfax County and then flows due south past MAXWELL. It is joined by the Vermejo River near FRENCH and shortly afterward by the Cimarron River. The river continues south serving as the boundary between Mora and Harding Counties and then flows through the Conchas Reservoir, turning eastward into the Texas Panhandle. The Conchas Dam is 235 feet (72 m) high and 1250 feet (380 m) long, and has been extended several times by earth dams up to a length of four miles (six km). The Canadian flows through the Ute Reservoir just before crossing into Texas. In the Panhandle the river runs through Lake Meredith and the Sanford National Recreation Area, heading northeast into Oklahoma. It is joined by the North Canadian River about 27 miles (43 km) northeast of the town of MCALESTER in eastern Oklahoma at the Eufaula Reservoir. The river is also known as the South Canadian because of its relatively southerly course in relation to its tributary the North Canadian. The Canadian drains an area of 29,700 square miles (76,009 sq km) and is totally unnavigable. Its primary use is for irrigation projects and flood control. The Canadian empties into the Arkansas River as one of its chief tributaries.

Candelaria, Guatemala
The Candelaria River rises in Guatemala near the border of Mexico. It crosses the border and flows for 130 miles (210 km) northwest and north through a dense tropical forest to enter the Laguna de Terminos on the Bay of Campeche. The Candelaria is navigable for 45 miles (72 km) and is utilized primarily for logging.

Caney, Kansas, USA
The Caney rises in southeastern Kansas. It is 165 miles (265 km) long and flows south and southeast into Oklahoma to join the Verdigris River east of TULSA. The Hulah Dam and Reservoir are located on the river northwest of the town of BARTLESVILLE and are extremely important flood control projects.

Caney Fork, Tennessee, USA
The Caney Fork River rises in central Tennessee and runs west and northwest to join the Cumberland River near the town of CARTHAGE. The large dams of Great Fall and Center Hill are located on its course. The river is 144 miles (232 km) long and flows through Tennessee's finest scenic countryside.

Caniapiskau, Quebec, Canada
Rising in northern Quebec, the Caniapiskau River flows from Lake Caniapiskau, which covers an area of 375 square miles (970 sq km), north-northwest to join the Larch River, southwest of Fort Chimo to form the Koksoak River. The Caniapiskau is 450 miles (720 km) long.

Canisteo, New York, USA

The Canisteo rises near Arkport, western Steuben County, New York. It flows south-southeast past HORNELL, CANISTEO and CAMERON. It is joined by the Tioga River and continues to merge with Cohocton River to form the Chemung River, a tributary of the Susquehanna River.

Cannon, Minnesota, USA

The Cannon River rises in the lake area of Rice County, Minnesota. It is 100 miles (160 km) long and flows west, south and northeast passing Cannon Falls before joining the Mississippi River. Its chief tributary is the Straight River, which is 40 miles (64 km) long at the town of FARIBAULT.

Cannonball, North Dakota, USA

The Cannonball rises in the Badlands of southwestern North Dakota. It is 295 miles (475 km) long and flows east-southeast past NEW ENGLAND, HAVELOCK, MOTT and BURT before receiving the Cedar Creek River. Its last leg is northeast past SHIELDS, BREIEN and SOLEN to enter Lake Oahe of the Missouri River.

Caonillas, Puerto Rico

The Caonillas River rises in central Puerto Rico in an area of lush vegetation. It is only 25 miles (40 km) long but is very important because of the hydroelectric station and lake which it runs. It is a chief tributary of the Arecibo River which along with Dos Bocas Reservoir and hydroelectric station provide the majority of the island's electrical power.

Cape Fear, North Carolina, USA

The Cape Fear River is formed by the confluence of the Deep and Haw Rivers just below the Hope Reservoir in the Piedmont Region of central North Carolina. The river is 200 miles (320 km) long and flows on a winding course generally south-southeast. It passes through Lee, Harnett and Cumberland Counties to the head of its navigation, the town of FAYETTEVILLE which has a population of 212,042. The Cape Fear is well known for its flooding and has been recorded to rise as much as 30 feet (nine m) in only 24 hours, inundating the adjacent farmland with its flood waters. Flowing across the agricultural coastal plain the river reaches ELIZABETHTOWN in Bladen County. The South River joins it above the port of WILMINGTON, which has a population of 107,292. Wilmington was a principal port for the Confederate States of America during the Civil War 1861–65. On the estuary is located the remains of several fortifications, notably Fort Caswell, Fort Johnson and Fort Fisher. On 15 January 1865 Fort Fisher fell before a tremendous assault from land and sea, and Wilmington, the last Confederate seaport, was evacuated on the 22 February. For the hardy hunter of memorabilia, the beaches still are exposed to the Atlantic winds which occasionally turn up skeletons and cannonballs, grim reminders of the Civil War. The river itself enters the Atlantic at Cape Fear.

Carson, Nevada-California, USA

The Carson River is formed by the confluence of the East and West Carson Rivers near the beautiful and scenic Lake Tahoe. It is 125 miles (200 km) long and flows northeast past the capital of Nevada, CARSON CITY, and the small town of FALLON before running into the Carson Sink, the remains of an ancient lake in western Nevada. The Carson Sink is 20 miles (32 km) long by 15 miles (24 km) wide and is between the Trinity and Stillwater Ranges. This section of Nevada was once the location of numerous lakes and waterways long since dried up, but their remains are quite evident.

Casas Grandes, Mexico

The Casas Grandes rises south of BUENAVEN-TURA in northern Mexico. It is 250 miles (400 km) long and flows north for the majority of its course, but nearing the US border it swings east then south to Lake Guzman.

Cataraqui, Ontario, Canada

The Cataraqui River rises in Rideau Lake, southern Ontario, Canada. It is 70 miles (113 km) long and runs southwest on a winding course to enter Lake Ontario at KINGSTON.

Catawba, North Carolina-South Carolina, USA

The Catawba is named for an Indian tribe of that name which used to dwell throughout this rich and forested region prior to the arrival of the white man. The river rises south of Mount Mitchell, which is 6684 feet (2039 m) high, and flows east passing the Rhodhiss Dam and reservoir. The Catawba then passes the beautiful country town of MOUNT HOLLY which has a population of 5617. It then flows into Wylie Lake and over the border into South Carolina. Between the Broad River in Cleveland County and the Catawba is the famous Revolutionary War battlefield of Kings Mountain. Along the river in York County is a small Indian reservation set aside for the Catawba tribe. The river continues southeast through the once important power center of GREAT FALLS, which has since been replaced by three larger hydroelectric stations in the vicinity providing power for the entire northeastern section of the state. Below Great Falls, the Catawba changes its name to the Wateree River and flows through Wateree Lake. It continues for another 75 miles (121 km) until it meets the Congaree River southeast of the state capital, COLUMBIA, to form the Santee River. The upper course of the Catawba is dammed continually to provide a series of reservoirs, including Hickory Lake, Lake James, Lookout Shoals Lake, and Mountain Island Lake, but the largest reservoir is Catawba Lake in South Carolina. The Catawba is 295 miles (475 km) long and provides a large proportion of hydroelectric power for both states. It is also one of the most scenic regions and waterways in the eastern United States. The Catawba's most famous stretch is the Ridgecrest, located west of the Blue Ridge Crest near Catawba Falls, where the headwaters cascade spectacularly from five different levels of rock.

Cauto, Cuba

The largest river in Cuba, the Cauto rises in the Sierra Maestra only 22 miles (35 km) west of SANTIAGO DE CUBA, the scene of famous fighting during the Spanish-American War in the last years of the nineteenth century. The Cauto is 150 miles (240 km) long and flows through swamps to enter the Gulf of Guacanayabo on which the important town of MANZANILLO is located. The river is navigable by small vessels for a short distance upstream, for approximately 40 miles (64 km), or one-third of the river's entire course.

Cedar, Minnesota-Iowa, USA

The Cedar River rises in southeastern Minnesota. It is 300 miles (480 km) long and flows south past AUSTIN, then swings southeast through Iowa. It continues past CHARLES CITY and CEDAR RAPIDS to join the Iowa River at COLUMBUS JUNCTION. The Cedar River is not navigable.

Cedar, Nebraska, USA

The Cedar River rises in Garfield County, central Nebraska. It is 120 miles (190 km) long and flows southeast past ERICSON, SPALDING, PRIMROSE, CEDAR RAPIDS, BELGRADE to join the Loup River at FULLERTON in Nance County. The Loup then flows north-northeast for a short distance before joining the Platte River, after COLOMBUS.

Cedar Creek, North Dakota, USA

Cedar Creek rises in Slope County, southwestern North Dakota. It is roughly 200 miles (320 km) long and flows through Bowman and Adams Counties and forms the boundary between Sioux and Grant Counties before joining the Cannonball River. The river is not navigable and there are no towns or cities along its course.

Chagres, Panama

The Chagres River rises in the Cordillera de San Blas of Panama and flows southeast through the manmade Lake Madden, to link up with the Panama Canal at GAMBOA on the Gatun Lake. It was the Chagres which gave the Spaniards the idea of an Atlantic-Pacific link via a canal. The king of Spain, Charles I, ordered a survey of the region to ascertain the feasibility of building a canal across the isthmus. The engineers stated in their report that such a gargantuan project was totally impossible. The modern Chagres is an integral part of the Panama Canal for the majority of its 30-mile (48-km) length. Leaving Gatun Dam it continues for the remainder of its short journey into the Caribbean Sea. The Chagres is only navigable in the canalized sections, otherwise the numerous rapids throughout its course makes it impossible to navigate. Many small streams flow into the Chagres, the principal ones are the Gatun, the Pequeni and the Gatuncillo. The lush tropical vegetation along its banks is truly remarkable, with over 2000 species being catalogued and identified, and the wildlife along its lower section is plentiful.

Chamelecon, Honduras

The Chamelecon River rises southwest of FLORIDA, Honduras. It is about 125 miles (201 km) long and flows east-northeast into the Sula Valley, then turns north to enter the Gulf of Honduras just northeast of PUERTO CORTES.

Chandalar, Alaska, USA

The Chandalar rises in three main head-streams in the Endicott Mountains of the Brooks Range in central Alaska. It is 280 miles (450 km) long and flows southeast to the town of VENETIE. The river continues on course to enter the Yukon River west of Fort Yukon. The chief tributary of the Chandalar is the East Fork River which flows southwest from northeastern Alaska to join the main river above VENETIE.

Chariton, Iowa-Missouri, USA

The Chariton River rises in south central Clarke County, Iowa. It is 280 miles (450 km) long and flows east-northeast through Lucas County before entering the Rathbun Reservoir. It emerges near the town of RATHBUN and flows south through Appanoose County before crossing over into the state of Missouri. The Chariton passes the towns of LIVONIA, WORTHINGTON, CONNELSVILLE, NOVINGER, YARROW and GIFFORD before joining the Missouri River at GLASGOW in Howard County.

Charles, Massachusetts, USA

The Charles is a small river rising in Norfolk County in northeastern Massachusetts. It is roughly 60 miles (97 km) long and flows generally east passing CAMBRIDGE and BOSTON. It then enters the west side of Boston Harbor, the famous harbor in American history where the Boston Tea Party occurred.

Chattahoochee, Georgia, USA

This river rises in northern Georgia at the southern end of the beautiful Great Smoky Mountains. The headstreams of the Chattahoochee begin in Habersham and White Counties which are located in the northeastern portion of Georgia. The river is 436 miles (702 km) long and flows southwest initially across north-central Georgia, but the once narrow valleys of the river are now covered by Lake Sidney Lanier. It continues southwest through Cobb, Fulton, Carroll, Coweta and Heard Counties to the town of FRANKLIN, where it enters the immense West Point Reservoir. The Chattahoochee now flows due south along the borders of Alabama and Georgia, through Lake Harding, Bartletts Ferry Dam, Goat Rock Lake, Goat Rock Dam, Lake Oliver and the Oliver Dam until it reaches the twin towns of COLUMBUS, Georgia and PHENIX CITY, Alabama. From here the river assumes a winding course passing Fort Benning, a major US Army installation. It then runs in a large curve before resuming its southerly course into the long and narrow Lake Eufaula emerging at Walter F George Dam. The Chattahoochee now runs for a short distance before entering Lake Seminole,

Above: Boston, Massachusetts and the Charles River.

Below: Lake Eufaula on the Chattahoochee River.

where it is joined by the Flint River. The river emerges at the Jim Woodruff Dam and becomes the Apalachicola River. It serves as the border between Alabama and Georgia for over 200 miles (320 km) and is also the boundary for the Central and Eastern Time Zones.

Chaudière, Quebec, Canada

This river is famous for its 130-foot (40-m) falls, located approximately four miles (six km) from its mouth with the St Lawrence River opposite Quebec. The river rises in Megantic Lake and runs northeast for 115 miles (185 km) before joining the St Lawrence.

Chehalis, Washington, USA

The Chehalis rises in Lewis County, southwestern Washington. It is 115 miles (184 km) long and flows northeast past FORDS PRAIRIE, GALVIN, OAKVILLE, PORTER, MELBOURNE, CENTRAL PARK, COSMOPOLIS and ABERDEEN before emptying into Grays Harbor of the Pacific Ocean. Its chief tributary is the Wynoochee River which joins it between MONTESANO and Melbourne.

Chenango, New York, USA

The Chenango rises southwest of UTICA in Oneida County, New York. It is around 90 miles (145 km) long and flows south and southwest past the towns of SHERBURNE, NEW BERLIN, OXFORD and GREENE before joining the Susquehanna River at BINGHAMTON. Its principal tributary is the Tioughnioga River which joins it at CHENANGO FORKS.

Cheyel, Guatemala

See Grijalva, Guatamala-Mexico.

Cheyenne, Wyoming-South Dakota, USA

The Cheyenne is formed at the confluence of Lodgepole Creek and the South Fork at a point located practically in the center of the border between Weston and Niobrara Counties in northeastern Wyoming. The river flows east across the border into South Dakota, passing EDGEMONT, a town of 1174, and then swings slightly southward and northward before entering the Angostura Reservoir which was made possible by the large Angostura Dam and provides irrigation and flood control for over 16,000 acres of arid landscape. The river then heads northeast up through the center of South Dakota's Badlands region. It is joined by Lame Johnny Creek, French Creek, Battle Creek, Spring Creek, Boxelder Creek, Elk Creek and the Belle Fourche River, all of which flow from the west and drain a large proportion of the famous Black Hills of South Dakota. From PEDRO in Pennington County the river flows east by northeast and forms for its last 100 miles (160 km) the border of the Cheyenne Indian Reservation. The Cheyenne is 527 miles (848 km) long and enters Lake Oahe of the Missouri River. It is one of the truly natural western rivers of the United States with lovely scenery along its winding course.

Chickasawhay, Mississippi, USA

The Chickasawhay rises in east-central Mississippi and parallels the Alabama border for the majority of its course southward. It is roughly 210 miles (340 km) long and passes the towns of CHICORA and LEAKSVILLE before joining the Leaf River in George County to form the Pascagoula River.

Chicopee, Massachusets, USA

This river rising in north-central Massachusetts is formed by three headstreams, the Ware, Swift and Quaboag. It flows west past LUDLOW to enter the Connecticut River at the town of CHICOPEE.

Chikaskia, Kansas-Oklahoma, USA

The Chikaskia rises in northern Barber County near the town of ISABEL, Kansas. It is 145 miles (233 km) long and flows south, east, northeast and finally southeast before crossing over into Oklahoma, passing BLACKWELL and joining the Salt Fork of the Arkansas River.

Chipola, Alabama-Florida, USA

This river rises in several branches near the town of DOTHAN in southeast Alabama. It is around 125 miles (201 km) long and flows south across northwestern Florida and through Dead Lake before joining the Apalachicola River.

Chippewa, Minnesota, USA

Rising in Douglas County, west-central Minnesota, it flows west, south, southwest and southeast past HOFFMAN, BENSON, BIG BEND to join the Minnesota River at MONTEVIDEO. It is over 100 miles (160 km) long.

Chippewa, Wisconsin, USA

The Chippewa rises in the lake district of north-central Wisconsin. It is about 200 miles (320 km) long and flows south and southwest past the large hydroelectric plant at CHIPPEWA FALLS and DURAND to join the Mississippi River at the southeastern end of Lake Pepin.

Chitina, Alaska, USA

The Chitina rises at the foot of the Logan Glacier in the St Elias Mountains of southern Alaska. It is 120 miles (190 km) long and flows through a large copper producing region to join the Copper River at the town of CHITINA.

Chixoy, Guatemala

The Chixoy rises initially as the Rio Negro in central Guatemala. It is 250 miles (400 km) long and flows east past SACAPULAS. The river then winds northward to join the Pasion River at the Mexican border to form the Usumacinta River. The Chixoy is navigable for approximately 140 miles (230 km).

Choctawhatchee, Alabama-Florida, USA

The Choctawhatchee River rises in Barbour County, southeastern Alabama. It is 174 miles (280 km) long and flows south-southwest to GENEVA where it is joined by the Pea River. It then proceeds southward into Florida and west and east to enter Choctawhatchee Bay. The river is only navigable in its lower course.

Choluteca, Honduras

The Choluteca rises west of TEGUCIGALPA in Honduras. It is roughly 175 miles (282 km) long and flows east initially, then turns southwest to enter the Gulf of Fonseca just southwest of CHOLUTECA.

Churchill, Newfoundland, Canada

The Churchill is the largest river in Labrador. Including the Ashuanipi River, it has a length of 600 miles (960 km), and drains an area of 30,000 square miles (80,000 sq km). The river was at first named after Sir Charles Hamilton, Governor of Newfoundland in 1821 but changed to Churchill in 1965. The upper portion of the Hamilton is called the Ashuanipi, which rises in Lake Ashuanipi and runs to the Grand Falls. These falls are at the edge of the interior plateau where the water tumbles 245 feet (75 m) down a spectacular cataract; in 16 miles (26 km) of canyons the total fall is 1038 feet (317 m). The hydroelectric potential of this river is vast. The main settlements are near the mouth of the river at Lake Melville.

Churchill, Saskatchewan-Manitoba, Canada

The Churchill is one of northern Canada's primary rivers. It is 1000 miles (1600 km) long and rises in Methy Lake at an altitude of 1460 feet (445 m) in northwestern Saskatchewan. The mouth of the Churchill was discovered in 1619 by Jens Munck, but it was not until 1774–76 that the upper stretches were explored by Pond, Henry and the Frobisher brothers. A fur trading post was established at Frog Lake by the North West Company, and during the next 180 years the Churchill became one of the principal fur-trading routes of north-central Canada. The Indian name for the Churchill was Missinipi which meant 'Big River.' After the coming of Europeans it was often referred to as the English river, as it was one of the main routes utilized by the Hudson Bay Company to reach the interior of Canada. The river flows southeast initially to Peter Pond Lake, which covers an area of 302 square miles (782 sq km). The Churchill continues on to Churchill Lake which is 213 square miles (552 sq km) in area, then to Ile-à-la-Crosse, covering 187 square miles (484 sq km) before turning east and northeast toward Frobisher Lake. Thomas Frobisher discovered the lake that bears his name – a body of water which is 1382 feet (422 m) high, 24 miles (39 km) long and 17 miles (27 km) wide. The Churchill is the chief connecting link between the large network of lakes in this region of Canada. Granville Lake, Southern Indian Lake and Northern Indian Lake, together covering an area of 1350 square miles (3500 sq km), are the others on its route to the principal railway and seaport terminus on the west coast of Hudson Bay, CHURCHILL. The regularity of the Churchill is one of its great assets. It has been developed somewhat with the hydroelectric stations at Island Falls and Granville Falls supplying electricity to the nearby mining areas, but the river is otherwise virtually undeveloped and has great potential.

Cimarron, New Mexico-Colorado-Kansas-Oklahoma, USA

The Cimarron rises in Colfax County east of Raton in the northeastern section of New Mexico. It is called the Dry Cimarron in its early stages through the arid, semi-desert region of this part of New Mexico. Just below Black Mesa, a peak 4973 feet (1517 m) high in Cimarron County, Oklahoma, the river flows through KENTON flowing east-northeast across the border into Colorado. The Cimarron only runs through Colorado for a short distance before crossing into Kansas, where it picks up its first sizeable tributary, the North Fork. At the boundary of Stevens, Haskell and Seward Counties, the river turns southeast to curve into Oklahoma twice before slowing down to flow between the North Canadian and the Salt Fork Rivers. The upper Cimarron was an important alternative route for the famous Santa Fe Trail. The river is not navigable due to the shallowness of the channel. During the flood season the mile-wide Cimarron, normally a meandering river, is so full that its appearance changes completely. The river runs through one of the great wheat producing areas of Oklahoma, and the oil wells, derricks, refineries and other related oil industries surround the Cimarron for miles. The Cimarron joins the Arkansas River at the Keystone Reservoir, only 17 miles (27 km) west of Tulsa. It is 692 miles (1113 km) long.

Clark Fork, Montana-Idaho, USA

Initially called Silver Bow Creek, this river rises near the town of BUTTE, Montana on the Continental Divide. Silver Bow Creek is separated from another creek which runs into the Jefferson River and then the Missouri by Pipestone Pass just above Butte. The river is 499 miles (803 km) long including the Pende Oreille River. It flows northwest and is joined by the Blackfoot River near the town of MISSOULA, famous for its Forest Fire Fighting Service. Just past Missoula it is joined by the Bitterroot River and passes the towns of FRENCHTOWN, HUSON, ALBERTON, SUPERIOR and ST REGIS. The river swings east at St Regis and continues on this course and is joined by its principal tributary, the Flathead River, in Sanders County. It then passes through another chain of mountains, crosses over the border into Idaho, and passes CLARK FORK before entering Lake Pende Oreille in the northern most section of Idaho. Lake Pende Oreille is 40 miles (64 km) long, 2500 feet (763 m) deep and covers an area of 125 square miles (324 sq km), making it the largest lake in the state. The outflow of the lake is the Pende Oreille River which flows north through the northeastern portion of Washington State. It crosses the Canadian border and makes a loop west to join the Columbia River just as it begins to cross into Washington.

An aerial view of the harbor as the Coatzacoalcas River emerges into the Gulf of Mexico.

Clearwater, Idaho, USA

This river rises in central Idaho at the confluence of the Middle Fork which is 100 miles (160 km) long, and the South Fork which is 80 miles (129 km) long at the town of KOOSKIA. It is 90 miles (145 km) long and flows north-northwest past OROFINO, then turns west to join the Snake River at LEWISTON. The chief tributary is the North Fork which is 120 miles (190 km) long.

Clearwater, Minnesota, USA

The Clearwater River rises in Clearwater County in northwestern Minnesota. It is 205 miles (330 km) long and joins the Red Lake River at RED LAKE FALLS.

Clinch, Virginia, USA

The Clinch rises in Tazewell County, southwestern Virginia. It is approximately 300 miles (480 km) long and flows southwest through the Great Appalachian Valley into Tennessee. The river is then dammed to form the Norris Reservoir and later the Watts Bar Reservoir, both of the TVA.

Coatzacoalcas, Mexico

The Coatzacoalcas River rises north of IXTEPEC in southeastern Mexico. It is about 175 miles (282 km) long and flows on a winding course, passing MINATITLAN on its way north-northeast to the Gulf of Campeche. The most important river in the Tehuantepec Isthmus, it is navigable for 125 miles (201 km).

Coco, Honduras-Nicaragua

The Coco rises in the high mountains between the Central American countries of Honduras and Nicaragua. It flows east-northeast for the majority of its course of 300 miles (480 km) before emptying into the Caribbean Sea. It passes the commercial and manufacturing town of OCOTAL; TELPANECA, the center of the coffee growing region; the gold mining town of BOCAY, where the Bocay River joins the Coco;

and SANSANG, the terminal point of navigation on the lower section of the river also noted for its gold deposits. The Coco enters the Caribbean Sea at CABO GRACIAS A DIOS, which is situated on an island in the river's delta and is the capital of northeastern Nicaragua. The river is navigable for 140 miles (230 km) below Sansang. The Coco was known also as the Segovia, and its chief tributaries are the Jicaro, the Poteca, the Esteli and the Huaspuc.

Cohocton, New York, USA

The Cohocton rises in Livingstone County, New York. It flows southeast past the towns of ATLANTA, COHOCTON, WALLACE, AVOCA, BATH and COOPERS PLAIN before joining the Canisteo River at CORNING in Steuben County to form the Chemung River.

Coldwater, Mississippi, USA

This river rises in Marshall County, northwestern Mississippi. It is 220 miles (350 km) long and flows southwest, west and finally south to enter the Tallahatchie River in Quitman County.

Colorado, Western USA

One of the most famous rivers of the American West, the Colorado is best known for its spectacular Grand Canyon of Arizona. The Colorado is 1360 miles (2190 km) long and begins its long journey to the Gulf of California in Grand County, Colorado on the Continental Divide. Here in the beautifully forested mountains, the Colorado and its tributaries receive an abundance of water from the melting snow high in the Rocky Mountains. These snows keep the river so full that a portion is siphoned off through the Continental Divide via the Adams Tunnel to the Big Thompson River. This water provides a much needed boost to the irrigation projects of the South Platte River Valley in northeastern Colorado. The river heads west-southwest through northwestern Colorado, past HOT SULPHUR SPRINGS, PARSHALL, RADIUM, MCCOY,

Lee's Ferry on the Colorado River.

GLENWOOD SPRINGS, RIFLE and GRAND JUNC-
TION, where it is joined by the Gunnison
River before crossing into Utah. The chief
tributaries on this stretch of the Colorado are
the Gunnison, Roaring Fork, Eagle, Blue and
Williams Fork Rivers. The spring thaw in this
region of Colorado results in a rapid run-off
from the mountains, some of which are well
over 14,000 feet (4270 m) high. There are
numerous reservoirs to help in flood control
and to provide water in the late Indian
summers which favor this part of the country.

Nearby in southwestern Colorado are the
remains of the cliff dwellings of the Pueblo
Indians on the Mancos River, a tributary of the
San Juan River. The Pueblo Indians first
occupied this area in the very early Christian
era and they reached their height of advance-
ment between 1100–1300 AD – a period
referred to as the 'Classical Pueblo Period.'
The weather was to be the downfall of the
Pueblo Indians, for in 1276 a drought began in

the Colorado and San Juan River basins which
was to last for 24 years. The result of this was a
full-scale migration to a more suitable location
having an adequate water supply. Therefore,
by the beginning of the 14th century, the
magnificent cliff dwellings which took years to
build were abandoned. After entering Utah,
the Colorado flows southwest through Grand
County forming the eastern boundary of
Arches National Park. It is then joined by the
Green River in the Orange Cliffs just before
Cataract Canyon. The river continues through
the Glen Canyon National Recreation Area
and Lake Powell formed by the Glen Canyon
Dam to emerge in Arizona at Marble Canyon.
Between the Vermilion Cliffs on the west and
the Echo Cliffs on the east, the river runs
southwest through Coconin County and is
joined by the Little Colorado River on the east
central boundary of the Grand Canyon
National Park. It then bends west to form a
spectacular sight, the Grand Canyon of
Arizona. The distance from Marble Canyon to
the very end of the Grand Canyon is 217 miles

(349 km). The region the river flows through is
so arid and barren that it only receives one
tributary during this stretch of its course, and
it is dry in the summer. The Colorado carries
away half a million tons of dirt and sediment
each day, creating for itself a canyon slightly
over one mile (1610 m) in depth and between
four and 18 miles (six and 29 km) wide.

The first Europeans to have seen this sight
were the Spanish explorers in 1540. The Ives
expedition in 1858 believed they were the first
to have discovered the Grand Canyon but the
Spanish claims were later verified through
historical sources. The first man to actually go
through the rapids of the Grand Canyon was
Major Powell in 1869. The Colorado twists
and turns its way through the canyon, west,
southwest and west again, passing through the
Hualapai Indian Reservation, before entering
the Lake Mead National Recreation Area on
the northwestern border of Arizona and
southeastern tip of Nevada. Lake Mead is
formed by the Hoover Dam which backs up
the river's water far into Arizona. Once past

the great dam the Colorado is well controlled. Davis Dam has formed Lake Mohave, and it generates power and provides water for irrigation projects along the ' river. The Colorado then flows generally on a southerly course forming the border between California and Arizona. The next manmade impediment is Parker Dam at the southern end of Lake Havasu where the Bill Williams River joins the Colorado. Here at Parker Dam is the beginning of the Colorado River Aqueduct, which brings water 242 miles (389 km) across the Mohave Desert and mountains to the city of LOS ANGELES. Besides distributing water to Los Angeles, extensions of the aqueduct also carry water to other large cities in southern California. Departing from Parker Dam the river resumes its twisting course, flowing through the Colorado River Indian Reservation and past the western edge of the Chocolate Mountains in Yuma County before reaching Imperial Dam. Here the water is again backed into another manmade lake, the Imperial Reservoir. Immediately south is the

Laguna Dam which forms the Laguna Reservoir.

These last two reservoirs on the Colorado have enabled successful irrigation farming of a region completely made up of desert. The area around YUMA is one of the hottest places in the United States, averaging between 110° to 130°F (43° to 54°C) in the summer months. The town of Yuma is on the Arizona side of the Colorado and nearby is the remains of the once infamous Territorial Prison of Yuma. At Imperial Dam water is also taken via the All-American Canal to the Imperial and Coachella Valleys in southern California. The two valleys are located in the Salton Depression which is 241 feet (74 m) below sea level and extremely hot during the summer. This area is cut off from the Gulf of California by the deltaic deposits of the Colorado River. Under natural conditions the Salton Sea is subjected to periodic inundations as the distributaries of the Colorado fill up with silt and sediment, and new channels have been opened up by flood waters. Periods of serious flooding are

The Grand Canyon on the Colorado River.

followed by the expected drying out periods. This caused no problems until a farmer near the river started tapping into the water supply without utilizing sluices or any other supports, but the Hoover Dam and the All-American Canal now controls the flooding which used to plague the region. The Imperial Valley is so fertile that it doubles crops every year. Although the Colorado River is one of the longest rivers in the United States and drains a large area of 242,900 square miles (629,000 sq km), it has few important cities along its banks. In fact the only towns on the river between Grand Junction, Colorado and Yuma, Arizona are those utilized as stopovers for major transcontinental highways and railroads. The river itself is not a promoter of regional growth. Once past GADSDEN, Arizona, the river crosses the international border into Mexico and divides Baja California from the rest of Mexico. The Colorado is one of the great rivers of the United States.

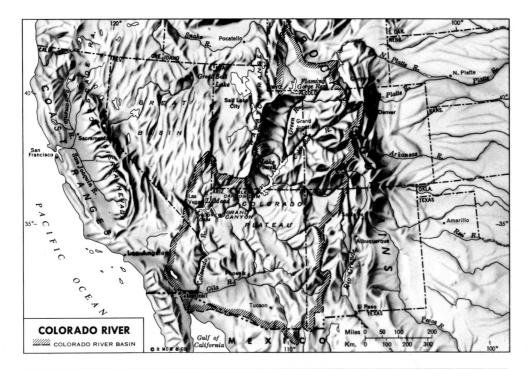

COLORADO RIVER
///// COLORADO RIVER BASIN

Colorado, Texas, USA

The Colorado River of Texas rises to a height of 3000 feet (915 m) in the Llano Estacado in the western Great Plains of Texas. It begins in several intermittent headstreams which are for the majority of the year dry. The river is 970 miles (1560 km) long and flows mainly southeast for its entire journey to the Gulf of Mexico. The Colorado runs through exceedingly dry terrain composed primarily of hills and flats in west-central Texas. Below COLORADO CITY in Mitchell County, the river is joined by Beals Creek which flows from the west. It then runs through the towns of ROBERT LEE, BALLINGER and AUSTIN, the state capital. The chief tributaries are the Concho, San Saba, Llano and Pedernales Rivers. The river is sapped by the Buchanan Dam, Marshall Ford Dam and the Austin Dam to provide hydroelectric power for this region of the state. The Colorado is lined by orchards of pecan trees in its lower course and the surrounding hills are utilized to graze the large herds of cattle. The river has formed an elongated delta across Matagorda Bay before entering the Gulf of Mexico.

Columbia, Canada-Northwestern USA

The Columbia is 1243 miles (2000 km) long and drains an area of 258,000 square miles (668,000 sq km). The river is second only to the Mississippi in volume of water carried. It rises only 80 miles (129 km) from the US border in British Columbia, high in the Canadian Rockies. For its first 150 miles (240 km) the river flows northwest past the towns of NICHOLSON, GOLDEN, DONALD and ROGERS, before receiving the Canoe River. The Columbia then turns southeast to flow between the Selkirk and the Monashee Mountains, past Mt Revelstoke National Park, BIG EDDY and REVELSTOKE before entering Upper Arrow Lake. It emerges to run south past East Arrow Park and Burton before entering Lower Arrow Lake. The Columbia then twists and turns for a short distance before finally crossing over into northeastern Washington State. Between the border and where the Snake River joins it, the Columbia takes its famous 'Great Bends.' The river acts as the boundary between Ferry and Stevens Counties. It flows through Lake Franklin Roosevelt and the Grand Coulee National Recreation Area to reach the Grand Coulee Dam where it is joined by the Okanogan River. On the initial stretch of its course, the chief tributaries are the Spokane, Sanpoil, Colville, Kettle, Canoe and Okanogan Rivers. The river now flows due south into its second Big Bend before flowing 200 miles (320 km) to receive the Snake River, its largest tributary and a mighty river in its own right. The river is dammed at Priest Rapids by the Priest Rapids Dam on the bend below SCHAWANA as it heads for the junction with the Snake. After absorbing the waters of the Snake, the Columbia turns west toward the Pacific Ocean and acts as the border between Oregon and Washington for the remainder of its course. The river flows through Wallula Lake which

The Grand Canyon and the Colorado River as seen from the Toroweap Overlook, which is near North Rim. This is near the beginning of the canyon.

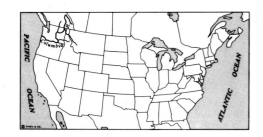

was formed by the McNary Dam, then is joined by the Umatilla River at UMATILLA. Continuing on course the Columbia passes Blalock Island, BOARDMAN and WILLOWS, where it is joined by Willows Creek. It then enters Umatilla Lake and emerges at John Day Dam to continue into Celilo Lake and past The Dalles Dam. The Columbia then enters Bonneville Lake, which was formed by the construction of the Bonneville Dam in 1933.

The head of the Columbia's tidewater is Bonneville Dam, located 144 miles (232 km) above the river's mouth and 40 miles (64 km) east of the city of PORTLAND. When the dam was first built it impeded the normal cycle of salmon returning up river to spawn in their pools. Therefore, a ladder and lock was constructed at the northern end of the spillway to help the fish climb above the dam. The Columbia is one of the most important salmon rivers in North America and as such has received additional protection to insure the safety of its valuable fishing. The chief tributaries on this portion of the river are the Deschutes, John Day, White Salmon, Willamette and Hood Rivers. The Columbia continues west past HOOD RIVER, CAMAS, VANCOUVER, PORTLAND, RAINIER and ASTORIA before entering the Pacific Ocean. The river is navigable for large vessels as far as Portland and Vancouver. It is a vast source of hydroelectric power which is only being partially tapped and a beautiful natural resource. The Columbia is quite unique in that it was named for a ship. Captain Gray of Boston sailed his ship, the *Columbia*, to the mouth of the river in 1792.

Colville, Alaska, USA
The Colville River rises in the Brooks Range of northern Alaska. It is roughly 375 miles (603 km) long and flows east-northeast, when not frozen, to the Beaufort Sea of the Arctic Ocean. The chief tributaries are the Anaktuvuk and Killik Rivers.

Conchos, Mexico
The Conchos rises in the Sierra Madre de Occidente at a height of 8000 feet (2440 m) in northern Mexico. It is 350 miles (560 km) long and drains an area of 30,000 square miles (77,700 sq km). The river is the most important Mexican tributary of the Rio Grande. It flows east from its source across Chihuahua State, past Nonoava and through the Presa La Boquilla. It then turns north toward the Texas border and the Rio Grande, first flowing through some of the most arid and barren

The Connecticut River as seen from Mt Tom near Northampton, Massachusetts. This is part of beautiful Hampshire County.

terrain in northern Mexico. The volume of the Conchos is not very great as evaporation and irrigation reduce the supply of water. Once past the town of OJINAGA, the Conchos enters the Rio Grande. The chief tributaries are the Rio Florido and Chuviscar Rivers.

Concord, Massachusetts, USA
Rising in east-central Massachusetts, the Concord River flows east through Middlesex County. It is joined by the Assabet River at the town of CONCORD, famous for the Battle of Concord which occurred on 19 April 1775. The river continues north to join the Merrimack River near the town of LOWELL, moving from a very heavily industrialized area of Massachusetts into the scenic countryside of New Hampshire. (See illustration on pages 270–71).

Conecuh, Alabama, USA
The Conecuh River begins near UNION SPRINGS, Alabama. It is 231 miles (372 km) long and flows southwest. It joins Escambia Creek at the border with Florida to form the Escambia River which flows into Pensacola Bay. It is navigable for a short distance on its lower course and is dredged to keep it clear.

Congaree, South Carolina, USA
The Congaree is a small river rising in Lexington County of central South Carolina and flowing for 55 miles (88 km) southeast to join the Wateree River to form the Santee River south of the state capital, COLUMBIA.

Connecticut, New England, USA
The largest river in the New England states, the Connecticut River rises in the Connecticut Lakes of Coos County in northeastern Vermont. The river is 345 miles (555 km) long and drains an area of 11,000 square miles

(28,490 sq km), a substantial area for a medium-sized river. It flows south from a height of 2000 feet (610 m) to form the Vermont and New Hampshire border, past the towns of BEECHER FALLS, STEWARTSTOWN, CANAAN, GUILDHALL and SOUTH LUNENBURG before entering a reservoir created by the Moore Dam. It emerges to flow southwest for a short distance into another reservoir created by the Comerford Dam before resuming its southward course. It runs past MCINDOE FALLS, WELLS RIVER, WOODSVILLE, ELY, NORTH THETFORD and HANOVER before encountering the Wilder Dam. The river continues past WINDSOR, CHARLESTOWN and BELLOWS FALLS prior to crossing over into Massachusetts. The chief tributaries on the upper course of the Connecticut River are the Mohawk, Nulhegan, Moore, Ammonoosac, Wells and White Rivers. Upon entering Massachusetts, the Connecticut River flows past EAST NORTHFIELD and NORTHFIELD FARMS before winding westward through central Franklin County. The river comes out of its bend after a short distance to resume its southerly course, through Hampshire and Hampden Counties to cross over into the state of Connecticut. It winds over lovely lowlands and the most scenic spot on this stretch of the river is the Enfield Falls above HARTFORD. Continuing toward the Long Island Sound the river passes NAUBUC, MIDDLE HADDAM and ESSEX before finally entering the Atlantic Ocean. The Connecticut River has been made navigable up to Hartford, but the prime effort has gone into flood control and hydroelectric projects.

Coosa, Georgia-Alabama, USA

The Coosa is formed by the confluence of the Etowah and the Oostanaula Rivers at ROME, Georgia, which has a population of 30,498. It is 286 miles (460 km) long and flows southward through the Appalachian Ridge into the Gulf Coastal Plain at WETUMPKA, Alabama. The river's course is southwest into Cherokee County where it is joined by the Chattooga River. It then flows on past GADSDEN, CHILDERSBURG and TALLADEGA SPRINGS to finally meet the Tallapoosa River to form the Alabama River.

Coppermine, Northwest Territories, Canada

The Coppermine rises north of the Great Slave Lake in the Lac de Gras. It is 525 miles (845 km) long and flows northwest through Point and Itchen Lakes, over numerous rapids and through the Copper Mountains before running over Bloody Falls and into Coronation Gulf on the Arctic Ocean. The Coppermine was discovered in 1771 by Samuel Hearne who explored it to its mouth and was named for the Copper Eskimos who live along side its banks. They were named the Copper Eskimos because of the copper tools they utilized.

Copper, Alaska, USA

The Copper River rises on the northern slopes of the Wrangell Mountains of southern Alaska. It is 300 miles (480 km) long and flows to the Pacific Ocean just east of the town of CORDOVA. The river was named for the copper mining region through which it flowed.

Cottonwood, Kansas, USA

The Cottonwood River rises in northwestern Marion County, central Kansas. The Cottonwood flows north, southeast, northeast and east past DURHAM, through Marion Reservoir, MARION, CLEMENTS, ELMDALE and COTTONWOOD FALLS to join the Neosho River in east-central Lyon County, Kansas. It is 140 miles (230 km) long.

Cowlitz, Washington, USA

This river rises in the Cascade Range of southwestern Washington State. It is 130 miles (210 km) long and flows west and south past the town of KELSO to join the Columbia River near LONGVIEW.

Crooked, Oregon, USA

The Crooked River rises in the Blue Mountains of central Oregon. It is 105 miles (169 km) long and flows west and north past PRINEVILLE before resuming its westerly course to join the Deschutes River north of REDMOND.

Croton, New York, USA

The Croton River is formed by the junction of three headstreams; the West, Middle and East

Turners Falls in Franklin County, Massachusetts on the Connecticut River.

The Old North Bridge over the Concord River in Massachusetts. In 1655 the British fled across this bridge only to be picked off on the other side by American marksmen.

branches, which flow through Putnam County to meet near Westchester County. The river then runs southwest to the Hudson River. The Croton Dam forms the Croton Reservoir which supplies the metropolitan New York City area with its water.

Crow, Minnesota, USA
The Crow River is formed by the North and South Fork Rivers near the town of ROCKFORD in Minnesota. It is 30 miles (48 km) long and flows northeast to join the Mississippi River near ANOKA.

Crow Wing, Minnesota, USA
The Crow Wing River rises in central Minnesota and flows for 100 miles (160 km) past the towns of MOTLEY and PILLAGER to join the Mississippi near BRAINERD. Its chief tributaries are the Long Prairie and Leaf Rivers.

Cuatitlan, Mexico
Part of the Panuco River system, the Cuatitlan rises in central Mexico. It is only a small river, 35 miles (56 km) in length, but drains Lakes Texcoco and Zumpango before joining the Tula River via the Tequixquiac Tunnel.

Cumberland, Kentucky-Tennessee, USA
The Cumberland is one of the eastern United States' most beautiful and scenic rivers, and evokes scenes of the early American settlement of the western wilderness by such famous pioneers as Daniel Boone and Davy Crockett.

The Cumberland rises in south-central Kentucky in the Cumberland Plateau. It was named after the victor of Culloden, William, Duke of Cumberland. The river descends rapidly from about 1200 feet (364 m) to flow southwest through a narrow valley which is also a primary route utilized by the railroads and highways. The valley of the Cumberland is quite beautiful, especially in the spring when the dogwood, azaleas, rhododendrons and forsythia bloom to cover the slopes. Beneath this vivid scenery lies a thick seam of bituminous coal which has been continuously mined since 1911 and is a large part of the state's economy. Upon reaching the town of PINEVILLE the Cumberland cuts its way through the Pine Mountains, the western ridge of the Appalachians. The surrounding land is not very fertile although hardy farmers have managed to eke out a living from this portion of the Cumberland Plateau.

As the river flows through Cumberland Falls State Park, it drops 68 feet (21 m) in a large fall 125 feet (38 m) wide. The river is joined by the South Fork at the town of BURNSIDE and then turns southwest. The Cumberland is a major source of hydroelectric power for the surrounding region and Wolf Creek Dam is the head of navigation, located 460 miles (740 km) from the mouth. Crossing over into Tennessee, the river flows past CELINA, through the Cordell Hull Reservoir to emerge near CARTHAGE. The river now starts its westward stretch through the northern part of Tennessee through Old Hickory Lake, formed by the Old Hickory Dam, before flowing through NASHVILLE, the capital of Tennessee. The Cumberland leaves Nashville and flows northwest through Cheatham Lake, formed by the Cheatham Dam. The river widens considerably as it approaches CLARKSVILLE at the confluence with the Red River. The Cumberland crosses back into Kentucky and runs across the Pennyroyal Plateau of southwestern Kentucky through Lake Barkley before passing Barkley Dam to join the Ohio River approximately ten miles (16 km) above its confluence with the larger Tennessee River. The dams along the Cumberland and its tributaries are an integral part of the great TVA system which provides the majority of hydroelectric power for this section of Kentucky, Tennessee, Alabama and Georgia. The river is 720 miles (1160 km) long, and drains an area of 18,080 square miles (46,830 sq km).

Current, Missouri-Arkansas, USA

The Current River rises in the Ozark Plateau of south-central Missouri. It is 225 miles (362 km) long and flows south-southwest past the towns of VAN BUREN and DONIPHAN before crossing over into Arkansas to join the Black River.

Dan, Virginia-North Carolina, USA

The Dan rises in southern Virginia and runs southeast, east, northeast through the textile manufacturing center of DANVILLE. The river then winds in and out of Virginia and North Carolina before swinging past SOUTH BOSTON and into the series of lakes along the Virginia and North Carolina border. The Dan is 180 miles (290 km) long and finally joins the Roanoke River in eastern Halifax County.

Delaware, Eastern USA

The Delaware was one of the most beautiful rivers of the eastern seaboard before the Industrial Revolution. Now its banks are lined with large industries and chemical plants which only detract from the natural beauty of this river. The Delaware is formed by the confluence of the East and West Branches at HANCOCK, New York in the lovely Catskill Mountains. The river is 390 miles (630 km) long and drains an area of 11,440 square miles (29,630 sq km). From Hancock the Delaware runs southeast past the small towns of DAMASCUS, MILANVILLE, LACKAWAXEN and SHOHOLA, marking the border between New York and Pennsylvania. Upon reaching PORT JERVIS, the river turns southwest and forms the border between Pennsylvania and New Jersey as it flows through the Delaware Water Gap National Recreation Area. This is one of the scenic wonderlands of eastern Pennsylvania. To the west are the gorgeous Pocono Mountains, and nearby in Pike County is the great fishing reservoir, Lake Wallenpaupack. The river continues past SHAWNEE ON DELAWARE, then through the most stunning stretch of its course, the Delaware Water Gap in Monroe County. The river cuts through the Kittatinny Mountains between Mount Tammany and Mount Minsi to shape the Gap and heads south-southeast past EASTON, RIEGELS-VILLE, ERWINNA, WASHINGTON CROSSING, TREN-TON, PHILADELPHIA, CAMDEN and NEW CASTLE before entering its estuarine inlet to join the Atlantic Ocean. At WILMINGTON, Delaware the river is spanned by Delaware Memorial Bridge, which is three and half miles (six km) long and one of the longest bridges in the east coast of the United States. The river is a prime source of hydroelectric power for the surrounding regions and provides the majority of cheap power for eastern Pennsylvania and western New Jersey. The chief tributaries are the Neversink, Musconetcong, Schuykill and Lehigh Rivers. The Delaware was first explored by Henry Hudson in 1609 and Cornelis Hendrickson in 1614. The initial settlements along the river were of Dutch and Swedish origin.

Deep, North Carolina, USA

The Deep rises near the town of KERNERSVILLE in central North Carolina. It is 125 miles (201 km) long and flows southeast past RANDLEMAN and FRANKLINVILLE to join the Haw River near HAYWOOD to form the Cape Fear River. The Deep runs through one of the most scenic regions of North Carolina.

Deep Fork, Oklahoma, USA

The Deep Fork River rises in Okmulgee County in central Oklahoma. It is the chief tributary of the North Canadian River which it joins after flowing for 263 miles (423 km), northeast, east and southeast in Oklahoma County.

Deschutes, Oregon, USA

The Deschutes rises in the beautiful Cascade Range of central Oregon. It flows for 240 miles (390 km), north-northeast past the towns of BEND and REDMOND to join the Columbia River near CELILO, where it forms the boundary between Oregon and Washington.

Des Lacs, North Dakota, USA

This is a small river which issues forth from Upper Des Lacs Lake near the Canadian border in northeastern Burke County, North Dakota. It flows southeast past KENMARE, DONNEYBROOK, CARPIO and FOXHOLM before joining the Souris River at BURLINGTON.

Des Plaines, Wisconsin-Illinois, USA

This river rises in the extreme southeastern section of Wisconsin. It is 110 miles (180 km) long and flows south into Illinois, running through the suburbs of CHICAGO to FOREST VIEW. The Des Plaines then heads southwest to join the Kankakee River to form the Illinois River.

Des Moines, Minnesota-Iowa, USA

Rising in Lake Shetak in north-central Murray County, western Minnesota, the Des Moines River flows south-southeast past WINDOM, JACKSON and PETERSBURG before crossing into Iowa. North of the town of HUMBOLDT, Iowa the river is alternatively known as the West Fork. It continues on its southeasterly course past ESTHERVILLE, WAL-LINGFORD, BRADGATE, RUTLAND and HUM-BOLDT, then joins the East Fork before entering Webster County. The Des Moines runs past FORT DODGE, LEHIGH, FRASER and MOINGONA, then enters the Saylorville Res-ervoir to emerge in central Polk Country. It flows on to DES MOINES where it is joined by the Raccoon River, and heads southeast to OTTUMWA where it is dammed to provide hydroelectric power. The Des Moines enters the Mississippi River south of KEOKUK, an old fur trading establishment. The river forms the border between Iowa and Missouri for its last 25 miles (40 km). It is not navigated today, but up to 1860 the river was utilized by steamboats. It is 535 miles (861 km) long.

Detroit, Michigan-Ontario, USA-Canada

The Detroit River is the drainage outlet for Lake St Clair on the Michigan and Ontario border. It is only 31 miles (50 km) long but forms an important and integral part of the Great Lakes shipping lane. It passes DETROIT and WINDSOR, both large industrial cities, and links Lake St Clair with Lake Erie, while the St Clair River links Lake Huron and Lake St Clair to the north.

Devils, Texas, USA

The Devils River rises in Sutton County in southwestern Texas. It is 100 miles (160 km) long and flows south to join the Rio Grande northwest of DEL RIO. Large dams form Lakes Hamilton and Walker in its lower course.

Diquis, Costa Rica

Also known as the Rio Grande de Terraba, the Diquis rises in southeastern Costa Rica. The Diquis is 100 miles (160 km) long, which includes its headstreams, the Brus and General Rivers. It runs past PUERTO CORTES, the head of navigation, to form a large and swampy delta at Coronado Bay on the Pacific Ocean.

One of the first modern bridges over the Detroit.

East, New York, USA
The East River is a navigable tidal strait located in NEW YORK CITY. It is 16 miles (26 km) long and links Upper New York Bay and Long Island Sound. The East River is also connected to the Hudson River by the Harlem River. It is spanned by several highway bridges, and has extensive port facilities.

Eastmain, Quebec, Canada
The Eastmain River rises in Lake Naococane on the border between Nouveau Quebec Territory and Mistassini Territory and flows west forming the boundary between these territories. The river is joined by the Opinaca River as it runs west to pass EASTMAIN before entering James Bay, near the Eastmain trading post which was founded by the Hudson Bay Company in 1665. It is 375 miles (603 km) long.

Eau Pleine, Wisconsin, USA
Rising in central Wisconsin, the Eau Pleine River flows southeast to join the Wisconsin River approximately 17 miles (27 km) south-southwest of WAUSAU. It widens at its mouth to form the Big Eau Pleine Reservoir below MOSINEE in Marathon County.

Edisto, South Carolina, USA
The Edisto River rises south of ORANGEBURG, South Carolina at the confluence of the North and South Forks. It is 90 miles (145 km) long and flows southeast and south to enter the Atlantic Ocean, dividing to form Edisto Island. The river is navigable and drains an area of 6150 square miles (15,930 sq km), a large area for such a small river.

Eel, California, USA
The Eel River rises in the famous wine growing county of Mendocino located in northwestern California. It is 200 miles (320 km) long and flows southeast and west to Lake Pillsbury, then swings west and northwest past SCOTIA to enter the Pacific Ocean south-southwest of EUREKA.

Dix, Kentucky, USA
The Dix River rises in Rockcastle County in central Kentucky. It is 77 miles (124 km) long and flows north to join the Kentucky River at High Bridge. This is Kentucky Bluegrass country at its best.

Dolores, Colorado, USA
The Dolores rises in the San Miguel Mountains of southwestern Colorado. It is roughly 250 miles (400 km) long and flows southwest and north-northwest past the towns of DOLORES and GATEWAY to join the Colorado River, just northeast of MOAB, Utah. Its chief tributary is the San Miguel River.

Dubawnt, Northwest Territories, Canada
The Dubawnt River rises northeast of Lake Athabasca in the Northwest Territories of Canada. It is 580 miles (930 km) long and flows northeast through Dubawnt Lake. It joins the Thelon River just west of Aberdeen Lake.

Duck, Tennessee, USA
The Duck River rises north-northwest of MANCHESTER in central Tennessee. It is 250 miles (400 km) long and flows south and west-northwest past COLUMBIA and CENTERVILLE to join the Tennessee River at Kentucky Lake in Humphreys County.

Eagle, Colorado, USA
The Eagle River rises in the Sawatch Mountains of central Colorado. It is 70 miles (113 km) long and flows northwest and west past AVON, EDWARDS, EAGLE and GYPSUM to join the Colorado River at DOTSERO.

Ekwan, Ontario, Canada
This river rises in the Patricia District of northern Ontario. It is 300 miles (480 km) long and flows northeast and east to enter James Bay opposite Akimiski Island.

Elk, Kansas, USA
The Elk rises in Greenwood County, Kansas. It flows southeast past HOWARD, LONGTON, OAK VALLEY and through the Elk City Reservoir to join the Verdigris in central Montgomery County, Kansas.

Elk, Tennessee, USA
The Elk River rises in the beautiful Cumberland Mountains of southern Tennessee. It is 200 miles (320 km) long and meanders west-southwest past FAYETTEVILLE to join the Tennessee River, where it is dammed to form the Wheeler Reservoir.

Elk, West Virginia, USA
This river rises in the Allegheny Mountains of central West Virginia. It is 172 miles (277 km) long and flows north and west past WEBSTER SPRINGS and SUTTON, then southwest to join the Kanawha River at CHARLESTON.

Elkhorn, Nebraska, USA
The Elkhorn River rises in Rock County, northeastern Nebraska. The Elkhorn River is 333 miles (536 km) long and flows east-southeast and south past O'NEILL, NORFOLK and WEST POINT to join the Platte River near OMAHA.

Elota, Mexico
The Elota River rises in the Sierra Madre Occidental of western Mexico. It is 100 miles (160 km) long and flows southwest through the fertile lowlands of Sinaloa to enter the Pacific Ocean just southwest of LA CRUZ.

Elwha, Washington, USA
The Elwha rises in central Olympia National Park in Jefferson County. It flows north to enter the Juan de Fuca Strait.

Embarrass, Illinois, USA
The Embarrass River rises near URBANA in eastern Illinois. It is 185 miles (298 km) long and flows south and southeast past NEWTON and LAWRENCEVILLE to join the Wabash River. Its chief tributary is the North Fork, which is 55 miles (88 km) long and which it joins southeast of Newton.

Escambia, Alabama-Florida, USA
See Conecuh, Alabama, USA.

Escatawpa, Alabama-Mississippi, USA
The Escatawpa River rises in northwestern Washington County near COPELAND, Alabama. It is 90 miles (145 km) long and flows south past FRUITDALE, ESCATAWPA, VINEGAR BEND and DEER PARK before entering Pascagoula Bay in southeastern Mississippi.

Esclavos, Guatemala
This river rises in the highlands of southern Guatemala near MATAQUESCUINTLA. It is 75 miles (120 km) long and flows south past Santa Rosa to enter the Pacific Ocean east-southeast of SAN JOSE.

Escondido, Nicaragua
The Escondido is formed by the confluence of the Siquia, Rama and Mico Rivers at the town of RAMA in southeastern Guatemala. It is 60 miles (96 km) long and flows east to enter Bluefields Bay of the Caribbean Sea. The river is navigable and is utilized to ship cargoes of banana, rubber and coconuts downstream.

Estero Real, Nicaragua
The Estero River rises northeast of LEON in western Nicaragua. It is 60 miles (96 km) long

and flows west-northwest to enter the Gulf of Fonseca on the Pacific Ocean.

Etowah, Georgia, USA
The Etowah rises in the scenic Blue Ridge Mountains of northwestern Georgia. It is 141 miles (227 km) long and flows southwest to ROME where it joins the Oostanaula River to form the Coosa River. The river is dammed east of CARTERSVILLE by the Allatoona Dam to form the Allatoona Reservoir.

Exploits, Newfoundland, Canada
The Exploits River rises in the southwestern portion of Newfoundland. It is 200 miles (320 km) long and flows east-northeast through a series of lakes starting with King George IV, Lloyds and Red Indian Lakes, then runs past GRAND FALLS to enter the Bay of Exploits on the Atlantic at BOTWOOD. The chief tributaries are the Victoria River and numerous small streams which flow into Red Indian Lake in central Newfoundland.

Fall, Kansas, USA
The Fall River rises in northwestern Greenwood County of southeastern Kansas. It is 90 miles (145 km) long and flows basically southeast on a diagonal course across Greenwood County, passing EUREKA. It is dammed near Fall River to form the Fall River Reservoir which is utilized mainly for various irrigational projects. The Fall continues past NEW ALBANY and NEODESHA before joining the Verdigris River.

Fawn, Ontario, Canada
The source of this river is Big Trout Lake, Kenora territory district in northern Ontario. It flows northeast through a sparsely inhabited region, then swings slightly northwest before joining the Severn River.

Feather, California, USA
The Feather River rises near the California border with Nevada just below Honey Lake near the town of CHILCOOT in the Sierra Nevada Mountains. It flows west-southwest through the central Sacramento River Valley to join the Sacramento River north of SACRAMENTO.

Finlay, British Columbia, Canada
See Peace, British Columbia-Alberta, Canada.

Flambeau, Wisconsin, USA
The Flambeau River rises in the lake region near the border with Michigan in northern Wisconsin. It is 115 miles (185 km) long and flows northwest through the Flambeau Reservoir, then southwest past PARK FALLS and LADYSMITH to join the Chippewa River.

Flathead, British Columbia, Canada
This river rises in southeastern British Columbia and flows south into Montana just east of the Whitefish Range. It is 240 miles

(390 km) long and flows south-southeast, south and west through Flathead Lake which covers an area of 189 square miles (490 sq km) before joining the Clark River near the town of PARADISE. The chief tributaries are the North Fork which is 85 miles (137 km) long and the South Fork which is 80 miles (129 km) long.

Flint, Georgia-Florida, USA
The Flint rises south of ATLANTA in western Georgia. It is 330 miles (530 km) long and flows south past ALBANY which is the head of navigation into Florida. It joins the Apalachicola River at CHATTANOOCHEE, on the Florida border.

Florido, Mexico
The Florido River rises near Hidalgo del Parral, northern Mexico. It is roughly 140 miles (230 km) long and flows in a semicircle past VILLA CORONADO, VILLA LOPEZ and JIMENEZ to join the Conchos River at CAMARGO.

Fort George, Quebec, Canada
The Fort George River rises in Nichicun Lake, located in central Quebec. It is 520 miles (840 km) long and flows west to enter James Bay at FORT GEORGE.

Fort Nelson, British Columbia, Canada
The Fort Nelson River rises in northeastern British Columbia. It is 100 miles (160 km) long and flows northwest to join the Liard River at NELSON FORKS.

Fox, Wisconsin, USA
This river rises in the Wisconsin lake district in the central portion of the state. It is 176 miles (283 km) long and flows northeast past OSHKOSH, then drains Lake Winnebago and continues to Green Bay on Lake Michigan. It is connected with the Wisconsin River via the Portage Canal.

Fraser, British Columbia, Canada
The Fraser is the longest river in British Columbia. It is 850 miles (1370 km) long and drains an area of 84,000 square miles (217,560 sq km). Originally it was a main fur trading route to the north, and as early as 1827 a trading post was built at Fort Langley, later

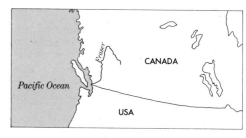

Vancouver. One of the chief assets of the river is its salmon which come in three varieties: sockeye, spring and coho salmon. The Fraser rises near Mt Robson, a peak 12,972 feet (3956 m) high in the Canadian Rockies of eastern British Columbia. It flows northwest on a 'S' shaped course past the towns of

British Columbia's Fraser River near the town of Hope.

DUNSTER, MCBRIDE, LAMMING MILLS, GOAT RIVER, LOOS, PENNY, UPPER FRASER and swings south through the Cariboo Mountains of central British Columbia. The chief tributaries are the Nechako, Quesnel and Thompson Rivers. Once past the Thompson junction, the river runs through the 70 mile (113 km) long Fraser Canyon and cuts through the Coast Ranges. The river then enters its lowlands, a large flood plain covering 900 square miles (2330 sq km). The Fraser is surrounded by rich farmlands and then reaches its wide delta to divide into two main channels around Lulu Island before passing through VANCOUVER and NEW WESTMINSTER into the Georgia Strait of the Pacific Ocean. The Fraser is noted for its sawmills and paper and pulp factories at New Westminster. The river was named after Simon Fraser who founded Fort George in 1807 at the confluence of the Nechako River.

French Broad, North Carolina, USA
The French Broad is formed by the confluence of several headstreams in the Blue Ridge Mountains of western North Carolina. This portion of the state is one of the most beautiful and most scenic areas of the eastern seaboard. The river is 204 miles (328 km) long and flows northeast past BREVARD, then swings northwest across the Tennessee border and west to join the Holston River just above KNOXVILLE to form the Tennessee River. Its chief tributaries are the Nolichucky and Pigeon Rivers.

Frenchman, Saskatchewan, Canada
The Frenchman River rises in the Cypress Hills of southwestern Saskatchewan, Canada. It is roughly 250 miles (400 km) long and flows southeast across the border into Montana to join the Milk River east-northeast of MALTA.

Frio, Texas, USA
The Frio River rises on the Edwards Plateau in Real County in southwestern Texas. It is 220 miles (350 km) long and flows south-southeast past LEAKEY, KNIPPA, LOS ANGELES, TILDEN and THREE RIVERS before joining the Nueces River. The chief tributary is the Atascosa River, which is 90 miles (145 km) long.

Fuerte, Rio del, Mexico
Formed by the confluence of the Rio Verde and the Urique Rivers, the Rio del Fuerte is 350 miles (560 km) long. It flows west into SINALOA, then southwest past EL FUERTE to enter the Gulf of California at Lechuguilla Island. The length of the Rio del Fuerte is inclusive of the Verde River, which is its longest tributary headstream.

Gallatin, Wyoming-Montana, USA
The Gallatin rises in the scenic Yellowstone National Park in northwestern Wyoming. It is 120 miles (190 km) long and flows north through a deep canyon to reach Three Forks, where it is joined by the Jefferson and Madison Rivers to form the Missouri River.

Gander, Newfoundland, Canada
The Gander rises in eastern Newfoundland at the junction of the Northwest and Southwest Gander Rivers at Gander Lake, which covers an area of 46 square miles (119 sq km). It is 110 miles (180 km) long and flows northeast to enter the Atlantic Ocean approximately 25

miles (40 km) north of GANDER. Gander has a very large airfield which is utilized by the Royal Canadian Air Force and the USAF.

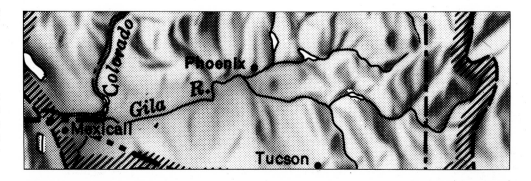

Gasconade, Missouri, USA
The Gasconade River rises in the Ozark Mountains of central Missouri. It is 265 miles (426 km) long and flows northeast to become a tributary of the Missouri River. The river is navigable during the summer for approximately 40 miles (64 km) upstream.

Gatineau, Quebec, Canada
The Gatineau River rises in the Laurentian Mountains of southwestern Quebec. It is 230 miles (370 km) long and flows south through Lake Baskatong to join the Ottawa River at HULL.

Gauley, West Virginia, USA
The Gauley River begins in Nicholas County, West Virginia and flows west-southwest. It is 104 miles (167 km) long and is the boundary for a time between Nicholas and Fayette Counties before turning southward at BELVA. It then proceeds to GAULEY BRIDGE where it joins the New River.

Genesee, Pennsylvania-New York, USA
The Genesee River rises in Potter County, Pennsylvania. It is 158 miles (254 km) long and flows generally northward until it reaches ROCHESTER on Lake Ontario. The falls and gorges of the Genesee are noted for their beauty.

George, Quebec, Canada
The George River rises on the border of Labrador in northern Quebec. It is 365 miles (587 km) long and flows northwest through Indian House Lake until it reaches Ungava Bay on the Atlantic Ocean.

Gila, New Mexico-Arizona, USA
The Gila rises in the Elk Mountains of western New Mexico. It is 630 miles (1010 km) long and one of the most important rivers in the American southwest. The Gila flows through some of the most arid and desert-like country in the United States. In 1928 the Coolidge Dam was constructed on the Gila with a reservoir of 6000 million cubic feet (171,428,570 cubic m) capacity and along with the Roosevelt Dam and Reservoir on the Salt River, irrigate a huge portion of southern Arizona. The irrigation projects of the Gila and the Salt Rivers utilize the entire water capacity of both streams, so that below the dams the flow of water is minute and sometimes the bed of Gila is dry to its confluence with the Colorado River north of YUMA. Yuma is one of the hottest places in the United States and once was the site of the Territorial Prison of Arizona. The Gila's initial course is southwest through a canyon where there are four magnificently preserved cliff dwellings, now a part of the Gila Cliff Dwelling National Monument in Catron County, New Mexico. Near the town of VIRDEN, the Gila twists into Arizona flowing northwest and receives the San Francisco River which comes down from the northeast. The Gila alternates its course from southwest to northwest in stretches of 20 to 60 miles (32 to 96 km) in length. It passes the towns of SAFFORD, FORT THOMAS, GERONIMO, CHRISTMAS, HAYDEN, RIVERSIDE STAGE STOP, and FLORENCE before entering the Gila Indian Reservation in Pinal County. Due north of Riverside Stage Stop, population 418 are the famous Superstition Mountains where the Lost Dutchman's gold mine is supposed to be located. The chief tributaries of the Gila are the San Simon, San Pedro, San Carlos, Santa Cruz, Salt, San Francisco, Agua Fria and Hassayampa Rivers; the river also receives numerous intermittent streams and creeks but because of the low annual rainfall these hardly ever run. The Gila continues southwest passing through the Bighorn Mountain and Maricopa Mountains, and AGUA CALIENTE, DOME and Yuma to finally join the Colorado River south of the Laguna Dam. The Gila has a great economic value to Arizona agriculturally because it irrigates thousands of acres of land.

Goascaran, El Salvador-Honduras
The Goascaran rises on the border between El Salvador and Honduras. It is 75 miles (121 km) long and flows south along the Inter-American Highway past Goascaran to enter the Gulf of Fonseca.

Grande Ronde, Oregon, USA
The Grande Ronde is a small river rising in the Blue Mountains of northeastern Oregon. It is 180 miles (290 km) long and flows northeast past LA GRANDE to join the Snake River in southeastern Washington State.

Grand, Iowa, USA
The Grand River rises near CRESTON, Iowa. It is 215 miles (346 km) long and winds southeast to join the Missouri River below BRUNSWICK, Missouri. Its chief tributaries are the Locust and Medicine Creeks.

Grand, Michigan, USA
The Grand rises only 100 miles (160 km) from Lake Michigan but has a very winding course for a total of 260 miles (420 km) before actually entering the lake. It is navigable for about 40 miles (64 km) from its mouth at GRAND HAVEN to GRAND RAPIDS. One mile above Grand Rapids a fall of 6 yards (1.8 m) in one mile has been used for a hydroelectric power station.

The Ottawa Indians were the original inhabitants of this region. In 1726 Louis Campeau established a trading post on the river at Grand Rapids which later grew into a large town. The accessibility of the logging industry on the river made Grand Rapids into the 'furniture capital of America.'

Grand, Ontario, Canada
This river rises northwest of ORANGEVILLE in southern Ontario. It is 165 miles (265 km) long and flows south past KITCHENER and BRANTFORD to enter Lake Erie at PORT MAITLAND. The Grand is navigable for approximately 70 miles (113 km).

Grand, South Dakota, USA
This river is formed by the confluence of the North and South Forks in northwestern South Dakota. It is 209 miles (336 km) long and flows east-southeast to join the Missouri River near the town of MOBRIDGE.

Great Miami, Ohio, USA
The Great Miami River is formed by several headstreams in Shelby County, Ohio and is 160 miles (260 km) long. It flows south past PIQUA, TROY, TIPP CITY and DAYTON and then swings southwest past MIAMITOWN, MIDDLETOWN and HAMILTON to join the Ohio River in southwestern Hamilton County.

Great Whale, Quebec, Canada
The Great Whale rises in the central lake district of Quebec in Lake Bienville. The river is 230 miles (370 km) long and is virtually one long stretch of rapids for its entire course. The last 20 miles (32 km) of the river is filled with sand bars and sandy beaches before it flows into Hudson Bay. The Great Whale settlement has had a Hudson Bay Company Trading Post for over 100 years and Eskimos and Indians travel miles to trade there. The region around Great Whale, which is one of the most sparsely populated areas of Quebec, has large iron ore deposits but the accessibility to the area is limited.

Green, Kentucky, USA
The Green River rises in central Kentucky. It is 370 miles (600 km) long and flows south-southwest and west through Mammoth Cave National Park, then northwest to join the Ohio River southeast of EVANSVILLE, Indiana. Its chief tributaries are the Nolin, Barren and Rough Rivers.

Green, Wyoming-Colorado-Utah, USA
The Green River rises at an altitude of 13,700 feet (4179 m) in the Wind River Range of the Rocky Mountains in the Continental Divide near Fremont and Gannet Peaks. The river is 730 miles (1175 km) long and is one of the major waterways of the western United States. It is a beautiful, scenic and historic river. The Green is joined by Horse Creek, which rises near Deadman Mountain, 10,365 feet (3161 m) in altitude, in the Wyoming Range of western Wyoming east of DANIEL. The river flows mainly on a southerly course, winding its way to Fontenelle Reservoir, and is joined by La Barge Creek, Middle Piney Creek and South Piney Creek between the towns of BIG PINEY and GREEN RIVER. The Green runs due south once past Green River, into the Flaming Gorge Reservoir and National Recreation Area. It flows west through the Flaming Gorge Dam in the northeastern corner of Utah and passes into Colorado for a short distance before turning southwest back into Utah for its final run to the Colorado River. The Green River cuts a picturesque canyon through the Dinosaur National Monument, a 298 square mile (772 sq km) tract of land set aside in Utah and Colorado which contains dinosaur fossils throughout. The Strawberry River, Price River, Rafael River, and Salaratus Wash are the chief tributaries of the Green as it heads to its confluence with the Colorado River in Orange Cliffs. The last section of the Green passes through a spectacular valley called Labyrinth Canyon, which curves in and out until the confluence with the Colorado. The Great Oregon Trail passes to the north of the Green in southwestern Wyoming and was the greatest of all the transcontinental wagon trails.

Greenbrier, West Virginia, USA
The Greenbrier River rises in northern Pocahantas County, West Virginia. It flows southwest through Pocahantas County, passing CASS, STONY BOTTOM, MARLINTON and BEARD. It then crosses over into Greenbrier County and passes RENICK, ANTHONY and RONCEVERTE before swinging across the tip of northwestern Monroe County into Summers County. The Greenbrier joins the New River near HINTON.

Greybull, Wyoming, USA
The Greybull River rises in south-central Park County, Wyoming. It flows from the central Absaroka Range east-northeast, past MEE-TEETSE and OTTO, to join the Bighorn River south of GREYBULL in Bighorn County. The Greybull is roughly 95 miles (153 km) long.

Grijalva, Guatemala-Mexico
The Grijalva rises in the Sierra Madre of Guatemala. It is 200 miles (320 km) long and was named for the Spanish explorer Juan de Grijalba. In 1518 Grijalba commanded the first exploratory group into southeastern

The Turk's Head on the Green River, Utah.

Mexico and explored the river to just below VILLAHERMOSA. The river is navigable for 70 miles (113 km) with an average depth of six feet (two m). The lower portion of the Grijalva has changed its course so many times that it is believed that Grijalba followed the Rio Seco channel in 1518 and not the present day channel. The river has many names and is called the Cheyel or Chejel at its very beginning in the Sierra de Chuchumatanes near GUATEMALA CITY. It then flows northwest, passing through hill country in Chiapas, Mexico where it is known as the Rio Grande de Chiapa. In the vicinity of TUXTLA GUTIERREZ the river flows for 25 miles (40 km) through a magnificent canyon, the walls of which rise to a height of 6000 feet (1830 m) and render the region inaccessible. It receives numerous tributaries from the west as it reaches LAS PALMAS, where it turns northeast as the Rio Mezcalapa. The Grijalva flows past the port city of Villahermosa and then into the Usumacinta.

Guadalupe, Texas, USA
The Guadalupe River rises on the Edward Plateau, Texas. It is 458 miles (737 km) long and flows southeast past KERRVILLE, GONZALES and VICTORIA to enter the head of San Antonio Bay of the Gulf of Mexico. Its chief tributaries are the Comal, San Marcos and San Antonio Rivers.

Guantánamo, Cuba
The Guantánamo is famous for the huge American Naval Base at Guantanamo Bay, the scene of much speculation during the Cuban crisis of the 1960s. The river rises east of SANTIAGO DE CUBA in eastern Cuba and flows for only 50 miles (80 km) before entering Guantánamo Bay. It is navigable for small vessels on its lower reaches.

Guayape, Honduras
The Guayape is a small river approximately 150 miles (240 km) long rising in central Honduras. It flows southeast past GUAYAPE, then heads east-northeast and south to join the Guayambre River, southeast of JUTICALPA to form the Patuca River.

Gunnison, Colorado, USA
The Gunnison is formed by the confluence of the East and Taylor Rivers near ALMONT in Gunnison County, central Colorado. It is 180 miles (290 km) long and flows west and northwest to join the Colorado River at GRAND JUNCTION. The Gunnison flows through Black Canyon just west of SAPINERO before joining the Colorado River.

Guyandot, West Virginia, USA
The Guyandot River rises in Raleigh County, West Virginia. It is 166 miles (267 km) long and flows southwest, west and north-northwest past GILBERT, LOGAN and BARBOURSVILLE, before joining the Ohio River at HUNTINGTON on the Ohio border.

Hackensack, New York-New Jersey, USA
The Hackensack River rises in Rockland County, New York. It is 45 miles (72 km) long and flows past ORADELL, New Jersey where it is dammed to form a reservoir. It then runs through Hackensack Meadows, which covers an area of 50 square miles (133 sq km), and emerges to enter Newark Bay just west of JERSEY CITY. The river is tidal and navigable to NEW MILFORD. This is one of the most populated areas of the northeastern United States.

Hams Fork, Wyoming, USA
The Hams Fork River rises in the Salt River Range of southwestern Wyoming. It is 100 miles (160 km) long and flows south past KEMMERER, then east past OPAL to the Blacks Fork of the Green River at GRANGER.

Hanalei, Kauai, Hawaii, USA
The Hanalei River rises on the northeastern slopes of Mt Waialeale, a peak 5080 feet (1549 m) high. It flows north and then west to the eastern side of Hanalei Bay.

Hare Indian, Northwest Territories, Canada
This small river rises west of Great Bear Lake in the Northwest Territories of Canada. It is 120 miles (190 km) long and flows west to join the Mackenzie River.

The Gunnison River flows through Black Canyon.

Harlem, New York, USA
The Harlem is a small, navigable, tidal channel which separates the Bronx from Manhattan. It is eight miles (13 km) long and joins the East River at the Hell Gate. The Harlem is linked to the Hudson River by the Spuyten Duyvil Creek.

Harpeth, Tennessee, USA
The Harpeth River rises in Rutherford County, central Tennessee. It is 117 miles (188 km) long and flows northwest past FRANKLIN to join the Cumberland River.

Harricana, Quebec, Canada
The Harricana River rises near VAL D'OR in western Quebec. It is 250 miles (400 km) long and flows northwest to James Bay of Hudson Bay in Ontario. The Harricana is navigable for 50 miles (80 km) upstream from its mouth.

Hatchie, Mississippi, USA
The Hatchie River rises in northern Mississippi and flows north-northwest into Tennessee. It is 175 miles (282 km) long and runs west-northwest to join the Mississippi River just north of MEMPHIS, Tennessee.

Haw, North Carolina, USA
The Haw River rises between the Blue Ridge and the Piedmont Plateau of North Carolina. It is 110 miles (180 km) long and flows east-southeast to join the Deep River near the town of HAYWOOD to form the Cape Fear River.

Hay, British Columbia-Alberta-Northwest Territories, Canada
The Hay rises in northeastern British Columbia. It is 350 miles (560 km) long and flows into Alberta, then north-northeast into the Northwest Territories to enter the Great Slave Lake. The Hay is especially noted for the scenic Alexandra Falls which is 150 feet (46 m)

high and located approximately 30 miles (48 km) above its mouth.

The mouth of the Hay River where it enters Great Slave Lake.

Hayes, Manitoba, Canada

The Hayes River rises north of Lake Winnipeg in Manitoba. It is 300 miles (480 km) long and flows northeast through several lakes to enter Hudson Bay at YORK FACTORY.

Heart, North Dakota, USA

Rising in southwestern North Dakota, the Heart flows northeast and east past GLADSTONE, where it is joined by the Green River. It is 180 miles (290 km) long and joins the Missouri River at MANDAN.

Henrys Fork, Idaho, USA

This river rises in Henrys Lake in southeastern Idaho. It is 110 miles (180 km) long and flows south and southwest past ST ANTHONY to join the Snake River.

Hiwassee, Georgia-North Carolina-Tennessee, USA

The Hiwassee River rises in the beautiful Blue Ridge Mountains of northern Georgia. It is 132 miles (212 km) long and flows north past HAVESVILLE, then northwest past MURPHY to the Chickamauga Reservoir on the Tennessee.

Hoh, Washington, USA

The Hoh River rises in the Olympia National Park in Jefferson County, Washington. It flows southwest, west and southwest to enter the Pacific Ocean south of Hoh Head.

Holston, Tennessee, USA

The Holston is formed by the confluence of the North Fork, which is 120 miles (190 km) long and the South Fork, which is 110 miles (180 km) long, just west of KINGSPORT, northeastern Tennessee. It is 115 miles (185 km) long and flows southwest to join the French Broad River above KNOXVILLE to form the Tennessee River.

Hondo, Guatemala

The Hondo River rises in Guatemala and flows for 130 miles (210 km) along the Mexican-Belize border to enter Chetumal Bay of the Caribbean Sea.

Hood, Oregon, USA

The Hood is a small river of northern Oregon. It rises on the eastern slopes of Mt Hood, a peak 11,235 feet (3427 m) high in Hood County. The river flows north past PARKDALE and Mt Hood to join the Columbia River at HOOD RIVER.

Hoosic, Massachusetts, USA

The Hoosic rises in the Taconic Mountains in northwestern Massachusetts. It is 70 miles (113 km) long and flows north, northwest and west, past ADAMS, WILLIAMSTOWN and HOOSICK FALLS to join the Hudson River approximately 14 miles (23 km) above TROY, New York.

Horse Creek, Wyoming, USA

The Horse Creek River rises in the Laramie Mountains of southeastern Wyoming. It is 136 miles (219 km) long and flows east, north and east past LA GRANGE to North Platte River near the town of MORRILL, Nebraska.

Horton, Northwest Territories, Canada

The Horton River rises north of the Great Bear Lake in the Canadian Northwest Territories. It is 275 miles (440 km) long and flows northwest to enter Franklin Bay in the Amundsen Gulf.

Housatonic, Massachusetts-Connecticut, USA

The Housatonic River rises in the Hoosac Range in the northwestern corner of Massachusetts, not far from Mt Greylock, a peak standing 3491 feet (1065 m) high. The Housatonic flows south, running parallel to the nearby Berkshire Hills. The river is 130 miles (208 km) long and drains an area of 1933 square miles (5066 sq km). The river crosses into Connecticut near ASHLEY FALLS, Massachusetts. Its chief tributaries are the Blackberry, Hollenbeck, and the Shepaug Rivers in its middle course. The river swings southeastward on its last leg to Long Island Sound, and is joined by its principal tributary the Naugatuck River at DERBY. The natural falls of the Housatonic provided power for the mills which developed along its banks.

Huahua, Nicaragua

Also known as the Wawa, the Huahua rises approximately 15 miles (24 km) east of BONANZA in northeastern Nicaragua. It is 100 miles (160 km) long and flows east-southeast to form the Carata Lagoon, 11 miles (18 km) south-southwest of PUERTO CABEZAS.

Hudson, New York, USA

In 1524 Giovanni da Verrazano, the great Florentine navigator sailed for a short distance up the Hudson River, but it was not until 1609 that the famous Dutch navigator, Henry Hudson, explored the river. Settlement of the Hudson Valley began 20 years later, but title to the land was withheld under the patroon system for over 200 years. During the 19th century the Hudson River traffic flourished, and further prospered after the opening of the Erie, the Delaware and the Hudson-Champlain Canals which linked NEW YORK CITY with the Great Lakes, the Delaware and St Lawrence River systems. The Hudson River Valley is famous for its lovely scenery and is the center for a large dairy and fruit-growing industry. The river is 306 miles (492 km) long, drains an area of 13,370 square miles (34,630 sq km) and is ranked 26th in volume of water carried of the US rivers. The Hudson is located entirely within New York State and originates in several small post glacial lakes in Essex County, near Mt Marcy, the highest point in the state at 5344 feet (1630 m). For the initial stage of its journey the river follows a winding course, southeast past the town of CORINTH in Saratoga County, then northeast to the Hudson Falls at the northern end of the Hudson River Valley. From there it runs south without any significant change in the gradient to the Battery at the head of New York City's Upper Bay. The Hudson continues for a further 150 miles (240 km) through a great subterranean canyon before finally flowing into the Atlantic Ocean. The chief cities on the Hudson are NYACK, TARRYTOWN, HAVERSTRAW, OSSINING, PEEKSKILL, NEW-BURGH, POUGHKEEPSIE, KINGSTON, SAUGERTIES, CATSKILL, ALBANY, TROY and GLENS FALLS. Tides reach as far as Troy, and the river varies in width from three-quarters of a mile to three miles (one to five km) at Haverstraw Bay. The most important tributary is the Mohawk River, and together with the Hudson, forms one of the world's greatest river systems. The shallow gradient of these two rivers has been for centuries the chief route through the Appalachian Mountains. The Hudson is spanned in numerous locations by some of the most famous bridges in the world: the Rip Van Winkle built in 1935 at Catskill, the Kingston-Rhinecliff built in 1957, the Mid-Hudson built in 1930 at Poughkeepsie, the Bear Mountain built in 1924 at Peekskill, the Tappan Zee built

in 1956 at Tarrytown, the George Washington built in 1931 in New York City and the Verrazano Narrows Bridge built in the 1960s.

Humber, Newfoundland, Canada

The Humber issues forth from Alder Lake in Newfoundland. It is 75 miles (121 km) long and flows southwest through Deer Lake, past CORNER BROOK to the Bay of Islands in the Gulf of the St Lawrence.

Humboldt, Nevada, USA

The Humboldt rises in the Ruby Mountains of Elko County, northeastern Nevada. It is 300 miles (480 km) long and flows west-northwest past CARLIN, PALISADE, BEOWAWE, DUNPHY, BATTLE MOUNTAIN, RED HOUSE and WIN-NEMUCCA, the latter being the first trading center established along the Humboldt Trail. The river was named for the great explorer Baron Alexander von Humboldt by John C Fremont, and was an integral part of the 'California Trail.' The Humboldt swings southwest past MILL CITY into the Rye Patch Reservoir, then continues past OREANA to enter the Humboldt Sink. The annual rainfall in this region of Nevada is extremely low, and accounts for the small volume of the river as it flows from the mountains to the desert. The Humboldt Sink is 11 miles (18 km) long and four miles (six km) wide, and is an intermittent dry lake bed or playa. It is the last remnant of a

Two views of New York City: left – The Hudson flows into the Upper New York Bay; below left – the Queensboro Bridge over the East River.

once large lake called Lake Lahontan which was formed in the last glacial period and covered a wide expanse of present-day Nevada. The lower part of the Humboldt is a desert area where only greasewood grows.

Humptulips, Washington, USA
This is a small river rising in northern Grays Harbor County in the Coast Range of Washington State. It flows southwest past the town of HUMPTULIPS and COPALIS CROSSING to enter Grays Harbor of the Pacific Ocean.

Huron, Michigan, USA
The Huron River rises in southeastern Michigan, and flows southwest and south to DEXTER, then southeast past ANN ARBOR and BELLEVILLE before entering Lake Erie. The river is 97 miles (156 km) long.

Huron, Ohio, USA
The Huron River rises in central Huron County near the town of FITCHVILLE, Ohio. It flows west and northeast, past NORTH FAIR-FIELD, MILAN and HURON, before entering Lake Erie.

Iditarod, Alaska, USA
See Innoko, Alaska, USA.

Illinois, Illinois, USA
The Illinois is formed by the confluence of the Des Plaines and the Kankakee Rivers near the boundary of Grundy and Will Counties in northeastern Illinois. It is 273 miles (439 km) long, and drains an area of 28,000 square miles (72,520 sq km). The river was first explored by Louis Joliet and Jacques Marquette in 1673. The original inhabitants of the Illinois Valley were the Fox, Kaskaskia and Sauk tribes. The Illinois flows west initially past MORRIS, SENECA, MARSEILLES and OTTAWA, where it is joined by the Fox River. It turns southwest near the town of DEPUE, Illinois, then passes PEORIA, the principal city on the river, EAST PEORIA, CREVE COEUR, PEKIN, HAVANA and HARDIN, before joining the Mississippi River approximately 38 miles (61 km) above ST LOUIS. The chief tributaries are the Vermilion, Spoon, Sangamon, La Moine and Macoupin Rivers.

Indian, New York, USA
The Indian River rises in Lewis County, northern New York State. It is 80 miles (129 km) long and flows northwest past ANTWERP, then southwest past PHILADELPHIA before swinging north past THERESA to enter the southern portion of Black Lake. The river has cut beautiful limestone caves and a bridge at NATURAL BRIDGE and is a prime tourist area during the summer season.

Innoko, Alaska, USA
The Innoko River rises in the western part of Alaska. It is 450 miles (720 km) long and flows north initially before winding southwest to the Yukon River opposite HOLY CROSS. Its chief tributary is the Iditarod River which is 150 miles (240 km) long.

Iowa, Iowa, USA
The Iowa is formed by the confluence of the East and West Branches near the town of BELMOND. It is 329 miles (529 km) long and flows southeast past IOWA FALLS, MARSHALL-TOWN and IOWA CITY before joining the Mississippi River approximately 20 miles (32 km) south of MUSCATINE.

James, North Dakota, USA
Sometimes referred to as the Dakota River, the James rises in central North Dakota and is 710 miles (1140 km) long. It flows south-southeast past JAMESTOWN and into South Dakota past the towns of HURON and MITCHELL to join the Missouri River at Yankton. The James is not navigable.

James, Virginia, USA
The James is formed by the confluence of the Jackson and Cowpasture Rivers in Botetourt County. It is 340 miles (550 km) long and flows southeast past BUCHANAN, then turns northeast past NATURAL BRIDGE, BIG ISLAND, COLEMAN FALLS to emerge through the Blue Ridge at LYNCHBURG. The river twists and turns for the remainder of its course through east-central Virginia. The James then passes through the state capital of RICHMOND, which also was the capital of the Confederate States of America during the American Civil War. The river finally concludes, after travelling through a long and wide estuary, at NEWPORT NEWS and into the end of the Chesapeake Bay before it enters the Atlantic Ocean. The rapids above Richmond have been harnessed for hydro-electric power, and the city is the head of navigation for large vessels. The lower reaches of the river are rich in American history, for here on 13 May 1607 at Jamestown the first English colony was established on the shores of North America. It was on the lower James River that the Federal troops dug the Dutch Gap Canal to finally take Richmond in April 1865. Today Richmond is one of the loveliest cities of the American South.

Jefferson, Montana, USA
Known initially as the Red Rock River, the Jefferson rises in the Gravelly Range of southwestern Montana. It is 207 miles (333 km) long and flows west through the Red Rock Lakes, then swings north past DILLON where it becomes the Beaverhead River. The river is joined by the Big Hole and the Ruby Rivers at TWIN BRIDGES, and continues for the remainder of its course as the Jefferson. It meets the Madison and Gallatin River at THREE FORKS to form the Missouri River.

John Day, Oregon, USA
The John Day rises in several headstreams in the Strawberry Mountains of northeastern Oregon. It is 281 miles (452 km) long and flows west and north to join the Columbia River east-northeast of THE DALLES.

Jordan, Utah, USA
The Jordan rises in Lake Utah, central Utah. It is 60 miles (97 km) long and flows north through SALT LAKE CITY to enter the Great Salt Lake near BOUNTIFUL.

Judith, Montana, USA
The Judith is a small but beautiful river which rises in the southwestern corner of Fergus County, central Montana. The river flows generally northward for its entire course to join the Missouri River on the boundary of Chouteau and Fergus Counties.

Kalamazoo, Michigan, USA
The Kalamazoo River is formed by the confluence of the North and South Branches at ALBION, Michigan. It is 138 miles (222 km) long and flows past MARSHALL, OTSEGO and ALLEGAN to enter Lake Michigan.

Kanawha, West Virginia, USA
The Kanawha rises at GAULEY BRIDGE, West Virginia at the junction of the New and Gauley Rivers. It is 97 miles (155 km) long and flows northwest past CHARLESTOWN to join the Ohio River at POINT PLEASANT.

Kansas, Kansas, USA
The Kansas is formed by the confluence of the Republican and the Smoky Hill Rivers in east-central Kansas. Both of these rivers flow virtually parallel to each other as they drain rolling great open spaces and short grasses of the Great Plains. The Kansas River is 170 miles (270 km) long and flows east through north-central Kansas. The river passes BELVUE, ST MARYS, WILLARD, the state capital of TOPEKA, LAWRENCE and BONNER SPRINGS to join the Missouri River at KANSAS CITY, Kansas. The river is sometimes called the Kaw River and flows through wide bottomlands ringed in by rugged hills. The valley is noted for its production of excellent melon and potato crops. The river has serious floods every year, especially when the rainfall has been exceedingly heavy. The major floods this century have been in 1903, 1908, 1923, 1935 and 1951, all which resulted in great property damage and loss of life and livestock. For a time the Kansas was utilized by small river steamers but the railroads soon supplanted them. Today the Atchison, Topeka and Sante Fe run along the south bank, while the Union Pacific runs parallel along the north bank. At one of the greatest confluences in the midwest, the Kansas joins the Missouri River at KANSAS CITY, Kansas and KANSAS CITY, Missouri. The twin cities are large meat-packing centers as well as railway hubs.

Kaskaskia, Illinois, USA
The Kaskaskia rises near URBANA in east-central Illinois. It is 320 miles (510 km) long and flows southwest to join the Mississippi River, northwest of Kaskaskia.

Kazan, Northwest Territories, Canada

The Kazan River rises in the southeastern section of the Mackenzie District of the Canadian Northwest Territories. It is 445 miles (716 km) long and flows into Keewatin District, then through Ennadai and Yathkyed Lakes to enter Baker Lake.

Kennebec, Maine, USA

The Kennebec rises in Moosehead Lake, central Maine which is near the source of the Penobscot. It flows south to join the Androscoggin River 25 miles (40 km) below AUGUSTA on Merrymeeting Bay. The river is 150 miles (240 km) long.

Kentucky, Kentucky, USA

The Kentucky River is formed by the North Fork River, 168 miles (270 km) long, and the Middle Fork River, 97 miles (156 km) long, at BEATTYVILLE, Kentucky. It is 259 miles (417 km) long and flows northwest to join the Ohio River at CARROLLTON.

Kickapoo, Wisconsin, USA

The Kickapoo River rises in Monroe County, west-central Wisconsin. It flows southwest past ONTARIO, LA FARGE, SOLDIERS GROVE, GAYS MILLS and WAUZEKA before joining the Wisconsin River.

Kissimmee, Florida, USA

The Kissimmee has its source in Lake Tohopekaliga in central Florida. It is 140 miles (220 km) long and flows south-southeast through Hatchineha and Kissimmee Lakes to enter Lake Okeechobee just southwest of OKEECHOBEE.

Klamath, Oregon-California, USA

The Klamath rises in Upper Klamath Lake in Klamath County in southwestern Oregon. It is 250 miles (400 km) long and flows southwest initially, curving abruptly northward for a short distance before making its swing southwest into California. The river is joined by Spencer Creek just as it turns southward into California. The Klamath then flows through Copco Lake and Iron Gate Reservoir, situated in north-central California. The Klamath's entire course in California is through high mountains approximately 7000 feet (2135 m) in altitude and has a very deeply cut, narrow but beautiful valley. The slopes of the valley are covered with cedar, pine, fir and redwood forests. The upper stretches of the Klamath are utilized for irrigation and hydroelectric projects. The river heads west passing the town of HORSE CREEK, then runs through the Siskiyou Range to HAPPY CAMP and CLEAR CREEK flowing south. The Klamath swings northwest through Humboldt and Del Norte Counties and enters the Pacific Ocean at the town of REQUA in the Redwood National Park, which runs along the northwestern section of the Pacific coast of California. The chief tributaries are the Trinity, the Scott and the Salmon Rivers. The Klamath used to be joined to the Lower Klamath Lake but when the river was closed the lower lake dried up.

Frankfort, Kentucky's capital city, rests on the northern bank of the Kentucky River.

Klondike, Yukon Territory, Canada

The Klondike is one of the most famous rivers in Canada although it is only a mere 100 miles (160 km) long. This small and totally inconsequential subarctic river would not have been given a second glance except for the discovery of gold. On 17 August 1896 a few prospectors struck gold in Bonanza Creek, a small tributary of the Klondike just southeast of DAWSON. In four years the annual yield of this precious metal was in excess of 22 million dollars. The main deposits were discovered along the tributaries of the Klondike and the Indian River, another small tributary of the Yukon. The most famous of the gold-bearing creeks were Bonanza, Eldorado, Dominion, Hunker and Gold Run. By 1906, ten years after the first strike was made, the gold had run out and the Klondike once again resumed its normal role as a quiet, unassuming, subarctic river.

Knife, North Dakota, USA

The Knife River rises in the Killdeer Mountains of North Dakota. It is 165 miles (265 km) long and flows due east to join the Missouri River near the town of STANTON.

Kobuk, Alaska, USA

The Kobuk River rises in the Brooks Range, Alaska. It is 300 miles (480 km) long and flows west to Hotham Inlet east-southeast of KOTZEBUE.

Kokolik, Alaska, USA

The Kokolik River rises in the De Long Mountains just north of Tingmerkat Mountain, which is 3787 feet (1155 m) high, in northwestern Alaska. It flows north and northeast to enter the Arctic Ocean at Point Lay.

Kokosing, Ohio, USA

This river rises in east-central Morrow County near CHESTERVILLE, Ohio. It flows eastward past MOUNT VERNON, GAMBIER, HOWARD and MILLWOOD before joining with the Mohican River at the town of Walhonding in Coshocton County to form the Walhonding River.

Koksoak, Quebec, Canada

This small river rises in northern Quebec at the confluence of the Larch and Caniapiskau Rivers. It is only 90 miles (145 km) long, but its name in Eskimo means 'Big River.' At the confluence the Koksoak is over one mile (1610 m) wide and by the time it reaches its mouth at Ungava Bay of the Hudson Strait, the river is three miles (five km) wide. The tides reach 36 miles (58 km) upstream and attain a height of over 40 feet (12 m) on occasions. In 1830 the Hudson Bay Company established a trading post at FORT CHIMO on the east bank of the river about 30 miles (48 km) upstream from its mouth. Today the Company trading post is located on the west bank and near the Fort Chimo airport. The Caniapiskau River is an untapped source of hydroelectric power.

Kootenay, British Columbia-Montana, Canada-USA

The Kootenay rises in southeastern British Columbia and is 448 miles (721 km) long. It flows across the border into Montana near the town of EUREKA. A section of the Kootenay is utilized as a fish hatchery. Further downstream the river passes a large sawmill at LIBBY before turning west and northwest into northeastern Idaho. It continues on course and re-enters British Columbia at the south end of Lake Kootenay. This lake is 64 miles (103 km) long and very narrow covering 191 square miles (495 sq km). The lake is a large extension of the river. The river drains out of the west arm of the lake. The principal town on the river is NELSON which is the center of a large mining region known for its gold, copper, silver, lead and zinc ores. The river is highly developed for hydroelectric power, and is rich in game and scenery. In British Columbia, 543 square miles (1406 sq km) of land bordering the river has been established as the KOOTENAY NATIONAL PARK. The river finally joins the Columbia approximately 20 miles (32 km) below Nelson.

Koyukuk, Alaska, USA

The Koyukuk River rises on the southern slopes of the Brooks Range, Alaska. It is 500 miles (800 km) long and flows southwest to join the Yukon River at the town of KOYUKUK. Its chief tributaries are the Alatna and John Rivers.

Kukpowruk, Alaska, USA

The river rises in the De Long Mountains of northwestern Alaska. It flows north to enter the Arctic Ocean south of POINT LAY.

Kuskokwim, Alaska, USA

The river rises in four separate branches in the Alaska Range of western Alaska. It is 600 miles (970 km) long and flows southeast past MCGRATH to enter Kuskokwim Bay of the Bering Sea. The river is navigable as far as McGrath.

La Have, Nova Scotia, Canada

The river rises in Lake La Have, 30 miles (48 km) east-northeast of ANNAPOLIS ROYAL in western Nova Scotia. It is 60 miles (96 km) long and flows southeast through a series of small lakes past BRIDGEWATER, the .head of navigation, to enter the Atlantic Ocean southsouthwest of LUNENBURG. Surrounding areas are noted for their superb fisheries.

Laramie, Colorado-Wyoming, USA

The Laramie River is one of the best known of the western rivers. It rises in the Front Royal Range of Colorado and flows for 216 miles (348 km) north and northeast through Laramie Plains and Wheatland Reservoirs, before joining the North Platte River at FORT LARAMIE.

Larch, Quebec, Canada

The Larch rises in northern Quebec in the Lower Seal Lakes, north of Clearwater Lake. It is 270 miles (430 km) long and flows northeast to Caniapiskau River to form the Koksoak River southwest of FORT CHIMO.

L'Assomption, Quebec, Canada

This river rises in the Laurentian Mountains of southern Quebec. It is 100 miles (160 km) long and flows southeast past JOLIETTE, then south past L'ASSOMPTION to join the St Lawrence River at the north end of Montreal Island.

Lavaca, Texas, USA

The Lavaca rises in Fayette County, southern Texas. It is 100 miles (160 km) long and flows south-southeast to Lavaca Bay. Its chief tributary is the Navidad River.

Leaf, Mississippi, USA

The Leaf rises in Scott County, south-central Mississippi. It is 180 miles (290 km) long and flows first south, and then southeast before joining the Chickasawhay River to form the Pascagoula River.

Leaf, Quebec, Canada

The Leaf River rises in Lake Minto in northern Quebec. It is 300 miles (480 km) long and flows northeast through Leaf Lake which is tidal. The Lake covers an area 30 miles (48 km) long and 15 miles (24 km) wide. The river proceeds to Ungava Bay approximately 65 miles (105 km) north-northwest of FORT CHIMO.

Lehigh, Pennsylvania, USA

The Lehigh rises in the Pocono Mountains of eastern Pennsylvania. It is 120 miles (190 km) long and flows southeast, south and east, past JIM THORPE, LEHIGTON and BETHLEHEM, before joining the Delaware River.

Lemhi, Idaho, USA

The Lemhi rises between the Lemhi Range and Beaverhead Mountains in Lemhi County, northern Idaho. It flows northwest past LEADORE, LEMHI, TENDOY and BAKER, before joining the Salmon River at SALMON.

Lempa, Guatemala-Honduras-El Salvador

The Lempa rises near ESQUIPULAS, Guatemala. It is 200 miles (320 km) long and flows south through the tip of Honduras across the border and into El Salvador. It winds south, east and south again to enter the Pacific Ocean eastsoutheast of LA LIBERTAD.

Leon, Texas, USA

The Leon River rises in several headstreams in Comanche County, Texas. It is 145 miles (233 km) long and flows southeast past the town of GATESVILLE with the Cowhouse Creek it forms the Belton Reservoir and then flows on to join the Lampasas River to form the Little River south of TEMPLE.

Lerma, Mexico

See Santiago, Mexico.

Lewes, Yukon, Canada

The Lewes issues forth from Lake Tagish in the southern Yukon Territory, Canada. It is 338 miles (544 km) long and flows north through Marsh Lake, past the town of WHITEHORSE, the head of navigation, then through Lake Laberge. It turns northwest past the Carmacks to join the Pelly River at FORT SELKIRK to form the Yukon River. Its chief tributary is the Teslin River.

Liard, Yukon-British Columbia-Northwest Territory, Canada

The Liard rises in the Yukon Territory, east of WHITEHORSE and runs east-southeast into British Columbia. The river is 570 miles (920 km) long. At NELSON FORKS, one of the many Hudson Bay Company's trading posts, it is joined by the Fort Nelson River. The Liard then turns north and northeast into the great Northwest Territories of Canada, passing FORT LIARD on the way to FORT SIMPSON, where it joins the Mackenzie River. The river is navigable from its mouth to Fort Liard by small vessels only. A large part of the river's course is closely followed by the Alaskan Highway. In its upper course, the Liard has worn one of the widest gaps through the Rocky Mountains and this pass has been used as the chief link between the Yukon and Alaska for many years. This region of Canada is interesting and scenic but is sparsely inhabited.

Licking, Kentucky, USA

The Licking River rises in Magoffin County, Kentucky. It is 320 miles (520 km) long and flows northwest past FALMOUTH to join the Ohio River opposite CINCINNATI. The chief tributaries are the North and South Fork Rivers.

Lièvre, Quebec, Canada

The Lièvre rises in Kempt Lake in the Laurentian Mountains of southwestern Quebec. It is 225 miles (362 km) long and flows due south past the town of BUCKINGHAM to join the Ottawa River. The river is noted for its scenic 130-foot (40-m) High Falls, located 22 miles (35 km) north-northwest of Buckingham.

Little, Oklahoma, USA

This river rises in the Ouachita Mountains of Oklahoma. It is 220 miles (350 km) long and flows southwest and southeast past WRIGHT CITY to join the Red River just west of FULTON, Arkansas.

Little Bighorn, Wyoming-Montana, USA

The Little Bighorn is 90 miles (145 km) long. It begins in the Bighorn Mountains of windswept northern Wyoming and flows in a generally northeasterly direction until it reaches the larger Bighorn River at HARDIN, near the Crow Indian Reservation. In the late

19th century, the Little Bighorn became famous when on 25 June 1876 the 7th US Cavalry, commanded by brevet Major General George Armstrong Custer, was utterly defeated by the Sioux nation. To this day, the Battle of the Little Bighorn still ranks as the largest massacre of a field unit on North American soil and the site of the battlefield is marked by a commemorative stone.

Little Colorado, New Mexico, USA
The river rises in New Mexico and flows west-northwest into Apache County, Arizona, where it is joined by the Zuni River. The river is 315 miles (507 km) long and flows past WOODRUFF, HOLBROOK, JOSEPH CITY, LEUPP, then heads across the Painted Desert to its ultimate destination, the Colorado River, which it meets in the Grand Canyon.

Little Kanawha, West Virginia, USA
The river rises in Upshur County, West Virginia. It is 160 miles (256 km) long and flows west and northwest to join the Ohio River at PARKERSBURG.

Little Miami, Ohio, USA
This river rises in east-central Clark County, Ohio. It flows southwest into Greene County and past YELLOW SPRINGS, then curves through Warren County. It reaches KINGS MILLS, where it turns south to join the Ohio River near FORT THOMAS.

Little Missouri, Wyoming-North Dakota, USA
The river rises in Crook County, northeastern Wyoming. It is 560 miles (900 km) long and flows into North Dakota, through the Badlands, to join the Missouri River at Lake Sasakawea.

Little Muskingum, Ohio, USA
The Little Muskingum rises in Monroe County, Ohio. It flows southwest through southern Monroe County and diagonally through northeastern Washington County, before joining the Ohio River opposite RENO, West Virginia.

Little Platte, Missouri-Iowa, USA
The Little Platte rises near the town of CRESTON, Iowa. It is 170 miles (270 km) long and flows south to join the Missouri River below LEAVENWORTH, in Platte County, Missouri.

Little Sioux, Minnesota-Iowa, USA
This river rises in Jackson County, Minnesota. It is 221 miles (356 km) long and flows south and southwest through northwestern Iowa to join the Missouri River near the town of LITTLE SIOUX, Iowa. The chief tributaries are the Maple, West Fork and Ocheyedan Rivers.

Little Wabash, Illinois, USA
The Little Wabash rises near MATTOON, Illinois. It is 200 miles (320 km) long and flows south and southeast to join the Wabash River near NEW HAVEN, Illinois.

Little Weiser, Idaho, USA
The river rises in Adams County, Idaho. It flows west past Indian Valley to join the Weiser River at CAMBRIDGE in· Washington County.

Lodgepole Creek, Wyoming-Nebraska-Colorado, USA
This small river rises at a height of 8000 feet (2440 m) in southeastern Wyoming. It is 212 miles (341 km) long and flows east through Nebraska eventually to become a tributary of the South Platte River near JULESBURG, Colorado.

Lost, West Virginia, USA
See Cacapon, West Virginia, USA.

Loup, Nebraska, USA
The Loup is formed by the confluence of the North and Middle Loup Rivers in Howard County, Nebraska. It is 68 miles (109 km) long and runs east to join the Platte River at COLUMBUS.

Mackenzie, Northwest Territories, Canada
The Mackenzie is the second largest river system in North America; only the Mississippi is larger. It is 2635 miles (4240 km) long and drains an area of 682,000 square miles (1,766,000 sq km). It flows through one of the most sparsely inhabited regions of the world. The most distant headstream of the Mackenzie is the Finlay River which rises in British Columbia. The name Mackenzie is given to the overflow of the Great Slave Lake which flows northwest to the Beaufort Sea, an arm of the Arctic Ocean. The river was explored by Sir Alexander Mackenzie for the North West Company in 1789. The delta and the coastline

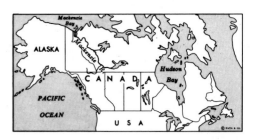

of the Beaufort Sea were not charted until 1825–26 by Sir John Franklin. Today, as in 1789, the river is the only route through the Mackenzie Territory. The river steamer *Mackenzie* began operations on the river in 1902 and carried all the required supplies to the far northern outposts. On the middle course of the Mackenzie it is four miles (six km) wide in places. A particularly scenic section of the great river is a five mile (eight km) stretch called the Ramparts, where the river flows through a channel 500 yards/m wide and between 200-foot (61-m) high cliffs. As the river reaches the far northern stretches of its course, it meanders and has a wide channel with shifting sandbars. The delta is in excess of 100 miles (160 km) in length, and requires expert and exceedingly careful navigation. The northern terminus of the Mackenzie is located at TUKTOYAKTUK on the Arctic Ocean where the open water season is only four months long. The chief tributaries of the Mackenzie are the Bear, Hare, Indian, Slave, Hay, Fort Nelson, Liard, Root, Redstone, Keele, Carcajou, Ramparts, Arctic Red and the Peel Rivers. The Hudson Bay Company stopped all freight traffic to the delta quite some time ago, but the service has since been replaced by the Mackenzie River Transport and Northern Transport Companies. The total tonnage of these two companies has seldom exceeded 40,000 tons per annum, but as the Arctic is opened up and its natural resources made accessible, the trade should increase in volume.

This photograph, taken in 1929, shows the Mackenzie River as it flows northwest past the Ramparts on its way to the Beaufort Sea.

Mackinaw, Illinois, USA
This small river rises in Ford County, Illinois. It is 130 miles (210 km) long and flows west, southwest and north to join the Illinois River just below PEKIN.

Madison, Wyoming, USA
The Madison rises in the Yellowstone National Park, Wyoming. It is 183 miles (294 km) long and flows due west through Hebgen Lake, then turns north to join the Gallatin and Jefferson Rivers at THREE FORKS to form the Missouri River.

Magdalena, Mexico
The Magdalena River rises southeast of NOGALES in northwestern Mexico. It is approximately 200 miles (320 km) long and flows southwest and west to enter the Gulf of California, northwest of Cape Tepoca. Its chief tributary is the Altar River.

Manicouagan, Quebec, Canada
The Manicouagan rises in Manicouagan Lake in Quebec Province, Canada. Manicouagan means 'where there is bark' in Indian. The river is 310 miles (500 km) long and flows due south for its entire journey to the St Lawrence River near the town of BAIE COMEAU. Its chief tributary is the Toulnustouc River. To the west is the mouth of the Outardes River which is only separated from the Manicouagan by a fan-shaped peninsula. The Manicouagan and the Outardes have highly developed hydroelectric power stations along their courses. Power is carried via under-river cable to the Gaspe copper mining center of MURDOCH-VILLE. This part of Quebec was one of the earliest settled by the French.

Manistee, Michigan, USA
The river rises in lakes district of Otsego County, in northwestern Michigan. It is 170 miles (270 km) long and flows southwest to enter Lake Michigan west of the town of MANISTEE.

Maquoketa, Iowa, USA
This river rises in eastern Iowa and flows southeast past the towns of MANCHESTER and MONTICELLO before joining the Mississippi River southeast of BELLEVUE. The river is 130 miles (210 km) long. Its chief tributary is the North Fork River.

Marias, Montana, USA
The Marias rises in several headstreams on the Continental Divide in northwestern Montana. It is 210 miles (340 km) long and flows east and south to join the Missouri River northeast of FORT BENTON.

Mattaponi, Virginia, USA
Formed by the confluence of several head-streams in Caroline County, eastern Virginia, the Mattaponi is 120 miles (190 km) long and flows southeast to join the Pamunkey River at WEST POINT to form the York River.

Maumee, Indiana, USA
The Maumee is formed in Indiana by the confluence of the St Joseph and St Mary's Rivers. It is 130 miles (210 km) long and flows northeast past TOLEDO, Ohio to enter Maumee Bay on Lake Erie. The chief tributary is the Auglaize River.

Mayo, Mexico
The Mayo River rises in Chihuahua State, northwestern Mexico. It is 220 miles (350 km) long and flows southwest past NAVOJOA and ETCHOJOA to enter a lagoon in the Gulf of California southwest of HUATABAMPO.

Meadow, West Virginia, USA
The Meadow River rises in southwestern Greenbrier County near GRASSY MEADOWS, West Virginia. It flows north past DAWSON, then upon reaching CRAWLEY, it turns west running past RUPERT. The river moves northwest to CHARMCO, then bends southward for a short distance before turning northwest again and forming the boundary first between Greenbrier and Fayette Counties, and later between Fayette and Nicholas Counties before joining the Gauley River.

Meade, Alaska, USA
The Meade River rises south of POINT BARROW, Alaska, the furthest point north on mainland Alaska. It is 250 miles (400 km) long and flows north to enter the Arctic Ocean.

Meherrin, Virginia, USA
The Meherrin rises in Lunenburg County, Virginia, when several headstreams meet. It is 126 miles (203 km) long and flows east-southeast past EMPORIA, then runs southeast into North Carolina, past the town of MURFREESBORO, the head of navigation. It then joins the Chowan River which proceeds for a

further 50 miles (80 km) before emptying into Albemarle Sound.

Meramec, Missouri, USA
The Meramec River rises in the Ozark Mountains of eastern Missouri. It winds for 207 miles (333 km), north, northeast and southeast before joining the Mississippi River below ST LOUIS. Its chief tributary is the Bourbeuse River which is 138 miles (222 km) long.

Merrimack, New Hampshire-Massachusetts, USA
The Merrimack is formed by the confluence of the Pemigewasset and the Winnipesaukee Rivers just below the Franklin Falls Reservoir near the town of FRANKLIN in Merrimack County, New Hampshire. The river is 110 miles (180 km) long and flows south and east before entering the Atlantic Ocean near NEWBURYPORT, Massachusetts. The river valley is the major route north from BOSTON and the surrounding area. The Merrimack flows down through one of New Hampshire's most scenic and beautiful regions. The principal tributaries of the Merrimack are the Warner, the Souhegan, the Piscataquog, the Suncook and the Nashua Rivers. The river flows past the capital of New Hampshire, CONCORD, with a population of 31,000, then through MANCHESTER and NASHUA before crossing into Massachusetts. Now it passes the town of LOWELL, and heads due east into the Atlantic Ocean. The river in its last reaches flows through one of the northeastern United States' most heavily industrialized regions, noted for its boots, shoes, hosiery, woolen and textile products. The Merrimack is one of New England's major sources of hydroelectrical power.

Old mills at Pentacook, New Hampshire on the banks of a tributary of the Merrimack.

Middle Loup, Nebraska, USA

This small river rises as an intermittent stream in southwestern Cherry County, Nebraska. It is 221 miles (356 km) long and flows east-southeast across the corner of Hooker County, then into Thomas County and past SENECA, THEDFORD and HALSEY, before receiving the Dismal River at DUNNING. The Middle Loup then proceeds on course past MILBURN, COMESTOCK, ARCADIA, LOUP CITY and ROCK-VILLE, before being joined by the South Loup River near BOELUS. The river then swings northeast to join the North Loup to form the Loup River in Howard County.

Milk, Montana-Alberta, USA-Canada

The two headstreams of the Milk River rise in the Blackfoot Indian Reservation of Glacier County, northern Montana. The Milk is 625 miles (1006 km) long and flows from the southern section of Alberta, roughly eastward before turning southeast to cross the border back into the United States. It then runs through the Fresno Reservoir of Hill County, Montana and continues on an east-southeast course for the remainder of its course. It passes NORTH HAVRE, HAVRE, CHINOOK, FORT BELKNAP, SAVOY, and MALTA before making a curve northward and then abruptly turning south to join the Missouri River at the northern head of the Fort Peck Reservoir. The chief tributaries of the Milk River are the Sandy Creek, Beaver Creek, Porcupine Creek and Frenchman River. The river was discovered by the great explorer Meriwether Lewis in 1805 and named for the glacial cloudiness of its waters.

Minnesota, Minnesota, USA

The Minnesota River rises in Big Stone Lake, Big Stone County, Minnesota, on the border with South Dakota. It is 332 miles (534 km) long and flows southeast and northeast in a 'V' like course. The river runs through the wide valley carved by the Warren River, which in ancient times drained Lake Agassiz. When the last ice sheet retreated across the North American continent ten thousand years ago, a vast fresh water lake was formed in Saskatchewan called Lake Agassiz. This huge lake was an inland sea in all but name only. The valley of this glacial period lake still remains. The modern Minnesota River emerges from Big Stone Lake at ORTONVILLE and is dammed by the Big Stone Lake Dam and the Marsh Lake Dam, the latter where the Pomme de Terre River joins the main channel. Continuing southeast past ODESSA, the river enters Lac Qui Parle. The surrounding region was once the private hunting grounds of the Sioux nation, and the continued encroachment of their territorial lands led to the great Sioux Uprising of 1862. The Minnesota continues southeast past GRANITE FALLS, FRANKLIN, ST PETER, SHAKOPEE and joins the Mississippi between the twin cities of ST PAUL and MINNEAPOLIS. The chief tributaries are the Lac Qui Parle, Redwood, Earth and Cottonwood Rivers.

Mississippi, Central USA

Known as the 'Father of Waters,' the great river was named Misisipi by the Ojibwa

The Paddleford *takes tourists along the Mississippi waterfront of Minneapolis–St Paul.*

Inset: At autumn scene in Wisconsin on the banks of the Mississippi.

Indians. The Mississippi is a massive 2348 miles (3778 km) long, drains an area of 1,243,700 square miles (3,221,200 sq km), one-eighth of North America, and is one of the great rivers of the world. With its two principal tributaries, the Missouri, 2533 miles (4076 km) long and the Ohio, 976 miles (1570 km) long, its drainage basin covers an area including 31 American States and two Canadian provinces. The Mississippi has an average discharge of 640,000 cubic feet (1830 cu m) per second; 1.5 times greater than the mighty St Lawrence, eight times that of the beautiful Rhine and a staggering 30 times that of the English Thames. The greatest contributor to the Mississippi is the Ohio River, which contributes 3.5 times that contributed by the Missouri, the next largest. The largest waterfall on the river is located 500 miles (800 km) upstream from Minneapolis-St Paul with a drop of 700 feet (214 m). The Mississippi is one of the great natural assets of the North American continent, and it has played a profound part in the early settlement and growth of the United States.

The Mississippi has its origin in Lake Itasca, 1475 feet (450 m) above sea level in the northern lake district of Minnesota; two other great river systems, the St Lawrence and the Red River of the North, also have their sources in this area. The true source of the river was not discovered until 1832, when Henry R Schoolcraft followed the river to its furthest point. The principal towns and major cities along the river are ST CLOUD, MINNEAPOLIS-ST PAUL, RED WING, WINONA, DUBUQUE, CLINTON, DAVENPORT, FORT MADISON, KEOKUK, ST LOUIS, CAIRO, MEMPHIS, VICKSBURG, NATCHEZ, BATON ROUGE and NEW ORLEANS.

The Mississippi has been important to America's growth since its discovery. Keel-boats and flatboats carried tons of furs and produce downstream. Keelboatmen rowed, poled and towed their craft back to St Louis and then up the Missouri. Flatboats from the Ohio Valley were taken apart and sold for lumber; crews braved bandits and hostile Indians as they walked home up the famous Natchez Trace to Kentucky and Tennessee. This period saw the Great River turned into a veritable tree-lined boulevard. Rivermen returned home with tales of the magnificent plantations and the Old World luxury of New Orleans. These hardened men gaped even more when the first steamboat, belching smoke proceeded up river in 1811. The steamboat launched an era of spectacular floating palaces, filled with gamblers, greenhorns from the East and beautiful women. This was the Mississippi's 'Golden Age.' Samuel Clemens, a Missouri youngster, stored up his memories of the river for the day, when as Mark Twain he would write his way into American and world literature, with such famous books as *Tom Sawyer* and *Huckleberry Finn*.

The Mississippi became even more important during the American Civil War as a major artery. If the Federals could gain control of the river, it would mean that the Confederacy would be cut in half. 'Seize the Mississippi and isolate Arkansas, Louisiana and Texas, then drive straight into the heartland of the Confederacy' – that was the North's strategy. Major campaigns and battles were fought along the Mississippi as well as along its chief

tributaries, but the most important one was the seige of Vicksburg. General Grant, aided by the naval squadrons of Admiral Farragut, took six grim weeks to rout the Southern forces. After the Civil War, the river continued to be a major source of transportation until the arrival of the railroads.

The physiography of the river can be best evaluated by dividing it into three major sections – the northern section, including the headwaters; the middle section; and the lower section. The headwaters and the northern tributaries flow through an area recently released from the continental ice sheet which effects the character of the drainage and the soil. The northern section consists of the west lakes district of the central lowlands and the superior upland section of the Laurentian Shield. The great preponderance of lakes and swamps has reduced the number and severity of floods in this northern region. The chief tributaries are the Black, Chippewa, St Croix, Minnesota and the Wisconsin Rivers.

The middle section of the Mississippi is the region that gives the river basin its continentality. Its two largest tributaries, the Ohio from the east and the Missouri from the west, embrace very large areas. The principal tributaries in this section are the Rock, Illinois, Kaskaskia, Des Moines and Cedar Rivers. This portion of the Great River is more susceptible to flooding than the northern section due to the noticeable absence of lakes, the high rainfall and high percentage of run-offs from its far-flung tributaries. The accessibility of this region is a major reason for its rapid economic development. The lower Great Lakes and the St Lawrence River, the only deep-water outlet to the Atlantic Ocean, lie to the northeast. Eastward are the essential corridors through the northern Appalachian Mountains which allow access to the middle Atlantic port cities. To the far west are the mountain passes through the Rockies. To the south it drains into the Gulf of Mexico.

The southern or lower section of the Mississippi receives tributaries which are totally different from those above the Ohio River. Swollen by the waters of the Ohio, the Mississippi meanders for a thousand miles over a vast flood plain built directly above the coastal plain. The tributaries in this section tend to parallel the main channel and include the St Francis, Tensas, Yazoo, Arkansas and Red Rivers. After World War II manufacturing industries became attracted to the Mississippi River Valley. This was largely due to the vast improvements in the river and the rising costs of freight transportation.

The river serves as the boundary between various States and as the course of the river changes, so do the boundaries which can cause political problems. Floods have also been a serious problem throughout the valley, not only to navigation but to the settlement of the fertile lowlands as well. Much effort, money and labor have gone into controlling the river. The Tennessee Valley Authority and Miami Valley Conservancy have vastly improved flood control along the tributaries, and US Army engineers have constructed reservoirs, floodways, spillways, levees and distributary channels on the lower section of the river to alleviate a large part of the strain upon the main river.

Missouri, Northwestern USA

The Missouri is the longest river in North America and one of the chief tributaries of the Mississippi River. It is 2533 miles (4076 km) long, drains an area of 529,400 square miles (1,371,100 sq km) and is ranked eighth in volume of water carried by major US rivers. The Missouri is formed by the confluence of the Gallatin, Jefferson and Madison Rivers, near THREE FORKS, on the boundary of Gallatin and Broadwater Counties in south-central Montana, at a height of 8000 feet (2440 m) above sea level. The river flows north initially

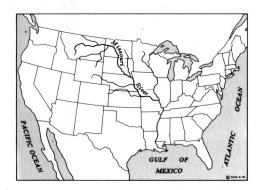

past LOMBARD, TOSTON and TOWNSEND, before entering first Ferry Lake, then Hauser Lake and Lake Helena, east of the State capital, HELENA. The river continues northward through Lewis and Clark County until it reaches CRAIG, where it begins to turn northeast across the Big Belt Mountains into Cascade County. It passes CASCADE, then is joined by the Smith River at ULM in the central portion of the county. The Missouri flows past GREAT FALLS, FORT BENTON, then is joined by the Teton and Marias Rivers near LOMA in Chouteau County. The river now begins to wind its way across the northern portion of Montana before being dammed by the Fort Peck Dam to form the Fort Peck Reservoir. On this stretch of the river it is joined by the Musselshell and Judith Rivers. After passing the Fort Peck Dam, the Missouri is joined by the Milk River, then proceeds due east into North Dakota. It runs past the Fort Union Trading Post National History Site near BUFORD where it is joined by the Yellowstone River. Shortly afterwards it enters a large manmade reservoir, Lake Sakakawea, formed by the Garrison Dam. Here the river turns south passing BISMARCK, the capital of North Dakota, before flowing into Lake Oahe, formed by the Oahe Dam and located in the State of South Dakota. The Missouri now heads southeast past PIERRE, the capital of South Dakota, through Lake Sharpe, the Lower Brulé Indian Reservation and emerges at the Big Bend Dam. From there the river enters Lake Francis Case, a large reservoir created by the construction of the Fort Randall Dam near the border of Nebraska. The Missouri forms the border between South Dakota and Nebraska below the Fort Randall Dam and SIOUX CITY, Iowa. It now winds its

Right: Vaguely reminiscent of Mark Twain's steam-powered paddle-wheelers which cruised up and down the Mississippi is this modern-day ferry which not only serves the citizens of St Louis but also ferries tourists and excursion groups along the river.

The Missouri River passes through the Gates of the Mountains near Helena, the capital city of Montana.

way south past OMAHA, NEBRASKA CITY and LEAVENWORTH, before turning east at KANSAS CITY, to flow east-southeast across the State of Missouri to join the Mississippi River just above ST LOUIS, Missouri.

The Missouri basin covers a tremendous area which varies in height from over 8000 feet (2424 m) above sea level to the Great Plains of the United States. There are four areas which stand out in sharp contrast to the famous Great Plains. First is the Sand Hills, located in the north central portion of Nebraska and consisting of low sand hills, small enclosed basins and small intermittent streams. Second, the Flint Hills of east central Kansas is an area of rolling terrain with thin limestone soil only fit for grazing livestock. Third is the Bad Lands of South Dakota, an eroded and windswept area of land in west central South Dakota. Last is the famous Black Hills of South Dakota, which is a verdant area, the majority of which is now protected as a national forest and is a prime tourist attraction.

The climate over the Missouri Basin is rather arid, with extreme temperature ranges, typical of mid-latitude continental interiors. The large cities of the basin are in the drier western region, including DENVER in Colorado, LARAMIE and CHEYENNE in Wyoming, and GREAT FALLS and HELENA in Montana. The highest wind velocity of the US interior is recorded on the Great Plains. Permanent settlement has been discouraged by such things as tornadoes, blizzards, heavy snows, extremely high temperatures and droughts which have lasted for several years at a time. The Missouri Basin remains one of the less populated regions of the American interior. It has a population of only 7,000,000, and although the population of the rest of the US has grown since 1945, the basin has declined in population.

The flow of the Missouri is varied with the lowest in the winter and the greatest between April-June. The average flow at the mouth is 64,000 cubic feet (1830 cu m) per second; the very minimum is 4200 cubic feet (120 cu m) and the maximum 900,000 cubic feet (25,700 cu m). The major problems of the river are caused by erosion and heavy silting due to the unprotected slopes and great fluctuations in flow.

The chief tributaries of the Missouri are the Yellowstone, Platte, Kansas, Musselshell, Milk, Little Missouri, James, Niobrara, Osage, Grand and Big Sioux Rivers. The principal crops grown in the basin are hay and sugar beets; the secondary ones are fruits, potatoes and other vegetables. The region is extremely rich in minerals especially in the Black Hills where gold, silver and lead have been mined since 1874.

The Missouri was discovered by Jacques Marquette and Louis Jolliet in 1673 as they paddled down the Mississippi on their great exploration trip. Later French fur traders began moving up the Missouri in the 18th century, and in 1764, St Louis was established as a trading center. But the first exploration of the Missouri was not accomplished until 1804–05, when the explorers Captains Meriwether Lewis and William Clark made their way west using the Missouri for most of their journey to the Pacific. The river was not used during the great settlement of the American West; instead the route over the South Pass in west central Wyoming was followed until the railroads were built further south. The first attempt to navigate the river by steamboat was in 1819. In 1830 the American Fur Company began using steamboats to transport furs,

Sunset on the Mississippi as a tug passes in front of St Louis' Gateway Arch.

trading goods and supplies on the Missouri. This river traffic reached its height in 1858, then began to decline swiftly with the completion of the Hannibal and St Joseph Railroad. By the end of the 19th century the river trade was a thing of the past. Although there is no equivalent central authority for the development of the Missouri as the TVA exists for the Mississippi, the potential of this river is overwhelming. Plans have been made by various State and federal governments for future development of the Missouri River.

Mistassibi, Quebec, Canada

The river rises in the northern part of Lac St Jean Ouest in Quebec. It is 200 miles (320 km) long and flows south to join the Mistassini River at DOLBEAU.

Mistassini, Quebec, Canada

The Mistassini River rises east of Lake Mistassini in central Quebec. It is 200 miles (320 km) long and flows south past DOLBEAU where it is joined by the Mistassibi River, and then continues on course to enter Lake St Jean.

Mohawk, New York, USA

The Mohawk rises in a small, hidden stream among the ferns north of the town of ROME in New York State. The Mohawk is 140 miles (224 km) long and is named after the once great Indian tribe of that same name. Reaching Rome, a town of 50,118, the Mohawk joins the famous Erie Canal, today known as the Barge Canal. The river then meanders eastward across the flat and dry bed of Lake Iroquois. The Mohawk passes YORKVILLE, UTICA, HERKIMER, MOHAWK, JOHNSVILLE, FORT JOHNSON, AMSTERDAM and SCHENECTADY before entering the Hudson. The ancient Mohawk River carved a steep valley through this portion of Upstate New York in the glacier age. Once past Schenectady the river widens out, meandering across the ancient dry bed of another of the many vanished lakes of this region and joins the Hudson at Cohoes Falls. This was once a spectacular falls but long since the waters have been diverted into the canal. The Mohawk, one of the swiftest flowing rivers in New York State, has been tamed by a series of steel locks which raise the large gas barges up the main water route through the Appalachians. The entire course of the Mohawk is followed by major roads and railway lines, and the whole valley is alive with various industries.

Mojave, California, USA

The river rises near the dry Soda Lake. This lake at one time was a large body of water stranded during a previous geological age with no outlet. The Mojave (Mohave) is roughly 100 miles (160 km) in length and flows west-southwest through the desolate landscape of the Mojave Desert, past YERMO, DAGGETT and BARSTOW. The river runs for a large part of its course underground, and settlers crossing the desert often died within yards of it without even knowing that it existed. The river flows past Cajon Summit, which is a major outdoor recreation area and accessible via major trunk roads from SAN BERNARDINO. The river ends somewhere in the dry southern region of the Mojave Desert.

Monongahela, West Virginia-Pennsylvania, USA

The Monongahela River is formed by the confluence of the Tygart and West Fork Rivers in Marion County, West Virginia. It is 128 miles (206 km) long and flows north-northeast past MORGANTOWN, then north into Pennsylvania passing BROWNSVILLE and CHARLEROI to join the Allegheny River at Pittsburgh where it forms the Ohio River. The river is a very important freight route.

Montmorency, Quebec, Canada

The Montmorency River rises in Laurentides Park in southern Quebec. It is 60 miles (97 km) long and flows south to join the St Lawrence River. The famous 275 feet (84 m) high Montmorency Falls is located just above the river's mouth and is quite a spectacular sight.

Montreal, Ontario, Canada

The Montreal River rises in central Ontario. It is 90 miles (145 km) long and flows south and southwest to enter Lake Superior, the largest of the Great Lakes. A major hydroelectric power station is located at Montreal Falls which is situated ten miles (16 km) above the mouth.

Moose, New York, USA

The Moose River rises in northern Herkimer County, New York. The Moose flows southwest and west for a short distance before joining the Black River at LYONS FALLS, Lewis County, New York.

Moreau, South Dakota, USA

The Moreau River rises in Perkins County, South Dakota at the junction of the North and South Forks. It is 289 miles (465 km) long and flows east to join the Missouri River just south of MOBRIDGE.

Motagua, Guatemala

The Motagua River rises south of QUICHE and is the longest river in Guatemala. It is 250 miles (400 km) long and flows east and east-northeast to enter the Gulf of Honduras approximately 25 miles (40 km) east of PUERTO BARRIOS. The river is navigable for 125 miles (200 km). Its chief tributary is the Chiquimula River.

Muddy Boggy Creek, Oklahoma, USA

This small American river rises east of ADA, Oklahoma. It is 110 miles (180 km) long and flows southeast to join the Clear Boggy Creek, approximately 18 miles (29 km) west of HUGO.

Muskegon, Michigan, USA

The Muskegon rises in Houghton Lake, Michigan. It is 227 miles (365 km) long and flows southwest past BIG RAPIDS and NEWAYGO to form Muskegon Lake, which covers an area five miles (eight km) long and two miles (three km) wide. The river finally enters Lake Michigan at the town of MUSKEGON.

Muskingum, Ohio, USA

The Muskingum rises in central and southeastern Ohio at the confluence of the Walhonding and Tuscarawas Rivers in the town of COSHOCTON. It is 112 miles (180 km) long and flows south past DRESDEN, the head of navigation, before joining the Ohio River at MARIETTA. The river is dammed as a safety measure for flood and navigation control.

Muskwa, British Columbia, Canada

The Muskwa River rises in the Stikine Mountains of northeastern British Columbia. It is 160 miles (260 km) long and flows northeast to Sikanni Chief River at FORT NELSON to form the Fort Nelson River.

Musselshell, Montana, USA

The Musselshell River rises in the Crazy Mountains of central Montana. It is 292 miles (470 km) long and flows east and north to the Fort Peck Reservoir of the Missouri River.

Nahualate, Guatemala

The Nahualate River rises in the mountains near NAHUALA in southwestern Guatemala. It is 100 miles (160 km) long and flows south past SANTA CATARINA to enter the Pacific Ocean southeast of TAHUESCO. The river runs through important coffee and sugar growing regions.

Namekagon, Wisconsin, USA

The river rises in Namekagon Lake in Wisconsin's beautiful lake district. It flows west, southwest and northwest past the towns of SEELEYS and HAYWARD before joining the St Croix River in Burnett County.

Nantahala, North Carolina, USA

The Nantahala River rises in the Nantahala Mountains southwest of ASHEVILLE, North Carolina. It is 40 miles (64 km) long and flows north-northwest and north through the beautiful Nantahala National Forest to enter the Fontana Reservoir on the Little Tennessee River. One of its most scenic stretches is on the lower course where the river passes through the Nantahala Gorge, which is eight miles (13 km) long and 2000 feet (610 m) deep.

Nanticoke, Delaware-Maryland, USA

The Nanticoke is formed by the confluence of the St Johns and the Gravelly Branches in Sussex County. It flows southwest, crosses into Maryland and enters a large estuary called Nanticoke Sound, an arm of Chesapeake Bay.

Nass, British Columbia, Canada

The Nass rises in the Coast Mountains of British Columbia. It is 200 miles (320 km) long and flows south and southwest to the Portland Inlet of the Pacific Ocean.

Natashquan, Newfoundland-Quebec, Canada

The Natashquan River rises in the southern portion of Labrador. It is 200 miles (320 km) long and flows south through Quebec to enter the Gulf of the St Lawrence.

Naugatuck, Connecticut, USA

This is a small river rising in Litchfield County, west-central Connecticut. It flows south past WATERVILLE, WATERBURY, BEACON FALLS and SEYMOUR to become a tributary of the Housatonic River at DERBY.

Nazas, Mexico

This river is formed by the confluence of the Rio del Oro and Ramos Rivers near EL PALMITO in northern Mexico. It is 180 miles (290 km) long and flows due east past the towns of RODEO and TORREON to enter the Laguna de Mayran. The river is important for navigation and irrigation projects.

Necaxa, Mexico

The Necaxa rises in northwestern Zacatlan, Mexico. It is 125 miles (201 km) long and flows northeast past HUAUCHINANGO to join the Tecuantepec becoming the Tecoluta which empties into the Gulf of Mexico.

Neches, Texas, USA

The Neches rises in the Sandy Hills of eastern Texas at a height of 500 feet (153 m). It is 416 miles (669 km) long and flows southeast to form the eastern boundary of the Davy Crockett National Forest and the southern boundary of the Angelina National Forest. Just east of ROCKLAND, the Neches swings south to enter Sabine Lake, its outlet. The chief tributary is the Angelina River. The main industry of the upper Neches is lumbering, while the lower reaches near BEAUMONT are noted for the vast pools of petroleum located there. The meandering course of the Neches provides Beaumont with its port facilities, and the Sabine-Neches Channel links Beaumont with Sabine Lake, which gives it access to Port Arthur and the Gulf of Mexico.

Nelson, Manitoba, Canada

The Nelson is the principal outlet for the Saskatchewan River system from Lake Winnipeg. It is 410 miles (660 km) long and runs generally northeast. In its upper course the river is connected by a series of irregular lakes, the most notable being Cross Lake and Sipiwesk Lake. These two lakes are connected by falls and rapids. Upon reaching Split Lake, the river is joined by the Burntwood and Grass Rivers before continuing through the flat forested lowlands of northeastern Manitoba to enter Hudson Bay. In 1682 the Hudson Bay Company realized the necessity of this short route to Lake Winnipeg and established a trading post at the mouth of the river called FORT NELSON. A large nickel ore deposit was discovered in the region in 1956 and resulted in a complete new town being built at THOMPSON. The Nelson provides a considerable amount of the much needed power for the area.

Neosho, Kansas-Oklahoma, USA

The Neosho River rises in Morris County, eastern Kansas. The Neosho is 460 miles (740 km) long and runs southeast through Council Grove Reservoir, past COUNCIL GROVE, DUNLAP, EMPORIA, NEOSHO RAPIDS, through the John Redmond Reservoir, then past NEOSHO FALLS, IOLA and OSWEGO before crossing into Oklahoma, where it is known as the Grand River. It continues south past MIAMI to join the Arkansas River near MUSKOGEE.

Neuse, North Carolina, USA

The Neuse is formed by the confluence of the Flat and the Eno Rivers in the lowland basin of the Piedmont region of North Carolina. Including its estuary, the Neuse is 275 miles (442 km) long and flows southeast to enter Pamlico Sound near the town of NEW BERN. Near the junction with the Little River is GOLDSBORO, with a population of 26,810 and the center of a large agricultural and light industry area. KINGSTON is the head of the river's navigation, and one can still see the remains of a sunken Confederate gunboat at low tide. Just below Kingston the river is joined by Contentnea Creek, where in 1713 the Colonials defeated the Tuscarora Indians in a major battle. The result for the Indians was the loss of their lands and hunting grounds. The Neuse enters Pamlico Sound of the Atlantic Ocean through a large estuary five miles (eight km) wide and 40 miles (64 km) long. Croatan National Forest is located on the south side of the estuary and comprises an area of 300,000 acres of swamps, cypress and red gum forests.

New, North Carolina, USA

The New River rises as the South Fork in Watauga County, North Carolina and is 320 miles (510 km) long. It flows north-northeast into southwestern Virginia, then north-northwest through the Allegheny Mountains into West Virginia to join the Gauley River at Gauley Bridge where it forms the Kanawha River.

Niagara, New York-Ontario, USA-Canada

The Niagara River was formed as the major outlet for Niagara Falls on the border between Ontario and New York. The word Niagara has its root in the North American Indian languages and means 'thundering of waters.' The falls are three-quarters of a mile (one km) wide and are divided by Goat Island in the middle. American Falls is 167 feet (51 m) high and 1060 feet (323 m) wide while Horseshoe or Canadian Falls to the west is 162 feet (49 m) high and 3000 feet (915 m) wide. The great cataracts were formed in the Quaternary Period during the last Ice Age, when the Dundas Valley became clogged with glacial debris and huge sections of ice. The Niagara River evolved to drain the overflow from the glacial waters occupying the region around Lake Erie, and cuts its way for 35 miles (56 km) to Lake Ontario. The river is extremely deep and flows through a canyon which is between 250–350 feet (76–107 m) deep for four miles (six km) before emerging at QUEENSTON. The fantastic gorge between NIAGARA FALLS, Ontario and NIAGARA FALLS, New York is spanned by the world famous Rainbow International Bridge. The region of the Niagara peninsula is noted for its peaches, plums, cherries and grapes. The Canadian side of the river is one continuous national park, with lookouts posted along the entire length of Niagara's course.

Ninnescah, Kansas, USA

This small river is formed by the junction of

Below and overleaf: Views of the spectacular Horseshoe and American Falls at Niagara.

the North Fork River, 87 miles (140 km) long and the South Fork River, 92 miles (148 km) long, six miles (ten km) southeast of CHENEY in southern Kansas. It is 49 miles (79 km) long and flows southeast to join the Arkansas River.

Niobrara, Wyoming-Nebraska, USA

The Niobrara rises is south-central Niobrara County, east-central Wyoming. It is 431 miles (693 km) long and drains an area of 13,000 square miles (33,700 sq km). It flows east-southeast, then basically east past LUSK, NODE and VAN TASSELL into Nebraska. The river continues east past AGATE, through Box Butte Reservoir, then swings northeast and east to join the Missouri River just west of NIOBRARA.

Noatak, Alaska, USA

The Noatak River rises in the Brooks Range of northwestern Alaska. It is roughly 400 miles (640 km) long and flows west to enter Kotzebue Sound, Chukchi Bay.

North Canadian, New Mexico-Oklahoma, USA

Rising in northeastern New Mexico, this river flows initially eastward into Cimarron County, Oklahoma. The North Canadian is 760 miles (1220 km) long and flows along an east-southeast line through Oklahoma to join the Canadian River at Eufaula Reservoir in the east-central portion of the state, not far from the Arkansas River. The chief tributaries of the North Canadian are the Wolf Creek, Goff Creek, Pony Creek, Coldwater Creek, Palo Duro Creek and Kiowa Creek.

North Loup, Nebraska, USA

This small river rises in central Cherry County, northern Nebraska. It flows east-southeast through Cherry County, past the town of BROWNLEE, into Blaine County and past PURDUM and BREWSTER before entering Loup County. The river continues past ALMERIA and TAYLOR, then receives the Calamus River at BURWELL. It proceeds past ORD, NORTH LOUP and ELBA to join the Loup River in Howard County. The river is 212 miles (340 km) long.

North Platte, Colorado-Wyoming-Nebraska, USA

The North Platte rises in Jackson County, northern Colorado, at the confluence of the Illinois River and Grizzly Creek. The river is 618 miles (994 km) long and flows north across the border into Wyoming. It winds northward through the Medicine Bow Range. The river flows through the Seminoe Reservoir, Seminoe Dam, Pathfinder Reservoir, turns slightly northeast and continues through the Alcova Reservoir and the town of CASPER before curving southward. The chief tributaries of the North Platte are the Encampment River, the Medicine Bow River, Poison Spider Creek, the Laramie River and Horse Creek. The river passes old FORT LARAMIE, which was the principal staging area and stopover for the pioneer journeying west. The remains of Fort Laramie have been made into a National

Historic Site. The river crosses into Nebraska and continues generally east-southeast passing NORTH PLATTE before meeting the South Platte River to form the Platte.

North Skunk, Iowa, USA

The North Skunk River rises on the boundary between Storey and Marshall Counties in central Iowa. It flows east-southeast to join the South Skunk to form the Skunk River.

North Saskatchewan, Alberta-Saskatchewan, Canada

This river rises in southwestern Alberta and flows east through Saskatchewan. It is 760 miles (1220 km) long and joins the South Saskatchewan River to form the Saskatchewan River.

Nottaway, Quebec, Canada

The Nottaway River issues forth from Mattagami Lake in western Quebec. It is 205 miles (330 km) long and flows northwest to enter James Bay of Hudson Bay. The chief headstream of the Nottaway is the Waswanipi River, which is 195 miles (314 km) long, and runs south and west-northwest into Mattagami Lake.

Nowitna, Alaska, USA

The Nowitna rises north of the North Fork of the Kuskokwim River in southwestern Alaska, near the von Frank Mountain, which is 1374 ft (419 m). It is 250 miles (400 km) long and runs north to the Yukon River.

Nueces, Texas, USA

The boundary dispute between Mexico and the United States over which river was to be the border separating Texas and Mexico resulted in the Mexican war. The Mexicans stated that the boundary was the Nueces River and not the Rio Grande, but the Texans claimed the opposite. The United States was the victor and established the border permanently as the Rio Grande, and gained substantial territory. The Nueces rises to an altitude of 2400 feet (732 m) in the Edwards Plateau of southwest Texas. The river flows through an area which is semi-arid, supporting very little aside from sagebrush. The Nueces is 315 miles (507 km) long and flows southeast for its entire journey across the coastal plain – cattle-ranching country. The river derives its name from the numerous pecan trees lining the river's banks on this inland section of its course. The main tributaries of the Nueces are the Frio and the Atascosa Rivers. At SANDIA the river is dammed to form Lake Corpus Christi, which provides fresh water to the nearby cities and for fishing. The Nueces enters Corpus Christi Bay of the Gulf of Mexico.

Nulhegan, New Hampshire, USA

The Nulhegan rises in Essex County, northeastern New Hampshire. It flows east to join the Connecticut River near the town of BLOOMFIELD.

Nushagak, Alaska, USA

This river rises in the Alaska Range of southwestern Alaska as the Mulchatna River. It is 280 miles (450 km) long and flows southwest to enter Nushagak Bay, Bristol Bay, east of DILLINGHAM.

Ochlockonee, Georgia-Florida, USA

The river rises southwest of SYLVESTER in southwestern Georgia. It is 150 miles (240 km) long and flows southward into northwestern Florida to enter Apalachee Bay on the Gulf of Mexico.

Ocmulgee, Georgia, USA

The river rises in central Georgia, southeast of ATLANTA at the junction of the South, Yellow and Alcovy Rivers in the Lloyd Shoals Reservoir. It runs for 225 miles (362 km) south-southeast to ABBEVILLE, then turns east to join the Oconee River to form the Altamaha River which continues for 137 miles (220 km) southeast past DARIEN to enter Altamaha Sound on the Atlantic Ocean.

Oconee, Georgia, USA

The Oconee rises near LULA in northeastern Georgia. It is 282 miles (454 km) long and runs south-southeast past the towns of ATHENS, MILLEDGEVILLE and DUBLIN to join the Ocmulgee River to form the Altamaha River near Hazlehurst.

Ogeechee, Georgia, USA

The Ogeechee River rises east of GREENSBORO in eastern Georgia. It is 250 miles (400 km) long and flows southeast past MAYFIELD, LOUISVILLE, MIDVILLE, HERNDON, MILLEN and ROCKY FORD, before entering Ossabaw Sound on the Atlantic Ocean.

Ogoki, Ontario, Canada

The Ogoki rises in the lake region of northwestern Ontario. It is 300 miles (480 km) long and flows northeast to the Albany River. The river is dammed at the Waboose Rapids to form an immense reservoir.

Ohio, Pennsylvania-Ohio-Indiana-Illinois, USA

The Ohio is formed by the confluence of the Allegheny and the Monongahela Rivers at PITTSBURGH, a city of 2,400,000. (The city was known as Fort Pitt during the colonial period, but after independence and the subsequent expansion of the United States, Pittsburgh grew into one of the leading producers of steel in the country.) The Ohio is 976 miles (1570 km) long and drains an area of 203,900

square miles (543,700 sq km). The principal tributaries of the Ohio are the Beaver, Big Sandy, Cumberland, Guyandot, Hocking, Green, Licking, Kentucky, Miami, Muskingum, Kanawha, Salt, Tennessee, Scioto and the Wabash Rivers. The Ohio flows through the middle of one of the United States's most populated regions which is the center of American industrial power. Unfortunately, the Ohio River is subject to regular flooding which often causes severe damage in this densely populated area. During the Great Ohio River Flood of 1937 the river rose 80 feet (24 m) above its banks. This was the worst flood in the Ohio Valley in recorded history. Rain fell unabated for two days and nights. Tributaries overflowed into the main river, swelling it even more. The land and fields which normally absorbed the rainfall were now concrete and unabsorbent. On 18 January 1937, the river passed its normal level, and continued to rise six inches (15 cm) every hour. By the end of the week, houses became completely submerged. On the 1–3 February the rains still continued to fall throughout the Ohio Valley. The Coast Guard now had boats patrolling the cities, as this was the only way for life-support and rescue teams to get to the trapped people. The National Guard was dispatched into the disaster area to help rescue cut-off families many of whom had spent days on top of their submerged houses. The town of JEFFERSONVILLE was completely underwater; 36,000 were homeless in EVANSVILLE, Indiana; and 100,000 were homeless in LOUISVILLE, Kentucky. On the 28th January, the crest was at its maximum. The 'lake' was seven miles (11 km) wide at CINCINNATI, Ohio. It took weeks for the water level to go down any appreciable amount.

Apart from the city of Pittsburgh, the other important commercial and industrial centers along the Ohio are MARIETTA, GALLIPOLIS, IRONTON, PORTSMOUTH, MADISON, JEFFERSONVILLE, LOUISVILLE, EVANSVILLE and WHEELING. The largest city on the river is CINCINNATI which is built on terraces above the river and has a population of 1,384,000. The Federal Government has built a series of dams, levees and reservoirs to control the Ohio and a tremendous amount of work has been done to improve the river's navigation.

Robert de la Salle discovered the Ohio in 1669, and its ownership was contested by both the English and the French colonialists. The Ohio flows northwest initially, then swings southwest for the remainder of its journey to meet the Mississippi at CAIRO, Illinois. The Ohio is one of America's great rivers and is a river of great beauty.

Oldman, Alberta, Canada

The Oldman rises in the Rocky Mountains near COLEMAN, Alberta. It is 250 miles (400 km) long including its longest headstream, and flows east past FORT MACLEOD and LETHBRIDGE to join the Bow River in forming the South Saskatchewan River approximately 45 miles (72 km) west of the town of MEDICINE HAT.

Olentangy, Ohio, USA

The river rises in southern Crawford County, Ohio. It flows west for a very short distance, then turns south past NEW WINCHESTER, CALEDONIA, WALDO, through the Delaware Reservoir, and DELAWARE, to finally join the Scioto River at COLUMBUS.

Oostanaula, Georgia, USA

The river rises in Gordon County in northwestern Georgia. It flows southwest past the towns of OOSTANAULA, MOUNT BERRY and RIVERSIDE, to join the Etowah River at ROME to form the Coosa River.

Osage, Kansas-Missouri, USA

The Osage is formed by the confluence of the Marais des Cygnes (which means 'swan marshes') and the Little Osage Rivers, in the low hill country of eastern Kansas. It is approximately 500 miles (800 km) long and flows east past the towns of OTTAWA and OSAWATOMIE, before crossing into the State of Missouri near PLEASANTON, Kansas. The river was named for the Osage Indian tribe which lived at its mouth in the late 17th century. The valley of the Osage is fertile and supports mixed agriculture: grain crops, of which corn is foremost, and livestock. Located downstream is the Bagnall Dam, which has created the Lake of the Ozarks [130 miles (210 km) long, 1300 miles (2080 km) in circumference]. The dam forms the head of navigation for the river and supplies the hydroelectric power for the surrounding region. The Osage swings northeast across Miller County, then continues on course forming the boundary between Cole and Osage Counties before joining the Missouri River as a tributary.

Otoskin, Ontario, Canada

See Attawapiskat, Ontario, Canada.

Ottauquechee, New Hampshire, USA

The river rises in Rutland County in central New Hampshire. It flows east past KILLINGTON, BRIDGEWATER and WOODSTOCK before joining the Connecticut River.

Ottawa, Ontario-Quebec, Canada

The Ottawa is a beautiful river of the Canadian northeast. It is 696 miles (1120 km) long and drains an area of 57,000 square miles (147,600 sq km). The river rises in the Hudson Bay and St Lawrence drainage area, and flows on an irregular course to join the St Lawrence at MONTREAL. The name of the river initially was the Grand River of the Algonquins, but its present name was derived from the French version or corruption of *Outaouak*, the name of an Algonquin tribe living in this region. The Ottawa provided an important early route to the interior of Canada. Etienne Brulé discovered the river in 1610, and the explorer, Samuel de Champlain, utilized it to reach Georgian Bay in 1613. Champlain opened what became the historic fur-trade route of the northeast. As the trade in animal pelts decreased, lumbering quickly took its place. The upper course of the Ottawa is made up of several lakes – Grand Lake Victoria, Lac Decelles and Lac Simard – all connected by rapids and short stretches of river. The Ottawa runs into the northern portion of Lake Timiskaming and emerges as a tremendously powerful river. At Deep River, the river is forced through a narrow gorge, 700 feet (214 m) in depth, and runs through five separate sets of rapids before arriving at the city of OTTAWA. The Ottawa Valley widens once past the city and flows through beautiful, extremely fertile farmland. Again there are rapids at LONG SAULT, and the river widens into numerous lake-like expanses before finally splitting into three distributaries to enter the St Lawrence. The chief tributaries are the Dumoine, Black, Coulange, Madawaska, Gatineau, Lièvre and Rouge Rivers.

Otter Tail, Minnesota, USA

This river rises in Clearwater County in western Minnesota. It is 150 miles (240 km) long and flows south through Pine, Rush and Otter Tail Lakes to BRECKENRIDGE where it joins the Bois de Sioux River to form the Red River of the North.

Ouachita, Arkansas-Louisiana, USA

The Ouachita rises in the heavily forested heights of the Ouachita Mountains in Arkansas. It is 605 miles (973 km) long and flows on a southeasterly course across Arkansas, passing the towns of CADDO GAP and GLENWOOD, the De Grey Reservoir, and then CAMDEN, EAST CAMDEN and SNOW HILL before crossing over into Louisiana. Camden is the head of the river's navigation. The surrounding region is thickly forested and provides the raw materials for booming furniture and pulp and paper industries. As the river flows through Louisiana, it separates the cottonlands from the cattle country to the west. The Ouachita joins the Red River a short distance south of the town of ACME in Concordia County. The river is known as the Black River after receiving the Tensa River.

Outardes (Rivière aux), Quebec, Canada

The Rivière aux Outardes rises in the Otish Mountains of central Quebec. It is 300 miles (480 km) long and flows south through Pletipi Lake. It joins the St Lawrence River 18 miles (29 km) southwest of BAIE COMEAU.

Owyhee, Nevada-Idaho-Oregon, USA

The river rises in Elko County, Nevada and flows through the Wild Horse Reservoir, past RIO TINTO and MOUNTAIN CITY into the Duck Valley Indian Reservation and across into Idaho. The river crosses through the southwestern corner of Owyhee County, and is joined by Battle Creek, Deep Creek, Little Fork and South Fork before crossing into Oregon. It flows northwest and north, through Malheur County between the border and the town of ROME, it is joined by the Little Owyhee River, Antelope Creek and the North Fork. The Owyhee runs through the center of Malheur County heading north to Lake Owyhee, then north-northeast to meet the Snake River south of NYSSA. The river is 300 miles (480 km) long.

Above: The paddlewheeler Mike Fink *docked on the Ohio river at Cincinnati.*
Right: The Canadian parliament buildings overlook the Ottawa River.

Pahsimeroi, Idaho, USA
The river rises in northeastern Custer County in the Lost River Range of Idaho. It flows northwest past MAY, then forms the boundary between Lemhi and Custer Counties before joining the Salmon River at ELLIS.

Palouse, Idaho, USA
The Palouse River rises in Latah County, northern Idaho. The Palouse is 140 miles (224 km) long and runs on a westerly course past the town of COLFAX to join the Snake River northwest of DAYTON. Near the mouth of the river is located PALOUSE FALLS, which is 198 feet (60 m) high.

Pamlico, North Carolina, USA
See Tar, North Carolina, USA

Panuco, Mexico
Formed by the confluence of the Moctezuma and Tamuin Rivers in northern Vera Cruz,

Mexico, the Panuco is 100 miles (160 km) long and flows east-northeast past PANUCO and TAMPICO to enter the Gulf of Mexico. At Tampico the river is 100 yards/meters deep and 400 yards (360 m) wide and can support large ocean-going vessels.

Papaloapam, Mexico

One of the primary rivers of Mexico, the Papaloapam is formed by several headstreams near TUXTEPEC in Vera Cruz State. It assumes a winding course, running northeast past TLACOJALPAN, COSAMALOAPAN and TLACOTALPAN to enter the Alvarado Lagoon. Including its longest headstream, the Tuxtepec River, the Papaloapam is 200 miles (320 km) long and is navigable for 150 miles (240 km).

Pascagoula, Mississippi, USA

The river rises in southeastern Mississippi at the junction of the Leaf and the Chickasawhay Rivers. It is 90 miles (144 km) long and flows south to the port of PASCAGOULA on the Mississippi Sound.

Passaic, New Jersey, USA

The Passaic rises southwest of MORRISTOWN in northeastern New Jersey. It is 80 miles (128 km) long and flows past MILLINGTON, then swings north and northeast to PATERSON, then south and east past the towns of PASSAIC and NEWARK to enter Newark Bay of the Atlantic Ocean.

Patoka, Indiana, USA

This small river rises in Orange County, Indiana. It is 138 miles (221 km) long and flows west past JASPER, WINSLOW and PATOKA before becoming a tributary of the Wabash River opposite Mt Carmel.

Patuca, Honduras

The Patuca is formed by the confluence of the Guayape and the Guayambre Rivers, 23 miles (37 km) southeast of JUTICALPA in eastern Honduras. The river is 200 miles (320 km) long and flows northeast to enter the Caribbean Sea at Patuca Point.

Payette, Idaho, USA

The river is formed by the confluence of the North Fork, 110 miles (176 km) long and the South Fork, 70 miles (112 km) long in Boise County of western Idaho. It is 70 miles (112 km) long and flows west to the Snake River.

Pea, Alabama, USA

The Pea River rises in Bullock County in southeastern Alabama. It is 140 miles (224 km) long and flows southwest forming the boundary between Pike and Barbour Counties. The river then cuts through the corner of northwestern Dale County to run diagonally across Coffee County, past the town of ELBA and then turns due south into Geneva County. From here it swings gradually eastward to join the Choctawhatchee River at the town of GENEVA.

Peace, British Columbia-Alberta, Canada

The Peace rises in the Stikine Mountains of northern British Columbia as the Finlay River. The Finlay flows southeast to Finlay Forks where it joins the Parsnip River to form the Peace. It is 1054 miles (1686 km) long and flows eastward through the Rocky Mountains of Canada into Alberta. The river flows past the town of PEACE RIVER, then turns north to FORT VERMILION, with a final course change east-northeast to the Slave River, just north of Lake Athabaska. The river valley is extensively wooded and lumbering is a primary industry. The soil is extremely fertile and crops have short growing seasons. The Peace River received its name from Peace Point, where the Cree and Beaver Indian tribes settled their border disputes. The arrival of the first whitemen in 1786 saw the river opened up as a major trading route. The river has great potential and is virtually untapped as a source of hydroelectric power.

Pearl, Mississippi-Louisiana, USA

The Pearl rises in the Red Hills of central

Below: A tributary of the Peace River runs beside a forestry road north of Grand Cache, Alberta.

Mississippi. It is 485 miles (780 km) long and winds generally south and southeast past JACKSON (the state capital), BYRAM, ROCKPORT, MONTICELLO, MORGANTOWN and COLUMBIA before crossing into Louisiana. The Pearl forms the border between the two states for the remainder of its course. In the early trading days, Jackson was the head of the river's navigation, but today the river is navigable as far as BOGALUSA, Louisiana. Near PICAYUNE, about 30 miles (48 km) from its mouth, the river divides into two parallel channels separated by Honey Island Swamp. This area of the river is noted for its excellent hunting and fishing. The main channel of the river is the East Pearl River which empties into Lake Borgne, an inlet of the Gulf of Mexico. The other channel, the West Pearl River, enters the Rigolets, another channel which drains into Lake Pontchartrain. The river was named for the bountiful pearl oysters to be found along its banks by the local Indian tribes.

Pecos, New Mexico-Texas, USA

The Pecos is one of the most famous of the old rivers of the American West. Judge Roy Bean, a famous western personality, once stated that he was 'the only law west of the Pecos,' which at the time was most probably true. It rises in the Sangre de Cristo Mountains of north-central New Mexico and flows for a total of 926 miles (1490 km). It runs southeast through San Miguel and Guadalupe Counties, and is joined in this early initial stage by various intermittent streams, the most notable being the Gallinas River, Tescolate Creek, and Pintada Creek. It passes through SANTA ROSA, a town of 2485, then heads due south. The river is flanked by the Llano Estacado on one side and the mountains on the other as it continues through a large depression which is underlined by porous rock formations. The Pecos is 1000 feet (305 m) below the surrounding surface land, and occasionally disappears from sight for long stretches only to reappear from numerous underground channels. This behavior is somewhat commonplace in rivers which flow through hot and semi-arid terrain. The Pecos is joined by numerous intermittent rivers and streams on its course adding to its already heavy load of silt and mineral deposits. In Chaves County the Rio Felix River, Macho Creek and the Rio Hondo River join the main channel. The river crosses into Eddy County near the town of LAKE ARTHUR where it picks up the Rio Penasco and Seven River as it flows through Lake McMillan. It turns slightly southeast as it runs through the Avalon Reservoir and heads towards CARLSBAD, which has a population of 21,297. Nearby and close to the border with Texas is the famous CARLSBAD CAVERNS NATIONAL PARK. The Pecos now begins to wind and curve as it crosses into Texas at Red Bluff Lake to emerge at the dam of that same name. The river now flows southeast through the Stockton Plateau at the head of the Amistad Reservoir to join the Rio Grande. This last leg of the Pecos is through a scenic steep-sided, winding canyon, which is one of Texas' most scenic areas. The principal activities in the lower Pecos Valley are mining, tourism and cattle ranching. The Pecos drains an area comprising 38,300 square miles (99,200 sq km).

Peel, Yukon-Northwest Territories, Canada

The river rises in the Yukon in Canada. It is 365 miles (587 km) long and flows east and north to join the Mackenzie River approximately 40 miles (64 km) south-southeast of AKLAVIK in the Northwest Territories. The lower course of the Peel serves as the boundary for a huge game sanctuary.

Pelly, Yukon, Canada

The Pelly rises in the Mackenzie Mountains of the central Yukon in Canada. It is 330 miles (530 km) long and flows west-northwest passing the town of ROSS RIVER before joining the Yukon River at FORK SELKIRK.

Pembina, Alberta, Canada

The Pembina rises to the east of beautiful Jasper National Park in the Rocky Mountains of Alberta. It is 350 miles (560 km) long and flows northeast to join the Athabaska River, approximately 40 miles (64 km) west of ATHABASKA.

Pembina, Manitoba-North Dakota, Canada-USA

The river rises in the Turtle Mountains and then drifts across the prairies of southern Manitoba. It is roughly 275 miles (442 km) long and flows northeast, southeast across the border into North Dakota and finally east to join the Red River of the North at the town of PEMBINA.

Pemigewasset, New Hampshire, USA

The source of the Pemigewasset is Lake Profile in the White Mountains of New Hampshire. It is 70 miles (113 km) long and, with the Winnipesaukee River, forms the Merrimack River near FRANKLIN, New Hampshire. The region surrounding the Pemigewasset Valley is a well-known tourist area.

Pende Oreille, Montana, USA

See Clark Fork, Montana-Idaho, USA.

Penobscot, Maine, USA

The Penobscot River is the largest river in the State of Maine. It has a length of 350 miles (560 km) and flows south to enter Penobscot Bay of the Atlantic Ocean. The region of the Penobscot was first explored by Samuel de Champlain in 1604. But the Pilgrims were the first to establish a permanent settlement on Penobscot Bay in the 1620s. The river is named after the Penobscot Indian tribe who inhabited this part of Maine prior to European colonization. The entire upper region of the Penobscot River was the scene of intense and bitter fighting between the French and British from 1673 to 1759; and later between the Americans and British until in 1815 a treaty was ratified which settled the Maine question once and for all. BANGOR, located in Penobscot County, was the world's leading timber exporting port for years. Most of Maine's white pine was dispatched to the British fleet to be utilized as masts. In its early days, the

Penobscot was also noted for its excellent salmon fishing but this has since been eliminated by the intense lumber and pulp industries which have grown up along the banks of this once beautiful and scenic river. Along the West Branch of the Penobscot can be found large glacial lakes such as Seboomook, Chesuncook and Pemadumcook, while its East Branch is more regular and easy flowing. The river's chief tributary is the Mattawamkeag River which joins it at the town of MATTAWAMKEAG in northeastern Penobscot County. The river is tidal as far as Bangor, 23 miles (37 km) from the Atlantic.

Peribonca, Quebec, Canada

The Peribonca begins in the Otish Mountains of central Quebec, Canada. It flows south through Peribonca Lake to the St John Lake after a 300-mile (480-km) journey.

Pine Creek, Pennsylvania, USA

This small river rises in Potter County, northern Pennsylvania. The stream is 75 miles (121 km) long and flows south-southeast through the Grand Canyon of Pennsylvania, which is 1000 feet (305 m) deep, to join the west branch of the Susquehanna River.

Pipestem, North Dakota, USA

The Pipestem is a small river which rises in south-central Wells County, North Dakota. It flows east and southeast past SYKESTON, through the southwestern corner of Foster County into Stutsman County and joins the James River at JAMESTOWN.

Pit, California, USA

This small river rises in Goose Lake, northeastern California. It is 200 miles (320 km) long and flows southwest to enter Lake Shasta, which was formed by the damming of the upper Sacramento River.

Platte, Nebraska, USA

The Platte is formed by the 'Y'-like confluence of the North and South Platte Rivers in Nebraska. It flows in a curve southeast through south central Nebraska before turning northeast and then southeast into the Missouri River at PLATTSMOUTH. The Platte is 310 miles (500 km) long and has a drainage area of 90,000 square miles (233,000 sq km). The chief tributaries are the Elkhorn and the Loup Rivers. The river occupies a wide channel studded with islands, in a flat valley lying below the level of the surrounding country. The valley of the Platte River has been utilized as a major route to the West for decades. Trappers, mountain men, Oregon settlers and the Mormons used it to settle the interior of the country; it was also used by the Union Pacific Railroad in the 1870s during the railroad expansionist movement – nowadays US Highway 30 runs through the Platte Valley. It was named Platte by the French Mallet brothers in 1739, perhaps because the valley was so flat. This region is one of great historical significance to Americans as it was the backcloth for the move West.

Polochic, Guatemala

This small river of central Guatemala rises east of TACTIC. It is 150 miles (240 km) long and flows east past the towns of TUCURU and PANZOS through a small delta into Lake Izabel. The chief tributary is the Cahabon River.

Popo Agie, Wyoming, USA

The Popo Agie rises in the Wind River Range in west-central Wyoming. It is 60 miles (97 km) long and flows northeast along the border of the Wind River Indian Reservation to join the Wind River at the town of RIVERTON to form the Bighorn River.

Porcupine, Yukon-Alaska, Canada-USA

The Porcupine rises on the western slopes of the Mackenzie Mountains in the northern Yukon. It is 525 miles (845 km) long and runs for the majority of its course north, then swings west-southwest into Alaska to join the Yukon River at FORT YUKON.

Potomac, East-central USA

The Potomac rises on Meadow Mountain in the Appalachian Mountains of West Virginia. It is 287 miles (462 km) long of which 117 miles (188 km) are tidal, and drains an area of 14,500 square miles (37,600 sq km). It has two headstreams, the North and South Branches, which join 15 miles (24 km) below CUMBERLAND, Maryland. Its chief tributary is the

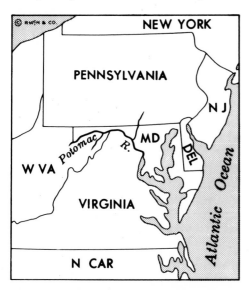

Shenandoah River which joins the Potomac at HARPERS FERRY. Here John Brown made his famous raid on the Federal Arsenal, and was subsequently captured and hanged in December 1859. Abolitionists made Brown into a martyr, but his raid crystallized the issues that were then tumbling the nation toward Civil War.

After flowing southeast through a series of watergaps, it is joined by the Monocacy River in the PIEDMONT region, and by the Anacostia River at WASHINGTON DC. For a 12-mile (19-km) stretch above Washington, the river descends from the Piedmont to the Coastal Plain in a series of rapids and waterfalls, of which the Great Falls is the highest at 35 feet (11 m). The Chesapeake-Ohio Canal which runs parallel to the river, was completed in 1850 from GEORGETOWN to Cumberland. Although traffic ceased on the canal at the turn of the 20th century, it is now the center of a large scenic recreational area. The Potomac forms the border between Maryland and West Virginia from its source to Harpers Ferry, and from there to its mouth, the border between Maryland and Virginia. Washington DC, the Federal capital of the United States, lies at the head of the tidewater on the left bank of the Potomac. Minor port facilities are located at Washington and ALEXANDRIA, Virginia. Once past Washington the river continues southeast until it enters Chesapeake Bay.

Powder, Wyoming-Montana, USA

The Powder River rises in the Bighorn Mountains of Wyoming. It is 486 miles (782 km) long and flows northward through dry ranching country. The river was named 'Powder' because the black sand along its banks resembles gunpowder. The river runs through Johnson and Sheridan Counties in Wyoming before crossing over into Montana. It continues northeast through Powder River, Custer and Prairie Counties to join the Yellowstone River just south of TERRY, Montana. The upper basin of the Powder is extremely rich in bituminous coal, and nearby are the Teapot Dome petroleum fields. The Powder River Valley is primarily a cattle ranching region and has been for the last hundred years.

Price, Utah, USA

The Price rises in the Wasatch Range of central Utah. It is 130 miles (210 km) long and flows southeast past the town of PRICE to meet the Green River, north-northeast of GREEN RIVER. The Price is dammed very near its source to provide water for the adjacent irrigation projects.

Prinzapolca, Nicaragua

The river rises in the Cordillera Isabelia in eastern Nicaragua. It is 120 miles (190 km) long and flows due east to enter the Caribbean Sea at the town of PRINZAPOLCA.

Provo, Utah, USA

The tiny river rises in the Uinta Mountains of central Utah. The Provo is 70 miles (113 km) long and runs southwest past CHARLESTON to enter Utah Lake. This is the center of the principal irrigation project supporting SALT LAKE CITY.

Purgatoire, Colorado, USA

The Purgatoire is formed by the junction of the North and Middle Fork Rivers which rise in the Sangre de Cristo Mountains of southeastern Colorado. It is 186 miles (299 km) long and flows past the town of TRINIDAD, then through a long canyon to join the Arkansas River just east of LAS ANIMAS.

Qu'Appelle, Saskatchewan-Manitoba, Canada

The river rises northwest of MOOSE JAW in southern Saskatchewan. It is 270 miles (430 km) long and flows east through Buffalo Pound Lake to join the Assiniboine River northeast of MOOSOMIN, Manitoba.

Queets, Washington, USA

This small river rises in west-central Olympia National Park in Jefferson County, Washington. It flows west-southwest to enter the Pacific Ocean at the town of QUEETS.

Quinault, Washington, USA

This river rises in southern Olympia National Park in Jefferson County, Washington. It flows west-southwest through Lake Quinault, emerges near Amanda Park and runs through the Quinault Indian Reservation to enter the Pacific Ocean at TAHOLAH.

Quinebaug, Connecticut, USA

This small river rises in Windham County in northeastern Connecticut. It flows south-southwest past JEWETT CITY to join the Yantic River in forming the Thames River near NORWICH.

Quinnipiac, Connecticut, USA

The river rises in northern New Haven County in Connecticut. It flows southwest through New Haven to enter New Haven Harbor of Long Island Sound.

Raccoon, Iowa, USA

The Raccoon rises in Buena Vista County, northwestern Iowa. It is 200 miles (320 km) long and flows south-southeast past SAC CITY, JEFFERSON, DAWSON, ADEL and VAN METER before joining the Des Moines River at DES MOINES, the capital of Iowa. The chief tributaries are the South Raccoon, 50 miles (80 km) long, and the Middle Raccoon, 76 miles (122 km) long.

Raisin, Michigan, USA

This is a small river beginning southeast of JACKSON in southeastern Michigan. It is approximately 115 miles (185 km) long and flows northeast past the town of DUNDEE to enter Lake Erie at MONROE.

Ramos, Mexico

Called the Santiago in its upper course, this river rises in the Sierra Madre Occidental of northwestern Mexico. It is 125 miles (201 km) long and flows north and northeast past Santiago Papasquiaro to join the Rio del Oro to form the Nazas River near the town of EL PALMITO. The Rio del Oro is also known as the Sestin River.

Rapid, Alberta-Saskatchewan, Canada

See Saskatchewan, Alberta-Saskatchewan, Canada.

Rapidan, Virginia, USA

The Rapidan rises in the Blue Ridge

Mountains of Virginia. It is 90 miles (145 km) long and flows south-southeast. This river forms the boundary between Greene, Madison, Culpepper and Orange Counties before joining the Rappahannock River.

Rappahannock, Virginia, USA

The Rappahannock rises in the Blue Ridge Mountains of Virginia at a height of 950 feet (290 m) in the Manassas Gap. This region in colonial times was the location of the great Powhatan Indian Confederation. The river is 185 miles (298 km) long and flows southeast through the Piedmont plateau of Virginia. It is joined by its principal tributary, the Rapidan, 20 miles (32 km) above FREDERICKSBURG. Below Fredericksburg is located the Salem Church Dam which provides hydroelectric power and flood control for the Rappahannock region. Upon nearing the coast the river widens out into a 50-mile (80-km) wide estuary. The real mouth of the Rappahannock is a drowned valley which was covered by the sea in post-glacial times.

Raquette, New York, USA

The Raquette River issues forth from Raquette Lake in the Adirondack Mountains

Top left: The North Platte River in Nebraska.
Center left: The Watergate apts on the Potomac.

of northern New York State. The Raquette is 140 miles (230 km) long and flows through New York's most scenic region. It heads northeast through Long Lake, then north and northwest through Raquette Pond, north and northeast past POTSDAM and MASSENA to enter the St Lawrence River west of HOGANSBURG.

Above: The Potomac River farther upstream.
Top right: The Red Deer River in Alberta.

Raritan, New Jersey, USA

The Raritan rises in the Schooley Mountains in Morris County, northwestern New Jersey. It flows southwest, east, northeast and east, past MIDDLE VALLEY, HIGH BRIDGE, THREE BRIDGES, RARITAN and HIGHLAND PARK to enter Raritan Bay of the Atlantic Ocean.

Rattlesnake Creek, Kansas, USA

This river is formed by the confluence of several headstreams northeast of GREENSBURG, Kansas. It is 122 miles (196 km) long and runs northeast to join the Arkansas River west of STERLING.

Red, Southwestern USA

The Red River rises in the high plains of the Texas panhandle in several headstreams. It is 1270 miles (2040 km) long, drains an area of 93,244 square miles (241,500 sq km) and is ranked tenth in volume of water carried of the

large American rivers. It flows east into Arkansas, then turns southeast through Louisiana to its junction with the Old River, which links the Mississippi River with the Atchafalaya River. Although technically the Red is a tributary of the Mississippi, the

majority of its water is discharged into the Gulf of Mexico via the Atchafalaya River. For approximately half of its total distance the river forms the border between Texas and Oklahoma. The chief tributaries are the North Fork of the Red, Kiamichi, Little and Black Rivers. FULTON, Arkansas, 455 miles (732 km) upstream, is considered the modern head of navigation but all the river's one million tons of traffic is on its first 35 miles (56 km). The Red River is one of the major rivers of the American West.

Red Cedar, Wisconsin, USA

This river issues forth from Red Cedar Lake, which is formed by a small dam in northwestern Wisconsin. It is 85 miles (137 km) long and flows south past RICE LAKE, SAND CREEK, COLFAX and MENOMONIE before joining the Chippewa River.

Red Deer, Alberta, Canada

The Red Deer rises in the Rocky Mountains of the Banff National Park, Alberta. It is 385 miles (619 km) long and flows northeast past RED DEER, south to DRUMHELLER, then turns southeast and east past EMPRESS to join the South Saskatchewan River.

Red Lake, Minnesota, USA

This river is the principal tributary of the Red River of the North. It rises in Lower Red Lake, northwestern Minnesota. The river is 196 miles (315 km) long and flows west to Thief River Falls, then south and west past Red Lake Falls to the Red River of the North at East Grand Forks. The chief tributaries are the Thief and Clearwater Rivers.

Red River of the North, USA-Canada
Formed by the confluence of the Bois de Sioux and the Otter Tail Rivers, which meet at BRECKENRIDGE, Wilkins County, west-central Minnesota. The river forms the border between North Dakota and Minnesota as it flows due north, past KENT, WOLVERTON, MOREHEAD, HALSTAD, GRAND FORKS, OSLO, ST VINCENT and NOYES before crossing over into Manitoba, Canada for the remainder of its course. Its chief tributaries are the Buffalo, Wild, Rice, Red Lake, Sand, Snake, Middle, Tamarac, Maple, Sheyenne, Elm, Goose, Park and Forest Rivers, all of which join the Red River of the North in the USA. Entering Canada the river passes EMERSON, ST JEAN BAPTISTE, MORRIS, ST VITAL, WINNIPEG and SELKIRK before it runs into Lake Winnipeg after a 545-mile (877-km) journey northward. The river flows through the extremely flat bed of the ancient glacial waterway called Lake Agassiz, which was once a vast inland sea.

Republican, Colorado-Nebraska-Kansas, USA
The Republican rises in eastern Colorado and joins the Arikaree east of BENKELMAN in Nebraska. It is 422 miles (679 km) long and flows east and southeast past MAX, STRATTON, through Swanson Lake, TRENTON, MCCOOK, INDIANOLA, through Harlan County Reservoir, FRANKLIN, RIVERTON, RED CLOUD and BOSTWICK. The river then crosses over into Kansas and continues on to JUNCTION CITY where it joins the Smoky Hill River to form the Kansas River.

Restigouche, New Brunswick, Canada
The Restigouche River rises east of EDMUNDSTON, northwestern New Brunswick. It is 130 miles (210 km) long and flows on a winding course northeast picking up the Matapedia River west of CAMPBELLTON, then turns east-northeast to Chaleur Bay at DALHOUSIE through a 24-mile (39-km) long tidal estuary.

Richelieu, Quebec, Canada
The Richelieu River rises at the northern end of Lake Champlain in southern Quebec. It is 75 miles (121 km) long and flows north past ST JEAN to join the St Lawrence River at SOREL. It is a principal part of the Hudson-St Lawrence waterway link.

Rio Grande de Matagalpa, Nicaragua
The Rio Grande rises southwest of MATAGALPA in central Nicaragua. It is 200 miles (320 km) long and flows east past EL CAMARON, LOS EN CUENTROS, TARICA and LA CRUZ to enter the Caribbean Sea. The Rio Grande is navigable for a distance on its lower course. The chief tributary is the Tuma River.

Rio Grande, Southwestern USA
The Rio Grande is the fifth longest river in the United States. It rises in the snow fields and alpine meadows of the San Juan Mountains of southwestern Colorado. It comes to life as a beautiful clear mountain stream at a height of 12,000 feet (3660 m). It is 1885 miles (3033 km) long and drains an area of 171,585 square miles (444,405 sq km). The Rio Grande flows southeast and south for 175 miles (282 km) through Colorado, then turns due south for 470 miles (760 km) through New Mexico, and southeast for its remaining 1240 miles (1995 km) between Texas and the Mexican states of Chihuahua, Coahuila, Nuevo Leon and Tamaulipas before entering the Gulf of Mexico. Once it leaves the high slopes of the San Juan Mountains, the river flows through a canyon abounding in fir, spruce and aspen forests before entering the San Luis Valley of Colorado. The river then flows through the Rio Grande gorge and White Rock Canyon before running into open country. Before entering the Gulf Coastal Plain, the Rio Grande cuts three canyons between 1500–1700 feet (458–519 m) deep across the faulted area of the 'big bend.' On the Texas side of the border this large area has been included in the Big Bend National Park. On the last phase of its course the river flows sluggishly across the coastal plain to enter the Gulf of Mexico. The principal tributaries are the Pecos, Devils, Chama, Puerco, Conchos, Salado and San Juan Rivers. Irrigation has been going on in the Rio Grande Basin since prehistoric times. The flow of the river has suffered greatly from the large amounts of water tapped from its main channel and tributaries. In some places the depth of the Rio Grande has been recorded to vary from 60 feet (18 m) to a mere trickle. In numerous stretches from the New Mexico-Colorado border to BROWNSVILLE there has been no surface water at all. The Rio Grande Basin has been developed considerably to provide hydroelectric power for the surrounding area.

Red Rock, Montana, USA
See Jefferson, Montana, USA.

Roanoke, Virginia-North Carolina, USA
The Roanoke rises in the Blue Ridge Mountains of west central Virginia at an altitude of 1000 feet (305 m). The river is 410 miles (660 km) long and flows south-southeast for the majority of its course to the sea. The Roanoke cuts through the Blue Ridge in a narrow gap which is also occupied by the important manufacturing city of ROANOKE with a population of 181,000. It flows past HARDY and into Smith Mountain Lake heading southeast. The river, also known as the Staunton River, passes LEESVILLE, ALTIVISTA, LONG ISLAND and BROOKNEAL before receiving the Dan River. Below CLARKSVILLE is the large J H Kerr Dam, which is an important part of the flood and irrigation control projects along the river. The dam causes the waters of the Roanoke to back up for 30 miles (48 km) in a long lake with many arms. The river flows across the border into North Carolina and passes ROANOKE RAPIDS. Its chief tributaries are the Dan, Big Otter, Pigg Rivers and Goose

Summer tourists are encouraged to take a five day boat ride

from Grants Pass Oregon to the ocean down the Rogue River and through Hellgate Canyon.

Creek. The Roanoke continues on course past PALMYRA, HAMILTON, WILLIAMSTON, and PLY-MOUTH before entering Albemarle Sound. The last leg of the river was the scene of intense fighting during both the Revolutionary War and the Civil War.

Roaring Fork, Colorado, USA
This river rises in southeastern Pitkin County, central Colorado. It flows northwest past the town of ASPEN, then continues on through SNOWMASS and BASALT before joining the Colorado River near GLENWOOD SPRINGS.

Rock, Wisconsin-Illinois, USA
The Rock River rises in the lake country just south of FOND DU LAC in eastern Wisconsin. It is 285 miles (459 km) long and flows south and southwest in a wide glacial channel cut by the melted water draining from Green Bay and Lake Winnebago. The original settlers in the valley were from Scandinavia and they inundated the area. The first inhabitants of this rich valley were the Winnebago Indians in the north and the Sauk Indians to the south. The Black Hawk War, 1831–32 saw the tribes all but wiped out. The river passes ROCKFORD, BYRON, OREGON, DIXON, ROCK FALLS, ERIE and MILAN before entering the Mississippi River south of ROCK ISLAND, Illinois.

Rogue, Oregon, USA
The Rogue rises in the Cascade Range, northwest of the blue waters of Crater Lake in southwestern Oregon. It is 200 miles (320 km) long and flows southwest and west through the Klamath Mountains, past GRANTS PASS to enter the Pacific Ocean at GOLD BEACH.

Romaine, Quebec, Canada
The Romaine River rises in eastern Quebec on the border with Labrador. The Romaine is 250 miles (400 km) long and flows south through Lac Long, which is 20 miles (32 km) long, and Burnt Lake to enter the St Lawrence River opposite Mingan Island.

Roseau, Minnesota-Manitoba, USA-Canada
This river is formed by the junction of two small forks in Roseau County, northwestern Minnesota. It is 140 miles (230 km) long and flows west and northwest across the border into Canada to join the Red River of the North.

Rupert, Quebec, Canada
This river rises in western Quebec in Lake Mistassini. It is 380 miles (610 km) long and flows west through Nemiscau Lake, past RUPERT HOUSE to enter James Bay of Hudson Bay.

Sabine, Texas-Louisiana, USA
The Sabine River rises in Titus County, northeastern Texas. It rises some 50 miles (80 km) northwest of Dallas. It is 578 miles (930 km) long and flows southeast through a country of low rolling hills. The region of the

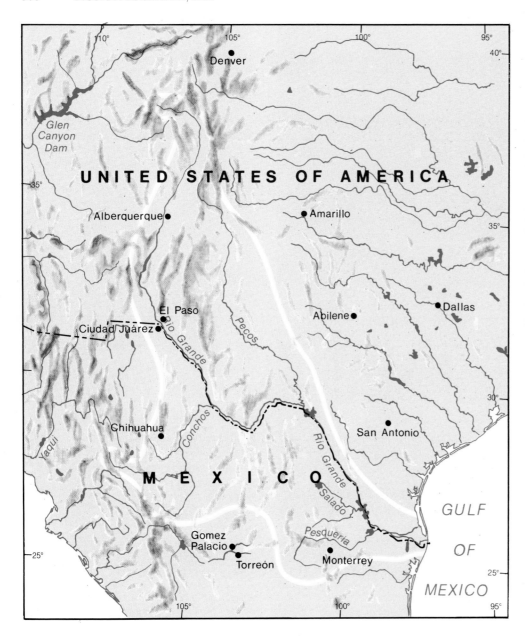

upper Sabine was once the home of the Caddo Indian tribe. Near the town of LOGANSPORT in Louisiana the river forms the boundary between Texas and Louisiana, curving southward through the Toledo Bend Reservoir. It then flows along the eastern boundaries of the Sabine National Forest. The only important town on this stretch of the course is ORANGE, which is also the head of navigation. Orange is a deep water port and is in the middle of a rich oil, lumber and rice growing region. The city is linked by a deepwater channel with nearby Sabine Lake, which is connected with the Gulf of Mexico by the Sabine Pass.

Sacandaga, New York, USA
The Sacandaga River is formed by the confluence of several headstreams in Hamilton County, northeastern New York State, south of WELLS in the Adirondack Mountains. It is 12 miles (19 km) long from its source to where it enters the Great Sacandaga Lake, which covers an area of 250 square miles (648 sq km). The river then runs for a further seven miles (11 km) to join the Hudson River, south of HADLEY and Lake Luzerne.

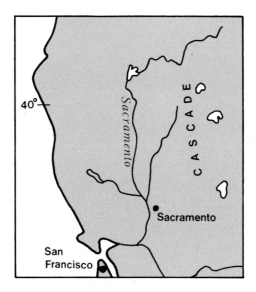

Sachigo, Ontario, Canada
The Sachigo River rises in small lakes in northern Kenora Territorial District, northern Ontario. The Sachigo flows northeast, east and northeast through a sparsely populated

region of northern Ontario as it makes its way to join the Severn River approximately 100 miles (160 km) south of FORT SEVERN.

Sacramento, California, USA
The Sacramento River is the largest and most important river in California. It is 380 miles (611 km) long and flows basically on a southward course. It rises in the Klamath Mountains near Mt Shasta and runs south for the majority of its length before turning west below the state capital of SACRAMENTO. The river then is joined by the northward flowing San Joaquin River near PITTSBURG to flow through Suisun and San Pablo Bays, the San

Above: Sunset on the Saguenay River, Quebec, Canada.
Left: Santa Elena Canyon on the Rio Grande.

Pablo Strait and into San Francisco Bay. It is navigable for 250 miles (400 km) of its course by small vessels. The chief tributaries are the Cottonwood, Thames, Stony and Cache Creeks which all rise on the Coast Ranges to the west. The principal tributaries which rise in Sierra Nevadas are much larger and faster flowing, namely the Battle, Antelope, Mill, Deer, Big Chico and Butte Rivers. There are numerous dams along the river and its chief tributaries have revived the Central Valley Project which provides irrigation water and fresh drinking water for a large population. In 1848 the Sacramento and its tributaries were the scene of the famous California Gold Rush. The Sacramento and the San Joaquin Rivers together form the great Central California Valley, one of the richest agricultural regions in the world.

Sajua la Grande, Cuba
This river rises south of SANTA CLARA in central Cuba. It flows for 75 miles (121 km) due north past Santo Domingo to Nicholas Channel at the town of ISABELA DE SAJUA.

Saguenay, Quebec, Canada
The Saguenay rises in Lake St John and is its outlet to the St Lawrence. It is 110 miles (177 km) long and flows south, dropping over 300 feet (92 m) on its initial 35 miles (56 km) to CHICOUTIMI. Its major tributaries are the Au Sable, Chicoutimi, Shipshaw and Valin Rivers. The three largest hydroelectric power stations in this region are located at Isle Maligne, Shipshaw and Chute à Caron, which together have an output of well over one million kilowatts. The Saguenay then flows southeast through the Canadian Shield in a fjord like channel. By the time the river reaches ETERNITY and TRINITY, the walls rise to a height of 1000 feet (315 m) and the depth of the river is over 800 feet (242 m). The river was formed during the great continental glacier period of North America. It enters the St Lawrence River just past the town of TADOUSSAC, population 1010.

Saint Croix, Wisconsin, USA
The St Croix River rises in the lake district of Douglas County, Wisconsin. It is 164 miles (264 km) long and flows southwest and south through Lake St Croix to become a tributary of the Mississippi River at PRESCOTT.

Saint Francis, Missouri-Arkansas, USA
The St Francis rises to the north of Mt Taum Sauk, 1772 feet (540 m) high, in the St Francois Mountains of east-central Missouri. It is 475 miles (764 km) long and flows northeast, south, and south-southeast through the Clark National Forest, Lake Wappapello and is the boundary between Butler and Stoddard Counties. It continues south and is the border between Arkansas and Missouri for a distance of some 50 miles (80 km). It turns slightly westward as it enters Arkansas in the southeastern corner of Greene County. The St Francis winds and twists its way south passing TULOT, MARKED TREE, MADISON and SOUDAN before joining the Mississippi below MEMPHIS, Tennessee. A large area along the banks of the St Francis is prime peach country.

Saint Francis, Quebec, Canada
This river rises in Lake St Francis, approximately 30 miles (48 km) northwest of MEGAN-TIC, Quebec. It is 150 miles (240 km) long and flows southwest through Lake Aylmer, past LENNOXVILLE, and then heads northwest past RICHMOND and PIERREVILLE to Lake St Peter, a part of the St Lawrence River, 12 miles (19 km) east-northeast of SOREL.

Saint John, Maine-New Brunswick, US-Canada
This river rises in the northern part of Somerset County, Maine. It is 400 miles (640 km) long and flows northeast and east. Initially it flows through a rather sparsely inhabited area of northern Maine, and is joined by the Big Black in northwestern Aroostook County and by the Little Black at the town of ALLAGASH. It continues on its basically northeasterly course past ST FRANCIS and is joined by the St Francis River shortly afterward. The river now runs east and forms

the boundary between the United States and Canada for a distance. It passes the towns of CONNORS, ST JOHN, FORT KENT, FRENCHVILLE and EDMUNDSTON, all of which are located on the border before turning southeast. The St John practically runs parallel with the New Brunswick and Maine border as it heads south. It receives the Grand, Salmon and Tobique Rivers before reaching WOODSTOCK where it widens as it turns eastward. The river continues east past FREDERICTON, the capital of New Brunswick, but gradually begins to swing south. It flows into the Long Reach, located in Kings County, and heads west for a short distance, then enters Grand Bay to flow past the city of ST JOHN, New Brunswick into the Bay of Fundy.

Saint Johns, Florida, USA

The St Johns River has its source in the swamps of central northeastern Florida, at an altitude of less than 20 feet (six m). The river is 285 miles (459 km) long and flows north through Lakes Washington, Winder, Harney, Jessup, Monroe, Dexter, and George before arriving at the town of PALATKA which has a population of 9310. Besides the famous citrus orchards which abound in this region, the agricultural produce of the St Johns area includes excellent potato crops. Just south of Palatka the river is joined by the Oklawaha River, which helps to drain this swampy and lake studded region of northeastern Florida. North of Palatka the river is a wide estuarial river and a major section of the Intracoastal Waterway. The St Johns then flows past Jacksonville Naval Air Station and the Fort Caroline National Monument before entering the Atlantic Ocean. JACKSONVILLE is a major port and industrial city and has a population of 528,850.

Saint Joseph, Michigan, USA

The St Joseph River rises near HILLSDALE in southern Michigan State. It is 210 miles (338 km) long and flows northwest initially, then turns west and southwest past SOUTH BEND, Indiana and northwest into Lake Michigan.

Saint Lawrence, Canada-USA

The St Lawrence River is the greatest North American river draining east to the Atlantic Ocean. The St Lawrence was discovered in 1535 by the French explorer, Jacques Cartier. The river is one of the principal routes through the highlands of eastern North America, and is the center of Canada's most important economic and cultural region – the St Lawrence Lowlands. These lowlands lie between the Laurentian Upland or Canadian Shield to the north and the Appalachian Highlands and Adirondack Mountains to the south. It extends from the city of QUEBEC west to the Thousand Islands near the head of the river. At the head of the St Lawrence is the Great Lakes Basin which has a joint land and water area of 291,000 square miles

Top right: The Saint Lawrence in Quebec.
Right: Looking down the Saint Lawrence.
Far right: Thousand Islands on the Saint Lawrence.

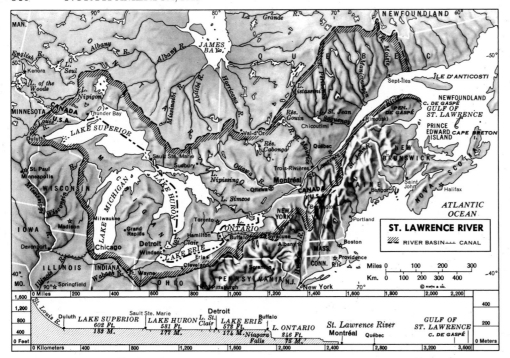

ST. LAWRENCE RIVER
▨▨ RIVER BASIN ─··─ CANAL

Miles 0   100   200   300
Km. 0 100 200 300 400

| LAKE SUPERIOR 602 Ft. 183 M. | LAKE HURON 581 Ft. 177 M. | L. St. Clair | LAKE ERIE 572 Ft. 174 M. | L. ONTARIO 246 Ft. 75 M. | St. Lawrence River Montréal Québec | GULF OF ST. LAWRENCE c. DE GASPÉ |

Riverside view of Fredericton, the capital of New Brunswick, Canada. Fredericton on the Saint John River is the head of navigation for small sea-going vessels.

(567,000 sq km). The drainage area of the St Lawrence extends as far as the headwaters of the St Louis River, which flows into Lake Superior at its westernmost extremity, but the St Lawrence River has its head at the easternmost end of Lake Ontario. The river is the link between the Great Lakes and the Atlantic Ocean. The total estimated drainage area in Canada, excluding the Great Lakes section, is 198,000 square miles (513,000 sq km). There have been various lengths assigned to the St Lawrence, but the one preferred by geographers places the mouth between Point des Monts and Cap Chat, 595 miles (957 km) downstream from Lake Ontario. For easy analysis the river is divided into three parts: the upper river, the middle river and the lower river or estuary section.

Upper River: This section of the St Lawrence runs for 182 miles (293 km) from KINGSTON at the outlet of Lake Ontario to MONTREAL. From Kingston for 114 miles (183 km) the river forms the international border between the United States and Canada, the remainder lies wholly within Canada. At Lake Ontario, the river is 245 feet (75 m) above sea level and at Montreal 20 feet (six m). A large international dam and two smaller control dams, part of the seaway development project, have eliminated some of the rapids, the most famous being the Long Sault Rapids. These were replaced with a manmade body of water 100 square miles (259 sq km) in area called Lake St Lawrence. Further downstream the river widens in two areas to form Lake St Francis, 28 miles (45 km) long and Lake St Louis, 15 miles (24 km) long. At the head of Lake St Louis is the confluence of the Ottawa River, which served as an outlet to the sea for the post glacial Great Lakes.

Middle River: Montreal is the beginning of the St Lawrence's middle course. It was established at the head of navigation for the river, where further progress upstream was impeded by the Lachine Rapids. The construction of the St Lawrence Canal in the 1800s and the St Lawrence Seaway in 1959 permitted medium-sized vessels to continue upriver, but the port of Montreal is still the

terminus for larger ocean-going vessels. Montreal is one of the great seaports of the world and is open for ocean-going vessels two-thirds of the year. At Trois Rivières (Three Rivers), mean sea level is reached, and this becomes the limit of tidal conditions. Forty-five miles (72 km) downstream from Montreal is SOREL at the mouth of the Richelieu River and the head of Lake St Peter. The Richelieu-Lake Champlain route provides a shallow-draft waterway which connects the Hudson River to the St Lawrence. The middle section of the St Lawrence ends at QUEBEC.

Lower or Estuary Section: The estuary section begins at Quebec, the capital of Canada's largest province. Here the decisive battle of the French and Indian War was fought between the British Army of General Wolfe and the French Army under General Montcalm, in which both commanders were killed. Tidal action is very fierce in this funnel-shaped estuary with the Spring Tide reaching a height of 19 feet (six m) and the neap tide 13 feet (four m). The estuary is navigable to Quebec throughout the year and has a length of 253 miles (407 km) to Point des Monts, to Anticosti Island an added 130 miles (210 km).

The establishment of the St Lawrence Seaway was a joint international undertaking by the United States and Canada and enabled navigation to be extended from Montreal to Lake Erie and the other great Lakes.

Saint Louis, Minnesota, USA
The river rises in St Louis County, north-eastern Minnesota. It is 160 miles (260 km) long and runs southwest to FLOODWOOD, then swings southeast and eastward to an estuary on Lake Superior, the largest of the Great Lakes, to form a harbor for the port cities of DULUTH and SUPERIOR.

Saint Maurice, Quebec, Canada
The river rises in central Quebec and flows southeast and south through Gouin Reservoir, past LA TUQUE and SHAWINIGAN FALLS to join the St Lawrence River at TROIS RIVIÈRES.

Salinas, California, USA
This Salinas rises in the Coast Range, east of SAN LUIS OBISPO in western California. It is 150 miles (240 km) long and runs northwest past the towns of PASO ROBLES and KING CITY before entering Monterey Bay on the Pacific Ocean.

Salinas, Mexico
This Salinas rises near SALTILLO in the Sierra Madre Oriental of northern Mexico. It is 150 miles (240 km) long and flows north and east past HILDALGO, SALINAS, VICTORIA and GENERAL ZUAZUA to join the Pesqueria River, which continues for 110 miles (180 km) to become a tributary of the San Juan River.

Saline, Arkansas, USA
The Saline rises in the Ouachita Mountains west of LITTLE ROCK, Arkansas. It is 300 miles (480 km) long and runs south-southeast to join the Ouachita River just west of CROSSETT.

Saline, Kansas, USA
Formed by the junction of two small headstreams near the town of OAKLEY in northwestern Kansas, the Saline is 342 miles (550 km) long and runs east past SYLVAN GROVE and LINCOLN to join the Smoky Hill River east of SALINA.

Salmon, Idaho, USA
The Salmon rises in central Idaho in the Salmon River Mountain Range between Lone Pine Peak, 9652 feet (2944 m) and Bald Mountain, 10,315 feet (3146 m). The river flows north initially, and is joined by the Pahsimeroi River near the town of ELLIS which has a population of only 75. Upon reaching SALMON, which has a population of 2910, the river begins to curve westward, near the foot of the Continental Divide. It continues on past CARMEN, NORTH FORK and SHOUP as it heads west across the Clearwater Mountains of north-central Idaho. Reaching RIGGINS, a small town of 533, the Salmon abruptly turns north passing LUCILE, and runs parallel with the Seven Devils Mountains. The Salmon is joined by Slate Creek between Lucile and WHITE BIRD, the last town of any note before the river turns west again and enters the Snake River slightly above the High Mountain Sheep Reservoir. The Salmon is 420 miles (676 km) long, and is only separated from the Grand Canyon of the Snake by the Seven Devils Mountains on the last leg of its course.

Salt, Arizona, USA
The Salt River is formed by the confluence of the White and the Black Rivers on the Apache Indian Reservation in the high plateau region of eastern Arizona between the Mogollon Mesa and the Gila Mountains. The river flows southwest crossing Gila County and enters Theodore Roosevelt Lake, near the TONTO NATIONAL MONUMENT. It departs through the Theodore Roosevelt Dam and continues on

Left: Rapid riders on the Salmon River, Idaho, pass through majestic scenery.

Saluda, South Carolina, USA

The Saluda rises in the Blue Ridge Mountains of South Carolina. This picturesque river begins at a height of 3560 feet (1086 m) high on Sassafras Mountain. It flows south-southeast past PIEDMONT, WARE SHOALS, through Lake Greenwood to emerge at Buzzards Roost Dam, then continues as the boundary between Saluda and Newberry Counties before entering Lake Murray, which is formed by the Saluda Dam. The river continues on course to join the Broad River at COLUMBIA, the capital of South Carolina. They form the Congaree River.

Samala, Guatemala

The Samala rises west of SAN FRANCISCO in southwestern Guatemala. It is 75 miles (121 km) long and flows south-southwest past ZUNIL and SANTA MARIA to enter the Pacific Ocean at PLAYA GRANDE.

San Antonio, Texas, USA

This famous river in Texas rises in several small springs in SAN ANTONIO, Texas. The Battle of the Alamo was fought nearby during Texas' fight for independence from Mexico. The river is 195 miles (314 km) long and runs southeast to join the Guadalupe River.

Sandusky, Ohio, USA

The Sandusky rises in Crawford County, Ohio. It flows west-southwest, north and northeast, past the towns of BUCYRUS, UPPER SANDUSKY, OLD FORT and FREMONT, to empty into Sandusky Bay of Lake Erie.

San Francisco, Arizona-New Mexico, USA

The San Francisco rises in Apache County in eastern Arizona. It is 160 miles (260 km) long and flows due east into New Mexico, then south and west back into Arizona to join the Gila River southwest of CLIFTON.

San Gabriel, California, USA

This small river rises in the San Gabriel Mountains of southern California, northeast of LOS ANGELES. It is formed by the junction of three tiny headstreams and is 75 miles (121 km) long. The river flows south-southwest to enter Alamitos Bay.

course across Maricopa County, through Lake Apache and Canyon Lake. The chief tributary of the Salt is the Verde River where the Bartlett Dam is located. Water is at a premium in this part of the American southwest; Indians have used the Salt River to irrigate the nearby fields for hundreds of years. The dams along the Salt and its tributary the Verde, allow thousands of acres of land to be irrigated and to produce crops. The principal city on the river is PHOENIX, the capital of Arizona, with a population of 967,522. The Salt is 200 miles (320 km) long and flows into the Gila River about 15 miles (24 km) southwest of Phoenix.

Salt, Kentucky, USA

This Salt River rises west of DANVILLE in northern Kentucky. It is 125 miles (200 km) long and runs west past SHEPHERDSVILLE, the head of its navigation, then north to become a tributary of the Ohio River at WEST POINT.

Salt Fork, Kansas-Oklahoma, USA

Formed by the junction of several headstreams in Comanche County in southern Kansas, the Salt Fork River is 192 miles (309 km) long and flows southeast past ALVA, Oklahoma, then east past POND CREEK to join the Arkansas River.

Sangamon, Illinois, USA

The Sangamon River rises in central Illinois in the morainic ridges to the northwest of Champaign and Ford Counties. The river is 250 miles (400 km) long and flows in a shallow curve first south, west and northwest. It runs through Platt County, then through Macon County into Lake Decatur, and emerges to flow through the northern tip of Christian County. It then enters Sangamon County to continue on its northwesterly course. The Sangamon is best known as the home of Abraham Lincoln. In the 1820s Lincoln's

family moved from Kentucky to Illinois and he lived for over a year in a small log cabin overlooking the bluffs of the river west of DECATUR. Lincoln studied law at NEW SALEM, a small town on the banks of the Sangamon, and it was here that he began his great political career. In fact, the President's fondest memories were of his year on the Sangamon and the long walks along the bluffs of the river. Below SPRINGFIELD, the capital of Illinois, the river is joined by Salt Creek and the South Fork. It finally joins the Illinois River.

San Jacinto, Texas, USA
Sam Houston, the father of Texas, defeated the Mexican Army of General Santa Ana on the banks of this river to insure Texas' bid for independence. It rises in Walker County in southeastern Texas at the junction of the West Fork, 80 miles (129 km) long, and the East Fork, 65 miles (105 km) long. The San Jacinto is 50 miles (80 km) long and flows south to enter Galveston Bay on the Gulf of Mexico.

San Joaquin, California, USA
The San Joaquin is the second most important river in California and the chief stream of the southern portion of the Great Central Valley. In its natural condition the San Joaquin valley

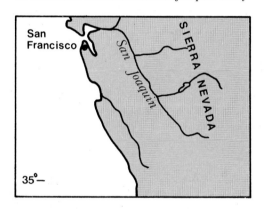

is arid and barren. The agriculture of the valley depends entirely upon the various irrigation projects. The northern, Sacramento River section, has an average rainfall of 25 inches (64 cm) per annum and although irrigation is still required, less is necessary. The waters of the San Joaquin are dammed at the foot of the Sierras and are led off to the arid lands in the Bakersfield region instead of being allowed to flow into the sea. Utilizing the power of the Shasta Dam, surplus water is brought from the Sacramento River to be pumped into the Delta-Mendota Canal, and then conveyed by gravity up the San Joaquin valley to be fed into the river as it starts its journey northward. The major engineering project in this half of the valley was the FRIANT DAM, which was constructed in 1944. The Friant-Kern Canal takes San Joaquin water into the southern section of the valley, where there is a basin of interior drainage. The southern Sierras are drained by the Kings, Kaweah and Kern Rivers, which at one time emptied into Lake Tulare, once 50 miles (80 km) long and 35 miles (56 km) wide. This large body of water is now a thing of the past; it is now being farmed, and the rivers which used to feed it are being used for irrigation projects.

San Juan, Colorado-New Mexico-Utah, USA
The San Juan rises in several headstreams in the San Juan Mountains of southwestern Colorado. It is 400 miles (640 km) long and flows southwest into New Mexico, passing the impressive AZTEC RUINS NATIONAL MONUMENT. The river passes the towns of FRUITLAND, KIRTLAND, FARMINGTON, WATERFLOW and SHIPROCK as it flows west through San Juan County. It turns northwest through the corner of New Mexico, near FOUR CORNERS, (the only place in the United States, where four states border each other). There are no major towns or cities along the San Juan's course. It is unnavigable because of the numerous rapids which are strewn throughout its entire length. The river flows through desert terrain, with many scenic views. Its chief tributaries are mostly intermittent streams but the notable ones are McElmo Creek, Montezuma Creek, Cottonwood Wash and Comb Wash. The San Juan flows west through the southern portion of Utah as it heads towards the Colorado River, which it joins near the RAINBOW BRIDGE NATIONAL MONUMENT. The river is at its panoramic best as it flows through Gooseneck Canyon, which is 1500 feet (458 m) deep, in a series of five tight bends over 25 miles (40 km) – five miles (eight km) as the crow flies.

San Juan, Nicaragua
This San Juan River issues forth from the southeastern end of Lake Nicaragua. It is 120 miles (190 km) long and runs east-southeast past EL CASTILLO to the Caribbean Sea at SAN JUAN DEL NORTE. Its chief tributaries are the San Carlos and the Sarapiqui Rivers.

San Miguel, Colorado, USA
The San Miguel rises near the town of OPHIR in

Homemade dugout on the Santa Maria River, Mexico.

southeastern San Miguel County in southwestern Colorado. It is 90 miles (145 km) long and flows northwest past SAW PIT and PLACERVILLE to join the Dolores River in northwestern Montrose County.

San Pablo, Panama
The San Pablo River rises ten miles (16 km) west-northwest of SANTE FE in southwestern Panama. It is 50 miles (80 km) long and flows south past CANAZAS, SAN PABLO and SONA to enter Montijo Gulf of the Pacific Ocean.

San Pedro, Mexico (1)
See Armeria, Mexico.

San Pedro, Mexico (2)
Also known as the Tuxpan, the river rises in the Sierra Madre Occidental in western Mexico. It is 250 miles (400 km) long and flows south past NOMBRE DE DIOS and MEZQUITAL, then west past TUXPAN to coastal lagoons draining into the Pacific Ocean.

Sanpoil, Washington, USA
This small river rises in Ferry County, northeastern Washington. It flows northeast to the town of REPUBLIC, then turns south through the Colville Indian Reservation to join the Columbia River south of KELLER.

Santa Maria, Mexico
The Santa Maria rises in the Sierra Madre Oriental of Mexico. It is 200 miles (320 km) long and flows east to join the Moctezuma River to form the Panuco River.

Santee, South Carolina, USA

The Santee River is formed by the confluence of the Congaree and the Watree Rivers at Lake Marion in central eastern South Carolina. The river is 143 miles (230 km) long and flows basically southeast to the Atlantic Ocean. It is the principal river of South Carolina. The Santee is navigable, but its primary purpose is as a source of hydroelectric power for this region of the state. The Santee Dam, located 15 miles (24 km) south of the town of MANNING and which forms Lake Marion, not only provides hydroelectric power, but flood control and navigational control for this stretch of the river. The Santee is linked by a canal to Lake Moultrie, another reservoir formed by the Pinopolis Dam on the nearby Cooper River. The Santee enters the Atlantic Ocean through two mouths, the North and South Santee 15 miles (24 km) south of GEORGETOWN.

Santiago, Mexico

The Santiago is the chief river of Mexico. It rises under the name of Lerma in central Mexico, southeast of TOLUCA, and runs northwest and west. It has a total length of 600 miles (960 km). Close to the town of LERMA there is excellent trout fishing. The river flows past IXTLAHUACA, noted for its silver mining, ACAMBARO, SALVATIERRA, SALAMANCA and PUEBLO NUEVO to enter the eastern side of Lake Chapala, which covers an area of 417 square miles (1080 sq km). Lake Chapala is the largest body of fresh water in Mexico and is famous for its numerous islands and oustanding fishing. At OCOTLAN, the Lerma becomes the Santiago and flows west-northwest past JUANACATLAN. At Juanacatlan a massive horseshoe-shaped falls – 524 feet (160 m) wide and 70 feet (21 m) high – is located. A large hydroelectric power station has been built here to provide electricity to the surrounding

The San Juan River in Utah as it bends dramatically through Gooseneck Canyon at Mexican Hat.

region. The Santiago flows through the valuable Mexican silver- and gold-mining region, past YAGO and SANTIAGO IXCUINTLA. The river enters the Pacific Ocean ten miles (16 km) northwest of SAN BLAS. The principal tributaries are the Apaseo, Laja, Turbeo, Juchipila and the Bolanos. The Lerma and the Santiago are not navigable rivers, but they both provide water for the large-scale irrigation projects and hydroelectric plants along their courses.

Saskatchewan, Alberta-Saskatchewan, Canada

Also known as the Rapid, the Saskatchewan is the largest river system in Alberta and Saskatchewan. In the fur trading days, the river system was a principal route north and an easy means of transportation. Numerous forts and trading posts were established along the banks of the river: the most notable were FORT PITT, FORT BATTLEFORD, CUMBERLAND HOUSE and CARLTON HOUSE. The two branches or forks of the Saskatchewan begin at the Columbia ice field in the eastern Rocky Mountains. The North Saskatchewan is 760 miles (1220 km) long, while the South Saskatchewan has a length of 890 miles (1430 km). This river system is the fourth largest in Canada and has a drainage area of 136,000 square miles (352,000 sq km) which includes all of southern Alberta and Saskatchewan. The actual meaning of the name is 'swift-flowing river' as translated from the Cree Indian word, *kisiskatchewan*. It was discovered in 1690 by Henry Kesley of the famous Hudson Bay Company, but was not fully explored until 1741 when La Verendrye traced it to its source. The North Saskatchewan runs north, then east to cut its way

through high mountains. After receiving the Brazeau River, it flows northeast across a wide forested valley, opening up to the northern prairies. The river is a fast-flowing, winding river, incising itself well into the valley to a depth of 200–300 feet (61–91 m). The South Saskatchewan is formed by the confluence of the Oldman and Bow Rivers. After leaving the mountains, like its northern counterpart, it turns eastward to flow through a deeply entrenched valley, which widens out to the east of the Missouri Coteau. The river is broad and shallow, with numerous sand bars. The chief towns on its banks are LETHBRIDGE, CALGARY, DRUMHELLER, MEDICINE HAT and SASKATOON. The potential of the South Saskatchewan is tremendous, and hydroelectric projects are being expanded and built at an amazing rate. The river continues on course until east of PRINCE ALBERT it joins the North Saskatchewan to form the Saskatchewan River. The last leg of the Saskatchewan is 369 miles (594 km) long and flows east to enter Lake Winnipeg. The chief tributaries are the Battle, North Branch, the Bow, Belly and Red Deer, South Branch and the Sturgeon Weir and Carrot Rivers. The river was navigated by steamers during the early days of settlement, but today it is only navigated on its lower course.

Satilla, Georgia, USA

The Satilla rises near FITZGERALD in southeastern Georgia. It is 200 miles (320 km) long and flows east past the town of WOODBINE to enter the Atlantic Ocean south of BRUNSWICK. Its chief tributary is the Little Satilla River which is 70 miles (113 km) long.

Savannah, Georgia-South Carolina, USA

The Savannah is one of the South's principal

The Saskatchewan River as it flows through Jasper National Park, Alberta. The Saskatchewan River system is the fourth largest in Canada.

rivers. Its source is Hartwell Lake on the South Carolina-Georgia border. The Savannah is 314 miles (505 km) long and forms most of the border between Georgia and South Carolina. Above AUGUSTA the river is halted by the Clark Hill Dam and is pushed back for 40 miles (64 km) to form the Clark Hill Reservoir. The river flows southeast to the sea. Augusta is the head of the river's navigation, and prior to the coming of the railroads, shallow-bottomed vessels were used to transport cotton and tobacco downstream to SAVANNAH. Flowing across the wide coastal plain, the Savannah has made a broad, swampy valley. On the South Carolina side of the river, the US Atomic Energy Commission has over 202,000 acres of land. Nearing its delta, the river reaches the once great port of Savannah, a city of 125,000 people. The city is situated on a bluff overlooking the river, and has eight miles (13 km) of wharves from which ocean-going vessels are loaded with cotton, tobacco and other cargo. Savannah has many other industries such as sugar refining, pulp and paper mills and shipbuilding. The river leaves the city and flows through a delta, which is now a wildlife refuge area, before entering the Atlantic Ocean.

Schuylkill, Pennsylvania, USA

The river rises in southeastern Pennsylvania. It is 130 miles (210 km) long and flows southeast past POTTSVILLE, READING and NORRISTOWN to join the Delaware River at the colonial capital of PHILADELPHIA. The upper Schuylkill is beautiful and flows through some of Pennsylvania's most scenic countryside, in the foothills of the Appalachians. Early pioneers used the river for transportation.

Scioto, Ohio, USA

The river rises west of KENTON in southern Ohio. The Scioto is 237 miles (381 km) long and flows southeast and south past COLUMBUS and CHILLICOTHE to join the Ohio River at PORTSMOUTH. The Ohio River forms the border between Ohio, Kentucky and West Virginia.

Segovia, Honduras-Nicaragua

See Cacō, Honduras-Nicaragua.

Severn, Ontario, Canada

The Severn issues forth from Sandy Lake in northern Ontario. It is 610 miles (980 km) long and flows northward through northwestern Kenora Territorial District, past the town of BEARSKIN LAKE and through Severn Lake, before entering Hudson Bay at FORT SEVERN. The chief tributaries are the Sachigo and the Fawn Rivers. The river was named by Captain Thomas James in 1631 and was known initially as the New Severn. Although trappers used the Severn as a secondary route to Lake Winnipeg, the route never became permanent because of the inordinate number of rapids found along the river's course.

Sevier, Utah, USA

The Sevier rises in southwestern Utah at the junction of the Panguitch and Assay Rivers, north of the town of PANGUITCH. It is 325 miles (523 km) long and flows north and southwest past DELTA, through the Sevier Desert to enter Sevier Lake, the dry-bed remains of a once great ancient lake. Several reservoirs are built on the Sevier.

Shenandoah, West Virginia-Virginia, USA

The Shenandoah is the loveliest and most scenic of the smaller rivers of the eastern seaboard. Upstream from the mountain town of FRONT ROYAL where the Blue Ridge Mountains Skyline Drive begins, the river is made up of a North Fork and a South Fork divided by the Massanutten Mountain. The actual headwaters rise at an altitude of 4000 feet (1220 m) before making their way down to join one of the main channels. The river is very shallow and is broken by numerous rapids. During the summer season, many a weary tourist has stopped along the road to cool his feet in the waters of the Shenandoah. Some of the finest apples and apple cider are to be found in the nearby Blue Ridge Mountains. The river meanders, taking 34 miles (55 km) to cover 12 miles (19 km). Because of this meandering course cut through the floor of the limestone vale, the river is often completely hidden from view. Breathtaking scenic views can be obtained from the Blue Ridge Skyline Drive, a road which was built during the Roosevelt era, running along the crest of Blue Ridge Mountains in the Shenandoah National Park. The principal towns along the river are Front Royal and WAYNEBORO. The Shenandoah flows northeast to join the Potomac River near HARPERS FERRY. In 1859 John Brown, a fierce abolitionist, organized and led a raid in Harpers Ferry in protest against slavery. He was tried and executed for this act.

Sheyenne, North Dakota, USA

The Sheyenne rises in central North Dakota in Sheridan County. It is 325 miles (523 km) long and flows east and south past VALLEY CITY and LISBON before turning northeast to join the Red River of the North.

Shoshone, Wyoming, USA

The Shoshone rises in the Absaroka Range of northwestern Wyoming when the two chief headwaters, the North Fork and the South Fork, merge in central Park County to form the Buffalo Bill Reservoir. Emerging at the Buffalo Bill Dam, the Shoshone flows for 100 miles (160 km) northeast past the towns of RALSTON, BYRON and LOVELL before entering Bighorn Lake to join the Bighorn River.

Sico, Honduras

Also known as the Rio Negro or Rio Tinto, it rises in the Sierra de Agalta of eastern Honduras. It is 150 miles (240 km) long and flows northeast past GUALACO and SAN ESTEBAN to enter the Caribbean Sea east of IRIONA.

Silver Bow, Montana, USA

See Clark Fork, Montana-Idaho, USA.

Similkameen, Washington-British Columbia, USA-Canada

The river rises in the Cascade Range of northern Washington State. It is 140 miles (230 km) long and flows through northern Washington into British Columbia, past Copper Mountain to join the Okanogan River at OROVILLE.

Sinaloa, Mexico

The Sinaloa rises in the Sierra Madre Occidental in northwestern Mexico. It is 200 miles (320 km) long and flows southwest past the towns of SINALOA and GUASAVE to enter the Gulf of California approximately 17 miles (27 km) southwest of ANGOSTURA.

Siquia, Nicaragua

This small river rises near CAMOAPA in southern Nicaragua. It is 100 miles (160 km) long and flows east past SANTO DOMINGO to join the Mico and Rame Rivers at RAMA to form the Escondido River.

Sixaola, Costa Rica

The Sixaola River rises in the Cordillera de Talamanca of southeastern Costa Rica. It is 85 miles (137 km) long and runs north and east to enter the Caribbean Sea, southeast of LIMON. The river is navigable on its lower course and forms the border between Panama and Costa Rica.

Skagit, British Columbia-Washington, Canada-USA

The Skagit rises in the Cascade Range of British Columbia. It is 163 miles (262 km) long and flows southwest through WASHINGTON to enter Puget Sound.

Skeena, British Columbia, Canada

This medium sized river rises in the Skeena Mountains of north-central British Columbia. The Skeena is 360 miles (580 km) long and flows southeast, south and finally west before emptying into the Channel Sound of the Pacific Ocean. The chief tributaries are the Babine, Bulkley, Sustut, Kispiox and Kitsumgallum Rivers. The Skeena is navigable for approximately 100 miles (160 km) of its lower course but is seldom utilized; consequently traffic is very light. In 1872 a Hudson Bay trading post was established at HAZELTON, 150 miles (240 km) from the mouth and is still in operation today. Hazelton is of note now because it is the point where the Canadian National Railroad spans the river by a high suspension bridge, before continuing up the Babine Valley southeast. Another fact worthy of note is that all five species of Pacific salmon can be caught in the Skeena's waters. The value of the sockeye catch alone is in excess of $2 million annually. The fisheries and canneries between the mouth and Prince Rupert provide jobs for 2000 people. Besides Hazelton, there is only one other settlement on the river and that is located at TERRACE, 80 miles (129 km) from the mouth of the river.

Skunk, Iowa, USA

Formed by the junction of the North and South Skunk Rivers in central and southeastern Iowa, the Skunk River is 264 miles (425 km) long and runs southeast past AMES to join the Mississippi River seven miles (11 km) south of BURLINGTON.

Slate, Colorado, USA

The Slate River rises in northwestern Gunnison County, Colorado. It flows southeast through central Gunnison County to join the Taylor River near ALMONT, to form the Gunnison River.

Slave, Alberta-Northwest Territories, Canada

The Slave rises in northeastern Alberta, Canada. It is 258 miles (415 km) long and flows north-northwest past FORT FITZGERALD and FORT SMITH to enter the Great Slave Lake.

Smoky, Alberta, Canada

The Smoky rises in the Rocky Mountains of Alberta. It is 245 miles (394 km) long and winds its way north-northeast to join the Peace River.

Smoky Hill, Colorado-Kansas, USA

Smoky Hill and North Fork of Smoky Hill converge just west of RUSSELL SPRINGS in Kansas. The Smoky Hill is 560 miles (900 km) long and flows east into Wallace County, west Kansas, passing the towns of WALLACE and RUSSELL SPRINGS. It is joined by Ladder Creek near the boundary between Logan and Gove Counties. The river continues on its easterly course through the Cedar Bluff Reservoir in Trego County, and passes SCHOENCHEN, PFEIFER and ELLSWORTH, before entering the Kanopolis Reservoir. Reaching LINDSBORG,

the river turns north, then turns east-northeast at SALINA, a town of 37,714, and through the greatest wheat-belt in the world. At the town of SOLOMON, the Solomon River joins the Smoky Hill, and then heads past the great old cattle town of ABILENE. The first cattle town in Kansas was Abilene, and it was the destination of the great Texas cattle drives for over 50 years. The only other important tributary of the Smoky Hill is the Saline River which links up with the main river at SALINA. At JUNCTION CITY, Kansas, the Smoky Hill joins with the Republican River to form the Kansas River.

Snake, Nebraska, USA

The Snake rises as an intermittent stream in east-central Sheridan County, Nebraska. It runs east across central Cherry County, through the Merritt Reservoir and emerges to head north to join the Niobrara River not far from the South Dakota border.

Snake, Northwestern USA

The Snake is one of the most important rivers of the American northwest and is the principal tributary of the Columbia River. The Snake is 1038 miles (1670 km) long, drains an area of 109,000 square miles (282,000 sq km) and is ranked twelfth in volume of water carried of major US rivers. The river begins in southeastern Yellowstone National Park in Teton County, northwestern Wyoming. This mountainous region is extremely beautiful and tourists come here from all over North America just to see the spectacular wildlife and parklands. It heads southwest toward Idaho, passing through Jackson Lake in the Grand Teton National Park. Overlooking the river is the towering Grand Teton Peak, rising to a height of 13,766 feet (4199 m). The wildlife is typically North American: antelope, bison, bear, beaver, elk, deer, and moose, as well as other numerous species of animals and birds. Near the confluence with the Greys River, the Snake swings northwest and crosses into Idaho. Upon reaching the town of HEISE, the river leaves the mountains and enters southern Idaho in a large snakelike curve that ends near the junction of the Boise River. Heading north it forms the Oregon-Idaho border for 216 miles (346 km). From the northeastern part of Oregon, it flows along the border of Washington-Idaho as far as LEWISTON, Idaho, before swinging west to link with the Columbia River near the town of PASCO, Washington. The Snake drains 50 percent of the Columbia River Basin in the United States, including sections of Wyoming, Idaho,

Utah, Oregon, Nevada and Washington. The river is regulated by Jackson Lake, Palisades, American Falls, Minidoka and the Milner Reservoirs. The chief tributaries of the Snake are the Salmon, Henry Fork, Blackfoot, Portneuf, Raft, Little Wood and the Big Wood Rivers. The Snake River Plain is an immense hidden underground reservoir. The lower Snake, between WEISER and the confluence with the Columbia, flows through a deep gorge, known as Hells Canyon, and is one of the deepest gorges in North America. Southern Idaho has four main towns located on the Snake River: IDAHO FALLS, POCATELLO, TWIN FALLS and NAMPA. Besides its valuable water supply and scenic value, the Snake has one other great natural resource: the Pacific salmon which spawns in its waters. The Federal Government is taking action to protect this valuable asset.

Soleduck, Washington, USA
The river rises in the Olympic National Park in Clallam County in northwestern Washington. It flows northwest, west and southwest, past SAPPHO and BEAVER, to enter the Pacific Ocean at LA PUSH.

Below: Hell's canyon on the Snake River.

Solomon, Kansas, USA
The Solomon River is formed by the confluence of the North Fork, 210 miles (338 km) long and the South Fork, 150 miles (240 km) long, west of BELOIT in north Kansas. It is 140 miles (230 km) long and flows southeast to join the Smoky Hill River at the town of SOLOMON.

Sonora, Mexico
The Sonora begins very close to the US border in northwestern Mexico near the town of CANANEA. It is 250 miles (400 km) long and flows south and southwest past ARIZPE and HERMOSILLO to enter the Gulf of California opposite Tiburon Island. Its chief tributary is the San Miguel River.

Souris, Saskatchewan, Canada
The Souris rises in the southeastern part of Saskatchewan. It is 435 miles (700 km) long and flows southeast into North Dakota, past MINOT, then turns north into Manitoba to join the Assiniboine River.

Below: The Snake River.

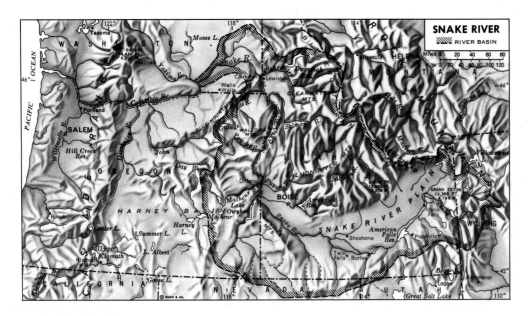

South Fork, Eel River, California, USA
The South Fork rises in Mendocino County in northwestern California. It is 90 miles (145 km) long and flows northwest to join the Eel River near WEOTT.

South Loup, Nebraska, USA
The South Loup River begins as an intermittent stream in central Logan County near STAPLETON, Nebraska. It is 152 miles (246 km) long and flows east, southeast and east-northeast to join the Middle Loup River near the town of BOELUS, Nebraska.

South Nahanni, Northwest Territories, Canada
This river rises in the mountains on the Yukon-Mackenzie border of the Canadian Northwest Territories. The river runs southeast for 250 miles (400 km) to become a tributary of the Liard River. The South Nahanni has some beautiful waterfalls called the Virginia Falls, which reach a height of 316 feet (96 m).

South Fork Skunk, Iowa, USA
This small river rises in Hamilton County in central Iowa. It flows south and southeast past CAMBRIDGE, COLFAX, REASNOR and PEORIA before joining the North Fork Skunk in Keokuk County to form the Skunk River.

South Platte, Colorado-Nebraska, USA
The South Platte rises in central Colorado in the Front Range of the Rocky Mountains. It is 424 miles (682 km) long and runs northeast from near the Florissant Fossil Beds National Monument. It flows through Lake Cheesman, and passes DECKERS, LITTLETON and between SHERIDAN and ENGLEWOOD, before entering the 'Mile High' city of DENVER, capital of Colorado. The chief Colorado tributaries of the South Platte are the Thompson River, Tarryall Creek, Boxelder Creek, Kiowa Creek, Bijou Creek, Pawnee Creek and Owl Creek. Between the towns of EVANS and KERSEY the river swings east, then takes a shallow southward dip, before steadying onto an easterly course across the border and into Nebraska. It passes through BIG SPRINGS, BRULE, OGALLALA, ROSCOE and PAXTON before joining the North Platte in the center of Lincoln County to form the Platte River.

Spanish, Ontario, Canada
The Spanish River issues forth from Spanish Lake in central Ontario. The river flows for 153 miles (246 km) south through Biskotasi and Agnew Lakes to ESPANOLA before turning west to enter Lake Huron.

Spoon, Illinois, USA
The Spoon rises in northern Stark County in northwestern Illinois. It flows south, southwest and southeast, past the towns of WYOMING and LONDON MILLS before joining the Illinois River opposite HAVANA.

Stewart, Yukon, Canada
The Stewart rises in the Mackenzie Mountains of the central Yukon. It is 320 miles (512 km) long and flows west past MAYO to join the Yukon River.

Staunton, Virginia, USA
See Roanoke, Virginia-North Carolina, USA.

Stikine, British Columbia-Alaska, Canada-USA
The Stikine rises near Mount Gunanoot in northern British Columbia. It is 335 miles (539 km) long and flows first north, then turns west through the Cassiar Mountains. The river flows through a 68-mile (109-km) long stretch which is known as the Grand Canyon of the Stikine before turning southwest across the Coast Ranges and the Alaskan Panhandle to enter the Pacific Ocean. The chief tributaries are the Klappan, the Tuya and the Iskut Rivers. The Stikine is navigable for 168 miles (270 km) of its course. This region is sparsely inhabited and can only boast of three small towns, WRANGEL in Alaska, and GLENORA and TELEGRAPH CREEK in British Columbia. The Stikine was utilized for a time as a route to the Klondike during the short-lived gold-rush days.

Sunflower, Mississippi, USA
The river rises in Coahoma County in northwestern Mississippi. It is 240 miles (390 km) long and runs south to join the Yazoo River in southwest Yazoo County.

Susitna, Alaska, USA
The Susitna rises on the glaciers high on Mount Hayes in the Alaskan Range of south Alaska. It is 300 miles (480 km) long and winds generally southwest past Curry, then swings south past TALKEETNA, CHULITNA and SUSITNA to enter the head of Cook Inlet approximately 25 miles (40 km) west of ANCHORAGE. Its chief tributaries are the Talkeetna and Yentna Rivers.

Susquehanna, Eastern USA
The Susquehanna is the largest river in the eastern seaboard of the United States. It rises in Otsego Lake, central New York State. It flows southwest into Chenango County, New York, then heads south into Susquehanna County of northeastern Pennsylvania. The river is 444 miles (714 km) long, drains an area of 27,570 square miles (71,410 sq km), and is ranked fourteenth in volume of water carried of major US rivers. The Susquehanna turns northwest to enter south central New York for a short distance before changing direction again, heading southward into Bradford County, Pennsylvania. The river flows southeast through the Allegheny Plateau, then enters the Ridge and Valley provinces, just north of Wilkes-Barre, before turning southwest through a large valley. Reaching SUNBURY, the North Fork is joined by the West Branch to form the main channel of the Susquehanna. The river turns southeast, crosses five ridges and forms several water-gaps, before flowing across the Piedmont Plateau to empty into the Chesapeake Bay at HAVRE DE GRACE, Maryland. The chief left-bank tributary is the Lackawanna and the chief right-bank tributaries are the Juniata and the Bald Eagle Rivers. Prior to the Pleistocene Ice Age, the Susquehanna drained most of New York State, but morainal deposits across the state blocked off the northern tributaries of the river. A large submarine channel at the mouth indicates the presence of a former valley extending eastward across the continental shelf. All major rivers of the eastern United States have large submarine valleys which extend well out into the Atlantic across the Continental Shelf. This, according to geologists, proves that this portion of North America was once well above present sea level. The chief cities along the river are BINGHAMTON, New York, WILKES-BARRE, Pennsylvania and HARRISBURG, Pennsylvania. The Susquehanna is not navigable due to numerous rock obstructions and its shallowness.

Sustut, British Columbia, Canada
The Sustut rises on the western Continental

Divide south of Thutade Lake in north-central British Columbia. The river flows southwest and west to join the Skeena River before that river cuts its way through the Skeena Mountains.

Suwannee, Georgia-Florida, USA

This river was made famous for all time by a song 'Swannee' written by Stephen Foster, and is believed to be a Black corruption of the Spanish *San Juanee* which means 'little St Johns.' The Suwannee rises in the dangerous Okefenokee Swamp in southern Georgia. It is 250 miles (400 km) long and flows southwest into Florida. The chief tributaries of the Suwannee are the Alapaha, Sante Fe and Withlacoochee Rivers, and Suwanoochee Creek. It winds through Florida forming the boundary between Hamilton and Columbia Counties, then passes WHITE SPRINGS, heading west between Hamilton and Suwannee Counties. It turns south at the tri-border of Hamilton, Suwannee and Madison Counties near the town of ELLAVILLE. Once past DOWLING PARK the river swings southeast, and is again the boundary between two counties, this time Suwannee and Lafayette Counties. As it passes BRANFORD, the Suwannee swings southwest to the Gulf of Mexico, which it enters near the town of SUWANNEE. In the 19th century the region surrounding the river was rich in cedar forests which have long since been cut down.

Tallahatchie, Mississippi, USA

This river is formed by the confluence of the Coldwater and the Little Tallahatchie Rivers in eastern Quitman County, northern Mississippi. It is 230 miles (370 km) long and flows southwest and south to join the Yalobusha River north of GREENWOOD to form the Yazoo River.

Tallapoosa, Georgia-Alabama, USA

The Tallapoosa River rises southwest of DALLAS in northwestern Georgia. It is 268 miles (431 km) long and flows west and southwest into Alabama, then south near HEFLIN and through Martin Lake, and finally west to join the Coosa River to form the Alabama River.

Tamesi, Mexico

This is a small river rising in the Sierra Madre Oriental, west of CIUDAD VICTORIA in northeastern Mexico. It is 250 miles (400 km) long and flows southeast and east past XICOTENCATL to enter the Gulf of Mexico through small lagoons northwest of TAMPICO.

Tanana, Alaska, USA

The Tanana River rises in the western Yukon on the northern slopes of the Wrangell Range of southeastern Alaska. It is 600 miles (970 km) long and flows basically west-northwest along the northern side of the Alaska Range. It passes the towns of TANACROSS, DOT LAKE and BIG DELTA at the confluence of the Delta River, RICHARDSON, Eielson AFB and NORTH POLE before reaching FAIRBANKS. This city is the

The Tar River of North Carolina near the town of Rocky Mount.

commercial center and supply hub for interior Alaska as well as the terminus of the Alaskan Railroad and Highway. Once past Fairbanks the river heads for NENANA, where it is joined by the Nenana River and is spanned by a 700-foot (214-m) railroad bridge. It then turns north to the small town of MINTO, approximately 40 miles (64 km) west of Fairbanks, then past MANLEY HOT SPRINGS. The river makes its final directional change, flowing west-northwest to join the Yukon River at the town of TANANA. The chief tributaries of the Tanana are the Delta, Nenana, Nabesna and the Kantishana Rivers.

Tar, North Carolina, USA

The Tar rises east of ROXBORO, North Carolina. It is 217 miles (349 km) long and flows southeast past LOUISBURG, GREENVILLE, the head of navigation and WASHINGTON to enter Pamlico Sound. Its estuary is called the Pamlico River below Washington and is 38 miles (61 km) long, and between one and five miles (one and a half and eight km) wide.

Taylor, Colorado, USA

The Taylor rises on the boundary of Gunnison and Pitkin Counties near Taylor Peak, 13,419 feet (4066 m) high, in Colorado. It flows southeast through Taylor Park Reservoir and emerges to head southwest to join the East River near ALMONT to form the Gunnison River.

Tempisque, Costa Rica

The Tempisque River rises on the slopes of the

Orosi volcano in northwestern Costa Rica. It is 80 miles (129 km) long and flows south and southeast past the towns of PALMIRA, FILADELFIA and BOLSON to enter the Pacific Ocean approximately 30 miles (48 km) northwest of PUNTARENAS.

Tennessee, East-central USA

The Tennessee River is the largest tributary of the Ohio River. It is 652 miles (1049 km) long, and drains an area of 40,910 square miles (105,960 sq km). The river derives its name from a Cherokee Indian village which was located on the Little Tennessee River, called 'Tennassee' or 'Tanase.' The Tennessee was thoroughly explored during the long period of rivalry between the French and the English, because both nations wanted the rich, virgin territory west of the Appalachian Mountains.

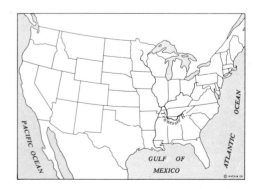

The territory along the Holston and Watauga Rivers, which is considered the upper valley of the Tennessee, was settled between 1770–80s. The role of the river was minute in comparison to that of the Ohio River. From the beginning the Tennessee was navigated with great difficulty, and then only by shallow-draft boats

Above: Visitors to Point Park can view the city of Chattanooga on the banks of the Tennessee River.

Above: A section of Canada's transcontinental train service follows British Columbia's Thompson River.

and rafts. The upper course of the river was extremely shallow, and filled with numerous short rapids which impeded navigation, except at high water. Also the run-offs from the Tennessee's mountain tributaries varied according to the season, resulting in periods of insufficient water for navigation and frequent downstream flooding. The middle section of the river through the Cumberlands was exceedingly dangerous, filled with whirlpools and the famous Muscle Shoals. The only section relatively easy to navigate was the lower section. During the American Civil War, the Tennessee was of great importance, as its valley offered the premier invasion route into the western Confederacy. Downstream the river is paralleled by the Cumberland River on which Fort Donelson was built, and only 12 miles (19 km) away was its sister base, Fort Henry, on the Tennessee. There are only two cities of importance on the Tennessee: KNOXVILLE located at the head of navigation; and CHATTANOOGA, a transportation and communication center as well as a beautiful city. Other large towns on the river are GUNTERSVILLE, DECATUR, FLORENCE and TUSCUMBIA. There are numerous dams and reservoirs along the river valley, all integral parts of the Tennessee Valley Authority Project (TVA), including the Barkley, Kentucky, Pickwick, Wilson, Wheeler, Tims Ford, Cheatham, Old Hickory, J P Priest, Center Hill, Wolf Creek, Dale Hollow, Great Falls, Chickamauga, Guntersville, Nickajack, Apalachia, Blue Ridge, Chatuge, Ocoee, Hiwassee, Fontana, Watts Bar, Tellico, Melton Hill, Norris, South Holston, Fort Loudoun, Douglas, Watauga, Fort Patrick Henry, Boone and the Cherokee. The TVA is the most extensive river project in the world, and was initiated in 1933 to control the river, prevent flooding and provide hydroelectric power for the seven state area of Alabama, Georgia, Kentucky, Tennessee, Mississippi, North Carolina and

Virginia. The present day capacity of the TVA is in the region of 12,000,000 kilowatts. The chief tributaries of the Tennessee are the Clinch, Elk, Rock, Emory, Little Tennessee and the Hiwassee Rivers. The river is actually formed by the confluence of the Holston and the French Broad Rivers approximately four miles (six km) above the city of Knoxville, Tennessee. The river flows south-southeast initially to Chattanooga, then turns west through the Cumberland Plateau. It heads into northeastern Alabama, then turns north forming the border between Alabama and Mississippi for a distance before crossing into Tennessee and Kentucky to join the Ohio River at PADUCAH, Kentucky.

Teton, Montana, USA
The Teton is a beautiful river rising in the northwestern region of Teton County on the eastern Continental Divide, Montana. It is 143 miles (242 km) long and flows generally eastward across Teton County, past CHOTEAU and COLLINS, then into Choteau County where it joins the Marias River near LOMA. The Teton flows through some of Montana's most scenic countryside.

Thames, Ontario, Canada
The Thames River rises north-northwest of WOODSTOCK in southern Ontario. It is 160 miles (260 km) long and flows southwest past WOODSTOCK, LONDON and CHATHAM to enter Lake St Clair.

Thelon, Northwest Territories, Canada
The Thelon rises to the east of the Great Slave Lake in the Canadian Northwest Territories.

This region is one of tundra and is a sparsely populated area. The Thelon is 550 miles (880 km) long and widens out into a series of lakes at the border of Keewatin District. The four chief bodies of water, Lakes Beverley, Aberdeen, Schultz and Baker cover an area of 1100 square miles (2850 sq km) before running into the slim 140-mile (230-km) long Chesterfield Inlet of Hudson Bay. The chief tributaries are the Dubawnt River, which is 580 miles (930 km) long, and the Kazan or White Partridge River, which is 455 miles (732 km) long. The first inhabitants of this region were the Caribou or Keewatin Eskimos who for centuries lived off a basic diet of caribou meat. Later settlements forced a change in the migratory route of the caribou and the great depletion of the natural wildlife resources has led to the relocation of some of the Eskimo families. The main settlements are located at Baker Lake and Chesterfield Inlet where Hudson Bay Company trading posts are located, as well as a small landing strip and Canadian Mounted Police post.

Thompson, British Columbia, Canada
The Thompson is formed by the confluence of the North and South Thompson Rivers at the town of KAMLOOPS, British Columbia. It is 304 miles (489 km) long and flows west and south to join the Fraser River at LYTTON. The length of the Thompson is measured from its furthest headstream, the North Thompson River.

Tioughnioga, New York, USA
This river rises in northwestern Cortland County, New York. It is 70 miles (113 km) long and flows south-southeast past the towns of CORTLAND, TRUXTON, LISLE and WHITNEY

POINT before joining the Chenango River at CHENANGO FORKS.

Tioga, Pennsylvania-New York, USA

The Tioga rises in Tioga County, northern Pennsylvania. It flows north past BLOSSBURG, COVINGTON and TIOGA before crossing into New York State to join the Canisteo River in Steuben County.

Tippecanoe, Indiana, USA

The Tippecanoe rises in Kosciusko County, Indiana and flows west-northwest initially. The name of the river comes from the Miami Indian word for 'place of buffalo fish.' The river flows generally southwest passing through Marshall, Fulton, Pulaski and White Counties before running through Lake Shaefer and Lake Freeman to join the Wabash River. The river was the scene of a major battle in 1811 between the US troops of William Henry Harrison, later a president of the United States, and a confederation under the Shawnee chief, Tecumseh. The Tippecanoe is 180 miles (290 km) long and flows through what is now one of the most heavily populated areas of the state.

Tombigbee, Mississippi-Alabama, USA

The Tombigbee rises in Prentiss County, Mississippi and flows for a total of 384 miles (618 km) in a southeasterly direction. The main headwaters of the Tombigbee are the East and West Forks which flow down from the fall line hills of northeastern Mississippi. The river runs south through Itawamba, Monroe and Lowndes Counties before crossing into Alabama at the northeastern corner of Lowndes and Noxubee Counties. The Tombigbee is crossed by two famous old roads of the region, the Natchez Trace and Gaines Trace. In the heyday of the cotton trade, the river was utilized to ship the white gold of the South from such old river ports as COTTON GIN PORT and PLYMOUTH. The river now flows southeastward receiving the Noxubee River before entering Demopolis Lake. The main tributaries of the Tombigbee are the Sipsey, which runs from northwestern Alabama and flows south and southwest to join the main channel at the borders of Pickens, Greene and Sumter Counties; the Black Warrior, which links the Tombigbee with the BIRMINGHAM industrial area; and the Buttahatchee, which rises in northwestern Alabama and flows southwest to enter the Tombigbee in Lowdnes County near COLUMBUS, Mississippi. The river is canalized by numerous dams and locks, such as the Demopolis Dam, located at the southwestern terminus of the two rivers, and the Warrior Dam, situated just below EUTAW, Alabama. The Tombigbee for its size carries a tremendous load of traffic between MOBILE and Birmingham. Along the fertile river valleys are large mounds which date back to 1000 BC. Below JACKSON, in Clarke County, Alabama, the river flows through the Tombigbee National Forest which is a huge forest and swamp area extremely bountiful in game. The Tombigbee River joins the Alabama to form the twin rivers of the Mobile and the Tensaw which make a combined delta in Mobile Bay.

Tongue, Wyoming, USA

The Tongue rises on the precipitous eastern slopes of the Bighorn Mountains near the town of SHERIDAN, Wyoming. It is 246 miles (396 km) long and joins the Yellowstone River at MILES CITY, Montana. Near ASHLAND, Montana is the Tongue Indian Reservation, home of the Northern Cheyenne.

Touchet, Washington, USA

The Touchet rises in the Blue Mountains of Columbia County in southeastern Washington. It flows north to DAYTON, then west and south to join the Walla Walla River at the town of TOUCHET, which flows through Oregon for much of its length.

Trinity, Texas, USA

The Trinity is formed by the confluence of the West and the Clear Forks in northeastern Texas. The river is 510 miles (820 km) long. The West Fork rises in several intermittent streams south of WICHITA FALLS, a city of 127,100. It then flows southeast to FORT WORTH, which has a population of 762,000 and is the largest sheep market in the United States. The Clear Fork begins in Parker County, and flows southeast, then swings northeast to join the West Fork at Fort Worth. The Trinity now flows east to DALLAS, which is one of the leading cities of Texas with a population of 1,555,000. At Dallas the Trinity receives the Elm Fork, which is 100 miles (160 km) long and rises in Montague County. The river continues on a generally south-southeast course, passing through Lake Livingstone before entering Trinity Bay, the northeastern arm of Galveston Bay. The river is navigable for approximately 40 miles (64 km) upstream by shallow-bottomed vessels as far as LIBERTY.

Truckee, California-Nevada, USA

The Truckee River rises on the border between California and Nevada in *Lake Tahoe*, one of the most beautiful lakes of the Pacific West. It is 120 miles (190 km) long and flows northeast past TRUCKEE and RENO to enter Pyramid Lake. In bygone days Pyramid Lake was a huge body of water, and the local Indian tribes relied heavily on it for their food supply and livelihood, but today it is only a shadow of its once great size.

Tucannon, Washington, USA

The Tucannon rises in the Blue Mountains of southeastern Columbia County, Washington State. It flows northwest past STARBUCK to join the Snake River. Its chief tributary is Pataha Creek which rises at the town of PATAHA in Garfield County.

Tuira, Panama

The Tuira is the longest river in Panama with a length of 125 miles (201 km). It rises in the Darien Highlands and flows northwest and north past the towns of PINOGANA, EL REAL and CHEPIGANA to enter the San Miguel Gulf of the Pacific Ocean, to form the Puerto Darien estuary at LA PALMA. The river is navigable for 80 miles (129 km) above the mouth.

Tuscarawas, Ohio, USA

The Tuscarawas River rises in northern Tuscarawas County in east-central Ohio. It flows south and west past NEW PHILADELPHIA, MIDVALE, TUSCARAWAS and PORT WASHINGTON before crossing into Coshocton County. It then proceeds westward to join the Walhonding River to form the Muskingum River at COSHOCTON.

Tuxpan, Mexico

See San Pedro, Mexico (2).

Twisp, Washington, USA

The Twisp rises at Twisp Pass on the eastern slopes of the Cascade Range. It flows east-southeast through central Okanogan County to join the Chewack River at TWISP, Washington.

Ulua, Honduras

The Ulua rises east of MARCALA in western Honduras. It is approximately 200 miles (320 km) long and flows north past PORTER-ILLOS and EL PROGRESO to enter the Gulf of Honduras east-northeast of PUERTO CORTES.

Uncompaghre, Colorado, USA

The Uncompaghre rises in southern Ouray County, Colorado. It flows northwest past OURAY, PORTLAND and RIDGWAY to join the Gunnison River at DELTA, Colorado.

Usumacinta, Guatemala-Mexico

This river rises as the Rio Salinas in the Sierra de los Altos of Huehuetenango Department in north-central Guatemala. The Usumacinta is 270 miles (430 km) long and is navigable for 250 miles (400 km). It flows north through the Indian highlands. Once past the town of SALINAS, it becomes the Chixoy River. The river does not actually assume the name of Usumacinta until after the Rio de la Pasion joins it on the border of Mexico. Now the Usumacinta forms the boundary between Mexico and Guatemala for slightly over 185 miles (298 km). It leaves the border and continues northward passing the towns of TENOSIQUE DE PINO SUAREZ and BALANCAN in Tabsco State before entering the Gulf of Mexico. Some of Mexico's most valued archeological sites are adjacent to the river: BONAMPAK which is renowned for its priceless murals, and YAXCHILAN which is situated on the banks of the Usumacinta and known for its beautiful ancient temples.

Verde, Arizona, USA

The Verde rises 30 miles (48 km) southeast of the town of SELIGMAN in central Arizona. It is 190 miles (310 km) long and flows south past CLARKDALE and COTTONWOOD to join the Salt River east-northeast of PHOENIX. The Verde Valley is rich in ancient Indian artifacts and remains, especially at Montezuma Castle.

Verdigris, Kansas, USA

The Verdigris River rises southwest of

EMPORIA in southeastern Kansas. It is 351 miles (565 km) long and flows south-southeast past ALTOONA, then south past COFFEYVILLE and into Oklahoma to join the Arkansas River northeast of MUSKOGEE. It provides the water for two reservoirs, the Toronto and the Oologah.

Virgin, Utah, USA

The Virgin is formed by the confluence of the North and South Virgin Rivers in southwestern Utah. It is 200 miles (320 km) long and flows southwest through the northwestern part of Arizona to enter Lake Mead in southeastern Nevada.

Wabash, Ohio, USA

The Wabash rises in Grand Lake in western Ohio. The river was once a spillway of the ancient glacial Lake Maumee – Lake Erie is today's small remnant. The Wabash is 529 miles (851 km) long, drains an area of 33,000 square miles (85,500 sq km) and flows westward across Indiana, then swings south near the western border of the state. It is the boundary between Indiana and Illinois for about 200 miles (320 km). During the 18th century it was widely utilized as a major transportation route between Louisiana and Quebec. The river is navigable, but has not been much used since the coming of the railroads. The chief tributaries of the Wabash are the White, Tippecanoe, Vermilion, Little Wabash and the Embarrass Rivers. In Indian times the Wabash supported a large indigenous population and was the most accessible route between Lake Erie and the Ohio Valley. The Indians called the river 'water over white stones' and the French equivalent was Oubache. The Wabash is one of the most historical of American rivers. During the American Civil War, the Battle of Vincennes was fought on its banks. Walks along the Wabash in the spring and the summer months take one through some memorable American countryside.

Waccamaw, North Carolina, USA

This small river rises in Lake Waccamaw in southeastern North Carolina. It is 140 miles (224 km) long and flows southwest to enter Winyah Bay near GEORGETOWN, South Carolina.

Waimea, Kauai, Hawaii, USA

The Waimea River rises on the northwestern slopes of Mt Waialeale, a peak which is 5080 feet (1550 m) high. It flows northwest, and northeast to enter Hanalei Bay near WAINIHA. Although only a tiny stream, it is surrounded by the lovely scenery which only the Hawaiian islands can offer.

Walnut, Kansas, USA

This river is formed by several headstreams in Butler County in southern Kansas. It is 121 miles (195 km) long and flows southwest past EL DORADO, then south past AUGUSTA and WINFIELD to join the Arkansas River at ARKANSAS CITY.

Wapsipinicon, Iowa, USA

This river rises north-northwest of MCINTIRE in Mitchell County in northeastern Iowa. It is 225 miles (362 km) long and flows southeast past ELMA, FREDERICKA, TRIPOLI, LITTLETON, OTTERVILLE, TROY MILLS, PARIS, CENTRAL CITY, WAUBEEK, STONE CITY, ANAMOSA, HALE, OXFORD JUNCTION, OXFORD MILLS and TORONTO, before joining the Mississippi River northeast of DAVENPORT.

Wateree, South Carolina, USA

The Wateree is in reality only an extension of the Catawba River between Wateree Lake and its junction with the Congaree River approximately 30 miles (48 km) southeast of Columbia, South Carolina. The Wateree is 75 miles (121 km) long and with the Congaree forms the Santee River which continues southeast to enter the Atlantic Ocean.

Weiser, Idaho, USA

The Weiser River rises in central Adams County, Idaho. It flows south and west, past FRUITVALE, COUNCIL, CAMBRIDGE and WEISER. It joins the Snake River at WEISER on the Oregon border.

White, Indiana, USA

The White River rises in two branches in Indiana; the West Fork begins in Randolph County in southwestern Indiana and flows 255 miles (410 km) west and southwest past Indianapolis to join the East Fork, which is 282 miles (454 km) long, near PETERSBURG. The White River then flows 52 miles (84 km) southwest to join the Wabash River opposite MOUNT CARMEL, Illinois.

White, Nebraska-South Dakota, USA

The White River rises in the Pine Ridge Hills of northwestern Nebraska and is 507 miles (816 km) long. It flows northeast passing the old frontier towns of CRAWFORD and CHADRON, the rail point for the Chicago and North Western Railroads. The river is utilized to irrigate the nearby potato, alfalfa and grain fields. Upon entering South Dakota, the White flows northeast through lush grassy hills of the Pine Ridge Indian Reservation, a large center of the Sioux Nation. The White borders the southern edge of the Badlands of South Dakota. The scene of many Western motion pictures, the Badlands are made up of bright and colorful rocks, which have been sculpted into various shapes and sizes by wind and water erosion. The chief tributary of the river is the Little White River or South Fork, which joins the main channel at the town of WESTOVER. The White becomes a tributary of the mighty Missouri southwest of CHAMBERLAIN.

Wichita, Texas, USA

The Wichita River rises in several intermittent streams in north-central Texas. It is 250 miles (400 km) long and flows east and northeast past WICHITA FALLS to join the Red River. Below Wichita Falls large dams have created Lake Kemp and Diversion Reservoir.

Willamette, Oregon, USA

The Willamette Valley was one of the first regions to be settled in the Oregon Territory, and is today the most densely populated area of the state. The river is 270 miles (430 km) long and drains an area of 11,200 square miles (29,000 sq km), and is ranked fifteenth in size of the large rivers of the United States in order of average discharge. It rises at the confluence of the Coast Fork and the Middle Fork in the Cascade Range near the town of EUGENE, Oregon. The principal tributaries, of which the Mckenzie and the Santiam Rivers are the most notable, rise in the eastern Cascades at a height of 10,000 feet (3050 m). These small rivers are dammed to provide power and flood control for the Willamette Valley. The main city on the river is PORTLAND (with a population of 1,009,129) located near the mouth of the Willamette before its confluence with the Columbia River. The Willamette Valley is noted for its dairy cattle and fine agricultural products.

Wind, Wyoming, USA

The Wind rises in the Wind River Range of the Rocky Mountains in the west-central region of Wyoming. It is so named because of the severe winds along its upper section. The Wind River is 110 miles (180 km) long and flows southwest through some of Wyoming's loveliest countryside before joining the Bighorn River.

Winnipeg, Manitoba, Canada

The Winnipeg rises in the Lake of the Woods, is 475 miles (764 km) long and drains an area of 48,880 square miles (126,600 sq km). It was discovered by Pierre de la Verendrye and Christopher de la Jemeraye in 1733. The waterfalls and rapids on the lower course of the river supply most of the power for Manitoba. The chief hydroelectric stations on the river are the Seven Sisters and Great Falls, Point du Bois and Slave Falls, and Pine Falls and McArthur Falls.

Wisconsin, Wisconsin, USA

The Wisconsin River rises in the Superior Uplands of northern Wisconsin near the borders of Michigan in an area literally studded with small and beautiful lakes. It is 430 miles (690 km) long and flows south through the 'cutover lands.' Once the greatest coniferous forests in North America. The forests were cut down in the 1880s and 1890s without today's knowledge of conservation. Soon wind and water eroded the unprotected landscape. Recently the replanting of trees and conservation has rectified the situation somewhat.

There are over 50 hydroelectric power stations on the Wisconsin. In the upper region of the river's course are the large pulp-and-paper-mill towns of RHINELANDER, TOMAHAWK, WAUSAU and WISCONSIN RAPIDS, all of which were built near waterfalls where dams now provide power for the mills. The Wisconsin continues southward through Petenwell Flowage and Castle Rock Flowage, then shifts slightly southeastward through the Wisconsin Dells, near the Fox River's source. The ancient route, the Fox-Wisconsin, was utilized by the Indians for centuries, and was traveled by the famous French explorers Louis Jolliet and Jacques Marquette in 1673. Upon reaching the town of PORTAGE, which has a population of 7821, the river turns southwest passing PRAIRIE DU SAC, SAUK CITY, LONE ROCK and BRIDGEPORT before joining the Mississippi below the once important French trading post of PRAIRIE DU CHIEN, which is today only a small agricultural town with a population of little over 5000.

Wolf, Wisconsin, USA
The Wolf rises in Forest County in northeastern Wisconsin. It is 220 miles (354 km) long and flows south past the towns of SHAWANO and NEW LONDON, then through Lake Poygan. It finally joins the Fox River above OSHKOSH.

Wood, Wyoming, USA
The Wood rises at the foot of Mt Crosby, a peak 12,435 feet (3793 m) high, in Park County, Wyoming. It is roughly 40 miles (64 km) long and flows east-northeast to join the Greybull River.

Yadkin, North Carolina, USA
The Yadkin River rises in northwestern North Carolina. It flows south-southeast through High Rock Lake and Lake Tillery. The river is considered to be the upper course of the Pee Dee River, which flows from the border of South Carolina southeast to enter the Atlantic Ocean near GEORGETOWN. The total length of both rivers is 435 miles (700 km).

Yakima, Washington, USA
This river rises in the Cascade Range of southern Washington State. It is 203 miles (327 km) long and flows southeast past ELLENSBURG and YAKIMA to join the Columbia River near the town of KENNEWICK.

Above right: The Yellowstone River in Wyoming.
Below: Yellowstone National Park is also noted for fishing especially for trout.

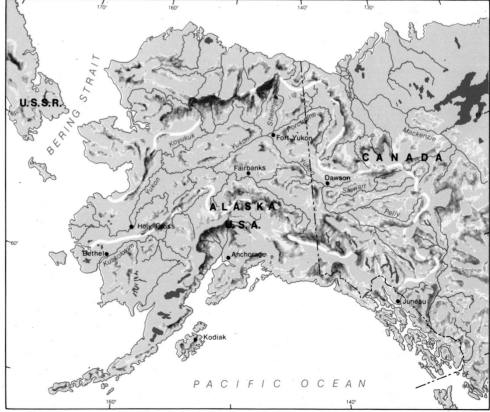

Yaqui, Mexico

The Yaqui rises in northern Sonora State at the confluence of the Bavispe River and other smaller streams just north of SAHUARIPA in northwestern Mexico. It is 420 miles (680 km) long including its longest tributary. It flows south and southwest through a large delta to enter the Gulf of California 28 miles (45 km) southeast of GUAYMAS.

Yampa, Colorado, USA

The Yampa rises near STEAMBOAT SPRINGS, Routt County in the Rocky Mountains of northwestern Colorado. It is 250 miles (400 km) long and flows westward past MILNER, CRAIG, MAYBELL, SUNBEAM and through DINOSAUR NATIONAL MONUMENT, before joining the Green River. Its chief tributaries are the Elk River, Trout Creek and Williams Fork.

Yazoo, Mississippi, USA

The Yazoo River rises in central Mississippi at the confluence of the Tallahatchie and Yalobusha Rivers north of GREENWOOD. It is 189 miles (304 km) long and flows south-southwest through the Yazoo flood plain to join the Mississippi River at the town of VICKSBURG. The Yazoo Valley is noted for its cotton. Vicksburg was the scene of a great victory for the Federal forces under Ulysses S Grant during the American Civil War.

Yantic, Connecticut, USA

The Yantic rises on the boundary between Toland and New London Counties in central Connecticut. It flows south-southeast through BREWSTER POND, past GILMAN, FITCHVILLE and YANTIC to join the Quinebaug River in forming the Thames River near NORWICH.

Yellowstone, Wyoming-Montana, USA

The Yellowstone rises near the Continental Divide of the Absaroka Range of northwestern Wyoming. It flows north through Yellowstone Lake located in the Yellowstone National Park, which is the home of some of the finest wildlife specimens in the West, and the famous geyser, 'Old Faithful,' named for its predictability. This region is full of volcanic activity; hot springs and geysers are the commonest examples. The river leaves Yellowstone Lake at LAKE FISHING BRIDGE-BRIDGE BAY, a tiny town of 167 people. It then flows through the town of CANYON, swings northeast near Mt Washburn, a peak 10,243 feet (3124 m) high. Inspiration Point and Artist Point are the two main lookout points over the Grand Canyon of the Yellowstone, which is famous for its beautiful coloring. The river turns north past TOWER and Tower Falls and is joined by the Lamar River a few miles further on. It crosses over into Montana and runs past GARDINER, the Gateway to Yellowstone National Park, situated in the greatest elk hunting region in America. The Yellowstone continues on past Corwin Springs, then curves northeast again, passing the towns of PRAY, LIVINGSTON and SPRINGDALE in Park County, Montana. Between Livingston and Springdale is the confluence with the Shields River, which comes down from the northern part of Park County. It now flows east-northeast for the remainder of its course, passing BIG TIMBER and GREYCLIFF in Sweet Grass County, REEDPOINT and COLUMBUS in Stillwater County, BILLINGS, NIBBE and CUSTER in Yellowstone County, then past FORSYTH, MILES CITY, GLENDIVE, SAVAGE and CRANE before reaching FORT UNION where it joins the Missouri River. The chief tributaries of the Yellowstone are the Stillwater, the Tongue, the Powder and the Bighorn Rivers. The Yellowstone is 671 miles (1080 km) long, drains an area of 70,000 square miles (181,300 sq km), and irrigates over 20,000 acres of land.

Yockanookany, Mississippi, USA

The Yockanookany rises in Choctaw County, central Mississippi. It flows southwest past the towns of WEIR, MCCOOL, ETHEL and OFAHOMA before joining the Pearl River.

Yukon, Yukon Territory-Alaska, Canada-USA

The Yukon is the fifth longest river in North America with a total length of 1979 miles (3184 km). It is navigable for 1775 miles (2856 km). The Yukon is formed by the confluence of the Lewes and the Pelly Rivers at FORT SELKIRK. The Lewes is sometimes referred to as the Upper Yukon and the

farthest headstream of the river is the Nisutlin River which has its source in British Columbia. The drainage basin of the Yukon is 320,000 square miles (828,800 sq km) of which 127,000 square miles (204,300 sq km) are located within Canada. The river heads north past DAWSON, where it is slightly more than a mile (1610 m) wide, then swings northwest past FORTY MILE and across into Alaska to FORT YUKON. The river then moves west and southwest across Alaska to enter the Bering Sea through several channels, one of which is navigable. Between Selkirk and Dawson the river is sprinkled with islands of all shapes and sizes. From the Stewart River to Dawson, the river flows in long wide stretches bordered on both sides by mountains. Once past Dawson the Yukon flows across the border into Alaskan Territory and is bordered by hills and has only one principal channel. The Yukon has great hydroelectric potential in its upper reaches. Because of the uniform gradient of the river and its numerous tributaries, the Yukon could, with proper planning and direction, become the prime source of hydroelectric power in northwestern North America. The chief tributaries of the Yukon are the Tanana, Koyukuk, Innoko, Chandalar, Stewart, Klondike, Porcupine and White Rivers plus numerous small creeks and streams. The Yukon River is best remembered for its gold rush days, but as a long-term natural resource it will continue to play a major role in the development of the Pacific Northwest.

Zuni, New Mexico-Arizona, USA

The Zuni River rises in the Zuni Mountains in McKinley County in northwestern New Mexico. It flows southwest through the Zuni Indian Reservation, past the town of ZUNI, (population 3,958) and crosses into Arizona to join the Little Colorado River in south-central Apache County.

Left and below: The Yukon River crosses the vast expanses of Alaska.
Right: The Iguaçu Falls on the Iguaçu River.

South America

Abuná, Bolivia

The Abuná rises near the border of Bolivia and Brazil to the southwest of the town of SANTA ROSA. The river is 210 miles (340 km) long, and runs on a northeasterly course to join the Madeira River at MANOA as a tributary. The Abuná is navigable for its entire length.

Acará, Brazil

The Acará River rises in the eastern region of Pará state, Brazil. The river is 207 miles (333 km) long, and flows east to join the Guajara River south of the port of BELEM, a city of over 560,000 and one of Brazil's major seaports. The Acará becomes a tributary of the much larger Pará River which continues on into the Atlantic Ocean.

Aconcagua, Chile

This river flows through one of the finest natural agricultural valleys in Chile. It is noted for wheat, numerous fruits and excellent tobacco. The river is 120 miles (190 km) long, and flows from the foot of the Aconcagua massif, which is 22,831 feet (6961 m) high, to where it enters the Pacific Ocean at CONCON, northeast of the city of VALPARAISO, which has a population of over 300,000.

Acre, Peru

The river rises in the mountains along the Peruvian-Brazilian borders near the Brazilian state of Acre. The river runs northeast, first passing the border town of Brasiléia, then continues on past RION BRANCO and PORTO ACRE. Finally it reaches XAPURI, the head of the river's navigation. The Acre is slightly over 400 miles long (640 km), and joins the larger Purús River after leaving BOCA DO ACRE.

Aguapeí, Brazil

The Aguapeí rises in the western portion of São Paulo State to the west of the town of PIRAJUI. It is slightly over 200 miles (320 km) long, and flows on a northwesterly course to become a tributary of the Paraná River. The Aguapeí is navigable for a short distance on its lower course.

Amacuro, Venezuela

The Amacuro rises high on the borders between Guyana and Venezuela in the northeastern tip of the South American continent. The river is slightly over 102 miles (164 km) long. It flows along the border for a short distance before swinging to a northwesterly course. The outlet of the Amacuro is one of the mouths of the Orinoco River which flows into the Atlantic Ocean.

Amambaí, Brazil

The Amambaí rises in the southern region of the Mato Grosso, the great plains area of western Brazil. Small compared to its giant neighbors, it is 150 miles (240 km) long. The river flows from the Paraguay border to join the Paraná River above the Guaíra Falls. The Guaíra Falls or Sete Quedas Falls are spectacular cataracts of great beauty on the

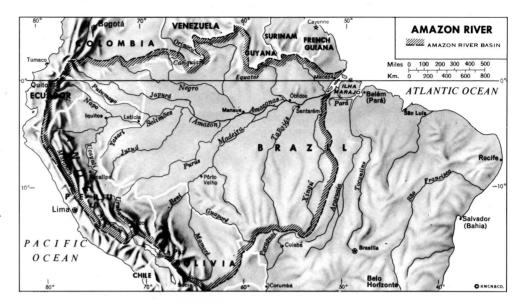

The floating village of Belén in Iquitos, Peru on the Amazon.

Alto Paraná River near the Brazil-Paraguay border. In total there are 18 cataracts, the highest falling over 100 feet (30 m).

Amazon, Brazil

This river has an aura of mystery and intrigue about it and has been the subject chosen by many great writers for works of fact and fiction alike. It is the largest river system in the world not only in respect of the volume of water carried but also in drainage area. The Amazon is 3915 miles (6299 km) long and drains an area 2,722,000 square miles (7,499,000 sq km) which encompasses over 50 percent of the entire South American continent, and supports the largest tropical rainforest in the world. The Amazon's discharge rate is seven times greater than North America's Mississippi River.

The source of the Amazon is high in Lake Lauricocha at a height of over 13,000 feet (3939 m) in the Andes Mountain Range of

Peru. The river rises as the Marañón, only 125 miles (201 km) northeast of the Peruvian capital of LIMA. It runs on a northwesterly course for a distance before turning northeasterly down a series of large cataracts and *pongos* (the native word for gorges) breaking through into the vast plains below at the Pongo de Manseriche. This huge gorge is over 2000 feet (600 m) deep and is a true natural wonder. Once the river leaves Peruvian territory, the name changes to Solimões, a name it retains until its confluence with the Negro River. The major tributaries of the Amazon are in their own right some of the major rivers of the world:

Xingu 1304 miles (2098 km)
    Navigable
Tapajós 807 miles (1298 km)
    Navigable for 188 miles (302 km)
Madeira 2013 miles (3239 km)
    Navigable for 807 miles (1298 km)
Purús 1995 miles (3210 km)
    The most crooked river in the world.
Juruá 621 miles (999 km)
    Navigable

The Amazon near Manaus

Javari 656 miles (1056 km)
    Navigable
Ucayali 1000 miles (1609 km)
    Partly navigable

From the high Andes extending in an arc running 1500 miles (2410 km) from the Colombian border to Bolivia, numerous tributaries swell the waters of the river. The Amazon is very much like a human heart: it collects all the water from the tributaries and carries it to the central dispatching station, the Atlantic Ocean. The major tributaries and largest are the Madeira and Negro Rivers which, for all practical purposes, drain the huge expanses of the Brazilian and Guiana massifs before joining the Amazon near the interior city of MANAUS. A city of over 285,000, Manaus which is located 1000 miles (1600 km) upstream on the banks of the Negro, is the focus of commerce for the entire upper Amazonian basin. Further upstream from the Negro, tributaries of note are the Japurá, Putumayo and the Napo which all flow on an easterly course. Once past the port of Manaus, the tributaries of the northern regions become much shorter in length. This is due primarily to the fact that they are flowing from the neighboring Guiana massif and consequently do not have a long distance to run before joining the Amazon. During the month of June, the Amazon is in its flood stage, caused by the increased volume of water which the Huallaga, Ucayali, Purús, Juruá, Tapajós and Xingu (the first four from the Andes and the latter two from the high Brazilian plateau) bring down into the already flooding river. At one time in past ages, the Tocantins-Araguaia River system was part of the Amazon system and added its water to the larger river, but this is no longer the case, as the Tocantins system is now classified as a separate and distinct system.

It was not until the years 1541–42 that the Amazon became known to the world. It was then that Francisco de Orellana made his famous exploration trip from the confluence of the Napo River to the Amazon. Later settlements were very limited as only sites located near major river confluences were considered suitable for development. This left the dense tropical forests virtually unexplored. Today, these same forests are still largely unexplored and unmapped. But with the advent of modern technology, man is reducing the unexplored Amazon frontier and in the not too distant future will eventually conquer the entire basin. The modern capital of Brazil, BRASILIA, is a prime example of how to open up the interior of the country and utilize its virtually untapped natural resources. Brasília, the new capital, with a population of over 500,000 is only the first stepping stone in the conquest of the Brazilian interior.

The Amazon is an example of a reversed drainage system. Long ago the river flowed from its source near OBIDOS westward to the Pacific Ocean but this pre-dated the rise of the Andes Mountains which caused the river to flow east through an already filled basin of immense proportions. The flat saucer-shaped area of the upper basin and its large meandering rivers are explained by the rise of the Andes. This also explains why there is so little fall in altitude on the Amazon on its run to the sea from IQUITOS. The fall, spread over 2300 miles (3700 km) of length, is negligible especially as it is only 350 feet (106 m). The Amazon has one of the most immense flood plains in the world, averaging between 30 to 40 miles (48 to 64 km) wide in its lower reaches. This area is particularly prone to flooding, especially during the heavy tropical rainfalls in the upper basin which, by the time it reaches Iquitos, is 20 feet (six m) high; at Manaus it amounts to 40 feet (12 m). Consequently any settlements close to the river and not built upon high ground would be washed away. Owing to the weight of the sheer volume of water it carries, the current of the river is only two to three miles (three to five km) per hour, but the river makes up for this slowness by its immense width. The Amazon is between four to six miles (six to ten km) wide on long stretches and is between 75 feet (23 m) deep at Manaus and measures over 200 feet (60 m) deep at Obidos. The one thing which the river truly lacks is a proper delta. The reason for this is because of land subsidence near the mouth of the river. The Amazon has an estuary-like mouth caused by the rise of the Andes Range which forced the continent to tilt eastward resulting in interconnecting channels through whatever land is above water level. In the mouth of the river is one of the great riverine islands of the world, Marajo Island, which is slightly over 180 miles (290 km) long and 100 miles (160 km) wide, encompassing a large area of land. The Amazon is navigable for ocean-going vessels as far as Iquitos in Peru but the chief seaport of the river is BELEM, a city of over 450,000 people, located on the Rio do Pará. The Amazon region is noted for rubber plantations and jungles. Its high humidity and extreme heat together with the daily falls of rain make it one of the most unhealthy climates in the world. The local swamps are infested with crocodiles, anacondas, electric eels and the most voracious of fish, piranhas. A school of piranhas has been known to strip an entire cow in less than one minute. It is no wonder that human settlement is sparse within the interior of the Amazonian basin. The margins of the basin have been exploited commercially for rubber, cinchona (utilized for making quinine) and cattle ranching. The ranches in this part of Brazil more than rival any other would-be producers. Although history does not record the rise and fall of great cities and civilizations along the banks of the Amazon, it still ranks as the world's major river system.

Anauá, Brazil

The Anauá has its source east of Serra Iaravarune in Brazil on the Guyana border. It flows for 175 miles (282 km) west by southwest to the Rio Branco.

Apa, Brazil

The Apa rises near Cordillera de Amambay in the southern Mato Grosso of Brazil. It is 160 miles (260 km) long and flows on a westerly course by the town of BELA VISTA and then flows along the Paraguay border until it enters the Paraguay River as a tributary.

Apaporis, Colombia

This river is 550 miles (880 km) long and rises in the southeastern portion of Colombia. It runs on a southeasterly course to become a tributary of the Japurá-Caquetá River.

Approuague, French Guiana

This river rises in the Guiana Highlands of the northeastern tip of South America. It flows for a total of 175 miles (280 km) through a dense tropical forest until it reaches a navigable estuary on the Atlantic at POINT BÉHAGUE.

Apure, Venezuela

The Apure is one of the larger rivers of the northern portion of South America. It rises near SAN CRISTOBAL in the Cordillera de Mérida near the border between Colombia and Venezuela. The river runs through central Venezuela to become a tributary of the Orinoco River. The Apure is over 500 miles (800 km) long and is navigable.

Apurimac, Peru

The Apurimac rises in the south central portion of the Peruvian Andes. The Apurimac is also known as the Ene River and Tambo River in its lower reaches. It flows northwest to join the Mantaro and Perene Rivers, which along with the Urubamba River, 450 miles (720 km) long, form the Ucayali River. The Ucayali River is one of the main headstreams of the Amazon.

Araçuai, Brazil

Alternatively known as the Arassuahy River, it rises east of DIAMANTINA, located in the State of Minas Gerais on the eastern coast of Brazil. The river is 150 miles (240 km) long and becomes a tributary of the Jequitinhonha River just below ARACUAI CITY.

Araguaia, Brazil

The Araguaia rises in the central plateau of Brazil and flows for a distance of 1000 miles (1600 km) before becoming a tributary of the Tocantins River. At one time in the long past history of the continent, the Araguaia and Tocantins systems were not independent as they are today. Before the gradual submergence of the eastern continental shelf by the rise of the Andes Mountains, the Araguaia-Tocantins system was a tributary of the Amazon. The Araguaia flows 800 miles (1290 km) through a deep valley cut out of the great Brazilian plateau. Just like its sister river, the Araguaia is plagued by rapids which extend as far downstream as 120 miles (190 km) from its confluence with the Tocantins. An interesting geographical feature of the Araguaia occurs along its middle course where it splits into two separate branches to form Bananal Island. The river is navigable in its lower course.

Araguari, Brazil

The Araguari begins near the French Guiana border of northern Brazil. It runs for a total of 250 miles (400 km) passing FERREIRA GOMES on the way to enter the Atlantic Ocean. The river is navigable only below Ferreira Gomes.

Arapey Grande, Uruguay

The Arapey Grande is formed by the confluence of three small rivers in the northwestern portion of Uruguay very near the Brazilian border. It is 125 miles (200 km) long and becomes a tributary of the Uruguay River northeast of the town of CONSTITUCION.

Arassuahy, Brazil

See Araçuai, Brazil.

Arauca, Colombia-Venezuela

This Colombian River rises in the Cordillera Oriental. It is over 500 miles (800 km) long and runs east past the towns of ARAUQUITA and EL AMPARO before crossing into Venezuela. The Arauca becomes a tributary of the much larger Orinoco River in central Venezuela.

Arinos, Brazil

The river rises in the Mato Grosso State of Brazil and flows north by northwest for over 400 miles (640 km). The Arinos is the longest headstream of the great Tapajós River. It continues on course until the confluence with the Juruena River to form the Tapajós River.

Aripuana, Brazil

The lower course of the Aripuana is known as the Roosevelt River. The Aripuana rises in the northwest portion of Mato Grosso State in Brazil and flows 410 miles (660 km) to become a tributary of the Madeira River. It is navigable for a distance on the lower course.

Atrato, Colombia

The Atrato rises in western Colombia and follows a meandering course as it flows through the center of the local platinum mining area. The river passes QUIBDO and continues on its 375 mile (600 km) long trip to enter the Gulf of Urabá.

Atuel, Argentina

The Atuel rises in the high Andes on the borders of Chile. It flows southeast for 300 miles (480 km) before becoming a tributary of Rio Salado just southeast of SANTA ISABEL.

Balsas, Brazil

The Balsas is 200 miles (320 km) long. It rises near the border of Maranhão Province in eastern Brazil. The river runs northeast past the towns of BALSAS and LORETO to join the Parnaíbo River at BENEDITO LEITE.

The Beni and the Madre de Dios Rivers merge at Riberalta in central Bolivia.

Barama, Guyana

The Barama rises near the Venezuelan border of Guyana. It flows through the gold region of the North West District of Guyana. Between the Barama and Barima Rivers are great natural deposits of manganese. The Barama is 120 miles (190 km) long and runs east then northeast before joining the Waini River.

Barima, Guyana-Venezuela

The Barima rises in Guyana and flows in a great curve first eastward, then north, before turning finally to a west by northwest direction into Venezuela. The Barima is linked by the very short Mora Passage to the Waini River mouth on the Atlantic Ocean. The river is navigable for 52 miles (84 km), and becomes a tributary of the Orinoco River at its mouth. The Barima's navigability has given access to the rich gold regions of Guyana, which would have been otherwise practically inaccessible.

Beni, Bolivia

The Beni is formed in the Cordillera Real and augmented by many tributaries including the Boopi and Altamachi Rivers. The Beni is one of the principal rivers of Bolivia and is navigable for 500 miles (800 km). It flows northwest, then north and finally northeast for over 600 miles (960 km) before becoming a tributary of the Madeira River, one of the chief tributaries of the Amazon.

Berbice, Guyana

This river rises in Guyana and flows for a total distance of 350 miles (565 km). It runs through a region rich in timber forests, diamonds and bauxite. The main tributary of the Berbice is the Canje River, whose length is 156 miles (251 km). The river is navigable for 100 miles (160 km) as far as the town of PARADISE. It enters the Atlantic Ocean at NEW AMSTERDAM, a large port on the seacoast.

Bermejo, Argentina (1)

The source of the Bermejo is high in the mountains at a height of 6500 feet (1970 m) in the northwest of Argentina and for much of its course is a natural border between Argentina and Bolivia. The Bermejo is 650 miles (1050 km) long. It is known as the Teuco River in its central course. It eventually becomes a tributary of the Paraná River near PILAR.

Bermejo, Argentina (2)

The Bermejo rises in the northern portion of La Rioja State of Argentina. It runs for 250 miles (400 km) on a southerly course to the Huanacache lakes. Afterwards it becomes the Desaguadero River and further on the Rio Salado; it flows through some of the finest regions of Argentina.

Bío-Bío, Chile

The Bío-Bío rises in the lakes of Cautin State in the Andes Mountains of Chile. It is one of the primary rivers of Chile with a length of 240 miles (380 km). The principal tributary of the Bío-Bío is the Laja River which provides hydroelectric power for Concepción State. The river flows northwest to enter the Bahía de Arauco to the west of CONCEPCIÓN. The Bío-Bío is navigable as far as Concepción.

Blanco, Bolivia

The Rio Blanco rises near the town of YOTAU in the Santa Cruz Department of Bolivia. It is 330 miles (530 km) long and runs on a northerly course to FORTE PRINCIPE DE BEIRA in Brazil. The chief tributaries are the Negro and San Martin Rivers. The Rio Blanco becomes a tributary of the Guaporé River close to Forte Principe de Beira.

Bogotá, Colombia

The Bogotá River is 124 miles (199 km) long and rises north of CHOCONTA in central Colombia. The river is famous for the spectacular falls west of CHARQUITO called TEQUENDAMA FALLS. It continues on a southwesterly course to join the Magdalena River.

Branco, Brazil

The Rio Branco is formed by the confluence of several streams in the northern portion of Brazil. It is 350 miles (560 km) long and runs south past the towns of BOA VISTA and CARACARAI before entering the Rio Negro near MOURA. The river is partly navigable.

Calchaqui, Argentina

The Calchaqui is one of the headstreams of the Rio Salado in Argentina. It is 126 miles (203 km) long and flows to join the Santa Maria River northeast of CAFAYATE to form the Pasaje River.

Calle-Calle, Chile

The source of the Calle-Calle is Rinihue Lake in south-central Chile. It only runs for 60 miles (96 km) on a westerly course past the town of VALDIVIA. Its chief tributary is the Cruces River. For the rest of its course the river continues through an 11-mile (18 km) estuary to Corral Bay on the Pacific Ocean. The coastline along this section of Chile is particularly beautiful.

Camaquã, Brazil

The Camaquã is navigable for 80 miles (129 km) of its 206 mile (331 km) length. It rises north of BAGE in Rio Grande do Sul in Brazil and flows east to Lake Patos, 50 miles (80 km) from the town of PELOTAS.

Cañete, Peru

This river rises in the Lima Department of Peru in the high Andes approximately 18 miles (29 km) west-northwest of the town of MATUCANA. It runs for 120 miles (190 km) first south, then southwest before flowing into the Pacific Ocean near the town of CANETE. The river is a source for irrigation projects along its short course.

Canindé, Brazil

This river rises to the southwest of PAULISTANA, in the Serra dos Dois Irmaos in northeastern Brazil. It is 210 miles (340 km) long and flows in a northwesterly direction. Its chief tributary is the Piauí River. The Canindé becomes a tributary of the Parnaíba River and is not navigable.

Canõas, Brazil

The Canõas is one of the chief headwaters of the Uruguay River. It rises in the Serra do Mar of southern Brazil and flows west to join the Pelotas River southwest of CAMPOS NOVOS. The river is over 200 miles (320 km) long.

Canumã, Brazil

The Canumã is also known in its upper reaches as the Secunduri River. It rises on the border between the Mato Grosso and Amazonas States. The river is a major tributary of the Madeira River which it joins approximately 82 miles (132 km) southeast of the large inland city of MANAUS. The Canumã is 350 miles (560 km) long.

Capanaparo, Colombia-Venezuela

This river rises in the northeastern portion of Columbia and runs on an easterly course through Apure Territory, Venezuela. It is 355 miles (570 km) long and parallels the Arauca River before becoming a tributary of the Orinoco.

Capiberibe, Brazil

The Capiberibe is an intermittent river of northeastern Brazil. It flows from the Serra dos Cariris Velhos for 150 miles (240 km) eastward to the Atlantic at RECIFE.

Caquetá-Japurá, Colombia

The Caquetá rises in the Colombian Andes south of PARAMO DEL BUEY and is the largest river in Colombia. It flows virtually unmarked and unexplored through dense tropical forests, across the equator and then runs east-southeast through Cauca, Putumayo, Caquetá and Amazonas districts. The chief tributaries of the river are the Apaporis, Caguán, Yarí, Orteguaza and the Miritiparaná. It is not navigable. Once the Caquetá reaches the Brazilian border, it becomes the Japurá River which continues on course for another 400 miles (640 km) before joining the Amazon above TEFE in central Amazonia. The combined Caquetá-Japurá River has such a winding course that it is practically impossible to measure its length, but reliable sources estimate it between 1300 and 1750 miles (2090–2820 km). The Japurá is navigable for a distance in Brazil depending on the season.

Carcarañá, Argentina

The Carcarañá is formed by the confluence of the Cuarto and Tercero Rivers in Córdoba Province. It is 130 miles (210 km) long and runs eastward past CRUZ ALTA to become a tributary of the much larger Paraná River. Hydroelectric power stations are being developed along its route.

Carinhanha, Brazil

This Brazilian river rises in the central regions of the country. It forms the border between the states of Bahia and Minas Gerais, is 175 miles (280 km) long and flows on a northeasterly course before joining the São Francisco River above the town of CARINHANHA.

Caroni, Venezuela

The source of the Caroni River is high on Mt Roraima in the Guiana Highlands. The river runs for a total length of 430 miles (690 km) first west, then north before it enters the Orinoco River near SAN FELIX. The chief tributary of the Caroni is the Paragua River. Along its course is one of the great natural wonders of the world, the spectacular ANGEL FALLS, which, at 3050 feet (930 m), is the highest in the world, and falls uninterrupted for that entire distance. The lower course of the Caroni is navigable.

Carrenleufu, Argentina

See Palena, Argentina

Casanare, Colombia

The Casanare rises south of the Sierra Neveda de Cocuy in eastern Colombia. The river is navigable for small vessels and is 200 miles (320 km) long. It runs eastward to the Meta River which is its outlet.

Casiquiare, Venezuela

This waterway links the great Orinoco and Amazon basins. It rises in the Amazonas Territory of southern Venezuela and leaves the Orinoco River approximately 20 miles (32 km) west of the town of ESMERALDA. It then flows for 140 miles (230 km) first southwest, then west to join the Rio Negro near the town of CARLOS, thus completing the link between the two great rivers of South America.

Above: A stream merges into the Caroni river of Venezuela.
Right: Angel Falls on the Caroni are more than half a mile high and are the highest in the world.

Catatumbo, Colombia

The Catatumbo River flows through some of the richest oil regions in the world. With its tributary the Tarra River, which is 50 miles (80 km) long, it flows from the Cordillera Oriental in Colombia through the Venezuelan foothills. It turns eastward into the lowlands close to the oil-bearing regions. The river continues on course until it enters the great Maracaibo Lake and finally the Caribbean Sea. The river is 210 miles (340 km) long. The major towns along the lower reaches of the river are CUCUTA and ENCONTRADOS which are connected by railways.

Cauca, Colombia

The Cauca is the chief tributary of the Magdalena River. It rises at the foot of PARAMO DEL BUEY in the Andes and is 610 miles (980 km) long. It runs through some of the most fertile land in South America, noted for its agricultural produce, cattle and gold mines. The Cauca is only partly navigable. It flows through a wide valley, receiving the Nechi River in the Caribbean lowlands, and finally joins the left arm of the Magdalena River, the Brazo de Loba, southeast of the town of MAGANGUE.

Cayari, Brazil
See Uaupes, Brazil

Cebollatí, Uruguay
This river rises south of ILLESCAS in south-eastern Uruguay and flows east, then northeast to Mirim Lake which is located 40 miles (64 km) east of the town of TREINTA Y TRES. The river is 130 miles (210 km) long and is only navigable in its lower reaches.

César, Colombia
This river flows through rich pasture lands, after rising in the Sierra Neveda de Santa Marta of northern Colombia. It is 200 miles (320 km) long and meanders on a southwesterly course to become a tributary of the Magdalena River at EL BANCO.

Chadileufu, Argentina
See Salado, Argentina (3)

Chama, Venezuela
The source of the Chama is the foot of the Piedras Blancas massif in northwest Venezuela. The Chama is 100 miles (160 km) long. It flows southwest through the fertile valley to the town of LAGUNILLAS, then swings north past EL VIGIA to enter Lake Maracaibo.

Chamaya, Peru
See Huancabanba, Peru.

Chanchan, Ecuador
This river rises east of ALAUSI in the Andes of central Ecuador. It is only 60 miles (97 km) long. The river flows west through a steep valley to become a tributary of the Chimbo River. On its upper reaches is the famous, *Nariz del Diabolo* or Devil's Nose gorge.

Chapecó, Brazil
This Brazilian river rises in western Santa Catarina and runs for 170 miles (270 km) on a west-southwesterly course. It flows into the Uruguay River west of the city of CHAPECO.

Chasicó, Argentina
The Arroyo Chasico, as it is known locally, rises at a height of 1400 feet (427 m) in the Sierra de Curumalan in Buenos Aires State. It is 80 miles (129 km) long and flows in a southwesterly direction to enter Chasico Lake, 40 miles (64 km) west of BAHIA BLANCA.

Chicamocha, Colombia
This river of north central Colombia rises west of LAGUNA DE TOTA. It is 150 miles (240 km) long and flows first north, then northwest before joining the Suarez River in forming the Sogamoso River near the town of ZAPATOCA.

Chico, Argentina (1)
This Rio Chico, the first of two rivers of the same name, rises in Lake Colhué Huapi in

southern Argentina. It is 175 miles (282 km) long and flows through the immense Patagonia highlands to the Chubut River southeast of LAS PLUMAS.

Chico, Argentina (2)
This Chico River rises in the very southern tip of Argentina in the lower Andes Range. It flows for a total of 260 miles (420 km) on a southeasterly course to enter the Santa Cruz estuary only 15 miles (24 km) from the Atlantic Ocean. The Rio Chico is Argentina's most southerly river.

Chimbo, Ecuador
The Chimbo rises in the Andes of southern Ecuador near the town of CHIMBORAZO. It is 125 miles (201 km) long and flows south past GUARANDA. The river then turns westward to join the Guayas River near YAGUACHI.

Chira, Peru
This river is formed by the confluence of the Catamayo and Macara Rivers on the Peruvian-Ecuador border. It is 100 miles (160 km) long and flows southwest through one of the major cotton-growing regions in the country. It finally enters the Pacific Ocean near VICHAYAL.

Chubut, Argentina
The source of the Chubut is in the high eastern Andes of Argentina. It is 430 miles (690 km) long and flows south for a while before breaking through the foothills into the Patagonian plateau. The Chubut occupies a great valley which was once the home of a large glacial river. It finally empties into the Atlantic Ocean by its main branch, while a secondary one flows into Bahía Nueva.

Cinzas, Brazil
The Rio das Cinzas River rises in northeastern Paraná State, Brazil. It flows for 300 miles (480 km) on a north by northwesterly course, passing the town of TOMAZINA on the way to join the Paranapanema River. The Cinzas flows through one of the richest coal deposits in Brazil.

Colorado, Argentina
The Colorado River of Argentina rises in northern Patagonia at the confluence of the Barrancas and Grande Rivers. The river is over 530 miles (850 km) long and flows southeast for the majority of its course before entering the Atlantic approximately 70 miles (113 km) south of BAHIA BLANCA. The only tributary of note which the Colorado receives is the Curicó which drains the saline basin of the State of La Pampa. The region the Colorado flows through is extremely arid and this is the reason why the other small tributaries are very uncertain streams. The rate of evaporation is higher than the actual rate of precipitation. The Colorado derives its name from the distinctive color of the reddish clays through which it flows. The actual width of the present-day river is small compared to

its great valley. The original valley was made by a much larger ancestor of the present Colorado when the ice caps of the Andes began to recede. The region surrounding the river is primarily utilized for ranching as it is unsuitable for agriculture. The Colorado has no great port at its mouth like the other Patagonian rivers which is due to the stifling influence of Bahía Blanca north of the river.

Commewijne, Surinam
This river rises north of DAM in eastern Surinam (Dutch Guiana) and runs for a total of 100 miles (160 km). The upper course of the Commewijne is noted for its great gold deposits. The chief tributary of the Commewijne is the Cottica River, itself 100 miles (160 km) long and noted for its bauxite deposits. The river flows east to the mouth of the Surinam River at the city of NIEUW AMSTERDAM. It is navigable in its lower reaches.

Copiapó, Chile
The source of the Copiapo is in the Andes Hills of northern Chile. The river flows for 110 miles (180 km) due west past the town of COPIAPO to enter the Pacific Ocean south of

The desolate canyon of Argentina's Colorado River shows the rugged terrain of Patagonia which is mostly unsuitable for agricultural use.

CALDERA. The Copiapó Valley is noted for its produce throughout Chile and the local farmers take great pride in living up to their reputation. The river also flows through some of the richest silver and copper mining regions in Chile.

Coppename, Surinam
Two small headstreams in the Wilhelmina Mountains join together to form the Coppename River. It is 256 miles (412 km) long and flows due north to enter the Atlantic Ocean southwest of the mouth of the Saramacca River. It is linked naturally with the Nickerie River. The Coppename is navigable by small vessels for approximately 60 miles (97 km).

Corrente, Brazil
The Corrente rises in the Serra Geral de Goiás in southwest Bahía State, Brazil. The river is navigable below SANTA MARIA DA VITORIA. It is 180 miles (290 km) long and flows northeast to the São Francisco River.

Corrientes, Ecuador-Peru
This Peruvian river rises in the foothills of the Andes Range within Ecuador. It is navigable for 85 miles (137 km). The river is 350 miles (560 km) long and runs southeast initially, then turns due east to join the Tigre River just north of SARGENTU LOROS.

Corumbá, Brazil
This river rises near Corumbá de Goiás in the central region of Brazil. It is noted for the diamonds and gold found along its course. It is 200 miles (320 km) long and flows due south to become a tributary of the Paranaíba River above the town of ITUMBIARA.

Cotingo, Brazil
This Brazilian river flows from the far north and forms as one of the chief headstreams of the Rio Branco. It is noted for its gold and diamonds. The river is 180 miles (290 km) long and flows south to join the Tacutu River approximately 50 miles (80 km) above the town of BOA VISTA.

Courantyne, Guyana
The Courantyne River rises on the borders of Brazil and Guyana in the Serra Acarai situated in the northernmost watershed of the Amazon basin and forms for most of its length a natural border between Guyana and Surinam. The river is 450 miles (720 km) long, and flows north through tropical rainforests. Large ocean-going vessels can navigate the river as far as the village of OREALLA, known for its kaolin and bauxite. Farther upstream beyond Orealla are the famous COW FALLS, a spectacular natural wonder which begins approximately 125 miles (201 km) from the Atlantic outlet. The river enters the Atlantic Ocean west of NIEUW NICKERIE, a major port on the Nickerie River in northwest Surinam.

Cuiabá, Brazil
The Cuiabá is noted for the gold washings found in its headwaters. It rises along the Amazon-Paraguay watershed in central Mato Grosso Province of Brazil. It is over 300 miles (480 km) long and flows south-southwest past the town of CUIABA to CORUMBA. At Corumbá, the river joins the São Lourenço River which becomes a tributary of the much larger Paraguay River, 80 miles (129 km) north of Corumbá.

Cumina, Brazil
See Erepecuru, Brazil.

Curaco, Argentina
See Salado, Argentina (3).

Curaray, Ecuador
The lower course of the Curaray is navigable. The river rises northeast of the town of PUYO on the eastern slopes of the Andes Mountains in northeastern Ecuador. It is over 500 miles (800 km) long and flows east-southeast to join the Napo River in northeastern Peru. The river runs through some of the finest forests of South America.

Cuyuni, Venezuela-Guyana
The Cuyuni is noted for the gold and diamonds which can be found along its course. The river rises in the Guiana Highlands of Venezuela and flows for 350 miles (560 km), first north and then east into Guyana. It flows through tropical forests, past the town of AURORA to the Mazaruni River, just before joining the Essequibo River near BARTICA.

Dagua, Colombia
The Dagua rises northwest of the town of CALI (population 900,000) in western Colombia. It is 60 miles (97 km) long and flows to the Pacific Ocean at the city of BUENAVENTURA.

Daule, Ecuador
The Daule rises west of the capital city of Ecuador, QUITO, which has a population of well over 600,000, on the high slopes of the Andes Mountains. It flows due south through extremely fertile lowlands to the Guayas River at the port of GUAYAQUIL. The river is 175 miles (282 km) long and navigable.

Morning on lake Titicaca. The Desaguadero is the only outlet for this, the world's highest lake.

Demerara, Guyana
The Demerara River rises in the dense jungle of Guyana and flows for a total of 208 miles (335 km) to the Atlantic Ocean at GEORGE-TOWN. The river is noted for its bauxite, kaolin, gold, timber and especially sugar cane (note demerara sugar). It is navigable for ocean-going vessels for 65 miles (105 km).

Desaguadero, Argentina
See Salado, Argentina (3).

Desaguadero, Bolivia
The Desaguadero is the only outlet of the highest lake in the world, Lake Titicaca. This lake is 130 miles (210 km) long and 35 miles (56 km) wide, encompassing an area of 3500 square miles (9060 sq km), and stands at a height of 12,500 feet (3810 m) above sea level. The river flows southeast to the saline Lake Poopó. Its chief tributary is the Mauri River. The river is 200 miles (320 km) long.

Deseado, Argentina
The Deseado rises in southern Argentina in the Andean hills and flows for a total of 380 miles (610 km) before emptying into the Atlantic Ocean at Puerto Deseado.

Diamante, Argentina
The source of the Diamante is a small lake at the foot of the Maipo volcano in the Andes of Mendoza State, Argentina. The river is 200 miles (320 km) long and runs east to join the Rio Salado. It provides hydroelectric power for the province and water for the vast irrigation projects throughout the region.

Doce, Brazil
The Rio Doce rises above PONTE NOVA in Minas Gerais State of eastern Brazil. It flows northeast to GOVERNADOR VALADARES, then swings southeast to enter the Atlantic Ocean northeast of VITORIA. The river is 360 miles (580 km) long and is hazardous due to the rapids along its course. The chief tributary of the Rio Doce is the Piracicaba River.

Dulce, Argentina
The Rio Dulce begins as the Sali River in northern Argentina's Tucuman State. The river is primarily used for irrigation. It flows 400 miles (640 km) southeast past the towns of TUCUMAN and SANTIAGO DEL ESTERO through Lake Porongos to empty into Mar Chiquita.

Duvida, Brazil
See Roosevelt, Brazil.

Elqui, Chile
This river rises in north-central Chile at the town of RIVADAVIA where the Rio Turbio and Rio Claro meet. It flows on a westerly course past VICUNA to enter the Pacific Ocean at Coquimbo Bay. The river is 130 miles (210 km) long.

Erebato, Venezuela
The Erebato rises in the state of Bolivar in Venezuela and flows for 150 miles (240 km) due north through a large tropical rainforest. It becomes a tributary of the Caura River.

Erepecuru, Brazil
The Erepecuru or Cumina River rises in the Brazilian State of Pará in the Serra Tumucu-maque adjacent to the border of Surinam. It is not navigable and flows into the Trombetas River.

Essequibo, Guyana
The Essequibo is by far the largest river in Guyana. It rises in the Serra Acarai near the border of Brazil and drains more than 60 percent of Guyana. The river is 600 miles (970 km) long, and flows north to the Atlantic Ocean, west-northwest of the capital city of GEORGETOWN in what can be best described as a huge estuary over 20 miles (32 km) wide. It is navigable for a distance on the lower course but due to waterfalls and rapids, large vessels can not navigate past BARTICA. The Essequibo flows through a region rich in timber, gold, diamonds and other natural resources. The chief tributaries are the Potaro, Rupununi and Mazaruni-Cuyuni Rivers.

Gallegos, Argentina
The source of the Gallegos is in southern Patagonia. It flows due east to PUERTO GALLEGOS on the Atlantic Ocean and is 200 miles (320 km) long.

Garças, Brazil
This river rises in the eastern Mato Grosso of Brazil and flows for 160 miles (260 km), northeast to become a tributary of the Araguaia River at BARRO DO GARCAS. There are some local mining industries along the river but the chief export is derived from the excellent diamond washings.

Grajaú, Brazil
The river rises in Maranhão, northeastern Brazil and runs for over 300 miles (480 km) on a north-northeast course. It passes the town of GRAJAU, the head of the river's navigation, to

A home on the banks of the Essequibo River in Guyana. In the foreground are racks covered by thatched roofs on which fish and the like may be dried.

enter the Mearim River south of BAIXO MEARIM.

Gualeguay, Argentina
The river rises west-northwest of CHAJARI, in Entre Rios State of Argentina. It flows for 220 miles (350 km) due south to an arm of the Paraná River, the Paraná Ibicuy, to the southwest of GUALEGUAY.

Guama, Brazil
A tributary of the Pará River, the Guama rises in eastern Pará State and runs for a total of 200 miles (320 km) due north before emptying into the Pará at BELEM.

Guanare, Venezuela
The Guanare has two separate arms which flow on slightly different courses before ultimately rejoining. The river rises in western Venezuela to the south of the town of EL TOCUYO. It runs for a total of 205 miles (330 km) due east to the Portuguesa River at the town of LA UNION. The Guanare Viejo River, the other arm of the main stream, flows from GUANARITO for a distance of 110 miles (180 km) before rejoining the main branch at a location 30 miles (48 km) from the mouth.

Guanipa, Venezuela
The Guanipa rises northeast of PARIAGUAN, in northeastern Venezuela. The river runs for 175 miles (282 km) east-northeast to enter the Gulf of Paria on the Atlantic Ocean. The chief tributary is the Amana River. It is partly navigable for a short distance up stream.

Guapay, Bolivia
See Rio Grande, Bolivia.

Guaporé, Brazil
Sometimes called the Iténez, the Guaporé rises in the Mato Grosso State of Brazil and flows northwest. It is 750 miles (1210 km) long and runs past MATO GROSSO city on its way to the Bolivian border and the Mamoré River. The Guaporé carries a large volume of water as many large tributaries (the Rio Verde, Rio Banco, Paraguá and Itonamas Rivers) empty into it.

Guárico, Venezuela
The Guárico rises in northern Venezuela to the west of the town of BELEM. It flows for 300 miles (480 km) first due east, then south, passing the towns of BARBACOAS and CALABOZO to an arm of the Apure River near SAN FERNANDO. The chief tributary of the river is the Orituco.

Guasco, Chile
See Huasco, Chile.

Guaviare, Colombia
Known as the Guayabero River to some locals, the river rises in the Cordillera Oriental of central Colombia. It is 653 miles (1051 km) long and flows due east to join the mighty Orinoco River at SAN FERNANDO ATABAPO. Its chief tributary is the Ariari River, 160 miles (260 km) long.

Guayas, Ecuador
Although not such a popular river of South America as the Amazon or Orinoco, it is still the largest river system on the Pacific coast of South America. It is formed by numerous headstreams high in the Andes; the most notable are the Vinces, Daule Chimbo and Babahoyo Rivers. The Guayas has a huge delta which is navigable for 40 miles (64 km) upstream by ocean-going vessels. GUAYAQUIL, a city of over 900,000 inhabitants, it is over two miles (three km) wide. It then enters the Pacific Ocean by the Gulf of Guayaquil.

Guayuriba, Colombia
The river rises south of the Colombian capital of BOGOTA which has a population of well over 3,250,000. It runs for 150 miles (240 km) in a wayward course, first southeast, then east and finally northeast before joining the Guatiquia River to form the Meta River.

Gurguéia, Brazil
This medium-sized river rises near the Bahía border, south of PIAUI in Brazil. It is 250 miles (400 km) long and runs past the town of BOM JESUS to join the Parnaíba River above FLORIANO.

Gurupi, Brazil
The Gurupi forms the Pará-Maranhão State border for its entire course of 300 miles (480 km). This region is noted for its bauxite deposits and gold washings, the latter so numerous that any amateur can find some examples. It flows north-northeast to enter the Atlantic Ocean below the town of VISEU.

Huallaga, Peru
The river rises south of Cerro de Pasco in the Peruvian Andes and flows for a total of 700 miles (1130 km). It runs due north past the towns of HUANUCO and TINGO MARIA, then swings northeast past YURIMAGUS and LAGUNAS to become a tributary of the Marañón River. It is navigable by large vessels to Lagunas and by small vessels to Tingo María.

Huancabamba, Peru
Also called the Chamaya River, it rises in the Cordillera Occidental of northwestern Peru. The river is 120 miles (190 km) long and flows south, then northeast past the town of HUANCABAMBA. It enters the Marañón River southeast of JAEN.

Huasco, Chile
Also known as the Guasco River, the Huasco rises southeast of the town of VALLENAR in northern Chile where two headstreams from the Sierra de Tatul meet. The river is over 140 miles (230 km) long and flows west-northwest to VALLENAR before entering the Pacific Ocean near HUASCO town.

Huaura, Peru
The source of the Huaura occurs in the high Andes of west central Peru near the town of YANAHUANCA. On its lower course the river is utilized for irrigation projects near HUACHO. The river takes a southwesterly course initially, then turns westward passing the towns of SAYAN and HUAURA before entering the Pacific Ocean.

Iaco, Peru-Brazil
This medium-sized river rises on the southeastern border of Peru and Amazonas State in Brazil. It runs for 250 miles (400 km) into Acre State of western Brazil on a northeasterly course to become a tributary of the Purús River below SENA MADUREIRA. It is partly navigable.

Ibicuí, Brazil
This navigable river rises in the southwestern portion of Rio Grande do Sul in Brazil. It flows for 300 miles (480 km) due west before joining the Uruguay River on the Argentina border just northeast of the town of URUGUAIANA.

Ica, Columbia
See Putumayo, Columbia.

Ica, Peru
This small river rises in the Cordillera Occidental near HUAYTARI in southwestern Peru. The Ica is 100 miles (160 km) long and flows due south to the Pacific Ocean.

Iguaçu, Brazil

Known alternatively as the Iguassu, the river rises in the Serra do Mar, east of the town of CURTIBA, Paraná State, in southeastern Brazil. It is over 820 miles (1320 km) long, and flows on a winding course westward to the Paraná River. The Iguaçu forms the boundary between Argentina and Brazil for its last 75 miles (121 km). The river is noted for the famous Iguaçu Falls which are located 14 miles (23 km) above the mouth. Its chief tributary is the Rio Negro.

Ijui, Brazil

The Ijui rises in the Serra Geral of northern Rio Grande do Sul in Brazil. The river is 225 miles (362 km) long, and runs due west to the Uruguay River, just east of Concepción de la Sierra in Argentina.

Imperial, Chile

The Imperial River rises in south-central Chile at the confluence of the Cautín and Quepe Rivers near Nueva Imperial. It is 135 miles (217 km) long and runs west past the towns of CARAHUE and PUERTO SAAVEDRA to enter the Pacific Ocean.

Inambari, Peru

The Inambari River rises in the Nudo de Apolobamba, Andes Range, of southeastern Peru. It is 210 miles (340 km) long and runs northwest, then northeast to the Madre de Dios River at INAMBARI.

Inirida, Colombia

This river rises north-northwest of CALAMAR in southeast Colombia and flows for 450 miles (720 km) east and northeast to become a tributary of the Guaviare River. It flows through one of the large rainforests of South America.

Ireng, Brazil

See Mau, Brazil.

Itajaí Acu, Brazil

This Brazilian River rises in the Serra do Mar. The Itajaí Acu flows east through a heavily populated region for 125 miles (201 km) past Blumenau to enter the Atlantic Ocean at ITAJAI. It is partly navigable.

Itapicuru, Brazil (1)

The Itapicuru rises in the Serra do Itapicuru in Maranhão State of northeastern Brazil. The river flows for over 400 miles (640 km) on a northeasterly course passing the towns of COLINAS and CAXIAS before turning to a northwesterly direction. The river valley is very important to the economy of the country. It enters São Luis Bay of the Atlantic below the city of ROSARIO.

Itapicuru, Brazil (2)

The Itapicuru rises near JACOBINA in Bahía State, Brazil. It flows east-southeast for 250 miles (400 km), passing QUEIMADAS and CIPOE to enter the Atlantic below CONDE.

Itata, Chile

The river rises in the foothills of the Andes to the west of YUNGAY in the south-central region of Chile. It is 110 miles (180 km) long and flows northwest to enter the Pacific Ocean northeast of TOME.

Ivai, Brazil

The Ivai rises in the Serra de Esperanca, central Paraná State, Brazil. The Ivai is 400 miles (640 km) long and flows northwest to become a tributary of the Paraná River above Guíara Falls.

Jacuí, Brazil

The river rises in the Serra Geral, northeast of Cruz Alta in the Rio Grande do Sul, Brazil. It is 280 miles (450 km) long and flows first due south past Cachoeira do Sul, then runs east through the large coal basin of São Jerónimo to Pôrto Alegre. Here together with the confluence of the Caí, Sinos and Gravitai Rivers, it forms the Guaíba Estuary at the northern end of Lake Patos.

Jaguarão, Brazil

This small river rises east of the town of BAGE in Rio Grande do Sul, Brazil. It is 135 miles (217 km) long, and flows southeast forming the border between Brazil and Uruguay before entering Lake Mirim.

Jaguaribe, Brazil

Rising in the Serra Grande of northeastern Brazil, the Jaguaribe flows first due east, then northeast past the town of LIMOEIRO DO NORTE before entering the Atlantic Ocean below

Above: The renowned Iguaçu Falls.

ARACATI. The river is noted for its irrigation projects and is 350 miles (560 km) long. It is partly navigable along its lower course.

Jamunda, Brazil

The Jamunda is sometimes called the Nhamundá River, and flows from the Guiana Highlands in northern Brazil for 400 miles (640 km) before becoming a tributary of the mighty Amazon near FARO.

Japurá, Brazil

See Caquetá-Japurá, Colombia.

Jari, Brazil

This Brazilian river rises in the Serra de Tumucumaque of northern Brazil. It flows 350 miles (560 km) southeast to join the Amazon delta at Gurupa Island.

Javari, Brazil

The river rises on the Peruvian-Brazilian border and runs for a total of 600 miles (970 km) northeast to the Amazon River near BENJAMIN CONSTANT. The Javari is navigable.

Jequitinhonha, Brazil

The river rises south of DIAMANTINA, Minas Gerais State, in eastern Brazil. It is over 500 miles (800 km) long, and flows northeast to the Atlantic Ocean to form a joint delta with the Rio Pardo.

Jiparaná, Brazil

The Jiparaná River, sometimes called the Machado, rises in Guapore State of western Brazil. It flows northwest to become a

Above: A tributary of the Jurua River.

tributary of the Madeira River near the border of Amazonas.

Jubones, Ecuador
The Jubones flows from the Andes near the town of CUENCA for 100 miles (160 km) past PASAJE to enter the Jambelí Canal.

Juramento, Argentina
See Salado, Argentina (2).

Juruá, Brazil
One of the major tributaries of the mighty Amazon, the Juruá rises in the Serra do Divisor, a subsidiary of the Andes Range near the Peruvian border. It is over 900 miles (1450 km) long and flows west on a meandering course to join the Amazon approximately 100 miles (160 km) above TEFE. It runs through swampy jungle-covered *varzea* or riverine flats which are susceptible to heavy flooding during the rainy season. The Juruá region is sparsely populated for this very reason but a few settlements have grown up on the barrancas along the river, despite the adverse conditions.

Juruena, Brazil
The Juruena rises in the Serra dos Parecis in the northern Mato Grosso, Brazil. It flows for 500 miles (800 km) north to join the São Manuel River in forming the Tapajós River.

Jutai, Brazil
A large tributary of the Amazon, the Jutai rises in Amazonas State of Brazil and flows on a northeasterly course. The river is over 800 miles (1290 km) long and navigable along its lower reaches.

Laja, Chile
The Laja rises in Lake Laja which takes in an area encompassing 40 square miles (104 sq km) in south-central Chile. It flows due west to the Bío-Bío River and has a length of 100 miles (160 km). The SALTO DEL LAJA FALLS are famous throughout this portion of South America.

Lambayeque, Peru
The Lambayeque River is formed by the confluence of the Cumbil and Chancay Rivers near the town of CHONGOYAPE. It irrigates major sugar cane plantations and runs for a total of 70 miles (113 km) to the Pacific Ocean near LAMBAYEQUE.

La Paz, Bolivia
The La Paz River rises in western Bolivia at the confluence of the Choqueyapu and Chuquiaguillo Rivers. It is the chief headstream of the Beni River and runs 100 miles (160 km) southeast and northeast through the Eastern Cordillera of the Andes. The river passes LA PAZ before joining the Tamampaya River to form the Boopi River, which continues for a further 50 miles (80 km) to the Beni River.

Leon, Colombia
The Leon River rises in the Serrania de Abibe in northwestern Colombia. It runs for only 75 miles (120 km) in a north-northwest direction before entering the Gulf of Urabá to the Caribbean Sea.

Limari, Chile
A river of central Chile, the Limari rises near the Argentinian border in the Andes Range. It flows for 125 miles (200 km) due west passing the town of SOTAQUI before entering the Pacific

Ocean approximately 30 miles (48 km) southwest of OVALLE

Limay, Argentina
The Limay River rises in Lake Nahuel Huapi, located in southwestern Argentina and flows northeast. The principal tributaries are the Collon Cura River and the Arroyo Picun-Leufú. The river is over 260 miles (420 km) long and joins the Neuquén River at the town of NEUQUEN to form the Rio Negro.

Lluta, Chile
The Lluta rises in Cerro de Tacora on the Peruvian border of northern Chile. It flows 105 miles (169 km) due south, then westsouthwest to the Pacific Ocean north of the town of ARICA.

Loa, Chile
The Loa rises at the foot of Mino volcano near the Bolivian border. It flows in a curve first south, then west and finally north through the Atacama Desert to the Pacific Ocean north of TOCOPILLA. The river is 275 miles (440 km) long.

Machodo, Brazil
See Juparaná, Brazil.

Madeira, Bolivia-Brazil
The Madeira is formed by the confluence of the Beni and Mamoré Rivers at VILLA BELLA, a small village located in the Beni Department of northern Bolivia. It flows north initially for slightly over 60 miles (96 km) before turning northeast into Brazilian territory which is still unexplored and for all practical purposes uninhabited. The river is 2013 miles (3239 km) long and is navigable for 807 of those miles (1298 km). It is one of the chief tributaries of the mighty Amazon and rivals that great river in volume of water carried. It continues on course passing the towns of HUMAITÁ and BORBA through 500 miles (800 km) of tropical rainforest to join the Amazon approximately 90 miles (145 km) east of the city of MANAUS. A smaller branch of the Madeira enters the Amazon 100 miles (160 km) northeast of the main river, and forms the massive and marshy island of Tupinambaranas. During the rainy season the Madeira rises more than 50 feet (15 m) and large ocean-going vessels can navigate as far as the ALTO MADEIRA FALLS over 1250 miles (2110 km) from the sea. The Alto Madeira Falls are composed of 19 cataracts and rapids which make navigation on the upper course of the river impossible for 260 miles (420 km). The last rapid is called the Guajará-Mirim, the Small Pebble, and is located below the union of the Guaporé River with the Mamoré. The chief tributaries of the Madeira are the Roosevelt and the Canuma Rivers. It drains an area larger than France and Spain combined.

Madre de Dios, Peru-Bolivia
This river is over 700 miles (1130 km) long and flows from the Amazon Mountain Range in

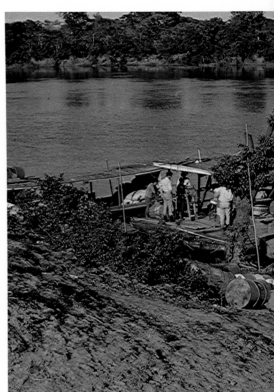

southern Peru on a northerly course initially, then shifts slightly to the northeast. Its chief tributaries are the Manu, Sena, Inambari and Tambopata Rivers. It joins the Beni River at RIBERALTA in Bolivia.

Magdalena, Colombia

The Magdalena rises in the foothills of the Paramo del Buey in the Cordillera Central in southwest Colombia. The river runs due north until it reaches the city of BARRANQUILLA which is on the left bank of the river. The Magdalena is over 1000 miles (1600 km) long. It flows between the Cordillera Central and the Cordillera Oriental as it heads for the alluvial lowlands. Once past Barranquilla the river spreads out into a wide and very irregular delta along the Caribbean coast. It is navigable from Barranquilla to HONDA, the latter a city in the Tolima Department of western Colombia. It is here that the famous Honda Falls obstructs all attempts to get above to the river's upper course. But man, undaunted by the falls, bypassed it and the rapids, to make the river navigable above the Honda Falls to the town of NEIVA. The Magdalena is the principal artery of Colombia, and its valley is extremely fertile. The chief crops of the region are sugar cane, cacao, cotton, tobacco and the all important coffee. The river passes the center of Colombia's oil fields, the city of BAR-RANCABERMEJA, located on the main highway to BOGOTA, the capital of Colombia. The chief tributary of the Magdalena is the Cauca River which also rises at the northern foot of the Paramo del Buey. In the Tertiary period, the Cauca Valley was the sight of an immense lake which explains why it is so fertile today. The valley although extremely humid has an abundant rainfall which is good for its bumper crops. The Magdalena also receives the San Jorge, Bogotá and Sogamoso Rivers.

Above: Bolivia's Madeira River is one of the chief tributaries of the Amazon.

Maipo, Chile

The Maipo rises at the foot of the Maipo volcano near the Argentinian border of central Chile. It is 155 miles (250 km) long and flows northwest and west to the Pacific Ocean a few miles south of SAN ANTONIO. Its chief tributary is the Mapocho River, 75 miles (121 km) long.

Majes, Peru

This medium-sized river rises in the Arequipa Department of southern Peru as the Colca River. It is slightly longer than 250 miles (400 km) and flows west and south to the Pacific Ocean, just west of the town of CAMANA.

Mamoré, Bolivia

Mamoré is formed by the confluence of the Chaparé and Ichilo Rivers in northern Bolivia. It is 1200 miles (1930 km) long. The Chaparé rises in the Cordillera de Cochabamba in Bolivia and runs northeast for 180 miles (290 km) before joining with the Ichilo, which itself flows for 170 miles (270 km) south of TRINIDAD. Twenty miles (32 km) later, the Mamoré is joined by the Rio Grande, a chief headstream of the river. [This Rio Grande, one of many South American rivers of that name, rises at the confluence of the Caine and Chayanta Rivers, and flows for 510 miles (820 km).] The Mamoré now continues on course due north to the Brazil-Bolivia border. There it is joined by the Guaporé River, which is 750 miles (1210 km) long and runs through the dense tropical forests of the Mato Grosso. The river continues until it reaches VILLA BELLA to meet the Beni River to form the Madeira. Most of the Mamoré basin is unexplored and unmapped.

Mana, French Guiana

The Mana River rises in the Chaine Granitique in western French Guiana. It is 200 miles (320 km) long, and flows north to enter the Atlantic Ocean at MANA.

Mantaro, Peru

The river rises in central Peru near Cerro de Pasco and flows 360 miles (580 km) before joining the Apurimac at PUERTO BOLOGNESI.

Manuripi, Peru-Bolivia

This river rises in southern Peru and flows northeast into Bolivia past SAN MIGUELITO to the Tahuamanu River at PUERTO RICO to form the Ortón River. The Manuripi River is 253 miles (407 km) long.

Marañón, Peru

The Marañón rises in the Peruvian Andes, only 100 miles (160 km) northeast of the capital city of LIMA, in a group of small lakes. The river is over 1000 miles (1600 km) long and flows through a deep valley on a northwest course. It heads for the border of Ecuador, and just as it is about to cross over the boundary takes a great curve to the northeast. The chief tributary of the Marañón is the Chinchipe River which joins it after flowing from southern Ecuador. The Marañón runs through the great Pongo de Manseriche or the Gorge of Parakeets, which is three miles (five km) long and slightly over 2000 feet (610 m) deep. This huge rent in the Andes narrows to a width of only 100 feet (30 m) in places, and the river travels through it at a rate of 15 miles (24 km) per hour. Once through the mountains the river flows on to join the Ucayali River in forming the Amazon, approximately 55 miles (88 km) upstream from the city of IQUITOS.

Above: A flat-bottomed riverboat on the Mamore.

Maroni, French Guiana
The Maroni rises in the Tumuc-Humac Mountains of French Guiana and is also known as the Marowijne. It is 450 miles (720 km) long, and flows north along the Surinam border to enter the Atlantic at Galibi Point.

Maú, Brazil
The Maú rises on the Brazilian-Guyana border in the Serra Pacaraima. It is sometimes called the Ireng River. The Maú flows through rich diamond deposits due south for 175 miles (282 km) to the Tacutu River.

Maule, Chile
The Maule rises in Lake Maule which has an area of 17 square miles (44 sq km) in central Chile. It flows for 175 miles (281 km) west-northwest to enter the Pacific Ocean at CONSTITUCION. Chief tributaries are the Rio Claro and Loncomilla River.

Mazaruni, Guyana
The Mazaruni River rises in the Guiana Highlands of northern Guyana. It runs for 350 miles (560 km) in a series of curves, flowing first north, then east and finally northeast before joining the Essequibo River at BARTICA near the junction with the Cuyuni River.

Mearim, Brazil
The Mearim River rises in several headstreams in Maranhão in northeastern Brazil. It has a winding course for 350 miles (560 km) as it runs through the Brazilian lake district and cotton region. Its main tributaries are the

Grajaú and Pindare Rivers. It enters São Marcos Bay of the Atlantic Ocean at the town of ANAJATUPA. The river is partly navigable.

Medellin, Colombia
See Porce, Colombia.

Mendoza, Argentina
The Mendoza rises in the Aconcagua massif of Argentina. It flows east past the towns of USPALLATA and LUJAN, then swings north to the Huanacache lakes. It is 200 miles (320 km) long and is utilized primarily for irrigation projects and as a source of power.

Meta, Colombia
The river rises at the confluence of the Upía River, 100 miles (160 km) long, and the Guayuriba River, 150 miles (240 km) long, east of the capital city of BOGOTA. The river is 650 miles (1050 km) long and flows northeast then east to become a tributary of the much larger Orinoco.

Morona, Ecuador-Peru
The Morona rises in the foothills of the eastern Andes Range of Ecuador, northeast of the town of MACAS. It is 260 miles (420 km) long and flows due south to the Marañón, approximately 25 miles (40 km) northwest of BARRANCA in Peru. The river is navigable.

Mortes, Brazil
The Rio das Mortes, sometimes called the Rio Manso, rises east of CUIABA in central Mato Grosso, Brazil. The river is 450 miles (720 km) long and flows through a diamond region to become a tributary of the Araguaia River.

Above: The Magdalena River near Honda.

Mucuri, Brazil
The Mucuri rises in Serra do Chifre, Minas Gerais, Brazil and flows east-southeast to the Atlantic Ocean southwest of the town of CARAVELAS. It is 150 miles (240 km) long.

Napo, Ecuador-Peru
The Napo rises near the Cotopaxi volcano in northeastern Ecuador. The chief tributaries are the Aguarico, Coca and Curaray Rivers. The river flows southeast past the town of NUEVO ROCAFUERTE into Peru and the upper Amazon near the city of IQUITOS. The Napo is 550 miles (880 km) long.

Negro, Argentina
The Rio Negro rises at the confluence of the Neuquén and Limay Rivers at the town of NEUQUEN. It is 400 miles (640 km) long and is navigable for slightly over 250 miles (400 km) from its mouth. The river runs east and southeast past ALLEN and FUERTE GENERAL ROCA to the Atlantic Ocean southeast of VIEDMA.

Negro, Colombia-Brazil
This Negro River rises in Highlands of Colombia and flows for a total of 1860 miles (2990 km) before emptying into the Amazon. It is one of the principal northern tributaries of the great river of South America. From its source in the watersheds between the Amazon and Orinoco Rivers, the Negro is known as the Guaina River until it reaches the Colombia-Venezuela boundary where it meets the Casiquiare River. The Negro crosses into Brazil at CUCUI, a small village, and flows northeast past the towns of TAPURUQUARA, BARCELOS and MOURA, before joining the

Amazon below MANAUS. The chief tributaries are the Içana, Uaupés and Branco Rivers. The Negro is navigable for 450 miles (720 km) above its mouth. The majority of the river's channel is so quiet and unassuming that one would hardly notice the slight flow of the water. Directly before meeting the Uaupés River, the Negro flows through a series of rapids, cataracts and whirlpools which are totally out of character with the rest of its course. It is connected with the Orinoco system through the Casiquaire River. As time goes by, it looks as if the Negro is slowly capturing the upper portions of the Orinoco, but no one can predict the end result of this change in the riverine structure of northern South America.

Negro, Brazil-Uruguay

This river rises just east of BAGE in Rio Grande do Sul. It is 500 miles (800 km) long and flows west-southwest through the center of Uruguay. The river passes the towns of SAN GREGORIO, PASO DE LOS TOROS, a river port and MERCEDES, a health resort. The Negro provides

The Limay River, one of the tributaries of the Negro, rises in Lake Nahuel Huapi, Argentina.

important hydroelectric power for this region of Uruguay. It divides into three distinct arms before actually joining the larger Uruguay River, approximately 18 miles (29 km) south-west of Mercedes at the town of SORIANO, the oldest settlement in the country. The principal tributaries are the Tacuarembó, Arroyo Salsipuedes Grande, Yi and Arroyo Grande Rivers. The river is only navigable for 45 miles (72 km) above Soriano.

Neuquén, Argentina
The Neuquén is formed on the Argentina-Chile border in the high Andes. It flows south and southeast for 320 miles (510 km) to join the Limay River in forming the much larger Rio Negro.

Nhaminda, Brazil
See Jamunda, Brazil.

Nickerie, Surinam
The Nickerie River rises in western Surinam in the Guiana Highlands. The river is 200 miles (320 km) long and runs north and northwest to the Atlantic Ocean at the mouth of the Courantyne River. It is linked with the Coppename River.

Orinoco, Brazil-Venezuela
The Orinoco is one of the largest rivers in South America. It was discovered by the great Italian explorer, Christopher Columbus, while exploring the Gulf of Paria in the year 1498. Columbus believed that he had discovered the entrance to Paradise. In 1530–31, Diego de Ordaz entered the Boca de Navios and managed to make his way as far as the junction with the Meta River. In doing this, Ordaz became the first white man to explore any portion of the Orinoco. However the Orinoco basin has attracted numerous exploration trips up river since. In 1744 Jesuit missionaries discovered the Casiquiare link between the Amazon and the Orinoco, and in 1800 the link was confirmed by Alexander von Humboldt. Although numerous exploratory trips had been conducted to find the source of the great river, it was not until 1951 that Risquez Iribarren actually discovered the source of the Orinoco high in the Guiana Highlands. The river crosses huge expanses of llanos or savannas and immense tropical forests. The entire tremendous basin of the Orinoco is sparsely inhabited. It is connected by two channels to the mighty Amazon, the Casiquiare and the Negro Rivers. The river is navigable for slightly over 1000 miles (1600 km) upstream from the delta. The river is divided into two sections by the Atures and Maipures cataracts which are located to the south of Puerto Ayacucho. The length of the river is 1281 miles (2061 km), although some estimates have been as high as 1700 miles (2740 km). The first is by far the most realistic. The source of the Orinoco is high in the Parima Mountain Range of the Guiana Highlands very close to the Brazilian border. It runs in a huge semicircle, first northwest, then north along the Colombian border, shifts itself through the very center of Venezuela, before finally turning north-northeast to the confluence of the Apure River and eastward to the Atlantic Ocean, south of TRINIDAD. The Orinoco has a tremendous delta. The principal tributaries of the river are the Guaviare which is 650 miles (1050 km) long, the Vichada which is 400 miles (640 km) long, the Meta which is 650 miles (1050 km) long, the Capanaparo which is 350 miles (560 km) long, the Arauca which is 500 miles (800 km) long; and the most important left-bank tributary, the Apure, which is 500 miles (800 km) long and formed

by the Uribante and Sarare Rivers. The chief right-bank tributaries are the Ventuari which runs from the Pakaraima Mountains and the Caura and Caroni Rivers which run in from the same region. The actual delta of the Orinoco takes in an area of roughly 7700 square miles (19,940 sq km) and begins 100 miles (160 km) out from the sea. Of the dozen or so arms of the river, the most important are the Mánamo, the Macareo, the Araguao and the Rio Grande; the latter forms the wide Boca de Navios estuary. The Orinoco's upper course is still virtually unmapped and unexplored.

Oyapock, Brazil
The Oyapock rises on the Brazil–French Guiana boundary and flows along the border between the two countries for its entire length of 260 miles (420 km). The Oyapock runs into the Atlantic Ocean at Cape Orange.

Pachitea, Peru
This Peruvian river rises east of CERRO DE PASCO and flows north past PUERTO VICTORIA to become a tributary of the Ucayali River. It is 220 miles (350 km) long, and the main headstream, the Pichis River is navigable. The Pachitea joins the Ucayali approximately 24 miles (39 km) south of the town of PUCALLPA.

Palena, Argentina-Chile
The Palena begins as the Carrenleufu River in Lake General Vittner in southwestern Argentina. It flows through a series of curves for 180 miles (290 km) north and west across the border of Chile to enter the Gulf of Corcovado on the Pacific Ocean at PALENA.

Pampas, Peru
The Pampas rises in the lakes of the Cordillera Occidental of central Peru. It is 200 miles (320 km) long and flows east-northeast past CANGALLO to become a tributary of the Apurimac River.

Pará, Brazil
The Pará is the southeastern arm of the Amazon delta, south of Marajó Island and it is navigable. It is noted for its famous tidal bore which is exceedingly strong. The port city of BELEM is on the right bank. The Tocantins River empties into the Pará.

Paracatu, Brazil
This Brazilian river rises in two small headstreams in western Minas Gerais on the Goias border. It is 200 miles (320 km) long and

runs east to join the São Francisco River above the town of SAO ROMAO.

Paragua, Venezuela
The Paragua River rises in the Pakaraima Mountains near the Brazilian border with Venezuela. The Paragua is 300 miles (480 km) long and runs north and north-northeast to join the Caroni River. It is not navigable.

Paraguaçu, Brazil
The Paraguaçu rises in the Serra do Sincora in Bahia Province, Brazil. It flows 300 miles (480 km) due east past the town of CACHOEIRA DO TODOS on the Atlantic Ocean above MARAGOGIPE. The river is noted for its black diamonds.

Paraguay, Brazil-Paraguay
The Paraguay River rises near the town of DIAMANTINO in the Serra dos Parecis of Brazil. The river is a long and sluggish stream with a length of over 1584 miles (2549 km). Before it reaches its ultimate destination, the Paraná River, the Paraguay runs through a huge swampy region. Passing through this basin, the river has multiple channels which all become flooded during the rainy season. This annual flooding covers an area which is in excess of 30,000 square miles (77,700 sq km).

The chief tributary of the Paraguay, on its first leg, is the winding Curiabá River. The Curiabá and other smaller tributaries add their diminutive waters to the already vast swamp area. The principal tributaries of the Paraguay are the Apa, Pilcomayo and Bermejo Rivers. Once the river passes the capital of Paraguay, ASUNCION, it acts as the border between Argentina and Paraguay. To the west of the river lies the Chaco Territory below CORUMBA, which is mainly in Paraguay but partly in Argentina and Bolivia. This huge expanse of land, through which the Pilcomayo and Bermejo rivers flow, is virtually uninhabited except for the wandering Chaco tribes. This territory has also been the scene of some of the worst fighting in the continent: first the invasion of Paraguay by Brazil and Argentina in 1870; second, the Civil War in 1904; and third the Chaco Wars of the 1930s between Paraguay and Bolivia. During those times of conflict, it was nothing for entire villages and towns to be burned to the ground. The remote character of the region around the Paraguay River has made it one of the locales deemed not worthy of colonization. The only major city of any consequence on the banks of the river is the capital, Asunción.

Paraíba do Noter, Brazil
This river rises in northeast Brazil in the Serra dos Cariris Velhos. It flows for 180 miles (290 km) east-northeast past the town of JOAO PESSOA to enter the Atlantic Ocean at CABEDELO. It is navigable.

Paraíba do Sul, Brazil
The river rises as the Paraitinga River in the Serra da Bocaina in São Paulo State. It is 600 miles (970 km) long and flows southwest to GUARAREMA which is only 40 miles (64 km) from the great Brazilian city of SAO PAULO. The river then turns northeast and runs between the Serra da Mantiqueira and the Serra do Mar. It acts as the border for the states of Rio de Janeiro and Minas Gerais for a distance. The river actually enters the Atlantic at SAO JOAO DA BARRA. The delta of the Paraíba do Sul is poorly drained, with lagoons and canals, and extends from CAMPOS to São Tomé Cape.

Paraná, Brazil-Paraguay-Argentina
The Paraná is one of the most important commercial waterways of South America. It is 1827 miles (2940 km) long and flows from the confluence of the Rio Grande and Paranaíba River in southeast Brazil as the Alto Paraná. The river runs south-southwest along the borders of Mato Grosso and São Paulo, and Mato Grosso and Paraná States. It penetrates

deep into the dark igneous rock which makes up the Paraná tableland before reaching URUBU-PUNGA FALLS, a series of large cataracts approximately seven miles (11 km) above the confluence with the Tiete River. Once below the falls, the Corumba-São Paulo railroad bridge spans the river, and it becomes navigable for small vessels as far as the Guáira

Falls, one of Brazil's natural wonders. The Guáira Falls are located on the borders of Brazil and Paraguay directly below PORTO GUAIRA. The Paraná is four miles (six km) wide at Porto Guáira, yet at the Falls it is compressed into a space only 200 feet (60 m) wide. The spectacular Guáira Falls are made up of 18 cataracts over 100 feet (30 m) high. The river is the border between Brazil and Paraguay to the influx of the Iguaçu River. It then turns southwest and west to become the border between Argentina and Paraguay for a distance. Upon reaching ENCARNACION, Paraguay, the river is again obstructed by cataracts for over 50 miles (80 km); these are the Apipe Rapids. The Paraguay River joins the Paraná below the Apipe Rapids and above CORRIENTES. The western banks of the river are extremely low and during the rainy season they flood continuously. The complex delta of the Paraná acts as the northern limit of the

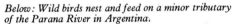
Below: Wild birds nest and feed on a minor tributary of the Parana River in Argentina.

Above: The Paraguay River near Asuncion.

Argentinian Pampa, which begins below the city of PARANA. The principal crop in this region is the famous 'green tea' which is believed to combat tropical fevers and is a favorite drink of native South Americans. The volume of the Paraná varies from season to season; it increases in the summer due to the heavy rains, and decreases in the winter months. The water level of the river rises over 15 feet (4·5 m) in the summer months. Ocean-going vessels can reach ROSARIO, PARANA and SANTE FE but smaller vessels can travel throughout the year to CORRIENTES and ASUNCION. The main crops of the Paraná region are corn, cattle, wheat, flax, alfalfa and

Above: The city of Asuncion on the Paraguay River.

maté. The Paraná is one of the great rivers of the world and on its upper course its waters provide a virtually untapped energy supply for future generations.

Paraná, Brazil

This smaller Paraná River is quite separate from the other Paraná and rises near BRASILIA in central Brazil and flows for 250 miles (400 km) on a north-northwest course. It becomes a tributary of the Tocantins River below the town of PARANA.

Below: Local women wash clothes in the Parana.

Paranaíba, Brazil

The Paranaíba River is the headstream of the great Paraná River and rises near SAO GOTARDO in Minas Gerais, Brazil. The river is over 500 miles (800 km) long and runs southwest, where together with the Rio Grande it forms the Paraná River.

Paranapanema, Brazil

The Paranapanema rises in São Paulo State in southeastern Brazil and flows west-northwest for 500 miles (800 km) before joining the Paraná River.

Parapeti, Bolivia

The Parapeti River rises east of AZURDUY in central Bolivia. It flows for 220 miles (350 km) due east through a heavily industrialized petroleum region before turning northeast into the large swamp area called Banados de Izozog, approximately 70 miles (113 km) east of the town of CABEZAS.

Pardo, Brazil (1)

The Pardo rises in the Serra do Espinhaco, northeastern Minas Gerais, Brazil. It flows for over 400 miles (640 km) east to the Atlantic to a delta shared with the Jequitinhonha River.

Pardo, Brazil (2)

The Rio Pardo rises northwest of POUSO ALEGRE in eastern São Paulo, Brazil. It flows 300 miles (480 km) northwest to the Rio Grande, north of the town of BARRETOS. Its chief tributary is the Mogi-Guaçu River which is 220 miles (350 km) long.

Parnaíba, Brazil

The Parnaíba rises in the Serras dos Tabatinga of northeastern Brazil and separates the neighboring states of Maranhão and Piauí. The river is 600 miles (970 km) long and flows northeast to its outlet the Atlantic Ocean. The Parnaíba drains a bottle-shaped basin on its way to the ocean in its upper course. The main town along its course is situated at the exist from the upper course, TERERSINA, the capital of Piauí State. The town is the main distribution and collection center for the region. It is connected with the port of PARNAIBA by a navigable waterway at the head of the delta. The river loses much of its tributary waterfall from the surrounding serras because of the intense rate of evaporation in this region.

Paru, Brazil

The Paru River rises in Serra de Tumucu-maque in central Pará, Brazil. It is 370 miles (600 km) long and runs south-southeast to become a tributary of the mighty Amazon above ALMERIM.

Pastaza, Ecuador-Peru

The river is formed by the confluence of the Patate and Chambo Rivers near BANOS in the Ecuadorian Andes. It has a length of 400 miles (640 km) and flows southeast and south through dense tropical forests to join the Marañón River in Peru. The Pastaza's chief tributary is the Bobonaza River.

Below: The delta of the Parana near Buenos Aires.

Left: The Sucre bridge over the Pilcomayo River.

Piquiri, Brazil

A tributary of the Paraná River, the Piquiri rises northwest of GUARAPUAVA in Paraná State, Brazil. The river is 356 miles (573 km) long and flows west and northwest before joining the Paraná River above PORTO GUAIRA.

Piranhas, Brazil

The river rises in Paraíba, northeastern Brazil and is noted for very important salt deposits near its mouth. The river is also known as the Acu on its lower course. It is 250 miles (400 km) long and flows northeast past ACU to finally enter the Atlantic Ocean through four separate mouths just west of MACAU.

Piray, Bolivia

The Piray River rises near SAMIPATA in central Bolivia and flows due north past SANTA CRUZ for 160 miles (260 km). It joins the Rio Grande approximately 20 miles (32 km) above its mouth.

Pisco, Peru

The source of the Pisco is in the Cordillera Occidental in southwestern Peru. It flows southwest and west for 150 miles (240 km) past the town of HUMAY to the Pacific Ocean just north-northwest of PISCO. The river runs through one of Peru's chief cotton- and wine-growing regions.

Piura, Peru

The Piura rises in the Cordillera Occidental near the town of HUARMACA. It flows for 150 miles (240 km) northwest and southwest through a major cotton-producing region, passing the towns of CHULUCANAS, TAMBO GRANDE and PIURA before entering Sechura Bay of the Pacific Ocean.

Plata (or Plate), Uruguay-Argentina

This extremely large estuary in the southernmost area of South America was discovered by Juan Dias de Solis in 1516 while he was attempting to find a route to the Pacific Ocean. He was killed by the Charrua Indians. The Rio de la Plata is comprehensively the mouth of an enormous drainage basin which includes the Paraguay, the Paraná and the Uruguay Rivers as well as numerous other small tributaries. It drains the majority of southern South America for a total of 1,679,535 square miles (4,349,975 sq km) and is the fourth largest river system in the world. It drains all of Paraguay, the southeastern section of Bolivia, Uruguay, southern Brazil and a large proportion of Argentina. It is second only to the Amazon in the volume of water carried to the ocean. The estuary gradually widens from 63 miles (101 km) to a massive 140 miles (230 km) at its mouth. During World War II, the German Pocket Battleship, *Graf Spee*, was forced to take refuge in MONTEVIDEO Harbor at the mouth of the Rio de la Plata after engaging three British cruisers, the *Ajax*, *Achilles* and the *Exeter*. The German captain requested political asylum for his ship and crew but was

Piquiri, Brazil

The Piquiri rises near the Goias border in central Mato Grosso, Brazil. It runs due west for 100 miles (160 km) before joining the Itiquira river which flows into the São Lourenço River.

Pilcomayo, Bolivia

The Pilcomayo rises at a height of 13,000 feet (3965 m) in the Cordillera de los Frailes in the eastern Andes, north-northeast of the town of RIO MULATO in Bolivia. The river is 700 miles (1130 km) long and flows north of POTOSI, once famous for its great silver mines, through the mountains and across the great Chaco Plains on a southeasterly course. Its principal tributary is the Pilaya River which joins the Pilcomayo in southern Bolivia. Below the junction of the two rivers is the Guarapetendi Falls, which is 23 feet (seven m) high. The river widens out to between 500–1000 feet (150–300 m) just below the falls but the numerous side channels quickly disperse the waters from the main stream, aided by the high rate of evaporation. The river meanders through the huge expanses of the Estero Patino swamp, approximately 70 miles (113 km) from the confluence with the Paraguay River. The Pilcomayo has no principal channel as it wanders through the great swamp. On the upper course of the river, it is a chief source of hydroelectric power for the region. It finally joins the Paraguay River at the town of PUERTO PILCOMAYO just south of the capital city of Paraguay, ASUNCION.

Pindaré, Brazil

The Pindaré rises in Serra do Piaui in northeastern Brazil. It flows northeast past the towns of PINDARE-MIRIM and MONCAO to join the Mearim River above ANAJATUBA. It is over 250 miles (400 km) long.

Right: Inhabitants of Buenos Aires crowd the beaches of the Rio de la Plata.

refused and only given enough time to refuel and provision his ship. Knowing that a reinforced British squadron was waiting for him to come out, he scuttled his ship, thus concluding the Battle of the Rio de la Plata.

Pomeroon, Guyana

The Pomeroon rises in the northern region of Guyana. It flows for 80 miles (129 km) on a northeast course to the town of CHARITY, then it swings north-northwest to enter the Atlantic Ocean. The river irrigates one of the large coconut-growing areas of South America.

Porce, Colombia

Sometimes called the Medellín River, it rises south of MEDELLIN in central Colombia. The alluvial soil surrounding the river is very rich in gold. GUADALUPE FALLS and a major hydroelectric station are located on the banks of one of its tributaries. The Porce flows for 150 miles (240 km) north-northeast past BELLO to join the Nechí River only six miles (ten km) south-southwest of ZARAGOZA.

Portuguesa, Venezuela

This river rises in the Andes, southeast of EL TOCUYO in western Venezuela. It flows for over 240 miles (390 km) southeast past the towns of PORTUGUESA and COJEDES before joining the Apure River near SAN FERNANDO. The river's chief tributaries are the Pão, Cojedes and Guanare Rivers.

Potaro, Guyana

The Potaro rises in the Guiana Highlands of central Guyana. It flows for 110 miles (180 km) first southeast, then northeast and finally eastward to join the Essequibo River. The Potaro is famous for the KAIETEUR FALLS which are located 60 miles (97 km) from the mouth.

Primero, Argentina

The Rio Primero rises in central Cordoba State, Argentina. It runs 125 miles (201 km) east and northeast past the towns of CORDOBA, RIO PRIMERO and SANTA ROSA before reaching the Mar Chiquita.

Pucara, Peru

See Ramis, Peru.

Purús, Peru-Brazil

The Purús is the most crooked river in the world, and its 1995 mile (3210 km) course makes it one of the longest rivers in the South American continent. The Purús rises on the eastern slopes of the Peruvian Andes. It flows northeast through Acre State and Amazonas, across the tropical rainforest with its large rubber-growing regions to join the Amazon 100 miles (160 km) west-southwest of MANAUS. The river passes BOCA DO ACRE, LABREA and BERURI before joining the Amazon. The chief tributary of the Purús is the Acre River. It is

navigable for a distance. An important feature of the Purús is the group of five parallel canals, called *furos* which the mighty Amazon dispatches to it from the northwest at regular intervals. These canals are not manmade but natural features of the Amazon system and as such are extremely interesting to the geographer. The canals cut the region into five distinct islands which are set in very low-lying country.

Putumayo, Colombia

The Putumayo rises east of PASTO, the large Colombian city on the high Andean Plateau, and runs along the boundaries of Colombia and Ecuador, and Colombia and Peru. The river flows on a westerly course, practically parallel to the Japurá River, running through densely forested plains populated almost exclusively by native Indian tribes. The climate is extremely humid and typically tropical. The chief tributary of the Putumayo is the San Miguel River. The river is navigable for a large part of its course which is over 1000 miles (1600 km) long. It becomes a tributary of the Amazon at SANTO ANTONIO DO ICA. On the lower course of the river's journey, it is sometimes called Içá River by the natives. The indigenous Indian population gathers rubber, balata gums, resins, fine woods, medicinal plants and nuts to sell to the white men who come up river expressly for that purpose.

Quarai, Brazil-Uruguay

The river runs southwest of RIVERA in Brazil and forms the border between Brazil and Uruguay. It flows 160 miles (260 km) northwest to join the Uruguay River near BELLA UNION in Uruguay. Bella Unión is unique in that it is the meeting point of three countries: Argentina, Brazil and Uruguay.

Ramis, Peru

Also known as the Pucara River, the Ramis rises in the Cordillera de Vilcanota of southeastern Peru. The river is 110 miles (180 km) long and flows southeast to the highest lake in the world, Lake Titicaca.

Ribeira de Iguape, Brazil

The river rises east of PONTA GROSSA in Paraná and flows for slightly over 200 miles (320 km) on an east-northeast course. It flows through a region rich in gold, lead, silver, copper and phosphate deposits. Its passes ELDORADO and RIBEIRA to join the Juquiá River above Registro to form the Iguape River.

Rimac, Peru

This Peruvian river rises in the lofty Western Cordillera of the country. The river is only 80 miles (129 km) long, but its importance to Peru is far out of proportion to its actual size and volume of water. The name of the river is believed to have been bastardized to LIMA, the name of the capital city of Peru. The city is built in the river's lower valley, and the chief port of the country, CALLAO is located at its mouth. When the Central Peruvian Railroad was being built, the Rimac was utilized to solve the great engineering difficulties in reaching a height of 15,800 feet (4820 m) to reach the town of OROYA from the capital, Lima. This feat of stupendous engineering was completed through a series of tunnels, great bridges and spiral loops. The Rimac is also known as San Mateo above its confluence with the Santa Eulalia River.

Rio Grande, Argentina

This river rises in the Andes Range near PLANCHON PEAK, Mendoza State, Argentina. It runs for 80 miles (129 km) southeast and south

Above: The Rimac River of Peru.
Right: The mines of Tamboraque on the Rimac.

to join the Barrancas River, 75 miles (121 km) long, to form the Rio Colorado.

Rio Grande, Bolivia

Called the Guapay by some natives, this Rio Grande rises in central Bolivia at the confluence of the Caine River, 140 miles (230 km) long, and the Chayanta River, 80 miles (129 km) long. The Rio Grande of Bolivia runs for over 510 miles (820 km), east, north and northwest passing through Santa Cruz Department before joining the Mamoré River. The chief tributaries are the Azero, Mizque and Piray Rivers. It is navigable for slightly over 100 miles (160 km).

Rio Grande, Brazil (1)

This river rises in the Serra da Mantiqueira in the southern part of Minas Gerais, 40 miles (64 km) from the coast. The Rio Grande flows westward for over 650 miles (1050 km) before joining with the Parnaíba River to form the third largest river in the entire South American continent, the Paraná River. It flows through a region rich in mineral resources for the first leg of its course, then it runs through rich grassland to form the border between the states of Minas Gerais and São Paulo.

Rio Grande, Brazil (2)

This river rises in the Serra Geral de Goias in

western Bahia, Brazil. It is 300 miles (480 km) long, and flows northeast to join the São Francisco River at the town of BARRA. Its chief tributary is the Rio Preto.

Rio Grande, Peru
This river rises east of ICA in southwestern Peru and runs for a total of 120 miles (190 km) first south and then southwest. It enters the Pacific Ocean approximately 14 miles (23 km) northwest of SAN NICOLAS.

Roosevelt, Brazil
The Roosevelt rises in the Mato Grosso of western Brazil. It is 400 miles (640 km) long and runs due north to join the Aripuaná River. It is also known as the Rio da Duvida.

Rupununi, Guyana
The river rises in the Guiana Highlands of Guyana. The river flows 250 miles (400 km) north and east to become a tributary of the Essequibo River.

Salado, Argentina (1)
The Rio Salado rises in Lake Chanar, northwest of General Arenales, Buenos Aires State in eastern Argentina. It flows for 400 miles (640 km) southeast past JUNIN to enter Samborombon Bay on the Atlantic.

Salado, Argentina (2)
The Rio Salado del Norte rises in the Andes Mountains of central Argentina at the confluence of the Toro and Guachipas Rivers southwest of SALTA. The river is 150 miles (240 km) long and runs east and south as the Juramento River, then becomes the Rio Salado del Norte. It then flows for 1100 miles (1770 km) to join the Parana River at SANTE FE.

Salado, Argentina (3)
The Salado rises as the Bermejo River in western La Rioja State and runs south for 250 miles (400 km) before reaching the Huanan-cache Lakes, 75 miles (121 km) southeast of SAN JUAN. The river continues southward as the Desaguadero River to the swamps south of Lake Bebedero, forming the border between Mendoza and San Luis States. It becomes the Salado and runs south across a marshy area into LA PAMPA, then swings southeast to become a tributary of the Colorado River, approximately 150 miles (240 km) west of the important port of BAHIA BLANCA. The river is over 600 miles (970 km) long and is also known as Chadileuvu River below LIMAY MAHUIDA and the Curacó River below PUELCHES. The major tributaries of this river are the Atuel, Diamante and the Tunuyán Rivers.

San Javier, Argentina
The river rises north of RECONQUISTA in Argentina and flows over 200 miles (320 km) due south past ROMANG, HELVECIA and CAYASTA to an arm of the Paraná River approximately 30 miles (48 km) northeast of SANTE FE.

San Juan, Bolivia
The San Juan rises in the Cordillera de Lipez in southwestern Bolivia. It runs 170 miles (270 km) east past SUIPACHA then swings north to join the Cotagaita River near VILLA ABECIA to form the Pilaya River.

San Juan, Argentina
This river is formed by the confluence of the Castaño River and the Rio de Los Patos, north of CALINGASTA, San Juan State, Argentina. The river is 150 miles (240 km) long and flows east and south past the towns of SAN JUAN and VILLA INDEPENDENCIA to enter the Huanan-cache Lakes.

San Juan, Colombia
The river rises in Chocó Department of western Colombia and runs for 200 miles (320 km) southwest past TADO and ISTMINA to a broad delta on the Pacific Ocean. Navigable for its entire length, the San Juan flows through regions rich in gold and platinum.

São Miguel, Bolivia
This river rises in Lake Concepción in southeastern Bolivia. It flows for 340 miles (550 km) on a north-northwest course passing SANTA ROSA DEL PALMAR before becoming the Itonamas River.

Santa, Peru
The Santa rises in the Cordillera Occidental of central Peru. It flows for 200 miles (320 km) north-northwest passing the towns of HUARAZ and HUALLANCA before turning westward to enter the Pacific Ocean northwest of SANTA.

Santa Lucia, Uruguay
A tributary of the Plate River, the Santa Lucia rises northeast of MINAS in southern Uruguay. It flows west and south past SANTA LUCIA to join the Plate at a location west of the capital city of Uruguay, MONTEVIDEO.

São Francisco, Brazil
This river rises in the Serra da Canastra of eastern Brazil. The São Francisco is a major river of Brazil with a length of 1800 miles (2900 km). It flows northeast through Minas Gerais and Bahia, then swings across the *sertao*, the desert of northwest Bahia. The next directional change is east-southeast to become the border between Bahia and Pernambuco States, then in turn of Alagoas and Sergipe. In 1949 a tremendous project, modeled upon the Tennessee Valley Authority (TVA), was initiated for the São Francisco River Valley starting near the PAULO ALFONSO FALLS to provide electrical power for northeastern Brazil. This has been a huge success and includes the tributaries of the river. The São Francisco enters the Atlantic Ocean 60 miles (97 km) northeast of the town of ARACUJU. The chief tributaries are navigable, and include the Paracatu, the Carinhanha, the Rio Grande, the Rio das Velhas and the Corrente Rivers. The São Francisco River system is the principal interior waterway of northeastern Brazil. The

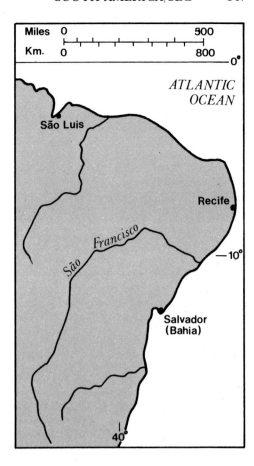

main river is navigable for 850 miles (1370 km) of its course.

São Lourenço, Brazil
The river rises near POXOREU in the central Mato Grosso, Brazil. It flows 300 miles (480 km) southwest to become a tributary of the Paraguay River north of CORUMBA. Chief tributaries of the São Lourenço River are the Cuiabá and Pequiri Rivers.

São Manuel, Brazil
The river rises in the Mato Grosso of Brazil and flows for 700 miles (1130 km) north-northwest. It joins the Juruena River to form the Tapajós River.

Saramacca, Surinam
The river rises in the Guiana Highlands of Surinam and flows for 250 miles (400 km). It is linked by the Saramacca Canal to the Surinam River. The river flows north and west near the large city of PARAMARIBO, the capital of Surinam, to the Atlantic near the mouth of the Coppename River.

Secunduri, Brazil
See Canuma, Brazil.

Segundo, Argentina
The Rio Segundo rises in central Córdoba, Argentina. It flows on an easterly course, then swings northeast passing PILAR, VILLA DEL ROSARIO and CONCEPCION to enter the Chiquita Lake. The river is 200 miles (320 km) long.

Senguerr, Argentina

The Senguerr rises in Lake Fontana in Patagonia near the border with Chile. It flows east and southeast, then turns north-northeast to Lake Musters, west of the town of SARMIENTO. Its chief tributaries are the Mayo and Genoa Rivers. Total length of the Senguerr is 210 miles (340 km).

Sinu, Colombia

The river rises in the Cordillera Occidental of northern Colombia. It flows for 250 miles (400 km) north to the Gulf of Morrosquillo.

Sogamoso, Colombia

The river rises in Santander Department, central Colombia. It flows over 100 miles (160 km) on a west-northwest course from where the Suarez River joins it to the Magdalena River north of the town of BARRANCABERMEJA.

Surinam, Surinam

This river rises in the Wilhelmina Mountain Range of Surinam. The Surinam flows north through a heavily forested region before descending into the savannas and then into the Atlantic Ocean approximately 14 miles (23 km) from the capital, PARAMARIBO. The chief tributaries are the Commewijne and Cottica Rivers. The river flows through an area rich in sugar cane, rice and coconuts on its way to the sea. It is 230 miles (370 km) long, and navigable for the last 40 miles (64 km) which allows ocean-going vessels to navigate as far as PARANAM, the bauxite center of the country. Surinam, formerly Dutch Guiana, does not have numerous roads or railroads, but this is partly alleviated by the numerous small rivers which crisscross the country making all parts of the country accessible to small ships

Tahuamanu, Peru-Bolivia

The river rises in the Madre de Dios Department of eastern Peru. The Tahuamanu flows due east for 250 miles (400 km) into Bolivia to join the Manuripi River at Puerto Rico to form the Ortón River, a chief tributary of the Beni River.

Tapajós, Brazil

This river is formed by the confluence of the Juruena and São Manuel Rivers. The Juruena rises in the Serra dos Parecis and the São Manuel in the Planalto of the Mato Grosso. The Tapajós is one of the great rivers of the southern interior of the Brazilian Plateau. It is 1200 miles (1930 km) long and empties into the Amazon. The only large town on the river is SANTAREM, which is in reality on the Amazon. There are small settlements along the river's course but they are extremely limited and with a very small population. The so-called Great Interior of Brazil is almost inaccessible because of the rapids and cataracts which

Ferries on the São Francisco River at Propria.

predominate the river's course. The surrounding savannas are utilized primarily for ranching by the few hardy souls who have eked out a home in this huge wilderness. These cataracts are called *cachoeiras* by the natives, and the lowest one is the Cachoeiro Maranhão Grande located only 170 miles (270 km) from the river's confluence with the Amazon. This one stretch of the river is the only navigable section in the entire 1200-mile (1930-km) course. The mouth of the Tapajós is even larger than the mouth of the Amazon, extending to a width of eight to ten miles (13 to 16 km).

Taquari, Brazil

The Taquari River rises near Alto Araguaia, in the central Mato Grosso, Brazil. It flows west-southwest for 350 miles (560 km) to enter the Paraguay River east of CORUMBA.

Taquarí, Brazil

The Taquarí rises in the Serra do Mar in northeastern Rio Grande do Sul in Brazil as the Rio das Antas. It runs for slightly over 200 miles (320 km) west and south to join the Jacuí River at BOM JESUS DO TRIUNFO.

Tarra, Colombia

See Catatumbo, Colombia.

Tebicuary, Paraguay

The Tebicuary rises near TAVAI in southern Paraguay. The river is 250 miles (400 km) long and winds its way past the town of FLORIDA to join the Paraguay River north-northeast of PILAR.

Tefé, Brazil

This Brazilian river rises in central Amazonas and flows for 550 miles (880 km) north-northeast to become a tributary of the Amazon River near TEFE where it forms a lake.

Tibagi, Brazil

The Tibagi rises west of CURITIBA in eastern Paraná, Brazil. It flows 270 miles (440 km) north-northwest to the Paranapanema River north of LONDRINA.

Tietê, Brazil

The river rises in the Serra do Mar, São Paulo, Brazil. It flows northwest for 500 miles (800 km) past MOGI DAS CRUZES and SAO PAULO city finally to join the Paraná River. The river is an important source of hydroelectric power.

Tocantins, Brazil

The Tocantins rises on the Planalto Central of the Brazilian Plateau between GOIANIA, the capital of Goias State and BRASILIA, the federal capital of Brazil. The river is not navigable and has a length of 1678 miles (2700 km). The Tocantins flows north for over 700 miles (1130 km), and then runs through a double bend before running another 500 miles (800 km) into its tidal estuary. The mouth of the Tocantins is over eight miles (13 km) wide. The Tocantins-Araguaia system is still described by some as a tributary of the mighty Amazon but this is not the case. The Tocantins and Araguaia together form an independent system with a separate estuarine mouth which was the result of the gradual submergence of the coast. The river itself is extremely old, just like the Brazilian Plateau and the other large rivers which drain it. The river falls from a height of 3000 feet (915 m) through a series of rapids and cataracts before reaching the sea. Because of these numerous obstructions along the entire course of the river (except for approximately 100 miles [160 km] of free navigable river upstream from the mouth) the Tocantins is not navigable. The climate of the Tocantins basin is totally different from the Amazon's. The Tocantins has a very distinct dry season which makes it far more habitable for humans despite its nearness to the equator. The primary crop of the region is a natural one, the Brazil nut, which is harvested and exported worldwide. The chief seaport in the area is BELEM located on the Rio do Pará. The Tocantins receives numerous small tributaries on the way to the sea but the most important one is the Araguaia River, which parallels the main river for a distance before actually running into it.

Tocuyo, Venezuela
The Tocuyo River rises in the Andes of northwestern Venezuela and flows over 200 miles (320 km) north passing EL TOCUYO and SIQUISIQUE before entering the Caribbean Sea near TOCUYO DE LA COSTA.

Trombetas, Brazil
The river rises near the Guyana border in northwestern Pará, Brazil. The river is 470 miles (760 km) long and runs due south to the Amazon above OBIDOS.

Uaupés, Colombia-Brazil
Also known as the Cayari River or the Vaupés River, the Uaupés rises in southeastern Colombia. It flows east-southeast into Amazonas in Brazil below MITU, then continues on to the Rio Negro near UAUPES after a journey of 500 miles (800 km).

Ucayali, Peru
The Ucayali is the principal river of Peru and the second largest tributary of the mighty Amazon. It is only second in size to the Madeira. The Ucayali drains the majority of the Peruvian Andes from CERRO DE PASCO to within 70 miles (113 km) of Lake Titicaca and a large area of the adjacent lowlands as well. The headstreams of the river, the Urubamba, Apurimac and Mantaro, rise at a height of 12,000 feet (3660 m) and run through gorges and rapids to finally break out of the mountains to form the Ucayali River. The river is navigable for its 400 mile (640 km) northward journey to join the Amazon, but this is twice the actual distance due to the steady meandering and loops of the river. The basin of the Ucayali takes in an area over 150,000 square miles (388,500 sq km) and is sparsely populated. The rainfall in the high uplands and the heavy snowfall in the Andes contribute to the immense volume of water which the headstreams carry down to the Ucayali. The sierra region is more populated than the other portions of the basin and has been since pre-Inca times. Today the population is primarily concerned with the area's mineral wealth while the tourists only care about seeing the remains of the Inca centers. The capital of Peru in the Inca days was CUZCO and it is still a principal market town. Leaving the sierra country, one notices the striking contrast; the Amazonian region is rainy and waterlogged. There are a few settlements but for the most part these are only small outposts of civilization and nothing more. The most important event of this century was the discovery of oil and the erection of an oil refinery for processing at GANSO AZUL on the Pachitea River. The Ucayali River has immense possibilities which have not yet been considered.

Uraricoera, Brazil
This river rises in the Serra Pakaraima, Roraimo Territory, Brazil very near the Venezuelan border. It is 300 miles (480 km) long and flows due east to join first the Parima River and then the Tacutu River above BOA VISTA to form the Rio Branco.

Urubamba, Peru
The river rises in central Peru as the Vilcanota River, which was the sacred river of the Inca nation. The river is 450 miles (720 km) long and flows northwest, north and west-northwest through the Andes, passing the towns of URCOS, SICUANI and QUILLABAMBA before joining the Apurimac River to form the Ucayali River.

Uruguay, Brazil-Uruguay
This river is formed by the confluence of the Pelotas and Canoas Rivers which both rise in the Serra do Mar of Brazil. The Uruguay is one of the most interesting and important rivers in South America. It flows for 250 miles (400 km) through Brazilian territory before turning southwest to form the boundary between Brazil and Argentina. The river is 1000 miles (1600 km) long, but this course is

actually more than double what it would have been if the river had run in a straight line. It flows through the ancient Brazilian massif, and the river itself is extremely old as witnessed by its deep valley. The main town on the river is URUGUAIANA, located in Brazil near the border with Uruguay. No other major towns have grown up along the river because the surrounding land tends to be utilized primarily for pasture for large herds. Also the wide mouth of the river is too shallow for large vessels to navigate. The current of the Uruguay is extremely fast which makes the upper portion of the river totally unnavigable. Once the river passes Uruguaiana, it runs straight along the border between Argentina and Uruguay as it heads for the Rio de la Plata. The river has one set of rapids known as the Salto Grande, 'a great leap,' where the river falls 27 feet (nine m) in two miles (three km), and flows through a gorge which compresses the normal 1500 feet (460 m) width to a mere 100 feet (30 m). Therefore, the town of SALTO is the upper limit of navigation for small river-craft which ply the waters of the Uruguay. The principal tributaries of the river are the Ijui, Ibicui, Quarai and the Negro Rivers. The tributaries mentioned are all left bank ones, as the nearby giant Paraná River takes all the available rivers within the adjacent belt into its system.

Vaupés, Colombia
See Uaupés, Colombia.

Velhas, Brazil
The Rio das Velhas rises north of OURO PRETO in central Minas Gerais, Brazil. It runs for over 500 miles (800 km) north-northwest to join the São Francisco River below the town of PIRAPORA.

Vichada, Colombia
The river rises in the Meta Comissary of eastern Colombia and winds for the majority of its 400 mile (640 km) journey to join the Orinoco River on the Venezuelan border.

Vilcanota, Peru
See Urumbamba, Peru.

Vitor, Peru
The river rises in the Cordillera Occidental as the Chili River in southern Peru. It flows southwest past AREQUIPA to the Pacific Ocean at QUILCA. The river is 160 miles (260 km) long.

Xingu, Brazil
The Xingu is one of the chief tributaries of the Amazon. It is 1230 miles (1980 km) long and rises in several headstreams in the Serra do Roncador in the Mato Grosso of Brazil. It flows northward, through the Brazilian State of Pará, to join the Amazon below PORTO DE MOZ at the head of the Amazon delta. The Xingu is one of the relatively unknown rivers of Brazil and this is so even today. Numerous expeditions have gone up other tributaries, but due to the excessive wildness of the Xingu basin, the inability to cope with the terrain, and the wet and torrid climate, this region has been the deathbed of many a would-be explorer. As the Xingu reaches its mouth, the river widens out into a series of lakes which become one immense lake at the mouth. The lakes are interconnected with the Amazon by natural canals called *canos*, which wind through a dense and wooded archipelago. The chief tributary of the Xingu is the Iriri River which enters the river from the left. At a point 105 miles (169 km) from where the Xingu enters the Amazon, is a large bend to the east as the river attempts to find its way across the rocky barrier. Here lies the great cataract of ITAMARACA. This great cataract falls for over a distance of three straight miles (five km) before tumbling over the Falls of Itamaraca. The Xingu is even more interesting as an unexplored river than the Amazon. It is a river of mystery which seems to be shrouded and protected by the dense tropical jungle surrounding its banks. The Upper Xingu is an uncommonly dry area where the Waura Indians use fires as a hunting technique to drive wild monkeys and deer from the savannas. The Indians along the Xingu are hardy and most adept at utilizing darts tipped with that most awesome of vegetable poisons, curare which can kill a full grown deer within a range of 120 feet (36 m).

Yari, Colombia
The Yari rises southeast of the town of NEIVA in southern Colombia. It is 300 miles (480 km) long and flows southeast through a dense tropical forest before joining the Caquetá River.

The Ucayali and the Maranon Rivers merge to form the Amazon River south of Iquitos. Jungle, swamps and marshes dominate this part of Peru. It is very sparsely populated with few roads and no railroads. The rivers serve as the major means of transportation.

ACKNOWLEDGMENTS

Page 1   **Colourviews**
Page 2-3   **Bruce Coleman Limited**
Page 4-5   **J Allan Cash**
Page 6   **Bruce Coleman Limited**
Page 7   **J Allan Cash**

Aerofilms Library: 26, 79 (right 2), 99 (bottom), 123, 130 (top), 138/139 (both), 160 (bottom left), 163 (bottom), 173, 178, 187, 190, 199 (bottom 2), 211 (top), 214/215, 217 (bottom), 218 (top), 234 (bottom left), 235 (bottom right), 240/241 (bottom), 243, 264, 265, 293, 325.

Argentinian Embassy: 336, 342 (bottom left), 343 (bottom right).

Australian Information Service, London: 110/111 (both), 113 (both), 114, 116/117 (all 3), 118/119 (all 3), 120/121 (both), 122 (top right and center).

Barnaby's Picture Library: 28 (top left), 258; Peter S Dole 285; T R Evans 19; Helen Grant 261 (top); Hubertus Kanus 28 (bottom left), 31 (top), 39 (bottom), 42, 43; Robert Mitchinson 275; Mavis Ronson: 78/79 (center); M L Rule 41; Alfred K Schroeder 267; E J Ziesman 16 (top left), 22/23, 39 (top).

British Tourist Authority: 129 (top), 136, 149 (bottom), 157, 160 (top left), 161 (bottom), 165, 180, 200/201, 219 (top), 226, 227, 231 (top right and bottom right), 234/235 (center bottom), 240/241 (top), 242, 251.

Belgian National Tourist Office: 216 (bottom 3).

J Allan Cash: 9 (both), 11, 14/15, 22 (left), 27, 28/29 (center), 30, 60 (bottom), 66/67, 74/75, 81, 104/105, 107, 112, 122 (top left), 130 (bottom), 131, 133, 137, 142, 144/145 (all 3), 149 (top and center), 153 (top), 154/155, 162, 168/169, 179, 182, 184/185, 188 (bottom) 189, 193, 194, 199 (top), 205, 207, 210 (top), 212, 213, 215 (top right), 216 (top), 217 (inset), 220/221, 222, 224/225, 229, 230 (top left, top center and center bottom), 235 (top), 238/239, 246/247 (top), 248/249 (both), 250, 252, 259, 279, 287 (inset), 294 (extreme left inset), 295 (extreme right inset), 298 (bottom), 302 (top left), 303 (top right), 308 (both), 311, 314 (top left), 323 (top).

Bruce Coleman: Bill Brooks 299, Bruce Coleman 314/315 (center); J A L Cooke 266; Gerald Cubitt 29 (right), 33; M Freeman 68/69 (top), 72 (bottom); Prato 64, 77 (right).

Colourviews: 25 (bottom), 44/45 (both), 46 (both), 61 (bottom), 85 (right), 129 (bottom), 140, 141 (both), 150/151, 156 (both), 163 (top), 172, 181, 188 (top), 209/210 (bottom 2), 246/247 (bottom), 346 (top).

David Eldred: 208/209 (top).

Noel Habgood: 143.

Tom Hanley: 60 (top), 61 (top), 68 (bottom), 69 (bottom), 72 (top), 93, 95, 257.

Peter Weller: 76/77 (bottom center).

Susan and John Linsley: 56/57, 80 (both), 161 (top right).

Nick McIver: 160/161 (top center).

MacLennan Collection: 208 (bottom left), 294/295 (center 3 insets).

MacQuitty Collection: 25 (top), 76/77 (top center), 92 (top), 96/97.

Marion Morrison: 327, 334 (top left), 339 (right).

Tony Morrison: 338/339 (left and center), 342 (top), 343 (top), 344, 345, 349 (center and bottom).

Novosti: 51, 52/53, 54/55, 63, 78 (left), 84/85 (center), 89 (bottom), 97 (bottom), 100/101, 102/103 (all 3), 134/135, 146/147 (all 3), 148, 175, 183, 191, 192, 195, 197, 203 (both), 236/237, 244/245 (all 3).

Popperfoto: 18, 31 (bottom), 36 (both), 38, 47, 59, 86/87 (both), 89 (top), 92 (bottom), 97 (top), 98/99 (top 2), 263, 273, 284, 307 (top right), 312, 319, 320 (right), 324 (both), 328, 329, 331 (top), 332/333, 334/335 (center), 337, 340, 342/343 (center bottom), 346 (bottom), 348, 349 (top), 351.

Michael Powell: 12, 13.

Jürgen Schadeburg: 16/17, 37.

Slater Picture Library: 126/127, 164, 209 (bottom right), 232/233.

Swiss National Tourist Office (and Swiss Federal Railways): 204 (both), 206, 206/207, 208/209 (bottom), 210/211 (bottom 2).

US Geological Survey: 302/303 (center).

US Travel Service: 253, 261 (bottom), 268/269, 270/271, 277, 278, 282, 286/287, 289, 290, 291, 294/295, 298 (top), 304/305 (both), 306/307 (center), 309, 312, 316/317 (both), 320 (left), 323 (bottom).

Venezuelan Embassy: 331 (bottom).

A special thank you to Susan de la Plain for her efforts in locating and obtaining the photographs used in this volume.

Maps on pages 21, 24, 32, 44, 209, 289, 306, were drawn by Pica Designs.